FROMMER'S

COMPREHENSIVE
TRAVEL GUIDE

Ireland

1st Edition

by Patricia Tunison Preston
and John J. Preston

MACMILLAN • USA

ABOUT THE AUTHORS

Patricia Tunison Preston and John J. Preston are a husband-and-wife writing team who reside in New York State. In addition to *Frommer's Ireland,* they are the authors of *Frommer's Dublin, Frommer's Tampa & St. Petersburg,* and *Frommer's Delaware & Maryland.* They also contribute to *Frommer's Europe* and *Frommer's Florida.* Patricia is also the author of the coffeetable picture book, *Reflections of Ireland,* a fitting result of her being a regular visitor to Ireland for the last 30 years, including more than 15 years as public relations director for the Irish Tourist Board. Articles by the Prestons appear regularly in major magazines and newspapers throughout North America and in Ireland. In their spare time, the Prestons use their knowledge of Ireland to plan and escort tours around the Emerald Isle.

MACMILLAN TRAVEL

A Prentice Hall Macmillan Company
15 Columbus Circle
New York, NY 10023
Copyright © 1995 by Simon & Schuster, Inc.

Macmillan is a registered trademark of Macmillan, Inc.

ISBN 0-028600 75-4
ISSN 1080-9104

Design by Robert Bull Design
Maps by Geographix Inc.

SPECIAL SALES

Bulk purchases (10+ copies) of Frommer's Travel Guides are available to corporations at special discounts. The Special Sales Department can produce custom editions to be used as premiums and/or sales promotion to suit individual needs. Existing editions can be produced with custom cover imprints such as corporate logos. For more information write to: Special Sales, Prentice Hall, 15 Columbus Circle, 15th Floor, New York, NY 10023.

Manufactured in the United States of America

Contents

List of Maps

*This book is dedicated to
our Galway-born friend,
Fr. Charlie Coen,
who brings Irish smiles, joy,
and music
into our everyday life*

Acknowledgments

Thank you, dear people of Ireland, for being your great selves. Your help and encouragement have made this book possible.

Thanks, in particular, to friends at Aer Lingus (John Bastable, Bernie Lynch, James Lyndon, Paul Murphy, Pat Hanrahan, and many more); friends at the Irish Tourist Board in Ireland (Matt McNulty, Joe Byrne, James Larkin, Joe Lynam, Paddy Derivan, and many more), in New York (Niall Millar, Marie Fullington, Simon O'Hanlon, Orla Carey, Ruth Moran, and many more), and in London (Margaret Cahill); friends at CIE/Ireland's Transport Company in Ireland (Ciaran O'Leary and many more) and in the U.S. (Brian Stack, Dennis Savage, Joe Fallon, Jim Kelly, and many more); friends at Shannon Development Company at Shannon (Nandi O'Sullivan, Tom O'Donnell, and many more) and in New York (Lorraine Grainger and Bridget Clarke); and in the Northern Ireland Tourist Board in Belfast (Eamonn McArdle and Rosemary Evans) and in New York (David Boyce, Maebeth Fenton, and Louise McKeown).

Thanks also to our stalwart Irish friends over the years—Patricia Barry; Mary Crotty and Derek Sherwin; Alan and Angela Glynn; Paddy Fitzpatrick and all the Fitzpatrick family; Margaret Doyle; Billy Kingston; Joan Ennis; Fr. Michael Coen and all the Coens at Lorrha and Drimnamuckla; Eamonn and Carole McKeon; Brian and Anne Cronin; John, Stella, and Simon Doyle; Brenda Weir, Vivienne Flanagan, Peter Harbison, and Mary O'Sullivan, and many more. And to those who have left us—Eithne Fitzpatrick, P.V. Doyle, and Fr. James McDyer.

Thank you to Peter Katucki, our editor, for his guidance and expertise in producing this book.

What the Symbols Mean

 Frommer's Favorites   Hotels, restaurants, attractions, and entertainments you should not miss

$ Super-Special Values   Really exceptional values

Abbreviations in Hotel and Other Listings

The following symbols refer to the standard amenities available in all rooms:

A/C   air conditioning
MINIBAR   refrigerator stocked with beverages and snacks
TEL   telephone
TV   television

The following abbreviations are used for credit cards:

AE   American Express
CB   Carte Blanche
DC   Diners Club
DISC   Discover
ER   enRoute
EU   Eurocard
JCB   Japan Credit Bank
MC   MasterCard
V   VISA

Trip Planning with this Guide

USE THE FOLLOWING FEATURES

What Things Cost   To help you plan your daily budget

Calendar of Events   To plan for or avoid

Suggested Itineraries   For seeing the regions or cities

What's Special About Checklist   A summary of a city's or region's highlights

Easy-to-Read Maps   Walking tours, city sights, hotel and restaurant locations—all referring to or keyed to the text

Fast Facts   All the essentials at a glance: currency, embassies, emergencies, safety, taxes, tipping, and more

OTHER SPECIAL FROMMER FEATURES

Famous People   The country's greats

Impressions   What others have said

Invitation to the Readers

In researching this book, we have come across many wonderful establishments, the best of which we have included here. We are sure that many of you will also come across appealing hotels, inns, restaurants, guesthouses, shops, and attractions. Please don't keep them to yourself. Share your experiences, especially if you want to comment on places that have been included in this edition that have changed for the worse. You can address your letters to:

Patricia and John Preston
Frommer's Ireland, First Edition
c/o Macmillan Travel
15 Columbus Circle
New York, NY 10023

A Disclaimer

Readers are advised that prices fluctuate in the course of time and travel information changes under the impact of the varied and volatile factors that affect the travel industry. Neither the author nor the publisher can be held responsible for the experiences of readers while traveling. Readers are invited to write to the publisher with ideas, comments, and suggestions for future editions.

Safety Advisory

Whenever you're traveling in an unfamiliar city or country, stay alert. Be aware of your immediate surroundings. Wear a moneybelt and keep a close eye on your possessions. Be particularly careful with cameras, purses, and wallets, all favorite targets of thieves and pickpockets.

Telephone Number Advisory

As of this writing, telephone numbers in the United Kingdom are scheduled to change on April 16, 1995. On this date, the digit 1 will be added to the beginning of all area codes for the six counties that compose Northern Ireland. For example, Belfast's current area code of 232 will be changed to 1232. This change does not affect any of the area codes in the 26 counties of the Irish Republic.

Getting to Know
Ireland

THE MOST POETIC IMAGES COME TO MIND WHEN ONE MENTIONS IRELAND TO someone who has stepped upon the shores of the Emerald Isle—from "land of heart's desire" to "a terrible beauty." That "cloud in the west" has also been referred to as a romantic lady, a bride, a mother, and an old woman. This island basking in Gaelic traditions is very much a part of the new Europe. It's a country of paradoxes—mystical but modern, beautiful yet bleak, proud and vulnerable, peaceful yet divided, rich in talent but poor in resources, foreign and friendly.

What draws visitors to this little island in the north Atlantic? For millions of people around the world, thoughts of Ireland touch the heartstrings in a compelling and often sentimental way. Millions of emmigrants and their descendants in far-flung countries yearn to go back, to see their homeland, to claim their roots.

Still others are attracted to the mystic charms of Ireland—the legends, the leprechauns, and the lure of the forty shades of green. Ireland—idyllically, intrinsically green—fresh and natural, thriving and lush, pure and unpolluted. For centuries, "green" has been almost another way of saying "Ireland." No other country has such an instant identification with one single image. Ireland is a paradise of verdant scenery, "a little bit of heaven," as the old song goes.

For many North Americans, Ireland is also an affordable and comfortable way to ease into Europe. There are no language barriers and the transatlantic journey is less than six hours, yet there are lots of things to do and see that are different from home—ancient prehistoric ruins, romantic medieval castles, stately manors and gardens, thatched-roof cottages, traditional music and song, time-honored crafts, folksy pubs, and miles of Ireland's own open countryside for horseback riding, golf, and just meandering.

But the greatest attraction of all in Ireland is her people—exuberant and enthusiastic folk known far and wide for their hospitality. "There are no strangers in Ireland," the old Irish saying goes, "only friends we have yet to meet."

Within a few seconds of your arrival on Irish soil, you'll see that a smile comes as naturally to the Irish as taking a breath. And when the people want to express their welcome for you, they do it in a grand and heartfelt way. *Cead Mile Failte* ("one hundred thousand welcomes") is the customary greeting. Not just one or two welcomes, or even a few dozen—only a hundred thousand will do. And after you settle in, the Irish will beguile you with their intangible assets, from quick wit and ready conversation to lilting music and song.

Where but in Ireland can you stroll the broad and narrow streets of Dublin's Fair City, watch the sun go down on Galway Bay, view the Mountains of Mourne that sweep down to the sea, kiss the Blarney Stone, hike the hills of Donegal, find the Rose of Tralee, or discover that it's not such a long way to Tipperary? Only in this Emerald Isle can you experience Beauty's Home, otherwise known as Killarney, dream your fondest dreams on the Lake Isle of Innisfree, and see Irish eyes smiling everywhere.

IMPRESSIONS

In Ireland the inevitable never happens, and the unexpected constantly occurs.
—Sir John Pentland Mahaffy (1839–1919)

1 Geography, History & Politics

GEOGRAPHY

Edged by the Atlantic on the western fringe and just eastward across the sea from Britain, Ireland's 1,970-mile coastline follows a path of various natural indentations, resulting in a pattern that places no part of Ireland more than 70 miles from the sea.

The total area of the island is 32,525 square miles, about the size of the state of Maine. Of this, 27,136 square miles belong to the Republic of Ireland and 5,459 square miles compose Northern Ireland. The greatest width of the island is 171 miles, and the greatest length is 302 miles.

Ireland's topography has the shape of a saucer—a broad limestone plain in the center, rimmed almost completely by coastal mountains and highlands. The central plain, largely bogland and farmland, is broken in places by low hills and dotted by hundreds of lakes and rivers, including the Shannon, which at 230 miles in length is the longest river in Ireland or even Britain. The Shannon passes through or beside 11 Irish counties, from County Cavan at its source southward to Counties Clare and Kerry. The Emerald Isle's largest lake is Lough Neagh in Northern Ireland at 153 square miles.

The island of Ireland is divided into four geographic provinces, dating back to their origins as medieval kingdoms: Leinster in the east, Munster in the south, Connaught in the west, and Ulster in the north. The exact breakdown is as follows:

Leinster (12 counties): Dublin, Carlow, Kildare, Kilkenny, Laois, Longford, Louth, Meath, Offaly, Westmeath, Wexford, and Wicklow.

Munster (6 counties): Clare, Cork, Kerry, Limerick, Tipperary, and Waterford.

Connaught (5 counties): Sligo, Mayo, Galway, Roscommon, and Leitrim.

Ulster (9 counties): Antrim, Armagh, Derry, Down, Fermanagh, Tyrone, Cavan, Donegal, and Monaghan. This province takes in both political parts of Ireland—the first six counties comprise Northern Ireland; the last three are part of the Republic of Ireland.

As you travel around, you will find that there is little distinction among the provinces, only a small sign to alert you that you have passed from one county to the next. The border between the Irish Republic and Northern Ireland is sometimes patroled, and you may have to pass through a customs post at some large border crossings.

Although it is difficult to separate one part of such a small island from another, the 26 counties of the Republic are usually referred to as Ireland and the six counties of Northern Ireland are commonly called The North or simply Ulster.

HISTORY

The Earliest Times

THE FIRST EVIDENCE OF HUMAN LIFE IN Ireland can be traced back as far as 6,000 B.C., when people from Scotland probably crossed the narrow 13-mile channel between Scotland and Ulster and settled along Ireland's eastern coast. The Neolithic or New Stone Age people reached Ireland around 3,500 B.C., and they introduced the practices of growing grain, keeping domestic animals for food and hides, and making pottery.

Dateline

- 6,000 B.C. Earliest evidence of human life in Ireland.
- 3,500 B.C. Neolithic people reach Ireland.
- 1,800 B.C. First metalworkers come to Ireland.

➤

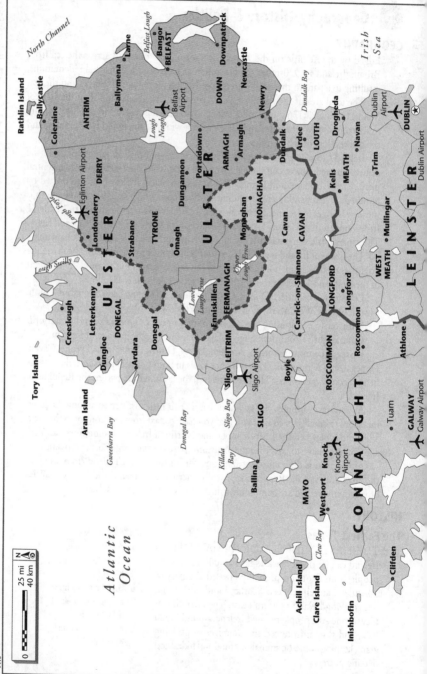

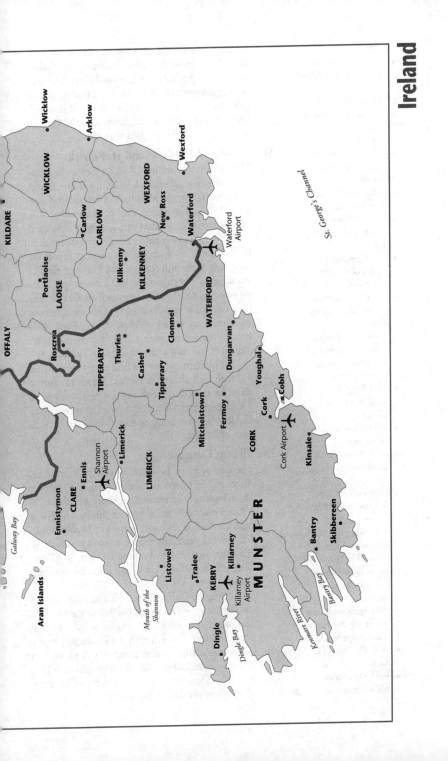

Ireland

Dateline

- 1,200 B.C. Late Bronze Age people produce gold ornaments.
- 700 B.C. Celts arrive.
- 130–180 First published accounts of Dublin by Ptolemy.
- 432 St. Patrick introduces Christianity to Ireland.
- 500 Start of Ireland's "Golden Age."
- 841 The Norse build a seafort on the River Liffey.
- 853 Danes take possession of the Norse settlement.
- 988 Dublin officially recognized as an Irish city.
- 1014 At the Battle of Clontarf, Irish high king Brian Boru triumphs over the Danes.
- 1038 King Sitric establishes Christ Church.
- 1162 Normans come to rule Ireland.
- 1172 Henry II lands at Dublin and proclaims rule.
- 1204 Dublin Castle becomes base of British power.
- 1297 First parliamentary sessions in Dublin.
- 1534–1552 Henry VIII begins suppression of Catholic Church in Ireland.
- 1601 Spain sends army to help the Irish but it is defeated at Kinsale.
- 1607 The flight of the Earls.
- 1603 The Articles of Confederation ➤

The next wave of settlers came around 1,800 B.C., as the first metalworkers arrived to tap the land's copper deposits, particularly in Cork and Kerry. Irish axes and daggers were exported to mainland Europe, as were gold ornaments. During the Late Bronze Age, which began around 1,200 B.C., artisans produced decorative bronze shields and more gold ornaments.

The Coming of the Celts and St. Patrick

The Celts arrived around 700 B.C.; they spoke a language akin to modern Irish and utilized iron implements for farming. Celtic Ireland was divided into about 150 local kingdoms, each ruled by a king or *ri*. Governing the local realms were provincial Kings, and a high King, or *ard-ri*, held authority over these rulers. Niall of the Nine Hostages, who ruled at Tara at the beginning of the fifth century, may have held the first ard-ri title. Celtic culture was based on a simple agrarian economy and the unit of currency was the cow. The Celts excelled at horse-racing and a field sport that was a precursor to hurling. *Brehons* (lawyers) and *filidh* (poets) rounded out society. The filidh were the custodians of Irish history, mythology, and genealogy.

The next turning point in Irish history came in A.D. 432 with the arrival of St. Patrick. As Ireland's patron saint, he is credited with converting the island to Christianity. From A.D. 500 to 800, Ireland enjoyed a Golden Age of learning and sent missionaries to all parts of Europe.

The Vikings Conquer

The days of glory, however, were to be short-lived. Although Ireland was spared the Roman and Teutonic Saxon invasions that reached neighboring England, the Vikings eventually sailed to Irish shores. The Norse built a seafort on the banks of the River Liffey in A.D. 841, and 12 years later the Danes took possession of the town that was to become Dublin. Wicklow, Wexford, Waterford, Cork, and Limerick were also founded by the Vikings.

During the 10th century, Irish kings laid claim to the settlement of Dublin, and in 988, it was officially recognized as an Irish city—thanks to the efforts of Mael Sechnaill II—although the Danes still kept a considerable grip. Danish power began to wane in 1014, however, when Irish chieftain and high king Brian Boru was victorious at the Battle of Clontarf, although he perished in the process.

Following Boru's demise, other local kings squabbled among themselves for power. The two dominant dynasties ruled from Tara and Cashel.

The Normans Arrive and Settle In

In the 12th century, Dermot MacMurrough, a deposed local chieftain anxious to regain his authority, enlisted the aid of a band of warriors from western Britain led by Richard FitzGilbert de Clare, commonly referred to as Strongbow. These new arrivals, known as Normans, were actually descendants of the same Viking invaders who had attacked Ireland and other lands three centuries earlier. Having settled in northern France, in the area known as Normandy, they were called Normans when they came to Britain with William the Conquerer. By 1162, Dermot had complete control over Dublin and the Normans had firmly planted their feet on Irish soil. In the centuries that followed, the Normans conquered and prevailed in Ireland.

Although the Normans were generally considered benevolent overseers, who gradually intermarried with the native population and became "more Irish than the Irish," their coming also signaled a new wave of subjugation for the Irish: The Normans recognized the King of England as their overlord.

800 Years of Domination

The chain of events that led to British domination over Ireland, which would last for more than eight centuries, officially began in 1172 when King Henry II landed at Dublin and claimed power over the Irish isle. By 1204 Dublin Castle was established as the administrative center of English rule, and an Irish Parliament was launched in 1297. In the countryside, the feudal system of government was introduced; it granted land to those who paid homage and dues to the crown. Each major landlord divided his holding among lesser lords, who, in turn, had sub-tenants.

Throughout the Middle Ages, a succession of English kings landed briefly in Dublin to exert their power. The most telling years, 1534 to 1552, came during the reign of Henry VIII, who sought to suppress the Catholic religion of the native Irish while imposing his self-appointed supremacy as head of the Church of England and Ireland. Monasteries were dissolved and churches were destroyed or handed over from Catholic to Protestant clerics.

Dateline

introduced and the "plantation" of Ulster commences.

- 1642 The Confederation of Kilkenny formed.
- 1649 Oliver Cromwell crushes Irish rebellion.
- 1654 Cromwell sends Irish "to hell or Connaught."
- 1690 The Battle of the Boyne is fought.
- 1695 Penal Laws passed and "Wild Geese" flee.
- 1791 Wolfe Tone founds the United Irishmen.
- 1798 English defeat French fleet at Killala Bay.
- 1803 Robert Emmet fails in his rebellion attempt.
- 1829 Daniel O'Connell secures passage of Catholic Emancipation Act.
- 1841 Daniel O'Connell is named Lord Mayor of Dublin.
- 1845 The Great Famine scourges Ireland.
- 1867 The Fenian uprising is put down.
- 1884 Gaelic Athletic Association is formed to preserve native sports.
- 1893 The Gaelic League is founded to restore Irish language.
- 1904 Establishment of Abbey Theatre.
- 1916 Padraic Pearse leads an armed uprising to proclaim the Irish Republic on Easter Monday.

➤

Dateline

- 1919 A Declaration of Independence from Britain is declared and an Irish provisional government is formed with Eamonn De Valera as president of the parliament.
- 1919–1921 The Anglo-Irish War is waged, ending with 26 of Ireland's 32 counties becoming the Irish Free State (Eire), separate from Britain.
- 1926 Irish Free State's first broadcasting network is launched.
- 1927 First general election in Irish Free State.
- 1937 Ireland's 26 counties adopt a new constitution, abandoning membership in British Commonwealth.
- 1938 Douglas Hyde inaugurated as Eire's first president.
- 1939 Dublin is bombed by Germany at start of World War II, but Ireland remains neutral.
- 1949 Eire formally declares itself as the Republic of Ireland.
- 1955 Ireland is admitted into the United Nations.
- 1963 U.S. President John F. Kennedy visits Dublin.
- 1969 Violence breaks out in Northern Ireland.
- 1972 British Embassy is burned in Dublin. ➤

Religious persecution continued under Elizabeth I to the point where many of the local Irish earls and leaders took to rebellion. Hugh O'Neill, the Earl of Tyrone, sought help from Spain but when the Spanish army landed at Kinsale in 1601, the Spanish-Irish alliance was sorely defeated. The Gaelic chieftains were forced to sign the treaty of Mellifont which, although conciliatory in tone, reinforced that English garrisons were here to stay. In 1607, the Irish earls O'Neill, O'Donnell, and 90 other Ulster chiefs sailed into voluntary exile on the continent.

The Plantation Years

This "flight of the earls" enabled the English government to confiscate their lands. Within two years, the Articles of Plantation followed. These laws put a half-million acres of "profitable land" into the hands of English and Scottish settlers who were charged with setting up towns and villages. The so-called plantation gave the northeast corner of the island a largely Protestant population in contrast to the overwhelmingly Catholic population of the rest of Ireland. The agriculture of Derry was put in the hands of a group of London guilds, and hence the name became Londonderry.

Soon unrest among the oppressed Irish began to ferment. In 1642 leading Catholics met in Kilkenny and set up a provisional government, laying plans for a general assembly, the Confederation of Kilkenny. An Irish rebellion followed, but it was ruthlessly crushed by Oliver Cromwell, who arrived in 1649 as commander-in-chief of the English forces. Cromwell took the original Ulster plantation a step further by commanding "all transplantable [Irish] persons" to move west of the Shannon River by May 1, 1654, under pain of death. Their lands were to be given to English soldiers and other adventurers. "To hell or to Connaught" was the cruel theme. Catholic priests were outlawed and the Irish parliament was abolished. Although this plantation was not as successful as the one in Ulster—the English soldiers found that they needed the native Irish to farm the land and many married Irish women—it instilled a new bitterness in the hearts of the Irish along with a renewed determination to reclaim their country.

The Battle of the Boyne & The Wild Geese

A ray of hope in the Irish developed during the late 17th century when James II, a Catholic, ascended the English throne. He appointed an Irishman, the Earl of Tyrconnell, as Lord Lieutenant of Ireland. This spurred many English soldiers to return to England to prevail on the Protestant William of Orange to seek the monarchy. The struggle

Dateline
- 1972 Ireland joins the European Union.
- 1994 IRA declares a complete cease-fire on August 31. Peace talks commence.

for power between the two men culminated on Irish soil at the Battle of the Boyne in July of 1690. William's larger force triumphed over James's, and Ireland was left in the hands of a Protestant ascendancy. In 1695 the Penal Laws were passed: Roman Catholics could no longer serve in the government, armed forces, or legal profession; nor could Catholics teach, send their children to school, bear arms, or buy land. Many Catholic soldiers who were formerly in the Irish army were given the choice of taking an oath of allegiance to William and returning to civilian life, joining the English army, or sailing for France. Most of them chose the latter, and became known as the Wild Geese, fleeing to join the Irish brigades of Europe's armies. Many of the Wild Geese melded quickly into Europe and especially into the enterprises of France and hence the name of Hennessy on a French brandy and wineries with names like Château McCarthy, Dillon, Phelan, Lynch, Barton, and Kirwan. This was the start of the Irish Diaspora that would flare to much greater proportions in the following centuries.

Rebellions and Risings

It's not surprising that the native Irish also began to look for help from abroad. Inspired by both the American and French revolutions, the Irish began to hatch plots of their own. In 1791 a young lawyer in Dublin, Theobold Wolfe Tone, founded a society known as the United Irishmen. He enlisted the help of the French and sailed into Bantry Bay with a French fleet in 1796, but high winds prevented the troops from landing. In 1798, French expeditions also arrived at Killala Bay and at Lough Swilly, but both were defeated and Tone himself was captured and condemned for high treason. Even though Tone's efforts had failed, others took up the cause. In 1803 Robert Emmet planned an insurrection in Dublin, hoping to seize Dublin Castle, but was unsuccessful. At his trial, his speech at the dock became an inspiration for others to continue the quest. Another ill-fated uprising followed in 1867 led by the Irish Republican Brotherhood, known as Fenians.

In the midst of these failed coups, the Kerry-born Daniel O'Connell secured the 1829 passage of the Catholic Emancipation Act, a restoration of civil rights for Catholics. For his efforts, O'Connell became known as the Liberator.

The Great Famine

Ireland's attempts to win freedom came to an abrupt halt in 1845 with the onset of the Great Famine, a failure of the potato crop, the staple diet of the masses of rural Irish people. In less than four years, Ireland's population of eight million fell to five million, 1¹/₂ million died of starvation and the rest emigrated to distant lands. This disaster also underscored the growing contrast between Ulster and the other Irish provinces. Ulster had a thriving linen industry and was in the throes of the Industrial Revolution, while the rest of Ireland barely survived. The results of the famine produced a growing agitation for both land reform and home rule.

Dawn of National Pride and The Easter Rising

Toward the close of the 19th century, national pride reawakened in the Irish; this spirit in some ways fueled the ultimate rebellion. In 1884 the Gaelic Athletic Association was formed to preserve and cultivate native sports. To restore the Irish language, the Gaelic League was founded in 1893. A literary renaissance blossomed, ushering in the 20th century with the writings of William Butler Yeats and the foundation of the Abbey Theatre.

Spurred by a new unity, the Irish sought to end the long chronicle of England's domination. The eight centuries of hardships and heroes, repressions and rebellions, conflicts and compromises finally reached a crescendo in 1916 when the Irish Volunteer movement, under Padraic Pearse, organized an armed rising and declared the Irish Republic. Headquartered in the General Post Office on O'Connell Street in Dublin, the revolt was put down in a week and most of the leaders were executed but the tide had been turned. In 1919 a national parliament (Dail Eireann) was convened at Dublin and proclaimed a Declaration of Independence, forming a provisional Irish government. The American-born revolutionary, Eamonn De Valera, was elected president of the parliament.

A Free State and Republic

Peace, alas, was still elusive. From 1919 to 1921, Ireland launched a final thrust for total independence from England, the Anglo-Irish War. It ended with only a partial victory for the Irish—the signing of a treaty establishing the Free State of Ireland (Eire) made up of 26 of the total of 32 countries, leaving the other six counties to remain part of Britain, and henceforth known as Northern Ireland.

In 1926 the Irish Free State's first broadcasting network was launched and the first general election took place in the following year. In 1937 the 26 counties of Ireland adopted a new constitution abandoning membership in the British Commonwealth. Douglas Hyde was inaugurated as Eire's first president in 1938. The following year, with the outbreak of World War II in Europe, Ireland chose to remain neutral, although German bombs twice were dropped on Dublin.

In 1949, Eire formally declared itself a republic, and in 1955 it was admitted into the United Nations.

Ireland Today

Since coming into its own as a free nation, Ireland has been thrust into the world spotlight on several occasions, including the visits of two U.S. Presidents of Irish ancestry, John F. Kennedy in 1963 and Ronald Reagan in 1984. Pope John Paul II visited the Emerald Isle in 1979, and each year more than four million tourists come to its shores.

Amid the shining moments has been pain. Since 1969, violent events in the North have had a chilling spinoff effect on all of Ireland. With the exception of the burning of the British Embassy in Dublin in 1972, isolated car bomb explosions from 1973 to 1976, and scattered border skirmishes, the Republic of Ireland has rarely been drawn into the conflict, although the Dublin-based Irish government is committed to peaceful negotiations with counterparts in Belfast. At presstime, talks continue, but progress is slow in bringing about a permanent peace.

On a brighter note, in 1972 Ireland joined the European Union (EU), opening up many new avenues of trade and economic partnership. A new Financial Services Centre has recently been launched in Dublin, attracting dozens of international banks and investment firms. Ireland has one of the lowest inflation rates of the EU, and Ireland's economy has the second-highest growth rate among the world's industrialized nations.

One of the most significant events in Irish history that will affect Ireland's future took place on August 31, 1994, when the IRA called for a complete cease-fire. Through its political wing, Sinn Fein, the IRA agreed to join in talks geared toward the negotiation of a permanent peace. As we go to press, the cease-fire is holding and the prospects seem bright.

POLITICS

The island of Ireland is divided into two distinct political parts—the Republic of Ireland and Northern Ireland. The Republic, of which Dublin is the capital, takes up four-fifths of the land and is composed of 26 of the island's 32 counties. The Republic of Ireland is a parliamentary democracy, with a duly elected President, a largely ceremonial role, and a Prime Minister, called the Taoiseach (pronounced *teé-shock*), who is the head of the government. The Irish Parliament has two houses, a House of Representatives, called the Dail (pronounced *dawl*), and a Senate. The remaining six counties, designated as Northern Ireland, are part of the United Kingdom; their capital city is Belfast.

2   The Irish People

No book on Ireland would be complete without a special mention of her friendly people—north, south, east, and west. Time and time again, "friendly people" is given as a top reason for visiting Ireland.

Without a doubt, Ireland's greatest asset is her people, far above the scenery, the castles, the country manors, the pints of Guinness, the rainbows, a winning day at the races, or even a hole-in-one on the golf course. No matter what other experiences you have in Ireland, it is the friendliness of the people that will long linger in your mind.

No matter how hectic their lives or how harsh the elements around them, the Irish can always find time for a gesture of goodwill to friend and stranger alike. Drive the open roads and watch the farmers saving the hay, stacking the turf, or tending their sheep, or the neatly uniformed children walking home in bunches from school. Invariably, they will stop for a moment to wave at a passing car, whether they know the occupants or not. If their hands are busy with shovels or filled with books, at least there will be a nod of the head or a wink of the eye. Even in the big cities, a smile comes much easier to the Irish than a scowl or a stare.

As Ireland is such a small country (the population of the Republic is 3,523,401; 1,589,400 live in the North), it seems like everybody knows everybody else, or that they know of one another. It's a kind of national familiarity that holds true equally within the hubbub of the cities and the tranquillity of the countryside. Quite simply, the Irish people are genuinely interested in one another, and for visitors, this makes for a very congenial atmosphere.

IMPRESSIONS

The great Gaels of Ireland
Are the men that God made mad,
For all their wars are merry,
And all their songs are sad.
—G. K. Chesterton, "The Ballad of the White Horse," 1911

Taking time for a chat is second nature to the Irish. No business transaction, no request for directions, and no visit to a pub can ever be completed without a bit of a chat. This is what Ireland and her people are all about—close encounters of the human kind.

3 Ireland's Famous People

Samuel Beckett (1906–1989) Playwright and novelist, Beckett is one of three Irish winners of the Nobel Prize for Literature (1969). A native of Dublin, he taught French at Trinity College, Dublin. In 1938, he moved to France, where he served as a secretary to James Joyce, became involved in the French Resistance, worked with the Irish Red Cross, and wrote. His most performed play *Waiting for Godot* (1952) remains one of the definitive plays of the Theatre of the Absurd genre, which Beckett popularized. Beckett used a minimalist style—paring words and gesture to the bone.

Brendan Behan (1923–1964) Playwright, travel writer, journalist, IRA activist, and raconteur, Behan is remembered for his boisterous behavior as well as his writings. His best works include his autobiography *Borstal Boy* (1958) and the plays *The Quare Fellow* (1954) and *The Hostage* (1958), first written in Irish. The streets of his native Dublin are the setting for many of his works.

George Berkeley (1685–1753) Born in Kilkenny but educated at Trinity, Dublin, this bishop and philosopher traveled widely throughout Europe and was hailed for his masterpiece, "A Treatise Concerning the Principles of Human Knowledge" (1710). It's said that Berkeley, California, is named in his honor.

Brian Boru (c.940–1014) Born in north Munster, the youngest son of a local chieftain, Boru claimed the kingship of all of Munster. The first Irish ruler to assemble a fleet to extend his territory, he eventually claimed at least the northern half of Ireland. Boru led a triumphant battle at Clontarf in 1014 against the Vikings but lost his life in the process.

Dionysius Boucicault (1820–1890) Well known for his melodramas, this Dublin-born playwright and actor wrote three plays that are still performed today, *The Colleen Bawn* (1859), *Arrah na Pogue* (1864), and *The Shaughraun* (1875). He was a pioneer in the touring-company approach to theater.

Elizabeth Bowen (1899–1973) A novelist and short-story writer, Bowen was born in Dublin but spent a major part of her adult life in England. Her impressions of her early life in Dublin are recorded in *Seven Winters* (1942).

Christy Brown (1932–1981) Novelist and poet, this Dubliner was born with severe physical disabilities, but was educated at home by his mother, who taught him to write with his left foot. His autobiography, *My Left Foot* (1954), was adapted into the Oscar-winning film of the same name. His other works include *Down All the Days* (1970) and *Wild Grow the Lillies* (1976).

Edmund Burke (1729–1797) Parliamentarian, journalist, and philosopher, Burke was born in Dublin, studied at Trinity, but went on to edit a literary-political journal in London. His "Reflections on the Revolution in France" (1790) is said to have spurred Thomas Paine to write "The Rights of Man."

Eamon de Valera (1882–1975) This Irish nationalist politician was born in New York of an Irish mother and Spanish father and raised in Co. Limerick. He joined the Irish Volunteers and participated in the 1916 Easter Rising, for which he received a death sentence, later commuted (because of his American birth). De Valera went on to become the first president of Dail Eireann, the Irish Parliament, and the first Taoiseach (Prime Minister). From 1959–73, he served as President of Ireland.

John Field   (1782–1837) Composer and pianist, Field was born in Dublin but spent most of his life in Europe and Russia. He is credited with creating the piano nocturne, made famous by Chopin. He wrote over 20 nocturnes as well as concertos and other pieces.

Percy French   (1854–1920) Born in Co. Roscommon, French was educated at Trinity to become a civil engineer, but "showed a preference for the banjo." He was appointed to the Board of Works and bicycled throughout the country. His rural travels inspired him to write sentimental and comic songs, from "Phil the Fluter's Ball" to "The Mountains of Mourne." One of his most famous pieces, "Are Ye Right There, Michael?" tells the tale of the West Clare Railway.

Oliver St. John Gogarty   (1878–1957) Poet, wit, surgeon, senator, and athlete, Gogarty served as a model for the Buck Mulligan character in *Ulysses,* written by his friend James Joyce. His own writings include *As I Was Going Down Sackville Street* (1937), *Tumbling in the Hay* (1939), and *I Follow Saint Patrick* (1939). He was born in Dublin but spent most of his life in Connemara.

Oliver Goldsmith   (1728–1774) Born in Co. Longford, he studied medicine at Trinity but left to travel Europe. Goldsmith worked as a physician, schoolmaster, and chemist's assistant before turning to writing. Although he lived most of his life in London, many of his works, such as *The Deserted Village* (1770) and *Sweet Auburn,* were inspired by his early years in the Irish midlands.

Arthur Guinness   (1725–1803) Born in Co. Kildare, Guinness began brewing ale as a young man and within eight years became a master of his trade in Dublin. In 1778, he started to brew porter, a darker beer containing roasted barley. By 1799, his brewery at St. James' Gate had become the largest porter and stout brewery in the world. Ten of his 21 children lived to carry on the business that today produces Ireland's national drink—Guinness.

Seamus Heaney   (b. 1938) Born and educated in Derry, this contemporary poet is often referred to as Ireland's Robert Frost. Heaney's poems about his homeland in the North of Ireland can be found in his collections *North* (1975), *Field Work* (1979), and *Station Island* (1984).

Evie Hone   (1894–1955) One of Dublin's great contemporary artists, Hone specialized in stained-glass work. Her windows are featured in many churches and public buildings in Dublin, including the National and Hugh Lane Galleries, and as far away as Eton College in England.

Nathaniel Hone   (1831–1917) An engineer who turned to art, Hone is one of Ireland's foremost and most prolific painters of the 19th century. Principally a landscape and seascape artist, this Dubliner painted in a muted color range, and his works are considered a precurser to Impressionism. A large collection of his works is found at the National Gallery.

Rex Ingram   (1893–1950) Born Reginald Ingram Hitchcock, he left Dublin for the U.S. in 1911, becoming a film director in Hollywood, with such films to his credit as *The Four Horsemen of the Apocalypse* (1921) and *The Prisoner of Zenda* (1922). Both Rudolph Valentino and Roman Navarro were introduced into the movie world in Ingram-directed works.

James Joyce (1882–1941) Although born in Dublin, he left the city at age 22 and spent most of his life outside the country, yet Joyce used Dublin as the setting for all of his writings, including his masterwork, *Ulysses* (1922). Joyce's other writings include *Portrait of the Artist as a Young Man* (1916), *Dubliners* (1914), and *Finnegans Wake* (1938). Although his imaginative stream-of-consciousness works were banned in Ireland when they were first published, he eventually was recognized as a great 20th-century novelist by his own people.

Sheridan Le Fanu (1814–1873) Novelist and journalist, this Dubliner is considered one of the founding fathers of the Gothic novel. His 16 novels include *The House by the Churchyard (1863), Uncle Silas (1864)* and *In a Glass Darkly (1872).*

Hugh Leonard (b. 1926) Born John Keyes Byrne, this master playwright is one of the most successful of Dublin's contemporary writers. *Da* (1975) dramatizes his relationship with his maddeningly selfless foster father, and *A Life* (1981) reflects his own experience in Dublin.

Constance Markievicz (1868–1927) Born in London but raised at Lissadell, Co. Sligo, she studied in Paris and married Count Casimir Dunin-Markievicz who returned with her to live in Ireland. Inspired by the cause of Irish freedom, she joined the Irish Citizen Army and participated in the 1916 Rising and was president of Cumann na mBan, the women's auxiliary force of the Irish Volunteers. She later became the first woman elected to the Parliament in Westminster but chose to serve instead in the first Irish Dail (Parliament) and became Ireland's first Minister for Labor.

Richard Martin (1754–1834) A member of one of Galway's leading families, or tribes, Martin was a lawyer, magistrate, and member of Parliament who divided his time between Connemara and London. He was a founder of the Society for the Prevention of Cruelty to Animals and was such a staunch advocate of animals that King George IV of England nicknamed him "Humanity Dick."

Brian Merriman (c.1747–1805) Born in west Co. Clare, he became a teacher and was also an accomplished fiddler. Merriman is best remembered for a single poem of 1,206 lines written in the Irish language, "The Midnight Court."

Thomas Moore (1779–1852) Poet and songwriter of the Romantic period, this Dubliner wrote many airs and poems that have become national favorites, such as "Believe Me If All Those Endearing Young Charms" (1807) and "The Last Rose of Summer." He also wrote biographies, including *Life of Byron* (1824).

Sean O'Casey (1880–1964) Born into poverty as John Casey in Dublin, this Abbey Theatre playwright based three of his greatest works on his early life in Dublin tenements—*The Shadow of a Gunman* (1923), *Juno and the Paycock* (1924), and *The Plough and the Stars* (1926).

Turlough O'Carolan (1670–1738) Born in Co. Meath and raised in Co. Roscommon, O'Carolan was blinded at the age of 18 and took up the harp as a profession. He became one of Ireland's foremost composers and music makers, performing at the great houses of Ireland.

Grace O'Malley (c.1530–1603) Born of a seafaring family in Co. Mayo and known by the Irish equivalent of her name, Grainne, she gained fame as a pirate on the Irish seas.

Saint Patrick (c.390–416) Raised in Britain, this saint was kidnapped at 16 by raiders who sold him into slavery in Ireland. After six years he escaped to Gaul but later returned to Ireland as a bishop. Based at Armagh, he traveled widely and converted many local chieftains and their people to Christianity. His writings include "Confession" and "Letter to Coroticus." He is credited with banishing snakes from Ireland and using the three-leafed shamrock to teach the doctrine of the Trinity.

Patrick Pearse   (1879–1916) Trained as a lawyer in Dublin, Pearse was an educator and poet, who worked in the cause of Irish freedom. As Commander-in-Chief of the Irish Republican Brotherhood and Volunteers, he led the 1916 Easter Rising and was shot after its suppression. His poems such as "The Rebel" and "The Mother" found together in *Collected Works* (1917) have brought him further acclaim in recent years.

Augusta Persse/Lady Gregory   (1852–1932) Born in Co. Galway, she married Sir William Gregory of Coole Park. Influenced by a childhood familiarity with Irish folklore, she developed an interest in literature and a friendship with W. B. Yeats; together, they founded the Abbey Theatre. She wrote over 30 plays including *Spreading the News* (1904) and *Goal Gate* (1906) and made Coole Park the headquarters of the Irish Literary Revival.

George Bernard Shaw   (1856–1950) Author of *Man and Superman (1903), Major Barbara (1905), Pygmalion (1912), Candida (1903),* and *St. Joan (1923),* Shaw won the Nobel Prize for Literature in 1926. Although he left school at age 15, Shaw spent a great deal of time at the National Gallery in Dublin and later credited the institution with providing the best part of his early education (and he bequeathed one-third of his royalties to the gallery). His birthplace, at 33 Synge St., is a museum in his honor.

Richard Brinsley Sheridan   (1751–1816) This Dubliner was a member of Parliament but is best remembered for his satirical comedies of manners such as *The Rivals* (1775) and *School for Scandal* (1777) written for the stage.

Bram Stoker   (1847–1912) Born in Dublin and educated at Trinity, he worked first as a civil servant but his heart was always in the theater. Eventually Stoker became a drama critic and then began to write novels, many based on his experiences in the West of Ireland. His most famous work, *Dracula* (1897), was based on research he had done on Transylvania.

Jonathan Swift   (1667–1745) This brilliant poet and satirist is best remembered for *Gulliver's Travels* (1726) and *A Modest Proposal* (1729). Swift's proud and sensitive temperment made him intolerant of human vice and stupidity. From 1713 to 1745, he served as Dean of St. Patrick's Cathedral, where his self-written epitaph is inscribed.

John Millington Synge   (1871–1909) Noted Abbey Theatre playwright and one of the founders of the Irish Literary Revival, Synge was born in Dublin but is best remembered for plays that reflect rural life in Ireland, such as *The Shadow of the Glen* (1903), *Riders to the Sea* (1904), and *Playboy of the Western World* (1907).

Oscar Wilde   (1854–1900) The son of a well-known Irish surgeon and an eccentric poetess, Wilde had a keen wit and was a brilliant conversationalist. As a playwright, he is best remembered for *The Importance of Being Earnest* (1895).

William Butler Yeats   (1865–1939) Poet and dramatist, Yeats was also a founding member of the Abbey Theatre. His poems and plays, which deal with mystic and Celtic legendary themes, won him a Nobel Prize for Literature in 1923. Yeats served in the Irish Senate but rejected a knighthood in 1915. He was born in Dublin and summered in the West, particularly in Sligo, where he is buried.

4 Language & Religion

LANGUAGE

Ireland has two official languages, Gaelic (or Irish, as it's commonly known) and English. Just about everyone speaks English in everyday life, but Irish is still very much in evidence in public places. Irish is still taught in schools and is required for some government positions. You'll hear Irish used on national radio and television at certain times of the day. Newspapers feature articles written in Irish, but most communication is in English. Street signs in large cities like Dublin are printed in English, although some signs use both English and Irish. Some older signs use only Irish, but these are usually accompanied close by with an English sign. (In the North, signage is in English only.)

Irish is a Celtic language, related to Scottish Gaelic, Welsh Breton, and ancient Gaulish. Ogham, a script dating from the 5th and 6th centuries, is the earliest known written form of Irish. Ogham can still be seen on ancient stones through the countryside.

Well into the 17th century, Ireland was an Irish-speaking nation, but with the increasing domination by the English, the native Irish people learned English to improve their socio-economic positions. The survival of Irish is a major national priority, especially since it's instrinsically linked to the music and folklore of the land. Certain rural parts of Ireland are classified as Gaeltacht regions, where Irish is the everyday language. These Gaeltacht areas are located primarily in counties Donegal, Mayo, Galway, Kerry, and Cork, with smaller pockets in Meath and Waterford. The Gaeltacht population numbers about 50,000, about half of whom are farmers; the remainder earns their living from fishing or from native crafts like weaving.

There's a music to the English language when Irish people speak it, conveyed by their special lilting accent. As you travel around the country, you'll hear a variety of accents. In Cork, the people have a distinctive sing-song pattern. It's often said that the best enunciated English in the world is heard in Dublin.

RELIGION

Christianity, which has shaped the Irish national psyche over the centuries, arrived in the fifth century A.D. with the indefatigable St. Patrick, who is said to have traveled the length and breadth of the country—from Down to Dublin, from Clew Bay to Cashel, from the Hills of Tara to Slane, and all the towns in between.

It was at Tara that Patrick plucked a three-leaf clover, or shamrock, from the grass to illustrate the doctrine of the Trinity. The spellbinding saint not only converted the High King Laoire but made such an impression on the assembled crowd that the shamrock has been blessed to the Irish ever since.

No sooner had the Irish embraced Christianity then they excelled in spreading the word. Monasteries sprang up in such far-flung locations as Glendalough in County Wicklow and Clonmacnois in County Offaly; beautifully illuminated manuscripts of the Bible, Ireland's first written documents, were produced here. Princes, nobles, and prelates from England and other nations flocked to these centers of learning for training. Through the years 500 to 1000 as Ireland was drawing scholars to its shores, missionaries embarked to convert and educate people all over Europe. To this day, the names of Irish monks are associated with religious sites throughout the continent, including St. Virgil/Feargal (Salzburg), St. Colman (Melk), St. Killian (Wurzburg),

St. Martin (Tours), and St. Columbanus (Bobbio). It's no wonder that Ireland earned the title "Isle of Saints and Scholars."

Today the country is still overwhelmingly Christian. In the Republic of Ireland, 90% of the people identify themselves as Roman Catholic and about 5% as Protestant. The remainder are a diverse mixture of everything from Amish and Jews to Muslims and Hare Krishnas. The population of Northern Ireland is approximately 55% Protestant and 43% Catholic, and 2% other religions.

The city of Armagh in the North is considered the spiritual capital of Ireland since it is the seat of both the Catholic and Anglican archbishops. St. Patrick is said to be buried in the North, at Down Cathedral in Downpatrick.

5 Art, Architecture & Crafts

ART

Three-dimensional, geometric figures etched onto prehistoric granite slabs and burial tombs in the Irish countryside are the earliest specimens of Irish art. The sixth century saw delicate enamel work and manuscript illumination produced at monasteries. The Tara Brooch, the Ardagh Chalice, and the Cross of Cong are just three of Ireland's early artistic gems ensconced at the National Museum in Dublin.

Without question, *The Book of Kells*, on view at Trinity College in Dublin, is Ireland's greatest treasure. Dating back to the late eighth or early ninth century, *The Book of Kells* is an elaborate version of the four Gospels of the Bible. It was produced at the monastery of Kells in County Meath, which was famous for its scholarship. Made of vellum, the pages of this book are prized for their hand-lettering and colorful illustration. Its distinctively Irish script is bold and well rounded, semi-uncial in shape. The book is ornamented with fanciful abstract designs and charming little animals, all intertwined with the foliage of plants and tendrils of vines. This thousand-year-old manuscript has inspired much of Irish art and craftsmanship since its creation.

The decorative arts flourished in Ireland in the 17th and 18th centuries. Beautiful silverware, plasterwork, cut glass, hand-carved furniture, and tapestries were created and filled the great Georgian and Palladian-style homes, built for the gentry who settled in Ireland from England.

The lush Irish countryside, with its varied colors and ever-changing skies, lends itself wonderfully to landscape painting. Among Ireland's great artists of this genre were James Arthur O'Connor and Paul Henry, the latter of whom studied at Whistler's studio in Paris before settling down to paint in Connemara.

Contemporary artists Brian Bourke and Camille Souter take a post-modern approach to landscapes. Patrick Hickey and Pauline Bewick are acclaimed for their distinctive graphic arts. North and South, Ireland boasts more than a hundred art galleries. In Dublin, no less than fifty galleries are found, and it seems more spring up each day. The relatively new Irish Museum of Modern Art (IMMA) also showcases contemporary creativity.

IMPRESSIONS

This [Ireland] has never been a rich or powerful country, and, yet, since earliest times, its influence on the world has been rich and powerful . . . and no larger nation has ever provided the world with more literary or artistic geniuses.
—John F. Kennedy, Addressing the Irish Parliament June 1963

ARCHITECTURE

Those stone walls that remain at least in part around towns and cities can be credited to the Normans, who also built great churches and cathedrals, but are best remembered for their castles. Many Norman castles are still occupied today, while others sit moss-covered in ruins but with their rectangular keeps, lichened towers, and time-worn turrets still leaving their mark on the Irish countryside.

The British also left an architectural legacy—from Dublin's, Limerick's and Armagh's Georgian avenues, squares, and public buildings to the countryside's sprawling "big houses." Built by the Anglo-Irish aristocracy and absentee landlords, these manor homes date from the 17th and 18th centuries and reflect a spirit of "spare no expense." More than forty of these great houses, originally occupied by the rich and powerful, are now open to the public as museums. Others have been converted into hotels.

Also dotting the rural landscape are simple stone-constructed, white-washed, thatched-roof cottages, the homes of farming people. Some of these cottages have been replaced by modern bungalows and two-story stucco homes.

Modern Irish architecture tends toward glass-and-concrete construction, but many newer buildings are designed to harmoniously blend in alongside Georgian, Edwardian, and Victorian landmarks.

CRAFTS

One of the most famous of Irish crafts is the thick bainin sweater, which was first hand-knit on the Aran Islands to protect the local fishermen against the elements. These oatmeal-colored garments are still knit in cottages on the islands and in homes all over the west of Ireland.

With all the sheep that graze on the Irish hillsides, it's not surprising that wool is a source for another major craft—handweaving. Weaving is done in homes and local factories, the latter of which are usually open to visitors, particularly in areas like Donegal and Connemara. Ireland's oldest hand-weaving mill, dating back to 1723, is found in a cluster of stone buildings at Avoca in Co. Wicklow. With mauve, heather, and teal tones, the Avoca tweeds reflect the colors of the local landscape; these tweeds are fashioned into capes, coats, ponchos, suits, jackets, bedspreads, and rugs.

Waterford is one of Ireland's most famous craft trademarks. A tour of the Waterford Crystal Factory seems almost impossible to resist for anyone coming within striking distance of Ireland's southeast coast. Every step of production can be viewed—from glass-blowing and shaping to hand-cutting and engraving to polishing and packaging. More than 3,000 visitors pass through the factory each workday. Other glass-making centers that welcome the public are located in Dublin, Tipperary, Galway, Cavan, Sligo, Killarney, Kinsale, Wexford, Cork, Belfast, and Tyrone.

Pottery- and porcelain-making is done in all parts of the Emerald Isle. Some of the leading names include Royal Tara China (Galway), Donegal Parian China (Ballyshannon), and the most famous of all Belleek (Fermanagh).

Basketry, hearldry, batik, patchwork, wood carving, doll making, enamel painting, lace making, pewter casting, candle making, gold and silver jewelry design, printmaking, stained glass, and beaten copper art are more of Irish crafts. Shopping on the Emerald Isle for these crafts often provides an opportunity to talk with the artisans and watch them practice their trades.

6   Literature, Music & Folklore

LITERATURE

Just as the Irish are known for their gift of gab, they're equally talented at putting pen to paper. G. K. Chesterton said on a visit more than seventy years ago, that the city of Dublin was a "paradise of poets."

From the 8th to 17th centuries, Ireland's literature was written, of course, in the Irish language. Many of the short poems had nature themes and described the sights and sounds of the land, sea, and sky. Longer poems, often of epic proportions, recounted the deeds of Ireland's high kings. Irish prose pieces varied from great historical annals to the sagas of early Irish heroes.

Ireland's most notable impact on the literary world has come during the last three-hundred years in Anglo-Irish literature, writings by Irish men and women in English. Many of these writers spent most of their adult life living and writing in England and other parts of Europe. Living abroad gave these writers access to major publishing houses and theaters and more artistic freedom.

Ahead of their times and mores, Irish writers were perhaps too critical of established systems. Embraced as genuises abroad, some Irish writers were initially censored or banned at home in Ireland. With time, all of these literary exiles eventually earned respect and approval in their homeland.

Individually and collectively, these writers continue to have a strong impact. Critics have often wondered aloud how a small island could generate such an abundance of significant writers: Johnathan Swift, the master of satire; Oscar Wilde, the incomparable wit; Ireland's three Noble Prize–winners for literature, George Bernard Shaw, William Bulter Yeats, and Samuel Beckett; as well as Oliver Goldsmith; Richard Brinsley Sheridan; Thomas Moore; James Stephens; George Russell; George Moore; Oliver St. John Gogarty; and James Joyce, the maverick novelist who forged the stream-of-conscious style of writing.

Home to the Abbey, the Gate, and dozens of other theatres, Dublin is known for its compelling drama, both classical and experimental. John Millington Synge, Sean O'Casey, Brendan Behan, Brian Friel, John B. Keane, and Hugh Leonard are a few of Ireland's noted playwrights.

Luckily, contemporary Irish writers do not have to go abroad for recognition. New ideas are welcomed, controversy is relished, and the writer is revered. An about-face migration has occurred with writers from the United States and other countries coming to Ireland to live and write. At various times, tax incentives have even been extended by the Irish government to encourage more writers to be in residence.

MUSIC

Music is second nature to the Irish. Wherever they gather—be it hearthside, in a pub, or in the middle of Dublin's Grafton Street—music invariably fills the air and is as common as conversation. As a people often conquered and oppressed, the Irish have always found music to be a source of joy and self-expression.

It may come as a shock to some folks, but "Mother Macree" and "When Irish Eyes Are Smiling" are not really examples of Irish music. Such songs can best be attributed to Irish-American origins. When you come to Ireland, you'll find an entirely different repertoire, ranging from patriotic melodies to spirited foot-tapping tunes.

As in most of Europe, music in Ireland can trace its beginnings back to the bards of medieval times, who traveled the countryside singing songs, usually to the accompaniment of a harp. So beloved was such music that the harp was adopted as part of the Irish coat of arms in the 17th century and remains the chief symbol of the country to this day.

Although the songs of the bards were seldom written down, the works of one such poet, harpist, and composer, Turlough O'Carolan, have survived and provide the basis for many modern-day airs.

First used almost 300 years ago, the uilleann pipe (pronounced *ill-un*) is often referred to as the Irish organ. This popular form of bagpipe is pumped with the elbow and produces a softer, more resonant sound that its Scottish counterpart. Other instruments used to produce the distinctive sounds of Irish music are the concertina (a smaller version of the accordian); fiddle; flute; tin whistle; and the bodhran (pronounced *bowrawn*), a hand-held drum that can be best described as a goat-skin tambourine. The Irish have also been known to improvise with anything from a washboard to a set of spoons. In recent years, groups like the Chieftans from Dublin and individual performers such as James Galway from Belfast and Phil Coulter from Derry have done much to popularize authentic Irish music throughout the world.

At any time, one of the best places to hear good Irish music is, of course, a pub. No matter when you visit, scheduled and spontaneous music sessions are on tap. Irish music is also featured at festivals, hotel cabarets, summer shows, and at venues dedicated to traditional entertainment such as the National Folk Theatre of Ireland in Tralee, An Taibhdhearc in Galway, the Bru Boru Center at Cashel, Culturlann na hEireann near Dublin, Cois na hAbhna in Ennis, and the Shannon Traditional Evening at the Bunratty Folk Park.

On the modern music scene, the Irish have also made a considerable contribution. The members of U2, concert organizer Bob Geldof, Sinead O'Connor, and Mary Black call Dublin home; Van Morrison lives in Belfast. The Cranberries from Limerick are making their mark on record charts, as are the Sawdoctors from Galway.

FOLKLORE

The origin of much of Ireland's folklore and mythology can be traced back to the coming of the Celts from continental Europe in 350 B.C. The natives wholeheartedly embraced Celtic culture, from the Gaelic language to epic-style art, music, and folklore. This age of horse-drawn chariots, provincial high kings, local clans, and larger-than-life heroes spawned most of the well-known facets of Irish superstition, mythology, and legend. Over the centuries, much of this lore has been passed by word of mouth from one generation to the next. Consequently, storytelling has always been respected as an art and was once a genuine profession. In the days before books and newspapers, a man traveling from area to area bringing news and telling tales was called a seanachie (pronounced *shan-ah-key*). He often had more than 400 stories in his repertoire. (There are still some seanachies in Ireland today; a few appear in traditional Irish cabarets and at local festivals.)

IMPRESSIONS

 No harp hath the sound so long and so melting as the Irish harp.
—Francis Bacon

Favorite tales spun by a seanachie include the heroics of Cuchulainn, the legendary hurler and strong man; the saga of the Children of Lir, four youngsters whose stepmother changed them into white swans; the desirable and elusive place called Tir na nOg, the land of youth; and the appearances of the Banshee, a woman who wails when death is near.

By far the most popular folk tradition focuses on the early inhabitants of Ireland, known variously as fairies, little people, or leprechauns. Legend has it that leprechauns are no more than 24 inches tall, wear bright green tunics, and live in round fairy forts hidden deep in the woods. These little people are skilled shoemakers by day. Late in the evening, when it is fully dark, they can sometimes be seen, dancing to the music of the wind as it sings through the trees.

It's said that each leprechaun possesses a crock of gold. If you're lucky enough to see one of these little people, you may be able to win his treasure by fixing a steely stare upon him. If you blink, however, he'll disappear and with him his pot of gold.

7 Sports & Recreation

Sports, in all its forms, are a year-round obsession for the Irish. For spectators, horses tear around the tracks for a photo finish more than 300 days a year. Greyhounds race, too. Soccer, rugby, polo, and other international games are played. But what sets the Irish sporting scene apart from other countries are its two native traditional games—hurling and Gaelic football.

Hurling, one of the world's fastest field sports, is played by two teams of 15, using wooden sticks and a small leather ball. Gaelic football, also played by two teams of 15, is a field game similar to rugby or soccer except that the ball is round and can be played with the hands.

With huge followings in all of Ireland's 32 counties, these all-amateur sports are played every weekend throughout the summer, culminating in September at Dublin's Croke Park with the All-Ireland Finals, an Irish version of the "Super Bowl."

The Irish sporting scene also invites participation by visitors. Known for its 40 shades of green, the Emerald Isle has greens in the form of more than 250 golf courses, all of which are open to the public. More than a dozen new 18-hole championship courses have opened in recent years, and plans call for 25 more by 1996.

Nothing beats a day's fishing to get you totally in tune with the gentle ebb and flow of the Irish lifestyle. To cast a rod on an Irish river is to enter a world set apart, where you can relax and forget pressures. Ireland offers excellent fishing for salmon, brown trout, and other types of fish.

With its 6 national parks, 12 forest parks, hundreds of miles of open countryside, and close to 2,000 miles of coastline, Ireland also provides many nature trails, sign-posted routes, and beachside paths—ideal for walking, bicycling, and other sports.

8 Food & Drink

FOOD

In the last 25 years, Irish cuisine has undergone a healthy metamorphosis. Previously—although it was recognized as one of the world's best-fed nations—Ireland wallowed in soggy culinary reputation for over-cooked meats, water-logged vegetables, piles of potatoes, and cream-on-cream desserts. But healthful preparation and appealing presentation of fresh natural ingredients are now the norm.

The transformation of Irish cuisine did not come about by chance. The basic assets had always been there—beef and lamb nurtured on Irish pastures, an abundance of freshwater fish and ocean seafood, a bounty of agrarian produce, and dairy goods straight from the local creamery—but it was travel that inspired Irish chefs. They learned the arts of French *nouvelle cuisine* and California *au courant*. At the same time, visitors came to Ireland in greater numbers and requested crisper vegetables and more seafood on the menus. In kitchens from Dublin to Donegal, the "new Irish cuisine" reigns. And to prove it, Irish chefs now bring home dozens of gold medals from the International Food Olympics.

MEALS & DINING CUSTOMS   Mealtimes in Ireland are similar to those in the United States, with most hotels and restaurants offering breakfast from 6 or 7am to around 10am; lunch from noon to 2 or 3pm; and dinner from 6 or 7pm to 10 or 11pm.

Breakfast in Ireland can be continental (juice, rolls or toast, coffee or tea) or "full Irish" (juice, fruits, yogurt, cereal, eggs, bacon, sausage, brown bread, toast, or scones, coffee or tea, and sometimes fish). If you choose the full breakfast, you'll probably be content with a snack for lunch.

In many rural parts of Ireland, the agrarian tradition of a big dinner at mid-day still holds, with a light supper, or high tea, at night. In the cities, lunch can be a light or full meal, and the evening meal is usually the main family dinner of the day. The upper-priced restaurants prefer to sell set lunches, usually three or four courses, but most other places offer snacks, sandwiches, salads, or a variety of hot and cold entrees.

Most restaurants have set three- or four-course dinner menus, known locally as table d'hôte, and an à la carte menu for picking and choosing. The set menus usually offer the best value, unless, of course, you want to skip an appetizer and dessert and just have a salad/soup and main course.

To all of this, add morning coffee, usually around 11am, and afternoon tea around 3 or 4pm. The latter can be as simple as a cup of tea on the run, or as formal as a sit-down gathering at a fine hotel with a brewed pot of tea, finger sandwiches, pastries, and other sweets arrayed on a silver tray and accompanied by piano or harp music. After a proper afternoon tea, some visitors have been known to skip dinner!

THE CUISINE   The star of most menus is seafood, formerly considered penitential fare. In particular, it's hard to equal wild Irish salmon, caught daily from local rivers. Served steamed or broiled with a wedge of lemon, it's pink, delicate, and sweet.

As an appetizer or starter (as the Irish say), salmon is slowly oak-smoked and thinly sliced with capers and lemon. Most visitors become so addicted to it that they take home at least a side of smoked salmon, vacuum-packaged for travel.

One of Ireland's most popular seafoods is the Dublin Bay prawn, a more tender version of a shrimp but a cousin to the Norway lobster in flavor. Plump and succulent, prawns are equally tempting served either hot with melted butter or cold with a light cocktail sauce.

And there's Galway Bay oysters, Kinsale and Wexford mussels, Kerry scallops, Dingle Bay lobster, and Donegal crab.

Exported to all parts of the world, Irish beef has always been a favorite with the natives as well as visitors. Today you'll not only get your choice of steaks, but you can also order filet of beef en croûte, stir-fry beef, beef stuffed with oysters, beef flambéed in Irish whiskey or sautéed in Guinness.

Those sheep that graze on the Irish hillsides produce a lot more than wool. Their offspring are the source of the lean racks and legs of lamb that are the pride of Irish chefs.

From the famous Limerick ham to thick country bacon or zesty homemade sausages, pork is served in hefty portions as part of the standard Irish breakfast.

Traditional roast chicken will usually be the tasty free-range variety, accompanied by lean Irish bacon or ham, and a herby bread stuffing. Breast of chicken wrapped around local mushrooms or smoked salmon mousse are also popular choices.

One of Ireland's most humble foods is also one of its greatest culinary treasures—brown bread. Made of stone-ground whole meal flour, buttermilk, and other "secret" ingredients, Irish brown bread is served on the tables of every restaurant in the country. Brown bread, be it light or dark, firm or crumbly, sweet or nutty, is always delicious—especially when the crust is crispy. For sheer ambrosia, add a little rich creamery butter or homemade raspberry jam.

Some traditional dishes adapted to the new lighter cuisine might include boxty (a potato pancake filled with meats, vegetables, or fish); crubeens (pig's feet); colcannon (potatoes mashed with scallions and cabbage); coddle (boiled bacon, sausages, onions, and potatoes); boiled bacon and cabbage (a precurser to the Irish-American St. Patrick's Day favorite, corned beef and cabbage); and, above all, the classic Irish lamb stew.

Irish desserts (sometimes called sweets) range from cakes (often called *gateaux*), pies, and American-style cheesecakes, to a seasonal array of fruit salads or simple dishes of fresh strawberries. With a little effort, you can still find some of the rich traditional dishes such as trifle, a fruit salad combined with custard and sherry-soaked cake, and then topped with rich cream; and plum pudding, a whiskey-based soft fruitcake usually reserved for Christmas and special occasions. Other native desserts include barm brack, a light and yeasty fruitcake, and raisin-filled soda cake.

Irish farmhouse cheeses offer a piquant alternative to rich and sweet confections. More than 60 cheeses are now produced throughout the land, and many restaurants pride themselves on the quantity and quality of their all-domestic cheeseboards.

DRINK

The story goes that Irish monks concocted the first brew of whiskey for medicinal purposes in the sixth century. These same inventive monks carried the recipe on a mission to Scotland. They called their brew *uisce beathe* (pronounced *ish-ka ba-ha*) which in Irish means "the water of life"; shortly afterward, it was Anglicized to whiskey. In 1608, a license to distill alcohol was granted to Old Bushmills; it remains the world's oldest distillery still in operation.

Irish whiskey differs from Scotch or English whisky in the method of distillation. While the Scottish/English mode requires the use of smoke-dried malted barley, the Irish use a combination of local malt and unmalted barley, which is allowed to dry naturally without the aid of heat and smoke. The result gives Irish whiskey a clear, smooth, and smokeless taste. Among the leading brands of Irish whiskey are the afore-mentioned Bushmills, John Jameson, Powers, Paddy, Tullamore Dew, Murphy, and Dunphy.

The Irish like to drink their whiskey "neat," which means without ice, water, or other mixers. Whiskey is also the sine qua non for Irish coffee, an after-dinner drink, made by adding some to a goblet of hot coffee mixed with sugar, and then topping it off with a dollop of fresh cream.

In recent years, Irish Coffee has found a bit of competition in sweet Irish whiskey–based drinks like Bailey's Irish Cream and Irish Mist. These after-dinner libations have, in turn, inspired desserts like Irish Mist soufflé and Bailey's Irish ice cream.

Guinness stout, a black yeasty ale with a foamy head, is the most widely consumed national drink. Brewed in Dublin, it's preferred on draft by the Irish and served in a large tumbler called a pint. Sipping a pint of Guinness is the favorite pastime in the pubs. First brewed by Arthur Guinness in 1759, it's considered to be a healthful drink, and an advertising slogan boldly proclaims "Guinness is good for you." The Guinness Company also produces a light lager beer called Harp and a non-alcoholic beer known as Kaliber. Other Irish beers include Smithwicks, brewed in Kilkenny, and Beamish and Murphys, produced in Cork.

Tap water in Ireland is both pure and plentiful. Sparkling Irish bottled waters, such as Ballygowan, Glenpatrick, and Tipperary, are readily available, rivaling Perrier and other international brands. Not surprisingly, Irish tea, strong and flavorful, is a drink that has no equal in the Emerald Isle. Barry's Tea is produced in Cork. For coffee drinkers, Bewley's is the name to remember.

9 Recommended Books & Periodicals

BOOKS

The Arts and Architecture

Arnold, Bruce, *A Concise History of Irish Art* (New York and Toronto: Oxford University Press, 1977).

Costello, Peter, *Dublin Churches* (Dublin: Gill and MacMillan, 1989).

deBreffny, Brian, and Ffolliott, Rosemary, *The Houses of Ireland* (London: Thames & Hudson, 1984).

Guinness, Desmond, *Georgian Dublin* (London: Batsford, 1979); and *Portrait of Dublin* (London: Batsford, 1967).

Harbison, Peter, *Guide to the National Monuments of Ireland* (Dublin: Gill & MacMillan, 1975).

Shaw-Smith, David, *Ireland's Traditional Crafts* (New York and London: Thames & Hudson, 1984).

Biography/The Irish People

Byrne, Matthew, *Dublin and Her People* (Dublin: Eason & Son, 1987).

Connery, Donald S., *The Irish* (New York: Simon & Schuster, 1970).

Finlay, Fergus, *Mary Robinson—President with a Purpose* (Dublin: O'Brien Press, 1992).

Joyce, James, *The Dubliners* (London: Grant Richards, 1914).

Llywelyn, Morgan, *Grania, the She-King of the Irish Seas* (New York: Crown, 1986).

McDyer, Fr. James, *An Autobiography* (Dingle: Brandon Press, 1982).

Mullally, Frederick, *Silver Salver: the Story of the Guinness Family* (London: Granada, 1981).

O'Donovan, Donal, *Dreamers of Dreams: Portraits of the Irish in America* (Bray, Co. Wicklow: Kilbride Books, 1984).

Shannon, Elizabeth, *Up in the Park* (New York: Atheneum, 1983).

Shannon, William F., *The American Irish* (New York: MacMillan, 1966).

Genealogy

DeBreffny, Brian, *Irish Family Names* (Dublin and New York: Gill & MacMillan, 1982).

MacLysaght, Edward, *The Surnames of Ireland* (Dublin: Irish Academic Press, 1980).

Pine, L. G., *The Genealogist's Encyclopedia* (New York: Collier, 1969).

History

Beckett, J. C., *The Making of Modern Ireland* (London and Boston: Faber and Faber Ltd., 1981).

Collins, James, *Life in Old Dublin* (Cork: Tower Books, 1978).

Conlin, Stephen, *Historic Dublin: From Walled Town to Georgian Capital* (Dublin: O'Brien Press, 1986).

Coogan, Beatrice, *The Big Wind* (Garden City, NY: Doubleday, 1969).

Foster, R. F., *Modern Ireland 1600–1972* (London and New York: Penguin, 1988).

Gilbert, John T., *History of the City of Dublin* (Dublin: Gill & MacMillan, 1978).

Moody, T. W., and Martin, F. X., *The Course of Irish History* (Cork: Mercier, 1987).

O'Connor, Ulick, *The Troubles: Ireland 1912–1922* (Indianapolis and New York: Bobbs Merrill, 1975).

Severin, Tim, *The Brendan Voyage* (New York: McGraw-Hill, 1978).

Literature and Music

Hogan, Robert, *Dictionary of Irish Literature* (Dublin: Gill & MacMillan, 1979); and *The Book of Kells: Reproductions from the Manuscript* (London: Thames & Hudson, 1974).

Joyce, James, *Ulysses* (Paris: Shakespeare & Co, 1922).

Kavanagh, Peter, *Irish Mythology: A Dictionary* (Newbridge, Co. Kildare: Goldsmith Press, 1988).

Kenny, Herbert A., *Literary Dublin: A History* (New York: Taplinger, Dublin: Gill & MacMillan, 1974 and 1991).

Kinsella, Thomas, *The New Oxford Book of Irish Verse* (Oxford, England and New York: Oxford University Press, 1986).

Norris, David, *Joyce's Dublin* (Dublin: Eason & Son, 1982).

O'Canainn, Thomas, *Traditional Music in Ireland* (Cork: Ossian Publications, 1993).

O'Faolain, Sean, *The Collected Stories* (Boston & Toronto: Little, Brown & Co., 1983).

Preston, Patricia Tunison, *Reflections of Ireland* (New York: Smithmark 1991, and Dublin: Eason & Son, 1992).

Yeats, W. B., *Selected Poetry* (London: Pan Books, 1990).

PERIODICALS

For the most up-to-date news on Ireland, consider a subscription to these two periodicals, both published in Dublin:

- *Inside Ireland* is a quarterly newsletter packed with the latest details on life in Dublin and happenings all over Ireland. Now in its 18th year, this publication also provides an information service, genealogical advice, regular updates on buying property and/or retiring in Ireland, shopping news, and coupons that entitle subscribers to discounts at hotels and restaurants. It's the next best thing to having your own correspondent in Dublin, for just $40 a year or $3 for a sample copy. Contact *Inside Ireland,* Rookwood, Stocking Lane, Ballyboden, Dublin 16, Ireland (☎ **01/493-1906**).

- *Ireland of the Welcomes* is a full-color bi-monthly magazine, published by the Irish Tourist Board, but it's not just another tourism promotion publication. It is a finely written, well-researched periodical that spotlights ongoing events and celebrations, new attractions, unique driving routes, legends and lore, flora and fauna, traditions and the arts, noteworthy trends, and interesting personalities. If you're planning a trip, it offers regular sections on where to stay and shopping. $21 a year. Contact *Ireland of the Welcomes,* P.O. Box 84, Limerick, Ireland.

Planning a Trip
to Ireland

2

IT IS OFTEN SAID THAT THE NEXT BEST THING TO BEING IN IRELAND IS PLANNING TO be there. To do your planning, there are some fundamental questions that you need answered: Where to get more information? When to go? How to get there? How to make the best arrangements? What to pack and prepare? What will the weather be like?

This chapter is designed to answer those questions—and more. The pages that follow will guide you in making arrangements to meet your particular needs, whether you are traveling on vacation or business, or if you have the special interests of a senior citizen, student, or disabled person.

1   Information, Entry Requirements & Money

SOURCES OF INFORMATION

To get your planning off to a sound start, contact the following offices of the Irish Tourist Board and/or the Northern Ireland Tourist Board.

In the U.S.A.

- **Irish Tourist Board,** 345 Park Avenue, New York, NY 10154 (☎ **212/418-0800** or toll free **800/223-6470** in U.S.; fax 212/371-9052).
- **Northern Ireland Tourist Board,** 551 Fifth Ave., Ste. 701, New York, NY 10176 (☎ **212/922-0101** or toll free **800/326-0036** in U.S.; fax 212/922-0099).

In Canada

- **Irish Tourist Board,** 160 Bloor St. E., Ste. 1150, Toronto, Ontario M4W 1B9 (☎ **416/929-2777;** fax 416/929-6783).
- **Northern Ireland Tourist Board,** 111 Avenue Rd., Ste. 450, Toronto, Ontario M5R 3J8 (☎ **416/925-6368;** fax 416/961-2175).

In the U.K.

- **Irish Tourist Board/Bord Failte,** 150 New Bond St., London W1Y OAQ (☎ **071/493-3201;** fax 071/493-9065).
- **Northern Ireland Tourist Board/All Ireland Desk,** British Travel Centre, 12 Regent St., Picadilly Circus, London SW1 4PQ (☎ **071/824-8000**).

In Australia

- **Irish Tourist Board,** 36 Carrington St., 5th level, Sydney, NSW 2000 (☎ **02/299-6177;** fax 02/299-6323).

In Ireland

- **Irish Tourist Board/Bord Failte,** Baggot Street Bridge, Dublin 2 (☎ **01/676-5871;** fax 01/676-4764).
- **Northern Ireland Tourist Board,** 16 Nassau St., Dublin 2, Ireland (☎ **01/679-1977** or toll free **1-800/230-230** in Ireland).

In Northern Ireland

- **Irish Tourist Board,** 53 Castle St., Belfast BT1 1GH (☎ **0232/327888;** fax 0232/240201).
- **Northern Ireland Tourist Board,** 59 North St., Belfast BT1 1NB (☎ **0232/246609;** fax 0232/240960).

ENTRY REQUIREMENTS

DOCUMENTS   For citizens of the United States, Canada, Australia, and New Zealand entering the Republic of Ireland for a stay of up to three months, no visas are necessary but a valid passport is required.

Citizens of the United Kingdom, when traveling on flights originating in Britain, do not need to show documentation to enter Ireland. Nationals of the United Kingdom and Colonies not born in Great Britain or Northern Ireland must have a valid passport or national identity document.

For entry into Northern Ireland, the same conditions apply.

CUSTOMS   Since the EU's introduction of a single market on January 1, 1993, goods brought into Ireland and Northern Ireland fall into two categories: (1) goods brought duty-paid and VAT-paid in other EU countries, and (2) goods bought as duty-free and VAT-free allowances at duty-free shops.

With regard to the first category, provided that the goods are for personal use, then there is no further duty or VAT to be paid. The limits for goods in this category are as follows: 800 cigarettes, 10 liters of spirits, 45 liters of wine, and 55 liters of beer. This category normally applies to Irish citizens, visitors from Britain, and travelers from other EU countries.

The second category, which primarily pertains to overseas visitors such as U.S. and Canadian citizens, allows the following duty-free and VAT-free items to be imported for personal use: 200 cigarettes, one liter of liquor, two liters of wine, and other goods (including beer) not exceeding the value of £34 ($42.70) per adult. There are no restrictions on bringing currency into Ireland.

The Irish and Northern Irish Customs systems operate on a Green, Red, and Blue Channel format. The first two choices are geared for passengers coming from the U.S. and non-EU countries. The Green Channel is for people who are not exceeding their duty-free allowances, and the Red Channel for those with extra goods to declare. If you are like most visitors, and bringing in only your own clothes and personal effects, choose the Green Channel.

The Blue Channel, the latest addition to the system, is exclusively for use by passengers coming into Ireland from another EU country.

In addition to your luggage, you can bring in sporting equipment such as golf clubs or tennis rackets for your own recreational use while in Ireland. Prohibited goods include arms, ammunition and explosives; narcotics; meat, poultry, plants, and their by-products; and domestic animals from outside the United Kingdom.

MONEY

CASH/CURRENCY   The 26 counties of the Republic Ireland have an independent currency system, even though now linked with several other currencies as part of the European Monetary System. The punt is the basic unit of currency, although most people refer to it as a pound, like Britain currency. Do not, however, automatically assume that all pounds are equal! The value of the Irish pound is about 3%–5% less than the British pound.

The six counties of Northern Ireland, on the other hand, use the British pound sterling currency system. The Irish pound is not accepted as legal tender in Northern Ireland.

In dollar terms, the Irish pound has fluctuated throughout most of 1994 between $1.45 and $1.55, while the British pound has been between $1.50 and $1.60. So, it will cost you less to buy an Irish pound than a British pound.

Both the Irish and British pounds are symbolized by a £ sign; each unit of paper currency is called a note. The pound notes, which are printed in denominations of £5, £10, £20, £50, and £100, come in different sizes and colors (the larger the size, the greater the value). There are still some £1 notes in circulation, although these are being phased out in favor of the £1 coin. Each pound is divided into 100 pennies ("p"); coins come in denominations of £1, 50p, 20p, 10p, 5p, and 1p.

The British currency used in Northern Ireland, identified by engravings of British royalty, follows the same pattern, with notes in the denominations of £5, £10, £20, £50, and £100. Coins are issued to the value of £1, 50p, 20p, 10p, 5p, 2p, and 1p.

Note: The value of the Irish and British pounds fluctuate daily, so it is best to check the exchange rate at the time of your visit. As we go to press, the Irish pound is approximately £1 Irish = $1.50 U.S., while the British £1 sterling = $1.53.

Irish Punt & U.S. Dollar Equivalents

Pence	U.S. $	Pounds	U.S. $
1	.02	1	1.50
2	.03	2	3.00
3	.05	3	4.50
4	.06	4	6.00
5	.08	5	7.50
10	.15	7.50	11.25
25	.38	10	15.00
50	.75	15	22.50
75	$1.08	20	30.00

Northern Irish/British Pound & U.S. Dollar Equivalents

Pence	U.S. $	Pounds	U.S. $
1	.02	1	1.53
2	.04	2	3.06
3	.05	3	4.59
4	.07	4	6.12
5	.08	5	7.65
10	.16	7.50	11.48
25	.38	10	15.30
50	.77	15	22.95
75	1.15	20	30.60

TRAVELER'S CHECKS   Traveler's checks (usually spelled "cheques") are readily accepted in the Republic of Ireland and Northern Ireland. In general, banks provide the best exchange rates, followed by bureaux de change. Most banks and bureaux usually post exchange rates in their front windows so you can shop around for the best rate.

Hotels, restaurants, and stores also accept traveler's checks, but their rate of exchange is usually less favorable than the banks. **Note:** personal checks, or cheques, even when presented with your passport, are not usually accepted by banks or places of business, unless you are a member of the Eurocheque scheme or have made prior arrangements in advance.

CREDIT CARDS   Leading international credit cards, such as American Express, Carte Blanche, Diners Club, Mastercard (also known as Access or Eurocard), and Visa (also known as Visa/Barclay), are readily acceptable throughout all 32 counties. Most establishments display the symbols or logos of the credit cards they accept on their windows or shopfronts.

What Things Cost in Dublin	U.S. $
Taxi from the airport to the city center (£13)	19.50
Express bus from airport to city center (£2.50)	3.75
Bus minimum fare (55p)	.83
Local telephone call (20p)	.30
Double room at the Shelbourne Hotel (deluxe) (£150)	225.00
Double room at Temple Bar Hotel (moderate) (£90)	135.00
Double room at Jurys ChristChurch (inexpensive) (£46)	.69
Double room at Avalon House (budget) (£26)	.39
Lunch for one at Terrace Bistro (moderate) (£7.50)	11.25
Lunch for one at Lane Gallery Restaurant (inexpensive) (£4.95)	7.43
Lunch for one at Bewley's (budget) (£3)	4.50
Dinner for one, without wine, at The Commons (deluxe) (£27.50)	41.25
Dinner for one at Roly's Bistro (moderate) (£18)	27.00
Dinner for one at DaVincenzo (inexpensive) (£10)	15.00
Pint of Guinness (£2)	3.00
Shot of Irish whiskey (£2.05)	3.08
Glass of Wine (£2)	3.00
Coca-Cola in a cafe (60p)	.90
Cup of coffee (80p)	1.20
Roll of ASA 100 color film, 36 exposures (£4.98)	7.47
Admission to the *Book of Kells* at Trinity College (£2.50)	3.75
Admission to the National Museum	Free
Movie Ticket (£4)	6.00
Ticket to the Abbey Theatre (£10)	15.00

What Things Cost in Galway	U.S. $
Bus flat rate fare (65p)	.98
Local telephone call (20p)	.30
Double room at the Great Southern Hotel (deluxe) (£102)	151.00
Double room at Ardilaun House Hotel (moderate) (£60)	90.00
Double room at Jurys Inn (inexpensive) (£39)	58.50
Lunch for one at House of Bards (moderate) (£5.95)	8.93
Lunch for one at Conlon & Sons (inexpensive) (£3.95)	5.93
Lunch for one at Bewley's (budget) (£3)	4.50
Dinner for one, without wine, at Park House (deluxe) (£20.45)	30.68
Dinner for one at Grapevine (moderate) (£15.95)	23.90
Dinner for one at G.B.C./Galway Baking Company (inexpensive) (£7.95)	11.95
Pint of Guinness (£2)	3.00
Shot of Irish Whiskey (£2.05)	3.08
Glass of Wine (£1.90)	2.85
Coca-Cola in a cafe (60p)	.90
Cup of coffee (60p)	.90
Roll of ASA 100 color film, 36 exposures (£5.98)	8.97
Admission to the Dun Guaire Castle (£2.10)	3.15
Admission to Galway Museum (60p)	.90
Cruise on Lough Corrib (£5)	7.50
Round-trip boat trip to Aran Islands (£15)	22.50
Ticket to the Druid Theatre (£7)	10.50

2 When to Go

CLIMATE

Contrary to the time-worn stereotype, the island of Ireland does not have constant precipitation. The average annual rainfall is 30 in. in the east around Dublin, 43 in. in the North, and 50 in. inc in the western mountainous areas. The driest area is the coastal strip near Dublin.

You are certainly apt to see some rain and occasional mist during your visit, but you are also likely to experience glorious sunshine, sweeping cloud formations, and beguiling rainbows. The weather can vary dramatically from day to day; it can also change from fair to showery and back again to fair in a matter of minutes.

The reasons for Ireland's erratic weather patterns are many. Being surrounded by water is certainly a contributing factor, as is the presence of mountains all along the Irish coast. In addition, Ireland lies in an area where mild southwesterly winds prevail. Most of the country also comes under the influence of the warm drifting waters of the Gulf Stream.

What Things Cost in Belfast	U.S. $
Taxi from the airport to the city center (£15)	23.00
Express bus from the airport to city center (£3.50)	5.35
Bus minimum fare (40p)	.60
City sightseeing tour (£4.50)	6.70
Local telephone call (10p)	.15
Double room at the Culloden (deluxe) (£185)	283.00
Double room at Dukes (moderate) (£92)	140.00
Double room at Ash Rowan (inexpensive) (£56)	85.00
Lunch for one at Saints & Scholars (moderate) (£6.95)	10.60
Lunch for one at Skandia (inexpensive) (£5)	7.65
Dinner for one without wine at Roscoff (deluxe) (£35)	53.00
Dinner for one without wine at Nick's Warehouse (moderate) (£20)	30.00
Dinner for one without wine at Harvey's (inexpensive) (£10)	15.30
Bottle of Beer (£1.50)	2.30
Shot of Bushmills Whiskey (£2)	3.06
Glass of Wine (£1.65)	2.50
Cup of Coffee (70p)	1.00
Admission to Ulster Museum (free)	–
Movie ticket (£3.50)	5.35
Ticket to Grand Opera House (£10)	15.30

On the plus side, all of these factors combine to make a mild and equable climate year-round. A former U.S. ambassador to Ireland described the country as "the land of perpetual springtime." The countryside is always green, even in January, and palm trees and other forms of sub-tropical vegetation flourish side-by-side with the native plants.

Snow is a rarity in the winter, and summertime temperatures that reach into the 70s or 80s F. are usually considered to be a heat wave by the locals.

Because of her northerly situation, the island of Ireland enjoys long daylight hours in the spring/summer months, with sunrise as early as 5am and sunset as late as 10pm. This gives a few bonus hours of daylight after dinner for a walk or a game of golf. May, June, and July have the longest days, with April, August, and September following close behind.

People frequently ask "What will the weather be like in Ireland in the month of X?" The answer most often heard on Irish radio weather reports is that the weather will be normal. And in Ireland that means unpredictable!

Come expecting the worst; bring a raincoat, umbrella, and waterproof footwear. Then count your blessings if you never have to unpack them. And don't forget a pair of sunglasses. The Irish sun can be blindingly brilliant, especially on a long summer's evening.

HOLIDAYS

Republic of Ireland	Northern Ireland
New Year's Day	New Year's Day
St. Patrick's Day (March 17)	St. Patrick's Day
Easter Monday	Easter Monday
May Day (first Monday in May)	May Day
Summer Bank Holidays	Spring Bank Holiday
(first Monday in June & August)	(last Monday in May)
Autumn Bank Holiday	Orangeman's Day/July 12
(last Monday in October)	Summer Bank Holiday
Christmas Day	(last Monday of August)
St. Stephen's Day (December 26)	Christmas Day
	Boxing Day (December 27)

Note: Good Friday, although not a statutory public holiday, is usually observed as a holiday in the Republic.

Ireland Calendar of Events

January

- **Pantomime Season, Belfast.** Traditional pantomime at the Grand Opera House and in Belfast theaters. End-December to early January.

February

- **Cavan Song Contest,** Cavan. An international competition for original (popular) songs. Early February.
- **Belfast Musical Festival.** Held every year since 1911, this is a competition in speech, music, and drama categories. Mid-February to mid-March.

March

✪ **St. Patrick's Day.**

Is there a better place to be other than Ireland on this Irish national holiday? This is a countrywide celebration of marching bands, continuous music, floats, and delegations from all over the world.
Where: All over Ireland. **When:** March 17. **How:** For tickets, schedules, and information on package tours from the U.S. and Canada, contact the Irish Tourist Board.

- **Guinness Roaring 1920s Festival,** Killarney. This is an exuberant gathering celebrating the 1920s era of glamour, fun, music, and glitz. Mid-March.
- **Limerick International Band Festival,** Limerick. Marching bands, concert bands, and drill and dance team bands from all over the world compete in this one-day event. Mid-March.
- **Annual Derry Feis,** Derry. For almost 100 years, this has been a major gathering at the Guildhall for performers and followers of Irish music. Third week of March.

April

- **Pan Celtic Festival,** Galway. Celts from all parts of Europe gather for a week of song, dance, and music with Celtic traditions. Early April.

★ **Punchestown Spring Horse Racing Festival.**
This country race track offers three days of exciting hurdle, steeplechase, and cross-country racing in a colorful and festive atmosphere.
Where: Naas, Co. Kildare. **When:** Tues–Thurs of last week of April.
How: For full details, contact the Manager, Punchestown Racecourse, Naas, Co. Kildare (☎ **045/97704**).

• **Cork International Choral Festival,** Cork. This is Ireland's premier choral event featuring international and national choirs and folk dance teams. Late April to early May.

May

• **Belfast Marathon.** This epic race attracts nearly 5,000 runners on a path all around the city. First Monday in May.
• **Apple Blossom Day,** Armagh. This annual spring festival celebrates the blooming of the colorful apple blossoms in this orchard-rich valley. Mid-May.

★ **Fleadh Nua.**
Singers, instrumentalists, and dancers from all over Ireland come to this annual cultural festival of Irish traditional music. The program includes concerts, ceilis, set dancing, lectures, and street entertainment.
Where: Ennis, Co. Clare. **When:** Late May. **How:** For ticket information, contact Terry Moorhead, The Crescent, Ennis, Co. Clare (☎ **065/20938**).

• **International Maytime Festival,** Dundalk. Theatrical groups from all over Ireland and abroad compete in this annual celebration of drama and of spring. Late May.

June

• **Listowel Writers Week.** This annual gathering of writers and would-be writers contains a heady mixture of workshops, lectures, readings, plays, discussions, and socializing. First week of June.
• **International Cartoon Festival,** Rathdrum, Co. Wicklow. Local and international cartoonists exhibit their works and draw for the public during this event. Early June.

★ **Budweiser Irish Derby.**
One of the richest races in Europe and widely accepted as the definitive European middle-distance classic, this race is Ireland's version of the Kentucky Derby or Royal Ascot. It's a fashionable gathering of racing fans from all over Ireland and abroad, all arriving for the day by the carloads and busload.
Where: The Curragh, Co. Kildare. **When:** Last Sunday in June or first weekend of July. **How:** For full information, contact the Irish Racing Board, Leopardstown Racecourse, Foxrock, Dublin 18 (☎ **01/289-2888**).

★ **Strawberry Fair.**
A feast of luscious and ripe Wexford-grown strawberries is the focus at this event which also includes kite flying, craft exhibitions, pub talent, photo and art exhibitions, sports, and open-air entertainment.

Where: Enniscorthy, Co. Wexford. **When:** Last week of June-first week of July. **How:** For details, contact Margot Hogan, Riverdale, Parklands, Enniscorthy, Co. Wexford (☎ 054/34623).

- **Castlebar Walking Festival,** Co. Mayo. This event offers four days of scenic walks and rambles through the Mayo countryside, with plenty of social gatherings and entertainment each evening. Late June to early July.

★ Irish Open Golf Championship.

This is Ireland's premier international golf event, televised to over 90 countries featuring the world's top players.
Where: St. Margaret's Golf Club, Dublin. **When:** Last weekend of June.
How: For details, contact the Irish Tourist Board.

July

- **Ballina Salmon Festival,** Co. Mayo. A week-long celebration in honor of Ireland's delicious game fish, along with music, song, pennyfarthing bicycle rides, street theater, and a traditional Irish wake. Mid-July.
- **Battle of the Boyne Commemoration.** This annual event, sometimes called Orangeman's Day, is a national day of parades and celebration in all of Northern Ireland, recalling the historic battle, fought between two 17th century kings. Twelfth of July.

★ Galway Arts Festival & Races.

This is a two-week feast of theatre, big top concerts, literary evenings, street shows, arts, parades, music, and more, in the streets of Galway, followed by five days of racing and more merriment, music, and song.
Where: Galway City and Racecourse. **When:** Last two weeks of July.
How: For information, contact the Ireland West Tourism Office, Aras Failte, Eyre Square, Galway (☎ 091/563081).

- **Lady of the Lake Festival,** Irvinestown, Co. Fermanagh. This ten-day event, in the heart of Lough Erne territory near Enniskillen, includes a vintage car rally, powerboat racing, motorcycle racing, raft racing, and music and dancing. End of July.
- **Youghal International Busking Festival,** Co. Cork. This event features street entertainers and musicians, with competitions for the best buskers. Late July into early August.
- **O'Carolan Harp & Traditional Irish Music Festival,** Keadue, Co. Roscommon. Staged in memory of the blind Turlough O'Carolan, Ireland's legendary harper, this event presents harp recitals, music, and dance. Late July into early August.

August

★ Letterkenny International Folk Festival.

For nearly 30 years, this event has drawn people to north Donegal for the music of top Irish and international artists, plus ceilis, workshops, and more.
Where: Letterkenny, Co. Donegal. **When:** Early August. **How:** For details, contact Judy Ball, Letterkenny Festival Office, Letterkenny, Co. Donegal (☎ 074/21752).

- **International Maiden of the Mournes Festival,** Warrenpoint, Co. Down. Held with the Mountains of Mourne as a setting, this festival includes concerts, music, dance, cabaret, banquets, and the crowning of the Maiden of the Mournes. Second week of August.

★ **Yeats International Summer School.**
For more than 35 years, this has been the benchmark of Ireland's many summer schools. Designed for literary enthuisiasts and followers of Yeats, it offers lectures, seminars, poetry, reading, tours, music, and more. **Where:** Sligo. **When:** Middle two weeks of August. **How:** For details, contact Mrs. Georgina Wynne, Yeats Society, Douglas Hyde Bridge, Sligo (☎ 71/42683).

- **Puck Fair, Killorglin,** Co. Kerry. Each year the residents of this tiny Ring of Kerry town carry on a centuries-old tradition by capturing a wild goat and enthroning it as "king" over two days of unrestricted merrymaking. Mid-August.
- **Connemara Pony Show,** Clifden, Co. Galway. Ireland's legendary and sturdy native pony is the focal point of this one-day gathering with the atmosphere of an old-fashioned horse fair. Late August.

★ **Rose of Tralee Festival.**
A carnival-like atmosphere prevails at this five-day event, with a full program of concerts, street entertainment, horse races, and beauty/talent pageant leading up to the selection of the Rose of Tralee. **Where:** Tralee, Co. Kerry. **When:** End of August. **How:** Contact the Festival of Tralee Office, Tralee, Co. Kerry (☎ 066/21322).

★ **Kilkenny Arts Week.**
This one-week festival features a broad spectrum of the arts, from classical and traditional music, to plays, one-person shows, readings, films, poetry, and visual arts exhibitions. **Where:** Kilkenny. **When:** Last week of August. **How:** For details, contact Mary Mooney, Kilkenny Arts Festival, Rothe House, Parliament St., Kilkenny (☎ 056/63663).

- **Fleadh Cheoil.** This is Ireland's major summer festival of traditional music, with competitions to select the All-Ireland champions in all categories of instruments and singing. The venue changes each year. Last weekend of August.
- **Oul' Lammas Fair,** Ballycastle, Co. Antrim. Chartered in 1606, this is Ireland's oldest traditional fair. Last weekend of August.

September

- **Waterford Festival of Light Opera,** Waterford. For nearly 40 years, this has been a major gathering for amateur music societies from all over Ireland the Britain. Last two weeks of September.

★ **Galway International Oyster Festival.**
First held in 1953, this event attracts oyster-aficionados from all over the globe. Highlights include the World Oyster-Opening Championship, golf

tournament, yacht race, art exhibition, gala banquet, traditional music and song, and lots of oyster-eating.

Where: Galway and environs. **When:** Last weekend of September. **How:** For details, contact Ireland West Tourism Office, Aras Failte, Eyre Square, Galway (☎ **091/563081**).

October

- **Kinsale Gourmet Festival,** Kinsale, Co. Cork. Participants feast on the best cuisine of the many restaurants in the Kinsale area during this three-day event.

⭐ **Wexford Opera Festival.**

For more than 40 years, this event has been highly acclaimed for its productions of 18th- and 19th-century operatic masterpieces plus classical music concerts, recitals, and more.

Where: Wexford. **When:** Last two weeks of October. **How:** Contact the Wexford Festival Office, Theatre Royal, High Street, Wexford (☎ **053/22400**).

- **Guinness Cork Jazz Festival,** Cork. Top names from the international jazz world converge on Cork for concerts, impromptu sessions, and "jazz on tap" pub gigs. Last weekend of October.

November

⭐ **Belfast Festival at Queens.**

As Ulster's best-known arts festival, this annual 19-day event attracts a huge following to enjoy drama, opera, music, and film events in and around Queens University.

Where: Queens University, Belfast. **When:** Mid-November. **How:** For details, contact the Northern Ireland Tourist Board.

- **Sligo International Choral Festival,** Sligo. A weekend of music performed by international choirs in concert and competition. First weekend of November.

Dublin Calendar of Events

January

- **International Rugby Championships.** These events, which spill into February, attract huge local crowds (and often book out hotels) to the Lansdowne Road Stadium, Ballsbridge, Dublin. Check with the Irish Tourist Board to see what the lineup is for 1995 and 1996.

February

⭐ **Dublin Film Festival.**

Over 100 films are featured, with screenings of the best of Irish and world cinema, plus seminars and lectures on film-making.

Where: Irish Film Centre and at various movie houses. **When:** Last week of February. **How:** For schedules and ticket information, contact the Irish Film Centre, 6 Eustace St., Dublin 2 (☎ **01/679-2937**).

March

★ St. Patrick's Day Parade.

Ireland's biggest and best parade in honor of the national patron saint—
a panorama of marching bands, drill teams, fife and drum corps, floats,
and delegations from all over the world.
Where: O'Connell Street, Dublin. **When:** March 17. **How:** For details,
contact the Irish Tourist Board.

April

★ Feis Ceoil.

In spite of its Gaelic name, this 11-day springtime event is not a traditional
music gathering. It is a mostly classical competitive music festival that covers
all instruments including voice. There are more than 150 categories featuring
orchestral and choral events, with duets, trios, and ensembles of all sizes.
Where: Royal Dublin Society, Ballsbridge. **When:** Between mid-March and
mid-April (dates change annually). **How:** For full information, contact Feis
Ceoil Office, 37 Molesworth St., Dublin 2 (☎ 01/676-7365).

• **Dublin Grand Opera.** A one-week program of classic works presented at the
Gaiety Theatre. Last week of April.

May

★ Springtime Home & Good Food Fair.

A festive week of events ranging from horse-jumping and sheepdog trials to
fashion shows and culinary demonstrations, all with much social merriment.
Where: Royal Dublin Society, Ballsbridge. **When:** First week of May. **How:**
For details, contact the Royal Dublin Society, Merrion Road, Ballsbridge,
Dublin 4 (☎ 01/490-0600).

• **Festival of Early Irish Music.** This program offers madrigals, liturgies,
clapping music, sacred music, chamber music, and early Irish traditional
music at various centers throughout Dublin. End April to early May.

June

★ Festival of Music in Great Irish Houses.

This is a continuous ten-day festival of classical music performed by leading
Irish and international artists in some of the Dublin area's great Georgian
buildings and mansions.
Where: Various venues throughout Dublin and neighboring Counties
Wicklow and Kildare. **When:** Mid-June for ten days. **How:** Contact the
Festival Committee, c/o Castletown House, Celbridge, Co. Kildare
(☎ 01/496-2021).

★ Bloomsday.

Dublin's unique day of festivity, commemorating 24 hours in the life of
Leopold Bloom, the central character of James Joyce's *Ulysses.* The whole
city—including the menus at restaurants and pubs—seeks to duplicate the
aromas, sights, sounds, and tastes of Dublin on June 16, 1904. Special
ceremonies are held at the James Joyce Tower and Museum and there are
guided walks of Joycean sights.

Where: Citywide. **When:** June 16. **How:** For full information, contact the Irish Tourist Board.

- **Dublin International Organ & Choral Festival.** A week of beautiful music rings out from church and concert halls.

July

- **Dun Laoghaire Festival.** A week-long celebration in the seafront suburb seven miles south of Dublin, with arts and crafts, concerts, band recitals, sports events, and talent competitions. Mid-July.
- **Summer Schools.** Study sessions meeting in Dublin include the Irish Theatre Summer School in conjunction with the Gaiety School of Acting at Trinity College; the James Joyce Summer School at Newman House; and the International Summer Schools in Irish Studies at Trinity College and National University of Ireland. July.

August

⚔ Kerrygold Dublin Horse Show.

This is the principal sporting and social event on the Irish national calendar attracting visitors from all parts of the world. More than 2,000 horses, the cream of Irish bloodstock, are entered for this show, with jumping competitions each day, dressage, and more. Highlights include a fashionable ladies day (don't forget your hat!), formal hunt balls each evening, and the awarding of the Aga Khan Trophy and the Nation's Cup by the President of Ireland. **Where:** Royal Dublin Society Showgrounds, Ballsbridge. **When:** First full week of August, Tuesday through Sunday, following the first Monday, except during Olympic years when it is held in mid-July. **How:** For ticket and schedule information, contact Royal Dublin Society, Merrion Road, Ballsbridge, Dublin 4 (☎ **01/668-0645**).

- **Temple Bar Blues Festival.** A three-day celebration of the blues at various sites in or near Temple Bar, including a free open-air concert at College Green and a "blues trail" of free live blues in 18 different pubs. Mid-August.
- **Summer Music Festival.** St. Stephen's Green is the setting for this series of free lunchtime band concerts of popular and Irish traditional music, as well as afternoon open-air performances of Shakespearean classic plays, sponsored by the Office of Public Works. Last two weeks of August.

September

⚔ All Ireland Hurling and Football Finals.

Tickets must be obtained months in advance for these two national amateur sporting events—the equivalent of Superbowls for Irish national sports. **Where:** Croke Park. **When:** First and second weekends in September. **How:** Contact the Irish Tourist Board for information on tickets and travel packages from the U.S.

October

⚔ Irish Life Dublin Theatre Festival.

Hailed as the major English-language event of its kind, this festival is a showcase for new plays by Irish authors and quality productions from abroad. **Where:** Theaters throughout Dublin. **When:** First two weeks of October.

How: For information and tickets, contact the Dublin Theatre Festival Office, 47 Nassau St., Dublin 2 (☎ **01/677-8439**).

★ **Golden Pages Dublin Marathon.**
More than a thousand runners from both sides of the Atlantic and the Irish Sea participate in this popular run through the streets of Dublin City. **Where:** Dublin city center. **When:** Last Monday in October. **How:** For entry forms and information, contact the Dublin Marathon Office, 12 Herbert Place, Dublin 2 (☎ **01/676-1383**).

November/December

• **Dublin Grand Opera.** This is the second half of Dublin's twice-yearly operatic fling, with great works presented by the Dublin Grand Opera Society at the Gaiety Theatre. Early December.

• **Christmas Horse Racing Festival,** Leopardstown Racetrack. Three days of winter racing for thoroughbreds. December 26–29.

3 Health, Insurance & Other Concerns

HEALTH   As a general rule, there are no health documents required to enter Ireland or Northern Ireland from the U.S., Canada, the United Kingdom, Australia, New Zealand, or most other countries. If a traveler has visited areas where an infectious, contagious disease is prevalent in the last 14 days, however, proof of immunization for such diseases may be required.

INSURANCE   When planning a trip, it is wise to consider insurance coverage for the various risk aspects of travel—health and accident, cancellation or disruption of services, and lost or stolen luggage.

Before buying any new coverage, check your own insurance policies (automobile, medical, and homeowner) to ascertain if they cover the elements of travel abroad. Also check the membership contracts of automobile and travel clubs, and the benefits extended by credit card companies.

If you decide you need further coverage, consult your travel agent or tour planner. In many cases, tour operators that sell packages to Ireland and Northern Ireland provide insurance as part of a package or offer coverage for a small optional fee. Alternatively, you may wish to contact one of the following companies, specializing in short-term policies for travelers:

• **Access America,** 600 Third Ave., P.O. Box 807, New York, NY 10163-0807 (☎ **212/490-5345** or toll free **800/284-8300**).

• **InsureAmerica/Travel Guard International,** 1145 Clark St., Stevens Point, WI 54481 (☎ **715/345-0505** or toll free **800/826-1300**).

• **Mutual of Omaha (Tele-Trip),** Mutual of Omaha Plaza, Omaha, NE 68175 (☎ **402/351-8000** or toll free **800/228-9792**).

• **Travel Insurance International,** Travelers Insurance Co., 1 Tower Sq., Hartford, CT 06183-5040 (☎ **203/227-2318** or toll free **800/243-3174**).

WHAT TO PACK

Comfortable and casual clothing is ideal. Slacks, sports clothes, and good walking shoes are *de rigueur* for both men and women; always pack a sweater or two, which you can add to or subtract from your outfits as required. It is wise for men to include a jacket and a tie for dinnertime, especially for Dublin or Belfast restaurants and theaters. Women should likewise take something dressy for evenings out at stylish places.

Light rainwear or all-weather coats are advisable at any time of year. Don't forget a folding umbrella, just in case. Sunglasses come in handy, too, especially when driving. Take a bathing suit, if you enjoy a swim and will be staying in a hotel with an indoor pool.

Don't panic if you forget your toothpaste or hair spray. The island of Ireland has just about everything you are used to, albeit sometimes with different brand names. Do remember to pack any prescription medicines you may have; and take along a copy of your prescription, just in case you need to get a refill. If you bring your hair dryer, don't forget transformer and converter plugs.

4 Tips for Special Travelers

FOR THE DISABLED

For the last 30 years, the **National Rehabilitation Board of Ireland,** based at 25 Clyde Road, Ballsbridge, Dublin (☎ **01/668-4181**), has encouraged facilities to accommodate the disabled. Consequently, some hotels and public buildings now have ramp or graded entrances, and rooms specially fitted for wheelchair access.

Unfortunately, many of the older hotels, guesthouses, and landmark buildings still have steep steps both outside and within. For a list of the properties that cater to the needs of the disabled, contact the National Rehabilitation Board in advance.

The **Irish Hotels Federation,** 13 Northbrook Rd., Dublin 6 (☎ **01/497-6459**), publishes an annual guide to hotels and guesthouses, with symbols indicating premises that are (*a.*) accessible for disabled persons, or (*b.*) suitable with the assistance of one helper. This booklet covers accommodations in all 32 counties of Ireland.

The **Irish Wheelchair Association,** Blackheath Drive, Clontarf, Dublin (☎ **01/833-8241**), loans free wheelchairs for travelers in Ireland. A donation is appreciated. Branch offices are located at Parnell Street, Kilkenny (☎ **056/62775**); White Street, Cork (☎ **021/966544**); Henry Street, Limerick (☎ **061/313691**); and Dominick Street, Galway (☎ **091/565598**).

For advice on travel to Northern Ireland, contact **Disability Action,** 2 Annandale Ave., Belfast (☎ **0232/491011**).

U.S. firms that operate tours to Ireland for the disabled include: **Evergreen Travel,** 4114 198th St. SW., Ste. 13, Lynwood, WA 98036 (☎ **206/776-1184** or toll free **800/435-2288**), and **Grimes Travel,** 54 Mamaroneck Ave., White Plains, NY 10601 (☎ **914/761-4550** or toll free **800/832-7778**).

FOR SENIOR CITIZENS

Seniors, known in Ireland and Northern Ireland as OAPs (Old Age Pensioners), enjoy a variety of discounts and privileges. Native OAPs ride the public transport system free of charge, but this privilege does not extend to tourists. Visitors can avail themselves of other discounts, particularly on admission to attractions and theaters. Always ask about a senior discount if special rates are not posted; the senior discount is usually 10%.

The Irish Tourist Board (see "Sources of Information," above) publishes a list of reduced rate hotel packages for seniors, **Golden Holidays/For the Over 55s.** These packages are usually available in the months of March to June, September, and October to November.

Some tour operators in the U.S., such as **CIE Tours,** 100 Hanover Ave., Cedar Knolls, NJ 07927-0501 (☎ **201/292-3438** or toll free **800/CIE-TOUR**), a company that operates tours covering Ireland and Northern Ireland, give senior citizens over age 55 cash discounts on selected departures of regular tour programs throughout the year. In addition, the following U.S. firms operate tours to Ireland specifically geared to seniors: **Elder Hostel,** 75 Federal St., Boston, MA 02110 (☎ **617/ 426-7788**); **Evergreen Travel,** 4114 198th St. S.W., Ste. 13, Lynnwood, WA 98036 (☎ **206/776-1184** or toll free **800/435-2288**); and **SAGA Tours,** 222 Berkeley St., Boston, MA 02116 (☎ **617/262-2262** or toll free **800/343-0273**).

FOR STUDENTS

With almost half of its population under age 25, Ireland is particularly geared to students. Most attractions have a reduced student-rate admission charge, obtainable on the presentation of a valid student identity card.

From north to south, the island of Ireland is also rich in university life. Dublin is home to three revered universities—Trinity College, University College-Dublin, and Dublin University—and many other fine schools and institutes of higher learning. Branches of the National University of Ireland are also located in Cork, Limerick, Galway, and Maynooth. In Northern Ireland, the leading universities are Queen's University in Belfast and Ulster University, with branches in Belfast, Coleraine, and Derry.

To find out about the various year-round, semester, and summer-school academic programs, contact the Irish Tourist Board or the Northern Ireland Tourist Board (see "Sources of Information," above).

For information on student flights, accommodations, travel, and discounts, plus application forms for student identity cards, contact the **Irish Student Travel Service (USIT),** 19 Aston Quay, Dublin 2 (☎ **01/677-8117**). In Northern Ireland, contact USIT at the University of Ulster, Shore Road, Jordanstown, Newtownabbey, Belfast (☎ **0232/365434**). In the U.S., USIT is located at 895 Amsterdam Ave., New York, NY 10025 (☎ **212/663-5435**).

U.S. firms offering educational programs to Ireland include: **Academic Travel Abroad,** 3210 Grace St. NW, Washington, DC 20007 (☎ **202/333-3355** or toll free **800/556-7896**); **Consortium for International Education (CIE),** 2021 Business Center Dr., Suite 209, Irvine, CA 92715 (☎ **714/955-1700**); **Cultural Heritage Alliance,** 107-115 S. Second St., Philadelphia, PA 19106 (☎ **215/923-7060** or toll free **800/323-4466**); and **Irish American Cultural Institute,** University of St. Thomas, 2115 Summit Ave., Mail #5026, St. Paul, MN 55105 (☎ **612/962-6040** or toll free **800/232-3746**).

5   Alternative/Adventure Travel

Surrounded by water and stroked by Gulf Stream breezes, Ireland enjoys a temperate climate year-round—ideal for all types of outdoor activities. To encourage visitors to share in the great outdoors, the Irish Tourist Board publishes a series of colorful brochures entitled *Only the Best,* covering golf, fishing, equestrian activities, bicycling, and walking. The Northern Ireland Tourist Board publishes a color brochure on golf and information bulletins on bicycling, fishing, horseback riding, and walking. All of this information is available free of charge (see "Sources of Information," above).

GOLF On both sides of the border, golf is a major sport; Ireland has more than 250 courses. Teeing off is a sporting way to see some of Ireland's most appealing sights. Courses are as varied as the landscape. Lahinch, one of the Irish circuit's most challenging championship courses, is nestled near the Cliffs of Moher on the Atlantic. The seaside links at Salthill overlook Galway Bay. Killarney's twin courses rest amid a panorama of lake and mountain vistas. In the North, Royal County Down sits "where the Mountains of Mourne sweep down to the sea."

Best of all, Ireland's golf facilities are seldom crowded, waiting times are rare, and greens fees are very affordable, averaging about £10 to £15 ($15 to $22.50) a day. A call in advance to the club secretary is all that is needed to arrange a game.

More than three-dozen tour operators offer golf vacation packages to both Ireland and Northern Ireland from the U.S. and Canada including **Aer Lingus Vacations,** 122 E. 42nd St., New York, NY 10168 (☎ **212/557-1110** or toll free **800/223-6537**); **Golf Getaways,** 30423 Canwood St., Suite 227, Agoura Hills, CA 91301 (☎ **818/991-7015** or toll free **800/991-9270**); **Golf International,** 275 Madison Ave., Suite 1819, New York, NY 10016 (☎ **212/986-9176** or toll free **800/833-1389**); **Ireland Golf Tours,** 251 E. 85th St., New York, NY 10028 (☎ **212/772-8220** or toll free **800/346-5388**); **Owenoak Tours,** 3 Parklands Dr., Darien, CT 06820 (☎ **203/655-2531** or toll free **800/426-4498**; and **Wide World of Golf,** Box 5217, Carmel, CA (☎ **408/624-6667**).

HORSEBACK RIDING Ireland is great horse country, and riding is easy to arrange. More than 50 riding stables offer horses for hire by the hour or the day. An hour's ride averages L10 ($15) in most locations. Some equestrian centers also operate guided point-to-point treks with overnight accommodations and meals included in the package.

Equestrian tours are available from **Destination Ireland,** 250 W. 57th St., Suite 2511, New York, NY 10019 (☎ **212/977-9629** or toll free **800/832-1848**), and **Keith Prowse USA,** 234 W. 44th St., New York, NY 10036 (☎ **212/398-1430** or toll free **800/669-7469**).

FISHING Angling, as the Irish call fishing, can be enjoyed almost year round. The seasons are as follows: salmon, January 1 to September 30; brown trout, February 15 to October 12; seatrout, June 1 to September 30; coarse fishing and sea angling, January to December.

Many hotels and guesthouses near rivers or lakes offer private salmon and trout fishing privileges to guests. Otherwise, the cost of a salmon and seatrout license is £3 ($4.50) for one day, £10 ($15) for 21 days, £12 ($18) for a season (one district) or £25 ($37.50) for a season (all-districts/all regions). A permit/ticket for brown trout is £5 ($7.50) per day or less depending on the area. A complete day's fishing can be arranged for about £40 to £50 ($60 to $75) per day, with boats and ghillies (guides).

Fishing trips to Ireland and Northern Ireland can be arranged through **Adventure Safaris,** 8 S. Michigan Ave., Suite 2012, Chicago, IL 60603 (☎ **312/782-4756**); **Fishing International,** Hilltop Estate, 4010 Montecito Ave., Santa Rosa, CA 95405 (☎ **707/542-4242** or toll free **800/950-4242**); and **Owenoak Tours,** 3 Parklands Dr., Darien, CT 06820 (☎ **203/655-2531** or toll free **800/426-4498**).

BICYCLING Except for cows and sheep, the roads in rural Ireland and Northern Ireland are relatively traffic-free, so biking is quite leisurely. Almost 100 rent-a-bike stations are scattered throughout the countryside. Suggested bicycle tours are available free of charge from bike shops and tourist offices. A day's rental averages £7 ($10.50).

Companies that arrange guided biking vacations include **Backroads Bicycle Touring,** 1516 Fifth St., Berkeley, CA 94710 (☎ 510/527-1555 or toll free **800/ 245-3874); Classic Bicycle Tours & Treks,** P.O. Box 668, Clarkson, NY 14430 (☎ 716/637-5930 or toll free **800/777-8090); Destination Ireland,** 250 W. 57th St., Suite 2511, New York, NY 10019 (☎ 212/977-9629 or toll free **800/832-1848);** and **Gerhard's Bicycle Odysseys,** P.O. Box 757, Portland, OR 97207 (☎ **503/ 223-2402).**

WALKING   The Irish countryside certainly lends itself to extended walks, especially on long summer days when the sun rises early in the morning and sets after 10pm.

Beautiful trails can be followed in Ireland's scenic area, its national parks, forest parks, and nature reserves. Many of Ireland's cities and towns also offer guided walking tours for visitors.

Walking-tour vacations are offered by **Brendan Tours,** 15137 Califa St., Van Nuys, CA 91411 (☎ 818/785-9696 or toll free **800/421-8446); Country Walks,** P.O. Box 180, Waterbury, VT 05676 (☎ 802/244-1387); **Destination Ireland,** 250 W. 57th St., Suite 2511, New York, NY 10019 (☎ 212/977-9629 or toll free **800/832-1848);** and **Irish Walking Trails/British Coastal Trails,** California Plaza, Suite 302, 1001 B Ave., Coronado, CA 92118 (☎ 619/437-1211 or toll free **800/945-2438).**

RURAL LIVING   One of the newest developments on the Irish tourism scene is Irish Country Holidays, a program that invites visitors to share everyday life with the Irish in communities usually off the tourist track. Visitors are put up in homes, farms, self-catering cottages, or hotels, and they're given the opportunity to take part in turf-cutting, bread-baking, cheese-making, butter-churning, salmon-smoking, wood-turning, and pottery-making. Leisure activities—such as fishing, canoeing, rock climbing, hill walking, cycling, and horse riding—is also part of the holiday. At night there's traditional Irish music, song, dance, and amateur drama productions. Each itinerary is custom-planned. For more information, contact Dervla O'Neill, **Irish Country Holidays,** Plunket House, 84 Merrion Sq., Dublin 2 (☎ 01/676-5790).

6   Getting There

About half of all visitors from North America arrive in Ireland via direct transatlantic flights to Dublin Airport, Shannon Airport, or Belfast Airport. The other half fly first into Britain or Continental Europe and then "back-track" into Ireland by air or sea.

BY PLANE

From the U.S.A.

The Irish national flag carrier, **Aer Lingus** (☎ toll free **800/223-6537),** is the leader in providing transatlantic flights to Ireland. The words *Aer Lingus* are Irish meaning "air fleet." With bright green shamrock logos on the tails of its jets, the carrier offers year-round daily scheduled flights from New York and Boston to Dublin and Shannon International Airports. A new fleet of widebody Airbus 330 aircraft was introduced in the summer of 1994. Connections are available from over 100 U.S. cities via American, TWA, or USAir.

In the high season, mid-June through August, Aer Lingus has more than a dozen weekly round-trip flights from New York and six from Boston.

Scheduled flights, on a more limited basis, are also offered by **Delta Airlines** (☎ toll free **800/241-4141**) from Atlanta to Dublin and Shannon, with feed-in connections from Delta's network of gateways throughout the U.S.

In addition, service to Shannon is offered by **Aeroflot** (☎ toll free **800/995-5555**) from Chicago, Washington, DC, and Miami. Service to Belfast is provided by **American Trans Air** (☎ toll free **800/221-0924**).

If you'd like your trip over the Atlantic to be more than just another airplane ride, however, we heartily recommend Aer Lingus. You'll feel like you have arrived in Ireland from the minute you step on board—from the welcoming smiles of the cabin crew to the lilting Irish music and the hearty meals with such delicacies as Irish smoked salmon, Bewley's breads, and Golden Vale cheeses. Aer Lingus has flown the Atlantic for over 40 years, and has an excellent record for service and year-round reliability.

Backtracking to Ireland

Many travelers opt to fly to Britain and backtrack into Dublin (see "From Britain," below). Carriers serving Britain from the U.S. include **Air India** (☎ toll free **800/442-4455**); **American Airlines** (☎ toll free **800/433-7300**); **British Airways** (☎ toll free **800/247-9297**); **Continental Airlines** (☎ toll free **800/231-0856**); **El Al** (☎ toll free **800/223-6700**); **Kuwait Airways** (☎ toll free **800/458-9248**); **Northwest Airlines** (☎ toll free **800/447-4747**); **TWA** (☎ toll free **800/892-4141**); **United** (☎ toll free **800/241-6522**); **USAir** (☎ toll free **800/428-4322**); and **Virgin Atlantic Airways** (☎ toll free **800/862-8621**).

From Britain

Air service from Britain into Dublin is operated by **Aer Lingus** (☎ toll free **800/223-6537** in the U.S. and **081/899-4747** in Britain) from Birmingham, Bristol, East Midlands, Edinburgh, Glasgow, Leeds/Bradford, London/Heathrow, Manchester, and Newcastle; **British Midland** (☎ toll free **800/788-0555** in U.S. or **0345-554554** in Britain) from London/Heathrow; **Brymon Airways** (☎ **0752/705151** in Britain) from Plymouth; **Manx Airlines** (☎ **0624/824313** in Britain) from Blackpool, Cardiff, Guernsey, Isle of Man, Jersey, and Liverpool; **Ryanair** (☎ toll free **800/365-5563** in the U.S. and **071/435-7101** in Britain) from Birmingham, Liverpool and London/Stansted; **SAS** from Manchester (☎ toll free **800/221-2350** in the U.S. and **061/499-1441** in Britain).

Air service from Britain to Shannon is operated by **Aer Lingus** from London/Heathrow. Service to Cork is provided by British Airways Express (☎ toll free **800/247-9297** from U.S. and **081/897-4000** in Britain) from Birmingham, Bristol, Manchester, and Plymouth; Orient Air (☎ **0452/855565** in Britain) from Coventry; Air Southwest (☎ **0392/446447** in Britain) from Cornwall; and Ryanair from London/Stansted.

Air service into Belfast International Airport is provided by AirUK (☎ **0279/680146** in Britain) from Leeds/Bradford; Brymon Airways from Birmingham; Britannia Airways (☎ **061/489-2084** in Britain) from London/Luton; and British Midland from East Midlands and Jersey. In addition, there is service into Belfast City Airport via Gill Air (☎ **091/286-9665**) from Aberdeen and Newcastle-upon-Tyne; Jersey European (☎ **0232/460630** in Britain) from Blackpool, Bristol, Guernsey, Isle of Man, Jersey, Teeside, London/Gatwick, Leeds/Bradford, Exeter, and Birmingham; Loganair from Edinburgh, Glasgow, Manchester, Jersey, Channel Islands, and

Blackpool; Manx Airlines from Isle of Man, Aberdeen, London/Luton, Cardiff, and Liverpool; and Yorkshire European (☎ **0345/626217**) from Southampton.

There are also regular services into regional airports such as Waterford via Manx Airlines from London/Stansted and Orient Air from Gloucester; Knock via Logan Air from Glasgow and Manchester, and Ryanair from London/Stansted and Liverpool; Donegal's Carrickfinn Airport via Loganair from Glasgow; and Derry's Eglinton Airport via Loganair from Glasgow and Manchester.

From the Continent

Major air connections into Dublin from the continent include service from Brussels via Aer Lingus and Sabena (☎ toll free **800/952-2000**); Copenhagen via Aer Lingus and SAS; Paris via Aer Lingus and Air France; Munich via Ryanair and Lufthansa (☎ toll free **800/645-3880**); Rome via Aer Lingus and Alitalia; Amsterdam via Aer Lingus; Lisbon and Faro via TAP Air Portugal (☎ toll free **800/221-7370**); and Zurich via Aer Lingus.

Service to Shannon includes Aer Lingus from Dusseldorf, Paris, and Zurich; and Aeroflot from Moscow and St. Petersburg. Flights into Cork are operated by Aer Lingus from Amsterdam, Paris, and Rennes; Brit Air (☎ **098/621022** in France) from Brest and Nantes; and KLM from Amsterdam.

Service into Belfast International includes KLM CityHopper from Amsterdam.

BEST-VALUE AIRFARES

Airfares are always changing, with the year, with the season, and sometimes with the month (for St. Valentine's Day, Aer Lingus recently offered a promotional fare of $479 for two round-trip tickets to Ireland from New York or Boston, or $239.50 one-way). Generally speaking, fares fall into the categories listed below. (**Note:** fares quoted are round-trip to Dublin; fares to Shannon are $30 less per round-trip.)

SUPER APEX   Normally the cheapest fare across the Atlantic to Dublin Super APEX is a highly restricted advance-purchase fare. In the high season (June 15 to September 15), the Super APEX fare to Dublin—as of this writing—is $663 weekdays and $683 weekend, plus $22.95 in taxes, based on a 14-day advance purchase. In the shoulder months of May to mid-June and mid-September through October, the fare is $573 weekdays, $593 weekend, plus taxes. In the off season, January to March and November to December, the fare drops to $529 or lower plus taxes weekdays and weekends.

APEX   The next lowest fare, APEX requires a 7-day advance purchase. In the high season, it costs $763 weekdays and $783 weekend plus taxes; and in the shoulder season, it is $673 weekdays and $693 weekends, plus taxes.

SALE FARES   Each year, to stimulate early bookings, Aer Lingus offers Sale Fares—reduced prices on spring and summer travel, if fares are booked and paid for by a certain set date, usually February 28. Under this arrangement, the transatlantic fare to Dublin in April and May is $458 weekdays and weekend; in June and September, it is $518 weekdays and $538 weekend; and in July and August, it is $578 weekdays and $598 weekends. Taxes are extra in all cases. Sale fares require a minimum stay of seven days, a maximum stay of six months, and carry a $125 penalty for changes made after February or cancellations.

WEEKEND FARES   In the November to April period, Aer Lingus offers weekend fares for off-season minitrips from Wednesday to Sunday, Thursday to Monday, or

Friday to Tuesday. These fares, usually pegged around $459 to Dublin from New York or Boston, carry certain penalties and restrictions, but can be a great bargain for those who crave a long weekend in Dublin's Fair City.

PREMIER/FIRST/BUSINESS CLASS FARES If the sky is the limit for your travel budget, treat yourself to Premier Class Service on Aer Lingus, priced at $1,244 one-way to Dublin from New York or Boston. Delta's one-way first class fare from Atlanta to Dublin is $2,942; business class is $1,630. Taxes are extra in all cases.

EURO-GREENSAVER PASS This pass is designed for those who want to combine a visit to Ireland with a trip to London or other European cities. When purchased in conjunction with a transatlantic ticket on Aer Lingus, it costs $60 to visit any city in the United Kingdom or $99 to visit any of the 11 other cities in Europe served by Aer Lingus. This pass must be purchased prior to departure from the U.S. and some restrictions apply.

Charters

From the U.S. The largest and most reliable charter program to Ireland is operated by **Sceptre Charters,** 101-13 101 Ave., Ozone Park, NY 11416 (☎ toll free **800/ 221-0924** or **718/738-9400**). Using American Trans Air, Sceptre offers charter seats from New York to Dublin or Shannon priced from $369 to $469 round-trip. This operator also flies to Shannon from Boston, Philadelphia, Chicago, and Los Angeles.

From Canada Several companies in Canada operate charter flights from Toronto to Ireland, including Adventure Tours (☎ **416/967-1112** or toll free in Canada **800/ 268-7063**); Air Canada Vacations (☎ **416/615-8000** or toll free in Canada **800/263-0882**); Air Transat Holidays (☎ **416/485-3377** or toll free in Canada **800/ 268-8805**); Regent Holidays (☎ **416/673-3343** or toll free in Canada **800/387-4860**); and Sunquest Vacations (☎ **416/482-3333** or toll free in Canada **800/268-8899**).

BY FERRY

If you're heading to the Emerald Isle from Britain or mainland Europe, you can travel there over sea by ferry. Several car/passenger ferries offer over a minicruise atmosphere, as they're equipped with comfortable furnishings or cabin berths, good restaurants, duty-free shopping, and spacious lounges.

Prices average $50 to $100 per person, depending on your route, time of travel, and other factors. It's best to check with your travel agent for up-to-date details.

From Britain

B & I Line (☎ toll free **800/221-2474** in U.S.) operates from Holyhead, Wales, to Dublin and from Pembroke, Wales, to Rosslare, Co. Wexford. **Sealink Stena Line** (☎ toll free **800/677-8585** in U.S.) sails from Holyhead to Dun Laoghaire, eight miles south of Dublin; from Fishguard, Wales, to Rosslare; and from Stranraer, Scotland, to Larne, Northern Ireland. **Swansea/Cork Ferries** (☎ **0792/456116** in Britain) links Swansea, Wales, to Cork. **P & O European Ferries** (☎ **201/768-1187** in U.S.) operates from Cairnryan, Scotland, to Larne, Northern Ireland. **Isle of Man Steam Packet Company** (☎ **0624/661661** in Britain) connects Douglas, Isle of Man, to Dublin and Belfast. **Seacat Scotland Ltd.** (☎ toll free **800/677-8585** in U.S.) ferries from Stranraer, Scotland, to Belfast.

From Continental Europe

Irish Ferries (☎ toll free **800/221-2474**) sails from Le Havre, France to Rosslare and Cork, and from Cherbourg, France, to Rosslare and Cork. **Brittany Ferries** (☎ **021/277801** in Cork) connects Roscoff and St. Malo, France, to Cork.

Note: Because the Irish Ferries company is a member of the Eurail system, you can travel free on the ferries between Rosslare and LeHavre, if you hold a valid Eurailpass.

BY BUS FROM BRITAIN

Even though no bridges have yet been built across the Irish Sea, a bus service links Dublin with London and other major cities in Britain, using the B & I or Stena Sealink ferry trips as part of the bus ride.

Operated jointly by Ireland's Bus Eireann and Britain's National Express, these Supabus routes operate daily. One-way fares between Dublin and London start at £18 ($30); round-trip fares start at £35 ($52.50), making this connection a true bargain.

For full details on the Supabus routes, contact CIE Tours International in the U.S. (☎ toll free **800/CIE-TOUR**).

PACKAGE TOURS

Some people think that a package tour has to involve a tour with a group. Many package tours are designed for individuals or couples traveling together. Such packages may include airfare, a car rental, and hotel accommodations or just a hotel room plus sightseeing—all for one price that's lower than if you purchased each element separately as an individual. Tour operators can negotiate the best rates because of business volume, and they pass the savings on to you.

In these days of fluctuating currencies, it's wise to pre-pay for a vacation package in U.S. dollars soon after you make reservations. Many tour operators guarantee no increase in the land costs of a tour package as soon as the deposit is paid. So, even if the dollar weakens, your price is locked in at the original rate.

The leading firms offering package tours of Ireland and Northern Ireland include the following:

* **Aer Lingus "Discover Ireland" Vacations** (☎ toll free **800/223-6537**), offers Dublin City packages, pub tours, shopping tours, golf tours, and self-drive vacations designed for individual travelers.
* **CIE Tours International** (☎ toll free **800/CIE-TOUR**) is Ireland's national tour company, established more than 60 years ago and the leader in escorted vacations to Ireland, as well as Dublin City–based packages, self-drive vacations, and Ireland/Britain combination trips. CIE also offers rail/bus touring arrangements within Ireland for individuals and for groups.
* **Grimes Travel** (☎ toll free **800/832-7778**) offers various travel packages year round but is best known for its travel arrangements coinciding with the annual Dublin Marathon in October.

Other tour operators include: **Brendan Tours** (☎ toll free **800/421-8446**); **Brian Moore International Tours** (☎ toll free **800/982-2299**); **Lismore Tours** (☎ **800/547-6673**); **Lynott Tours** (☎ toll free **800/221-2474**); and **Owenoak-Castle Tours** (☎ toll free **800/426-4498**).

3

Settling into Ireland

Oᴺᴄᴇ ʏᴏᴜ ʜᴀᴠᴇ ᴀʀʀɪᴠᴇᴅ ɪɴ Iʀᴇʟᴀɴᴅ, ᴛʜᴇʀᴇ ᴀʀᴇ ʟᴏᴛs ᴏғ ᴛʜɪɴɢs ᴛᴏ ᴄᴏɴsɪᴅᴇʀ: how to travel around, where to stay, where to eat and drink, and how to save money in the process. This chapter will help you to get to know Ireland and to feel at home once you are there.

1 Getting Around

BY PLANE   Since Ireland is such a small country, it is not likely that you'll be flying from place to place. If you do require an air transfer, however, Aer Lingus, Dublin International Airport, Dublin 1 (☎ **01/844-4777**) operates daily scheduled flights linking Dublin with Cork, Galway, Kerry, Knock, Shannon, and Sligo.

BY TRAIN   Iarnrod Eireann/Irish Rail, Travel Centre, 35 Lower Abbey St., Dublin 1 (☎ **01/836-6222**), operates a network of train services throughout Ireland. With the exception of flying, train travel is the fastest way to get around Ireland. Most lines radiate from Dublin to other principal cities and towns. From Dublin, the journey time to Cork is 3 hours; Belfast, 2 hours; Galway, 3 hours; Limerick, $2^1/4$ hours; Killarney, 4 hours; Sligo, $3^1/4$ hours; and Waterford, $2^3/4$ hours.

In addition to the Irish Rail service between Dublin and Belfast, Northern Ireland Railways, Central Station, East Bridge Street, Belfast (☎ **0232/230310**) runs trains from Belfast to Derry, Coleraine, Bangor, and Newry.

BY BUS   Bus Eireann, Busaras/Central Bus Station, Dublin 1 (☎ **01/836-6111**), operates an extensive system of express bus service on routes such as Dublin to Donegal ($4^1/2$ hours), Killarney to Limerick ($2^1/2$ hours), Limerick to Galway ($2^1/4$ hours), and Limerick to Cork (2 hours), as well as local service to nearly every town in Ireland.

For bus travel within Northern Ireland, contact Ulsterbus, Europa Bus Centre, 10 Glengall St., Belfast (☎ **0232/333000**).

Rail/Bus Travel Passes   For extensive travels by public transport, save money by purchasing a rail/bus pass or a rail-only pass. The options include:

Emerald Card   This pass is good for rail and bus services throughout Ireland and Northern Ireland, priced at $288 for 15 days, and $168 for 8 days.

Irish Rover   For use in the Republic of Ireland only, this pass entitles you to 5 days of rail travel for $112.

Irish Explorer   For use in the Republic of Ireland, this pass gives combined rail and bus services for 8 days, for $136, or rail only for $96.

The 5-day passes are good for any 5 days in a 15-day period; the 8-day passes for any 8 days in 15; and the 15-day passes are valid for any 15 days in 30. All of these passes can be purchased from a travel agent or by contacting CIE Tours International, 100 Hanover Ave., Cedar Knolls, NJ 07927-0501 (☎ toll free **800/243-7687**).

If you combine a visit to Ireland with a stay in Britain, consider purchasing a BritIreland Pass, offering unlimited standard class rail travel in Britain, Ireland, and Northern Ireland. This pass includes round-trip cruise-style ferry crossings of the Irish Sea. Valid for one month, it costs $269 for 5 days of travel or $419 for 10 days of travel. Further information is available from travel agents or from BritRail, 1500 Broadway, New York, NY 10036 (☎ **212/575-2667**).

In addition, if your visit is part of an overall European itinerary and you have purchased a Eurailpass, you can use your pass for unlimited rail travel within Ireland.

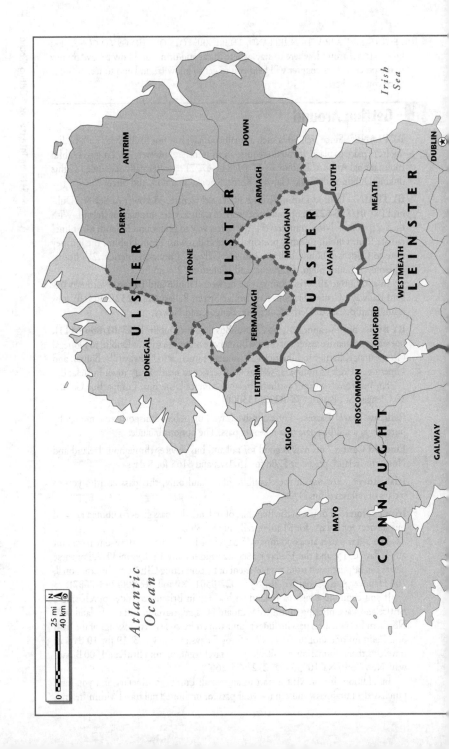

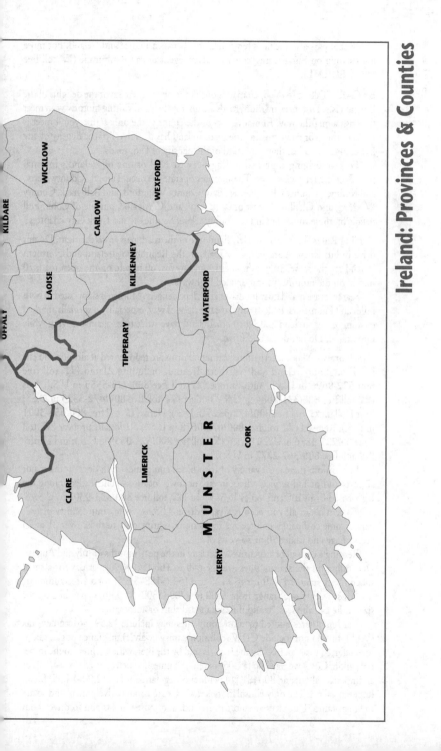

Ireland: Provinces & Counties

The Eurail pass also includes ferry transport between France and Ireland. For more information on Eurailpasses, contact a travel agent or call RailEurope (☎ toll free **800/4-EURAIL**).

BY CAR   Taking to the open road is one of the best ways to savor the delights of the Emerald Isle. Distances are short, roads are uncrowded, and visiting motorists can meet the Irish along the way. In many parts of the country, the only traffic you'll meet is herds of sheep or cows crossing the road. Ireland has the lowest traffic density of any EU country, and less than one-third of the density of U.S. roads.

To save driving time and mileage, try to avail of one of Ireland's internal passenger/car ferry crossings. These routes operate between Tarbert, County Kerry, and Killimer, County Clare; Passage East, County Waterford, and Ballyhack, County Wexford; and Glenbrook, east of Cork City, and Carrigaloe, outside of Cobh. Full details on these routes are in the County Clare, Southeast, and Cork City chapters.

Driving Rules   Drive on the left-hand side of the road; pass from the right. Do not drive in bus lanes. Speed limits for roads in the Republic of Ireland and Northern Ireland are the same: 30 m.p.h. in cities and towns, 60 m.p.h. on the open road, 70 m.p.h. on the motorways and divided highways.

Seat belts are mandatory for driver and all passengers. Mileage is signposted in both miles and kilometers. Pedestrians have the right of way, especially in specially marked crossing zones. Ireland and Northern Ireland have strict rules against driving while intoxicated. Do not drink and drive.

Car Rentals   Major international car rental firms are represented at airports and cities throughout Ireland and Northern Ireland, including Alamo (☎ toll free **800/522-9696** in U.S.); Auto-Europe (☎ toll free **800/223-5555** in U.S.); Avis (☎ toll free **800/331-1084** in U.S.); Budget (☎ toll free **800/472-3325** in U.S.); EuroDollar (☎ toll free **800/472-3325** in U.S.); Hertz (☎ toll free **800/654-3001** in U.S.); Kemwel (☎ toll free **800/678-0678** in U.S.); National/Europcar (☎ toll free **800/227-3876** in U.S.); Payless (☎ toll free **800/524-0555** in U.S.); and Thrifty (☎ toll free **800/367-2277** in U.S.).

In addition, there are a variety of Irish-based companies, with desks at the major airports and/or full-service offices in city or town locations. The leader among the Irish-based firms is Dan Dooley Rent-a-Car (☎ toll free **800/331-9301** in U.S.).

To rent a car, all you need is a valid driver's license from your country of residence; some companies enforce age restrictions, renting only to those over 21 or 23 years of age and under 70 or 75 years of age.

Renting a car can be expensive, especially in the peak months of July and August. Depending on the season, rates average £40 to £60 ($60–$90) per day for a small subcompact standard shift car to £125 to £150 ($188–$225) for a large automatic car. Most weekly rates range from £200 to £700 ($300–$1,050), depending on the size of the car, the season, and if it is standard shift or automatic.

Car rental rates quoted by most companies may include 12.5% government tax (VAT), but do not include CDW (collision damage waiver) insurance or gas. Gasoline, referred to as "petrol" by the Irish, is sold by the liter, with 4.5 liters to the imperial gallon. Costs average 70p ($1.05) per liter of unleaded petrol or £2.75 ($4.13) for an imperial gallon; and 80p ($1.20) per liter of regular petrol or £2.90 ($4.35) for an imperial gallon. The only consolation is that cars are comparatively small and so are their gas tanks. Distances are short in Ireland, and most tourists aim to drive about

Irish Rail Routes

100 to 150 miles a day, making a tank of gas last a lot longer than in the U.S. It might also cheer you up to know that a gallon in Ireland is an imperial measure, about a fifth more than the U.S. gallon.

Gas stations are plentiful throughout Ireland, in cities, towns, and in remote regions. Most stations usually accept major credit cards, especially MasterCard (also called Access) and Visa; they do not, as a rule, honor U.S. gasoline company cards. Gas stations usually do not have public rest rooms.

Some money-saving points: (1) The price of gas in Ireland can vary from brand to brand, station to station, and locality to locality. In other words, it pays to compare and shop around. (2) Irish car rental firms will give you a car with a tankful of gas, and they expect you to return it the same way. If you don't, they will add a refueling charge to your bill. Since the car rental firms usually charge the maximum rate per gallon for this, it is wise to find a competitive rate at a local station and fill up the tank before you return the car. You'll save at least a few pounds.

Parking When arriving in cities, be sure to observe local rules including where to park. Some small cities and most towns have free street parking, but larger cities confine parking to metered spaces or parking garages and lots. Disc-parking is also in effect in many places, requiring you to purchase a paper disc and display it for the time you are parked in a certain area. Discs usually cost from 20p to 40p (30¢ to 60¢) per hour of use; most shops, hotels, and tourist offices sell parking discs. Some towns also follow the "pay and display" system which means that you buy a parking voucher, usually from 20p to 40p (30¢ to 60¢) per hour, from a machine at the site and display the voucher for the time you are parked.

In Belfast and other large cities in the North, you will see signs stating Control Zone, indicating that no vehicle can be left unattended at any time. This means that if you are a single traveler, you cannot park and leave your car; if you are a traveling twosome, one person must remain in the car while it is parked. Unlocked cars are subject to a fine in the North of Ireland, for security reasons.

If you are renting a car in the Republic and taking it into the North and vice-versa, be sure to check with the car rental firm that the rental insurance provided covers cross-border transport. If not, you may be required to purchase extra insurance. If you rent a car in the Republic, it is best to return it to the Republic, and if you rent in the North, it is best to return it to the point of origin in the North, since some firms will charge extra for cross-border drop-offs.

2 Suggested Itineraries

To see all of Ireland and Northern Ireland, you need at least two weeks and possibly three. If you only have a week, however, you can certainly cover the main highlights.

Here are a few ideal itineraries, with the number of days suggested for each city or touring center indicated in parentheses. Each tour starts or finishes near Shannon or Dublin, the two main arrival/departure points. You can ask your travel agent to design a trip, based on your interests or the amount of time you can devote to Ireland.

One Week—Southern Coast   Shannon area (1), Kerry (2), Cork (2), Wexford (1), Dublin (1).

One Week—Main Highlights   Shannon area (1), Kerry (1), Cork (1), Waterford (1), Dublin (2), Galway (1).

Atlantic Ocean

North Channel

Portrush
Coleraine
Magherafelt
LONDONDERRY
Letterkenny
Larne
Ballybofey
Strabane
Donegal
Cookstown
BELFAST
Omagh
Ballyshannon
Dungannon
Portadown
Bundoran
Lough Derg
Newry
SLIGO
Enniskillen
Monaghan
Armagh
BALLINA
Ballinamore
Clones
C'Blayney
Carrick-on-Shannon
Cavan
Dundalk
Carrickmacross
Dooagh
Charlestown
Boyle
Virginia
Kells
Ardee
Achill
Castlebar
Knock
Mohill
Drogheda
Westport
Strokestown
Navan
Slane
Irish Sea
Claremorris
Ballyhaunis
LONGFORD
Leenane
Roscommon
Moylough
Mullingar
Kinnegad
Clifden
Tuam
ATHLONE
Roundstone
Oughterard
Ballinasloe
Moate
Rhode
DUBLIN
GALWAY
Loughrea
Edenderry
Bray
Gort
Portumna
Dr. Nua
Naas
Lahinch
Birr
Kildare
Wicklow
Miltown Malbay
Ennis
ROSCREA
Port Laoise
Athy
Arklow
Shannon Airport
Nenagh
Durrow
Carlow
Tullow
Gorey
Kilkee
Thurles
Kilrush
LIMERICK
Cashel
Kilkenny
Enniscorthy
Ballybunion
Adare
Tipperary
Callan
New Ross
WEXFORD
Listowel
Clonmel
Rosslare Harbour
Dingle
Rathluirc
Cahir
Carrick-on-Suir
Tralee
Mitchelstown
WATERFORD
Mallow
Fermoy
Cappoquin
Killarney
Dungarvan
Kenmare
Youghal
Glengarriff
Bandon
CORK
Bantry
Clonakilty
Skibbereen

St. George's Channel

0   25 mi
     40 km

N

One Week—East Coast   Dublin (3), Dundalk (1), Kilkenny (1), Waterford (1), and Wexford (1).

One Week—West Coast   Kerry (2), Galway and Connemara (2), Sligo (2), and Shannon area (1).

One Week—The North West   Shannon area (1), Sligo (2), Donegal (3), Shannon (1).

One Week—The North   Newcastle (1), Belfast (2), Antrim Coast (2), Derry (1), Enniskillen (2).

Two Weeks—The Coastal Circuit   Shannon (1); Kerry (2); Cork (1), Dublin (2), Belfast (2), Sligo (1), Donegal (2), Galway, Mayo, and Connemara (2), Shannon (1).

Three Weeks—The Complete Tour   Shannon (1), Kerry (2), Cork (1), Kilkenny (1), Waterford or Wexford (1), Dublin (3), Belfast (2), Portrush (1), Derry or Enniskillen (2), Sligo (1), Donegal (2), Mayo (1), Galway and Connemara (2), Shannon (1).

---

3   Where to Stay

From castles and country manors to modern high-rise hotels and motels, Ireland has a great variety of places to stay, priced to suit every budget.

All hotel accommodations throughout the Republic of Ireland are inspected, registered, and graded by the Irish Tourist Board. The board classifies each hotel into a category of from 1- to 5-stars, consistent with other European countries and international standards. Guesthouses are classified into categories of 1- to 4-stars.

In Northern Ireland, the Northern Ireland Tourist Board inspects and grades hotels according to a 1- to 4-star rating system, and guesthouses are divided into two categories, grade A and grade B.

As a rule, hotels offer full services, restaurants, coffee shops, bars, lounges, shops, currency exchanges, concierge desks, and more, while guesthouses provide more limited facilities—they may serve only breakfast, may or may not have a bar license, and often do not have elevators (this is often because of the historic nature of their structures).

The lodgings described on the following pages are hotels and guesthouses that we consider to offer the best facilities and value. Unless otherwise noted, they offer all rooms with private bath or shower. All are centrally heated, although the majority do not have air conditioning, since Ireland has a fairly equable climate and air conditioning is normally not required. Almost all of these lodgings provide car parking for customers, whether in secure garages or adjacent parking lots. This service is free for overnight guests.

RATES   All room charges quoted include 12.5% government tax (VAT) in the Republic of Ireland and 17.5% VAT in Northern Ireland, but do not include service charge, usually between 10% and 15%, with the majority adding 12.5%. Most hotels and guesthouses will automatically add the service charge onto your final bill, although in recent years, many family-run or limited-service places have begun the practice of not charging for service, leaving it as an option for the guest.

The rates quoted are in effect at presstime, but will probably increase slightly in 1995/1996. Rates are for room only, unless otherwise indicated.

We have classified hotels and guesthouses into categories of price. The price levels as specified below are an indication of what it costs for a double room for two people per night including tax but not service charge.

Very Expensive	£150 and up ($225 and up)
Expensive	£120–£150 ($180–$225)
Moderate	£60–£120 ($90–$180)
Inexpensive	£30–£60 ($45–$90)
Budget	Under £30 ($45)

RESERVATIONS   Many hotels can be booked through toll free 800 numbers in the U.S. For those properties that do not have a U.S. reservation number, the fastest way to reserve is by telephone or fax. Fax is preferable since you then have a printed confirmation. You can then follow up by sending a deposit check (usually the equivalent of one night's room rate) or giving your credit card number.

If you arrive in Ireland without a reservation, the staff members at the various tourist offices throughout the Republic and Northern Ireland will gladly find you a room via a computerized reservation service known as Gulliver. You can also call the Gulliver line directly yourself by dialing **1-800/600-800.** This is a nationwide and cross-border "freephone" facility for credit-card bookings.

BED-AND-BREAKFAST HOMES   In addition to hotels and guesthouses, Ireland and Northern Ireland have hundreds of private homes that rent rooms to visitors on a nightly basis. Usually referred to as bed-and-breakfasts, these homes are also inspected and registered, but are not graded. The number of rooms available at each house varies, but it is usually three to five, some of which may or may not have a private bath or shower. Most do not accept credit cards.

These houses can be booked in person at any tourist office or by phoning or writing to individual owners. Nightly per person rates average £14 to £17 ($21 to $25.50) with private bath and £12 to £5 ($18 to $7.50) without private bath. These rates include a full Irish breakfast and there is no service charge. For a list of homes available in advance of your visit, contact the Irish Tourist Board or the Northern Ireland Tourist Board (see "Sources of Information," in Chapter 2). Also refer to *Frommer's Ireland on $45 a Day* by Susan Poole for hundreds of recommendations personally inspected by the author.

A FEW TIPS   Many older hotels and guesthouses consider the lobby level as the ground floor (not the first floor); the first floor is the next floor up or what Americans would call the second floor. So, if your room is on the first floor, that means it is one flight up, not on ground level.

Elevators, readily available in hotels but not so plentiful in guesthouses, are called lifts. Remember to press "G" for the main floor or lobby, not "1."

Concierges or hall porters, as they are sometimes called, arrange all types of services, from taking luggage or delivering packages to your room to obtaining theater tickets, booking a self-drive or chauffeur-driven car, selling postage stamps and mailing letters/cards, dispensing tourist literature, or reserving taxis. Many of Dublin's concierges consider their craft a real art form and are members of the prestigious international organization known as Les Clefs d'Or. Be prepared to be pampered!

4 Where to Dine

Ireland has a wonderful variety of restaurants in all price categories. The settings range from old-world hotel dining rooms, country mansions, and castles to skylit terraces, shopfront bistros, riverside cottages, thatched-roof pubs, and converted chapels. Best of all, the food is fresh, varied, and delicious (see "Food & Drink," in Chapter 1). Before you hasten to book a table, here are a few things you should know.

RESERVATIONS   Except for self-service eateries, informal cafes, and some popular seafood spots, most all restaurants encourage reservations. The more expensive restaurants absolutely require reservations, since there is little turnover—once a table is booked, it is yours for the whole lunch period or for the evening until closing. Friday and Saturday nights (and Sunday lunch) seatings are often booked out a week or more in advance at some places, so have a few choices in mind if you are booking at the last minute.

Here's a tip for Americans who don't mind dining early. If you stop into or phone a restaurant and find that it is booked out from 8pm or 8:30pm onward, ask if you can dine early (at 6:30pm or 7pm), with a promise to leave by 8pm, and you will sometimes get a table. A few restaurants are even experimenting with early bird menus, with reduced prices, to attract people for early evening seating. Irish restaurateurs are just beginning to learn that it is a lot more profitable to have more than one seating a night.

TABLE D'HOTE OR A LA CARTE   In most restaurants, two menus are offered: *table d'hôte:* a set three- or four-course lunch or dinner, with a variety of choices, for a fixed price; and *à la carte:* a menu offering a wide choice of appetizers (starters), soups, main courses, salads or vegetables, and desserts (sweets), each individually priced.

With the former, you pay the set price whether you take each course or not, but, if you do take each course, the total price offers very good value. With the latter, you choose what you want and pay accordingly. If you are just a salad-and-entree person, then à la carte will probably work out to be less expensive, but if you want all the courses and the trimmings, then stick with the table d'hôte.

In the better restaurants, the table d'hôte menu is pushed at lunch time, particularly for the business clientele. In the evening, both menus are readily available. In the less expensive restaurants, coffee shops, and cafés, you can usually order à la carte at any time, whether it be a soup and sandwich for lunch or steak and salad at night.

Here's a tip for those on a budget: If you want to try a top-rated restaurant, but can't afford the dinner prices, then have your main meal in the middle of the day by trying the table d'hôte set lunch menu at the special restaurant. You'll experience the same great cuisine at half the price of a nighttime meal.

PRICES   Meal prices at restaurants include 12.5% VAT in the Republic of Ireland and a 17.5% VAT in Northern Ireland, but service charge is extra. In more than half of all restaurants, a set service charge is added automatically to your bill—this can range from 10% to 15%. In the remaining restaurants, it is now the custom not to add any service charge, leaving the amount of the tip up to you. Needless to say, this diversity of policy can be confusing for a visitor, but each restaurant normally prints its policy on the menu. If it is not clear, ask.

When no service charge is added, then you should tip as you normally would in the U.S.—up to 15% depending on the quality of the service. If 10% to 12.5% has already been added to your bill, then you should leave an appropriate amount that will total 15% if service has been satisfactory.

We have classified the restaurants described in this book into categories of price. The price levels are based on what it costs for a complete dinner (or lunch, if dinner is not served) for one person including tax and tip, but not wine or alcoholic beverages.

Very Expensive	£35 ($52.50) and up
Expensive	£25–£35 ($37.50–$52.50)
Moderate	£10–£25 ($15–$37.50)
Inexpensive	£5–£10 ($7.50–$15.00)
Budget	Under £5 ($7.50)

MONEY-SAVING TIP   Some restaurants, in all categories of price, offer a fixed-price three-course tourist menu during certain hours and days. These menus offer limited choices, but are usually lower in price than the restaurant's regular table d'hôte menu. Look for a tourist menu with a green Irish chef symbol in the window; there will also be a copy of the menu displayed and the hours when the prices are in effect.

SOME DINING TIPS   If you are fond of a cocktail or beer before or during your meal, be sure to check in advance if a restaurant has a full license—some restaurants are only licensed to sell wine.

Don't be surprised if you are not ushered to your table as soon as you arrive at a restaurant. This is not a delaying tactic—many of the better dining rooms carry on the old custom of seating you in a lounge or bar area while you sip an aperitif and peruse the menus. Your waiter then comes to discuss the choices and take your order. You are not called to the table until the first course is about to be served. It's a relaxed way of dining, designed to avoid having you sit at a table with empty dishes or glasses—and just another Irish way of making guests feel welcome.

5   Sightseeing Tips/Savings

Sightseeing on a budget? Ireland offers several ways to cut costs and stretch a dollar (or a pound). Here are a few ways to save on admission charges at major attractions.

A **Heritage Card** entitles you to unlimited admission into the more than 50 attractions all over Ireland operated by the Office of Public Works. These include castles, stately homes, historic monuments, national parks, and more. This card, which costs £10 ($15.00) adults, £7 ($10.50) seniors, and £4 ($6.00) children/students, is available from participating attractions or from the Office of Public Works, 51 St. Stephen's Green, Dublin 2 (☎ **01/661-3111** ext. 2386).

Heritage Island VIP Discount Entry Card entitles you to discounted admissions at more than 60 attractions in the Republic of Ireland and Northern Ireland. These sites range from castles, stately homes, and heritage centers to caves, planetariums, forts, national parks, museums, and abbeys. The card comes with a guide to the attractions, on sale for £3 ($4.50) at tourist offices and shops, or from Heritage Island, 37 Main St., Donnybrook, Dublin 4 (fax 01/260-0058). It is also available in the U.S. in advance of your trip by sending $10 to Heritage Island, 795 Franklin Ave., Franklin Lakes, NJ 07417.

Shannon Vacation Money is a $200 packet of vouchers in the format of fake currency that can be used at various attractions, hotels, restaurants, shops, golf courses, and historic sites in the Shannon and West of Ireland area. For example, you can save from £5 to £10 ($7.50 to $15) on greens fees at leading golf courses or have a free bottle of wine with dinner at designated restaurants, or use a voucher toward purchases at Shannon's Duty Free Shop. These vouchers are distributed free of charge to visitors who fly into Shannon Airport and embark on certain self-drive tours. This innovative program, due to run through mid-1995, may be extended or replaced by another type of discount program. For full details of what special offers may be in effect for the rest of 1995 and in 1996, contact Shannon Development Company, 345 Park Ave., New York, NY 10154 (☎ 212/371-5550).

The National Trust Visitors Guide, covering attractions in Northern Ireland, comes with vouchers offering free or reduced admission charges for one person at 16 properties ranging from castles and stately homes to the Giant's Causeway. Copies are available from the Northern Ireland Tourist Board (see "Sources of Information" in Chapter 2).

6 VAT Tax Refunds

When shopping in the Republic of Ireland and Northern Ireland, bear in mind that the price of most goods already includes VAT (Valued Added Tax), a government tax of just over 17%. The only exceptions are books and children's clothing/footwear which are not subject to VAT. VAT is a hidden tax—it is already included in the prices quoted to you and on the price tags.

Fortunately, as a visitor, you can avoid paying this tax, IF you follow a few simple procedures. (Note: EU residents are not entitled to a VAT refund on goods purchased.)

The easiest way to make a VAT-free purchase is to arrange for a store to ship the goods directly abroad to your home; such a shipment is not liable for VAT. However, you do have to pay for shipping, so you may not save that much in the end.

If you wish to take your goods with you, then you must pay the full amount for each item including all VAT charges. However, you can have that tax refunded to you in a number of ways. Here are the main choices:

STORE REFUND   At the time of purchase, obtain a full receipt showing name, address, and VAT paid (cash register tally slips are not acceptable by Customs); passports and other forms of identification (e.g., driver's license) may be required. When departing Ireland, go to the Customs Office at the airport or ferryport to have receipts stamped and goods inspected. Stamped receipts should then be sent to the store of purchase and the store will then issue a VAT refund check to you by mail to your home address. Most stores will deduct a small handling fee for this service.

Cashback   This is a private company that gives you a cash refund on purchases made at one or more of the 2,000 stores affiliated with its system. Refunds can be collected (in the currency of your choice) as you depart from Dublin or Shannon Airport. The fee for this service is calculated on the amount of money you spend in each store. If you spend £150 ($225) or less in a store, the fee is £3.35 ($5.03); if you spend between £150–£300 ($225–$450), the fee is £4.35 ($6.53); and if you spend over £300 ($450) in a store, the fee is £5.35 ($8.03).

To obtain a refund, you must do the following:

1. Purchases must be made from stores displaying a Cashback sticker; and each time you make a purchase, you must obtain a Cashback voucher from a participating shop.
2. Fill out each form with your name, address, passport number, and other required details.
3. When departing Ireland, if you have any vouchers with a value of over £200 ($300), you must have them stamped and validated by a customs official.
4. You can then go to the Cashback desk at Dublin Airport (Departures Hall) or Shannon Airport (in the Arrivals Hall), turn in your stamped Cashback forms, and receive cash payments in U.S. or Canadian dollars, British pounds sterling, or Irish punts, whatever you prefer.

If you are departing from Ireland via a ferryport, or if you don't have time to get to the Cashback desk before you leave, you can also mail your stamped receipts to the Cashback Headquarters at Spiddal Industrial Estate, County Galway (☎ 091/83258). Your refund, issued as a check, will be mailed to your home within 21 days. You can also request to have your VAT refund applied to your credit card account.

TaxBack   This company refunds the VAT after you leave Ireland by charging a flat fee averaging 2% of the gross price of goods purchased. On departure from Ireland, go to the TaxBack service desk at Shannon or Dublin Airport and turn in your receipts. Any receipts over £200 ($300) in value must first be stamped by a Customs official. If time is short, you can return home, have your receipts stamped by a notary public, and then mail them to TaxBack, P.O. Box 132 CK, 125 Patrick St., Cork City, Co. Cork (☎ 021/277010). If you charged your purchases on a credit card, TaxBack will arrange a credit to your account in the amount of the VAT refund; if you paid cash, then you will receive a check in U.S. dollars sent to your home with the refund.

7 A Primer on Pubs

The mainstay of Irish social life—both by night and by day—is unquestionably the pub. With more than 10,000 specimens spread throughout the Emerald Isle, there are pubs in every city, town, and hamlet, on every street at every turn.

The origin of pubs harks back several centuries ago to a time when there were no hotels or restaurants. In those days, neighbors would gather in a kitchen, often to sample some home brew. As a certain spot grew popular, word spread and people would come from all directions, always assured of a warm welcome.

Such places gradually became known as public houses or pubs, for short. In time, the name of the person who tended a public house was mounted over the doorway, and hence many pubs still bear a family or proprietor's name, such as Moran's, Kate Kearney's, Doheny & Nesbitt, or W. Ryan.

Many pubs have been in the same family for generations and have changed little in the last 200 years. A few may have added televisions, pool tables, and dartboards to their decor, but the true Irish pub is still basically a homey place—a unique hybrid of open hearth, news depot, and gathering spot.

In recent years, many pubs have shown their versatility by introducing pub grub, an inexpensive food service, primarily at lunchtime. Pubs have also led the way in providing musical entertainment in the evenings, whether it be spontaneous traditional tunes or a staged contemporary program.

Most of all, however, the pub is a friendly place where the art of conversation is king and strangers soon become friends.

PUB ETIQUETTE Before you set foot into one of these hallowed establishments, it is helpful to know about local habits. Rarely do people sit or drink alone in a pub. If you don't have your own family and friends traveling with you, you'll find that the Irish will draw you into their own conversations. If so, be warned that the round system often prevails. That means that each person in a group or conversation takes a turn buying a round of drinks; this can require great stamina if you happen to be in a large party. You also pay as you go, not running up a tab.

PUB HOURS In the Republic of Ireland, hours May through September are from 10:30am to 11:30pm on Monday through Saturday, closing a half-hour earlier during the rest of the year. On Sunday, bars are open from 12:30pm to 2pm and from 4pm to 11pm all year.

In the North, pubs are open year-round from 11:30am to 11pm on Monday through Saturday, and from 12:30pm to 2pm and 7pm to 10pm on Sunday.

DRINK PRICES Charges are more or less standardized throughout Ireland, with hotel bar prices sometimes being slightly higher than the norm. A pint of draft beer or stout average £2 ($3); bottle of beer £1.30–£2 ($1.95–$3); measure of whiskey £1.65–£2.05 ($2.48–$3.08); brandy from £1.85 ($3.78); or a glass of wine £1.60–£2.15 ($2.40–$3.23).

RAISING A GLASS The official toast is "*Slainte!*"—an Irish word meaning the equivalent of "To your health!" In the North, you'll also hear a lot of "Cheers!"

So head for a few pubs—and "*Slainte!*" or "Cheers!" to you.

8 Tracing Your Irish Roots

Whether your name is Kelly or Klein, you may have some ancestral ties with Ireland—about 44 million Americans do, and that's almost 10 times as many people as there are in all of Ireland today! From medieval times, the Irish have spread their influence (and their genes) all over the world—from London to Los Angeles, Montreal to Melbourne, and from Africa to Argentina.

If you are planning to visit Ireland to trace your roots, you'll enjoy the greatest success if you do some planning in advance. The more information you can gather about your family before your visit, the easier it will be to find your ancestral home or even a distant cousin once you arrive.

When in Ireland, you can do the research and foot-work yourself or you can use the services of a commercial agency. One of the best firms to contact is **Hibernian Research Co.,** P.O. Box 3097, Dublin 6 (☎ **01/496-6522;** fax 01/497-3011). These researchers, all trained by the Chief Herald of Ireland, have a combined total of over 100 years of professional experience in working on all aspects of family histories, no matter how complicated or compact. Among the cases that Hibernian Research has handled in the past were U.S. President Ronald Reagan and Canadian Prime Minister Brian Mulrooney. If your ancestors were from the North, a similar service is operated by the **Irish Heritage Association,** The Old Engine House, Portview,

310 Netownards Road, Belfast BT4 1HE (☎ **0203/455325**). Minimum search fees average £50 ($75).

If you prefer to do the digging yourself, be advised that Dublin City is the location for all of the Republic of Ireland's centralized genealogical records and Belfast is the place to go for Ulster ancestral hunts. Here are the major sources of information:

The Genealogical Office, 2 Kildare St., Dublin (☎ **01/661-8811**). It incorporates the office of the Chief Herald and operates a specialist consultation service on how to trace your ancestry. Minimum consultation fee is £20 ($30).

The National Library, Kildare Street, Dublin 2 (☎ **01/661-9911**). The resources include an extensive collection of pre-1880 Catholic records of baptisms, births, and marriages, plus other genealogical material, including trade directories, journals of historical and archaeological societies, local histories, and most newspapers. In addition, the Library has a comprehensive indexing system which will enable you to identify the material you need to consult.

Office of the Registrar General, Joyce House, 8/11 Lombard Street East, Dublin 2 (☎ **01/671-1000**). Here you will find the records for non-Catholic marriages dating from 1845, and of births, deaths, and marriages from 1864 onwards. A general search cost £12 ($18).

The National Archives, Bishop Street, Dublin 8 (☎ **01/478-3711**). Previously known as the Public Record Office, this facility was severely damaged by a fire in the early 1920s and many valuable source documents pre-dating that event were lost. However, numerous records rich in genealogical interest are still available here. These include Griffith's Primary Valuation of Ireland, 1848–1863, which records the names of all those owning or occupying land or property in Ireland at the time; the complete national census of 1901 to 1911; tithe listings, indexes to wills, administrations, licenses, and marriage bonds. In addition, there is also an ever-expanding collection of Church of Ireland Parish Registers on microfilm and partial surviving census returns for the 19th century. In addition, there are rebellion reports and records relating to the period of the 1798 rebellion; crime and convict records, and details of those sentenced to transportation to Australia.

Registry of Deeds, Henrietta Street, Dublin 1 (☎ **01/873-2233**). Its records date from 1708 and relate to all the usual transactions affecting property, notably leases, mortgages, and settlements, and some wills. A fee of £2 ($3) per day is charged which includes instruction on how to handle the indexes.

Public Record Office of Northern Ireland, 66 Balmoral Ave., Belfast BT 9 6NY (☎ **0232/661621**). This office has the surviving official records of Northern Ireland including tithe and valuation records from the 1820s and 1830s; copy wills from 1858 for Ulster; and copies of most pre-1900 registers of baptisms, marriages, and burial papers for all denominations in Ulster.

If you know the county or town that your ancestors came from, then you can also consult the various local genealogical centers, parish records, and libraries throughout Ireland and Northern Ireland.

Fast Facts: Ireland

Area Codes   Codes for cities and towns covered in this book are given at the beginning of each chapter, or with specific phone numbers.

Babysitters   With advance notice, most hotels and guesthouses will arrange for babysitting.

Business Hours   As a rule, banking hours throughout all of Ireland are from 10am to 12:30pm and 1:30pm to 3pm, Monday through Wednesday, and Friday; and from 10am to 12:30pm and 1:30 to 5pm on Thursday. In larger cities, some banks now remain open through the lunch hour as well.

Most business offices are open from 9am to 5pm, Monday through Friday. Stores and shops are open from 9am to 5:30pm Monday through Saturday. In some cities such as Dublin, Belfast, Cork, and Galway, stores remain open until 8pm or 9pm on Thursday or Friday; and in some country towns, there is an early closing day, meaning that shops will close one weekday afternoon per week. Some tourism-oriented stores also open on Sunday from 11am or noon until 5pm or later in many areas. For exact shopping hours, see each individual chapter.

Camera and Film   Film for color prints and slides is readily available in Ireland, on sale at camera shops and pharmacies. One-hour photo-developing services are also available in most major cities.

Climate   See "When to Go," in Chapter 2.

Currency   See "Information, Entry Requirements & Money," in Chapter 2.

Currency Exchange   A currency exchange service in Ireland is signposted as a Bureau de Change. There are bureaux de change at all banks and at many post office branches. In addition, many hotels and travel agencies offer bureau de change services, although the best rate of exchange is usually given at banks.

Customs   See "Entry Requirements," in Chapter 2.

Dentists   For a recommendation, look under "Dental Surgeons" in the Golden Pages of the Irish telephone book or in the Yellow Pages of the Northern Ireland telephone book.

Doctors   In an emergency, most hotels and guesthouses will contact a house doctor for you. You can also consult the Golden Pages of the Irish telephone book or the Yellow Pages of the Northern Ireland telephone book under "Doctors—Medical."

Documents Required   See "Information, Entry Requirements & Money," in Chapter 2.

Driving Rules   See "Getting Around," in this chapter.

Drugstores   Drugstores are usually called chemist shops or pharmacies. Look under "Chemists—Pharmaceutical" in the Golden Pages of the Irish telephone book or "Chemists—Dispensing" in the Yellow Pages of the Northern Ireland telephone book.

Electricity   The standard electrical current is 220 volts AC (50 cycles) in the Republic of Ireland and 240 volts (50 cycles) in Northern Ireland. Most hotels have 110 volt shaver points for use in bathrooms, but other 110 volt equipment such as hair dryers will not work. It is necessary to bring a transformer and plug adaptor.

Embassies/Consulates   The American Embassy is located at 42 Elgin Rd., Ballsbridge, Dublin 4 (☎ 01/668-8777); Canadian Embassy, 65/68 St. Stephen's Green, Dublin 2 (☎ 01/678-1988); British Embassy, 33 Merrion Road, Dublin 4 (☎ 01/669-5211); Australian Embassy, Fitzwilton House, Wilton Terrace, Dublin 2 (☎ 01/676-1517). In addition, there is an American Consulate at 14 Queen St., Belfast BT1 6EQ (☎ 0232/328239).

Emergencies   For police, fire, or other emergencies, dial **999.**

Etiquette   The Irish still observe chivalrous practices, such as males holding doors for females and younger folk giving up a seat on a bus for a senior citizen. They are inquisitive and will try to draw you into conversation; be polite and soft-spoken and you will fit right in. Avoid discussions of religion or politics, especially criticisms of Irish religious practices or politics in the North of Ireland. Common courtesies prevail; never use a demanding or demeaning tone of voice, avoid pushiness, and always stand in line, or queue, patiently.

Hairdressers/Barbers   Consult the Golden Pages or Yellow Pages under "Hairdressers—Ladies" and "Hairdressers—Men."

Holidays   See "When to Go," in Chapter 2.

Hospitals   See listings in individual chapters.

Information.   See "Information, Entry Requirements & Money," in Chapter 2.

Language   See the "Language" section in Chapter 1.

Laundry/Dry Cleaning   Most hotels provide same-day or next-day laundry and/or dry cleaning services. If you wish to make your own arrangements, look under "Dry Cleaners" in the Golden Pages or Yellow Pages of the telephone book.

Liquor Laws   Individuals must be age 18 or over to be served alcoholic beverages in Ireland. Ireland has very strict laws and penalties regarding driving while intoxicated, so don't drink and drive. For pub hours, see "A Primer on Pubs," in Chapter 3. Restaurants with liquor licenses are permitted to serve alcohol during the hours meals are served. Hotels and guesthouses with licenses can serve during normal hours to the general public; overnight guests, referred to as residents, can be served after closing hours. Alcoholic beverages by the bottle can be purchased at liquor stores, pubs displaying "off-license" signs, and at some supermarkets.

Mail Information   In Ireland, mail boxes are painted green with the word "Post" on top. In Northern Ireland, they are painted red with a royal coat of arms symbol. To mail a letter via airmail service to the U.S., from the Republic of Ireland it costs 52p (78¢) and 38p (57¢) for a postcard; from Northern Ireland, it costs 39p (56¢) and 34p (51¢) respectively. It takes about five days to a week for delivery. The best way to receive mail while in Dublin is to have it sent c/o your hotel or guesthouse. Otherwise, you can have mail sent to the main post office—this service is called poste restante, and should be addressed to your name, in care of the post office in the city you will be staying. All poste restante mail, which can be collected within normal opening hours, will be held for two weeks, then returned to sender if unclaimed. There is no charge for this facility.

Money   See "Information, Entry Requirements & Money," in Chapter 2.

Newspapers/Magazines   The main national daily newspapers in the Republic of Ireland are the *Irish Times, Irish Independent, Irish Press,* and *Cork Examiner.* The prime dailies in the North are the *Belfast Newsletter* and the *Belfast Telegraph.*

Police   In the Republic of Ireland, a law-enforcement officer is called a Garda Siochana (guardian of the peace); in the plural, it's Gardai (pronounced *gar'-dee*) or simply referred to as the Guards. Dial **999** to reach the gardai in an emergency. Except for special detachments, Irish police are unarmed and wear dark blue uniforms. In Northern Ireland, the police can be reached by dialing **999.**

Radio/TV   In the Republic of Ireland, RTE (Radio Telefis Eireann) is the national broadcasting authority with two TV channels, RTE 1 and Network 2, and three radio stations, RTE 1, 2FM, and Radio na Gaeltachta (all Irish language-programming). Besides RTE, there are other smaller local stations throughout Ireland (see individual chapter listings). In the North, there is Ulster Television, BBC-TV (British Broadcasting Corporation) and ITN-TV (Independent), plus BBC Radio 1, 2, and 3. Satellite programs, via CNN, SKY News, and other international operators, are also received.

Restrooms   Public restrooms are usually simply called Toilets, or are marked with international symbols. In the Republic of Ireland, some of the older ones still carry the Gaelic words *Fir* (Men) and *Mna* (Women). The newest and best kept rest rooms are found at shopping complexes and at multistory car parks—some cost 10p (15¢) to enter. In addition, free use of rest rooms is available to customers of sightseeing attractions, museums, hotels, restaurants, pubs, shops, theaters, and department stores. Gas stations normally do not have public toilets.

Safety   Although the Republic of Ireland enjoys a relatively low crime rate with little physical violence, normal precautions should prevail for travelers. In recent years, the larger cities have been prey for pickpockets, purse snatchers, car thieves, and drug traffickers. To alert visitors to potential dangers, the Garda Siochana (police) department publishes a small leaflet, *A Short Guide to Tourist Safety*, available at tourist offices and other public places. The booklet advises you not to carry large amounts of money or important documents like your passport or airline tickets when strolling around (leave them in a safety deposit box at your hotel). Do not leave cars, cameras, binoculars, or other expensive equipment unattended or unlocked. Be alert and aware of your surroundings, and do not wander in lonely areas alone at night.

   In the North of Ireland, safety is of more concern because of the political unrest that has prevailed for the past 30 years. Before traveling to Northern Ireland, visitors are advised to contact the U.S. State Department and the Northern Ireland Tourist Board to obtain the latest update about safety considerations.

Taxes   As in many European countries, sales tax is called VAT (value added tax) and is often included in the price quoted to you. In the Republic, VAT rates vary—for hotels, restaurants, and car rentals, it is 12.5%; for souvenir and gifts, it is just over 17%. In Northern Ireland, it is 17.5% across the board. VAT charged on services such as hotel stays, meals, car rentals, and entertainment, cannot be refunded to visitors, but the VAT charged on products such as souvenirs is refundable. For full details on VAT refunds for purchases, see "VAT Tax Refunds," section 6 in this chapter.

Telephone   To telephone Ireland, dial the international access code, then the country code—**353** for the Republic, and **44** for the North. In the Republic, the telephone system is known as Telecom Eireann; in Northern Ireland, it is British Telecom. For direct-dial calls to the U.S., dial the international access code (**00**), then the country code (**1**), followed by area code and number.

   Local calls from a phone booth cost 20p (30¢) within the Republic of Ireland, and 10p (15¢) in the North. The most efficient way to make calls from public phones is to use a Callcard in the Republic and a Phonecard in the North. Both are prepaid computerized cards that insert into the phone in lieu of coins. They can be purchased at phone company offices, post offices, and many retail outlets such as newsstands.

Time   Ireland follows Greenwich Mean Time (one hour earlier than Central European Time) from November through March; and British Standard Time (the same as Central European Time) from April through October. This translates to mean that Ireland is five time zones earlier than the eastern U.S. (that is, when it is noon in New York, it is 5pm in Ireland).

Tipping   Most hotels and guesthouses add a service charge to the bill, usually 12.5% to 15%, although some smaller places add only 10% or nothing at all. Always check to see what amount, if any, has been added to your bill. If it is 12.5% to 15%, and you feel it is sufficient, then there is no need for further gratuities. However, if a lesser amount has been added or if staff members have provided exceptional service, then it is appropriate to give additional cash gratuities. For restaurants, the policy is usually printed on the menu—either a gratuity of 10% to 15% is added to your bill, or, in some cases, no service charge is added, leaving it up to you. Always ask if you are in doubt. For porters or bellmen, tip 50p (75¢) to £1 ($1.50) per piece of luggage. For taxi drivers, hairdressers, and other providers of service, tip as you would at home, an average of 10% to 15%. As a rule, bar staff do not expect a tip, except for table service.

Water   Tap water throughout the island of Ireland is safe to drink. If you prefer bottled water, it is readily available at all hotels, guesthouses, restaurants, and pubs.

Yellow Pages   The classified section of telephone books in the Republic of Ireland is called the Golden Pages. In the North, it's *Yellow Pages.*

4

Dublin

Oｎｅ ｏｆ Ｅｕｒｏｐｅ'ｓ ｍｏｓｔ ｐｉｃｔｕｒｅｓｑｕｅ ｃａｐｉｔａｌｓ, Dｕｂｌｉｎ ｓｉｔｓ ｏｎ Iｒｅｌａｎｄ'ｓ ｅａｓｔ coast overlooking the Irish Sea. It is bisected by the River Liffey and sheltered on three sides by a crescent of the Dublin mountains.

Compact and easily walkable, Dublin harmoniously blends past and present in its narrow cobblestone lanes and wide one-way streets, medieval cathedrals and open-air markets, 18th-century townhouses and multi-story shopping centers, horse-drawn liveries and doubledecker buses.

For more than 1,000 years, this proud city has been the nation's nucleus—politically, economically, socially, and culturally. A major transportation center by land, air, and sea, Dublin is also the seat of the Irish government; headquarters of dozens of banks, financial institutions, and major international companies; and the hub of great theaters and museums. Yet the city exudes a friendliness, felt when one steps inside its neighborhood pubs.

The name "Dublin" is derived from the Irish or Gaelic *Dubhlinn,* meaning dark pool. Today, the city's official name, which appears on some street signs, is Baile Atha Cliath, which means "the town of the hurdle ford," a reference to the River Liffey that runs through Dublin. In earliest days, it was known by yet another name, Eblana, used by the geographer Ptolemy in the period A.D. 130–180.

Like a lot of cities and towns in Ireland, Dublin is believed to have been traversed around A.D. 448 by St. Patrick, who converted many of the inhabitants to Christianity. During the next four centuries a Christian community grew around the site of a primitive ford on the River Liffey and lived in relative peace until the Norwegian Vikings sailed onto its shores. The Norse built a seafort on the banks of the Liffey in A.D. 841, and the Danes took possession of the town 12 years later. During the tenth century, Irish kings laid claim to the settlement, and in A.D. 988, Dublin was officially recognized as an Irish city, largely due to the efforts of Mael Sechnaill II. Despite this Irish advance against Norse authority, the Danes still kept a considerable grip on the city. It wasn't until Irish high king Brian Boru attained victory at the Battle of Clontarf in 1014 that the Norse command of Dublin was finally broken. Tragically for the Irish, Boru perished in his moment of glory.

Following Boru's demise, other kings exerted authority over Dublin, including the Danish King Sitric, who is best remembered for helping to establish the original Christ Church Cathedral in 1038. For the next one hundred years, local kings squabbled among themselves for power.

During the 12th century, the Normans firmly planted their feet in Dublin, the first stage of the conquest of Ireland from neighboring Britain, a phase of history that would last for more than 800 years. The subjugation of Ireland by Britain officially started in 1171 when King Henry II landed at Dublin and claimed power. In 1174, Henry granted a city charter to Dublin and gave its merchants free trading rights throughout his dominions. In 1204, Dublin Castle was established as the administrative seat of English power in Ireland, and in 1229 the first Mayor of Dublin, Richard Muton, was appointed. Parliamentary sessions began in Dublin in 1297.

Throughout the Middle Ages, a succession of English kings came briefly to Dublin to exert their power. From 1534 to 1552, Henry VIII sought to suppress the Catholic religion of the native Irish while imposing his self-appointed supremacy as head of the Church of England and Ireland. Monasteries were dissolved and churches were destroyed or handed over from Catholic to Protestant clerics—hence, to this day, both of Dublin's prime cathedrals, Christ Church and St. Patrick's, are Protestant.

What's Special About Dublin

Buildings
- Dublin Castle, which boasts a 13th-century tower, a 19th-century chapel, elaborate ceremonial state apartments, and a medieval undercroft revealing excavations going back to Viking times.
- Custom House, with a long classical facade overlooking the River Liffey.
- Four Courts, a multi-columned and domed Georgian beauty.
- Leinster House, which served as a model for the design of the White House.

Museums/Art Galleries
- National Museum, which ensconces great treasures such as the Tara Brooch, Cross of Cong, and Ardagh Chalice.
- The Royal Hospital, home to Ireland's Museum of Modern Art.
- Chester Beatty Library and Gallery of Oriental Art, with its collection of Western, Middle Eastern, and Far Eastern manuscripts and art.

Parks/Gardens
- Phoenix Park, with over 1,700 acres of gardens, nature trails, pasturelands, and forests.

Ace Attractions
- *The Book of Kells,* an 8th-century, meticulously illuminated version of the Four Gospels.
- Merrion and Fitzwilliam Squares, wide Georgian streets and parks lined by rows of restored brick-fronted town houses.

City Spectacles
- "Dublinia," this re-creation of early Dublin includes a walk-through medieval maze, a diorama, prototypes of 13th- to 15th-century buildings, and a 360° wrap-around sight-and-sound show.
- "Dublin Experience," a multimedia sound-and-light show.

Cathedrals
- Christ Church Cathedral, at the heart of Dublin's Old City.
- St. Patrick's Cathedral, the longest church in Ireland. Among its distinguished deans was Jonathan Swift.

Literary Landmarks
- Dublin Writers Museum, a tribute to Dublin's great scribes with books galore, exhibits, paintings, sculptures, and memorabilia.
- Joyce Tower, a 40-ft. round granite seaside tower that once was home to the novelist.

Offbeat/Oddities
- St. Michan's Church, its underground burial vault holds mummified bodies that show no signs of decomposition.
- Whitefriar Street Carmelite Church, the final resting place for St. Valentine.
- Heraldic Museum, a perfect place to start a search for your ancestors.

In spite of its role as conqueror, over the years England did make positive contributions to the face of Dublin. It was Elizabeth I who in 1592 granted a charter for the founding of Trinity College in the heart of the city. During the reigns of the Kings George in the 18th century, Dublin acquired its glorious Georgian architecture of sweeping avenues, graceful squares, and rows of brick-fronted town houses, each with its own unique door.

Often referred to as the "Doors of Dublin," these elaborate entranceways have come to symbolize Dublin in all its past and present glory. Some doors have fanlights, arches, columns, or sidelights, others have decorative brass bells or knockers. Each is painted a different color—pink, red, yellow, green, lavender, and so on—a rainbow of classic individuality. Some of the city's grandest buildings date from the Georgian era, including the Four Courts, Custom House, Parliament House, and the National Gallery, Museum, and Library.

But buildings alone did not satisfy the Dubliners' desire to take their city back unto themselves. It is not surprising that the struggles for Irish independence culminated in the heart of Dublin on Easter Monday, 1916, when the Irish freedom fighters, headquartered at the General Post Office on O'Connell Street, proclaimed the Irish Republic. Although it took several years to achieve their goals, the rebels did eventually make Ireland a Free State in 1926 and a Republic in 1949, with Dublin as its capital.

In 1988 Dublin marked its millennium—one thousand years as an Irish city. The year-long program of celebration brought many welcome improvements to the face of the city, from the restoration of historic facades to making Grafton Street a pedestrian way—the prime shopping thoroughfare.

The city layout was permanently enhanced with the addition of ten new bronze sculptures by Irish craftspersons in public places, including a rendering of Dublin's legendary heroine, Molly Malone, at the juncture of Nassau and Grafton Streets; a replica of a Viking ship on Essex Quay; and a liberty bell in St. Patrick's Cathedral Park. O'Connell Street, the city's main thoroughfare, was perked up by an elaborate 40-spout fountain with a reclining nude in the center, representing the River Liffey and referred to as Anna Livia, the symbolic name that novelist James Joyce bestowed upon the river. Dubliners have a few good-natured names of their own for the eye-catching spectacle.

The Dublin skyline is also distinguished by the new green-tinted glass-and-concrete Financial Services Centre on Customs House Quay, a major urban renewal project being developed along the city's docks, and the 30-year-old Liberty Hall, a 17-story tower of reflective glass. Considered Dublin's only skyscraper, it is the headquarters for the Irish Transport General Workers Union.

In 1987 Dublin took a progressive leap among the world's major cities by electing a woman, Carmencita Hederman, as Lord Mayor. But, by 1990, even that feat was topped when Mary Robinson became the first woman president of Ireland. Today women are also employed as busdrivers and gardai (police).

IMPRESSIONS

In a little city like Dublin, one meets every person whom one knows within a few days. Around each bend in the road there is a friend. . . .
—James Stephens, *The Charwoman's Daughter,* 1912

To be sure, Dubliners are a special breed—well informed and interested in all that is happening in the world. They seem to be always reading a newspaper—indeed it is amazing that such a small city supports as many as three morning dailies and two evening tabloids. Dubliners will draw you into conversation and eagerly strive to make you a part of their city.

More than a million people reside in the Dublin metropolitan area—over a quarter of the entire Irish population. But still this a city where conviviality is the norm, and all of its inhabitants seem to know one another. Dubliners, young and old alike, rarely walk down a single street without stopping to chat briefly or give a friendly wave or greeting to others out for a stroll. Even visitors, after a few days, will be tempted to fall into this pattern of dropping a few affable words, a nod, a wink, or a smile. Simply put, Dublin is a cosmopolitan capital with the heart of a small village.

1 Orientation

Dublin is 138 miles NE of Shannon Airport, 160 miles NE of Cork, 104 miles S of Belfast, 192 miles NE of Killarney, 136 miles E of Galway, 147 miles SE of Derry, 88 miles N of Wexford.

ARRIVING IN DUBLIN

BY AIR   Regularly scheduled nonstop flights into Dublin International Airport are operated from New York and Boston by Aer Lingus, Ireland's national airline, and from Atlanta by Delta Airlines. In the summer months, charters also operate from other U.S. and Canadian cities (see "Getting to Ireland," in Chapter 2). Alternatively, you can fly from the U.S. to London or other European cities and backtrack into Dublin Airport (see "Getting to Ireland," in Chapter 2).

Dublin International Airport (☎ **01/837-9900**) is located seven miles north of the city center. Dublin Bus (☎ **01/873-4222**) provides express coach service from the airport into the city's central bus station, Busarus, Store Street. Service runs daily, 7:30am until 10:30pm, with departures every 20 to 30 minutes. One-way fare is £2.50 ($4.25) adults and £1.25 ($2.93) for children under age 12.

For speed and ease, a taxi is the best way to get directly to your hotel or guesthouse. Depending on your destination, fares average between £10 ($15) and £13 ($19.50). Taxis are lined up at a first-come, first-served taxi stand outside of the arrivals terminal.

Major international and local car rental firms operate desks at Dublin Airport (for a list of firms, see "Getting Around, by Car," below).

BY FERRY   Passenger/car ferries from Britain arrive at the Dublin Ferryport (**01/874-3293**), on the eastern end of the North Docks, and at the Dun Laoghaire Ferryport (☎ **01/280-1905**), about ten miles south of city center. There is bus and taxi service from both ports.

BY TRAIN   Irish Rail (☎ **01/836-6222**) operates daily train service into Dublin from Belfast in Northern Ireland and all major cities in the Irish Republic, including Cork, Galway, Limerick, Killarney, Sligo, Wexford, and Waterford. Trains from the south, west, and southwest arrive at **Heuston Station,** Kingsbridge, off St. John's Road; from the north and northwest at **Connolly Station,** Amiens Street; and from the southeast at **Pearse Station,** Westland Row, Tara Street.

BY BUS   Bus Eireann (☎ **01/836-6111**) operates daily express coach and local bus services from all major cities and towns in Ireland into Dublin's central bus station, Busaras, Store Street.

BY CAR   If you are arriving by car from other parts of Ireland or via car ferry from Britain, all main roads lead into the heart of Dublin and are well signposted to City Centre. If you are staying on the north side of the River Liffey, follow signs for North Ring, and if you are staying on the south side of the River, follow signs for South Ring.

TOURIST INFORMATION

Dublin Tourism operates year-round walk-in visitor offices at 14 Upper O'Connell St., Dublin 1 (☎ **01/284-4768**); 18 Eustace St., Temple Bar, Dublin 2 (☎ **01/671-5717**); Baggot Street Bridge, Dublin 2 (☎ **01/284-4768**); the Arrivals Hall of Dublin Airport (☎ **01/844-5387**); and at the ferry terminal, St. Michael's Wharf, Dun Laoghaire (☎ **01/280-6984**).

The first three outlets are open Monday through Friday from 9am to 6pm and on Saturday from 9am to 1pm, with extended hours during the May to October period. Airport and ferry offices are open to coincide with arrival and departure schedules.

CITY LAYOUT

Compared with other European capitals, Dublin is a relatively small metropolis and easy to get to know. The downtown core of the city, identified in Irish on bus destination signs as An Lar (The Center), is shaped somewhat like a pie, with the River Liffey cutting across the middle from east to west. The top half of the pie, or north side of the city, is rimmed in a semicircular sweep by the Royal Canal; and the bottom half, or south side, is edged in a half-circle shape by the waters of the Grand Canal.

To the north of the Royal Canal are the northside suburbs such as Drumcondra, Glasnevin, Howth, Clontarf, and Malahide; to the south of the Grand Canal are the southside suburbs of Ballsbridge, Blackrock, Dun Laoghaire, Dalkey, Killiney, Rathgar, Rathmines, and other residential areas.

Main Arteries, Streets, and Squares

The focal point of Dublin is the River Liffey, with no fewer than 14 bridges connecting its north and south banks. On the north side of the River, the main thoroughfare is O'Connell Street, a wide two-way avenue that starts at the riverside quays and runs northward to Parnell Square. Enhanced by statues, trees, and a modern spouting fountain, O'Connell Street of earlier days was the lifeblood of the city, and it is still important today although a little less fashionable than it used to be.

On the south side of the Liffey, Grafton Street is Dublin's main shopping street. Narrow and restricted to pedestrians, Grafton Street sits at the center of Dublin's commercial district, surrounded by smaller and larger streets where a variety of shops, restaurants, and hotels are situated. At the south end of Grafton Street is St. Stephen's Green, a lovely park and urban oasis ringed by rows of historic Georgian townhouses, fine hotels, and restaurants.

Nassau Street, which starts at the north end of Grafton Street and rims the south side of Trinity College, is noted not only for its fine shops, but because it leads to Merrion Square, another fashionable Georgian park noted for the historic brick-front townhouses which surround it. Merrion Square is also adjacent to Leinster House, the Irish House of Parliament, the National Gallery, and the National Museum.

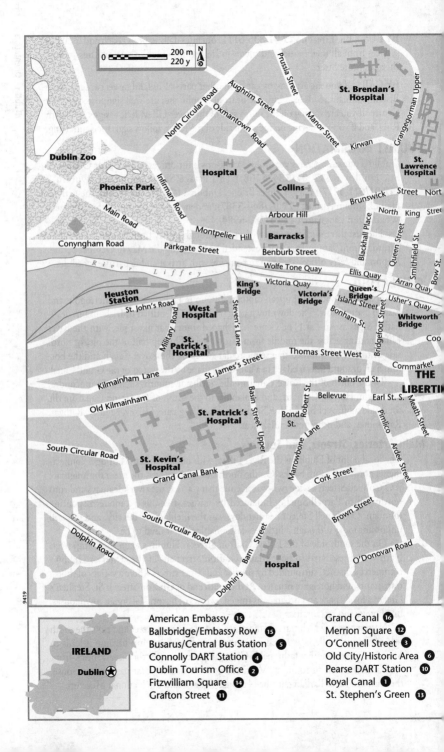

Dublin

0 — 200 m / 220 y

N

Dublin Zoo

Phoenix Park

Main Road

Conyngham Road

North Circular Road

Aughrim Street

Oxmantown Road

Prussia Street

Manor Street

St. Brendan's Hospital

Grangegorman Upper

Kirwan

St. Lawrence Hospital

Hospital

Collins

Arbour Hill

Brunswick   Street   Nort

North   King   Stree

Infirmary Road

Montpelier Hill

Barracks

Benburb Street

Blackhall Place

Queen Street

Smithfield St.

Bow St.

Parkgate Street

Wolfe Tone Quay

Ellis Quay

Arran Quay

River   Liffey

Victoria Quay

Queen's Bridge

Usher's Quay

Heuston Station

King's Bridge

Victoria's Bridge

Island Street

Bonham St.

Whitworth Bridge

St. John's Road

West Hospital

Steven's Lane

Bridgefoot Street

Military Road

St. Patrick's Hospital

Thomas Street West

Coo

Whitworth Bridge

Cornmarket

Kilmainham Lane

St. James's Street

Rainsford St.

THE LIBERTI

Old Kilmainham

Basin Street Upper

Robert St.

Bellevue

Earl St. S.

Meath Street

Pimlico

South Circular Road

St. Patrick's Hospital

Bond St.

Marrowbone Lane

Ardee Street

St. Kevin's Hospital

Grand Canal Bank

Cork Street

Brown Street

Grand   Canal

South Circular Road

Dolphin Road

Dolphin's   Barn Street

O'Donovan Road

Hospital

9419

IRELAND

Dublin ✪

American Embassy ⑮
Ballsbridge/Embassy Row ⑮
Busarus/Central Bus Station ⑤
Connolly DART Station ④
Dublin Tourism Office ②
Fitzwilliam Square ⑭
Grafton Street ⑪

Grand Canal ⑯
Merrion Square ⑫
O'Connell Street ③
Old City/Historic Area ⑥
Pearse DART Station ⑩
Royal Canal ①
St. Stephen's Green ⑬

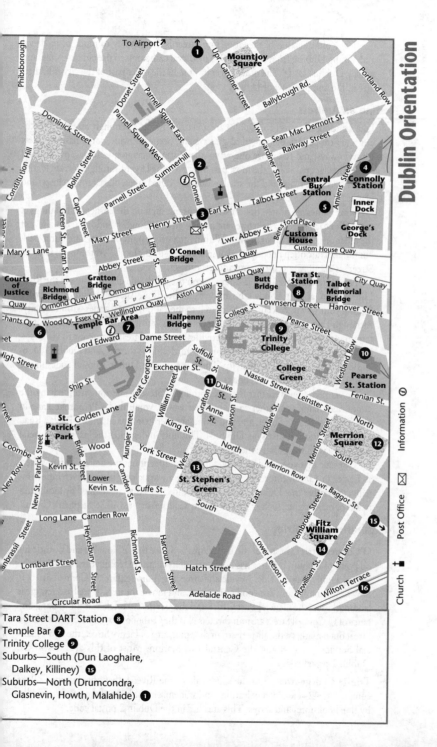

Dublin Orientation

To Airport ↗
Mountjoy Square
Phibsborough
Dominick Street
Constitution Hill
Bolton Street
Capel Street
Green St.
Arran St. E.
Dorset Street
Parnell Square West
Parnell Square East
Parnell Street
Summerhill
Upr. Gardiner Street
Ballybough Rd.
Portland Row
Sean Mac Dermott St.
Railway Street
Lwr. Gardiner Street
Talbot Street
Amiens Street
Connolly Station
Central Bus Station
Inner Dock
George's Dock
Henry Street
Earl St. N.
Mary Street
Mary's Lane
Abbey Street
O'Connell Bridge
Lwr. Abbey St.
Beresford Place
Customs House
Custom House Quay
Eden Quay
Gratton Bridge
Richmond Bridge
Courts of Justice
Ormond Quay Lwr.
Ormond Quay Upr.
Wellington Quay
Burgh Quay
Butt Bridge
Tara St. Station
Talbot Memorial Bridge
City Quay
Townsend Street
Hanover Street
Merchants Qy.
Wood Qy.
Essex Qy.
Temple Bar Area
Halfpenny Bridge
Aston Quay
Westmoreland
College Street
Pearse Street
Lord Edward
Dame Street
Suffolk St.
Exchequer St.
Trinity College
College Green
Nassau Street
Westland Row
Pearse St. Station
Fenian St.
High Street
Ship St.
Golden Lane
St. Patrick's Park
William Street
Great Georges St.
Duke St.
Anne St.
Grafton St.
Dawson St.
Kildare St.
Leinster St.
Merrion Street
Merrion Square
North
South
King St.
York Street
West
North
East
Merrion Row
St. Stephen's Green
Lwr. Baggot St.
New Row
Coombe
Kevin Street
Wood
Bride Street
New St.
St. Patrick Street
Aungier Street
Camden St.
Lower Kevin St.
Cuffe St.
South
Pembroke Street
Fitzwilliam St.
Fitz William Square
Lad Lane
Wilton Terrace
Hatch Street
Adelaide Road
Circular Road
Long Lane
Camden Row
Heytesbury Street
Richmond St.
Harcourt Street
Lombard Street
Lower Leeson St.

River Liffey

Church ✝   Post Office ✉   Information ⓘ

In the older section of the city, High Street is the gateway to much of medieval and Viking Dublin, from the city's two medieval cathedrals to the old city walls, and nearby Dublin Castle. The other street of note in the older part of the city is Francis Street, the antiques row of Dublin.

Finding an Address

Like London, the streets of Dublin are a maze of names, seemingly assembled without a logical pattern or numerical grid system. Some are wide, some narrow, a few run two ways, and many are one-way—they form rectangles, triangles, parallel and perpendicular angles. For the most part, however, the larger thoroughfares are identified as streets or roads and the smaller ones are called lanes, alleys, rows, closes, and places.

Most names are posted not on street signs but high on the corners of buildings at the end of each street. The names are usually given in English and Irish, but a few of the older ones have Irish signs only. Within each street, most buildings are numbered, but numbers are often not displayed or seldom used by the locals. "At the top of Grafton Street" is about as specific as any address can get.

For starters, always ask if an address is on the north side or south side of the River Liffey. Then, at least, you will be in the right direction. Another helpful strategy for finding your way is to acclimatize yourself to the various postal zones within the city. Although there are more than 20 different zones, most of the attractions—hotels, restaurants, pubs, shops, and other activities that are of greatest interest to visitors— lie within six zones: Dublin 1 and 9 on the north side of the city, and Dublin 2, 4, 6, and 8 on the south side of the city. There is a map of Dublin's postal zones in the front section of all telephone books.

Be warned, however, that there is nothing to prevent one zone from having the same street name as another zone. In other words, you'll find a Pembroke Lane in Dublin 2, off Baggot Street, and you'll find another Pembroke Lane off Raglan Road near the American Embassy in Dublin 4. This only underscores the fact that a general familiarity with the postal zones can be a great help.

One rule that you can depend on for further direction is the designation of streets as Upper or Lower. Streets that are Lower are always closer to the River Liffey. Finally, remember that Dubliners usually give directions that are defined by local landmarks or major sights, such as "beside Trinity College" or "just off St. Stephen's Green."

Neighborhoods in Brief

O'Connell Street (North of the Liffey Area) Once the fashionable and historic focal point of Dublin, this area has lost a little of its charm in recent years, but is still the core of Dublin's north side. A wide and sweeping thoroughfare, O'Connell Street is now rimmed by shops, fast-food restaurants, and movie theaters, as well as a few great landmarks like the General Post Office and the Gresham Hotel. Within walking distance of O'Connell Street are four theaters plus the Catholic Pro-Cathedral, the Moore Street open markets, the all-pedestrian shopping area of Henry Street, the new Financial Services Centre, and the Central Bus Station. Most of this area lies in the Dublin 1 postal code.

Trinity College Area On the south side of the River Liffey, the Trinity College complex is a 42-acre center of learning and academia in the heart of the city, surrounded by fine bookstores and shops. This area lies in the Dublin 2 postal code.

Temple Bar   Wedged between Trinity College and the Old City, this section has recently been spruced up and taken a new lease on life as Dublin's Left Bank, with a bohemian atmosphere and an assortment of unique shops, art galleries, recording studios, theaters, trendy restaurants, and atmospheric pubs. This area lies in the Dublin 2 postal code.

Old City/Historic Area   Dating back to Viking and medieval times, this cobblestoned enclave includes Dublin Castle, the city's two main cathedrals, Christ Church and St. Patrick's, and the remnants of the city's original walls. The adjacent Liberties section, just west of High Street, takes its name from the fact that the people who lived here long ago were exempt from the local jurisdiction within the city walls. Although it prospered in its early days, the Liberties fell on hard times in the 17th to 18th centuries and is only now feeling a touch of urban renewal. Highlights here range from the Guinness Brewery and Royal Hospital to the original Cornmarket area. Most of this area lies in the Dublin 8 zone.

St. Stephen's Green/Grafton Street Area   A visitor's focal point in Dublin, this district is home to some of the city's finest hotels, restaurants, and shops. There are some residential townhouses near the Green, but this area is primarily a business neighborhood. It is part of the Dublin 2 zone.

Fitzwilliam and Merrion Squares   These two little square parks are surrounded by fashionable brick-faced Georgian townhouses, each with its own distinctive and colorful doorway. Some of Dublin's most famous citizens once resided here, although today many of the houses have been turned into offices for doctors, lawyers, and other professionals. This area is part of the Dublin 2 zone.

Ballsbridge/Embassy Row   Situated south of the Grand Canal, this is Dublin's most prestigious suburb, yet it is within walking distance of downtown. Although primarily a residential area, it is also the home of some of the city's leading hotels, restaurants, and the embassies of Argentina, Austria, Belgium, China, Egypt, France, Britain, Italy, Japan, Korea, Netherlands, Poland, Spain, Switzerland, Turkey, and the United States. This area is part of the Dublin 4 zone.

2   Getting Around Dublin

PUBLIC TRANSPORTATION • By Bus   Dublin Bus operates a fleet of green double-decker buses, high-frequency single-deck buses, and minibuses, throughout the city and its suburbs. Most buses originate on or near O'Connell Street, Abbey Street and Eden Quay on the north side; and from Aston Quay, College Street, or Fleet Street on the south side. Bus stops are located every two or three blocks. Destinations and bus numbers are posted above the front windows; buses destined for the city center are marked with the Gaelic words "An Lar."

Bus service runs daily throughout the city, starting at 6am (on Sunday, at 10am), with last bus at 11:30pm, excluding Friday and Saturday nights, when there is a Nitelink service from city center to the suburbs running from midnight to 3am. Frequency ranges from every 10 to 15 minutes for most runs; schedules are posted on revolving notice boards at each bus stop.

Fares are calculated on distances traveled; minimum fare is 55p (83¢); maximum fare is £1.10 ($1.65). Nitelink fare is a flat £2 ($3). Buy your tickets from the driver as you enter the bus; exact change is not required. One-day, four-day, and weekly passes are available at reduced rates.

For more information, contact Dublin Bus, 59 Upper O'Connell St., Dublin 1 (☎ **01/873-4222**).

• **By DART** Although Dublin has no subway in the strict sense, there is an electrified train rapid transit system, known as DART (Dublin Area Rapid Transit). It travels mostly at ground level or on elevated tracks, linking the city center stations at Tara Street, Pearse Street, and Amiens Street with the residential suburb of Ballsbridge and the seaside communities of Howth on the north side and Dalkey and Dun Laoghaire to the south.

Service operates every 15 minutes (and every five minutes during rush hours), from 7am to midnight, Monday through Saturday, and from 9:30am to 11pm on Sunday. Minimum fare is 80p ($1.20). One-day, four-day, and weekly passes are available at reduced rates. For further information, contact DART, 35 Lower Abbey St., Dublin 1 (☎ **01/836-6222**).

BY TAXI Dublin taxis do not cruise the streets looking for fares; instead, they line up at ranks. Ranks are located outside all of the leading hotels, at bus and train stations, and on prime thoroughfares, such as Upper O'Connell Street, College Green, and the north side of St. Stephen's Green. You can also phone for a taxi. Some of the companies that operate a 24-hour radio-call service are: All Fives Taxi (☎ **01/455-5555** and **01/455-7777**); Access Taxis (☎ **01/668-3333**); Blue Cabs (☎ **01/676-1111**); Co-op Taxis (☎ **01/676-6666**); and National Radio Cabs (☎ **01/677-2222**).

Rates are fixed by law and posted in each taxi. Minimum fare for one passenger within the city is £1.80 ($2.70) for any distance not exceeding one mile or nine minutes; after that, it's 10p (15¢) for each additional one eighth of a mile or one minute. There are extra charges for additional passengers, luggage, and for hiring before 8am or after 8pm, all day Sunday, at the airport or by phone.

BY CAR Unless you are going to be doing a lot of driving from Dublin to neighboring counties, it is not logistically or economically advisable to rent a car. In fact, getting around the city center and its environs is much easier without a car.

If you must drive in Dublin, remember to keep to the **left-hand side of the road** and do not drive in bus lanes. The speed limit within the city is 30m.p.h. and seatbelts must be worn at all times by driver and passenger(s).

RENTALS All major international **car rental firms** are represented in Dublin, as are many Irish-based companies, with desks at the airport and/or full-service offices downtown. Depending on the season, daily rates average £40 to £60 ($60 to $90) per day for a small subcompact standard shift car or £125 to £150 ($188 to $225) for a large automatic car. Most weekly rates range from £200 to £700 ($300 to $1,050), depending on the size of the car and if it has a standard shift or automatic transmission.

International firms represented in Dublin include:

Avis/Johnson & Perrott, 1 Hanover St. E., Dublin 1 (☎ **01/677-4010**) and Dublin Airport (☎ **01/837-0204**).

Budget, at Dublin Airport (☎ **01/844-5919**).

Hertz, 149 Upper Leeson St., Dublin 4 (☎ **01/660-2255**) and at Dublin Airport (☎ **01/842-9333**).

National/Murray's Europcar, Baggot Street Bridge, Dublin 4 (☎ **01/668-1777**) and at Dublin Airport (☎ **01/844-4179**).

Thrifty, at Dublin Airport (☎ **01/844-4199**).

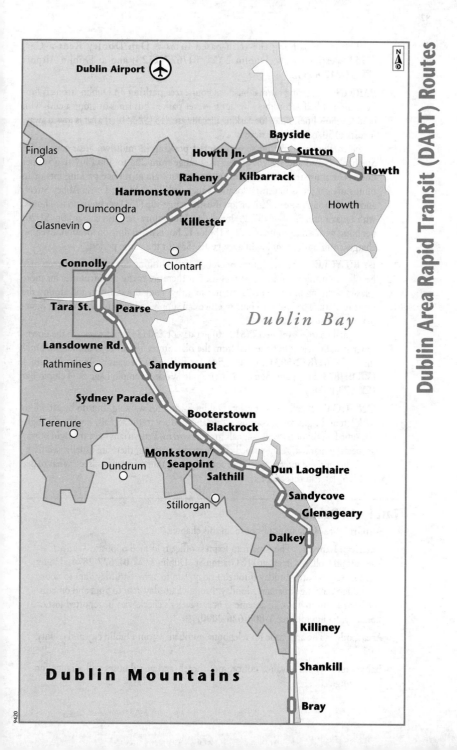

Dublin Area Rapid Transit (DART) Routes

The leader among the Irish-based firms is **Dan Dooley Rent-a-Car,** 42/43 Westland Row, Dublin 2 (☎ **01/677-2723**) and at Dublin Airport (☎ **01/842-8355**).

PARKING   During normal business hours, **free parking** on Dublin streets is limited, and marked accordingly by signs. Never park in bus lanes or along a curb with double yellow lines. Fines for parking illegally are £15 ($22.50); if a car is towed away, it costs £150 ($225) to retrieve it.

Normally you can find some **metered parking** in midtown areas such as St. Stephen's Green and Baggot Street; rates range from 20p to 50p (30¢ to 75¢) per hour. The most reliable and safest places to park are at surface parking lots or in multistory car parks in central locations such as Kildare Street, Lower Abbey Street, and Marlborough Street. Parking lots usually charge 50p (75¢) per hour, up to 4 hours, with a maximum of £4.50 ($7.25) for all day. Multi-story car parks charge 80p ($1.20) per hour, with a maximum of £12 ($18) for 12 hours depending on location. Evening charges from 6pm to midnight average £2 ($3) for the entire period.

BY BICYCLE   The steady flow of Dublin traffic rushing down one-way streets may be a little intimidating for most cyclists, but there are many opportunities for more relaxed peddling in residential areas and suburbs, along the seafront, and around the Phoenix Park. The Dublin Tourism office can supply you with bicycle touring information and suggested routes.

Rental charges average £7 ($10.50) per day or £30 ($45) per week. In the downtown area, bicycles can be rented from the Bike Store, 58 Lower Gardiner St., Dublin 1 (☎ **01/872-5931**); C. Harding for Bikes, 30 Bachelor's Walk, Dublin 1 (☎ **01/873-2455;** and Square Wheel Cycle Works, Temple Lane S., Temple Bar (☎ **679-0838**).

ON FOOT   Small and compact, Dublin is ideal for walking. But do be careful to look left and right for oncoming traffic and to obey traffic signals. Each traffic light has timed "walk/don't walk" signals for pedestrians. Pedestrians have the right of way at specially marked, zebra-striped crossings; as a warning, there are usually two flashing lights at these intersections. For some walking tour suggestions, see "What to See and Do" later in this chapter).

Fast Facts: Dublin

Airport   See "Orientation" above, in this chapter.

American Express   The American Express office is located opposite Trinity College, just off College Green, at 116 Grafton St., Dublin 2 (☎ **01/677-2874**). Hours for most services are Monday through Friday 9am to 5pm, Saturday 9am to noon; the foreign exchange operates Monday through Saturday 9am to 5pm and on Sunday from 11am to 4pm. In an emergency, traveler's checks can be reported lost or stolen by dialing toll-free **1-800/626-0000.**

Area Code   The area code for telephone numbers within Dublin city and county is **01.**

Babysitters   With advance notice, most hotels and guesthouses will arrange for babysitting.

Business Hours   Banks are open Monday through Wednesday and on Friday from 10am to 12:30pm and from 1:30pm to 3pm, on Thursday from 10am to 12:30pm and from 1:30 to 5pm. Some banks are beginning to stay open through the lunch hour. Most business offices are open from 9am to 5pm, Monday through Friday. Stores and shops are open from 9am to 5:30pm Monday through Wednesday and Friday to Saturday, and from 9am to 8pm on Thursday. Some bookshops and tourist-oriented stores also open on Sunday from 11am or noon until 4 or 5pm. During the peak season (May through September), many gift and souvenir shops post Sunday hours.

Car Rentals   See "Getting Around," above.

Currency Exchange   A currency exchange service in Ireland is signposted as a Bureau de Change. There are bureaux de change at all banks and at many branches of the Irish Post Office system, known as An Post. A bureau de change operates daily during flight arrival and departure times at Dublin Airport; a foreign currency note-exchanger machine is also available on a 24-hour basis in the main Arrivals Hall. In addition, many hotels and travel agencies offer bureau de change services, although the best rate of exchange is usually given at banks.

Dentist   For dental emergencies, contact the Irish Dental Council, 57 Merrion Sq., Dublin 2 (☎ **676-2226** or **676-2069**). See also "Dental Surgeons" in the Golden Pages of the telephone book.

Doctor   In an emergency, most hotels and guesthouses will contact a house doctor for you. You can also ask for a recommendation from the Irish Medical Organization, 10 Fitzwilliam Place, Dublin 2 (☎ **01/676-7273**) or consult the Golden Pages of the telephone book under "Doctors—Medical."

Drugstores   Centrally located drugstores, known locally as pharmacies or chemist shops, include Crowley's Pharmacy at 25 Nassau St., Dublin 2 (☎ **676-6261**) and 6 Lower Baggot St., Dublin 2 (☎ **678-5612**); Hamilton Long and Co., 5 Lower O'Connell St., Dublin 1 (☎ **874-3352**); and Smith's Pharmacy, 50 Grafton St., Dublin 1 (☎ **677-9288**).

Embassies/Consulates   The American Embassy is located at 42 Elgin Rd., Ballsbridge, Dublin 4 (☎ **668-8777**); Canadian Embassy, 65/68 St. Stephen's Green, Dublin 2 (☎ **478/1988**); British Embassy, 33 Merrion Road, Dublin 4 (☎ **269-5211**); Australian Embassy, Fitzwilton House, Wilton Terrace, Dublin 2 (☎ **676-1517**).

Emergencies   For police, fire, or other emergencies, dial **999.**

Eyeglasses   For one-hour service on glasses or contact lenses, try Specsavers, Unit 9, GPO Arcade, Henry Street, Dublin 1 (☎ **872-8155**) or look in the Golden Pages of the telephone book under "Opticians—Opthalmic."

Hairdressers/Barbers   The leading hairstyling names for women and men are Peter Mark, with over two dozen locations throughout Dublin and its suburbs, including 74 Grafton St., Dublin 2 (☎ **671-4399**) and 11A Upper O'Connell St., Dublin 1 (☎ **874-5589**); and John Adam, with shops at 13A Merrion Row, Dublin 2 (☎ **661-0354**), 112A Baggot St., Dublin 2 (☎ **661-1952**), and 39 Capel St., Dublin 1 (☎ **873-0081**). Also consult the Golden Pages under "Hairdressers."

Hospitals   For emergency care, two of the most modern health care facilities are St. Vincent's Hospital, Elm Park, Dublin 4 (☎ 269-4533) on the south side of the city; and Beaumont Hospital, Beaumont, Dublin 9 (☎ 837-7755) on the north side.

Hotlines   In Ireland, hotlines are called helplines. Some examples are for emergencies, police, or fire, dial **999;** Rape Crisis Centre (☎ 661-4911); Samaritans (☎ 872-7700); Alcoholics Anonymous (☎ 453-8998); and Narcotics Anonymous (☎ 830-0944).

Information   For information on finding a telephone number, dial **1190;** for visitor information, see "Tourist Information" under "Orientation," above.

Laundry/Dry Cleaning   Most hotels provide same-day or next-day laundry and/or dry cleaning services. If you wish to make your own arrangements, two centrally located choices are Craft Cleaners, 12 Upper Baggot St., Dublin 2 (☎ 668-8198) and Grafton Cleaners, 32 S. William St., Dublin 2 (☎ 679-4409). More are listed under "Dry Cleaners" in the Golden Pages of the telephone book.

Libraries   For research materials and periodicals, try the National Library of Ireland, Kildare Street, Dublin 2 (☎ 661-8811), or Dublin's Central Library, ILAC Centre, Henry St., Dublin 1 (☎ 873-4333).

Lost Property   Most hotels have a lost-property service, usually under the aegis of the housekeeping department. For items lost in public places, contact the police (known as garda) headquarters, Harcourt Square, Dublin 2 (☎ 873-2222).

Newspapers/Magazines   The three morning Irish dailies are the *Irish Times* (except Sunday), *Irish Independent,* and *Irish Press.* In the afternoon, two tabloids—*Evening Herald* and *Evening Press*—hit the stands. There are also two weeklies, *The Sunday World* and *The Sunday Tribune.* Papers from other European cities can also be purchased at Eason & Son, 40 Lower O'Connell St., Dublin 1. The leading magazine for upcoming events and happenings is *In Dublin,* published every two weeks.

Photographic Needs   For photographic equipment, supplies, and repairs, visit Camera Exchange, 63 S. Great George's St., Dublin 2 (☎ 478-4125), or City Cameras, 23A Dawson St., Dublin 2 (☎ 676-2891). For fast developing, try the Camera Centre, 56 Grafton St., Dublin 2 (☎ 677-5594) or One Hour Photo, 5 St. Stephen's Green, Dublin 2 (☎ 671-8578), 110 Grafton St., Dublin 2 (☎ 677-4472, and at the ILAC Centre, Henry Street, Dublin 1 (☎ 872-8824).

Police   Dial **999** in an emergency. The metropolitan headquarters for the Dublin Garda Siochana (Police) is at Harcourt Square, Dublin 2 (☎ 873-2222).

Post Office   The General Post Office (GPO) is located on O'Connell Street, Dublin 1 (☎ 872-8888). Hours are Monday through Saturday 8am to 8pm, Sunday and holidays 10:30am to 6pm. Branch offices, identified by the sign "Oifig An Post/Post Office," are open Monday through Saturday only, 8am to 5:30pm or 6pm.

Radio/TV   RTE (Radio Telefis Eireann) is the national broadcasting authority and controls two TV channels—RTE 1 and Network 2; three radio stations—RTE 1, 2FM, and Radio na Gaeltachta (all Irish-language programming). Besides RTE programming, there are other privately owned local stations including Anna Livia Radio on 103.8 FM, and Classic Hits Radio and Ireland Radio News on 98 FM. In addition, television programs from Britain's BBC-TV (British Broadcasting Corporation) and ITN-TV (Independent) can be picked up by most receivers in the Dublin area. BBC Radio 1, 2, and 3 can also be heard. Satellite programs, via CNN, SKY News, and other international operators, are also fed into the Dublin area.

Shoe Repairs   Two reliable shops in mid-city are O'Connell's Shoe Repair, 3 Upper Baggot St., Dublin 2 (no phone), and Rapid Shoe Repair, Sackville Place, off Lower O'Connell St., Dublin 1 (no phone).

Transit Info   Phone **873-4222,** Monday through Saturday, from 9am to 7pm.

Weather   Phone **01/842-5555.**

Yellow Pages   The classified section of the Dublin telephone book is called the Golden Pages.

3 Where to Stay

From legendary old-world landmarks to sleek glass-and-concrete high-rises, Dublin offers a contrasting variety of places to stay, priced to suit every budget.

Like the rest of Ireland, all hotels and guesthouses in Dublin are inspected, registered, and graded by the Irish Tourist Board/Bord Failte. In 1994, the board introduced a new grading system that classifies each hotel into a category that ranges from one to five stars, consistent with other European countries and international standards. Currently five hotels in Dublin merit the five-star rating: Berkeley Court, Conrad, Jurys, Shelbourne, and Westbury.

In general, rates for Dublin hotels do not vary with the seasons, as they do in the Irish countryside. Some hotels do charge slightly higher prices during special events, such as the Dublin Horse Show. For the best deals, try to reserve a room in Dublin over a weekend, and ask if there is a reduction or a weekend package in effect. Some Dublin hotels cut their rates by as much as 50% on Friday and Saturday nights, when business traffic is low.

HISTORIC OLD CITY & TEMPLE BAR/TRINITY COLLEGE AREA

Moderate

Blooms, Anglesea Street, Dublin 2. ☎ **01/671-5622** or toll free **800/44-UTELL** in U.S. Fax 01/671-5997. 86 rms (all with bath). TV TEL **Transportation:** DART to Tara Street Station or bus nos. 21A, 46A, 46B, 51B, 51C, 68, 69, 86.
Rates: £85 ($127.50) single, £95 ($142.50) double. Service charge 12.5%. AE, DC, MC, V.

Lovers of Irish literature will feel at home at Blooms. Named after Leopold Bloom, a character in James Joyce's *Ulysses,* this hotel is in the heart of Dublin, near Trinity College and on the edge of the artsy Temple Bar district. The bedrooms are modern and functional, with useful extras like garment presses and hair dryers.

Dining/Entertainment: For formal dining, reserve a table at the Bia restaurant, or for more informal fare, try The Anglesea Bar. Late-night entertainment is available in the basement-level nightclub known simply as M.

Services: Concierge, 24-hour room service, valet/laundry service.

Facilities: Enclosed private car park.

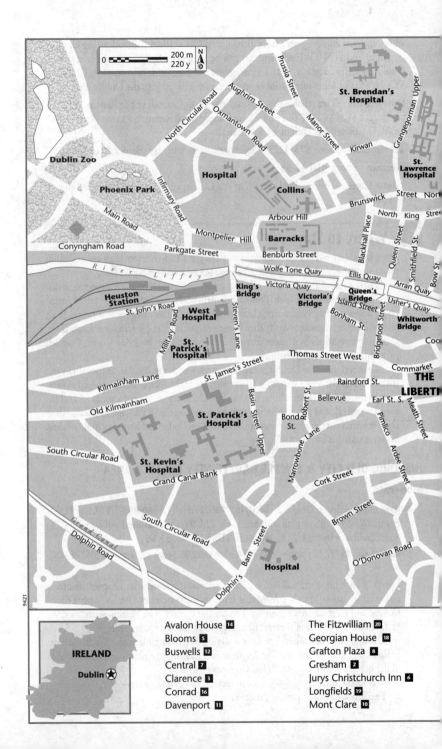

0 200 m
0 220 y
N

Prussia Street

St. Brendan's Hospital

Aughrim Street

Oxmantown Road

North Circular Road

Manor Street

Kirwan

Grangegorman Upper

St. Lawrence Hospital

Dublin Zoo

Phoenix Park

Infirmary Road

Hospital

Collins

Brunswick

Street Nor

Main Road

Arbour Hill

North King Stre

Blackhall Place

Queen Street

Smithfield St.

Bow St

Conyngham Road

Montpelier Hill

Barracks

Parkgate Street

Benburb Street

Wolfe Tone Quay

Ellis Quay

Arran Quay

River Liffey

King's Bridge

Victoria Quay

Victoria's Bridge

Queen's Bridge

Island Street

Usher's Quay

Heuston Station

St. John's Road

West Hospital

Steven's Lane

Bonham St.

Bridgefoot Street

Whitworth Bridge

Military Road

St. Patrick's Hospital

Thomas Street West

Coo

Kilmainham Lane

St. James's Street

Rainsford St.

Cornmarket

THE

Old Kilmainham

Basin Street Upper

Bellevue

Robert St.

Earl St. S.

Meath Street

LIBERTI

South Circular Road

St. Patrick's Hospital

Bond St.

Marrowbone Lane

Pimlico

Ardee Street

St. Kevin's Hospital

Grand Canal Bank

Cork Street

Brown Street

Grand Canal

South Circular Road

Dolphin Road

Dolphin's Barn Street

Hospital

O'Donovan Road

9421

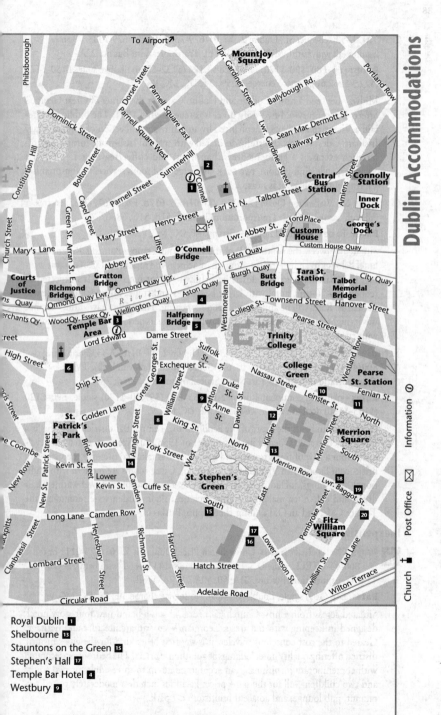

Dublin Accommodations

Royal Dublin **1**

Shelbourne **13**

Stauntons on the Green **15**

Stephen's Hall **17**

Temple Bar Hotel **4**

Westbury **9**

Church ✝ Post Office ⊠ Information ⓘ

Central, 1–5 Exchequer St., Dublin 2. ☎ **01/679-7302.** Fax 01/679-7303. 70 rms, 2 suites (all with bath). MINIBAR TV TEL **Transportation:** Bus no. 22A.

Rates: £60–£80 ($90–$120) single, £88–£124 ($132–$186) double, suites £150–£175 ($225–$262.50). Service charge 12.5%. AE, DC, MC, V.

Midway between Trinity College and Dublin Castle at the corner of Great George's Street, this century-old five-story hotel was renovated in 1991. The public areas retain a Victorian atmosphere, enhanced by an impressive collection of contemporary Irish art. Guest rooms, cheerfully decorated with colorful Irish-made furnishings, offer such extras as a garment press, hairdryer, and coffee/tea maker. There's a Victorian-style dining room, two bars, concierge, and room service. No on-premises parking but a public lot is nearby.

Clarence, 6/8 Wellington Quay, Dublin 2. ☎ **01/677-6178.** Fax 01/677-7487. 66 rms (all with bath). TV TEL **Transportation:** Bus nos. 51B, 51C, 68, 69, 79.

Rates: To be announced upon reopening. AE, DC, MC, V.

Situated between the south bank of the Liffey and Temple Bar, this Regency-style hotel belongs to an investment group that includes the rock band U2. As of this writing, the Clarence has been closed until July 1995 for renovation. It's expected to reopen as a 50-unit hotel with larger bedrooms and suites, all upgraded to deluxe standards. Rates will be announced upon reopening. The major draw at the Clarence was its nightclub, known as the Kitchen, where rock stars performed and often mingled with customers.

Temple Bar Hotel, Fleet Street, Temple Bar, Dublin 2. ☎ **01/677-3333** or toll free **800/44-UTELL** in the U.S. Fax 01/677-3088. 108 rms (all with bath). TV TEL **Transportation:** DART to Tara Street Station or bus nos. 78A or 78B.

Rates (including continental breakfast): £65–£80 ($97.50–$120) single, £90–£120 ($135–$180) double. No service charge. AE, DC, MC, V.

If you want to be in the heart of the action in the Temple Bar district, then this is a prime place to stay. Opened in the summer of 1993, this five-story hotel was developed from a row of town houses and great care was taken to preserve the Georgian brick-front facade with Victorian mansard roof. Guest rooms are modern with traditional furnishings, including amenities such as a garment press, towel warmer, hair dryer, and coffee/tea maker. Facilities include a skylit garden-style restaurant, the Terrace Cafe, and an Old Dublin-theme pub, Buskers.

Inexpensive

$ Jurys Christchurch Inn, Christchurch Place, Dublin 8. ☎ **01/475-0111** or toll free **800/44-UTELL** in the U.S. Fax 01/475-0488. 183 rms (all with bath). A/C TV TEL **Transportation:** Bus nos. 21A, 50, 50A, 78, 78A, 78B.

Rates: £46 ($69) single, double, or triple. No service charge. AE, CB, DC, MC, V.

Situated across from Christ Church Cathedral, this is a brand-new four-story hotel, designed in keeping with the area's Georgian/Victorian architecture and heritage. Geared to the cost-conscious traveler, it is the first of its kind for the city's historic district, offering quality hotel lodgings at guesthouse prices. The bedrooms, decorated with contemporary furnishings, can accommodate up to three adults or two adults and two children—all for the same price. Facilities include a moderately priced restaurant, pub lounge, and adjacent multistory car park.

ST. STEPHEN'S GREEN/GRAFTON STREET AREA

Very Expensive

Conrad, Earlsfort Terrace, Dublin 2. ☎ **01/676-5555** or toll free in the U.S.
800/HILTONS. Fax 01/676-5424. 188 rms and 9 suites (all with bath). A/C
MINIBAR, TV, TEL **Transportation:** DART to Pearse Station or bus nos. 11A, 11B,
13, 14A.
Rates: £145 ($217.50) single, £170 double ($255); £420–£583 ($630–$874.50) suites.
Service charge 15%. AE, CB, DC, MC, V.

A member of the international subsidiary of Hilton Hotels and one of the city's newest deluxe hotels, this seven-story red brick high-rise is situated opposite the National
Concert Hall and across from the southeast corner of St. Stephen's Green. The spacious public areas are rich in marble, brass, contemporary art, and lots of leafy plants.
Each guest room is outfitted with contemporary furnishings, blond woods, and pastel
tones, with extras such as electronic safety lock and three telephone lines.

   Dining/Entertainment: Choices include The Alexandra, a clubby room known
for a range of gourmet Continental and Irish fare; Plurabelle, a brasserie-style restaurant; The Lobby Lounge, for traditional afternoon tea or drinks with piano background
music; and Alfie Byrne's, a pub named for a former Lord Mayor of Dublin and serving light lunches.

   Services: 24-hour room service, concierge, valet, shoe-shine, express checkout.

   Facilities: Foreign-currency exchange, car parking garage, hairdressing salon.

★ **Shelbourne,** 27 St. Stephen's Green, Dublin 2. ☎ **01/676-6471** or toll free
800/CALL-THF in U.S. Fax 01/661-6006. 164 rms (all with bath). MINIBAR, TV,
TEL **Transportation:** DART to Pearse Station or bus nos. 10, 11A, 11B, 13, 20B.
Rates: £130–£143 ($195–$214.50) single, £150–£175 ($225–$262.50) double. Service
charge 15%. AE, CB, DC, MC, V.

With a fanciful red-brick and white-trimmed facade enhanced by wrought iron railings and window boxes brimming with flowers, this grand six-story hostelry stands
out on the north side of St. Stephen's Green. Built in 1824, it has played a significant
role in Irish history (the new nation's constitution was signed here in Room 112 in
1921), and it has often been host to international leaders, stars of stage and screen,
and literary giants. The public areas, replete with glowing fireplaces, Waterford chandeliers, and original art, are popular rendezvous spots for Dubliners. The guest rooms
vary in size, but all offer up-to-date comforts and are furnished with antique and period pieces; the front units overlook the bucolic setting of St. Stephen's Green.

   Dining/Entertainment: The Dining Room offers Irish/Continental cuisine, while
the Horseshoe Bar or Shelbourne Bar are both ideal for a convivial drink and The
Lord Mayor's Lounge is favored by the locals for a proper afternoon tea.

   Services: 24-hour room service, concierge.

   Facilities: Foreign-currency exchange, private enclosed car park.

Very Expensive/Expensive

Stephen's Hall, 14–17 Lower Leeson St., Earlsfort Terrace, Dublin 2. ☎ **01/661-0585** or
toll free **800/223-6510** in U.S. Fax 01/661-0606. 37 suites (all with bath). TV TEL
Transportation: DART to Pearse Station or bus nos. 14A, 11A, 11B, 13, 46A, 46B, 86.

Rates: £90–£130 ($135–$195) single, £130 ($195) double for one-bedroom suite; £95 ($142.50) single, £150 ($225) double for two-bedroom suite; £105 ($157.50) single, £170 ($255) for penthouse/townhouse suite. No service charge. AE, DC, MC, V.

With a gracious Georgian exterior and entranceway, this is Dublin's first all-suite hotel, situated on the southeast corner of St. Stephen's Green. It's ideal for visitors who plan an extended stay or who seek to do do their own cooking or entertaining. Furnished in a contemporary motif, each suite contains a hallway, sitting room, dining area, kitchen, bathroom, and one or two bedrooms. The luxury penthouse suites, on the upper floors, offer views of city, while the ground-level townhouse suites have private entrances.

Services: Concierge, maid service.

Facilities: Restaurant/coffee shop, underground parking

★ **Westbury,** Grafton Street, Dublin 2. ☎ **01/679-1122** or toll-free **800/223-6800, 800/42-DOYLE** or **800/44-UTELL** in the U.S. Fax 01/679-7078. 200 rms and 6 suites (all with bath). AC TV TEL **Transportation:** DART to Tara Street or Pearse Station or bus nos. 10, 11A, 11B, 13, 20B.

Rates: £146 ($219) single, £162–£227 ($243–$340.50) double, £275–£414 ($412.50–$621) suites, £450 ($725) presidential suite. Service charge 15%. AE, CB, DC, MC, V.

A tasteful hybrid of modern and traditional design, this relatively new midtown hotel blends a sleekly contemporary facade with a serene interior of soft pastel tones and antique furnishings. It sits in the heart of the city's fashionable shopping district and near all the major sights. The guest rooms, many with half-canopy or four-poster beds, are furnished with dark woods, brass trim, and floral designer fabrics. Many of the suites have Jacuzzis.

Dining/Entertainment: Choices include The Russell Room, a French/Irish restaurant; The Sandbank, a nautical-style pub serving fresh seafood; Charlie's Coffee Shop for a quick meal, and the Terrace Bar and Lounge, a favorite venue for afternoon tea or a drink, with live piano music.

Services: 24-hour room service, concierge, express checkout.

Facilities: Hairdressing salon, arcade of 20 shops, underground parking, fitness room, currency exchange.

Moderate

Buswells, 25 Molesworth St., Dublin 2. ☎ **01/676-4013** or **661-3888** or toll free **800/473-9527** in the U.S. Fax 01/676-2090. 67 rms (all with bath). TV TEL **Transportation:** DART to Pearse Station or bus nos. 10, 11A, 11B, 13, 20B.

Rates: £61 ($96.50) single, £98 ($147) double. Service charge 15%. AE, DC, MC, V.

Situated on a quiet street, even though only two blocks from Trinity College and opposite the National Museum, Library, and Art Gallery, and Leinster House, this vintage four-story hotel has long been a meeting point for artists, poets, scholars, and politicians. Originally two Georgian town houses (dating back to 1736), it was launched as a hotel in 1928 and has been managed by three generations of the Duff family ever since. The public rooms have period furniture, intricate plasterwork, Wedgwood flourishes, old prints, and memorabilia. All the bedrooms have been updated with a contemporary decor and Victorian touches, plus added amenities of tea/coffee makers and hair dryers. Facilities include a restaurant, two bars, concierge, and room service.

Grafton Plaza, Johnsons Place, off Lower Mercer Street, Dublin 2. ☎ **01/475-0888.**
Fax 01/475-0908. 75 rms (all with bath). TV TEL **Transportation:** Bus nos. 16A,
19A, 22A, 55, 83.

Rates: £50–£70 ($75–$105) single; £70–£90 ($105–$135) double. No service charge.
AE, DC, MC, V.

Taking its name from its proximity to Grafton Street, this new hotel has a graceful
Georgian town-house facade that fits right into the neighborhood. The lobby is small
and simple but the guest rooms are attractive, with Irish-made furniture and carpets,
as well as amenities such as garment press, hair dryer, coffee/tea-maker; some rooms
have minibars. The social focus at this hotel is Break for the Border, a bilevel American Southwest–themed restaurant/bar/nightclub serving Tex-Mex food and featuring live country bands at night.

$ **Stauntons on the Green,** 83 St. Stephen's Green, Dublin 2. ☎ **01/478-2300.**
Fax 01/478-2263. 32 rms (all with bath). TV TEL **Transportation:** DART to Pearse
Street Station or bus nos. 14A or 62.

Rates: £49–£53 ($73.50–$79.50) single, £62–£79 ($93–$118.50) double. No service
charge. AE, DC, MC, V.

Opened in 1993, this beautifully restored guesthouse occupies a four-story Georgian
townhouse on the south side of St. Stephen's Green, next door to the Irish Department of Foreign Affairs. As befits a landmark building, however, there is no elevator,
but there are rooms on the ground level. The guest rooms are decorated in traditional
style, enhanced by tall windows and high ceilings; front rooms overlook The Green
and rooms at the back have views of the adjacent Iveagh Gardens. Public areas include a parlor with open fireplace and breakfast room.

Moderate/Inexpensive

$ **Georgian House,** 20 Lower Baggot St., Dublin 2. ☎ **01/661-8832.**
Fax 01/661-8834. 33 rms (all with bath). TV TEL **Transportation:** DART to Pearse
Station or bus no. 10.

Rates (including full breakfast): £35–£48 ($52.50–$72) single, £52–£76 ($78–$104)
double. Service charge 10%. AE, DC, MC, V.

Located less than two blocks from St. Stephen's Green, this four-story, 200-year-old
brick townhouse sits in the heart of Georgian Dublin, within walking distance of most
major attractions. Bedrooms are smallish, but offer all the essentials and a colorful
decor with pine furniture. As at most small hotels in landmark buildings, there is no
elevator, but there is an enclosed car park at the rear, and a restaurant specializing in
seafood, The Ante Room, in the basement, and a lively in-house pub, Maguire's.

Budget

Avalon House, 55 Aungier St., Dublin 2. ☎ **01/475-0001.** Fax 01/475-0303. 42 rms
(7 with private bath), and 3 dorms. **Transportation:** Bus nos. 16, 16A, 19, 22.

Rates: £18–£18.50 ($27–$27.78) single, £26–£29 ($39.50–$43.50) double; £11–£13.50
($16.50–$20.25) per person in 4-bed room, £10–£10.50 ($15–$15.25) per person in
dorm-style room. No service charge. AE, MC, V.

With a four-story red sandstone facade, this strikingly ornate Victorian building was
erected in 1879 as a medical school, later used for commercial offices, and then

completely gutted and transformed into a custom-built hostel in 1992. Great care was taken to preserve original turf fireplaces, some of the more artistic wallpaper, and the wide windows, while at the same time to install the most modern equipment for showers, toilets, and other guest facilities. Rooms have two to eight beds. Geared for students and budget-conscious travelers, it is situated less than two blocks from St. Stephen's Green. Facilities include a coffee shop, study/reading room, bureau de change, TV lounge room, international payphones, lockers, luggage storage, self-catering kitchen, and guest laundry.

FITZWILLIAM/MERRION SQUARES AREA
Very Expensive/Expensive

Davenport Hotel, Merrion Square, Dublin 2. ☎ **01/661-6800** or toll free
800/44-UTELL in the U.S. Fax 01/661-5663. 120 rms (all with bath). A/C TV TEL
Transportation: DART to Pearse Station or bus nos. 5, 7A, 8, 62.

Rates: £110–£160 ($165–$240) single, £140–£180 ($210–$270) double. Service charge 12.5%. AE, DC, MC, V.

Opened as a hotel in 1993, this building incorporates the neoclassical facade of Merrion Hall, an 1863 church. Inside there is an impressive domed entranceway, with a six-story atrium lobby of marble flooring and plaster moldings, encircled by classic Georgian windows and pillars. The guest rooms, in a newly built section, have traditional furnishings, orthopedic beds, textured wall coverings, quilted floral bedspreads and matching drapes, and brass accoutrements. There are three telephone lines in each room plus a computer data line, work desk, personal safe, garment press, tea/coffee welcome tray, mirrored closet, and hairdryer. It is a sister hotel to the Mont Clare, which is across the street and shares valet car parking arrangements.

Dining/Entertainment: The Georgian-theme restaurant, Lanyon's, is named after a leading Irish architect of the 19th century; the clubby President's Bar, decorated with framed pictures of world leaders, past and present, serves drinks as well as morning coffee and afternoon tea.

Services: Room service, concierge, valet laundry.

Expensive

Mont Clare Hotel, Merrion Square, Clare St., Dublin 2. ☎ **661-6799** or toll-free
800/44-UTELL from U.S. Fax 01/661-5663. 74 rms (all with bath). AC MINIBAR
TV TEL **Transportation:** DART to Pearse Station or bus nos. 5, 7A, 8, 62.

Rates: £90–£150 ($135–$225) single, £120–£150 ($180–$225) double. Service charge 12.5%. AE, DC, MC, V.

Overlooking the northwest corner of Merrion Square, this vintage six-story brick-faced hotel was thoroughly restored and refurbished in recent years. It has a typically Georgian facade, matched tastefully inside by period furnishings of dark woods and polished brass. The guest rooms, decked out in contemporary style, offer every up-to-date amenity including hairdryer, tea/coffee maker, and garment press.

Dining/Entertainment: Named for one of Ireland's great writers, the main restaurant, Goldsmith's, has a literary theme. There is also a traditional lounge bar.

Services: 24-hour room service, concierge.

Facilities: Foreign currency exchange, private valet parking lot.

Moderate

Longfields, 9/10 Lower Fitzwilliam St., Dublin 2. ☎ **01/676-1367** or toll free **800/223-1588** from U.S. Fax 01/676-1542. 26 rms (all with bath). MINIBAR TV TEL **Transportation:** DART to Pearse Station or bus no. 10.

Rates (including full breakfast): £60–£120 ($90–$180) single, £80–£120 ($120–$180) double. No service charge. AE, DC, MC, V.

Created from two 18th-century Georgian townhouses, this smart little hotel is named after Richard Longfield, also known as Viscount Longueville, who originally owned this site and was a member of the Irish Parliament two centuries ago. Totally restored and refurbished several years ago, it combines Georgian decor and reproduction period furnishings of dark woods and brass trim. Bedrooms offer extras such as clock radios and hair dryers. Facilities include a restaurant with bar, room service, and foreign currency exchange, but no car park.

Moderate/Inexpensive

The Fitzwilliam, 41 Upper Fitzwilliam St., Dublin 2. ☎ **01/660-0048.** Fax 01/676-7488. 12 rms (all with bath). TV TEL **Transportation:** DART to Pearse Station or bus no. 10.

Rates (including full breakfast): £32–£40 ($48–$60) single, £49–£70 ($73.50–$105) double. Service charge 10%. AE, DC, MC, V.

Appropriately named for the wide thoroughfare it overlooks, this cozy guesthouse is a restored and refurbished 18th-century Georgian home. The entrance parlor has a homey atmosphere, with a marble fireplace and antique furnishings, while the bedrooms are outfitted with contemporary amenities including hair dryers and clock radios. Facilities include a French restaurant.

BALLSBRIDGE/EMBASSY ROW AREA

Very Expensive/Expensive

★ **Berkeley Court,** Lansdowne Road, Ballsbridge, Dublin 4. ☎ **01/660-1711** or toll free **800-42-DOYLE, 800/223-6800,** or **800/44-UTELL** in U.S. Fax 01/661-7238. 197 rms and 10 suites (all with bath). TV TEL **Transportation:** DART to Lansdowne Road or bus nos. 5, 7A, 8, 46, 63, 84.

Rates: £120–£132 ($180–$198) single, £135–£147 ($202.50–$220.50) double, £404–£472 ($606–$708) for suites, £1,350 ($2,025) for penthouse suite. Service charge 15%. AE, CB, DC, MC, V.

The flagship of the Irish-owned Doyle Hotel group and the first Irish member of Leading Hotels of the World, the Berkeley Court (pronounced Barkley) is nestled in a residential area near the American Embassy on well-tended grounds that were once part of the Botanic Gardens of University College. A favorite haunt of diplomats and international business leaders, the hotel is known for its posh lobby decorated with fine antiques, original paintings, mirrored columns, and Irish-made carpets and furnishings. The guest rooms, which aim to convey an air of elegance, have designer fabrics, semicanopy beds, dark woods, and bathrooms fitted with marble accoutrements.

Dining/Entertainment: Choices include the formal Berkeley Room for gourmet dining; the skylit Conservatory for casual meals; the Royal Court, a Gothic-style bar for drinks; and the Court Lounge, a proper setting for afternoon tea or a relaxing drink.

Services: 24-hour room service, concierge, laundry service, and express checkout.
Facilities: Foreign currency exchange, shopping boutiques, gym, and ample outdoor parking.

⭐ **Jurys Hotel,** Pembroke Road, Ballsbridge, Dublin 4. ☎ **01/660-5000** or toll free **800/843-3311** in U.S. Fax 01/660-5540. 390 rms (all with bath). TV TEL
Transportation: DART to Lansdowne Road Station or bus nos. 6, 7, 8, 18, 45, 46, 84.

Rates: Main hotel £105 ($162.50) single, £125 ($188) double; Towers wing (with continental breakfast) £150 ($225) single, £181 ($276.50) double. Service charge 12.5%. AE, DC, MC, V.

Setting a progressive tone in a city steeped in tradition, this unique hotel welcomes guests to a three story skylit-atrium lobby with a marble and teak decor. Situated on its own grounds opposite the American Embassy, this sprawling property is actually two interconnected hotels in one—a modern eight-story high-rise, and a new 100-unit tower with its own check-in desk, separate elevators, and private entrance, as well as full access to all of the main hotel's amenities. The guest rooms in the main wing, recently refurbished, have dark wood furnishings, brass trim, and designer fabrics. The Towers section—a first for the Irish capital—is an exclusive wing of oversized concierge-style rooms with bay windows. Each unit has computer-card key access, stocked minibar, three telephone lines, well-lit work area with desk, reclining chair, tile and marble bathroom, walk-in closet, and either a king or queen bed. Decors vary, from contemporary light woods with floral fabrics to dark tones with Far Eastern motifs. Towers guests also enjoy exclusive use of a private hospitality lounge with library, board room, and access to complimentary continental breakfast, daily newspapers, and coffee-tea service throughout the day.

Dining/Entertainment: Choices include the Embassy Garden for Irish/Continental cuisine; The Kish for seafood; and The Coffee Dock, Dublin's only around-the-clock coffee shop. This is also the home of Jurys Irish Cabaret Show, Ireland's longest-running evening entertainment; The Dubliner Bar, a pub with a turn-of-the-century theme; and the skylit Pavilion Lounge, overlooking the indoor-outdoor pool.

Services: 24-hour room service, concierge, foreign currency exchange, valet/laundry service, safety deposit boxes, and express checkout.

Facilities: Heated indoor/outdoor pool, therapeutic hot whirlpool, hairdressing salons, craft/clothes shop, Aer Lingus ticket office, and outdoor parking.

Expensive

⭐ **Hibernian Hotel,** Eastmoreland Place, Ballsbridge, Dublin 4. ☎ **01/688-7666** or toll free **800/447-7462** in the U.S. Fax 01/660-2655. 30 rms (all with bath). TV TEL
Transportation: Bus no. 10.

Rates (including full Irish breakfast): £85–£135 ($127.50–$202.50) single, £120–£135 ($180–$202.50) double. No service charge. AE, DC, MC, V.

Although it bears a similar name, this is not a reincarnation of the legendary Royal Hibernian Hotel that was ensconced on Dawson Street until the early 1980s. Instead, this handsome red-brick four-story Victorian building was originally part of Baggot Street Hospital. After a complete restoration, it was modeled into a hotel in 1993, and offers its guests up-to-date comforts with the charm of a country inn. The public areas are filled with antiques, graceful pillars, flowers, and plants, and classical music can often be heard discreetly in the background. The top floor sports a beautifully restored dome-shaped skylight. The bedrooms, of varying size and layout, are individually decorated with dark woods, floral fabrics, and specially commissioned paintings of Dublin and wildlife scenes. In-room conveniences include a full-length mirror, garment press, hairdryer, and coffee/tea-maker. Unlike some converted 19th-century buildings, it has an elevator.

Dining/Entertainment: On the lobby level, a cozy parlorlike room serves as guests' bar and conservatory-style restaurant with a Georgian decor.

Services: Room service, concierge, 24-hour butler, turn-down service, valet laundry.

Expensive/Moderate

$ **Burlington**, Upper Leeson Street, Dublin 4. ☎ **01/660-5222** or toll free **800/223-0888** or **800/44-DOYLE** in U.S. Fax 01/660-8496. 477 rms (all with bath). TV TEL **Transportation:** Bus nos. 10 or 18.

Rates: £88–£125 ($132–$188) single, £110–£125 ($165–$187.50) double. Service charge 15%. AE, CB, DC, MC, V.

A favorite headquarters for conventions, meetings, conferences, and group tours, this is the largest hotel in Ireland, situated a block south of the Grand Canal in a fashionable residential section within walking distance of St. Stephen's Green. It's a modern, crisply furnished seven-story property, constantly being refurbished. The bedrooms are outfitted with brass-bound oak furniture and designer fabrics. The good proportion of inter-connecting units are ideal for families.

Dining/Entertainment: Choices include the Sussex, a large formal dining room; a buffet restaurant; and a coffee shop for light meals. For a real old Dublin pub atmosphere, try Buck Mulligans, which serves a carvery-style lunch and light evening meals as well as drinks. Annabel's is the basement-level nightclub. From May to early October, the main ballroom offers Doyle's Irish Cabaret, a three-hour cabaret dinner show.

Services: 24-hour room service, concierge, valet/laundry service.

Facilities: Foreign-currency exchange, underground and outdoor parking, gift shops, newsstand, and hairdressing salons.

Moderate

Anglesea Town House, 63 Anglesea Rd., Ballsbridge, Dublin 4. ☎ **01/668-3877.** Fax 01/668-3461. 7 rms (all with bath). TV TEL **Transportation:** DART to Lansdowne Road Station or bus nos. 46, 63, 84.

Rates (including full breakfast): £45–£57 ($72.50–$85.50) single, £67–£90 ($100.50–$135) double. No service charge. AE, MC, V.

A true bed-and-breakfast experience is the best way to describe this 1903 Edwardian-style guesthouse. Located in the Ballsbridge section of the city, close to the Royal Dublin Showgrounds and the American Embassy, it is furnished with comfort in mind—rocking chairs, settees, a sun deck, and lots of flowering plants, as well as all modern conveniences in every guest room. You can count on a warm welcome from hostess Helen Kirrane and a breakfast of homemade goodies.

Ariel House, 52 Lansdowne Rd., Ballsbridge, Dublin 4. ☎ **01/668-5512.** Fax 01/668-5845. 28 rms (all with bath). TV TEL **Transportation:** DART to Lansdowne Road Station or bus nos. 5, 7A, 8, 46, 63, 84.

Rates: £39.50 ($58.75) single, £63–£100 ($94.50–$150) double. Service charge 10%. MC, V.

As Dublin guesthouses go, this one is the benchmark, opened over 25 years ago by Dublin-born and San Francisco-trained hotelier Michael O'Brien. With a historic mid-19th century mansion as its core, this bastion of hospitality has been expanded and enhanced continually over the years to its present capacity. Guests are welcome to relax in the drawing room, rich in Victorian style, with Waterford glass chandeliers, an open fireplace, and delicately carved cornices. The bedrooms are individually decorated, with period furniture, fine oil paintings and watercolors, and real Irish linens, as well as modern extras such as a hairdryer, garment press, and iron/ironing board. Facilities include a conservatory-style dining room that serves breakfast, morning coffee, and afternoon tea, a wine bar, and a private car park. It is conveniently located one block from the DART station.

⭐ **Doyle Montrose,** Stillorgan Road, Dublin 4. ☎ **01/269-3111** or toll free **800/42-DOYLE** or **800/44-UTELL** from U.S. Fax 01/269-1164. 190 rms (all with bath). TV TEL **Transportation:** Bus nos. 10, 46, 46A, 46B, 63.
Rates: £66–£94 ($99–$141) single, £85–£94 ($127.50–$141) double. Service charge 15%. AE, CB, DC, MC, V.

Nestled on its own palm tree–lined grounds in a residential neighborhood, across from the Belfield campus of Dublin's University College, this modern four-story hotel sits beside the main road (N 11) to the southeast of Ireland. The largest hotel on the southern outskirts of the city, it is a ten-minute drive from downtown, and offers ample outdoor car parking. Guest rooms are modern and functional, with colorful Irish-made furnishings.

   Dining/Entertainment: Facilities include a restaurant, The Belfield Room, plus a grill room, and skylit lounge bar.
   Services: Concierge, room service, laundry service.
   Facilities: Health center, souvenir shop, and full-service bank.

⭐ **Doyle Tara,** Merrion Road, Dublin 4. ☎ **01/269-4666** or toll free **800/42-DOYLE** from U.S. Fax 01/269-1027. 100 rms (all with bath). TV TEL **Transportation:** DART to Booterstown Station or bus nos. 5, 7, 7A, 8.
Rates: £66–£94 ($99–$141) single, £85–£94 ($127.50–$141) double. Service charge 15%. AE, CB, DC, MC, V.

Positioned along the coast road between downtown Dublin and the ferryport of Dun Laoghaire, this modern seven-story hotel offers wide-windowed views of Dublin Bay, just ten minutes from the city center in a residential area. It's an ideal place for car renters, as there is ample parking space; and for those who prefer to use public transport, it's within easy walking distance of major bus routes and a DART station. Guest rooms, with every modern convenience, have attractive Irish-made furnishings.
   Dining/Entertainment: There is a conservatory-style restaurant and a Joycean lounge bar.
   Services: Concierge, room service, laundry service.
   Facilities: Foreign-currency exchange, souvenir shop.

Moderate/Inexpensive

Glenveagh Town House, 31 Northumberland Rd., Ballsbridge, Dublin 4.
   ☎ **01/668-4612.** Fax 01/668-4559. 11 rms (all with bath). TV TEL **Transportation:**

DART to Lansdowne Road Station or bus nos. 5, 7, 7A, 8, 45.

Rates (including full breakfast): £36–£40 ($54–$60) single, £50–£70 ($75–$105) double. No service charge. AE, MC, V.

Fashioned into a guesthouse by the Cunningham family, this converted three-story Georgian residence is situated south of the Grand Canal on a quiet, tree-lined street. It offers a homey atmosphere with a glowing fireplace in the sitting room, high ceilings, and tall windows bedecked with floral drapery. Guest rooms are decorated with light woods, lots of frilly pastel fabrics, and all the modern conveniences. There is a private car park.

Lansdowne Lodge, 4 Lansdowne Terrace, Shelbourne Road, Ballsbridge, Dublin 4. ☎ **01/660-5755** or **660-5578.** Fax 01/660-5662. 12 rms (all with bath). TV TEL **Transportation:** DART to Lansdowne Road Station or bus nos. 5, 7, 7A, 8, 45.

Rates (including full breakfast): £35–£45 ($52.50–$72.50) single, £50–£100 ($75–$150) double. No service charge. MC, V.

With a lovely two-story brick townhouse facade, this guesthouse enjoys a very convenient location, between Lansdowne and Haddington Roads, and within a block of the DART station and major bus routes. Owner Finbarr Smyth offers a variety of individually styled bedrooms with armchairs and homey furnishings including decorative bed coverings and framed paintings; some rooms are on the ground floor. The grounds include a garden and private car park.

Inexpensive

$ Mount Herbert, 7 Herbert Rd., Ballsbridge, Dublin 4. ☎ **01/668-4321.** Fax 01/660-7077. 135 rms (all with bath). TV TEL **Transportation:** DART to Lansdowne Road Station or bus nos. 5, 7, 7A, 8, 46, 63, 84.

Rates: £33–£43 ($49.50–$64.50) single, £46–£56 ($69–$79) double. No service charge. AE, DC, MC, V.

Although technically classified as a guesthouse, this much-expanded three-story property is more like a small hotel. Originally the family home of Lord Robinson, it is a gracious residence set in its own grounds and gardens in a residential neighborhood near the DART station and major bus routes. Operated by the Loughran family, it offers bedrooms of various vintages and sizes, but all have standard amenities including a garment press. Guest facilities include a restaurant, wine bar, sauna, indoor solarium, gift shop, and guest car park.

Budget

Morehampton House, 78 Morehampton Rd., Donnybrook, Dublin 4. ☎ **01/668-8866.** Fax 01/668-8794. 85 beds (no private baths). **Transportation:** Bus nos. 10, 46A, 46B.

Rates: £11.50–£12.50 ($17.25–$18.75) per person single or double in twin-bed rooms; £8.95–£9.95 ($13.43–$14.82) per person in 4- to 8-bedded rooms; and £6.95–£7.95 ($10.43–$11.91) per person in 16-bed dorm room. MC, V.

In a residential area south of the city center and within a 15-minute walk from St. Stephen's Green, this four-story Victorian house has been recently converted into a hostel. Designed for the budget-minded traveler, it offers a choice of twin rooms and dorm-style accommodations. Facilities include a 24-hour reception desk, TV room, common room, self-catering kitchen, car and bike parking, and lovely gardens outside.

O'CONNELL STREET AREA
Expensive/Moderate

Gresham, 23 Upper O'Connell St., Dublin 1. ☎ 01/874-6881 or toll free **800/44-UTELL** in the U.S. Fax 01/878-7175. 202 rms and 6 suites. TV TEL
Transportation: DART to Connolly Station or bus nos. 40A, 40B, 40C, 51A.
Rates: £99–£140 ($132–$210) single or double, from £150 ($225) suite. Service charge 12.5%. AE, CB, DC, MC, V.

Centrally located on the city's main business thoroughfare, this Regency-style hotel is one of Ireland's oldest (1817) and best-known lodging establishments. Although much of the tourist trade in Dublin has shifted south of the River Liffey in recent years, the Gresham is still synonymous with stylish Irish hospitality and provides easy access to the Abbey and Gate Theatres and other northside attractions. The lobby and public areas are a panorama of marble floors, moulded plasterwork, and crystal chandeliers. With high ceilings and individual decors, guest rooms vary in size and style, with heavy emphasis on deep blue and pink tones, soft lighting, tile bathrooms, and period furniture including padded headboards and armoires. One-of-a-kind luxury terrace suites grace the upper front floors.

Dining/Entertainment: Choices include the bi-level Aberdeen Restaurant for formal meals and Toddy's, a trendy pub/lounge offering light meals all day. Another bar, Magnums, attracts a late-night crowd.

Services: Concierge, 24-hour room service, valet laundry service.

Facilities: Private parking garage, ice machines, foreign currency exchange.

Moderate

Royal Dublin, 40 Upper O'Connell St., Dublin 1. ☎ 01/873-3666 or toll free **800/528-1234** in the U.S. Fax 01/873-3120. 120 rms (all with bath). TV TEL
Transportation: DART to Connolly Station or bus nos. 36A, 40A, 40B, 40C, 51A.
Rates: £63–£81 ($94.50–$121.50) single, £78–£118 ($117–$177) double. No service charge. AE, DC, MC, V.

Romantically floodlit at night, this modern five-story hotel is positioned near Parnell Square at the north end of Dublin's main thoroughfare, within walking distance of all the main theaters and northside attractions. It combines a contemporary skylit lobby full of art deco overtones with adjacent lounge areas that were part of an original building dating back to 1752. These Georgian-theme rooms are rich in high moulded ceilings, ornate cornices, crystal chandeliers, gilt-edged mirrors, and open fireplaces. The bedrooms are strictly modern with light woods, pastel fabrics, and three-sided full-length windows that extend over the busy street below. Corridors are extremely well lit, with individual lights at each doorway.

Dining/Entertainment: Choices include the Cafe Royale Brasserie for full meals and Raffles Bar, a skylit clubby room with portraits of Irish literary greats, for snacks or drinks; and the Georgian Lounge for morning coffee or afternoon tea beside the open fireplace.

Services: 24-hour room service, concierge, laundry service.

Facilities: Bureau de change, underground car park, car rental desk.

4 Where to Dine

From formal old-world hotel dining rooms to casual bistros and wine bars, Dublin has a great variety of restaurants, in all price categories. As befits a European capital, there is plenty of continental fare, with a particular leaning toward French and Italian influences, plus a fine selection of international eateries, with recipes that come from as far away as Scandinavia, Russia, the Mediterranean, China, and even California.

So get ready for some good eating in Dublin's Fair City.

HISTORIC OLD CITY/LIBERTIES AREA

Expensive

Lord Edward, 23 Christ Church Place, Dublin 8. ☎ **454-2420.**

> **Cuisine:** SEAFOOD. **Reservations:** Required. **Transportation:** Bus nos. 21A, 50, 50A, 78, 78A, 78B.
> **Prices:** Lunch or dinner appetizers £2.95–£7.55 ($4.43–$11.33); lunch or dinner main courses £11.95–£15.95 ($17.93–$23.93). AE, DC, MC, V.
> **Open:** Lunch Mon–Fri noon–2:45pm, dinner 5–10:45pm; Sat dinner 5–10:45pm.

Established in 1890 and situated in the heart of the Old City opposite Christ Church Cathedral, this cozy upstairs dining room claims to be Dublin's oldest seafood restaurant. A dozen different preparations of sole including au gratin and Veronique are served, seven variations of prawns from thermidor to Provençale, and fresh lobster is prepared au naturel or in sauces, plus fresh fish from salmon and seatrout to plaice and turbot—grilled, fried, meunière, or poached. Vegetarian dishes are also available. At lunchtime, light snacks and simpler fare are served in the bar.

Expensive/Moderate

Old Dublin, 90/91 Francis St., Dublin 8. ☎ **454-2028** or **454-2346.**

> **Cuisine:** SCANDINAVIAN/RUSSIAN. **Reservations:** Recommended. **Transportation:** Bus nos. 21A, 78A, 78B.
> **Prices:** Set lunch £12.50 ($18.75); 3-course dinners £19–£25 ($27.50–$37.50). AE, DC, MC, V.
> **Open:** Lunch Mon–Fri 12:30–2:15pm, dinner Mon–Sat 6–11pm.

Located in the heart of Dublin's antiques row, this shopfront restaurant is also on the edge of the city's medieval quarter, once settled by Vikings. So it is not surprising that many recipes featured here reflect this background, with a long list of imaginative Scandinavian and Russian dishes. Among the best entrees are novgorod, a rare beef thinly sliced and served on sauerkraut with fried barley, mushrooms, garlic butter, sour cream, and caviar; salmon kulebjaka, a pastry filled with salmon, dill herbs, rice, egg, mushrooms, and onion; black sole Metsa, filled with mussels and served with prawn butter and white wine; and a varied selection of vegetarian dishes.

Budget

Leo Burdock's, 2 Werburgh St., Dublin 8. ☎ **454-0306.**

> **Cuisine:** FISH AND CHIPS/FAST FOOD. **Reservations:** Not accepted. **Transportation:** Bus nos. 21A, 50, 50A, 78, 78A, 78B.
> **Prices:** 70p–£2.50 ($1.05–$3.75). No credit cards.
> **Open:** Mon–Fri 12:30–11pm, Sat 2–11pm.

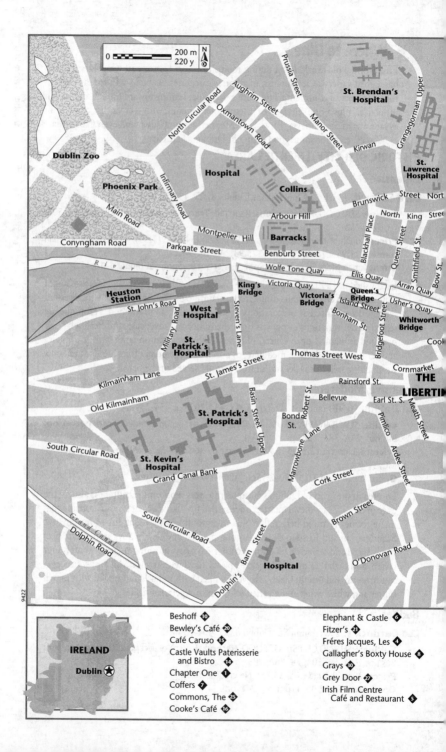

Beshoff ⑩

Bewley's Café ⑳

Café Caruso ⑮

Castle Vaults Paterisserie and Bistro ⑭

Chapter One ①

Coffers ⑦

Commons, The ㉓

Cooke's Café ⑯

Elephant & Castle ⑥

Fitzer's ㉑

Fréres Jacques, Les ④

Gallagher's Boxty House ⑧

Grays ㉚

Grey Door ㉗

Irish Film Centre Café and Restaurant ⑤

IRELAND

Dublin ★

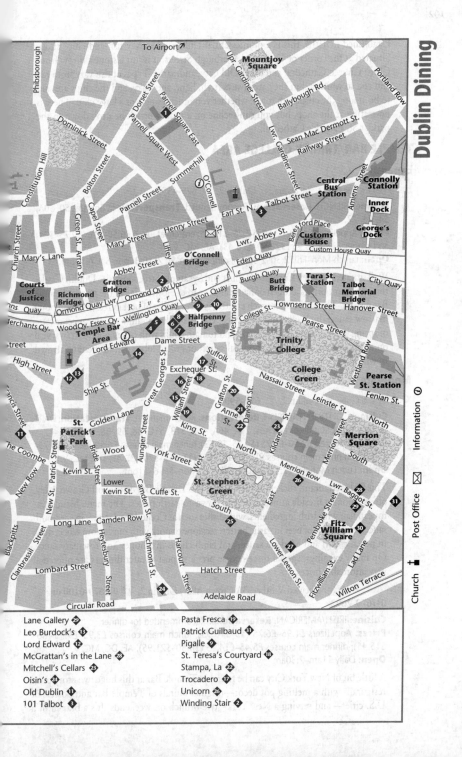

Dublin Dining

Church ✝ Post Office ☒ Information ⊘

Established in 1913, this is a quintessential Dublin take-away fish-and-chips shop. Situated at the corner of Castle and Werburgh Streets, it is just a stone's throw from Christ Church Cathedral and other Old City landmarks. Types of fish vary from ray and cod to whiting, but they are always fresh, light, and flaky, and the chips are said to be among the crispest in town, whether you order a single or a large chip. There is no seating at the shop, but you can recline on a nearby bench or stroll down to the park at St. Patrick's Cathedral.

TEMPLE BAR/TRINITY COLLEGE AREA

Expensive

Les Frères Jacques, 74 Dame St., Dublin 2. ☎ 679-4555.

Cuisine: FRENCH. **Reservations:** Recommended. **Transportation:** Bus nos. 50, 50A, 54, 56, 77.
Prices: Appetizers £4.50–£7.50 ($7.25–$11.25; entrees at lunch £6.50–£16 ($9.75–$24) and dinner £15–£18.95 ($22.50–$28.43). AE, MC, V.
Open: Lunch Mon–Fri 12:30–2:30pm; dinner Mon–Fri 7–10:30pm, Sat 7–11pm.

Well situated between Crampton Court and Sycamore Street opposite Dublin Castle, this restaurant brings a touch of haute cuisine to the lower edge of the trendy Temple Bar district. The menu offers such creative entrees as filet of beef in red wine and bone marrow sauce; duck suprême on a sweet corn pancake in tangy ginger sauce; rosette of spring lamb in meat juice sabayon and tomato coulis with crispy potato straws; veal on rainbow pasta with garlic and basil sauce; or grilled lobster from the tank flamed in whiskey.

Moderate

Coffers, 6 Cope St., Dublin 2. ☎ 671-5900.

Cuisine: CONTINENTAL/IRISH. **Reservations:** Recommended. **Transportation:** DART to Tara Street Station or bus nos. 21A, 46A, 46B, 51B, 51C, 68, 69, 86.
Prices: Appetizers £2.50–£5.75 ($4.25–$8.63); lunch main courses £6.50–£7.95 ($9.75–$11.83), dinner main courses £10.95–£13.95. ($16.43–$20.93). AE, DC, MC, V.
Open: Lunch Mon–Fri 12:15–2:30pm; dinner Mon–Sat 6–11pm.

This little restaurant, tucked in the heart of the Temple Bar district off Crown Alley, offers a homey fireside atmosphere and down-to-earth prices. The menu blends European flair with Irish ingredients, with dishes such as Coquille St-Jacques in vermouth sauce; medaillons of beef in garlic butter; escalope of pork with mushroom sauce; duck in peach cream and Madeira sauce; and lamb chops in a honey and rosemary sauce. On many evenings, special three-course pre- and post-theater dinners are offered at very affordable prices.

Eammon Doran, Licensed Vintner, 3A Crown Alley, Dublin 2. ☎ 01/679-0100 or 01/679-2692.

Cuisine: IRISH/AMERICAN. **Reservations:** Recommended for dinner.
Prices: Appetizers £1.95–£6.75 ($3–$10.95); lunch main courses £3.95–£9.95 ($6–$15.45); dinner main courses £5.45–£14.15 ($8.50–$21.95). AE, DC, MC, V.
Open: Daily 11am–2:30am.

A little bit of New York City can be found in Temple Bar at this huge two-story pub/restaurant with a melting pot decor—original murals of Temple Bar and posters of U.S. cities—and serving a New York–style brunch on weekends. It's a branch of a long-established mid-town Manhattan eatery—both are named for Eammon Doran, an Irish-born entrepreneur who flies back and forth across the Atlantic to tend to his business interests. Restaurant specialties include Gaelic steak, steak-and-kidney pie, shepherd's pie, chicken pot pie, fish and chips, and braised lamb stew. Universal favorites—roast duck flambée, rack of lamb, and chateaubriand—are offered along with a good selection of fresh seafood, pastas, sandwiches, salads, and omelets. The downstairs level is a venue for traditional music and plays.

⭐ **Irish Film Centre Cafe & Restaurant,** 6 Eustace St., Dublin 2. ☎ **677-8788** or **677-8099.**

Cuisine: IRISH/INTERNATIONAL. **Reservations:** Recommended for dinner. **Transportation:** Bus nos. 21A, 78A, 78B.
Prices: Appetizers £1.95–£4.95 ($2.93–$7.43), lunch main courses £1.50–£4.50 ($2.75–$6.75), dinner main courses $2.95–$8.95 ($4.43–$13.43). MC. V.
Open: Daily 12:30–11pm.

Hollywood prevails at this mezzanine-level restaurant—overlooking the central courtyard of the Irish Film Centre complex in Temple Bar. Black-and-white furnishings and walls lined with photos and posters of movie stars set the tone. The menu changes daily, but the creative cuisine often includes choices such as dry baked salmon with roasted pepper and balsamic vinaigrette; chicken breast with bananas and red and green peppers; spinach, walnut, and ricotta canelloni; minute steaks in pita bread; and smoked salmon and goat cheese pizza. Lunch, served in the lower-level bar area, includes omelets with seafood fillings, stir-fry dishes, and salad bar servings.

Pigalle, 14 Temple Bar, Dublin 2. ☎ **671-9262** or **679-6602.**

Cuisine: FRENCH. **Reservations:** Required on weekends. **Transportation:** DART to Tara Street Station or bus nos. 21A, 46A, 46B, 51B, 51C, 68, 69, 86.
Prices: Set lunch £11.50 ($17.25); set dinner £18.50 ($27.75). DC, MC, V.
Open: Lunch Mon–Fri 12:30–2:30pm; dinner Mon–Sat 7–10:45pm.

Overlooking Merchant's Arch and Crown Alley in the heart of Temple Bar, this upstairs restaurant attracted a loyal following long before the surrounding neighborhood was a hot spot. The decor is simple bistro style, with white walls, crisp linens, and plant-filled window ledges. The menu, which changes daily, is table d'hôte, with up to six courses on weekends. Entrées often include dishes such as fillet of beef with green peppercorn sauce; rack of lamb with fresh rosemary sauce; breast of duck with blueberry sauce, and wild salmon with capers, tomato, and shallots. The skills and service of the staff make it a true culinary outpost of France wedged in the midst of Dublin's own Left Bank.

Moderate/Inexpensive

Elephant & Castle, 18 Temple Bar, Dublin 2. ☎ **679-3121.**

Cuisine: CALIFORNIAN/INTERNATIONAL. **Reservations:** Not necessary. **Transportation:** DART to Tara Street Station or bus nos. 21A, 46A, 46B, 51B, 51C, 68, 69, 86.
Prices: Appetizers £2.25–£5.75 ($3.38–$8.63); lunch main courses £4.50–£7.95 ($6.75–$11.83), dinner £5.50–£10.50 ($8.25–$15.75). AE, DC, MC, V.
Open: Sun–Thurs 11:30am–11:30pm, Fri–Sat 11:30am–midnight.

Located in the heart of the Temple Bar district, this is an informal and fun restaurant, with simple pine wood tables and benches, and a decor blending modern art with statues of elephants and cartoon figures. The menu is eclectic, made up of exotic salads and multi-ingredient omelets, as well as guacamole and tortilla chips; sesame chicken with spinach and cucumber; fettuccine with shrimp, sun-dried tomatoes, and saffron; linguini with goat cheese, tomato, broccoli and thyme; and rare sliced steak with cracked pepper, watercress, and ginger vinaigrette; as well as smoked salmon salads, sandwiches, Stilton burgers, and a house-special Elephant burger with curried sour cream, bacon, scallions, cheddar, and tomato.

★ **Gallagher's Boxty House,** 20–21 Temple Bar, Dublin 2. ☎ **677-2762.**
Cuisine: TRADITIONAL IRISH. **Reservations:** Recommended. **Transportation:** DART to Tara Street Station or bus nos. 21A, 46A, 46B, 51B, 51C, 68, 69, 86.
Prices: Appetizers £1.70–£4.50 ($2.55–$6.75); lunch main courses £1.95–£3.50 ($2.55–$5.25), dinner £4.95–£9.95 ($7.43–$14.93). MC, V.
Open: Mon–Fri 11am–11pm, Sat–Sun 12:30–11pm.

Although native Irish cooking is sometimes hard to find in Dublin restaurants, here is one spot that keeps traditions alive, with a particular emphasis on Irish stew, bacon and cabbage, and a dish called boxty. Boxty is an Irish potato pancake grilled and rolled with various fillings, such as beef, lamb, chicken, fish or combinations like bacon and cabbage. Besides all types of boxty, salmon and steaks, there are hearty sandwiches served on open wedges of brown bread at lunchtime.

Inexpensive

Beshoff, 14 Westmoreland St., Dublin 2. ☎ **677-8026.**
Cuisine: SEAFOOD/FISH AND CHIPS. **Reservations:** Not necessary. **Transportation:** DART to Tara Street Station or bus nos. 7A, 8, 15A, 15B, 15C, 46, 55, 62, 63, 83, 84.
Prices: All items £1.90–£3.50 ($2.85–$5.25). No credit cards.
Open: Sun–Thurs 11:30am–11pm, Fri–Sat 11:30am–3am.

Little wonder that the Beshoff name is synonymous with fresh fish in Dublin—Ivan Beshoff settled here in 1913 from Odessa, Russia, and started a fish business that developed into this top-notch fish-and-chips eatery, reminiscent of an Edwardian oyster bar. The atmosphere is informal and the self-service menu is simple—crisp chips (French fries) are served with a choice of fresh fish, from the original recipe of cod, to classier variations using salmon, shark, prawns, and other local seafare—some days as many as 20 varieties of fish. The potatoes are grown on a 300-acre farm in Tipperary and freshly cut each day. A second shop is located at 5/6 Upper O'Connell St. in the International Food Court (☎ **874-3223**).

Budget

Castle Vaults Patisserie & Bistro, Dublin Castle, Palace Street, off Dame Street, Dublin 2. ☎ **677-0678** or **679-3713.**
Cuisine: INTERNATIONAL/SELF-SERVICE. **Reservations:** Not necessary. **Transportation:** Bus nos. 50, 50A, 54, 56A, or 77.
Prices: £1.30–£4.95 ($1.95–$7.43) for most items. No credit cards.
Open: Mon–Fri 8am–5pm, Sat–Sun 11:30am–5pm.

With stone walls, paned windows, and colorful medieval banners, the old vaults of Dublin Castle serve as the setting for this bustling indoor-outdoor cafe. The menu focuses on pastries, snacks, or light lunch items, such as homemade soups, pâtés, quiche, lasagnes, sausage rolls, stuffed baked potatoes, salads, and sandwiches.

ST. STEPHEN'S GREEN/GRAFTON STREET AREA

Very Expensive/Expensive

★ **The Commons,** 85–86 St. Stephen's Green, Dublin 2. ☎ **475-2597** or **478-0530.**
Cuisine: CONTINENTAL. **Reservations:** Required. **Transportation:** DART to Pearse
Station or bus nos. 62 or 14A.
Prices: Set lunch £16 ($24); set dinner £27.50 ($41.25); dinner appetizers £5–£12.50
($7.50–$18.75) and dinner main courses £16.50–£20 ($24.75–$30). AE, MC, V.
Open: Lunch Mon–Fri 12:30–2:15pm, dinner Mon–Sat 7–10pm.

Nestled on the south side of St. Stephen's Green, this Michelin-starred restaurant
occupies the basement level of Newman House, the historic seat of Ireland's major
university and comprised of two elegant townhouses dating back to 1740. The interior of the dining rooms is a blend of Georgian architecture, cloister-style arches, and
original contemporary artworks with Joycean influences. For an aperitif in fine weather,
there is a lovely stone courtyard terrace surrounded by a "secret garden" of lush plants
and trees. The inventive menu changes daily, but often dishes appear such as pan-fried
tuna with red wine; fish quartet, a selection of four fish with their appropriate sauces;
quail breasts with wild mushroom timbale honey sauce; rack of lamb; and tournedos
of beef in chive and Madeira juice.

Expensive/Moderate

★ **Cooke's Cafe,** 14 S. William St., Dublin 2. ☎ **679-0536.**
Cuisine: CALIFORNIA/MEDITERRANEAN. **Reservations:** Required. **Transportation:**
DART to Tara Street Station or bus nos. 16A, 19A, 22A, 55, 83.
Prices: Appetizers £1.95–£12.95 ($2.93–$19.43); lunch main courses £9.75–£16
($14.63–$24) or set lunch £11.95 ($17.93); dinner main courses £10.95–£16.95 ($16.43–
$25.43). AE, DC, MC, V.
Open: Mon–Fri 9am–midnight, Sat–Sun noon–3pm, 6pm–midnight.

IMPRESSIONS

We are the music makers,
And we are the dreamers of dreams,
Wandering by lone sea-breakers,
And sitting by desolate streams;
World-losers and world-forsakers,
On whom the pale moon gleams:
Yet we are the movers and shakers
Of the world forever, it seems.
—Arthur O'Shaughnessy (1844–81), "Ode"

She is a rich and rare land,
Oh! she's a fresh and fair land;
She is a dear and rare land—
This native land of mine.
—Thomas Davis, (1814–45), "Ireland—My Ireland"

Named for owner-chef Johnny Cooke, this shopfront restaurant is such a favorite with Dublin's fashionable set that reservations often have to be made weeks in advance. It is located opposite the Powerscourt Townhouse Center and two blocks from Grafton Street. The decor is dominated by an open kitchen and art murals on the walls; there is also seating outdoors on antique tables and chairs originally from Brighton Pier. Specialties include dry-aged filet of beef grilled with field mushrooms; grilled duck with pancetta, marsala balsamic sauce, and wilted endive; angel hair with clams, cockles, chili, and tomato; whole lobster with fine herb butter; sautéed brill and Dover sole with capers and croutons; and baked grouper with a ragout of mussels, clams, artichokes, and tomatoes.

La Stampa, 35 Dawson St., Dublin 2. ☎ 677-8611.

Cuisine: FRENCH/INTERNATIONAL. **Reservations:** Recommended. **Transportation:** DART to Pearse Station or bus nos. 10, 11A, 11B, 13, 20B.
Prices: Appetizers £3.95–£6.50 ($5.93–$9.75); set lunch £12.50 ($18.75); dinner main courses £8.95–£15.95 ($13.43–$23.93). AE, DC, MC. V.
Open: Lunch Mon–Sat noon–2:30pm, Sun 12:30–2:30pm; dinner Sun–Thurs 6–11:30pm, Fri–Sat 6pm–midnight.

A half-block from St. Stephen's Green and opposite the Lord Mayor's Mansion House, this trendy Renaissance-style restaurant is always busy and sometimes noisy, frequented by a glamorous clientele of politicians, senior government officials, models, and entertainers, not to mention visitors-in-the-know. It features a long and spacious dining room, with a glass-domed ceiling, tall pillars, and mirrors that make it seem even larger. In spite of its Italian name, the food is international, with an emphasis on French. House specialties are lobster ravioli; filet of cod on purée of potatoes rimmed with green beans and bacon; saddle of lamb stuffed with wild mushrooms and spinach; and grilled red mullet with a confit of fennel. The fish soup is not to be missed as a starter.

Moderate

$ Cafe Caruso, 47 S. William St., Dublin 2. ☎ 677-0708.

Cuisine: ITALIAN/INTERNATIONAL. **Reservations:** Recommended. **Transportation:** Bus nos. 16A, 19A, 22A, 55, 83.
Prices: Appetizers £1.95–£4.50 ($2.93–$6.75); main courses £6.95–£12.50 ($10.43–$18.75). AE, DC, MC, V.
Open: Mon–Sat 6pm–12:15am and Sun 6–11:15pm.

Skylit and plant-filled, this festive and airy eatery is just two blocks from St. Stephen's Green or Grafton Street. As its name implies, it brings a touch of Italy and beyond to this corner of the city. The menu features a variety of freshly made pastas as well such dishes as pork marsala and osso bucco. In addition, the choices often include steaks, seafood, lamb kidneys, chicken Kiev, rack of lamb, and traditional Irish stew. A resident pianist supplies background music in the mostly classical or blues genres.

Trocadero, 3 St. Andrew St., Dublin 2. ☎ 677-5545.

Cuisine: INTERNATIONAL. **Reservations:** Recommended. **Transportation:** DART to Tara Street Station or bus nos. 16A, 19A, 22A, 55, 83.
Prices: Appetizers £1.95–£3.60 ($2.93–$5.40); main courses £6.95–£11.95 ($10.43–$17.93). AE, DC, MC, V.
Open: Mon–Sat 6pm–12:15am, Sun 6–11:15pm.

In many ways the Troc is the Sardi's of Dublin, and has been for almost 20 years. Located close to the Andrews Lane and other theaters, it is a favorite gathering spot for theater-goers, performers, and press, particularly because it serves food after the theaters let out. Pre- and post-theater specials are also offered. As might be expected, the decor is theatrical, too, with subdued lighting, banquette seating and close-knit tables, and photos of entertainers on the walls. Steaks are a specialty, but the menu also offers rack of lamb, daily fish specials, pastas, and traditional dishes such as Irish stew or corned beef and cabbage with parsley sauce, as well as chicken Dijon, Kiev, or stuffed with cream cheese and chives.

Moderate/Inexpensive

Fitzers, 51 Dawson St., Dublin 2. ☎ **677-1155.**

Cuisine: INTERNATIONAL. **Reservations:** Recommended. **Transportation:** DART to Pearse Station or bus nos. 10, 11A, 11B, 13, 20B.
Prices: Appetizers £1.50–£2.95 ($2.25–$4.43); lunch main courses £4.95–£8.95 ($7.43–$13.43); dinner main courses £4.95–£10.95 ($7.43–$16.43). AE, DC, MC, V.
Open: Mon–Sat noon–11pm, Sun 5–11pm.

Wedged in the middle of a busy shopping street, this bright and airy Irish-style bistro has a multiwindowed shopfront facade and a modern Irish decor of light woods inside. The food is contemporary, tasty, and quickly served, with choices ranging from chicken breast with hot chili cream sauce or brochette of lamb tandoori with mild curry sauce, to gratin of smoked cod, burgers topped with avocado and sour cream, as well as a variety of steaks and pastas. To prove how popular this restaurant is, there is a branch just a few blocks away at the National Gallery, Merrion Square West (☎ **668-6481**), with service primarily during museum hours (Mon–Wed and Fri–Sat 11am–5:30pm, Thurs 11am–8:30pm, and Sun 2–5pm). A third branch is in the Ballsbridge section of the city at 24 Upper Baggot St. (☎ **660-0644**), open Mon–Sat 8:30am–11pm.

Mitchell's Cellars, 21 Kildare St., Dublin 2. ☎ **668-0367.**

Cuisine: IRISH/CONTINENTAL. **Reservations:** Not accepted. **Transportation:** DART to Pearse Station or bus nos. 10, 11A, 11B, 13, 20B.
Prices: Appetizers £1.50–£2.25 ($2.25–$3.38), entrees £4.75–£6.50 ($7.13–$9.75). AE, DC, MC, V.
Open: Oct–May, Mon–Sat 12:15–2:30pm; June–Sept, Mon–Fri 12:15–2:30pm.

Originally a wine cellar, this trendy 60-seat luncheon spot has lots of atmosphere, with barrel-shaped tables, tiled floors, a beamed ceiling, and red and white lights. A favorite with Dubliners, it's located close to Grafton Street, Trinity College, and St. Stephen's Green. Mitchell's often serves seafood and cold meat salads, country pâtés, vegetable quiche, sweet and sour pork, beef braised in Guinness, chicken à la Suisse, or fricassee of veal. It's very popular, so get here early.

IMPRESSIONS

There are no overall certitudes in Ireland any more. There's a lot of diversity of thinking, a lot of uncertainty, a lot of trying to assimilate to other cultures. It's a time when we need to take stock, to look into our hearts, and find a sense of Irishness, to find a pride in ourselves, that will make us sure of what we are.
—Mary Robinson (b. 1944), President of Ireland, quoted during the 1990 presidential campaign

Inexpensive

Pasta Fresca, 3/4 Chatham St., Dublin 2. ☎ **679-2402.**

> **Cuisine:** ITALIAN. **Reservations:** Suggested. **Transportation:** Bus nos. 10, 11A, 11B, 13, 20B.
> **Prices:** Appetizers £1.95–£3.95 ($2.93–$5.93); entrees £6.95–£11.95 ($10.43–$17.93). MC, V.
> **Open:** Lunch 11:30am–6pm, dinner Mon–Sat 6–11:30pm.

Situated just a block from Grafton Street and St. Stephen's Green and around the corner from the Gaiety Theatre, this trattoria is popular with shoppers and for pre- and post-theater dinners. The menu features a variety of pastas, from fettuccine or tagliatelle to lasagne, spaghetti, and ravioli, as well as veal and steak dishes.

Budget

Bewley's Cafe, 78/79 Grafton St., Dublin 2. ☎ **677-6761.**

> **Cuisine:** IRISH. **Reservations:** Not required. **Transportation:** DART to Pearse Station or bus nos. 15A, 15B, 15C, 46, 55, 63, 83.
> **Prices:** All items £1–£5 ($1.50–$7.50). AE, DC, MC, V.
> **Open:** Mon–Wed 7:30am–1am, Thurs–Sat 8am–2am, Sun 9:30am–10pm.

To experience the real flavor of Dublin, you have to sip a cup of coffee or tea at Bewley's, a three-story landmark founded in 1840 by a Quaker named Joshua Bewley. With a traditional decor of high ceilings, stained-glass windows, and dark woods, this busy coffeeshop-cum-restaurant serves breakfast and light meals, but is best known for its dozens of freshly brewed coffees and teas, accompanied by home-baked scones, pastries, or sticky buns. Other items on the menu range from soups and salads to sandwiches and quiches. There's a choice of self-service or waitress/waiter service, depending on which floor or room you choose. There are several branches throughout Dublin, including 11/12 Westmoreland St. (☎ 677-6761) and 13 S. Great George's St. (☎ 679-2078).

St. Teresa's Courtyard, Clarendon Street, Dublin 2. ☎ **671-8466** or **671-8127.**

> **Cuisine:** IRISH/SELF-SERVICE. **Reservations:** Not required. **Transportation:** DART to Tara Street Station or bus nos. 16, 16A, 19, 19A, 22A, 55, 83.
> **Prices:** All items 80p–£2 ($1.20–$3). No credit cards.
> **Open:** Mon–Sat 10:30am–4pm.

Situated in the cobbled courtyard of early–19th century St. Teresa's Church, this serene little dining room is one of a handful of new eateries inconspicuously springing up in historic or ecclesiastical surroundings. With high ceilings and an old-world decor, it's a welcome contrast to the bustle of Grafton Street a block away or Powerscourt Town House Centre across the street. The menu changes daily but usually includes homemade soups, sandwiches, salads, quiches, lasagnes, sausage rolls, hot scones and other baked goods.

IMPRESSIONS

> *This is the royal city and seat of Ireland, a famous town for merchandise, the chief Court of Justice, in munition strong, in buildings gorgeous, in citizens populous. . . . Seated it is in a right delectable and wholesome place: for to the south yee have hills mounting up aloft, westward an open champion ground, and on the east the seas at hand and in sight.*
> —William Camden, *Britain,* 1610

FITZWILLIAM/MERRION SQUARES AREA
Very Expensive

★ **Patrick Guilbaud,** 46 James Place, off Lower Baggot Street, Dublin 2.
☎ 676-4192.

Cuisine: FRENCH NOUVELLE. **Reservations:** Required. **Transportation:** DART to Pearse Station or bus no. 10.
Prices: Set lunch £16 ($24); appetizers £4–£13 ($6–$19.50); main courses £16–£19 ($24–$28.50). AE, DC, MC, V.
Open: Tues–Sat, lunch 12:30–2pm and dinner 7:30–10:15pm.

Tucked in a laneway behind a Bank of Ireland building, this modern skylit restaurant could be easily overlooked except for its glowing Michelin-star reputation for fine food and artful service. The menu features such dishes as casserole of black sole and prawns; steamed salmon with orange and grapefruit sauce; filet of spring lamb with parsley sauce and herb salad; filet of beef served with red wine and marrow bone sauce; roast duck with honey; and breast of guinea fowl with Madeira sauce and potato crust.

Expensive

★ **Dobbins Wine Bistro,** 15 Stephen's Lane, off Upper Mount Street, Dublin 2.
☎ 676-4679 and 676-4670.

Cuisine: IRISH/CONTINENTAL. **Reservations:** Recommended. **Transportation:** DART to Pearse Station or bus nos. 5, 7A, 8, 46, 84.
Price: Set lunch £14.50 ($21.75); dinner appetizers £3.95–£7.95 ($5.93–$11.83), dinner main courses £12.95–£16.95 ($19.43–$25.43). AE, DC, MC. V.
Open: Lunch Mon–Fri 12:30–3pm, dinner Tues–Sat 8pm–midnight.

Almost hidden in a laneway between Upper and Lower Mount Streets a block east of Merrion Square, this friendly enclave is a haven for inventive cuisine. The menu changes often, but usually includes such items as duckling with orange and port sauce; steamed paupiette of black sole with salmon, crab and prawn filling; fresh prawns in garlic butter; pan-fried veal kidneys in pastry; rack of lamb with a mint crust; and fillet of beef topped with crispy herb breadcrumbs with a shallot and Madeira sauce. You'll have a choice of sitting in the bistro, with checkered tablecloths and sawdust on the floor, or in the tropical patio, with an all-weather sliding glass roof.

Grey Door, 23 Upper Pembroke St., Dublin 2. ☎ 676-3286.

Cuisine: RUSSIAN/SCANDINAVIAN. **Reservations:** Required. **Transportation:** Bus nos. 46A, 46B, 86.
Prices: Set lunch £15 ($22.50); appetizers £4–£8 ($6–$12), entrees £11–£21 ($16.50–$31.50). AE, DC, MC, V.
Open: Lunch Mon–Fri 12:30–2:30pm, dinner Mon–Sat 7–11pm.

In a fine old Georgian townhouse with a gray front door, this place is known for its Northern and Eastern European delicacies. Specialties include seafood Zakuski in puff pastry; Kotlety Kiev, a variation of chicken Kiev stuffed with vodka butter; Galupsti Maskova, minced lamb wrapped in cabbage; and Scandinavian seafood combinations. Pier 32, the Grey Door's basement-level restaurant, has a more informal setting; it's like a country inn, complete with traditional music on many nights. Fresh seafood at modest prices is the emphasis here. The Grey Door and Pier 32 are located less than a block southwest of Fitzwilliam Square near the junction of Leeson Street.

Moderate

$ **The Lane Gallery**, 55 Pembroke La., off Pembroke Street, Dublin 2.
☎ **661-1829.**

Cuisine: FRENCH. **Reservations:** Recommended. **Transportation:** DART to Pearse Station or bus no. 10.
Prices: Set lunch £4.95 ($7.43); dinner appetizers £1.90–£4.50 ($2.85–$6.75), dinner main courses £9.50–£12.50 ($14.25–$18.75). MC, V.
Open: Lunch Mon–Fri 12:30–2:30pm, dinner Tues–Sat 7:30–11pm.

An ever-changing display of paintings and works by local artists is the focal point of this restaurant, tucked in a laneway between Baggot Street and Fitzwilliam Square, near the Focus Theatre. The decor compliments the art with skylight or candlelight, white-washed brick walls, and pastel linens. The menu is equally artistic, with choices such as filet of beef with smoked bacon and black pepper sauce; rack of lamb with tomato coulis and mint jus; prawns in chive and ginger sauce; salmon on a bed of leeks with spinach butter sauce; roast brace of quail with white and black pudding and whiskey sauce; Barbary duck, or breast of chicken stuffed with walnut mousse. There is live piano music most evenings from 9pm. The lunch and dinner specials offer great value.

McGrattan's in the Lane, 76 Fitzwilliam Lane, Dublin 2. ☎ **661-8808.**

Cuisine: IRISH/FRENCH. **Reservations:** Recommended.
Prices: Appetizers £2.95–£5.95 ($4.43–$8.93); lunch main courses £4–£8 ($6–$12), dinner main courses £10.50–£13.95 ($15.75–$20.93). AE, MC, V.
Open: Sun–Fri lunch noon–3pm; Mon–Sun dinner 6–11pm.

Out of view from the general flow of traffic, this restaurant is in a laneway between Baggot Street and Merrion Square. There is a lovely Georgian doorway at the entrance, and inside the decor ranges from a homey fireside lounge with oldies background music to a bright skylit and plant-filled dining room. The creative menu includes main dishes such as breast of chicken Fitzwilliam, stuffed with cheddar cheese in pastry; half of roast pheasant with wild mushrooms and red wine sauce; rack of spring lamb roasted in a crust of breadcrumbs and spices; salmon florentine or paupiette of salmon stuffed with scallop mousse, wrapped in a pancake of puff pastry; sole meunière; deep-fried prawn scampi; and charcoal-grilled steaks.

Inexpensive

Grays, 109D Lower Baggot St., Dublin 2. ☎ **676-0676.**

Cuisine: INTERNATIONAL/SELF-SERVICE. **Reservations:** Not required. **Transportation:** DART to Pearse Station or bus no. 10.
Prices: All items £1.50–£4.95 ($2.25–$7.43). MC, V.
Open: Breakfast and lunch Mon–Fri 7:30am–4pm.

A popular self-service eatery, this cozy converted mews has a decor that is eclectic, with choir benches, caned chairs, and lots of hanging plants, and seating is offered on ground and upstairs levels, including an outdoor courtyard for dining in fine weather. The menu choices concentrate on sandwiches and salads made to order, as well as pastas, quiches, curries, and casseroles.

BALLSBRIDGE/EMBASSY ROW AREA

Very Expensive

★ **Le Coq Hardi**, 35 Pembroke Rd., Ballsbridge, Dublin 4. ☎ **668-9070**.
Cuisine: FRENCH. **Reservations:** Required. **Transportation:** DART to Lansdowne Road Station or bus nos. 18, 46, 63, 84.
Prices: Set lunch £14.95 ($22.43); dinner appetizers £4–£9 ($8–$13.50), dinner main courses £10.75–£25 ($16.13–$37.50). AE, DC, MC, V.
Open: Lunch Mon–Fri 12:30–3pm, dinner Mon–Sat 7–11pm.

They say this is the only place in Dublin where Rolls-Royces vie nightly for parking places. Located on the corner of Wellington Road in a Georgian town-house setting close to the American Embassy and leading hotels such as Jurys and the Berkeley Court, this plush 50-seat restaurant has no trouble drawing a well-heeled local and international business clientele. Chef John Howard has garnered many an award by offering such specialties as Dover sole stuffed with prawns; darne of Irish wild salmon on fresh spinach leaves; filet of hake roasted on green cabbage and bacon with Pernod butter sauce; filet of prime beef in beef marrow and Beaujolais wine sauce with wild mushrooms; caneton à l'orange; and steaks flamed in Irish whiskey. The 700-bin wine cellar boasts a complete collection of Château Mouton Rothschild, dating from 1945 to the present.

Expensive

Kites, 17 Ballsbridge Terrace, Ballsbridge, Dublin 4. ☎ **660-7415**.
Cuisine: CHINESE. **Reservations:** Recommended. **Transportation:** DART to Lansdowne Road Station or bus nos. 5, 7, 7A, 8, 46, 63, 84.
Prices: Appetizers £4–£9.50 ($8–$13.75); lunch main courses £6.50–£12 ($9.75–$18), dinner main courses £8.50–£16 ($12.75–$24). AE, DC, MC, V.
Open: Lunch Mon–Fri 12:30–2pm, dinner daily 6:30–11:30pm.

Handily located between the American Embassy and the Royal Dublin Society Showgrounds, this Oriental-theme restaurant is housed in a Georgian townhouse just off Pembroke Road and diagonally across the street from Jurys Hotel. The menu features the usual chow meins, curries, and sweet and sour dishes, as well as a host of creative entrees such as king prawns with Chinese leaves in oyster sauce; stuffed crab claws; Singapore fried noodles; and birds nests of fried potatoes.

Lobster Pot, 9 Ballsbridge Terrace, Ballsbridge, Dublin 4. ☎ **668-0025**.
Cuisine: SEAFOOD. **Reservations:** Required. **Transportation:** DART to Lansdowne Road Station or bus nos. 5, 7, 7A, 8, 46, 63, 84.
Prices: Appetizers £2–£5.25 ($3–$7.88); lunch main courses £7–£10 ($10.50–$15), dinner main courses £9.95–£16.25 ($14.93–$24.38). AE, DC, MC, V.
Open: Lunch Mon–Fri 12:30–2:30pm, dinner Mon–Sat 6:30–10:30pm.

Positioned between the American Embassy and the Royal Dublin Society Showgrounds, almost opposite Jurys Hotel, this upstairs restaurant is known for its lobster dishes, as its name implies. Other entrees on the menu range from sole on the bone and coquilles St. Jacques, prawns mornay, and monkfish thermidor, to tableside preparations of steak Diane, prawns sautéed in garlic butter, pepper steak, and steak tartare.

Moderate

⭐ **Roly's Bistro,** 7 Ballsbridge Terrace, Dublin 4. ☎ 668-2611.

💲 **Cuisine:** IRISH/INTERNATIONAL. **Reservations:** Required. **Transportation:** DART to Lansdowne Road Station or bus nos. 6, 7, 8, 18, 45, 46, 84.

Prices: Appetizers: £1.95–£3.95 ($2.93–$5.93); set lunch £9.50 ($14.25); dinner main courses £6.50–£12.50 ($9.75–$18.75). AE, MC, V.

Open: Mon–Sat lunch noon–3pm, dinner 6–10pm; Sun brunch noon–3pm, dinner 6–9:30pm.

Opened in 1992, this two-story shopfront restaurant quickly skyrocketed to success, thanks to a magical blend of people and place—genial and astute host Roly Saul, master chef Colin O'Daly, a young and enthusiastic waiting staff, a trendy location between the American Embassy and the Royal Dublin Society, and, above all, excellent and imaginatively prepared food at mostly moderate prices. The main dining rooms, with a bright and airy decor and lots of windows, can be noisy with the din of a full house; but the nonsmoking section has a quiet enclave of booths laid out in an Orient Express-style for those who prefer a quiet tête-à-tête. The bistro serves roast breast of duck with vanilla and apricot sauce; medaillons of beef with green and red pepper sauce; sautéed monkfish with apple and dates in honey spiced sauce; roast whole spring chicken with diablo sauce; fillet of pork stuffed with eggplant and wrapped in bacon; seafood bake (salmon, haddock, cod, and clams in shellfish sauce); and a vegetarian dish of tomato, zucchini, and black olives with basil and rosemary in pastry.

Senor Sassi's, 146 Upper Leeson St., Dublin 4. ☎ 668-4544.

Cuisine: MEDITERRANEAN. **Reservations:** Recommended. **Transportation:** Bus nos. 10, 11A, 11B, 13, 46A, 46B.

Prices: Appetizers £1.90–£4.80 ($2.85–$7.20), lunch main courses £5.25–£9.50 ($7.88–$14.25), dinner main courses £6.25–£11.50 ($9.38–$17.25). AE, DC, MC. V.

Open: Lunch Tues–Fri noon–2:30pm and Sun noon–4pm; dinner Mon–Wed 6–11:30pm, Thurs–Sat 6:30–midnight, Sun 5:30–10:30pm.

New and innovative, this restaurant blends the simple and spicy flavors of Spain, Italy, southern France, and the Middle East, in its busy shopfront location at the juncture of Sussex and Mespil Roads within a block from the Burlington Hotel. The contemporary and casual setting includes slate floors, marble-topped tables, and walls painted a sunny shade of yellow; seating is also available in a conservatory extension overlooking a courtyard garden. The menu includes items such as Morroccan-style couscous; tagliatelle; prawns sauteed in rum with Creole sauce; charcoal steaks; tortilla Español, traditional omelet with potato and onions; and all-vegetarian dishes and warm salads. Be sure to try the olive bread, unusual for Dublin.

Inexpensive

💲 **Da Vincenzo,** 133 Upper Leeson St., Dublin 4. ☎ 660-9906.

Cuisine: ITALIAN. **Reservations:** Recommended. **Transportation:** Bus nos. 10, 11A, 11B, 46A, 46B.

Prices: Set lunch £6.50 ($9.75); dinner appetizers £1.95–£3.45 ($2.93–$5.18), dinner main courses £5.50–£11.25 ($7.25–$16.88). AE, MC, V.

Open: Mon–Fri 12:30pm–midnight, Sat 1pm–midnight, Sun 1–10pm.

Occupying a shopfront location within a block from the Hotel Burlington, this informal and friendly owner-run bistro offers ground level and upstairs seating, amid a casual decor of glowing brick fireplaces, pine walls, vases and wreaths of dried flowers, modern art posters, blue and white pottery, and a busy open kitchen. Pizza with a light pita-style dough is a specialty here, cooked in wood-burning oven. Other entrees range from pastas such as tagliatelle, lasagne, canelloni, spaghetti, and fettucine, to veal and beef dishes including an organically produced filet steak.

O'CONNELL STREET AREA

Expensive/Moderate

⭐ **Chapter One,** 18/19 Parnell Sq., Dublin 1. ☎ **873-2266** or **873-2281.**

Cuisine: IRISH. **Reservations:** Recommended. **Transportation:** DART to Connolly Station or bus nos. 10, 11, 11A, 11B, 12, 13, 14, 16, 16A, 19, 19A, 22, 22A, 36.
Prices: Set lunch £10 ($15); dinner appetizers £3–£5.25 ($4.50–$7.88), dinner main courses £9.30–£13 ($13.95–$19.50). AE, MC, V.
Open: Lunch Tues–Fri noon–2:30pm; dinner Tues–Sun 6–11pm.

A literary theme prevails at this restaurant, housed in the basement of the Irish Writers' Museum, just north of Parnell Square and the Garden of Remembrance. The layout is spread over three rooms and alcoves, all accentuated by stained-glass windows, paintings, sculptures, and literary memorabilia. The catering staff, affiliated with the Old Dublin Restaurant, have added a few Scandinavian influences. Main courses include filet of salmon on a bed of avocado with smoked tomato vinaigrette; black sole with citrus fruit and dill cucumber cream sauce; roast rib of beef with a mix of mushrooms; pot-roasted breast of chicken with onions, sage, garlic, and peapods; roast half-duck with apricot sauce; and a selection of fish with garlic, mango, fennel, cucumber and tomato salad.

Moderate/Inexpensive

$ **101 Talbot,** 101 Talbot St., Dublin 1. ☎ **874-5011.**

Cuisine: INTERNATIONAL/VEGETARIAN. **Reservations:** Recommended. **Transportation:** DART to Connolly Station or bus nos. 27A, 31A, 311B, 32A, 32B, 42B, 42C, 43, 44A.
Prices: Appetizers £1.50–£2.95 ($2.25–$4.43); lunch main courses £3–£6 ($4.50–$9), dinner main courses £6.90–£7.90 ($10.35–$11.85). MC, V.
Open: Mon 10am–3pm; Tues–Sat 10am–11pm.

Opened in 1991, this second-floor shopfront restaurant features light and healthy foods, with a strong emphasis on vegetarian dishes. The setting is bright and casual, with contemporary Irish art on display, big windows, yellow rag-rolled walls, ash-topped tables, and newspapers to read. Entrees include chicken breast with spinach mousse; plaice with lemon beurre blanc; medaillons of pork with brandy and mustard sauce; spanikopita (Greek spinach and feta cheese pie); parsnip stuffed with brazil nuts and vegetables in red pepper sauce; and various pastas. The lunch menu changes daily, and the dinner menu weekly. Expresso and cappuccino are always available for sipping, and there is a full bar. It's located at Talbot Lane near Marlborough Street, convenient to the Abbey Theatre.

Budget

The Winding Stair, 40 Lower Ormond Quay, Dublin 1. ☎ **873-3292.**

Cuisine: IRISH/SELF-SERVICE. **Reservations:** Not necessary. **Bus:** nos. 70 or 80.
Prices: All items £1–£3 ($1.50–$4.50). No credit cards.
Open: Mon–Sat 10:30am–6pm.

Retreat from the bustle of the north side's busy quays at this cafe-cum-bookshop, and join some customers in examining old books while others indulge in a light meal, and classical music plays gently in the background. There are three floors, each chock full of used books (from novels, plays, and poetry to history, art, music, and sports), and all connected by a winding 18th-century staircase. A cage-style lift serves those who prefer not to climb stairs. Tall and wide windows provide expansive views of the Ha'penny Bridge and River Liffey. The food is simple and healthy—sandwiches made with additive-free meats or fruits such as banana and honey, organic salads, home-made soups, natural juices.

SPECIALTY DINING

LOCAL FAVORITES/PUBS   In Dublin, pubs are a focal point for eating as well as drinking. Many pubs serve inexpensive fare (known locally as pub grub), particularly at lunchtime, ranging from soups and sandwiches to seafood platters and salads as well as hearty stews and meat pies. A good pub lunch will cost around £5 ($7.50) including beverage.

Descriptions of some of Dublin's best pubs are given in the "Evening Entertainment" section of this chapter. Among those recommended for good pub grub downtown south of the River Liffey are the **Castle Inn,** Christchurch Place, Dublin 8 (☎ 478-2933); **Davy Byrnes,** 21 Duke St., Dublin 2 (☎ 671-1298); **Kitty O'Shea's,** 23-25 Upper Grand Canal St., Dublin 2 (☎ 660-9965); **O'Dwyer's,** 8 Lower Mount St., Dublin 2 (☎ 676-1718); and **The Old Stand,** 37 Exchequer St., Dublin 2 (☎ 677-7220). On the north side, the standouts are **John M. Keating,** 14 Mary St., Dublin 1 (☎ 873-1567) and **W. Ryan,** 28 Parkgate St., Dublin 7 (☎ 677-6097).

MUSEUM/ART GALLERY COFFEE SHOPS   Many of Dublin's museums and art galleries operate excellent coffee shops and snack bars, offering good value, convenience, and an atmospheric setting. The menus, usually on chalkboards, feature homemade soups, salads, sandwiches, and daily hot plates. These eateries are normally open during the same hours as the attractions in which they are housed. Prices average £3–£5 ($4.50–$7.50) for a complete meal or £1–£2 ($1.50–$3) for snacks. Among the best are the **Dublin Writers Museum Coffee Shop,** 18/19 Parnell Sq. N., Dublin 1 (☎ 872-2077); **Hugh Lane Municipal Gallery of Modern Art Coffee Shop,** Parnell Square, Dublin 1 (☎ 874-1903); and the **National Gallery Restaurant,** Merrion Square West, Dublin 2 (☎ 668-6481).

AFTERNOON TEA   As in Britain, afternoon tea is a time-revered tradition in Ireland, especially in the grand hotels of Dublin. Afternoon tea in its fullest form is a sit-down event and a relaxing experience, not just a quick hot beverage taken on the run.

Properly presented, afternoon tea is also almost a complete meal—with a pot of freshly brewed tea accompanied by finger sandwiches, pastries, hot scones, cream-filled cakes, and other sweets arrayed on a silver tray. To enhance the ambience, there is usually live background music, provided by a pianist or harpist. Best of all, this sumptuous mid-afternoon pick-me-up is priced to please—averaging £5 to £6 ($7.50–$9) per head, even in the lobby lounges of the city's best hotels.

Afternoon tea hours are usually 3 to 4:30pm. Among the hotels offering this repast are the Berkeley Court, Conrad, Davenport, Gresham, Royal Dublin, Shelbourne, and Westbury (See "Dublin Accommodations," above, for full address and phone numbers of each hotel).

LATE NIGHT/24-HOUR   There is really only one restaurant in Dublin that approaches the 24-hour category—the **Coffee Dock at Jurys Hotel,** Ballsbridge, Dublin 4 (☎ **660-5000**). It is open 22.5 hours a day, from 6am until 4:30am. Bewley's at 78/79 Grafton St., Dublin 2 (☎ **677-6761**) is open Monday through Wednesday until 1am, Thursday through Saturday until 2am, and on Sunday until 10pm.

PICNIC FARE   The many parks of Dublin offer sylvan and relaxed settings for a picnic lunch. Most of the parks have plentiful benches or you can pick a grassy patch and spread open a blanket. In particular, try **St. Stephen's Green** at lunchtime (in the summer there are open-air band concerts); **Phoenix Park,** and **Merrion Square.** You can also take a ride on the DART to the suburbs of **Dun Laoghaire** (to the south) or **Howth** (to the north) and set up a picnic on along a bayfront pier or promenade.

In recent years, Dublin has fostered some fine delicatessens and gourmet foodshops, ideal for picnic fare. For the best selection of good picnic fixings, we recommend: **Gallic Kitchen,** 49 Francis St., Dublin 8 (☎ **454-4912**), for gourmet prepared food-to-go, from salmon en croûte to pastries filled with meats or vegetables, pâtés, quiches, sausage rolls, and homemade pies, breads, and cakes; **La Potinière,** Powerscourt Town House Center, 59 S. William St., Dublin 2 (☎ **671-1300**), for salads, sandwiches, nuts, mustards, teas, sodas, Irish cheeses, honey, sodas, and champagne; and **Magills Delicatessan,** 14 Clarendon St., Dublin 2 (☎ **671-3830**), for Asian and continental delicacies, meats, cheeses, spices, salads.

5   What to See & Do

Dublin is a city of many moods and landscapes—from medieval churches and majestic castles, to graceful Georgian squares and lantern-lit lanes, to broad boulevards and busy bridges, to picturesque parks and pedestrian walkways, to intriguing museums and marketplaces, to glorious gardens and galleries, and so much more.

To inhale the ambience of Ireland's number-one city, you should walk up Grafton Street, sip a cup of coffee at Bewley's, stroll through St. Stephen's Green, browse along the quays, step into a few pubs, and, above all, chat with the Dubliners. And that's just for starters.

You could devote a week, a month, or a lifetime to Dublin and still not see all the sights and savor all the experiences. But, by planning wisely, taking note of the suggestions on the following pages, and using a good map, you can spend a few days in Dublin and thoroughly relish the major highlights of this fair city.

Suggested Itineraries

If You Have 1 Day

Start at the beginning—Dublin's medieval quarter, the area around Christ Church and St. Patrick's Cathedrals. Tour these great churches and then walk the cobblestone streets and inspect the nearby old city walls at High Street. From Old Dublin, take a turn eastward and see Dublin Castle and then Trinity College with the famous *Book of Kells.* Cross over the River Liffey to O'Connell Street, Dublin's main thoroughfare. Walk up this wide street, passing the landmark General Post Office (GPO), to Parnell Square and the picturesque Garden of Remembrance. If time permits, visit the Dublin Writers' Museum, and then hop on a double-decker bus heading to the south bank of the Liffey for a visit to St. Stephen's Green for a relaxing stroll amid the greenery. Cap the day with a show at the Abbey Theatre and maybe a drink or two at a nearby pub.

If You Have 2 Days

Day 1   Spend Day 1 as above.

Day 2   In the morning, Take a Dublin Bus city sightseeing tour to give you an overview of the city—you'll see all of the local downtown landmarks, plus the major buildings along the River Liffey, and some of the leading sites on the edge of the city such as the Guinness Brewery, the Royal Hospital, the Irish Museum of Modern Art, and the Phoenix Park. In the afternoon, head for Grafton Street for some shopping. If time allows, stroll Merrion or Fitzwilliam Squares to give you a sampling of the best of Dublin's Georgian architecture.

If You Have 3 Days

Days 1 and 2   Spend Days 1 and 2 as above.

Day 3   Make this a day for Dublin's artistic and cultural attractions—visit some of the top museums and art galleries, from the National Museum and National Gallery, Natural History Museum, and Museum of Modern Art, to the Guinness Hop Store or a special interest museum, such as the Irish Jewish Museum, the Kilmainham Jail Museum, the Irish Whiskey Corner, or the Museum of Childhood. Save time for a walk around Temple Bar, the city's Left Bank district, lined with art galleries and film studios, interesting second-hand shops, and casual eateries.

If You Have 4 Days or More

Days 1–3   Spend Days 1 to 3 as above.

Day 4   Take a ride aboard DART, Dublin's rapid transit system, to the suburbs, either southward to Dun Laoghaire or Dalkey, or northward to Howth. The DART routes follow the rim of Dublin Bay in both directions, so you'll enjoy a scenic ride and get to spend some time in an Irish coastal village.

SAVINGS TIPS   If you are planning to visit Dublin's major cultural attractions, you can save money by purchasing a discount pass, "Dublin Alive Alive O: The Passport to Dublin's Heritage." Priced at £2 ($3), it provides a 10% discount off the admission charges at many of Dublin's top visitor attractions, including the Dublin's Writer's Museum, Dublin Zoo, Guinness Hop Store, Irish Museum of Modern Art, Malahide Castle, Newman House, and Trinity College. It's available at any tourist office or participating attractions.

For literary-minded visitors, the Dublin Writers Museum, 18 Parnell Sq., Dublin 1 (☎ 872-2077) offers a reduced-rate combination ticket that allows entry into the Dublin Writers Museum in conjunction with the James Joyce Tower or the George Bernard Shaw Birthplace for £3.80 ($5.70) adults, £2.80 ($4.20) seniors and students, £1.40 ($2.10) children ages 3–11.

IMPRESSIONS

The trees in St. Stephen's Green were fragrant of rain and the rainsodden earth gave forth its mortal odor, a faint incense rising upward through the mould of many hearts.
—James Joyce, *Portrait of an Artist as a Young Man,* 1916

A similar reduced-rate combination ticket allows entry into Trinity College's *Book of Kells* Exhibit in conjunction with admission to The Dublin Experience, for £5 ($7.50) adults, £4 ($6) seniors and students. It's available at the bookshop/visitor center at Trinity College, College Green, Dublin 2 (☎ **677-2941** ext. 1171).

THE TOP ATTRACTIONS

★ **Christ Church Cathedral,** Christ Church Place, Dublin 8. ☎ **677-8099.**

Standing on high ground in the oldest part of the city, this cathedral is one of Dublin's finest historic buildings. It dates back to 1038 when Sitric, Danish King of Dublin, built the first wooden Christ Church here. In 1171 the original simple foundation was extended into a cruciform and rebuilt in stone by Strongbow, although the present structure dates mainly from 1871 to 1878 when a huge restoration was undertaken. Highlights of the interior include magnificent stone work and graceful pointed arches, with delicately chiseled supporting columns. It is the mother church for the diocese of Dublin and Glendalough of the Church of Ireland.

Admission: Suggested donation £1 ($1.50) adults.

Open: Daily 10am–5pm (except Dec. 26). **Transportation:** Bus nos. 21A, 50, 50A, 78, 78A, and 78B.

★ **Dublin Castle,** Palace Street, off Dame Street, Dublin 2. ☎ **679-3713.**

Built between 1208 and 1220, this complex represents some of the oldest surviving architecture in the city, and was the center of British power in Ireland for more than seven centuries until it was taken over by the new Irish government in 1922. Highlights include the 13th-century Record Tower; the State Apartments, once the residence of English viceroys; and the Chapel Royal, a 19th-century Gothic building with particularly fine plaster decoration and carved oak gallery fronts and fittings. The newest developments are the Undercroft, an excavated site on the grounds where an early Viking fortress stood, and The Treasury, built between 1712 and 1715, believed to be the oldest surviving purpose-built office building in Ireland. It houses a visitor center in its vaulted basement which will also serve as an entrance to the medieval undercroft.

Admission: £1.75 ($2.63) adults, £1 ($1.50) for seniors, students, and children under 12.

Open: Mon–Fri 10am–12:15pm, 2–5pm; Sat–Sun 2–5pm. Guided tours are conducted every 20–25 minutes. **Transportation:** Bus nos. 54, 50, 50A, 56A, 77.

★ **Dublinia, Christ Church Place,** at High Street, Dublin 8. ☎ **679-4611.**

What was Dublin like in medieval times? Here is a historically accurate presentation of the Old City from 1170 to 1540, re-created through a series of theme exhibits, spectacles, and experiences. Highlights include an illuminated Medieval Maze, complete with visual effects, background sounds, and aromas, that lead you on a journey through time from the first arrival of the Anglo-Normans in 1170 to the closure of the monasteries in the 1530s. The next segment depicts everyday life in medieval Dublin with a diorama, as well as a prototype of a 13th-century quay along the banks of the Liffey. The finale takes you to The Great Hall for a 360-degree wrap-up portrait of medieval Dublin via a 12-minute cyclorama-style audio-visual.

Admission: £3.95 ($5.93) adults, £2.90 ($4.35) for children under 12.

Open: Daily 10am–5pm. **Transportation:** Bus nos. 21A, 50, 50A, 78, 78A, 78B.

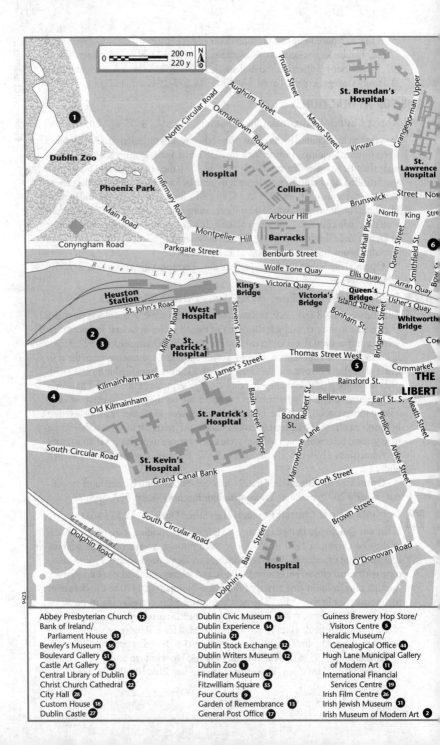

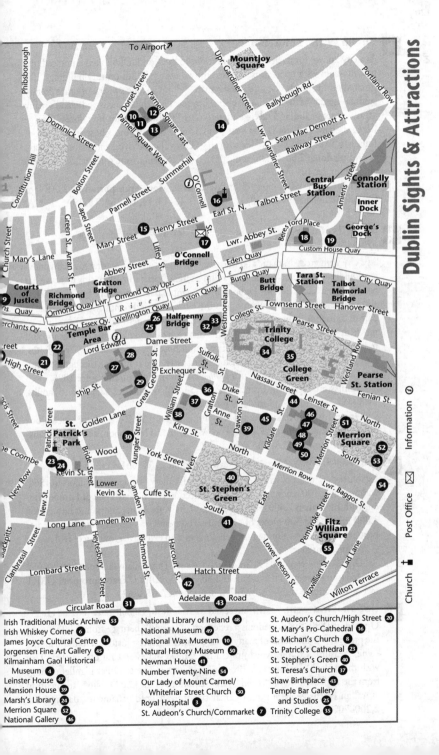

Dublin Sights & Attractions

To Airport ↗

Mountjoy Square

Irish Traditional Music Archive **53**
Irish Whiskey Corner **6**
James Joyce Cultural Centre **14**
Jorgensen Fine Art Gallery **45**
Kilmainham Gaol Historical
   Museum **4**
Leinster House **47**
Mansion House **39**
Marsh's Library **24**
Merrion Square **52**
National Gallery **46**

National Library of Ireland **48**
National Museum **49**
National Wax Museum **10**
Natural History Museum **50**
Newman House **41**
Number Twenty-Nine **54**
Our Lady of Mount Carmel/
   Whitefriar Street Church **30**
Royal Hospital **3**
St. Audeon's Church/Cornmarket **7**

St. Audeon's Church/High Street **20**
St. Mary's Pro-Cathedral **16**
St. Michan's Church **8**
St. Patrick's Cathedral **23**
St. Stephen's Green **40**
St. Teresa's Church **37**
Shaw Birthplace **43**
Temple Bar Gallery
   and Studios **25**
Trinity College **35**

Church ✚   Post Office ✉   Information ⓘ

⭐ **Dublin Writers Museum,** 18/19 Parnell Sq. N., Dublin 1. ☎ **872-2077.**

As a city known for its literary contributions to the world, Dublin has embraced this new museum with open arms. Housed in two restored 18th-century buildings, it is situated on the north side of Parnell Square, within a stone's throw of other literary landmarks, such as the Gate and Abbey Theatres. The exhibits focus on Ireland's many great writers including Dublin's three Nobel Prize winners for literature—George Bernard Shaw, William Butler Yeats, and Samuel Beckett, and a host of others from Jonathan Swift and Oscar Wilde to Sean O'Casey, James Joyce, and Brendan Behan.

Admission: £2.50 ($3.75) adults, £1.70 ($2.55) seniors and students, 80p ($1.20) children under 12.

Open: Daily 10am–5pm; Sept–May, closed Mon. **Transportation:** DART to Conolly Station or bus nos. 10, 11, 11A, 11B, 12, 13, 14, 16, 16A, 19, 19A, 22, 22A, 36.

⭐ **Irish Film Centre,** 6 Eustace St., Dublin 2. ☎ **679-5744;** cinema box office **679-3477.**

As a city with great dramatic and theatrical traditions and as a setting for many movies, Dublin is a natural location for a film center. Opened in 1993, this institute has fast become a focal point for Dublin's artsy Temple Bar district. The building itself is also of interest because it incorporates the city's historic Friends Meeting House as part of its layout. It houses several film components under one roof, including two movie theaters (cinemas), the Irish Film Archive, a library, film-theme bookshop and restaurant/bar, and eight film-related organizations. The center also displays photos, posters, and memorabilia of the Irish film industry, and from June through September, there are regular showings of *Flashback,* a history of Irish film since 1896.

Admission: Free to the Institute; £2–£4 ($3–$6) for cinemas; £2.30 ($3.45) adults, £1.80 ($2.70) seniors and students for *Flashback.*

Open: Institute daily 10am–11:30pm; cinemas daily 2–11:30pm; cinema box office daily 1:30–7:30pm; *Flashback* on Wed–Sun at 11am, noon, and 1pm. **Transportation:** Bus nos. 21A, 78A, 78B.

⭐ **National Gallery,** Merrion Square West, Dublin 2. ☎ **661-5133.**

Established by an act of Parliament in 1854, this gallery first opened its doors in 1864, with just over 100 paintings. Today the collection is considered one of Europe's finest, with more than 2,400 paintings; 15,200 drawings, watercolors, and miniatures; 3,000 prints; and 300 pieces of sculpture, vestments, and objets d'art. Every major European School of Painting is represented, as is an extensive grouping of Irish work.

Admission: Free.

Open: Mon–Wed and Fri–Sat 10am–5:30pm, Thurs 10am–8:30pm, Sun 2–5pm. Guided tours, Sat at 3pm and Sun at 2:30, 3:15, and 4pm. **Transportation:** DART to Pearse Station or bus nos. 5, 7, 7A, 8, 10, 44, 47, 48A, 62.

⭐ **National Museum,** Kildare Street and Merrion Row, Dublin 2. ☎ **661-8811.**

Opened in 1890, this museum is a reflection of Ireland's heritage from 2,000 B.C. to the present. It is the home of many of the country's greatest historical finds including "The Treasury" exhibit, which toured the United States and Europe in the 1970s with the Ardagh Chalice, Tara Brooch, and Cross of Cong. Other highlights range from the artifacts from the Wood Quay excavations of the Old Dublin Settlements to "Or," an extensive exhibition of Irish Bronze Age gold ornaments, dating from 2,200–700 B.C.

Admission: Free.

Open: Tues–Sat 10am–5pm, Sun 2–5pm. **Transportation:** DART to Pearse Station or bus nos. 7, 7A, 8, 10, 11, 13.

★ **Phoenix Park,** Parkgate Street, Dublin 7. ☎ **677-0095.**

This is Dublin's playground—the largest urban enclosed park in Europe, with a circumference of seven miles and a total area of 1,760 acres. Opened in 1747, it is also the home of the Irish President and the U.S. Ambassador to Ireland and assorted wildlife. Situated two miles west of the city center, it is traversed by a network of roads and quiet pedestrian walkways, and informally landscaped with ornamental gardens, nature trails, and broad expanses of grassland, separated by avenues of trees, including oak, beech, pine, chestnut, and lime. Livestock graze peacefully on pasturelands, deer roam the forested areas, and horses romp on polo fields.

Admission: Free.

Open: Daily 24 hours. **Transportation:** Bus nos. 10, 25, 26.

★ **St. Patrick's Cathedral,** Patrick's Close, Patrick Street, Dublin. ☎ **475-4817.**

It is said that St. Patrick baptized converts on this site and consequently a church has stood here since A.D. 450, making it the oldest Christian site in Dublin. The present cathedral dates from 1190, but because of a fire and a rebuilding in the 14th century, not much remains from the cathedral's foundation days. It is mainly early English in style, with a square medieval tower that houses the largest ringing peal bells in Ireland, an 18th-century spire, and a 300-ft.-long interior, making it the longest church in Ireland. St. Patrick's is closely associated with Jonathan Swift, who was dean here from 1713 to 1745 and whose tomb lies in the south aisle. Others who are memorialized within the cathedral include Turlough O'Carolan, a blind harper and composer and the last of the great Irish bards; Michael William Balfe, the composer; and Douglas Hyde, the first President of Ireland. St. Patrick's is the national cathedral of the Church of Ireland.

Admission: Suggested donations £1 ($1.50) adults and 40p (60¢) students and children under 12.

Open: April–Oct, Mon–Fri 9am–6pm, Sat 9am–5pm, Sun 10am–4:30pm; Nov–Mar, Mon–Fri 9am–6pm, Sat 9am–4pm, Sun 10:30am–4:30pm. **Transportation:** Bus nos. 50, 50A, 54, 54A, 56A.

★ **Trinity College and The Book of Kells,** College Green, Dublin 2. ☎ **677-2941.**

The oldest university in Ireland, Trinity was founded in 1592 by Queen Elizabeth I. It sits in the heart of the city on a 40-acre site just south of the River Liffey, with cobbled squares, gardens, a picturesque quadrangle, and buildings dating from the 17th to the 20th centuries. The college is best known as the home of the *Book of Kells,* an 8th-century version of the Four Gospels with elaborate scripting and illumination. This famous treasure and other early Christian manuscripts are on permanent view for the public in the Colonnades, a new exhibition area located on the ground floor of the Old Library. The complete Trinity College Library contains more than three million volumes, a figure that is always growing.

Admission: £2.50 ($3.75) adults, £2 ($3) students and seniors, free for children under 12.

Open: Mon–Sat 9:30am–5:30pm, Sun noon–5pm. **Transportation:** DART to Tara Street Station or bus nos. 5, 7A, 8, 15A, 15B, 15C, 46, 55, 62, 63, 83, 84.

MORE ATTRACTIONS

Art Galleries

Boulevard Gallery, Merrion Square West, Dublin 2.

The fence around Merrion Square doubles as a display railing on summer weekends in an outdoor display of local art similar to New York's Greenwich Village or Paris' Montmartre. Permits are given to local artists only to sell their own work, so this is a chance to meet an artist as well as to browse or buy.

Admission: Free.

Open: May–Sept, Sat–Sun 10:30am–6pm. **Transportation:** DART to Pearse Station or bus nos. 5, 7A, 8, 46, 62.

Hugh Lane Municipal Gallery of Modern Art, Parnell Sq., Dublin 1.
☎ 874-1903.

Housed in a finely restored 18th-century building known as Charlemont House, this gallery is situated next to the Dublin Writers Museum. It is named after Hugh Lane, an Irish art connoisseur who was killed in the sinking of the *Lusitania* in 1915 and who willed his collection (including works by Courbet, Manet, Monet, and Corot) to be shared between the government of Ireland and the National Gallery of London. With the Lane collection as its nucleus, this gallery also contains paintings from the Impressionist and post-Impressionist traditions, sculptures by Rodin, stained glass, and works by modern Irish artists.

Admission: Free; donations accepted.

Open: Tues–Fri 9:30am–6pm, Sat 9:30am–5pm, Sun 11am–5pm. **Transportation:** DART to Connolly Station or bus nos. 10, 11, 11A, 11B, 12, 13, 14, 16, 16A, 19, 19A, 22, 22A, 36.

Irish Museum of Modern Art (IMMA), Military Road, Kilmainham.
☎ 671-8666.

Housed in the splendidly restored 17th-century edifice known as the Royal Hospital, IMMA is a showcase of Irish and international art from the latter half of the 20th century. The buildings and grounds also provide a venue for theatrical and musical events, overlapping the visual and performing arts.

Admission: Free.

Open: Tues–Sat 10am–5:30pm, Sun noon–5:30pm. **Transportation:** bus nos. 24, 51, 63, 69, 78, 79, 90.

Temple Bar Gallery and Studios, 4–8 Temple Bar, Dublin 2. ☎ 679-9259.

Founded in 1983 in the heart of Dublin's "Left Bank," this is one of the largest studio/gallery complexes in Europe. More than 30 Irish artists work here at a variety of contemporary visual arts, from sculpture and painting to printing and photography. Only the gallery section is open to the public, but, with advance notice, appointments can be made to view individual artists at work.

Admission: Free.

Open: Mon–Fri 11am–5:30pm, Sat noon–4pm. **Transportation:** Bus nos. 21A, 46A, 46B, 51B, 51C, 68, 69, 86.

BREWERIES/DISTILLERIES

★ **Guinness Brewery Hop Store Visitor Centre,** Crane Street, off Thomas Street, Dublin 8. ☎ 453-6700, ext. 5155.

Founded in 1759, the Guinness Brewery is one of the world's largest breweries, producing the distinctive dark beer called stout, famous for its thick creamy head. Although tours of the brewery itself are no longer allowed, visitors are welcome to explore the adjacent Guinness Hop Store, a converted 19th-century four-story building. It houses the World of Guinness Exhibition, an audio-visual showing how the stout is made, plus a museum and a bar where visitors can sample a glass or two of the famous brew. The two top floors of the building also serve as a venue for a variety of art exhibits.

Admission: £2 ($3) adults, £1.50 ($2.25) seniors and students, 50p ($75¢) children under 12.

Open: Mon–Fri 10am–4pm. **Transportation:** bus nos. 21A, 78, 78A.

★ **Irish Whiskey Corner,** Irish Distillers, Bow Street, Dublin 7. ☎ 872-5566.

This museum illustrates the history of Irish whiskey, known as *uisce beatha* (the water of life) in Irish. Housed in a former distillery warehouse, it presents a short introductory audio-visual, an exhibition area, and a whiskey-making demonstration. At the end of the tour, whiskey can be sampled at an in-house pub. Since there is only one tour a day, it's wise to make a reservation in advance.

Admission: £3 ($4.50) per person.

Open: May–Oct, Mon–Fri tours at 11am and 3:30pm; Nov–Apr, Mon–Fri tours at 3:30pm. **Transportation:** bus nos. 34, 70, 80.

PLACES OF BUSINESS

★ **Bank of Ireland/Parliament House,** 2 College Green, Dublin 2. ☎ 661-5933, ext. 2265.

Although now a busy bank, this building was erected in 1729 to house the Irish Parliament, but it became superfluous when the British and Irish Parliments were merged in London. In fact, the Irish Parliament voted itself out of existence—the only recorded parliament in history to do so. Highlights include the windowless front portico, built to avoid distractions from the outside when Parliament was in session, and the unique House of Lords chamber—famed for its woodwork in Irish oak, 18th-century tapestries, golden mace, and a sparkling Irish crystal chandelier of 1,233 pieces, dating from 1765.

Admission: Free.

Open: Mon–Wed and Fri 10am–4pm, Thurs 10am–5pm; guided 45-minute tours of the House of Lords chamber on Tuesday at 10:30 and 11:30am, and 1:45pm (except holidays). **Transportation:** DART to Tara Street Station or bus nos. 15A, 15B, 15C, 21A, 46, 46A, 46B, 46C, 51B, 51C, 55, 63, 68, 69, 86, 78A, 78B, 83.

★ **General Post Office (GPO),** O'Connell Street, Dublin 1. ☎ 872-8888.

With a 200-ft.-long, 56-ft.-high facade of Ionic columns and pilasters in the Greco-Roman style, this is more than a post office; it is the symbol of Irish freedom. Built between 1815 and 1818, it was the main stronghold of the Irish Volunteers in 1916. Set afire, the building was gutted and abandoned after the surrender and execution of many of the Irish rebel leaders. It reopened as a post office in 1929 after the formation of the Irish Free State. In memory of building's dramatic role in Irish history, there is today an impressive bronze statue of Cuchulainn, the legendary Irish hero, on display.

Admission: Free.

Open: Mon–Sat 8am–8pm, Sun 10–6pm. **Transportation:** DART to Connolly Station or bus nos. 25, 26, 34, 37, 38A, 39A, 39B, 66A, 67A.

CATHEDRALS & CHURCHES

Our Lady of Mount Carmel/Whitefriar Street Carmelite Church,
57 Aungier St., Dublin 2. ☎ 475-8821.

One of the city's largest churches, it was built between 1825 and 1827 on the site of pre-Reformation Carmelite priory (1539) and an earlier Carmelite abbey (13th century). It has since been extended, with a new entrance from Aungier Street. This is a favorite place of pilgrimage on February 14th, because the body of St. Valentine is enshrined here, presented to the church by Pope Gregory XVI in 1836. The other highlight is the 15th-century black oak Madonna, Our Lady of Dublin.

Admission: Free.

Open: Mon and Wed–Fri 8am–6:30pm, Tues 8am–9:30pm, Sat 8am–7pm, Sun 8am–7:30pm. **Transportation:** Bus nos. 16, 16A, 19, 19A, 22, 22A, 55, 83.

St. Audeon's Church, Cornmarket, off High Street, Dublin 8. ☎ 677-8714.

Situated next to the only remaining gate of the Old City walls (1214), this church is said to be the only surviving medieval parish in Dublin. Although it is partly in ruins, significant parts have survived, including the west doorway, which dates from 1190, and the nave from the 13th century. In addition, the 17th-century belltower houses three bells cast in 1423, making them the oldest in Ireland. It is a Church of Ireland property.

Admission: Free.

Open: Fri–Wed 11:30am–1:30pm. **Transportation:** Bus nos. 21A, 78A, 78B.

St. Mary's Pro-Cathedral, Cathedral and Marlborough Streets, Dublin 1.
☎ 874-5441.

Since Dublin's two main cathedrals (Christ Church and St. Patrick's) belong to the Protestant Church of Ireland, St. Mary's is the closest the Catholics get to having a cathedral of their own. Tucked into a corner of a rather unimpressive back street, it is situated in the heart of the city's north side and is considered the main Catholic parish church of the city center. Built between 1815 and 1825, it is of the Greek Revival Doric style, providing a distinct contrast to the Gothic Revival look of most other churches of the period. The exterior portico is modeled on the Temple of Theseus in Athens, with six Doric columns, while the Renaissance-style interior is patterned after the Church of St. Philip de Reule of Paris. The church is noted for its Palestrina Choir, which sings every Sunday at 11am.

Admission: Free.

Open: Mon–Sat 8am–6pm, Sat 8am–9pm, Sun 8am–8pm. **Transportation:** DART to Connolly Station or bus nos. 28, 29A, 30, 31A, 31B, 32A, 32B, 44A.

St. Michan's Church, Church Street, Dublin 8. ☎ 872-4154.

Built on the site of an early Danish chapel (1095), this 17th-century edifice claims to be the only parish church on the north side of the Liffey surviving from a Viking foundation. Now under the Church of Ireland banner, it has some very fine interior woodwork and an organ (dated 1724) on which Handel is said to have played his *Messiah*. The most unique (and, in some ways, macabre) feature of this church, however, is the underground burial vault. Because of the dry atmosphere, bodies have laid for centuries without showing signs of decomposition. If you touch the skin of these corpses, you'll find it to be soft, even though it is brown and leathery in appearance. If you "shake hands" with the figure known as The Crusader, it is said you will always have good luck.

Admission: £1.20 ($1.80), £1 ($1.50) seniors, 50p ($75¢) children under 12.

Open: Mon–Fri 10am–12:45pm and 2–5pm, Sat 10am–12:45pm. **Transportation:** Bus nos. 34, 70, 80.

⭐ **St. Teresa's Church,** Clarendon Street, Dublin 2. ☎ 671-8466.

With its foundation stone laid in 1793, the church was opened in 1810 by the Discalced Carmelite Fathers, to be continuously enlarged until its present form was reached in 1876. This was the first post-Penal Law church to be legally and openly erected in Dublin, following the Catholic Relief Act of 1793. Among the artistic highlights are John Hogan's *Dead Christ,* a sculpture displayed beneath the altar, and Phyllis Burke's seven beautiful stained-glass windows.

Admission: Free; donations welcome.

Open: Daily 8am–8pm or longer. **Transportation:** Bus nos. 16, 16A, 19, 19A, 22, 22A, 55, 83.

HISTORIC BUILDINGS

⭐ **Custom House,** Custom House Quay, Dublin 1. ☎ 874-2961.

No view of the Dublin skyline is complete without a tableau of the Custom House, one of Dublin's finest Georgian buildings. Designed by James Gandon and completed in 1791, it is beautifully proportioned, with a long classical facade of graceful pavilions, arcades, columns, a central dome topped by a 16-ft. statue of Commerce, and 14 keystones over the doors and windows, known as the Riverine Heads because they represent the Atlantic Ocean and the 13 principal rivers of Ireland. Although burned to a shell in 1921, this building has been masterfully restored and its bright Portland stone recently cleaned.

Admission/Open: Not open to the public, but worth looking at the exterior. **Transportation:** Bus nos. 27A, 27B, 53A.

⭐ **Four Courts,** Inns Quay, Dublin 8. ☎ 872-5555.

The home of the Irish law courts since 1796, this fine 18th-century building overlooks the north bank of the River Liffey on the west side of Dublin. With a sprawling 440-ft. facade, it was designed by James Gandon and is distinguished by its graceful Corinthian columns, massive dome (64 ft. in diameter), and exterior statues of Justice, Mercy, Wisdom, and Moses (sculpted by Edward Smyth). The building was severely burned during the Irish Civil War of 1922, but has been artfully restored. The public is admitted only when court is in session, so it is best to phone in advance.

Admission: Free.

Open: Mon–Fri 11am–1pm, 2–4pm. **Transportation:** Bus nos. 34, 70, 80.

Leinster House, Kildare Street and Merrion Square, Dublin 2. ☎ 678-9911.

Dating back to 1745 and originally known as Kildare House, this building was once considered the largest Georgian house in Dublin, because of its 11-bay, 140-ft. facade. With an impressive central pediment and Corinthian columns, it is also said to have been the model from which the White House in Washington, D.C., was later designed by Irish-born architect James Hoban. It was sold in 1815 to the Royal Dublin Society, which developed it as a cultural center, with the National Museum, Library, and Gallery all surrounding it. In 1924, however, it took on a new role when it was acquired by the Irish Free State government as a parliament house. Since then, it has been the meeting place for Ireland's Dail Eireann (House of Representatives) and Seanad Eireann (Senate), which together constitute the Oireachtas (National Parliament). Tickets for admission when the Dail is in session must be arranged by writing in advance, or by contacting a member of Parliament directly.

Admission: Free.

Open: Oct–May, Tues–Thurs; hours vary. **Transportation:** DART to Pearse Station or bus nos. 5, 7A, 8.

Mansion House, Dawson Street, Dublin 2. ☎ **676-2852.**

Built by Joshua Dawson, this Queen Anne–style building has been the official residence of Dublin's Lord Mayors since 1715. It was here that the first Dail Eireann (Irish Parliament) assembled, in 1919, to adopt Ireland's Declaration of Independence and ratify the Proclamation of the Irish Republic by the insurgents of 1916.

Admission/Open: Not open to the public, but worth looking at the exterior. **Transportation:** DART to Pearse Station or bus nos. 10, 11A, 11B, 13, 20B.

★ **Newman House,** 85–86 St. Stephen's Green, Dublin 2. ☎ **706-7422** or **475-7255.**

Situated in the heart of Dublin on the south side of St. Stephen's Green, this is the historic seat of the Catholic University of Ireland, named for Cardinal John Henry Newman, the 19th-century writer and theologian, and first rector of the university. It is comprised of two 18th-century townhouses, dating back to 1740, that are decorated with outstanding Palladian and Rococo plasterwork, marble tiled floors, and wainscot panelling.

Admission: £1 ($1.50) adults, 75p ($1.08) seniors, students, and children under 12.

Open: May–Oct Tues–Fri 10am–4pm, Sat 2–4pm, Sun 11am–2pm. **Transportation:** Bus nos. 14, 14A, 15A, 15B.

LIBRARIES

★ **Chester Beatty Library and Gallery of Oriental Art,** 20 Shrewsbury Rd., Ballsbridge, Dublin 4. ☎ **269-2386.**

Bequeathed to the Irish nation in 1956 by Sir Alfred Chester Beatty, this collection contains approximately 22,000 manuscripts, rare books, miniature paintings, and objects from Western, Middle Eastern, and Far Eastern cultures.

Admission: Free.

Open: Tues–Fri 10am–5pm and Sat 2–5pm; free guided tours on Wed and Sat at 2:30pm. **Transportation:** DART to Sandymount Station or bus nos. 5, 7A, 8, 10, 46, 46A, 46B.

Marsh's Library, St. Patrick's Close, Upper Kevin Street, Dublin 8. ☎ **454-3511.**

This is Ireland's oldest public library, founded in 1701 by Narcissus Marsh, Archbishop of Dublin. It is a repository of more than 25,000 scholarly volumes, chiefly on theology, medicine, ancient history, maps, Hebrew, Syriac, Greek, Latin, and French literature.

Admission: Free, but a donation of £1 ($1.50) expected.

Open: Mon and Wed–Fri 10am–12:45pm and 2–5pm. Sat 10:30am–12:45pm. **Transportation:** Bus nos. 50, 50A, 54, 54A, 56A.

National Library of Ireland, Kildare Street, Dublin 2. ☎ **661-8811.**

For visitors who come to Ireland to research their roots, this library is often the first point of reference, with thousands of volumes and records yielding ancestral information. Opened at this location in 1890, this is the principal library of Irish studies, and is particularly noted for its collection of first editions and the works of Irish authors. It also has an unrivalled collection of maps of Ireland.

Admission: Free.

Open: Jan–Oct and Dec, Mon 10am–9pm, Tues–Wed 2–9pm, Thurs–Fri 10am– 5pm, Sat 10am–1pm. Closed Nov for inventory. **Transportation:** DART to Pearse Station or bus nos. 10, 11A, 11B, 13, 20B.

MORE MUSEUMS

Dublin Civic Museum, 58 S. William St., Dublin 2. ☎ **679-4260.**

Located in the old City Assembly House next to the Powerscourt Town House Centre, this museum focuses on the history of the Dublin area from medieval to modern times. In addition to old street signs, maps, and prints, you can see Viking artifacts, wooden watermains, coal covers, and even the head from the statue of Lord Nelson, which stood in O'Connell Street until it was blown up in 1965.

Admission: Free.

Open: Tues–Sat 10am–6pm, Sun 11am–2pm. **Transportation:** bus nos. 10, 11, 13.

Irish Jewish Museum, 3–4 Walworth Road, off Victoria Street, South Circular Road, Dublin 8. ☎ **497-4252.**

Housed in a former synagogue, this is a museum of Irish/Jewish documents, photographs, and memorabilia, tracing the history of the Jews in Ireland over the last 500 years.

Admission: Free; donations welcome.

Open: Oct–Apr, Sun 10:30am–2:30pm; May–Sept, Tues, Thurs, Sun 11am–3pm. **Transportation:** Bus nos. 15A, 15B, 47, 47B.

Natural History Museum, Merrion Street, Dublin 2. ☎ **661-8811.**

A division of the National Museum of Ireland, this complex focuses on the zoological aspect of Irish natural history, with collections illustrating wildlife, both vertebrate and invertebrate, ranging from Irish mammals and birds, to butterflies and insects.

Admission: Free.

Open: Tues–Sat 10am–5pm, Sun 2–5pm. **Transportation:** Bus nos. 7, 7A, 8.

Number Twenty Nine, 29 Lower Fitzwilliam St., Dublin 2. ☎ **702-6265.**

Situated in the heart of one of Dublin's fashionable Georgian streets, this is a unique museum—a restored four-story townhouse designed to reflect the lifestyle of a Dublin middle class family during the period 1790 to 1820. The exhibition ranges from artifacts and works of art of the time to carpets, curtains, decorations, plasterwork, and bell pulls. The nursery also includes dolls and toys of the era.

Admission: Free.

Open: Tues–Sat 10am–5pm, Sun 2–5pm; closed two wks before Christmas. **Transportation:** DART to Pearse Station or bus nos. 6, 7, 8, 10, 45.

A SIGHT-AND-SOUND SHOW

Dublin Experience, Trinity College, The Davis Theatre, Dublin 2. ☎ 677-2941.

An ideal orientation for first-time visitors to the Irish capital, this 45-minute multi-media sight-and-sound show traces the history of Dublin from the earliest times to the present. It is presented in the Davis Theater of Trinity College on Nassau Street.
Admission: £2.75 ($4.13) adults, £2.25 ($3.38) seniors and students, £1.50 ($2.25) children under 12.

Open: Daily mid–May to early Oct, 10am–5pm; continuous showings on the hour. **Transportation:** DART to Tara Street Station or bus nos. 5, 7A, 8, 15A, 15B, 15C, 46, 55, 62, 63, 83, 84.

COOL FOR KIDS

★ **Dublin Zoo,** Phoenix Park, Dublin 8. ☎ 677-1425.

Established in 1830, this is the third oldest zoo in the world (after London and Paris), nestled in the midst of the city's largest playground, Phoenix Park, about two miles west of the city center. This 30-acre zoo provides a naturally landscaped habitat for more than 235 species of wild animals and tropical birds. Highlights for youngsters include the Children's Pets' Corner and a train ride around the zoo. Other facilities include a restaurant, coffee shop, and gift shop.
Admission: £5.50 ($8.25) adults, £2.75 ($4.13) children under 12 and seniors.
Open: Mon–Sat 9:30am–6pm, Sun 11am–6pm. **Transportation:** bus nos. 10, 25, 26.

Museum of Childhood, The Palms, 20 Palmerston Park, Rathmines, Dublin 6. ☎ 497-3223.

Part of a large suburban house on the south side of Dublin, this museum specializes in dolls and doll houses of all nations, from 1730 to 1940. Among the unique items on display are doll houses that belonged to the Empress Elizabeth of Austria and Daphne du Maurier. In addition, there are antique toys, rocking horses, and doll carriages.
Admission: £1 ($1.50) adults, 75p ($1.08) children under age 12.
Open: July–Aug, Wed and Sunday 2–5:30pm; Sept and Nov–June, Sunday 2–5:30pm. **Transportation:** Bus nos. 13 or 14.

National Wax Museum, Granby Row, at Upper Dorset Street, off Parnell Square, Dublin 1. ☎ 872-6340.

For an overall life-size view of Irish history and culture, this museum presents wax figures of Irish people of historical, political, literary, theatrical, and sporting fame. In addition, there is also a wide range of tableaux featuring everything from the Last Supper and Pope John Paul II, to world leaders, as well as music stars like U2, Michael Jackson, and Elvis Presley. For younger children, there is also a Children's World, which depicts characters from fairytales such as *Jack and the Beanstalk, Sleeping Beauty,* and *Snow White.*
Admission: £3.50 ($5.25) adults, £2 ($3) children under age 12.
Open: Mon–Sat 10am–5:30pm, Sun 1–5:30pm. **Transportation:** Bus nos. 11, 13, 16, 22, 22A.

SPECIAL-INTEREST SIGHTSEEING

Tracing Ancestors

 Heraldic Museum/Genealogical Office, 2 Kildare St., Dublin 2. ☎ 661-8811.

Beautiful building

The only one of its kind in the world, this museum focuses on the uses of heraldry. Exhibits include shields, banners, coins, paintings, porcelain, and stamps depicting coats of arms. The office of Ireland's chief herald also offers a consulting service, for a fee of £20 ($30), on the premises, so this is the ideal place to start researching your own roots.

    Admission: Free.

    Open: Mon–Wed 10am–8:30pm, Thurs–Fri 10am–4:30pm, Sat 10am–12:30pm.

Transportation: DART to Pearse Station or bus nos. 5, 7A, 8, 9, 10, 14, 15.

Literary Centers

James Joyce Cultural Centre, 35 N. Great George's St., Dublin 1. ☎ 873-1984.

Located near Parnell Square and the Dublin Writers Museum, this newly restored Georgian townhouse, built in 1784, gives literary enthusiasts one more reason to visit Dublin's north side. Aiming to impart an increased understanding of the life and works of James Joyce, it contains various exhibits, a Joycean archive, reference library, and workshop. In addition, there are talks and audio-visual presentations daily; and Ken Monaghan, Joyce's nephew, conducts tours of the house and walking tours through the neighborhood streets of "Joyce Country" in Dublin's north inner city.

    Admission: £2 ($3) per person; with guided tour of house £5 ($7.50) per person; with walking tour of Joyce Country £5 ($7.50) per person.

    Open: Tues–Sat 10am–4:30pm, Sun 12:30–4:30pm. **Closed:** Mon. **Transportation:** DART to Connolly Station or bus nos. 1, 40A, 40B, 40C.

Shaw Birthplace, 33 Synge St., Dublin 2. ☎ 475-0854.

Situated off S. Circular Road, this simple two-story terraced house, built in 1838, was the birthplace in 1856 of George Bernard Shaw, one of Dublin's three Nobel Prize for Literature winners. Recently restored, it has been furnished in Victorian style to re-create the atmosphere of Shaw's early days. Rooms on view are the kitchen, maid's room, nursery, drawing room, and a couple of bedrooms, including young Bernard's.

    Admission: £1.90 ($2.85) adults, £1.50 ($2.25) seniors and students, £1 ($1.50) children ages 3–11.

    Open: May–Sept, Mon–Sat 10am–1pm and 2–5pm, Sun 10am–1pm and 2–6pm.

Transportation: Bus no. 55.

BUS TOURS

Dublin Bus, 59 Upper O'Connell St., Dublin 1. ☎ 703-3028.

This company operates several different tours. Seats can be booked in advance at the Dublin Bus office or through a hotel porter/concierge desk. All tours depart from the Dublin Bus office, but free pick-up from many Dublin hotels is available for morning tours. Tours include a three-hour **general sightseeing tour** via a unique double-decker bus, with either an open-air or glass-enclosed upper level. It's a great vantage point for picture-taking. The cost is £8 ($12) adults, £4 ($6) children under 16. It operates in January and February on Tuesday, Friday, and Saturday at 10:15am; in March through May and mid-September to mid-December daily at 10:15am and 2:15pm; and in June through mid-September at 10:15am, 2:15, and 6:15pm.

In addition, there is a full-day **Grand Tour,** which provides general sightseeing plus guided tours and admissions into attractions such as St. Patrick's Cathedral, Dublinia, Newman House, and Dublin Castle. The price is £16 ($24) adults, £8 ($12) children under 16. Departures are at 10:30am daily during July and August; and on Tuesday, Thursday, and Saturday during June.

For more flexible touring, there is a **Heritage Tour,** a continuous guided bus service connecting ten major points of interest including museums, art galleries, churches and cathedrals, libraries, and historic sites. For the flat fare of £5 ($7.50), you can ride the bus for a full day, getting off and on as often as you wish. It operates from mid-April through September daily from 10am–5pm.

Gray Line Tours—Ireland, 3 Clanwilliam Terrace, Grand Canal Quay, Dublin 2. ☎ **661-9666.**

A branch of the world's largest sightseeing organization, this company offers a range of full-day and half-day **sightseeing tours** of Dublin City from May through October, with a more limited service, subject to demand, in April and November to December. All tours depart from the Gray Line desk at the Dublin Tourism Office, 14 Upper O'Connell St. on Monday through Saturday; and from the Gray Line Office on Sunday. Pickups are also made from hotels. Reservations can be made through hotel porters and concierges or at the Gray Line desk in the Dublin Tourism office.

The selection of tours includes a two-hour **morning tour** that provides an overview of the city's historical sights and attractions. The price is £7 ($10.50) per person, with departures daily at 9 and 11am. A three-hour **afternoon city tour** includes admissions inside Trinity College Library to view the *Book of Kells,* the State Apartments of Dublin Castle, and St. Patrick's Cathedral. The price is £14 ($21) per person, with departures daily at 2:30pm.

In addition, there is a **full-day tour** that combines the morning and afternoon tours described above, making a seven-hour exploration of Dublin's highlights. The price is £18 ($28) per person, with departures daily at 10am.

WALKING TOURS

Small and compact, Dublin lends itself to walking tours. You can set out with a map on your own, but, in order not to miss anything, we recommend that you consider one of the following self-guided or escorted group tours.

Self-Guided Walking Tours

TOURIST TRAILS The Dublin Tourism Office, 14 Upper O'Connell St., Dublin 1 (☎ **284-4768**) has pioneered in the development of self-guided walking tours around Dublin. To date, there are four different tourist trails that have been mapped out and signposted throughout the city—Old City, Georgian Heritage, Cultural Heritage, and Rock 'n' Stroll/Music Theme. For each trail, the tourist office has also produced a handy booklet that maps out the route and provides a commentary about each place along the trail. The booklets covering the Old City, Georgian, and Cultural Tours each cost £1 ($1.50); the Rock 'n' Stroll booklet costs £1.95 ($2.93).

Escorted Group Walking Tours

Discover Dublin Tours, 82 Aungier St., Dublin 2. ☎ **478-0191.**

Walks with a literary or music theme are the specialty of this company. Tours include a two-hour literary/historical tour during which the costumed guide recites works from

Dublin's literary greats while walking beside the city's famous landmarks; a two-hour musical pub crawl which focuses on Irish music from traditional to rock. Departures from various venues; reservations required.

Price: £5 ($7.50) per person.

Schedule: Year-round daily by reservation.

Dublin Footsteps, Glendenning House, Wicklow St., Dublin 2. ☎ **845-0772** or **496-0641.**

This company offers a variety of themed two-hour tours including a Medieval Walk, Literary Walk, 18th-Century/Georgian Walk, and City Center Walk. The first three walks depart from the upstairs museum at Bewley's on Grafton Street; the fourth walk assembles at the Dublin Tourism Office at 14 Upper O'Connell St. No reservations required.

Price: £4 ($6) per person.

Schedule: June–Sept, daily starting at 10:30am, but hours vary depending on tour; call in advance for schedule.

Dublin Literary Pub Crawl. ☎ **454-0228.**

Walking in the footsteps of Joyce, Behan, Beckett, Shaw, Kavanagh, and other Irish literary greats, this guided tour rambles from pub to pub, with appropriate commentary in between stops. The tour assembles on Duke Street, and it can be booked in advance at the Dublin Tourism Office, 14 Upper O'Connell Street (☎ **874-7733**).

Price: £6 ($9) per person.

Schedule: Year-round Sun at noon; May and Sept daily 7:30pm; June–Aug daily at 3pm and 7:30pm; Oct–April Sat–Sun at 7:30pm.

Historical Walking Tours of Dublin. ☎ **845-0241** or **453-5730.**

This basic two-hour sightseeing walk takes in Dublin's historic landmarks, from Viking remains around Wood Quay and medieval walls to Christ Church, Dublin Castle, City Hall, and Trinity College. All guides are history graduates of Trinity College and participants are encouraged to ask questions. Tours assemble at the front gate of Trinity College; no reservations needed.

Price: £4 ($6).

Schedule: June–Sept, Mon–Sat 11am, noon, and 3pm, Sun 11am, noon, 2pm, 3pm; Oct–May, Sat–Sun noon and 3pm.

James Joyce's Dublin Walking Tours, 35 N. Great George's St., Dublin 1. ☎ **873-1984.**

Joycean fans, take note. You can walk in the footsteps of the great novelist with Joyce's nephew, Ken Monaghan, as your guide. Monaghan conducts walking tours through the streets of Dublin's north inner city. Tours depart from the James Joyce Cultural Centre (address above).

Price: £5 ($7.50).

Schedule: Tues–Sat 10am–5pm and Sun 12:30–5pm; call in advance for exact departures.

Old Dublin Walking Tours, 90 Meath St., Dublin 8. ☎ **453-2407** or **453-3423.**

This company offers guided walks in and around Old Dublin amid the city's medieval and Viking remains. Conducted by native Dubliners, these two-hour tours give visitors the opportunity to soak up the atmosphere and meet the people of the area. Tours assemble at the main gate of Christ Church Cathedral.

Price: £4 ($6) per person.

Schedule: Year-round Sun at 2pm and by appointment.

Trinity College Walking Tours, Tour Guides Ireland, 12 Parliament St., Dublin 2. ☎ **679-4291.**

This firm operates walking tours around Trinity College including admission to the Colonnades to see the *Book of Kells.* Tours depart every 15 minutes from Front Square of Trinity College. Reservations are not necessary, but appreciated.

Price: £3.50 ($5.25) adults per person; £3 ($4.50) seniors per person.

Schedule: May–Oct, Mon–Sat 9:30am–4:30pm, Sun noon–4pm.

BICYCLE TOURS

City Cycle Tours, 1A Temple La., Dublin 2. ☎ **671-5610.**

Peddle your way around Dublin via a three-hour narrated bicycle tour of Temple Bar and the surrounding area. The route covers over a dozen sightseeing landmarks and includes guided tours of the Royal Hospital, Kilmainham Gaol, and the National Gallery. Tours depart from 1A Temple Lane; reservations are not necessary but participants are asked to arrive at least 20 minutes before a tour departure. Bicycles and helmets are provided as part of the tour price.

Price: £10 ($15) per person.

Schedule: Mon–Sat 10:30am and 2:30pm; Sun 1:30pm.

HORSE-DRAWN CARRIAGE TOURS

Dublin Horse-Drawn Carriage Tours, St. Stephen's Green, Dublin 2. ☎ **453-8888** or **821-6463.**

Tour Dublin in style via a handsomely outfitted horse-drawn carriage. The driver commentates on the sights as you travel around the streets and squares of this Fair City. To arrange a ride, consult with one of the drivers stationed with carriages at the Grafton Street side of St. Stephen's Green. Rides range from a short swing around The Green to an extensive half-hour Georgian tour or an hour-long Old City Tour. Rides are available on a first-come basis, but can also be booked by phone in advance.

Price: £5 to £30 ($7.50–$45) for two to five passengers, depending on the duration of ride.

Schedule: April–Oct, daily and nightly, depending on weather.

6 Sports & Recreation

It is no secret that sporting events dominate the Irish national calendar and character—Ireland is indeed a sports-loving land—and Dublin is the hub. And if there's one thing Dubliners love more than participating, watching, wagering, and talking about their own athletic pursuits, it's sharing their sporting passion with visitors. Here are a few ways you can join in the fun.

SPECTATOR SPORTS

GAELIC GAMES If your schedule permits, don't miss attending one of Ireland's national games, hurling and Gaelic football. These two amateur sports are played every weekend throughout the summer at various local fields, culminating in September with the All-Ireland Finals, an Irish version of the Super Bowl. For schedules and admission charges, phone the Gaelic Athletic Assoc., Croke Park, Jones Road, Dublin 3 (☎ **836-3222**).

GREYHOUND RACING   Watching these lean and swift canines is one of the leading spectator sports in the Dublin area. Racing is held throughout the year at Shelbourne Park Stadium, Bridge Town Road, Dublin 4 (☎ **668-3502**) and Harold's Cross Stadium, 151 Harold's Cross Rd., Dublin 6 (☎ **497-1081**). For a complete schedule and details, contact Bord na gCon (The Greyhound Board), Shelbourne Park, Bridge Town Road, Dublin 4 (☎ **668-3502**).

HORSE RACING   Dublin's racing fans gather at Leopardstown Race Course, off the Stillorgan Road (N 11), Foxrock, Dublin 18 (☎ **289-3607**). Located six miles south of the city center, this is a modern facility with all-weather glass-enclosed spectator stands. Races are scheduled throughout the year, two or three times a month, on weekdays or weekends.

POLO   With the Dublin Mountains as a backdrop, polo is played during the May to mid-September period on the green fields of Phoenix Park, on Dublin's west side. Matches take place on Wednesday evenings, and on Saturday and Sunday afternoons. Any of these games can be attended free of charge. For full details, contact the All Ireland Polo Club, Phoenix Park, Dublin 8 (☎ **677-6248**), or check the sports pages of the newspapers.

RECREATION

BEACHES   The following beaches on the outskirts of Dublin offer safe swimming and sandy strands and can all be reached via city buses heading northward: Dollymount, 3.5 miles away; Sutton, 7 miles away; Howth, 9 miles away; and Portmarnock and Malahide, each ten miles away. In addition, the southern suburb of Dun Laoghaire, 7 miles away, offers a beach (at Sandycove) and a long bayfront promenade, ideal for strolling in the sea air. For more details, inquire at the Dublin Tourism Office.

GOLF   Dublin's courses welcome visitors on weekdays, but starting time on weekends can be difficult to arrange. Among the leading 18-hole courses in the Dublin area are:

Elm Park Golf Club, Nutley Lane, Dublin 4. ☎ **269-3438**.

Located on the south side of Dublin, this inland par-69 course is very popular with visitors because it is located within 3.5 miles of the city center and close to Jurys, Berkeley Court, and Burlington Hotels. Greens fees are £30 ($45) on weekdays and £35 ($52.50) on weekends.

 Portmarnock Golf Club, Portmarnock, Co. Dublin. ☎ **846-2968**.

Located ten miles from the city center on Dublin's north side, Portmarnock sits on a spit of land between the Irish Sea and a tidal inlet. First opened in 1894, this par-72 championship links has been the scene of leading tournaments during the years—from the Dunlop Masters (1959, 1965), Canada Cup (1960), Alcan (1970), and St. Andrews Trophy (1968), to many an Irish Open. Many experts consider this course as the benchmark of Irish golf. Greens fees are £40 ($60) on weekdays, £50 on weekends ($75).

⭐ **Royal Dublin Golf Club**, Bull Island, Dollymount, Dublin 3. ☎ **833-6346.**
Often compared to St. Andrews in layout, this par-73 century-old championship seaside links is situated on an island in Dublin Bay, 3.5 miles north of the city center.
Like Portmarnock, it has been rated among the top courses of the world and has also
hosted several Irish Open tournaments. The home base of Ireland's legendary champion, Christy O'Connor, Sr., the Royal Dublin is well known for its fine bunkers,
close lies, and subtle trappings. Greens fees are £35 ($52.50) on weekdays, £45 ($67.50)
on weekends.

St. Margaret's Golf Club, Skephubble, St. Margaret's, Co. Dublin. ☎ **864-0400.**
This par-72 parkland course is one of Dublin's newest championship golf venues,
located three miles west of Dublin Airport. At time of this writing, it's been announced
that St. Margaret's will host the 1995 Irish Open. Greens fees are £25 ($37.50) on
weekdays and £30 ($45) on weekends.

HORSEBACK RIDING   For equestrian enthusiasts, Dublin offers opportunities
to both experienced and novice riders, with almost a dozen riding stables within easy
reach. Prices average about £10 ($15) an hour, with or without instruction. Many
stables offer guided trail-riding as well as courses in show-jumping, dressage,
pre-hunting, eventing, and cross-country riding. Among the **riding centers** nearest
to downtown are Calliaghstown Riding Centre, Calliaghstown, Rathcoole, Co. Dublin
(☎ **458-9236**); Carrickmines Equestrian Centre, Glenamuck Road, Foxrock,
Dublin 18 (☎ **295-5990**); Spruce Lodge Equestrian Centre, Kilternan, Co. Dublin
(☎ **295-2109**); and Malahide Riding School, Ivy Grangge, Malahide, Co.
Dublin (☎ **846-3622**).

7   Savvy Shopping

As a country known the world over for its hand-made products and fine craftsmanship, Ireland is a shopper's paradise—and Dublin is a one-stop source for the country's
best wares.

Grafton Street is Dublin's Fifth Avenue, with a parade of fine boutiques, fashionable department stores, and specialty shops. Restricted to pedestrians, Grafton Street
often attracts street performers and sidewalk artists, giving it a festive atmosphere. The
smaller streets radiating out from Grafton are also lined with fine small book, handcraft,
and souvenir shops—Duke Street, Dawson Street, Nassau Street, and Wicklow Street.

Nearby is **Temple Bar,** the hub of Dublin's Left Bank artsy district, and the
setting for art and music shops, second-hand clothing stores, and a host of other
interesting boutiques.

On the north side of the Liffey, the **O'Connell Street** area is the main shopping
nucleus, along with its nearby off-shoots—Abbey Street for crafts, Moore Street for
its open-air market, and Henry Street, a pedestrian-only mecca of department stores
and indoor malls.

In general, Dublin shops are open from 9am or 9:30am to 5:30pm or 6pm, Monday through Saturday, with late hours on Thursday until 8pm. There are exceptions,
however, particularly in the tourist season (May through September or October), when
many shops also post Sunday hours, usually mid-morning through 4pm or 5pm.
Throughout the year, many bookshops are also open on Sundays.

Major department stores include Arnotts, 12 Henry St., Dublin 1, and 112
Grafton St., Dublin 2 (☎ **872-1111**); Brown Thomas, 15–20 Grafton St., Dublin

2 (☎ **679-5666**); Clerys, Lower O'Connell St., Dublin 1 (☎ **878-6000**); Marks and Spencer, 28 Grafton St., Dublin 2 (☎ **679-7855**) and 24 Mary St., Dublin 1 (☎ **872-8833**).

Dublin also has several clusters of shops, in the format of **multi-story malls** or ground-level arcades, ideal for indoor shopping on rainy days. These include the ILAC Centre, Henry Street, Dublin 1; Royal Hibernian Way, 49/50 Dawson St., Dublin 2; and St. Stephen's Green Shopping Complex, St. Stephen's Green, Dublin 2.

Art

Combridge Fine Arts, 24 Suffolk St., Dublin 2. ☎ **677-4652.**

In business over 100 years, this shop features works by modern Irish artists, as well as quality reproductions of classic Irish art. **Transportation:** DART to Pearse Station or bus nos. 15A, 15B, 15C, 55, 83.

The Davis Gallery, 11 Capel St., Dublin 1. ☎ **872-6969.**

Located one block north of the Liffey, this shop offers a wide selection of Irish watercolors and oil paintings, with emphasis on Dublin scenes, as well as wildlife and flora. **Transportation:** Bus nos. 34, 70, 80.

M. Kennedy & Sons Ltd., 12 Harcourt St., Dublin 2. ☎ **475-1749.**

If you are looking for a souvenir reflecting Irish art, try this interesting shop, established more than 100 years ago. It's a treasure trove of books on Irish artists and works, as well as fine-arts greeting and postal cards and bookmarks. There are all types of artists supplies as well, and an excellent art gallery on the upstairs level. **Transportation:** Bus no. 62.

Books

★ **Eason & Son Ltd.,** 40–42 Lower O'Connell St., Dublin 1. ☎ **873-3811.**

For over a century, Eason's has been synonymous with books at this central location and at its many branches throughout Ireland. This store offers a comprehensive selection of books and maps about Dublin and Ireland. **Transportation:** DART to Connolly Station or bus nos. 25, 34, 37, 38A, 39A, 39B, 66A, 67A.

Fred Hanna Ltd., 27–29 Nassau St., Dublin 2. ☎ **777-1255.**

Located across from Trinity College, this is a good bookshop for academic texts, as well as new, used, and antiquarian volumes on all topics. **Transportation:** DART to Pearse Station or bus nos. 5, 7A, 8, 62.

★ **Greenes Bookshop Ltd.,** 16 Clare St., Dublin 2. ☎ **776-2554.**

Established in 1843 and close to Trinity College, this is one of Dublin's treasures for bibliophiles. It's chock full of new and secondhand books on every topic from modern novels to religion. **Transportation:** DART to Pearse Station or bus nos. 5, 7A, 8, 62.

★ **Hodges Figgis,** 56/58 Dawson St., Dublin 2. ☎ **677-4754.**

This three-story landmark store has great charm and browse appeal. Although all topics are covered, there are particularly good sections on Irish literature, Celtic studies, folklore, and maps of Ireland. **Transportation:** DART to Pearse Station or bus nos. 10, 11A, 11B, 13, 20B.

Waterstone's, 7 Dawson St., Dublin 2. ☎ **679-1415.**

Less than a block south of Trinity College, this literary emporium has extensive sections on Irish interests, as well as crime, gay literature, health, new age, sport, women's studies, and wine. **Transportation:** DART to Pearse Station or bus nos. 10, 11A, 11B, 13, 20B.

China and Crystal

China Showrooms, 32/33 Abbey St., Dublin 1. ☎ **878-6211.**

Established in 1939, this shop is a one-stop source of fine china, such as Belleek, Aynsley, Royal Doulton, and Rosenthal; hand-cut crystal from Waterford, Tipperary, and Tyrone; and hand-made Irish pottery. **Transportation:** DART to Connolly Station or bus nos. 27B, 53A.

★ **Dublin Crystal Glass Company,** Brookfield Terrace, Carysfort Avenue, Blackrock, Co. Dublin. ☎ **288-7932.**

This is Dublin's own distinctive hand-cut crystal business, founded in 1764 and revived in 1968. Visitors are welcome to browse in the factory shop and to see the glass being made and engraved. **Transportation:** DART to Blackrock Station or bus no. 114.

Craft Complexes

★ **Powerscourt Townhouse Centre,** 59 S. William St., Dublin 2. ☎ **679-4144.**

Housed in a restored 1774 townhouse, this four-story complex consists of a central skylit courtyard and over 60 boutiques, craftshops, art galleries, snackeries, wine bars, and restaurants. The wares include all kinds of crafts, antiques, paintings, prints, ceramics, leatherwork, jewelry, clothing, hand-dipped chocolates, and Farmhouse cheeses. **Transportation:** Bus nos. 10, 11A, 11B, 13, 16A, 19A, 20B, 22A, 55, 83.

Tower Design Centre, Pearse Street, off Grand Canal Quay, Dublin 2. ☎ **677-5655.**

Located along the banks of the Grand Canal, this 1862 sugar refinery was beautifully restored in 1983 and developed into a nest of craft workshops. Watch the artisans at work and then purchase a special souvenir—from fine-art greeting cards and hand-marbled stationery to pewter, ceramics, pottery, knitwear, hand-painted silks, copper-plate etchings, all-wool wall hangings, silver and gold Celtic jewelry, and heraldic gifts. **Transportation:** DART to Pearse Station or bus nos. 2 or 3.

Fashion/Designers—For Women

★ **Cleo,** 18 Kildare St., Dublin 2. ☎ **676-1421.**

For more than 50 years, the Joyce family has been creating designer ready-to-wear clothing in a rainbow of vibrant tweed colors—elegant ponchos, capes, peasant skirts, coat-sweaters, decorative crios belts, and brimmed hats. **Transportation:** DART to Pearse Station or bus nos. 10, 11A, 11B, 13, 20B.

Pat Crowley, 3 Molesworth Pl., Dublin 2. ☎ **661-5580.**

The emphasis is on individuality by this designer, known for her exclusive line of tweeds and couture evening wear. **Transportation:** DART to Pearse Station or bus nos. 10, 11A, 11B, 13, 20B.

Sybil Connolly, 71 Merrion Square, Dublin 2. ☎ **676-7281.**

Irish high fashion is synonymous with this world-renowned made-to-measure designer. Evening wear and Irish linen creations are a specialty. **Transportation:** DART to Pearse Station or bus nos. 5, 7A, 8.

Fashion/Tailors—For Men

F.X. Kelly, 48 Grafton St., Dublin 2. ☎ **777-8211.**

A long-established men's ready-to-wear shop, this place blends old fashioned charm with modern design. It offers a handsome selection of styles, with emphasis on conventional clothing as well as creased linen suits, painted ties, and designer sportswear. **Transportation:** DART to Pearse Station or bus nos. 10, 11A, 11B, 13, 20B.

★ **Kevin and Howlin,** 31 Nassau St., Dublin 2. ☎ **677-0257.**

Located opposite Trinity College, this shop has specialized in men's tweed garments for over 50 years. The selection includes Donegal tweed suits, overcoats, and jackets. In addition, there is a wide selection of scarves, vests, Patch caps, and Gatsby, Sherlock Holmes, and Paddy hats. **Transportation:** DART to Pearse Station or bus nos. 5, 7A, 8, 15A, 15B, 46, 55, 62, 63, 83, 84.

★ **Louis Copeland,** 39–41 Capel St., Dublin 1. ☎ **872-1600.**

With a distinctive old-world shopfront, this store stands out on the north side of the River Liffey. It is known for high quality work in made-to-measure and ready-to-wear men's suits, coats, and shirts. Also located at 30 Pembroke St., Dublin 2 (☎ **661-0110**) and at 18 Wicklow St., Dublin 2 (☎ **677-7038**). **Transportation:** bus nos. 34, 70, 80.

Gifts/General Selection

Fergus O'Farrell Workshop, 62 Dawson St., Dublin 2. ☎ **677-0862.**

Irish design from the 5th to 15th centuries has been the inspiration for much of the craft work at this unique shop. These conversation-piece souvenirs range from *Book of Kells* art and bog-oak figurines to hand-carved fish boards and beaten copper wall hangings, as well as Irish road signs, handmade dolls and animals, and more. **Transportation:** DART to Pearse Station or bus nos. 10, 11A, 11B, 13, 20B.

★ **The Irish Times Collection,** 10–16 D'Olier St., Dublin 2. ☎ **671-8446.**

The general services department of *The Irish Times* operates this shop, featuring Irish-made crafts, many of which are commissioned by the newspaper for special offers to its readers. Items include jewelry and watches, as well as bog oak, silver, pewter, and bronze sculptures, and books on Ireland and Dublin written exclusively for the *Times*. **Transportation:** DART to Tara Street Station or bus nos. 14A or 54A.

House of Ireland, 37–38 Nassau St., Dublin 2. ☎ **671-4543.**

Located opposite Trinity College, this shop is a happy blend of European and Irish products, from Waterford and Belleek to Wedgewood and Lladro, as well as tweeds, linens, knitwear, Celtic jewelry, mohair capes, shawls, kilts, blankets, and dolls. **Transportation:** DART to Pearse Station or bus nos. 5, 7A, 15A, 15B, 46, 55, 62, 63, 83, 84.

The Kilkenny Shop, 6–10 Nassau St., Dublin 2. ☎ **677-7066.**

This modern multilevel shop is a showplace for original Irish designs and quality products including pottery, glass, candles, woolens, pipes, knitwear, jewelry, books, and prints. **Transportation:** DART to Pearse Station or bus nos. 5, 7A, 15A, 15B, 46, 55, 62, 63, 83, 84.

Weir & Sons, 96–99 Grafton St., Dublin 2. ☎ 677-9678.

Established in 1869, this is the grand-daddy of Dublin's fine jewelry shops, selling new and antique jewelry as well as silver, china, and glass items. A second branch is at the Ilac Centre, Henry Street (☎ 872-9588). **Transportation:** DART to Pearse Station or bus nos. 10, 11A, 11B, 13, 20B.

Heraldry

Heraldic Artists, 3 Nassau St., Dublin 2. ☎ 679-7020.

For over 20 years, this shop has been known for helping visitors locate their family roots. In addition to tracing surnames, it also sells all of the usual heraldic items, from parchments and mahogany wall plaques to crests scrolls, and books on researching ancestry. **Transportation:** DART to Pearse Station or bus nos. 5, 7A, 8, 15A, 15B, 46, 55, 62, 63, 83, 84.

House of Names, 26 Nassau St., Dublin 2. ☎ 679-7287.

This company offers a wide selection of Irish, British, and European family names, crests, and mottos, affixed to plaques, shields, parchments, jewelry, glassware, and sweaters. Also located at 8 Fleet St. (☎ 677-7034). **Transportation:** DART to Pearse Station or bus nos. 5, 7A, 8, 15A, 15B, 46, 55, 62, 63, 83, 84.

Knitwear

Blarney Woollen Mills, 21–23 Nassau St., Dublin 2. ☎ 671-0068.

A branch of the highly successful Cork-based enterprise of the same name, this shop is ideally located opposite the south side of Trinity College. Known for its competitive prices, it stocks a wide range of woolen knitwear made at the home base in Blarney, as well as crystal, china, pottery, and souvenirs. **Transportation:** DART to Pearse Station or bus nos. 5, 7A, 8, 15A, 15B, 46, 55, 62, 63, 83, 84.

Dublin Woollen Mills, 41 Lr. Ormond Quay, Dublin 1. ☎ 677-0301.

Situated on the north side of the River Liffey next to the Ha'penny Bridge, since 1888 this shop has been a leading source of Aran handknit sweaters, vests, hats, jackets, and scarves, as well as lambswool sweaters, kilts, ponchos, and tweeds. **Transportation:** Bus nos. 70 or 80.

★ **Monaghan's,** 15/17 Grafton Arcade, Grafton Street, Dublin 2. ☎ 677-0823.

Established in 1960 and operated by two generations of the Monaghan family, this store is a prime source of cashmere sweaters for men and women, with the best selection of colors, sizes, and styles anywhere in Ireland. Other items stocked include traditional Aran knits, lambswool, crochet, and Shetland wool products. Also located at 4/5 Royal Hibernian Way, off Dawson Street (☎ 679-4451). **Transportation:** DART to Pearse Station or bus nos. 10, 11A, 11B, 13, 20B.

Markets

★ **Moore Street Market,** Moore Street, Dublin 1.

For a flashback of what life was like for fishmonger Molly Malone, don't miss this Dublin enclave, full of streetside barrow vendors, and plenty of local color and chatter. It's the principal open-air fruit, flower, fish, and vegetable market of the city. **Transportation:** DART to Connolly Station or bus nos. 25, 34, 37, 38A, 66A, 67A.

Flea market

⭐ **Mother Redcaps Market,** Back Lane, off High Street, Dublin 8. ☎ **854-4655.**

Located in the heart of Old Dublin, this enclosed market is one of Dublin's best. The various stalls offer everything from antiques and used books and coins, to silver, handcrafts, leather products, knitwear, music tapes, furniture, and even a fortune teller! It's worth a trip here just to sample the wares at the Ryefield Foods stall (farm-made cheeses, baked goods, marmalades, and jams). **Transportation:** Bus nos. 21A, 78A, 78B.

Sheepskins/Leathers

Sheepskin Shop, 20 Wicklow St., Dublin 2. ☎ **671-9585.**

As its name indicates, this is a good place to find sheepskin jackets, hats, and moccasins, as well as suede coats and lambskin wear. **Transportation:** DART to Pearse Station or bus nos. 5, 7A, 8, 15A, 46, 55, 62, 63, 83, 84.

Shoes

Tutty's Handmade Shoes Ltd., 59 S. William St., Dublin 2. ☎ **679-6566.**

Located on the top floor of the Powerscourt Townhouse Center, this tiny shop specializes in made-to-measure shoes and boots, crafted from the finest leathers. **Transportation:** Bus nos. 10, 11A, 11B, 13, 16A, 19A, 20B, 22A, 55, 83.

Umbrellas/Walking Sticks

H. Johnston, 11 Wicklow St., Dublin 2. ☎ **677-1249.**

Just in case it rains, this centrally located shop is a good source for durable umbrellas. And if you are looking for an Irish blackthorn stick, otherwise known as a shillelagh, this spot has been specializing in them for more than 110 years. **Transportation:** DART to Pearse Station or bus nos. 5, 7A, 8, 15A, 46, 55, 62, 63, 83, 84.

---

8 Entertainment & Pubs

As the home of over 1,000 pubs plus the legendary Abbey Theatre and dozens of other entertainment venues, Dublin is lively and gregarious at night. Turn any corner and there is music or laughter in the air.

The best way to find out what is going on is to ask for current calendar listings at the Dublin Tourism Office at 14 Upper O'Connell Street (☎ **284-4768**), or consult the entertainment/leisure pages of *The Irish Times* and other daily newspapers. In addition, the tourist office and most hotels distribute copies of the bi-weekly *Dublin Event Guide*, a free newspaper listing entertainment and theater programs.

THE PERFORMING ARTS

The Major Concert/Performance Halls

⭐ **National Concert Hall,** Earlsfort Terrace, Dublin 2. ☎ **671-1533.**

This magnificent 1,200-seat hall is the setting for the classical music of the Concert Orchestra of Irish Television and the Irish Chamber Orchestra, as well as a variety of international performers. In addition, there are evenings of Gilbert and Sullivan, opera, jazz, and recitals.

Open: Box office, Mon–Sat 11am–7pm and Sun (if concert scheduled) from 7pm. Performances at 7:30pm or 8pm.

Admission: £6–£20 ($9–$30).

The Point, East Link Bridge, North Wall Quay, Dublin 1. ☎ **836-3633.**

With a seating capacity of 3,000, this is Ireland's newest large theater and concert venue, attracting top Broadway-caliber shows and international stars.

Open: Box office, Mon–Sat 10am–6pm; matinees at 2:30pm and evening shows 8pm.

Admission: £10–£50 ($15–$75).

Royal Dublin Society (RDS), Merrion Road, Ballsbridge, Dublin 2. ☎ **668-0645.**

Although best known as the venue for the Dublin Horse Show, this huge show-jumping arena is also the setting for major music concerts, with seating/standing room for over 6,000 people.

Open: Box office hours vary according to events; shows at 8pm.

Admission: £10–£30 ($15–$45).

Theaters

★ **Abbey Theatre,** Lower Abbey Street, Dublin 1. ☎ **878-7222.**

For over 90 years, the Abbey has been the national theater of Ireland and home of the world-famed Abbey Players. The original theater, destroyed in a 1951 fire, was replaced in 1966 by the current modern 600-seat building.

Open: Box office, Mon–Sat 10:30am–7pm; shows Mon–Sat 8pm.

Admission: £8–£14 ($12–$21).

Andrews Lane Theatre, 12/16 Andrews Lane, Dublin 2. ☎ **679-5720.**

This showplace consists of a 220-seat main theater, which presents contemporary work from home and abroad, and a 76-seat studio geared for experimental productions.

Open: Box office, Mon–Sat 10:30am–7pm; shows, Mon–Sat 8pm in theater and 8:15pm in studio.

Admission: £6–£12 ($9–$18).

City Arts Centre, 23–25 Moss St. at City Quay, Dublin 2. ☎ **677-0643.**

Opened in 1989, this is one of Dublin's newest lively arts venues, an affiliate of Trans Europe Halles, the European network of independent arts centers. It presents a varied program, from local drama groups performing original new plays, to theatrical discussions, comedies, readings by local writers, and touring companies from other parts of Ireland and abroad.

Open: Box office opens at 7:30pm; reservations can be made in advance, by phone only, Mon–Sat 9am–6pm; shows, Mon–Sat at 8pm or later.

Admission: £4–£6 ($6–$9).

Major Concert & Performance Halls: Box Offices

Abbey Theatre ☎ **878-7222**

Gaiety Theatre ☎ **677-1717**

The Gate ☎ **874-4045**

National Concert Hall ☎ **671-1533**

Olympia ☎ **677-7744**

The Point ☎ **836-3633**

Royal Dublin Society ☎ **668-0645**

Focus Theatre, 6 Pembroke Place, off Pembroke Street, Dublin 2. ☎ **676-3071.**

Nestled in a secluded alley two blocks south of St. Stephen's Green, this small, 70-seat theater presents a surprisingly varied repertoire of Irish and international plays including the great classics.
> **Open:** Box office, Mon–Sat 10am–7:30pm; shows, Mon–Sat 8pm.
> **Admission:** £7–£8 ($10.50–$12).

Gaiety Theatre, S. King St., Dublin 2. ☎ **677-1717.**

The Dublin Grand Opera Society performs its spring (April) and winter (December) seasons here. During the rest of the year, this very fine 19th-century theater of 1,100 seats stages musical comedy, ballet, revue, pantomime, and drama, all with Irish and international talent.
> **Open:** Box office, Mon–Sat 11am–7pm; shows, Mon–Sat 8pm.
> **Admission:** £7–£16 ($10.50–$24).

The Gate, 1 Cavendish Row, Dublin 1. ☎ **874-4045.**

Situated just north of O'Connell Street off Parnell Square, this recently restored 370-seat theater was founded in 1928 by Hilton Edwards and Michael MacLiammoir to provide a showing for a broad range of plays. This policy prevails today, with a program that includes a blend of modern works, as well as the classics.
> **Open:** Box office, Mon–Sat 10am–7pm; shows, Mon–Sat 8pm.
> **Admission:** £10–£12 ($15–$18).

New Eblana Theatre, Store Street, Dublin 1. ☎ **679-8404.**

Housed in the basement of Busaras (the central bus station), this 230-seat midtown theater presents a varied program of modern plays and events.
> **Open:** Box office (at Andrews Lane Theatre), Mon–Sat 10:30am–6pm, tickets also on sale on day of show if available from 7pm; shows, Mon–Sat 8pm.
> **Admission:** £6–£12 ($9–$18).

Olympia, 72 Dame St., Dublin 2. ☎ **677-7744.**

Dating back to the 1800s, this Victorian music hall–style theater has a capacity of 1,300. It presents an eclectic schedule of variety shows, musicals, operettas, concerts, ballet, comedy, and drama. As a variation, for the late night crowd, live bands are often featured after regular programs.
> **Open:** Box office, Mon–Sat 10am–6pm; shows, Mon–Sat 8pm; late-night shows, Fri–Sat midnight–2am.
> **Admission:** £7.50–£15 ($11.25–$22.50) for regular programs; £6–£10 ($9–$15) for late-night live bands.

Peacock, Lower Abbey St., Dublin 1. ☎ **878-7222.**

In the same building as the Abbey, this small, 150-seat theater features contemporary plays and experimental works including poetry readings and one-person shows, and plays in the Irish language.
> **Open:** Box office, Mon–Sat 10:30am–7pm; shows, Mon–Sat at 8:15pm.
> **Admission:** £8–£10 ($12–$15).

Project Arts Centre, 39 E. Essex St., Dublin 2. ☎ **671-2321.**

Located in the burgeoning Temple Bar district, this contemporary theater is part of a multipurpose arts complex. With a capacity of 180 seats, it specializes in experimental and new works, as well as performances by the Irish Modern Dance Theatre troupe. Depending on demand, it schedules lunchtime or late night shows.

Open: Box office, Mon–Sat 10am–6pm; shows, Mon–Sat 8pm.
Admission: £5–£9 ($7.50–$13.50).

Tivoli Theatre, 135–138 Francis St., Dublin 8. ☎ **454-4472.**

This 500-seat theater was originally a movie house that was refurbished and reopened in 1987. It presents Broadway and West End musicals and dramas.
Open: Box office, Mon–Sat 10am–6pm; shows, Mon–Sat 8pm; late night performances Fri–Sat 11pm.
Admission: £8–£15 ($12–$22.50).

Dinner Shows

⭐ **Abbey Tavern**, Abbey Road, Howth, Co. Dublin. ☎ **839-0307.**

A complete four-course meal, accompanied by Irish ballad music, with its blend of fiddles, pipes, tin whistles, and spoons, is on tap at this authentic old-world tavern.
Open: Box office, Mon–Sat 9am–5pm; dinner/show daily Mar–Oct and Mon–Sat Nov–Feb; dinner 7pm, show 9pm.
Admission: Dinner/entertainment £23–£28 ($34.50–$42); entertainment only £3 ($4.50).

Doyle's Irish Cabaret, Upper Leeson Street, Dublin 4. ☎ **660-5222,** ext. 1162.

Staged in the ballroom of the Hotel Burlington, this colorful dinner/show features some of Ireland's top performers in a program of Irish music, dancing, ballad singing, and storytelling.
Schedule: May–Oct, Mon–Sat dinner 7pm, show 8pm.
Admission: Dinner/show £30.90 ($46.35); show with two drinks £19.50 ($29.25).

⭐ **Jury's Irish Cabaret**, Pembroke Road, Ballsbridge, Dublin 4. ☎ **660-5000.**

As Ireland's longest running show (over 30 years), this production offers a unique mix of traditional Irish and international music, rousing ballads and Broadway classics, toe-tapping set dancing and graceful ballet, humorous monologues and telling recitations, and audience participation.
Schedule: May–Oct, Tues–Sun dinner 7:15pm, show 8pm.
Admission: Dinner/show £31.50 ($47.25); show with two drinks £19 ($28.50).

Traditional Irish Entertainment

The Castle Inn, 5–7 Lord Edward St, Dublin 8. ☎ **475-1122.**

Situated between Dublin Castle and Christ Church Cathedral, this recently rejuvenated bilevel pub exudes an "old city" atmosphere, with stone walls, flagstone steps, knightly suits of armor, big stone fireplaces, beamed ceilings, and lots of early Dublin memorabilia. It is also the setting for an Irish Ceili & Banquet featuring Irish traditional musicians and set dancers.
Schedule: May–Sept, preshow dinner 7:30pm, show at 8:45pm.
Admission: Show only, £7 ($10.50); show with Irish stew, £12 ($18); show with four-course dinner £21 ($36.50).

 Culturlann Na heireann, 32 Belgrave Sq., Monkstown, Co. Dublin.
☎ **280-0295.**

This is the home of Comhaltas Ceoltoiri Eireann, an Irish cultural organization that has been the prime mover in encouraging a renewed appreciation of and interest in Irish traditional music. The year-round entertainment programs include old-fashioned ceili dances on Fridays and informal music sessions on Fridays and Saturdays. In the summer months, an authentic fully costumed show featuring traditional music, song, and dance is staged. No reservations are necessary for any of the events.

Schedule: Year-round ceili dances, Fri 9:30pm–12:30am; informal music sessions, Fri–Sat 9:30–11:30pm; June–Sept, traditional music stage show, Sat–Thurs 9–10:30pm.

Admission: Ceilis, £4 ($6); informal music sessions, £1.50 ($2.25); stage shows, £5 ($7.50).

THE CLUB AND MUSIC SCENE

Although it has never been a nightlife mecca, Dublin has spawned a surprising number of after-hours clubs over the past 25 years. Initially, the focal point was Leeson Street, a one-block strip of basement-level discos off the southeast corner of St. Stephen's Green.

As in many cities, the Dublin audience has been fickle, always seeking something new, so the names and decor of these places have changed regularly, making it hard to keep track.

There are still a few trendy clubs along the Leeson Street strip, but the Dublin nightlife emphasis of the 1990s has been gradually shifting toward the Temple Bar District, now recognized as the city's cultural corner or Left Bank. Even the famed rock group, U2, has gotten into the act, by opening a nightclub in early 1994 called The Kitchen, in the heart of Temple Bar. Other current clubs of choice tend to be in areas near Temple Bar or in major hotels. A selection of those clubs currently in favor as we go to press follows.

Nightclubs/Discos

Annabel's, Upper Leeson Street, Dublin 4. ☎ 660-5222.

Located in the Burlington Hotel just south of the famed Lower Leeson Street nightclub strip, this club is one of the longest lasting in town. It welcomes a mix of tourists and locals of all ages to a disco party atmosphere.

Open: Tues–Sat 10pm–2am.
Admission: £7 ($10.50).

Club M, Anglesea Street, Dublin 2. ☎ 671-5622.

Housed in the basement of Blooms Hotel in the trendy Temple Bar district and close to Trinity College, this club boasts Ireland's largest hydraulic moving laser lighting system. It offers either disco or live music, for the over-23 age bracket.

Open: Tues–Sun 10pm–2am.
Admission: £4–£8 ($6–$12).

The Kitchen, 6/8 Wellington Quay, Dublin 2. ☎ 677-6178.

Housed in the basement of the Clarence Hotel in the heart of the Temple Bar district, this is one of Dublin's hottest nightclubs, partly owned by the rock group U2.

Open: Wed–Sun 11pm–2am.
Admission: £3–£8 ($4.50–$12).

Lillie's Bordello, 45 Nassau St., Dublin 2. ☎ 679-7539.

This place is designed to convey the fun-filled, slightly decadent atmosphere of yesteryear, with the music beats of today.

Open: Daily 10pm–1pm or later.
Admission: £7 ($10.50) weekdays, £8 ($12) weekends.

The P.O.D., Harcourt Street, Dublin 2. ☎ 478-0166.

Operated by John Reynolds, nephew of the former prime minister of Ireland, Albert Reynolds, this place is both politically correct and a lot of fun for dancing (P.O.D. stands for Place Of Dance), with a colorful Barcelona-inspired decor. It is located south of St. Stephen's Green, a block from the National Concert Hall, beneath the arches of the old Harcourt Street station.

Open: Wed–Sun 11pm–3am or later.
Admission: £6–£8 ($9–$12).

RI RA, Dame Court, off Dame Street, Dublin 2. ☎ 677-4835.

This club attracts a youngish crowd to hear guest DJs spin funk and reggae music weeknights and Saturdays. On Sunday, winding down the week, the mood shifts to a Sleep theme, with mellow instrumental sounds from the 70s.

Open: Wed–Sun 11:30pm–4am or later.
Admission: £4–£5 ($6–$7.50).

Country/Jazz/Blues

Bad Bob's Backstage Bar, 35–37 E. Essex St., Dublin 2. ☎ 677-5482.

This place specializes in live country music seven nights a week, drawing top international and local talent. It is situated next to the Project Arts Centre at Sycamore Street.

Open: Nightly 10pm–2am.
Admission: £6–£8 ($9–$12).

Break for the Border, Johnson Place, Dublin 2. ☎ 478-0300.

With a decor of Native American art and Western-style furnishings, this place has a Tex-Mex atmosphere, enhanced by performances of Cajun and country bands. It's located in the Grafton Plaza Hotel.

Open: Wed–Sat 11pm–2am or later.
Admission: £7–£8 ($10.50–$12).

Night Train, 7 Lower Mount St., Dublin 2. ☎ 676-1717.

Located in the basement of the traditional-style O'Dwyer's Pub, this enclave presents a varied program of jazz, Cajun, blues, soul, and rock, attracting a mostly over-25 crowd.

Open: Nightly 11pm–2am.
Admission: £6–£8 ($9–12).

Whelans, 25 Wexford St., Dublin 2. ☎ 678-0766.

Situated in a slightly off-the-beaten-track location between Camden and Aungier Streets yet within a block of St. Stephen's Green, this pub draws big crowds for its nightly programs of Cajun, blues, country, and other types of music.

Open: Nightly 9pm onward.
Admission: £3–£5 ($4.50–$7.50).

Rock

Baggot Inn, 143 Lower Baggot St., Dublin 2. ☎ 676-1430.

Located near St. Stephen's Green, this pub has long been a podium for emerging rock musicians and bands, including U2 in their early days.

Open: Nightly, shows from 9pm.
Admission: £3–£5 ($4.50–$7.50).

PUBS

The mainstay of Dublin social life—both by night and by day—is unquestionably the pub. More than 1,000 specimens are spread throughout the city; there are pubs on every street, at every turn. It was in *Ulysses* that James Joyce referred to the puzzle of trying to cross Dublin without passing by a pub, but then he abandoned the quest as fruitless, preferring instead to sample a few pubs in his path. Needless to say, most visitors should follow in Joyce's footsteps and drop in on a few pubs.

Pubs for Conversation and Atmosphere

★ **Brazen Head,** 20 Lower Bridge St., Dublin 8. ☎ **679-5186.**

This brass-filled and lantern-lit pub claims to be the city's oldest—and with good reason, considering that it was licensed in 1661 and occupies the site of an earlier tavern dating from 1198. Nestled on the south bank of the River Liffey, it is at the end of a cobblestone courtyard and was once the meeting place of Irish freedom fighters such as Robert Emmet and Wolfe Tone.

Davy Byrnes, 21 Duke St., Dublin 2. ☎ **677-5217.**

Referred to as a "moral pub" by James Joyce in *Ulysses,* this imbibers' landmark has drawn poets, writers, and lovers of literature ever since. Located just off Grafton Street, it dates back to 1873, when Davy Byrnes first opened the doors. He presided here for more than 50 years and visitors today can still see his likeness on one of the turn-of-the-century murals hanging over the bar.

Doheny and Nesbitt, 5 Lower Baggot St., Dublin 2. ☎ **676-2945.**

The locals call this Victorian-style pub simply Nesbitts. There are two fine specimens of snugs (a small room with a trap door where women were served a drink in days of old).

Flannery's Temple Bar, 48 Temple Bar, Dublin 2. ☎ **677-3807.**

Nestled in the heart of the trendy Temple Bar district on the corner of Temple Lane, this small three-room pub was established in 1840. The decor is an interesting mix of crackling fireplaces, globe ceiling lights, old pictures on the walls, and shelves filled with local memorabilia.

★ **John M. Keating,** 14 Mary St., Dublin 1. ☎ **873-1567.**

Situated north of the Liffey at the corner of Jervis Street, this bilevel pub is known for its old world decor, from its marble-top bar and spiral staircase to the upstairs loft.

The Long Hall, 51 S. Great George's St., Dublin 2. ☎ **475-1590.**

Tucked into a busy commercial street, this is one of the city's most photographed pubs, with a beautiful Victorian decor of filigree-edged mirrors, polished dark woods, and traditional snugs. The hand-carved bar is said to be the longest counter in the city.

IMPRESSIONS

Dublin is a state of mind as much as a city.
—Tom McDonagh (b. 1934), *My Green Age*

Mulligan's, 8 Poolbeg St., Dublin 2. ☎ 677-5582.

Established in 1782, this is a man's pub known for its superb pints and smoky Old Dublin atmosphere. The decor is rich in solid mahogany wood, gas lamps, and large wall mirrors.

Neary's, 1 Chatham St., Dublin 2. ☎ 677-8586.

Adjacent to the back door of the Gaiety Theatre, this celebrated enclave is a favorite with stage folk and theatergoers. Trademarks here are the pink and gray marble bar and the brass hands that support the globe lanterns at the entrance.

The Old Stand, 37 Exchequer St., Dublin 2. ☎ 677-7220.

In this sporting atmosphere with lots of camaraderie, participants and followers of rugby and Gaelic games meet for a pint.

Palace Bar, 21 Fleet St., Dublin 2. ☎ 677-9290.

This old charmer is decorated with local memorabilia, cartoons, and paintings that tell the story of Dublin through the years.

Stag's Head, 1 Dame Ct., off Dame Street, Dublin 2. ☎ 679-3701.

Mounted stags' heads and eight stag-theme stained glass windows dominate the decor, as its name implies, but there are also wrought iron chandeliers, polished Aberdeen granite, old barrels, skylights, and ceiling-high mirrors.

 W. Ryan, 28 Parkgate St., Dublin 7. ☎ 677-6097.

Three generations of the Ryan family have contributed to the success of this public house, located on the north side of the Liffey near Phoenix Park. Some of Dublin's best traditional pub features are a part of the scene here, from metal ceiling and domed skylight to beveled mirrors, etched glass, brass lamp holders, a mahogany bar, and four old-style snugs.

Pubs with Traditional/Folk Music

An Beal Bocht, 58 Charlemont St. off Harcourt Street at Albert Place W., Dublin 2. ☎ 475-5614.

Located between St. Stephen's Green and the Grand Canal, this cozy vintage pub offers a varied program of Irish traditional music on most nights and on Sunday from 12:30–2pm.

Admission: No cover charge.

Barry Fitzgeralds, 90–92 Marlborough St., Dublin 1. ☎ 874-0685.

Named for the Abbey actor who became a Hollywood movie star, this place has a theatrical atmosphere, with lots of thespian memorabilia lining the walls and alcoves. It offers live traditional music on Friday night and Sunday afternoon, and karaoke on Saturday. Music usually starts at 8:45pm.

Admission: No cover charge.

 Kitty O'Shea's, 23–25 Upper Grand Canal St., Dublin 4. ☎ 660-9965.

Situated just south of the Grand Canal, this pub is named after the sweetheart of 19th-century Irish statesman Charles Stewart Parnell. The decor reflects the Parnell era, with ornate oak paneling, stained-glass windows, old political posters, cozy alcoves, and brass railings. Traditional Irish music is on tap every night.

Admission: No cover charge.

Mother Redcaps Tavern, Back Lane, Dublin 8. ☎ **453-3960.**

A former shoe factory wedged in the heart of the Liberties section of the city, this large two-story pub exudes an old Dublin atmosphere, with eclectic mahogany and stripped pine furnishings, antiques and curios on the shelves, and walls lined with old paintings and newspaper clippings dating from the last century. On Sundays, there is usually a midday session of traditional Irish music, with everyone invited to bring an instrument and join in. On many nights, there is also traditional music on an informal basis or in a concert setting upstairs.

Admission: No cover charge except for concerts £5–£6 ($7.50–$9).

O'Donoghue's, 15 Merrion Row, Dublin 2. ☎ **661–4303.**

Tucked between St. Stephen's Green and Merrion Street, this smoke-filled enclave is widely heralded as the grand-daddy of traditional music pubs. At almost any time of the day or night, a spontaneous session is likely to erupt.

Admission: No cover charge for music.

Oliver St. John Gogarty, 57/58 Fleet St., Dublin 2. ☎ **671-1822.**

Situated in the heart of Temple Bar and named for one of Ireland's literary greats, this pub has an inviting old-world atmosphere, with shelves of empty bottles, stacks of dusty books, a horseshoe-shaped bar, and old barrels for seats. There are traditional music sessions on Saturday from 3:30 to 7pm, Sunday from 12:30 to 3pm, and every night from 9 to 11pm.

Admission: No cover charge for music.

Sean O'Casey, 105 Marlborough St., Dublin 1. ☎ **874-4294.**

Located a block from the Abbey Theatre and named for one of Dublin's great playwrights, this Tudor-style pub is appropriately decorated with playbills and posters. On most nights, there is traditional music or Irish ballads from 9pm.

Admission: £1 ($1.50) music cover charge.

Slattery's, 129–130 Capel St., Dublin 1. ☎ **872-7971.**

Located on the north side of the Liffey, this pub has a classic old-world facade and an interior of brass trim, dark wood, gas lamps, mirrors, and church pew benches. On Sundays, between 12:30 and 2pm, it is a focal point for traditional Irish music and ballads, with as many as 20 musicians playing in an informal sesson in the main bar. From Wednesday through Sunday nights, rock and blues music is featured in the upstairs lounge, from 9 to 11:30pm.

Admission: No cover charge for Irish music sessions; £3–£4 ($4.50–$6) cover charge for rock or blues.

9 Easy Excursions from Dublin

Fanning out a little over 12 miles in each direction, Dublin's southern and northern suburbs offer a variety of interesting sights and experiences, all easy to reach via public transportation or rental car.

Dublin's Southern Suburbs ————————————————

WHAT TO SEE & DO

Stretching southward from Ballsbridge, Dublin's prime southern suburbs, such as Dun Laoghaire, Dalkey, and Killiney, are on the edge of Dublin Bay. They offer lovely seaside views and walks. There is also a long promenade and bucolic park at Dun Laoghaire.

Thanks to DART service, these towns are very accessible from downtown Dublin. They are mostly residential areas, so there is a good selection of restaurants, and there are fine places to stay. A hillside overlooking Dublin Bay outside the village of Killiney is the setting for the Dublin area's only authentic deluxe castle hotel, Fitzpatrick Castle (see "Where to Stay," below).

For visitors to Ireland who travel by ferry from Holyhead, Wales, the first glimpse of Ireland they see is the port of Dun Laoghaire. Many people like it so much that they decide to stay and base themselves here, commuting into downtown Dublin each day.

The prime visitor attraction is the Joyce Tower, Sandycove, Co. Dublin (☎ **280-9265** or **280-8571**). Sitting on the edge of Dublin Bay about six miles south of the city center, this 40-ft. granite monument is one of a series of martello towers built in 1804 to withstand a threatened invasion by Napoleon.

The tower's greatest claim to fame, however, is that it was inhabited in 1904 by James Joyce, as the guest of Oliver Gogarty, who had rented the tower from the Army for an annual fee of £8 ($12). Joyce, in turn, made the tower the setting for the first chapter of his famous novel *Ulysses* and it has been known as Joyce's Tower ever since. Its collection of Joycean memorabilia includes letters, documents, first and rare editions, personal possessions, and photographs. Admission is £1.90 ($2.85) adults, £1.50 ($2.25) seniors and students, £1 ($1.50) children ages 3–11. It's open from April through October, Monday through Saturday from 10am to 1pm and from 2 to 5pm, Sunday from 2 to 6pm. To get there, take the DART to Sandycove Station or bus no. 8.

WHERE TO STAY

Expensive/Moderate

⭐ **Fitzpatrick's Castle,** Killiney Hill Road, Killiney, Co. Dublin. ☎ **01/284-0700.** Fax 01/285-0207. 88 rms (all with bath). TV TEL **Transportation:** DART to Dalkey Station or bus no. 59.

Rates: £70–£91.50 ($105–$137.25) single, £91.50–£115 ($137.25–$172.50) double. Service charge 15%. AE, CB, DC, MC, V.

With a fanciful Victorian facade of turrets, towers, and battlements, this restored 1741 gem is an ideal choice for those who want to live like royalty. A 15-minute drive from the center of the city, it is situated between the villages of Dalkey and Killiney, on nine acres of gardens and hilltop grounds, with romantic vistas of Dublin Bay. Two generations of the Fitzpatrick family pamper guests with 20th-century comforts in a regal setting of medieval suits of armor, Louis XIV–style furnishings, Irish antiques, original oil paintings, and specially woven shamrock-pattern green carpet. Most of the guest rooms have four-poster or canopy beds, and many have balconies with sweeping views of Dublin and the surrounding countryside. In spite of its size and exacting standards, the castle never fails to exude a friendly family-run atmosphere.

Dining/Entertainment: Choices include a Victorian-style French/Irish restaurant known as Truffles; the Castle Grill for informal meals; the Cocktail Bar for a relaxing drink in a posh setting, and The Dungeon for a pub/nightclub atmosphere.

Services: 24-hour room service, concierge, laundry service, courtesy minibus service to downtown and to the airport.

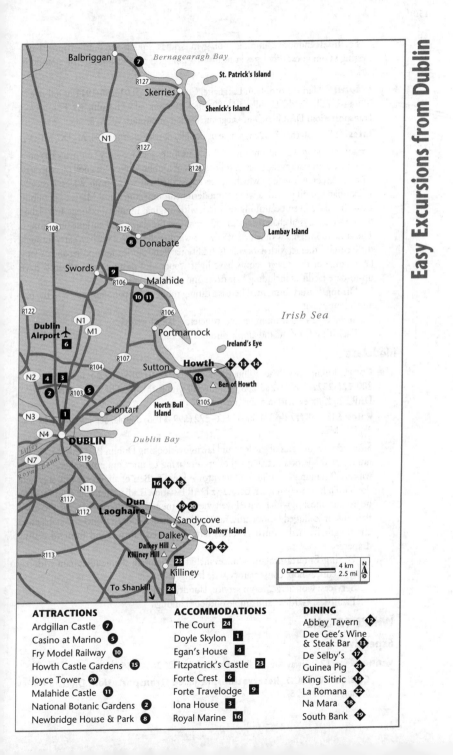

Easy Excursions from Dublin

ATTRACTIONS

Ardgillan Castle **7**
Casino at Marino **5**
Fry Model Railway **10**
Howth Castle Gardens **15**
Joyce Tower **20**
Malahide Castle **11**
National Botanic Gardens **2**
Newbridge House & Park **8**

ACCOMMODATIONS

The Court **24**
Doyle Skylon **1**
Egan's House **4**
Fitzpatrick's Castle **23**
Forte Crest **6**
Forte Travelodge **9**
Iona House **3**
Royal Marine **16**

DINING

Abbey Tavern **12**
Dee Gee's Wine & Steak Bar **13**
De Selby's **17**
Guinea Pig **21**
King Sitiric **14**
La Romana **22**
Na Mara **18**
South Bank **19**

Facilities: Indoor swimming pool, gym, saunas, squash and tennis courts; hairdressing salon; guest privileges at nearby 18-hole golf course; and extensive outdoor parking.

Royal Marine, Marine Road, Dun Laoghaire, Co. Dublin. ☎ **01/280-1911** or toll-free **800/44-UTELL** in the U.S. Fax 01/280-1089. 104 rms (all with bath). TV TEL **Transportation:** DART to Dun Laoghaire Station or bus nos. 7, 7A, 8.
Rates: £98–£150 ($147–$225) single or double. Service charge 15%. AE, DC, MC, V.

A tradition along the seafront since 1865, this four- and five-story landmark sits on a hill overlooking the harbor, seven miles south of Dublin City. It's a good place to stay for ready access to the ferry which travels across the Irish Sea to/from Wales. Basically a Georgian building, with a wing of modern bedrooms, the Royal Marine has public areas that have been beautifully restored, with original moulded ceilings and elaborate cornices, crystal chandeliers, marble-mantled fireplaces, and antique furnishings. The guest rooms, many of which offer wide-windowed views of the bay, carry through the Georgian theme, with dark woods, traditional floral fabrics, four-poster and canopy beds; some of the newer rooms have light woods and pastel tones. All units have up-to-date facilities including hair dryer and garment press.

Dining/Entertainment: There is a dining room with a panoramic view of the bay and a lounge bar.
Services: 24-hour room service, concierge, laundry service.
Facilities: Garden, and ample outdoor parking.

Moderate

The Court, Killiney Bay Road, Killiney, Co. Dublin. ☎ **01/285-1622** or toll free **800/221-2222.** Fax 01/285-2085. 86 rms (all with bath). TV TEL **Transportation:** DART to Killiney Station or bus no. 59.
Rates: £48–£58 ($72–$87) single, £66–£72 ($99–$108) double. Service charge 12.5%. AE, DC, MC, V.

Situated on four acres of gardens and lawns overlooking Dublin Bay, this three-story multigabled Victorian-style hotel offers a relaxing country inn atmosphere, yet it is within 20 minutes (12 miles) of downtown Dublin. Best of all, guests who stay here don't even have to rent a car, because a DART station is adjacent to the grounds. The bedrooms, most of which have lovely views of the bay, are decorated with Victorian flair, full of scalloped headboards, tasseled lampshades, Queen Anne–style tables and chairs, gilt-framed paintings, brass lamps, quilted fabrics, and floor-to-ceiling drapery.

Dining/Entertainment: Choices include a Victorian-theme restaurant with bay views, a coffee shop, conservatory-style lounge bar.
Services: Concierge, room service, laundry service.
Facilities: Gardens and ample outdoor parking.

WHERE TO DINE

Expensive

Guinea Pig, 17 Railway Rd., Dalkey, Co. Dublin. ☎ **285-9055.**
Cuisine: SEAFOOD. **Reservations:** Required. **Transportation:** DART to Dalkey Station or bus no. 8.

Prices: Set lunch £12.95 ($19.43); dinner appetizers £3–£8 ($4.50–$12), dinner main courses £11–£21 ($16.50–$31.50). AE, DC, MC, V.
Open: Sun lunch noon–3pm; Mon–Sat dinner 6–11:30pm.

Don't worry about the name of this restaurant; there is absolutely nothing experimental about the way guests are treated here. Emphasizing whatever is freshest and in season, the menu often includes a signature dish called symphony de la mer (a potpourri of fish and crustaceans), lobster newburg, crab au gratin, steak au poivre, roast stuffed pork, and rack of lamb. The culinary domain of chef-owner Mervyn Stewart, former Dalkey mayor, it is decorated in a stylish Irish country motif with Victorian touches. The early bird menu offers exceptional value, served between 6 and 8pm.

⭐ **Na Mara,** 1 Harbour Rd., Dun Laoghaire, Co. Dublin. ☎ **280-6767.**
Cuisine: SEAFOOD. **Reservations:** Recommended. **Transportation:** DART to Dun Laoghaire Station or bus nos. 7, 7A, 8.
Prices: Set lunch £15 ($22.50); dinner appetizers £2.95–£9.95 ($4.43–14.93), entrees £12–£29.50 ($18–$44.25). AE, DC, MC, V.
Open: Mon–Sat lunch 12:30–2:30pm and dinner 7–10:30pm.

Housed in a former Victorian railway station, this elegant eatery is located next to the ferry dock overlooking Dublin Bay and the Irish Sea. As its name (Na Mara means "of the sea") implies, it has a mostly seafood menu, with such dishes as lobster thermidor, sole bonne femme, prawns flamed in orange Curaçao and lobster sauce, or baked salmon in pastry. For those who prefer meat, there is always prime filet of beef, noisettes of lamb, or escalopes of veal.

Moderate

⭐ **South Bank,** 1 Martello Terrace at Islington Avenue, Dun Laoghaire, Co. Dublin. ☎ **280-8788.**
Cuisine: IRISH/CONTINENTAL. **Reservations:** Recommended. **Transportation:** DART to Sandycove Station or bus no. 8.
Prices: Set lunch £9.95 ($14.93); dinner appetizers £1.75–£6.95 ($2.63–$10.43); dinner main courses £10–£12 ($15–$18). MC, V.
Open: Dinner Tues–Sat 6–10:30pm; lunch Sun 12:30–3pm.

On the seafront across from the waterside promenade, this cozy 50-seat candlelit restaurant is one of the few Dublin eateries that offers glimpses of the sea. A relaxing atmosphere pervades as chamber music plays in the background. The eclectic menu changes often, but usually includes such dishes as maple chicken with grapefruit and watercress; breast of turkey with bourbon and peaches; pork steak with cider, nutmeg, and apple; roast duck with Cointreau and kumquat sauce; escalope of veal with mushrooms and mustard; strips of beef with mango, chili, and ginger; and fresh salmon in a dill and light lemon sauce.

Moderate/Inexpensive

$ **DeSelby's,** 17/18 Patrick St., Dun Laoghaire. ☎ **284-1761** or **284-1762.**
Cuisine: INTERNATIONAL. **Reservations:** Recommended. **Transportation:** DART to Dun Laoghaire Station or bus nos. 7, 7A, 8, 46A.
Prices: Appetizers £1.25–£4.95 ($1.93–$7.43), lunch main courses £3.25–£4.95 ($4.88–$7.43), dinner main courses £4.95–£9.95 ($7.43–$14.93). AE, DC, MC, V.
Open: Mon–Fri 5:30–11pm, Sat noon–11pm, Sun noon–10pm.

Named after a self-styled Dun Laoghaire philosopher in a Flann O'Brien book, this restaurant is in the center of the town, just off George's Street. The decor is eclectic and fun, starting with a portrait of the mythical DeSelby in the front window and paintings by local artists on the walls. The menu offers traditional Irish stew, beef stroganoff, rack of lamb, chicken stuffed with spinach and cheese, pastas, steaks, and a half-dozen types of fresh fish, as well as American-style burgers and Irish-style mixed grills. In good weather, light meals are also served outside in a country-village setting behind the restaurant. The outdoor fare features soups, salads, and sandwiches. It's a busy spot, especially on weekends, patronized by those enjoying a day's outing at the seaport.

La Romana, Castle Street, Dalkey, Co. Dublin. ☎ 285-4569.

Cuisine: ITALIAN. **Reservations:** Required for dinner. **Transportation:** DART to Dalkey Station or bus no. 8.
Prices: Appetizers £1–£4 ($1.50–$6), dinner main courses £3.95–£9.95 ($5.93–$4.93); bar menu £1.55–£6.95 ($2.33–10.43). MC, V.
Open: Dinner Mon–Sat 5:30–11:30pm, Sun 12:30–10pm; bar food daily noon–6pm.

Housed in the front section of the historic Queens Pub in the center of town, this informal trattoria has its own open kitchen, a contrast to the usual pub grub. The menu concentrates on pastas and pizzas, but also lists chicken breast stuffed with cream cheese and chives or pork escalope in Italian sherry with cream and mushroom sauce. In addition, there are daily specials and an interesting selection of antipasti. To create an Italian mood Pavarotti usually sings in the background (on disk only, thus far).

PUBS

P. McCormack & Sons, 67 Lower Mounttown Rd., off York Road, Dun Laoghaire. ☎ 280-5519.

If you rent a car and head toward the city's southern seaside suburbs, this is a great pub (with its own parking lot) to stop for refreshment, with a choice of three different atmospheres. The main section has an Old World feeling, with globe lamps, stained-glass windows, books and jugs on the shelves, and lots of nooks and crannies for a quiet drink. For a change of pace, there is a skylit and plant-filled conservatory area where classical music fills the air, and outdoors you'll find a festive courtyard beer garden. The pub grub here is top notch, with a varied buffet table of lunchtime salads and meats.

The Purty Kitchen, Old Dunleary Rd., Dun Laoghaire, Co. Dublin. ☎ 284-3576.

Housed in a building that dates back to 1728, this old pub has a homey atmosphere with open brick fireplaces, cozy alcoves, a large fish mural and pub poster art on the walls. Although there is often free Irish traditional music in the main bar area, many nights there is also blues and rock music upstairs in The Loft.
Open: Traditional music, schedule varies; live blues and rock Wed–Sat from 9pm, dance club with DJ Sun from 9pm.
Admission: Free for traditional music; £4–£5 ($6–$7.50) for blues and rock in The Loft.

The Queen's Pub, 12/13 Castle St., Dalkey, Co. Dublin. ☎ 285-4569.

If you venture south of the city, this is a good pub to know, in a delightful seaside suburb with palm trees. Situated on the main street, it has a decidedly 18th-century atmosphere, with dark-wood beams and pillars; oak and pine furnishings; floors of polished tile, rough timber, and coarse flag; and an authentic collection of memorabilia from copper jugs and urns, to lanterns and nautical bric-a-brac, all scattered amid nooks and alcoves and on fireplace mantles. In warm weather, seating is outside on an umbrella-shaded patio.

Dublin's Northern Suburbs

WHAT TO SEE & DO

Dublin's northern suburbs are best known as the home of Dublin International Airport, but there is also a delightful assortment of castles, historic buildings, and gardens to draw visitors. In addition, the residential suburbs of Drumcondra and Glasnevin offer many good lodgings en route to/from the airport.

Further north, the picturesque suburb of Howth is synonymous with panoramic views of Dublin Bay, beautiful hillside gardens, and many fine seafood restaurants. Best of all, it is easily reached via the DART.

Casino at Marino, Malahide Road, Marino, Dublin 3. ☎ 833-1618.

Standing on a gentle rise three miles north of the city center, this 18th-century building is considered to be one of the finest garden temples in Europe. Designed in the Franco-Roman style of neoclassicism by Scottish architect Sir William Chambers, it was constructed in the garden of Lord Charlemont's house by the English sculptor Simon Vierpyl. Work commenced in 1762 and it took 15 years to build. It is particularly noteworthy for its elaborate stone carvings and compact structure, which makes it appear to be a single story from the outside when it is actually two stories tall.

Admission: £1.50 ($2.25) adults, £1 ($1.50) seniors, 60p ($90¢) students and children under 12.

Open: Mid-June to mid-Sept, daily 10am–6:30pm. **Transportation:** Bus nos. 20A, 20B, 27, 27A, 32A, 42, 42B.

★ **Malahide Castle,** Malahide, Co. Dublin. ☎ 845-2337.

Situated about eight miles north of Dublin, Malahide is one of Ireland's most historic castles, founded in the 12th century by Richard Talbot and occupied by his descendants until 1976. Fully restored, the interior of the building is the setting for a *Wonderful* comprehensive collection of Irish furniture, dating from the 17th through the 19th centuries, and the walls are lined with one-of-a-kind Irish historical portraits and tableaux on loan from the National Gallery. The furnishings and art reflect life in and near the house over the past eight centuries.

After touring the house, you can can explore the 270-acre estate, which includes 20 acres of prized gardens with more than 5,000 species of plants and flowers. The Malahide grounds also contain the Fry Model Railway Museum (see below).

Admission: £2.65 ($3.98) adults, £2 ($3) seniors and students, £1.30 ($1.95) children under 12; gardens free.

Open: Apr–Oct, Mon–Fri 10am–5pm, Sat 11am–6pm, Sun 2–6pm; Nov–March, Mon–Fri 10am–5pm, Sat–Sun 2–5pm; gardens May–Sept daily, 10am–6pm. **Transportation:** Bus no. 42.

★ **Newbridge House and Park,** Donabate, Co. Dublin. ☎ 843-6534.

Situated 12 miles north of Dublin, this country mansion dates back to 1740 and was once the home of Dr. Charles Cobbe, an Archbishop of Dublin. Occupied by the

Cobbe family until 1984, the house is a showcase of family memorabilia such as hand-carved furniture, portraits, daybooks, and dolls, as well as a museum of objects collected on world travels. The Great Drawing Room, in its original state, is reputed to be one of the finest Georgian interiors in Ireland. The house sits on 350 acres, laid out with picnic areas and walking trails. The grounds also include a 20-acre working Victorian farm, stocked with farmyard animals.

Admission: £2.35 ($3.53) adults, £2 ($3) seniors and students, £1.25 ($2.93) children under 12.

Open: Apr–Oct, Tues–Fri 10am–1pm and 2–5pm, Sat 11am–6pm, Sun 2–6pm; Nov–March, Sat–Sun 2–5pm. **Transportation:** Bus no. 33B.

National Botanic Gardens, Botanic Road, Glasnevin, Dublin 9. ☎ 837-7596.

Established by the Royal Dublin Society in 1795 on a rolling 50-acre expanse of land north of the city center, this is Dublin's horticultural showcase. The attractions include more than 20,000 different plants and cultivars, a Great Yew Walk, a bog garden, water garden, rose garden, and an herb garden. There are also a variety of Victorian-style glass houses of tropical plants and exotic species.

Admission: Free.

Open: May–Sept, Mon–Sat 9am–6pm, Sun 11am–6pm; Oct–Apr, Mon–Sat 10am–4:30pm, Sun 11am–4:30pm. **Transportation:** Bus nos. 13, 19, 34, 34A.

The Fry Model Railway Museum, Malahide, Co. Dublin. ☎ 845-2758.

Housed on the grounds of Malahide Castle, this is an exhibit of rare hand-made models of more than 300 Irish trains, from the introduction of rail to the present. The trains were built in the 1920s and 1930s by Cyril Fry, a railway engineer and draughtsman. The complex includes items of Irish railway history dating back 1834, and models of stations, bridges, trams, buses, barges, boats, the River Liffey and the Hill of Howth.

Admission: £2.25 ($3.38) adults, £1.60 ($2.40) seniors and students, £1.20 ($1.80) children under 12.

Open: Apr–Sept 10am–1pm and 2–5pm, Sat 11am–1pm and 2–6pm, Sun 2–6pm; Jul–Aug, Fri 10am–1pm and 2–5pm; Oct–Mar Sat–Sun 2–5pm. **Transportation:** Bus no. 42.

Howth Castle Gardens, Howth, Co. Dublin. ☎ 832-2624.

Set on a steep slope about eight miles north of downtown, this 30-acre garden was first planted in 1875 and is best known for its two thousand varieties of rhododendron. Peak bloom time is in May and June. Note: the castle on the grounds is not open to the public.

Admission: Free.

Open: Daily 8am–sunset. **Transportation:** DART to Howth Station or bus no. 31

Ardgillan Castle & Park, Balbriggan, Co. Dublin. ☎ 849-2212.

Located between Balbriggan and Skerries, north of Malahide, this recently restored 18th-century castellated country house sits right on the edge of the Irish coastline. The house, home of the Taylour family until 1962, was built in 1738, and has some fine period furnishings and antiques. But the real draw here is the setting, right on the edge of the Irish Sea, with miles of walking paths and coastal views, as well as a rose garden and herb garden.

Admission: House, £2.50 ($3.75) adults, £1.50 ($2.25) seniors and students; park free.

Open: House Apr–Sept Tues–Sun 11am–6pm; Oct–Dec and Feb–Mar Wed and Sun 11am–4:30pm. Closed: Jan. Park year-round daily 10am–dusk. **Transportation:** Bus no. 33.

WHERE TO STAY

Moderate

Forte Crest, Airport Road, Dublin Airport, Co. Dublin. ☎ **01/844-4211** or toll free **800/225-5843** from U.S. Fax 01/842-5874. 195 rms (all with bath). TV TEL **Transportation:** Bus nos. 41, 41C; Express Airport Coach.

Rates: £73–£92 ($109.50–$138) single, £85–£94 ($127.50–$141) double. Service charge 15%. AE, DC, MC, V.

Formerly known as the Dublin International Hotel, this is the main lodging on the grounds of the airport, situated seven miles north of city center. With a modern three-story brick facade, it has a sunken skylit lobby, with a central courtyard surrounded by guest rooms. The bedrooms are contemporary and functional, with windows looking out into the courtyard or toward distant mountain vistas. Each unit is equipped with standard furnishings plus full-length mirror, hair dryer, coffee/tea making equipment, and garment press.

Dining/Entertainment: Choices include the Garden Room restaurant for Irish cuisine, Sampans for Chinese food (dinner only), and the Heritage Bar for drinks and snacks.

Services: 24-hour room service, concierge, valet laundry service, and courtesy coach between hotel/airport.

Facilities: Gift shop and outdoor parking.

Doyle Skylon, Upper Drumcondra Road, Dublin 9. ☎ **01/837-9121** or toll-free **800/42-DOYLE** or **800/44-UTELL** in the U.S. Fax 01/837-2778. 92 rms (all with bath). TV TEL **Transportation:** Bus nos. 3, 11, 16, 41, 41A, 41B.

Rates: £66–£94 ($99–$141) single, £85–£94 ($127.50–$141) double. Service charge is 15%. AE, CB, DC, MC, V.

With a modern five-story facade of glass and concrete, this hotel stands out on the city's north side, situated midway between downtown and the airport. Set on its own grounds in a residential neighborhood next to a college, it is just ten minutes from the heart of the city via several major bus routes that stop outside the door. The guest rooms have all the latest amenities, with colorful Irish-made furnishings.

Dining/Entertainment: For full-service dining, it's The Rendezvous Room, a modern plant-filled restaurant with an Irish/Continental menu; and for drinks, try the Joycean pub.

Services: Concierge, room service, laundry service.

Facilities: Gift shop and ample outdoor parking.

Inexpensive

Egan's House, 7/9 Iona Park, Glasnevin, Dublin 9. ☎ **01/830-3611.** Fax 01/830-3312. 23 rms (all with bath). TV TEL **Transportation:** Bus nos. 3, 11, 13, 13A, 19, 19A, 16, 41, 41A, 41B.

Rates: £20–£26.50 ($30–$39.75) single, £35–£43 ($52.50–$64.50) double. Service charge 10%. MC, V.

Located on the north side of the city between Botanic and Lower Drumcondra Roads, this two-story red-brick Victorian guesthouse is in the center of a pleasant residential neighborhood, within walking distance of the Botanic Gardens. Operated by John and Betty Egan, it offers bedrooms in a variety of sizes and styles including ground-floor rooms, with such conveniences as hair dryers and coffee/tea makers. The comfortable public rooms have an assortment of traditional dark woods, brass fixtures, and antiques. Car parking provided for guests.

Forte Travelodge, Pinnock Hill, Swords, Co. Dublin. ☎ **01/840-9233** or toll free **800/CALL-THF** in the U.S. 40 rms (all with bath). TV **Transportation:** Bus nos. 41, 43.

Rates: £31.95 ($47.53) per room. No service charge. AE, MC, V.

Located about ten miles north of downtown and 1.5 miles north of Dublin airport on the main N1 Dublin/Belfast Road, this new two-story motel offers no-frills accommodations at rock-bottom prices. The guest rooms, each with double bed, sofa bed, and private bath/shower, are basic but can sleep up to four people for one flat rate. The red-brick exterior blends nicely with the Irish countryside and the interior is clean and modern. Public areas are limited to a spartan reception area, public pay phone, and adjacent budget-priced Little Chef chain restaurant and lounge.

Iona House, 5 Iona Park, Glasnevin, Dublin 9. ☎ **01/830-6217.** Fax 01/830-6732. 11 rms (all with bath). TV TEL **Transportation:** Bus nos. 3, 11, 13, 13A, 19, 19A, 16, 41, 41A, 41B.

Rates (including full breakfast): £23–£27.50 ($39.50–$40.25) single, £46–£55 ($69–$82.50) double. No service charge. MC, V. Closed Dec–Jan.

A sitting room with a glowing open fireplace, chiming clocks, brass fixtures, and dark wood furnishings sets a tone of welcome for guests to this two-story red-brick Victorian home. Built around the turn of the century and operated as a guesthouse since 1963 by John and Karen Shouldice, it is located in a residential neighborhood, midway between Lower Drumcondra and Botanic Roads, within walking distance of the Botanic Gardens. The guest rooms offer modern hotel-style appointments and contemporary Irish-made furnishings. Facilities include a lounge, small patio, and outdoor parking for guests.

WHERE TO DINE

Very Expensive/Expensive

⭐ **King Sitric**, East Pier, Howth, Co. Dublin. ☎ **832-5235.**
Cuisine: SEAFOOD. **Reservations:** Required. **Transportation:** DART to Howth Station or bus no. 31.
Prices: Summer lunch main courses £5–£15.50 ($7.50–$23.17); dinner appetizers £2.80–£12 ($4.20–$18); dinner main courses £12.50–£21 ($18.75–$30.50). AE, DC, MC, V.
Open: Mon–Sat 6:30–11pm; July–Aug Mon–Sat noon–3pm.

Situated on the bay nine miles north of Dublin, this long-established restaurant is housed in a 150-year-old former harbormaster's building. On a fine summer's evening, it is well worth a trip out here to savor the finest of local fish and crustaceans, prepared and presented in a creative way. Entrees range from filet of sole with lobster mousse, and filet of brill Deauvillaise (in a cream and wine sauce), to grilled monkfish on a bed of aubergines (eggplant) topped with tomato coulis; lobster from the tank;

and Howth fish ragout, a signature combination of the best of the day's catch. For those who prefer meat, there is always a prime sirloin steak. In the summer months, an informal lunch is available in an upstairs oyster bar setting. Choices include oysters on the half-shell, plates of fresh Howth crab or Dublin Bay prawns, lobster mayonnaise, fisherman's platters, marinated or smoked salmon, or home-cooked ham.

Expensive/Moderate

Abbey Tavern, Abbey Street, Howth, Co. Dublin. ☎ 839-0307.

Cuisine: SEAFOOD/INTERNATIONAL. **Reservations:** Recommended. **Transportation:** DART to Howth Station or bus no. 31.
Prices: Appetizers £2.75–£8.25 ($4.13–$12.38); main courses £10.50–£18.50 ($15.75–$28.25). AE, DC, MC, V.
Open: Mon–Sat dinner 7–11pm.

Well known for its nightly traditional music ballad sessions, this old-world tavern also has a full-service restaurant upstairs. Although the menu changes by season, entrees often include such dishes as scallops Ty Ar Mor (with mushrooms, prawns, and cream sauce); filet of sole with prawns; crêpes fruit de mer; poached salmon; sole on the bone; duck with orange and Curaçao sauce; steak au poivre; and veal à la creme. After a meal, diners are welcome to descend to the lower level and join in the audience for some lively Irish music.

Moderate/Inexpensive

Dee Gee's Wine & Steak Bar, Harbour Road, Howth, Co. Dublin. ☎ 839-2641.

Cuisine: IRISH. **Reservations:** Recommended on weekends. **Transportation:** DART to Howth Station or bus no. 31.
Prices: Appetizers £1.50–£3.25 ($2.25–$4.88), lunch main courses £1.50–£4.50 ($2.25–$7.25), dinner main courses £4.45–£8.95 ($6.68–$13.43). MC, V.
Open: Daily lunch 12:30–2pm, dinner 6–10pm.

If you plan a day's outing at Howth, don't miss this place. Located opposite the local DART station and overlooking Dublin Bay across from the harbour, this informal seaside spot is ideal for a cup of coffee, a snack, or a full meal. A self-service snackery by day and a more formal table-service restaurant at night, it offers seating outdoors under umbrella-shaded tables as well as inside. The entrees at dinner range from steaks and burgers to shrimp scampi, pork à la crème, breast of chicken with mushroom sauce, and vegetable lasagne. At lunchtime, soups, salads, and sandwiches are featured. Relax here and watch all the activities of Howth from a front-row seat.

5

The East Coast

RIMMED BY THE IRISH SEA, IRELAND'S EAST COAST BECKONS VISITORS STAYING IN Dublin's Fair City to venture forth from the hustle and bustle and to savor the Irish countryside, for a few hours or for a few days.

Stretching inland to the south, west, and north of the Irish capital, this area forms a crescent around Dublin. To the south—the most traveled direction for visitors—County Wicklow presents a verdant and varied panorama of gardens, lakes, mountains, and seascapes, while to the east sit the flat plains of County Kildare, Ireland's prime horse country. Rounding out the crescent in the north are the counties of Meath and Louth, a small area packed with historic sites. No matter which way you go, Ireland's east coast will enchant you.

1 County Wicklow/The Garden of Ireland

County Wicklow extends from Bray, 12 miles S of Dublin to Arklow, 40 miles S of Dublin

GETTING THERE • By Train   Irish Rail (☎ 01/836-3333) provides daily train service between Dublin and Bray and Wicklow.

• By Bus   Bus Eireann (☎ 01/836-6111) operates daily express bus service to Arklow, Bray, and Wicklow towns. Both Bus Eireann and Gray Line Tours (☎ 01/661-9666) offer seasonal (May to September) sightseeing tours to Glendalough, Wicklow, and Powerscourt Gardens.

• By Car   Take N 11 south from Dublin City and follow turn-off signs for major attractions.

ESSENTIALS • Tourist Information   For information about County Wicklow, contact the Midlands-East Regional Tourism Organization, Ltd., Dublin Road, Mullingar, Co. Westmeath (☎ 044/48761); or the Wicklow Tourist Office, Fitzwilliam Square, Wicklow, Co. Wicklow (☎ 0404/96117). Both are open year round, Monday through Friday from 9:30am to 5pm and Saturday from 9:30am to 1pm, with extended hours in the summer months. Seasonal offices are also located in the following towns: Arklow (☎ 0404/32484) and Bray (☎ 01/286-7128), both open mid-June to August; and Laragh (☎ 0404/45482), open July and August.

• Area Code   Telephone numbers in the County Wicklow region use the codes 0404, 045, or 01.

The borders of County Wicklow start just a dozen or so miles south of downtown Dublin, and within this county is some of Ireland's best rural scenery. If you're based in Dublin, you can easily spend a day or afternoon in Wicklow and still return to Dublin in time for dinner and the theater, but you'll probably want to linger overnight at one of the many fine country inns.

Aptly described as the Garden of Ireland, Wicklow is a collage of tree-lined country lanes and nature trails, sloping hills and domed granite mountains, gentle glens and wooded valleys, endless lakes and rivers, and sandy seacapes. Welcoming visitors are villages with fanciful names like Annamoe, Laragh, Ballinalea, Blessington, Baltinglass, Glencree, Woodenbridge, and Hollywood—yes, Wicklow even has a Hollywood. Equally alluring are windswept mountain passes called Sally Gap, the Devil's Punch Bowl, Glenmalure, and Glen of the Downs.

What's Special About the East Coast

Monuments
- Hill of Tara, Co. Meath, its grassy mounds are remembered as the ancient religious and cultural capital of Ireland.

Buildings
- Killruddery House, Co. Wicklow, modeled after London's Crystal Palace.
- Castletown House, Co. Kildare, a showcase of Georgian furniture and paintings.

Parks/Gardens
- Powerscourt Gardens, Co. Wicklow, 1,000 acres of beautiful plantings, ornamental lakes, and statuary.
- Mount Usher Gardens, Co. Wicklow, with over 5,000 species of rare trees and plants.

For the Kids
- Newgrange Farm, Co. Meath, a working farm with aviaries of exotic birds and rare Jacob sheep.

Ace Attractions
- Glendalough, Co. Wicklow, the 6th-century monastic city of St. Kevin.
- Newgrange, Co. Meath, Ireland's version of Stonehenge.
- Irish National Stud, Co. Kildare, home of Ireland's future four-legged champions.
- The Curragh Racetrack, Co. Kildare, Ireland's Churchill Downs.

Natural Spectacles
- Great Sugar Loaf Mountain, Co. Wicklow, as it slopes to meet the Irish Sea.
- Powerscourt Waterfall, Co. Wicklow, the highest waterfall in Ireland.
- The Vale of Avoca, Co. Wicklow, immortalized by Thomas Moore.
- The Boyne River Valley, Counties Meath and Louth, the landscape where the battle that changed the course of Irish history was fought in 1690.

Shopping
- Avoca Handweavers, Co. Wicklow, Ireland's oldest hand-weaving mill dating back to 1723.

This verdant county is also home to many stately 18th-century estate houses and award-winning gardens, Ireland's third-highest mountain—Lugnaquilla (3,039 ft.)—countless lakes including the glistening Lough Luggala (also called Lough Tay) and Lough Dan, a sixth-century monastic site at Glendalough, a hand-weaving center dating back to 1723 at Avoca, and the 17th-century village of Roundwood. Situated beside the River Vartry deep in the mountains, Roundwood is said to be the highest village in Ireland (over 700 ft. above sea level).

The best way to explore Wicklow is to rent a car and follow one of two routes—either via the wide main road (N 11) that runs parallel to the Irish Sea coast, or by turning inland and traversing the twisting, scenic roads over the wooded mountains and valleys. If you are in a hurry or happen to be a beach lover, then take the main

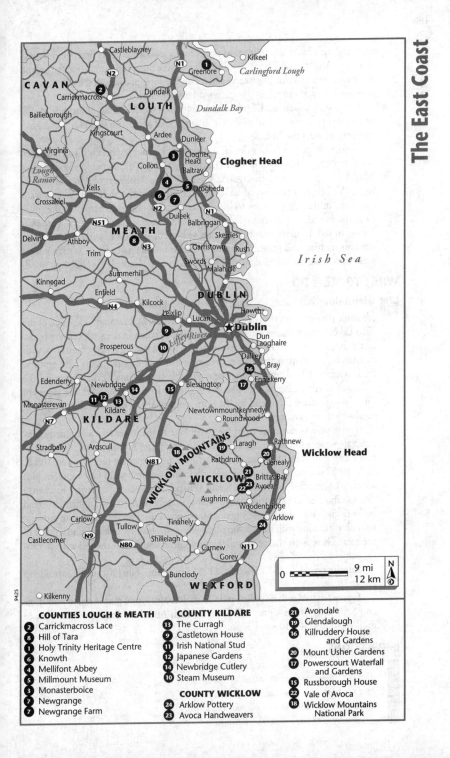

The East Coast

9425

COUNTIES LOUGH & MEATH
② Carrickmacross Lace
⑧ Hill of Tara
① Holy Trinity Heritage Centre
⑥ Knowth
④ Mellifont Abbey
⑤ Millmount Museum
③ Monasterboice
⑦ Newgrange
⑦ Newgrange Farm

COUNTY KILDARE
⑬ The Curragh
⑪ Castletown House
⑪ Irish National Stud
⑫ Japanese Gardens
⑭ Newbridge Cutlery
⑩ Steam Museum

COUNTY WICKLOW
㉔ Arklow Pottery
㉓ Avoca Handweavers

㉑ Avondale
⑲ Glendalough
⑯ Killruddery House
   and Gardens
⑳ Mount Usher Gardens
⑰ Powerscourt Waterfall
   and Gardens
⑮ Russborough House
㉒ Vale of Avoca
⑱ Wicklow Mountains
   National Park

road, and turn off, as time allows, to explore such seaside resorts as Bray, Greystones, Wicklow, Arklow, and Brittas Bay. If you have more time, and want to see the best of Wicklow, then head for Enniskerry and follow the interior roads all the way down to Avoca, where you can rejoin the main road for Wexford.

Either way, as you head south from Dublin into the Wicklow countryside, you'll be greeted by changing views of the Great Sugar Loaf Mountain (1,654 ft.), as it gently slopes to meet the Irish Sea.

If time allows, there is one detour you may wish to take, especially if you have ever wondered about the origin of the blackthorn walking stick known commonly as a "shillelagh" (pronounced *shi-lay-lee*). About 15 miles southwest of Avoca is the village of Shillelagh. Local legend has it that the bushes of the Shillelagh Woods were cut down in the 13th century to be used as weapons in a local battle. At the time, these sturdy cudgels were called "Shillelagh sticks," and eventually, just the word *shillelagh* evolved. In more recent times, they've become symbols of authority and been used for hunting and games. Not all the trees from this part of Co. Wicklow were made into sticks, the oak roofing of Dublin's St. Patrick's Cathedral is Shillelagh wood.

WHAT TO SEE & DO

★ **Glendalough,** County Wicklow. ☎ **0404/45325** or **45352.**

It's name derived from the Irish phrase *Gleann Da Locha,* meaning "The Glen of the Two Lakes," this secluded tree-shaded setting was chosen in the sixth century by St. Kevin for a monastery. Over the centuries, it became a leading center of learning, with thousands of students from Ireland, Britain, and all over Europe. In the 12th century, St. Lawrence O'Toole was among the many abbots to follow Kevin and spread the influence of Glendalough. But, like so many early Irish religious sites, the glories of Glendalough came to an end by the 15th century at the hands of the plundering Anglo-Norman invaders.

Today visitors can stroll from the upper lake to the lower lake and quietly contemplate what it must have been like in St. Kevin's day. Although much of the monastic city is in ruins, the remains do include a nearly perfect round tower, 103 ft. high and 52 ft. around the base, as well as hundreds of time-worn Celtic crosses, plus a variety of churches including St. Kevin's chapel, often called St. Kevin's Kitchen, a fine specimen of an early Irish barrel-vaulted oratory, with its own miniature round belfry rising from a stone roof. A new visitor center at the entrance to the site provides helpful orientation with exhibits on the archaeology, history, folklore, and wildlife of the area. There is no charge to walk around Glendalough, but there is a fee to view the exhibits.

Admission: £1.50 ($2.25) adults, £1 ($1.50) seniors, 60p (90¢) children/students under 16.

Open: Mid–Mar to mid–Apr and Oct daily 10am–5pm; mid–April to mid–June and Sept daily 10am–7pm; mid-June through Aug daily 9am–6:30pm; Nov to mid-Mar Tues–Sun 10am–4:30pm.

IMPRESSIONS

Still south I went and west and south again,
Through Wicklow from the morning till the night,
And far from cities, and the sites of men,
Lived with the sunshine and the moon's delight.
—John Synge (1871–1909), "Prelude"

Powerscourt Waterfall and Gardens, off main Dublin/Wicklow Road (N 11), Enniskerry, Co. Wicklow. ☎ 01/286-7676.

With Italian and Japanese themes, the gardens of this 1,000-acre estate is filled with splendid statuary, ornamental lakes, decorative iron-work, herbaceous borders, and a pet cemetery. Herds of deer roam a park. Until 1974, a fine 18th-century manor house stood on the grounds, then a fire gutted it. Future plans call for it to be rebuilt. Nearby (4 miles) is the highest waterfall in both Ireland and Britain. A cascade of water tumbles down from a 400-ft. cliff. Nestled beside the River Dargle, 12 miles south of Dublin.

Admission: Gardens £2.80 ($4.20) adults, £2.50 ($3.75) seniors and students, £1.70 ($2.55) children ages 5–16; free for children under 5; waterfall £1.50 ($2.25) adults, £1 ($1.50) seniors and students, 80p ($1.20) children ages 5–16; free for children under 5.

Open: Gardens, Mar–Oct daily 9:30am–5:30pm; waterfall, summer daily 9:30am–7pm, winter 10:30am–dusk.

★ **Wicklow Mountains National Park,** Glendalough, Co. Wicklow. ☎ 0404/45425.

As of this writing, a large area of County Wicklow is being designated as a new national park. The core area of the park is centered around Glendalough, including the Glendalough Valley and Glendalough Wood Nature Reserves. An information point is found at the Upper Lake at Glendalough. Completion of the park is expected by 1996. Year-round opening times and admission charges will be announced then.

Admission: To be announced.

Open: Late Apr to late Aug daily 10am–6:30pm; Sept Sat–Sun 10am–6:30pm.

Avondale House & Avondale Forest Park, Rathdrum, County Wicklow. ☎ 0404/46111.

In a fertile valley between Glendalough and the Vale of Avoca, this is the former home of Charles Stewart Parnell (1846–1891), one of the country's great political leaders. Built in 1779, the house is filled with Parnell memorabilia. The surrounding 523-acre estate, Avondale Forest Park, has been developed into a training school for the Irish Forest and Wildlife Service. The park is considered as the cradle of modern Irish forestry. Signposted nature trails lead alongside the Avondale River.

Admission: £2.50 adults ($3.75), £1.50 ($2.25) seniors and children under 16.

Open: Year–round daily 11am–5pm.

Killruddery House & Gardens, off the main Dublin/Wicklow Road (N 11), Killruddery, Bray, Co. Wicklow. ☎ 01/286-3405.

This estate has been the seat of the Earl of Meath since 1618. The original part of the mansion dates from 1820; the Victorian conservatory was modeled after the Crystal Palace in London. With a lime avenue, foreign trees and exotic shrubs, twin canals stretching for more than 500 ft., a round pond with fountains that's edged with beech hedges, and a sylvan theater—the gardens are the highlight here. It's said they have the only surviving 17th-century layout in Ireland.

Admission: House and garden tour £2.50 ($3.75) adults, £1.50 ($2.25) seniors and students over 12; garden only £1 ($1.50) adults, 50p (75¢) seniors and students over 12.

Open: May, June, and Sept daily 1–5pm.

⭐ **Mount Usher Gardens,** on the main Dublin/Wicklow Road (N 11), Ashford, Co. Wicklow. ☎ 0404/40116 or 0404/40205.

Encompassing 20 acres beside the River Vartry, this sylvan site is distinguished for its collection of more than 5,000 species of rare trees and plants, gathered from all parts of the world. Growing here are spindle trees from China, North American swamp cypress, and Burmese juniper tress, as well as fiery rhododendrons, fragrant eucalyptus trees, meandering green creepers, pink magnolias, and snowy camellias.

Admission: £2.80 ($4.20) adults, £1.80 ($2.70) seniors, students, and children ages 5–12.

Open: Mar 17–Oct Mon–Sat 10:30am–6pm, Sun 11am–6pm.

Russborough, off N81, Blessington, Co. Wicklow. ☎ 045/65239.

Ensconced in this Palladian house (1740–50) is the world famous Beit Art Collection, with paintings by Vernet, Guardi, Bellotto, Gainsborough, Rubens, and Reynolds. The house is furnished with European pieces and decorated with bronzes, tapestries, and some fine Francini plasterwork. It's 25 miles southwest of Dublin.

Admission: £2.50 ($3.75) adults, £1.50 ($2.25) seniors and students.

Open: Easter–May and Sept–Oct Sun 10:30am–5:30pm; June–Aug daily 10:30am–5:30pm.

Vale of Avoca, Route 755, Avoca, County Wicklow.

Basically a peaceful riverbank, the Vale of Avoca was immortalized in the writings of Thomas Moore, a 19th-century poet. It's here at the "Meeting of the Waters" that the Avonmore and Avonbeg Rivers join to form the Avoca River. It's said that the poet sat under "Tom Moore's Tree," looking for inspiration, and penned the lines: "There is not in the wide world a valley so sweet, as the vale in whose bosom the bright waters meet. . . ." The tree is a sorry sight now, as it's been picked almost bare by souvenir hunters, but the sight is worth a visit.

Admission: Free.

SPORTS & RECREATION

HORSEBACK RIDING With its secluded paths and nature trails, valleys and glens, County Wicklow is a natural territory for horseback riding. More than a dozen stables and equestrian centers offer horses for hire and instructional programs. Rates for horse hire average £10–£12 ($15–$18) per hour. Among the leading venues are Devil's Glen Equestrian Village, Ashford, Co. Wicklow (☎ 0404/40637); Calliaghstown Riding Centre, Glenmore, Blessington, Co. Wicklow (☎ 045/65538); Brennanstown Riding School, Hollybrook, Kilmacanogue, Co. Wicklow (☎ 01/286-3778); and the Laragh Trekking Centre, Laragh East, Glendalough, Co. Wicklow (☎ 0404/45282).

GOLF County Wicklow's verdant hills and dales provide lots of opportunities for golfing. Among the 18-hole courses welcoming visitors are the new Rathsallagh Golf Club, an 18-hole par-72 championship course at Dunlavin, Co. Wicklow (☎ 045/53112), with greens fees of £20 ($30) on weekdays and £29 ($43.50) on weekends; the seaside European Club, Brittas Bay, Co. Wicklow (☎ 0404/47415), a championship links with greens fees of £20 ($30) on weekdays and £25 ($37.50) on weekends; the parkland Glenmalure Golf Club, Greenane, Rathdrumm, Co. Wicklow (☎ 0404/46679), with greens fees of £12 ($18) on weekdays and £15 ($22.50) on weekends; and the Arklow Golf Club, an inland par-69 course, with greens fees of £12 ($18) on weekdays and £15 ($22.50) on weekends.

WALKING   The Wicklow Way is a signposted walking trail, following a path over the eastern flanks of the Dublin and Wicklow Mountains, the largest uninterrupted area of high ground in Ireland. The way follows sheep tracks, forest trails, old bog roads, private farmlands, and a wildlife area. An outline of the route is available from any Irish Tourist Office.

SAVVY SHOPPING

County Wicklow offers a wide array of wonderful craft centers and workshops. Here is a small sampling:

Arklow Pottery, South Quay, Arklow, Co. Wicklow. ☎ 0402/32401.

Situated in a busy seaside town, this is Ireland's largest pottery factory, and the home of Noritake's Celt Craft and Misty Isle lines. The pottery produced here ranges from earthenware, porcelain, and bone china tableware, to decorated teapots, casseroles, and gifts—in both modern and traditional designs. Free tours are available mid-June through August with the exception of the last week of July and first two weeks of August when the factory is closed for the staff's vacation. Open daily, 9:30am–4:45pm.

⭐ **Avoca Handweavers,** Avoca, Co. Wicklow. ☎ 0402/35105 or 35284.

Dating back to 1723, this cluster of whitewashed stone buildings and a weaving mill houses the oldest surviving handweaving company in Ireland. A wide range of tweed clothing, knitwear, and accessories is produced here. The dominant tones of mauve, aqua, teal, and heather reflect the landscape of the surrounding Co. Wicklow. Visitors are welcome to watch as craftspeople weave strands of yarn that has been spun from the wool of local sheep. A retail outlet and coffee shop are located on the complex. A second outlet/shop is on the main N 11 road at Kilmacanogue, Bray, Co. Wicklow (☎ 01/286-7466). Open Monday through Friday, 9:30am to 5:30pm; Saturday and Sunday, 10am to 6pm.

Bergin Clarke Studio, The Old Schoolhouse, Ballinaclash, Rathdrum, Co. Wicklow. ☎ 0404/46385.

Stop into this little workshop and see Yvonne Bergin knitting stylish and colorful apparel using yarns from Co. Wicklow, or Brian Clarke hand-fashioning silver jewelry and giftware. Open May through September daily, 10am to 8pm; October through April, Monday through Saturday, 10am to 5:30pm.

Glendalough Craft Centre, Laragh, Co Wicklow. ☎ 0404/45156.

In a converted farmhouse, this long-established craft shop offers handcrafts from all over Ireland, such as Penrose Glass from Waterford or Bantry Pottery. Books, jewelry, and a large selection of handknits from the area are also sold. Open daily 10am–6pm.

Wicklow Fly Fishers & Lady Fishers, The Old Schoolhouse, Newtownmount-Kennedy, Co. Wicklow. ☎ 01/281-9404.

As its name implies, this shop in a converted schoolhouse stocks a wide array of men's and women's sporting clothes—quilted jackets, waterproofs, footwear, blazers, and accessories. Open Monday through Saturday from 9:30am–5:30pm, Sunday 2–6pm.

WHERE TO STAY

Expensive

⭐ **Rathsallagh House,** Dunlavin, Co. Wicklow. ☎ 045/53112 or toll free 800/223-6510 in the U.S. Fax 045/53343. 14 rms (all with bath). TV TEL

Rates (including full breakfast): £65–£130 ($97.50–$195) single, £110–£170 ($165–$255) double. No service charge. DC, MC, V. **Closed:** Dec 23–31.

On the western edge of Co. Wicklow, this rambling ivy-covered country house sits amid 530 acres of parks, woods, and farmland. The original house on the property was built between 1702 and 1704, owned by a horse-breeding family named Moody. It was burned down in the 1798 Rebellion, and the Moodys moved into the Queen Anne–style stables, which were converted into a proper residence and served as a private home until the 1950s. It was purchased in 1978 by Joe and Kay O'Flynn and opened as a country house ten years later. Each room is individually decorated and named accordingly, from the Yellow, Pink, and Blue Rooms to the Romantic, Over Arch, Loft Rooms, and so on. Most rooms have a sitting area, huge walk-in closet, window seats, and some have a Jacuzzi. All have hair dryer, coffee/tea maker, vanity/desk, good reading lamps over the bed, and antique furnishings.

Dining/Entertainment: The dining room, under the personal supervision of Kay O'Flynn, is noted for its excellent food, using local ingredients and vegetables and herbs from the garden.

Facilities: 18-hole championship golf course, indoor heated swimming pool, sauna, hard tennis court, archery, croquet, billiards, and two-acre walled garden.

Expensive/Moderate

★ **Tinakilly House,** Off the Dublin/Wexford Road, on R 750, Rathnew, Co. Wicklow. ☎ **0404/69274** or toll free **800/223-6510** from the U.S. Fax 0404/67806. 29 rms (all with bath). TV TEL

Rates (including full breakfast): £75–£95 ($112.50–$142.50) single; £100–£140 ($150–$210) double. No service charge. AE, DC, MC, V. **Closed:** Dec 23–31.

Dating from the 1870s, this was the home of Capt. Robert Charles Halpin, commander of the *Great Eastern*, who laid the first successful cable connecting Europe with America. With a sweeping central staircase said to be the twin of the one built on the ship, Tinakilly is full of seafaring memorabilia and paintings, as well as Victorian antiques. Many of the individually furnished guest rooms have views of the Irish Sea. Opened as a hotel by the Power family in 1983, it is adjacent to the Broadlough Bird Sanctuary and a seven-acre garden of beech, evergreen, eucalyptus, palm, and American redwood trees.

Dining/Entertainment: The restaurant, known for fresh fish and local game, blends country house cooking with a nouvelle cuisine influence. Vegetables, fruits, and herbs come from the house gardens, and all breads are baked fresh daily on the premises.

Moderate

Glendalough Hotel, Glendalough, Co. Wicklow. ☎ **0404/45135** or toll free **800/365-3346** in the U.S. Fax 0404/45142. 16 rms (all with bath). TV TEL

Rates (including full breakfast): £40–£43 single ($60–$64.50), £60–£66 ($90–$99) double. AE, DC, MC, V. **Closed:** Nov to mid-Mar.

If location is everything, this hotel scores high. It sits in a wooded glen at the entrance to Glendalough, beside the Glendasan River. Dating back to the 1800s, it has recently been refurbished and updated with traditional Irish furnishings and every modern comfort. Public rooms include the Glendasan Restaurant overlooking the river and the Glendalough Tavern.

⭐ **Glenview Hotel,** Glen o' the Downs, Delgany, Dublin/Wexford Road (N 11), Co. Wicklow. ☎ **01/287-3399** or toll free **800/528-1234.** Fax 01/287-7511. 42 rms (all with bath). TV TEL

Rates: £39–£49 ($58.50–$73.50) single, £60–£90 ($90–$135) double. AE, DC, MC, V. **Closed:** Nov–Feb.

With the Sugar Loaf Mountain in the background and nestled in an idyllic setting overlooking the Glen of the Downs, this hotel has been a popular stopping-off place on the main road for over 50 years. Totally refurbished and enlarged in 1993, it has a striking new yellow facade and a bright and airy contemporary interior, while still maintaining much of its traditional charm in the guest rooms and public areas. The main dining room, the Malton Room, is noted for its wooden paneling and full set of Malton prints on the walls, while the Lodge Bar and Library Lounge enjoy panoramic views of County Wicklow countryside, including the hotel's 30 acres of gardens and woodlands. At presstime, plans call for a new leisure center with indoor swimming pool and other health facilities.

Inexpensive

💲 **Vale View Hotel,** Avoca, Co. Wicklow. ☎ **0402/35236.** Fax 0404/35144. 10 rms (all with bath). TV TEL

Rates (including full breakfast): £30 ($45) single, £60 ($90) double. AE, DC, MC, V.

Set on a hillside in the heart of the Avoca valley, this small family-run hotel is a great place to get away from it all. It has a faithful following of those who enjoy relaxing amid the natural beauty of the hotel's gardens and surrounding Wicklow scenery. The decor in the public rooms is homey, filled with a local art and Parnell memorabilia, while the guest rooms have standard furnishings. There is a restaurant and bar and patio for outdoor sitting when the weather is good. Innkeepers Mahon and Maureen O'Brien provide a warm welcome.

WHERE TO DINE

Moderate

⭐ **Mitchell's,** Laragh, Glendalough, Co. Wicklow. ☎ **0404/45302.**
Cuisine: IRISH/INTERNATIONAL. **Reservations:** Recommended.
Prices: Appetizers £1.40–£2.95 ($2.10–$4.43); lunch main courses £3.95–£6.95 ($5.93–$10.43); set dinner £14.50–£16.50 ($21.75–$24.75). AE, MC, V.
Open: Daily lunch 12:30–3pm, dinner 7:30–9pm. **Closed:** Good Friday and Christmas.

A 200-year-old former schoolhouse serves as the setting for this small restaurant in a garden in sight of the mountains. The unique cut-granite facade opens to a country-kitchen atmosphere, with pine furnishings and open log-burning fireplaces. In the summer, there is seating outdoors. The menu changes daily, but often includes pork tenderloin with apple and red currants; rack of Wicklow lamb with honey and rosemary sauce; roulade of chicken and smoked salmon on a spiced saffron-scented sauce; grilled filet of sea trout with sorrel sauce; or filet of beef with red wine and mushroom sauce. All breads and scones are made on the premises, as is an assortment of ice cream.

⭐ **Roundwood Inn,** Main Street, Roundwood, Co. Wicklow. ☎ **01/282-8107** or **282-8125.**

Cuisine: IRISH/CONTINENTAL. **Reservations:** Not necessary for lunch, advised for dinner.

Prices: Appetizers £1.95–£6.95 ($2.93–$10.43); lunch main courses £1.65–£9.75 ($2.48–$14.63); dinner main courses £9.95–£15.95 ($14.93–$23.93). MC, V.

Open: Tues–Sat lunch 1–2:30pm and dinner 7:30–9:30pm.

Dating back to 1750, this old coaching inn is the focal point of an out-of-the-way spot high in the mountains called Roundwood, said to be the highest village in Ireland. The old-world atmosphere includes open log fireplaces and antique furnishings. Menu choices range from steaks and sandwiches to traditional Irish stew, fresh lobster or smoked salmon salads, oysters on the half-shell, rollmops, and pickled herrings, as well as Hungarian goulash, smoked trout, and gravlax. Food is served all day in the bar, besides the normal meal times in the restaurant. It's located in the middle of village on the main road (R755).

Inexpensive

Wicklow Heather, Laragh, County Wicklow. ☎ **0404/45157.**

Cuisine: IRISH/INTERNATIONAL. **Reservations:** Recommended on weekends.

Prices: Appetizers £1–£4 ($1.50–$6); lunch main courses £3.50–£7.95 ($4.25–$11.83); dinner main courses £8.50–£11.95 ($13.25–$17.93). AE, MC, V.

Open: Daily 9am–9pm.

Situated just down the road from the entrance to Glendalough, this little cottage is surrounded by colorful rose gardens; seating is indoors or at picnic tables outside. The menu emphasizes local favorites such as Irish stew, sausage and beans, pork chops, and mixed grills, as well as lighter international fare such as smoked trout, pâté, salads, soups, and sandwiches. Reduced-price tourist menus are also available at certain times of the day. It's located on the main street between Laragh and Glendalough.

Budget

Poppies Country Cooking, Enniskerry, Co. Wicklow. ☎ **01/282-8869.**

Cuisine: IRISH/SELF-SERVICE. **Reservations:** Not required.

Prices: All items £1.50–£3.95 ($2.25–$5.93). No credit cards.

Open: Daily 9am–7pm.

Situated in the middle of town opposite the main square, this small ten-table shopfront eatery is popular for light meals and snacks throughout the day. The menu ranges from homemade soups and salads to shepherd's pie, sausage rolls, sandwiches, quiches, and lasagne.

PUBS

Cartoon Inn, Main Street, Rathdrum, Co. Wicklow. ☎ **0404/46774.**

With walls bedecked with the work of many famous cartoonists, this cottagelike pub claims to be Ireland's only cartoon-theme pub. This is also the headquarters for Ireland's Cartoon Festival, held in late May or early June each year. Pub grub is available at lunchtime.

The Coach House, Main Street, Roundwood. ☎ **01/281-8157.**

Adorned with lots of colorful hanging flower pots on the outside, this Tudor-style inn sits in the mountains in the heart of Ireland's highest village. Dating back to 1790, it is full of local memorabilia, from old photos and agricultural posters, to antique jugs and plates. It's well worth a visit to learn about the area or for some light refreshment.

The Meetings, Avoca, County Wicklow. ☎ 0402/35226.

This Tudor-style country-cottage pub stands idyllically at the "Meeting of the Waters," associated with poet Thomas Moore. An 1889 edition of Moore's book of poems is on display. Good pub grub is served every day. Every Sunday afternoon (from 4 to 6pm), traditional Irish music wafts from an open-air ceili; admission is free.

---

2 | Counties Meath & Louth/The Boyne River Valley

30 to 50 miles north and west of Dublin

GETTING TO COUNTIES LOUTH & MEATH • By Train   Irish Rail (☎ 01/836-3333) provides daily train service between Dublin and Drogheda.

• By Bus   Bus Eireann (☎ 01/836-6111) operates daily express bus service to Slane and Navan in Co. Meath, and Collon and Drogheda in Co. Louth. Both Bus Eireann and Gray Line Tours (☎ 01/661-9666) offer seasonal (March to October) sightseeing tours to Newgrange and/or the Boyne Valley.

• By Car   Take N 1 north from Dublin City to Drogheda and then N 51 west to Boyne Valley; N 2 northwest to Slane and east on N 51 to Boyne Valley; or N 3 northwest via Hill of Tara to Navan, and then east on N 51 to Boyne Valley.

ESSENTIALS • Tourist Information   For year-round information about Counties Meath and Louth, contact the **Midland-East Regional Tourism Organization,** Clonard House, Dublin Road, Mullingar, Co. Westmeath (☎ 044/48761); or the **Dundalk Tourist Office,** Market Square, Dundalk (☎ 042/35484). Both are open Monday through Friday from 9:30am to 6pm and Saturday from 9:30am to 1pm, with slightly longer hours in the summer months. **Seasonal information offices** are also open at Newgrange (☎ 041/24274) from Easter to October and in Drogheda (☎ 041/37070) from June through August.

• Area Codes   Telephone area code for County Lough is 041 and for County Meath 042.

Less than 30 miles north of Dublin along Ireland's east coast runs the River Boyne, surrounded by the rich and fertile countryside of Counties Meath and Louth. More than any other river in the country, this meandering body of water has been at the center of Irish history.

The banks of the Boyne are lined with reminders from almost every phase of Ireland's past—from the prehistoric passage tombs of Newgrange to the storied Hill of Tara, seat of the High Kings, to the early Christian sights associated with the preachings of St. Patrick. This land was also the setting for the infamous Battle of the Boyne, when on July 1, 1690 (the 12th of July by modern calendars), King William III defeated the exiled King James II for the crown of England. If the River Boyne could talk, what a story it would tell.

County Meath/The Royal County

The southern portion of the Boyne belongs to County Meath, an area that consists almost entirely of a rich limestone plain, with verdant pasturelands and occasional low hills. Once a separate province that included neighboring County Westmeath,

Meath was usually referred to as the Royal County Meath since it was ruled by the kings of pagan and early-Christian Ireland, from the Hill of Tara near Navan.

While the chief town of County Meath is Navan, nearby Kells is better known to the traveler because of its association with the famous *Book of Kells,* the hand-illustrated gospel manuscript on display at Trinity College in Dublin.

The town of Kells, known as *Ceanannus Mor* in Gaelic (meaning "Great Residence"), was originally the site of an important sixth-century monastic settlement founded by St. Colmcille and occupied for a time by monks driven from Iona by the Vikings. *The Book of Kells* was created here, at least in part, during the ninth century. The monastery was dissolved in 1551, but remnants of buildings and high crosses can still be seen.

A focal point of County Meath is Slane, a small crossroads village and gateway to prehistoric Newgrange. Nearby is the Hill of Slane, a lofty mound (500 ft.) that overlooks one of the loveliest parts of the Boyne Valley. This hill knew its greatest moment in 433, when St. Patrick lit the paschal fire, proclaiming Christianity throughout all of Ireland.

Even though Meath is primarily an inland county, it is also blessed with a short, six-mile stretch of Irish coastline and two fine sandy beaches, Bettystown and Laytown. In County Meath, however, always be prepared to find an occasional piece of history even on the beach—it was at Bettystown in 1850 that the Tara Brooch was found. Often copied in modern jewelry designs, the brooch is one of Ireland's finest pieces of early Christian gold-filigree work embelished with amber and glass; it's on view at the National Museum in Dublin.

WHAT TO SEE & DO

★ **Hill of Tara,** off the main Dublin Road (N 3), Navan, Co. Meath. ☎ **046/25903.**
This glorious hill is best remembered as the royal seat of the High Kings in the early centuries after Christ. Every three years a *feis* (a banquet reaching the proportions of a great national assembly) was held. It's said that more than a thousand people—princes, poets, athletes, priests, druids, musicians, and jesters—celebrated for a week in a single immense hall. As the poet Thomas Moore wrote: "The harp that once through Tara's halls,/ the soul of music shed. . . . " A feis wasn't all fun, though: laws were passed, tribal disputes settled, and matters of peace and defense were decided.

If you rally to Tara's halls today, you won't see any turrets or towers, nor moats and crown jewels; in fact, you won't even see any halls. All that remains of Tara's former glories are grassy mounds and some ancient pillar stones. Tara's decline is associated with the arrival of Christianity, and the last feis was held in A.D. 560. All the wooden halls rotted long ago. Bring your imagination to visit Tara along with good walking shoes. The hill rises 300 ft. above the surrounding countryside, and the views are surely as awesome as they were 1,500 years ago.

Tara can take credit for those shamrocks seen every March 17th. It all began in the 5th century when St. Patrick preached from Tara's heights. To convert High King Laoire, the spell-binding Patrick plucked a three-leaf clover, or shamrock, from the grass and illustrated the doctrine of the Trinity. The shamrock has since become synonymous with Ireland and the Irish all over the world.

A new visitor center, with exhibits and an audio-visual presentation, is located in the old church beside the entrance to the archaelogical area.

Admission: £1 ($1.50) adults, 70p ($1.05) seniors, 40p (60¢) children and students; no access to interior.

Open: Mid–June to early Oct daily 9:30am–6:30pm; early May to mid-June daily 9am–4:30pm.

Knowth, Slane, Co. Meath. ☎ 041/24824.

Dating from the Stone Age and currently under excavation, this great mound is believed to have been a burial site for the High Kings of Ireland. Archaeological evidence points to occupation from 3000 B.C. to A.D. 1200. Located one mile northwest of Newgrange between Drogheda and Slane, Knowth is more complex than Newgrange (see below), with two passage tombs, surrounded by another 17 smaller satellite tombs. Knowth has the greatest collection of passage tomb art ever uncovered in Western Europe. At the time of this writing, work is in progress and there is not yet access to the interior, but you may stroll the grounds by guided tour.

Admission: £1.50 ($2.25) adults, £1 ($1.50) seniors, 60p (90¢) students and children under 12.

Open: Mid-June to mid-Sept daily 9:30am–6:30pm; May to mid-June daily 10am–5pm; mid-Sept through Oct daily 10am–5pm.

⭐ **Newgrange,** off N 51, Slane, Co. Meath. ☎ 041/24488.

Known in Irish as *Brugh na Boinne* (the Palace of the Boyne), Newgrange is Ireland's best-known prehistoric monument and one of the finest archaeological wonders of western Europe. Dating from 3,000 B.C., Newgrange was built as a passage tomb in which Stone Age men buried the cremated remains of the dead. It's 500 years older than the Pyramids of Egypt and 1,500 years older than Stonehenge. The huge mound—36 ft. tall—consists of 200,000 tons of stone, a six-ton capstone, and other stones weighing up to 16 tons each. Many of the stones were hauled from as far away as County Wicklow and the Mountains of Mourne, it's thought. Each stone fits perfectly in the overall pattern and the result is a water-tight structure—an amazing feat of engineering. Early art is carved into the stones—spirals, diamonds, and concentric circles.

Curiosity about Newgrange reaches a peak each winter solstice. That day at 8:58am, as the sun rises to the southeast, sunlight pierces the inner chamber with an orange-toned glow for about 17 minutes. This occurrence is so remarkable that, as of this writing, the wait list for viewing extends through the year 2004. Admission to Newgrange is by guided tour only. Located two miles east of Slane, off N 51.

Admission: £2 ($3) adults, £1.50 ($2.25) seniors, £1 ($1.50) students and children over 12.

Open: Nov to mid-Mar Tues–Sun 10am–1pm and 2–4:30pm; mid-Mar through May and mid-Sept through Oct daily 10am–1pm and 2–5pm; June to mid-Sept daily 10am–7pm.

⭐ **Newgrange Farm,** off N 51, Slane, Co. Meath. ☎ 041/24119.

A contrast to all the surrounding antiquity in the Boyne Valley, this busy 333-acre farm is very much a 20th-century attraction. Farmer Willie Redhouse and his family invite visitors on a 1$^1/_2$ hour-tour of their farm, which grows wheat, oats, barley, oil seed rape, corn, and linseed (flax). You can throw feed to the ducks, groom a calf, or bottle-feed the baby lambs or kid goats. Children can hold a newborn chick, pet a pony, or play with the pigs. In the aviaries are pheasants and rare birds. In the fields romp horses, donkeys, and rare Jacob sheep.

Demonstrations of sheepdog working, threshing, and farrier work are given. The Redhouses spin and dye their own wool and have put together an exhibit of the fibers produced and the dyes, from beets, carrots, gorse, yew, and sage, used to color them. At the herb garden, visitors receive a lesson on picking edible plants and herbs. Many of the farm buildings are from the 17th-century. There's a coffee shop (see below) and indoor and outdoor picnic areas. Located two miles east of Slane, signposted off N 51 and directly west of Newgrange monument.

Admission: £2 ($3) per person; special reduced rates for parents with children.

Open: Apr–June and Sept Mon–Fri 10am–5:30pm and Sun 2–5:30pm; July–Aug Mon–Fri 10am–5:30pm, Sat–Sun 2–5:30pm.

SAVVY SHOPPING

Mary McDonnell Craft Studio, Newgrange Mall Studio, Slane, Co. Meath. ☎ 041/24722.

Mary McDonnell, textile artist, welcomes visitors to watch as she creates beautiful leather items, ceramics, jewelry, quilts, cushions, and wall hangings. Her shop also stocks the work of other local artisans. Dried flower art, candles, and lace are for sale. It's worth a detour.

Open: July–Aug Mon–Sat 10am–6pm, Sun 2–6pm; Sept–June Tues–Sat 10am–6pm, Sun 2–6pm.

WHERE TO STAY

Inexpensive

⭐ **Conyngham Arms Hotel,** Main Street, Slane, Co. Meath. ☎ **041/24155** or toll free **800/447-7462** from the U.S. Fax 041/24205. 16 rms (15 with bath). TV TEL

$ **Rates** (including full breakfast): £25–£36.95 ($38.75–$57.25) single, £45–£59.90 ($67.50–$89.85) double. No service charge. AE, DC, MC, V. **Closed:** Jan–Mar.

In the heart of one of the Boyne Valley's loveliest villages, this three-story stone-faced inn dates back to 1850 and has been run by the same family for more than 60 years. The current proprietors, Kevin and Vonnie Macken, work hard to blend old world charm and personal attention with 20th-century efficiency and innovative innkeeping. The guest rooms offer traditional dark wood furnishings, some with part-canopy beds, rich primary-color fabrics, good reading lights, and wildlife art. Other features include good writing desks, towel warmers, mirrored closets, and hairdryers, but, in keeping with the building's character, no elevator.

Dining/Entertainment: Exceptionally good bar food is available all day in the lounge. Dinner is served in the adjacent Flemings restaurant, two rooms with a lot of character and Irish memorabilia.

WHERE TO DINE

Inexpensive

$ **Newgrange Farm Coffee Shop,** off N 51, Slane, Co. Meath. ☎ **041/24119.**

Cuisine: SELF-SERVICE/IRISH. **Reservations:** Not necessary.

Prices: All items £1.50–£4.50 ($2.25–$6.75). No credit cards.

Open: Apr–June and Sept Sun–Fri 10am–5:30pm; July–Aug daily 10am–5:30pm.

Located on the premises of a working farm (see above), this family-run restaurant is housed in a converted cowhouse, now whitewashed and skylit. It has an open fireplace and local art on the walls. Ann Redhouse and her family oversee the baking and food preparation each day, using many ingredients grown on the farm or locally. The ever-changing blackboard menu ranges from homemade soups and hot scones or biscuits to sandwiches, with tempting desserts like apple tart and cream, carrot cake, and fruit pies. Food can also be enjoyed in an outdoor picnic area and there is often live Irish traditional music in the summer months.

County Louth/Cuchulainn Country

To the north and east of Meath is Louth, the smallest of Ireland's counties but possessing a diversity of scenery, historic treasures, and early Christian landmarks.

With more than 30 miles of coastline overlooking the Irish Sea, County Louth extends from the banks of the Boyne to a hilly stretch of land known as the Cooley Peninsula and the Northern Ireland border. With the Mountains of Mourne on its northern horizon, the Louth panorama includes the busy market town of Dundalk as well as little seacoast resorts and fishing villages such as Baltray, Blackrock, Gyles Quay, and Greenore.

In the ancient town of Drogheda (pronounced *Drah-ah´-da*), a complex of walls, gates, and churches was established as a permanent fortified settlement by the Danes in 911. Drogheda quickly ranked with Dublin and Wexford as a trading center. By the 14th century, it was one of the four principal towns in Ireland, and Drogheda continued to prosper until Oliver Cromwell took it by storm in 1649 and massacred its 2000 inhabitants. Happily, the population has grown to ten times that number today, and the town is a thriving port and industrial center.

Carlingford, one of Ireland's heritage towns, is set on a spur of the Cooley Mountains, overlooking Carlingford Lough and the Irish Sea at the most northerly point on Ireland's east coast south of Northern Ireland. Established by the Vikings, it is still very much a medieval town dominated by a massive 13th-century castle. Long before the Vikings came, however, legend has it that Carlingford was part of the hunting grounds of warriors. On the heights above the town, folk hero Cuchulainn is said to have singlehandedly defeated the armies of Ulster in an epic battle.

WHAT TO SEE & DO

Mellifont Abbey, off T 25, Collon, Co. Louth. ☎ **041/26459.**

Ireland's "Big Monastery" was set up in 1142 by St. Malachy of Armagh. Although little more than foundations survive here, this tranquil spot is worth a visit for a few moments of quiet. Remnants of a 14th-century chapter house, an octagonal lavabo dating from around 1200, and several Romanesque arches remain. The abbey is on the banks of the Mattock River, six miles west of Drogheda.

Admission: £1 ($1.50) adults, 70p ($1.05) seniors, 40p (60¢) students and children under 12.

Open: Mid-June to mid-Sept daily 9:30am–6:30pm; May to mid-June Tues-Sat 9:30am–1pm and 2–5:30pm, Sun 2–5pm; mid-Sept to end-Oct daily 10am–5pm.

Monasterboice, off the main Dublin Road (N 1), near Collon, Co. Louth.

Once a great monastery and now little more than a peaceful cemetery, this site is dominated by Muiredeach's High Cross. At 17 ft. tall, it's one of the most perfect crosses in Ireland. Dating back to the the year 922, the cross is ornamented with sculptured panels of scenes from the Old and New Testaments. On the monastery grounds are the remains of a round tower, two churches, two early grave slabs, and a sundial. It's located six miles northwest of Drogheda.

Admission: Free.

Open: Daylight hours.

★ **Holy Trinity Heritage Centre,** Carlingford, Co. Louth. ☎ **042/73454.**

In a beautifully restored medieval church, this center has exhibits that detail the town's history from its Norman origins. A visit here includes a guided walking tour of the town and a look at King John's Castle, the Mint, The Tholsel, and a Dominican friary. The center overlooks the south shore of Carlington Lough, at the foot of Sliabh Foy, the highest peak of the Cooley Mountains.

Admission: £1 ($1.50) adults, free for children under 16.

Open: Mar–Apr and Sept–Oct Sat 11am–6pm, Sun 2–6pm; May–Aug Mon–Fri 10:30am–6pm, Sat–Sun 2–6pm.

Millmount Museum, Duleek Street, off the main Dublin (N 1) Road, Drogheda, Co. Louth. ☎ **041/36391** or **33097.**

In the courtyard of 18th-century Millmount Fort, this museum offers exhibits on the history of Drogheda and the Boyne Valley area. A Bronze Age oracle, medieval tiles, and a collection of 18th-century guild banners are on display. Domestic items are showcased, too, such as spinning, weaving, and brewing equipment; antique gramophones; mousetraps; and hot-water jars. A geological exhibit contains specimens of stone from every county in Ireland, every country in Europe, and beyond.

Admission: 50p (75¢) adults, 20p (30¢) children under 12.

Open: May–Sept Tues–Sun 2–6pm; Oct–Apr Wed and Sat–Sun 3–5pm.

WHERE TO STAY & DINE

Moderate/Inexpensive

Ballymascanlon House, off the Dublin/Belfast Road (N 1), Dundalk, Co. Louth. ☎ **042/71124** or toll free **800/528-1234** from the U.S. Fax 042/71598. 36 rms (all with private bath). TV TEL

Rates (including full breakfast): £46–£50 ($69–$75) single, £70–£75 ($105–$112.50) double. No service charge. AE, DC, MC, V.

A stone-faced Victorian mansion dating back to the early 1800s, Ballymascanlon was formerly the home of Baron Plunkett, converted into a hotel by the Quinn family in 1947 who have extended it several times since. It stands on 130 acres of award-winning gardens and grounds—a peaceful oasis just three miles south of the Northern Ireland border. Rooms vary in size, but are decorated in traditional style, with some Victorian or antique touches.

Dining/Entertainment: The Dining Room specializes in local meats and seafood, using vegetables from the hotel gardens; the Cellar Bar offers light refreshment and usually traditional Irish music on weekends.

Facilities: Indoor heated swimming pool, two floodlit all-weather tennis courts, two squash courts, sauna, solarium, and gym, nine-hole golf course.

Inexpensive

💲 **McKevitts Village Inn,** Market Square, Carlingford, Co. Louth. ☎ **042/73116** or toll free **800/447-7462** from U.S. Fax 042/73144. 13 rms (all with bath). TV TEL

Rates (including full breakfast): £33–£35 ($49.50–$52.50) single, £46–£60 ($69–$90) double. No service charge. AE, DC, MC, V.

Situated right in the heart of a lovely medieval village, this is a great hotel for unwinding and taking long walks along the shores of Carlingford Lough. It's a vintage two-story property that has been updated and refurbished in recent years. Guest rooms vary in size and shape, but all have standard Irish furnishings and are very comfortable, with nice views of the town. The public areas include an old-world bar and a very good restaurant that specializes in local seafood and produce. It makes a great base for day trips into Northern Ireland and the surrounding Boyne Valley countryside.

An Easy Excursion from County Louth

The town of Carrickmacross in County Monaghan is famous for its tradition of lace making from 1820. Five miles from County Louth's northwest border—it's well worth a detour to the Lace Gallery of the **Carrickmacross Lace Co-op** on Main Street, Carrickmacross (☎ **042/62506**). On view here are the beautiful and intricate hand-made laces produced in the area. Occasionally demonstrations are given.

It's open May through October on Monday, Tuesday, Thursday, and Friday from 9:30am to 12:30pm and 1:30 to 5:30pm, on Wednesday and Saturday from 9:30am to 12:30pm only.

WHERE TO STAY & DINE

Nuremore, Ashbourne/Slane/Ardee Road (N 2), Carrickmacross, Co. Monaghan.
☎ **042/61438.** Fax 042/61853. 69 rms (all with bath). TV TEL

Rates (including breakfast): £70–£95 ($105–$142.50) single, £100–£140 ($150–$210). No service charge. AE, DC, MC, V.

In a town so famous for its lace, this modern three-story hotel is equally well known, for its hospitality and high standards. Set amid 100 acres of parkland and woods (including three lakes), it has been totally refurbished and updated in recent years. The decor is traditional with dark woods, marble fireplaces, and antique framed prints of the area. Most of the bedrooms feature bright colors, reproduction furniture, and semi-canopy beds; some have light woods and more contemporary styles. They all enjoy lake or garden views. Public areas include a restaurant and lounge bar. Facilities include an 18-hole championship golf course, heated indoor swimming pool, squash court, two tennis courts, sauna, steam room, gym, whirlpool, and trout fishing on privately stocked hotel lake.

3 County Kildare/Ireland's Horse Country

15 to 30 miles west of Dublin

GETTING THERE • By Train   Irish Rail (☎ **01/836-3333**) provides daily train service to Kildare town.

• **By Bus**   Bus Eireann (☎ **01/836-6111**) operates daily express bus service to Kildare.

• **By Car**   Take the main Dublin-Limerick road (N 7) west of Dublin to Kildare; or the main Dublin-Galway road (N 4) to Celbridge, turning off on local road R 403.

ESSENTIALS • Tourist Information   For information about County Kildare, contact the Midlands-East Regional Tourism Organization, Clonard House, Dublin Road, Mullingar, Co. Westmeath (☎ **044/48761**). It is open year round on Monday through Friday from 9:30am to 6pm and Saturday from 9:30am to 1pm, with extended hours in the summer. Seasonal information offices are located at Athy, Co. Kildare (☎ **0507/31859,** open July through August; and in Kildare Town (☎ **045/71011**) open mid-June through August.

• **Area Code**   The telephone area codes used in County Kildare are 01, 045, 0503.

County Kildare and horseracing go hand-in-hand, or should we say neck-and-neck; it's home of the Curragh racetrack, where the Irish Derby is held each June, and other smaller tracks at Naas and Punchestown. County Kildare is also the heartland of Ireland's flourishing bloodstock industry. In this panorama of open grasslands and limestone-enriched soil many of Ireland's 300 stud farms are found.

Just west of Dublin, County Kildare is the only totally inland county of Ireland's east coast. What it lacks in seashore, it more than makes up for in turf.

Historically, County Kildare's chief town is Naas (pronounced *Nay-se*). Taking its name from a Irish word that means "the assembly place of the kings," Naas was once the seat of the kings of the province of Leinster. An ancient royal palace stood in Naas where St. Patrick is said to have spent some time.

County Kildare's Newbridge, alias Droichead Nua, is a small manufacturing and market town. Kildare is famed as the birthplace of Brigid, Ireland's second patron saint. It's said that Brigid was a bit ahead of her time as an early exponent for women's equality; she founded a coed monastery in Kildare in the fifth or sixth century.

WHAT TO SEE & DO

 The Curragh, Dublin/Limerick Road (N 7), Curragh, Co. Kildare. ☎ **045/41205.**
Often referred to as The Churchill Downs of Ireland, this is the country's best-known racetrack, just 30 miles west of Dublin. Majestically placed at the edge of Ireland's central plain, it's home to the Irish Derby held each year at the end of June/early July. Horses race here at least one Saturday a month from March to October.

Admission: £6 ($9) for most races; £7–£25 ($10.50–$37.50) for Derby.
Open: Varies; first race usually 1pm.

 Irish National Stud & Japanese Gardens, off the Dublin/Limerick Road (N 7), Tully, Kildare, Co. Kildare. ☎ **045/21617.**
Some of Ireland's most famous horses have been bred and raised on the grounds of this government-sponsored stud farm. A prototype for other horse farms throughout this horse-happy country, it has 288 stalls to accommodate the mares, stallions, and foals. Visitors are welcome to walk around the 958-acre grounds and see the noble steeds being exercised and groomed.

A converted groom's house has exhibits on racing, steeplechasing, hunting, and show jumping, plus the skeleton of Arkle, one of Ireland's most famous equine heroes.

The Japanese garden is considered to be among the finest Oriental gardens in Europe. Laid out in 1906–1910, its design symbolizes the life of man. This is one place in Ireland where the bonsai trees outnumber the shamrocks. A Japanese-style visitor center has a restaurant and craft shop.

Admission: £4 adults ($6), £3 ($4.50) seniors, students, and children over 12; £2 ($3) children under 12.
Open: Mar 17–Oct daily 9:30am–6pm.

⭐ **Castletown House,** R. 403, off main Dublin/Galway Road, Celbridge, Co. Kildare. ☎ **01/628-8582.**
Although a little removed from the heart of Kildare horse country, this great house deserves a detour; it's ten miles northeast of Naas. One of Ireland's architectural gems, Castletown is a 1722 Palladian-style mansion designed by Italian architect Alessandro Galilei for William Connolly, then Speaker of the Irish House of Commons. It's known for its long gallery laid out in the Pompeian manner and hung with Venetian chandeliers; its main hall and staircase with elaborate Italian plasterwork; and an 18th-century print room. It's decorated with Georgian furniture and paintings.

Admission: £2.50 ($3.75) adults, £2 ($3) seniors and students; £1 ($1.50) children under 12.

Open: Apr–Sept Mon–Fri 10am–6pm, Sat 11am–6pm, Sun 2–6pm; Oct Mon–Fri 10am–5pm and Sun 2–5pm; Nov–Mar Sun 2–5pm.

Steam Museum, off Dublin/Limerick Road (N 7), Straffan, Co. Kildare.
☎ **01/627-3155.**

In a converted church, this museum is a must for steam-engine buffs. It contains two collections: The Richard Guinness Hall has more than 20 prototypical locomotive engines, dating from the 18th century; the Power Hall has rare industrial stationary engines. A bookshop stocks a variety of recent books and videos on the Irish Railway.

Admission: £3 ($4.50) adults, £2 ($3) seniors, children, and students.

Open: Feb–Mar Sun 2:30–4:30pm, Easter to May and Sept–Oct Sun 2:30–5:30pm, June–Aug Tues–Sun 2:30–5:30pm.

Newbridge Cutlery, off Dublin/Limerick Road, Newbridge, Co. Kildare.
☎ **045/31301.**

The craft of silversmithing dates back to the time of Ireland's High Kings. For the past 60 years, this company has been one of Ireland's leading manufacturers of fine silverware—you'll often see Newbridge products used at Ireland's fine hotels and restaurants. In the visitor center, you can see a display of silver place settings, bowls, candelabras, trays, frames, and one-of-a-kind items. A video on silvermaking is also shown. Silver pieces are sold here, including "sale" items.

Admission: Free.

Open: Mon–Fri 9am–5pm, Sat 11am–5pm, Sun 2–5pm.

SPORTS & RECREATION

GOLFING The flat plains of Kildare provide some lovely settings for parkland courses, including two new 18-hole championship courses. The par-72 Kildare Country Club, Straffan, Co. Kildare (☎ **01/627-3111**), charges £50 ($75) per day for greens fees to those staying at the hotel and £70 ($105) per day to day visitors. The par-71 Kilkea Castle Golf Club, Castledermot, Co. Kildare (☎ **0503/45156**), charges £25 ($37.50) on weekdays, and £30 ($45) on weekends.

For a slightly less costly game, try the par-72 championship course at the Curragh Golf Club, Curragh, Co. Kildare, with greens fees of £13 ($19.50) weekdays, and £16 ($24) on weekends; the two par-72 courses at Bodenstown Golf Club, Sallins, Co. Kildare (☎ **045/97096**), with greens fee of £10 ($15); or the par-73 Castlewarden Golf & Country Club, Kill, Co. Kildare (☎ **01/589254**), with greens fees of £12 ($18).

HORSEBACK RIDING Visitors who want to go horseback riding can expect to pay an average of £10 to £15 ($15 to $30) per hour for trekking or trail riding in the Kildare countryside. To arrange a ride, contact the Donacomper Riding School, Celbridge, Co. Kildare (☎ **01/628-8221**), or the Kill International Equestrian Centre, Kill, Co. Kildare (☎ **045/77208**).

WHERE TO STAY

Very Expensive/Expensive

Kildare Hotel & Country Club, Straffan, Co. Kildare. ☎ **01/627-3333** or toll free in U.S. **800/221-1074.** Fax 01/627-3312. 45 rms (all with bath). MINIBAR TV TEL

Rates (including full breakfast): £135–£170 ($202.50–$255) single, £160–£245 ($240–$367.50) double. No service charge. AE, DC, MC, V.

Located 20 miles west of Dublin, this 330-acre resort is a favorite with Ireland's sporting set. The focal point of the estate is Straffan House, a 19th-century mansion that now serves as the core of the hotel, with an adjacent new west wing that is a replica of the original building. The bedrooms are spread out among the main hotel, courtyard suites, and a lodge. High ceilings, bow windows, wide staircases, antiques and period pieces are all enhanced by hand-painted wall coverings and murals. The house overlooks a one-mile stretch of the River Liffey.

Dining/Entertainment: The main restaurant is the Bryerley Turk, featuring French food, while lighter fare including afternoon tea is available in the Gallery; the Legends bar overlooks the golf course.

Services: 24-hour room service, nightly turndown, concierge, laundry/valet service.

Facilities: 18-hole Arnold Palmer–designed championship par 72-golf course; private access to salmon and trout fishing, 2 indoor and 2 outdoor tennis courts, 2 squash courts, gym, indoor swimming pool, sauna, and solarium.

Expensive

⭐ **Kilkea Castle,** Castledermot, Co. Kildare. ☎ **0503/45156** or **45100.**
Fax 0503/45187. 40 rms (all with bath). TV TEL
Rates: £65–£105 ($97.50–$157.50) single, £90–£170 ($135–$255) double. Service charge 12.5%. AE, DC, MC, V.

Nestled beside the River Greese and surrounded by lovely formal gardens, this tall, multiturreted stone castle is a stand-out in the flat farmland of Co. Kildare. Considered the oldest inhabited castle in Ireland, it dates back to 1180 and was built by Hugh de Lacy, an early Irish governor, for Walter de Riddlesford, a great warrior. The castle later passed into the ownership of the legendary Geraldines and it is still supposed to be haunted by the 11th Earl of Kildare. Every seven years, the Earl—dressed in full regalia and accompanied by his knights, is said to gallop around the castle walls.

Fully restored as a hotel in recent years, it is decorated with suits of armour and medieval banners, as well as a mix of Irish antiques and Oriental tables, chests, and urns. About a third of the bedrooms are in the original castle building, with the rest in a newer courtyard addition. The furnishings include dark woods, semicanopy beds, armoires, chandeliers, brass fixtures, gilt-framed paintings and mirrors, and floral designer fabrics; each has a modern tile and brass bathroom. The castle is approximately 2.5 miles from Castledermot and is well signposted from the town.

Dining/Entertainment: The main dining room is de Lacy's, named for the castle's originator, specializes in innovative Irish cuisine. The Geraldine Bar conveys a 12th-century atmosphere, with original stone walls, stained-glass windows, and huge fireplace crowned by a copper flue.

Services: Room service, concierge.

Facilities: 18-hole golf course, indoor heated swimming pool, exercise room, saunas, spa pool, steam rooms, sunbed, toning table; fishing for brown trout on the adjacent River Greese, 2 floodlit hard tennis courts, clay pigeon shooting, and an archery range.

Expensive/Moderate

Hotel Keadeen, off Dublin/Limerick Road (N 7), Newbridge, Co. Kildare.
☎ **045/31666.** Fax 045/34402. 33 rms. (all with bath). TV TEL

Rates (Including full breakfast): £90 ($135) single, £140 ($210) double. No service charge.
AE, DC, MC, V.

Situated less than two miles east of The Curragh racetrack, this small country-style
hotel is a favorite with the horsey set. Although just off the main road, it is set back in
its own eight acres of grounds in a quiet garden setting. Equestrian art dominates the
public rooms. The guest rooms are up-to-date, with light woods, floral fabrics, and
brass fixtures. Facilities include the Derby Room restaurant and lounge.

WHERE TO DINE

Moderate/Inexpensive

Silken Thomas, The Square, Kildare, Co. Kildare. ☎ **045/22232.**

Cuisine: IRISH/INTERNATIONAL. **Reservations:** Not required for lunch.
Prices: Appetizers £1–£4.75 ($1.50–$7.13); lunch main courses £4.25–£8 ($6.38–$12),
dinner main courses £5–£11 ($7.50–$16.50). AE, MC, V.
Open: Daily lunch 12:30–3pm; dinner 6–10pm.

Formerly known as Leinster Lodge, this historic inn offers an old world pub-restaurant,
with open fire and dark woods. It is named after a character in Irish history, a member of the Norman Fitzgerald family, whose stronghold was in Kildare. He led an
unsuccessful rebellion against Henry VIII and some of the decor recalls his efforts.
The menu offers a good selection of soups, sandwiches, burgers, and salads as well as
steaks, roasts, mixed grills, and fresh seafood platters. It is located on the main square
in Kildare town.

6

The Southeast

WEXFORD, WATERFORD, AND KILKENNY ARE OFTEN REFERRED TO AS IRELAND'S sunny southeast, because these counties usually enjoy more hours of sunshine than the rest of the country. No matter what the weather, however, they also provide a varied touring experience—from the world-famous Waterford Crystal Factory, to the Viking streets of Wexford, and the medieval buildings of Kilkenny.

1 County Wexford

Wexford Town is 88 miles S of Dublin, 39 miles E of Waterford, 56 miles S of Wicklow, 116 miles E of Cork, 133 miles SE of Shannon Airport

GETTING THERE • By Rail   Daily train service into Wexford and Rosslare Pier is provided by Irish Rail into O'Hanrahan Station, Redmond Place, Wexford (☎ **053/22522**).

• By Bus   Daily bus service to Wexford and Rosslare is operated by Bus Eireann, into O'Hanrahan Station and Bus Depot, Redmond Place, Wexford (☎ **053/22522**).

• By Car   From Dublin and points north, take N 11 or N 80 to Wexford; from the west, take N 25 or N 8. Two bridges lead into Wexford from points north—the Ferrycarrig Bridge from the main Dublin Road (N 11) and the Wexford Bridge from R 741. The Ferrycarrig Bridge takes you into town from the west, while the Wexford Bridge leads right to the heart of town along the quays.

• By Ferry   Ferry service from Britain to Rosslare Harbour, 12 miles south of Wexford Town, is operated from Fishguard by Sealink (☎ **053/33115**) and from Pembroke by B & I Lines (☎ **053/33311**). Service from Le Havre and Cherbourg, France, is operated by Irish Ferries (☎ **053/33311**).

Within Ireland, the Passage East Car Ferry, Barrack Street, Passage East, Co. Waterford (☎ **051/82488** or **82480**), operates a car ferry service across Waterford Harbour, linking Passage East, about ten miles east of Waterford, with Ballyhack, about 20 miles southwest of Wexford. This shortcut saves about an hour's driving time between the two cities. Crossing time averages ten minutes and service is continuous. It's a drive-on, drive-off service, with no reservations required. The fares for car and passengers are £3.50 ($5.25) one-way, £5.50 ($8.25) round-trip. It operates April through September, Monday through Saturday, 7:20am until 10pm, and on Sunday, 9:30am until 10pm; October through March, Monday through Saturday, 7:20am until 8pm, and Sunday, 9:30am until 8pm.

TOURIST INFORMATION   Year-round information services are provided by the **Wexford Tourist Office,** Crescent Quay, Wexford (☎ **053/23111**), and the **Rosslare Harbour Tourist Office,** Ferry Terminal, Rosslare Harbour (☎ **053/33622**). The Wexford Town office is open April and May, September and October on Monday through Saturday, 9am to 6pm; January through March and in November, Monday through Friday from 9am to 5:15pm. In July and August it is open Monday through Saturday from 9am to 6pm and on Sunday from 10am to 5pm. The Rosslare Harbour Office opens daily to coincide with ferry arrivals. **Seasonal offices,** open June through August, are maintained at Enniscorthy, Town Centre (☎ **054/34699**); Gorey, Town Centre (☎ **055/21248**); New Ross, Town Centre (☎ **051/21857**), and Rosslare (☎ **053/33232**).

TOWN LAYOUT   Rimmed by the River Slaney, Wexford is a small and compact town. Four Quays (Custom House, Commercial, Paul, and the semicircular Crescent)

What's Special About the Southeast

Beaches
- Rosslare, Co. Wexford, a resort on a wide bay with a 6-mile curve of sandy beach.
- Tramore, Co. Waterford, a 3-mile-long sandy beach with a boardwalk and amusements galore.

Monuments
- John Barry Monument, Wexford, commemorating the Father of the American Navy.

Buildings
- West Gate Heritage Tower, Wexford, incorporating Wexford's original Viking/Norman walls.
- Reginald's Tower, Waterford, an 11th-century circular tower with walls 10-feet thick.
- Lismore Castle, Co. Waterford, a 12th-century fairy-tale castle once owned by Sir Walter Raleigh.
- St. Canice Cathedral, Kilkenny, with flooring using the four marbles of Ireland.

Museums
- Irish Agricultural Museum, Wexford, for a look at the importance of farming in Ireland.

Parks/Gardens
- John F. Kennedy Park, Co. Wexford, 600 acres of trees from around the world, in memory of the 35th U.S. president.
- Irish National Heritage Park, Wexford, reflecting 9,000 years of Irish history with full-scale replicas of early buildings.

Ace Attractions
- Waterford Crystal Factory and Gallery, Waterford, where the famous glass is made by hand.
- Rock of Cashel, Co. Tipperary, seat of Irish kings from the 4th century and ecclesiastical hub of Ireland in medieval times.
- Kilkenny Castle, Kilkenny, a medieval fortress whose art collection dates back to the 14th century.
- Bru Boru, Cashel, Co. Tipperary, features traditional Irish music all day long.

Natural Spectacles
- Glen of Aherlow, Co. Tipperary, Ireland's greenest valley.
- "The Vee," Counties Waterford and Tipperary, an 11-mile zigzag drive through the Knockmealdown Mountains.

Activities
- Walking Tours of Wexford, Waterford, and Kilkenny.
- Seeing the Waterford sights on board the Galley, Ireland's only floating restaurant.

Shopping
- Kilkenny Design Centre, Kilkenny; the stables of this 18th-century castle hums with the craft-making of local artisans.

TV and Film Locations
- Cahir Castle, Co. Tipperary, 13th-century setting for *Barry Lyndon* and *Excalibur.*

Offbeat/Oddities
- The Bull Ring, Wexford, used for the sport of bull-baiting in the 17th century, and now an open market.
- The Twin Churches, Wexford, two identical 19th-century structures built within a few blocks of each other.
- Jack Meades, Co. Waterford, Ireland's only "fly-over" pub.
- The Ronald Reagan, Co. Tipperary, a pub named for the 40th U.S. president.
- Smithwick's Brewery, Kilkenny, a brewery on the site of a 12th-century abbey.
- Kyteler's Inn, Kilkenny, 14th-century home of an Irish witch, now a pub.

run beside the water, with Cresent Quay marking the center of town. One block inland is Main Street, a long, narrow thoroughfare that can be easily walked. All of Wexford's shops and businesses are on either on North or South Main Street or on one of the many smaller street that fan out from it.

GETTING AROUND • By Public Transport Since Wexford is small and compact, with narrow streets, there is no local bus transport. Bus Eireann (☎ **053/22522**) operates daily service between Wexford and Rosslare. Other local services operate on certain days only to Kilmore Quay, Carne, and Gorey. If you need a **taxi,** call Bryne's Taxis (☎ **053/46777**), Williams Taxi (☎ **053/46666**), or Andrew's Taxi Service (☎ **053/45933**).

• **By Car** To see Wexford town, walk. Park your car along the Quays; parking is operated according to the disc system, at 30p (45¢) per hour. Discs are on sale at the tourist office or many of the shops. There is free parking off Redmond Square, beside the train/bus station. You'll need a car to reach Wexford County attractions outside of town.

If you need to rent a car, contact Budget at Rosslare Ferryport, Rosslare (☎ **053/33318**); Murrays Europcar, Wellington Place, Wexford (☎ **053/22122**) or at the Rosslare Ferryport, Rosslare (☎ **053/33634**); or Hertz at Ferrybank, Wexford (☎ **053/23511**) or at Rosslare Ferryport, Rosslare (☎ **053/33511**).

• **On Foot** The best way to see the town is by walking the entire length of North and South Main Street, taking time to detour up and down the various alleys and lanes that cross the street. The tourist office will supply you with a free map.

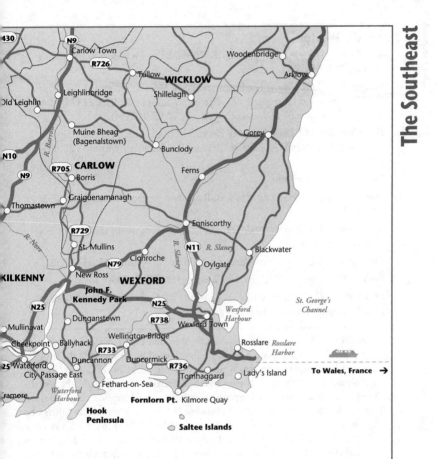

430

N9
Carlow Town
R726
Tullow
WICKLOW
Woodenbridge
Arklow
Leighlinbridge
Shillelagh
Old Leighlin
Muine Bheag
(Bagenalstown)
Gorey
Bunclody
N10
CARLOW
Ferns
N9
R705
Borris
Graiguenamanagh
Thomastown
R729
Enniscorthy
St. Mullins
N11
R. Slaney
Blackwater
Clonroche
R. Slaney
Oylgate
N79
New Ross
WEXFORD
KILKENNY
John F.
Kennedy Park
N25
St. George's
Channel
Dunganstown
Mullinavat
R738
Wexford
Harbour
Cheekpoint
Wellington Bridge
Wexford Town
Ballyhack
Rosslare
Rosslare
Harbor
R733
Duncannon
Duncormick
Waterford
R736
To Wales, France →
City Passage East
Tomhaggard
Lady's Island
ramore
Waterford
Fethard-on-Sea
Harbour
Fornlorn Pt. Kilmore Quay
Hook
Peninsula
◯ **Saltee Islands**

C e l t i c   S e a

0 ▬▬▬ 10 mi
16 km
N

Fast Facts: Wexford

Area Code   The telephone area code for Wexford Town is **053;** the surrounding areas use **051, 053, 054,** and **055.**

Drugstores   John Fehily/The Pharmacy, 28 S. Main St., Wexford (☎ **053/ 23163**); Sherwood Chemist, 2 N. Main St., Wexford (☎ **053/22875**); and Fortune's Pharmacy, 82 N. Main St., Wexford (☎ **053/42354**).

Dry Cleaning and Laundry   My Beautiful Launderette, St. Peter's Square, Wexford (☎ **053/24317**), Marlow Cleaners, 7 S. Main St., Wexford (☎ **053/ 22172**).

Emergencies   Dial **999.**

Hospital   Wexford General Hospital, Richmond Terrace, Wexford (☎ **053/ 42233**).

Newspaper   The *Wexford People* is the weekly newspaper covering town and county events and entertainment.

Photographic Services   Photo Centre, 6 N. Main St., Wexford (☎ **053/45502**).

Police   Garda Station, Roches Road, Wexford (☎ **053/22333**).

Post Office   General Post Office, Anne Street, Wexford (☎ **053/22587**), open Monday through Saturday from 9am to 5:30pm.

When it comes to scenery, Wexford is one of Ireland's most versatile counties. It's rich in fertile farm and pasture lands, yet also rimmed by the waters of the Irish Sea and the Celtic Sea. On the north, Wexford is bounded by the hills of County Wicklow and on the west by the River Barrow and the Blackstairs Mountains. All the best elements of the Irish countryside are tied up in one neat little package in County Wexford, yet it's often missed by those dashing between Dublin and Waterford, or others who bypass the entire southeast coast in their rush to get from Dublin to Cork or vice versa.

Wexford is a hotbed of history. In the second century, one of Ptolemy's maps marked the site as a place called Menapia, after a Belgic tribe that is believed to have settled here in prehistoric times. The Irish called the area Loch Garman, but that name is so old that its origin was disputed even in early Christian times.

The modern English name of Wexford evolved from Waesfjord, which is what the Viking sea-rovers called it when they settled here in the ninth century. It literally means the harbor of the mud-flats. Like the rest of Ireland, Wexford was under Norman control by the 12th century, and in 1649 Oliver Cromwell captured it and massacred most of the inhabitants.

The county's most shining hours occurred in 1798 when Wexford men rallied to lead a full-scale rebellion to protest the oppressive penal laws of the 18th century and the cruel treatment of the local people by English landlords.

Led by two priests, Fr. John Murphy of Boolavogue and Fr. Michael Murphy of Ballycanew, the insurgents were mostly farmers—poorly trained and ill equipped— who came with their enthusiasm and their pikes in hand. Eventually called the pikemen, these brave rebels met with success at first. They took Enniscorthy and Wexford town, and defeated several detachments of the militia sent to disperse them. After securing control of most of the county, they drove west and north but were halted at New Ross and Arklow.

Ultimately, the English militia columns converged on Vinegar Hill beside Enniscorthy where the pikemen had pitched their main camp, and after a fiercely fought

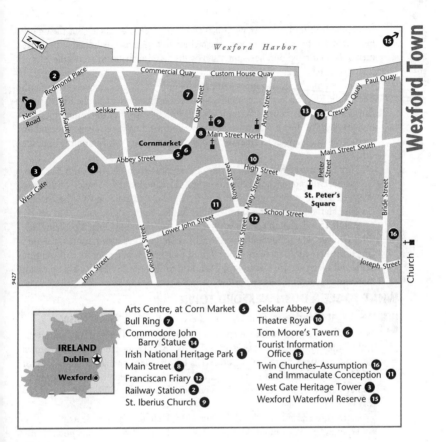

Arts Centre, at Corn Market **5**
Bull Ring **7**
Commodore John
  Barry Statue **14**
Irish National Heritage Park **1**
Main Street **8**
Franciscan Friary **12**
Railway Station **2**
St. Iberius Church **9**

Selskar Abbey **4**
Theatre Royal **10**
Tom Moore's Tavern **6**
Tourist Information
  Office **13**
Twin Churches–Assumption **16**
  and Immaculate Conception **11**
West Gate Heritage Tower **3**
Wexford Waterfowl Reserve **15**

IRELAND
Dublin ★
Wexford ●

9427

IMPRESSIONS

I am glad to be here. It took 115 years to make this trip, and 6,000 miles, and three generations. . . . In Ireland I think you see something of what is so great about the United States, and I must say that in the United States, through millions of your sons and daughters and cousins—25 million, in fact—you see something of what is great about Ireland. . . . I am proud to have connected . . . the coat of arms of Wexford, the coat of arms of the kingly and beautiful Kennedys, and the coat of arms of the United States. That is a very good combination.
—President John F. Kennedy, Wexford, June 1963

battle, the Irish insurgents were crushed and their leaders, executed. But their glory lives on in Wexford, as evidenced by the memorials and statues dedicated to the brave men of 1798 throughout the county, and by the haunting ballads that tell the tales of their heroic rebellion.

Today Enniscorthy is a quiet and peaceful little town, picturesquely set on both sides of the River Slaney. Fifteen miles south of Enniscorthy, where the River Slaney enters Wexford Harbour, is Wexford Town, the chief town of the county (population 15,000). In this ancient town of narrow and winding streets, you can stand on the sidewalk of many of its laneways and shake hands with a friend on the opposite side.

Near the town of Wexford lie a string of sandy beach resorts—Rosslare, Courtown, Curracloe, Duncannon, and Fethard-on-Sea. Rosslare, located 11 miles southeast of Wexford Town, is the largest, with a wide bay and a six-mile curve of beach. The Rosslare Harbour ferryport is just five miles farther south.

About 15 miles southwest of Rosslare Harbour is Kilmore Quay, a peaceful little fishing village, which looks out onto the Saltee Islands. These islands contain Ireland's largest offshore bird sanctuary. The town of Ballyhack is noted for its 15th-century castle and a ferry service that connects Wexford to Waterford. New Ross is a pleasant marketing town on the River Barrow.

WHAT TO SEE & DO IN WEXFORD TOWN

⭐ **West Gate Heritage Tower,** Westgate Street, Wexford. ☎ **053/46506.**
West Gate once guarded the western entrance of Wexford Town. It was built in the 13th century by Sir Stephen Devereux on instructions of King Henry. Like other town gates, it consisted of a toll-taking area, cells for offenders, and accommodations for guards. Fully restored and reopened in 1992 as a heritage center, it houses artifacts, displays, and a 27-minute audio-visual presentation depicting Wexford's varied history.

Admission: £1.30 ($1.95) adults, 80p ($1.20) children and students.
Open: Daily year-round, Mon–Sat 9:30am–1pm and 2–5pm, Sun noon–4pm.

Selskar Abbey, off Temperance Row at Westgate St., Wexford.
Said to be one of the oldest sites of religious worship in Wexford, this abbey dates back to at least the 12th century. It was often the scene of synods and parliaments. The first Anglo-Irish treaty was signed here in 1169, and it's said that Henry II spent the Lent of 1172 at the abbey doing penance for having Thomas à Becket beheaded. Although the abbey is mostly in ruins, its choir is now part of a Church of Ireland edifice, and a portion of the original tower is a vesting room. Check the sign on the gate, which is often locked, for information on access.

Cornmarket, off Upper George's Street, Wexford.
Until a century ago, this central marketplace buzzed with the activity of more than 20 businesses from cobblers to publicans. Today it's just a wide street. The Wexford Arts Centre, in a structure dating from 1775, dominates the street.

The Bull Ring, off N. Main Street, Wexford.
In the 17th century, this town square was a sporting venue for bull-baiting, introduced by the butcher's guild. Tradition has it that, after a match, the hide of the ill-fated bull was presented to the mayor and the meat was used to feed the poor. Ireland's first declaration as a Republic was made here in 1798. A statue here memorializes the Irish pikemen of 1798. Currently, the activity at the ring is much tamer—a weekly outdoor market.

Admission: Free.
Open: Market, Fri–Sat 10am–4:30pm.

St. Iberius Church, North Main Street. ☎ 053/22936.

Erected in 1760, St. Iberius was built on hallowed ground; the land had been used for previous houses of worship dating from Norse times. The church has a lovely Georgian facade and an interior known for its superb acoustics. Free guided tours are given according to demand.
Admission: Free; donations welcome.
Open: May–Sept daily 10am–5pm; Oct–Apr Tues–Sat 1pm–5pm.

★ **The Twin Churches—Church of the Assumption & Church of the Immaculate Conception,** Bride and Rowe Streets, Wexford ☎ 053/22055.

These twin Gothic structures (1851–8) were designed by architect Robert Pierce, a pupil of Augustus Pugin. Their spires rise 230 ft. and dominate the skyline of Wexford. Cobbled on the main door of both churches are mosaics showing relevant names and dates.
Admission: Free; donations welcome.
Open: Daily 8am–6pm.

John Barry Monument, Crescent Quay, Wexford.

This bronze statue—a gift from the American people in 1956—faces out to the sea as a tribute to John Barry, a favorite local son who became the Father of the American Navy. Born at Ballysampson, Tacumshane, ten miles southeast of Wexford town, Barry emigrated to the colonies while still in his teens and volunteered for the cause of the American Revolution. One of the U.S. Navy's first commissioned officers, he became captain of the *Lexington.* In 1797 George Washington appointed him Commander-in-Chief of the U.S. Navy.

★ **Irish National Heritage Park,** off the Dublin/Wexford Road (N 11), Ferrycarrig, Co. Wexford. ☎ 053/41733.

Two miles north of Wexford Town and overlooking the River Slaney, this theme park gazes back on 9,000 years of history—from man's first settlements in Ireland around 7,000 B.C. to the 12th-century Norman period. On the river estuary in the woodlands, marshlands, and mountains, this heritage park contains full-scale replicas of homesteads, burial sites, and places of worship. You'll see a crannog (an early lake dwelling), a ring fort, and a souterrain. Also here are a Viking ship, round tower, dolmen, horizontal mill, and a *fulacht fiadh* (an ancient cooking place which used hot stones).
Admission: £3 ($4.50) adults, £2 ($3) children.
Open: Mar–Nov daily 10am–7pm.

Wexford Wildfowl Reserve, Wexford Harbor. ☎ 053/23129.

This nature reserve is part of the Sloblands on the northern shore of Wexford Harbour, 3 miles east of Wexford town. About 10,000 Greenland white-fronted geese—more than one-third of the world's population—spend the winter here, as do Brent geese, Bewick swans, and wigeon. The area is immensely attractive to other wildfowl and birds; more than 220 species have been recorded seen here. The reserve has a visitor center and an observation tower.
Admission: Free.
Open: Mid-April–Sept daily 9am–6pm; Oct–mid-April daily 10am–5pm.

Sightseeing Tours

⭐ **Walking Tours of Wexford**, c/o Seamus Molloy, "Carmeleen," William Street. ☎ 053/22663.

Proud of their town's ancient streets and vintage buildings, the people of Wexford spontaneously started to give tours to visitors more than 30 years ago. Eventually organized as the Old Wexford Society, this core of local folk has developed a real expertise over the years and continue to give tours on a regular basis. All tours depart from West Gate Heritage Tower.

Price: £2.50 ($3.75) adults, 50p (75¢) children.

Schedule: Mon–Sat at 11:30am and 2:30pm.

NEARBY COUNTY WEXFORD ATTRACTIONS

⭐ **John F. Kennedy Park**, Dunganstown, New Ross, Co. Wexford. ☎ 051/88171.

Dedicated to the memory of the 35th U.S. president, this 600-acre park is located near a hill known as Slieve Coilte. The park overlooks the simple thatched cottage that was the birthplace of John F. Kennedy's great-grandfather. Opened in 1968, the park was a joint undertaking by a group of Irish Americans and the Irish government. More than 4,500 species of plants and trees from five continents grow here. Facilities include an information center and a picnic area. A hilltop observation point (at 888 ft.) presents a sweeping view of County Wexford, plus neighboring Waterford, the Saltee Islands, the Comeragh Mountains, and parts of the Rivers Suir, Nore, and Barrow. It's located off the Duncannon Road, R 783, about 20 miles west of Wexford.

Admission: £1 ($1.50) adults, 40p (60¢) children.

Open: Apr and Sept daily 10am–6:30pm; May–Aug daily 10am–8pm; Oct–Mar daily 10am–5pm.

Kennedy Centre, The Quay, New Ross, Co. Wexford. ☎ 051/25239.

At the time of this writing, the Kennedy Centre is slated to open in mid-1995. Housed in twin 18th-century grain mills, it tells the story of the Irish Diaspora—their lives and achievements abroad. It begins with the Irish monks who went to Europe in the sixth century and continues to the present day. A data bank for tracing County Wexford roots contains more than four million names in a computer system that's being developed with the Ellis Island Immigration Museum in New York and other immigration centers as far away as Australia and Argentina. A section will be devoted to John F. Kennedy, 35th president of the United States, descended from a Wexford County family. His 1963 speech to the Irish Parliament will be highlighted.

Admission: Not final at presstime.

Open: Year-round Mon–Fri 9am–5pm.

Enniscorthy Castle/Wexford County Museum, Castle Hill, Enniscorthy, Co. Wexford. ☎ 054/35926.

Overlooking the River Slaney at Enniscorthy, 15 miles north of Wexford Town, this castle was built by the Prendergast family in the 13th century. It's said that it was once owned briefly by the poet Edmund Spenser. Remarkably well preserved and restored, it's now home to the Wexford County Museum. The museum focuses on the area's ecclesiastical, maritime, folk, agricultural, industrial, and military traditions. Displays include an old Irish farm kitchen, early modes of travel, nautical memorabilia, and items connected with Wexford's role in Ireland's struggle for independence.

At the eastern end of Enniscorthy is Vinegar Hill (390 feet), where the Wexford men of 1798 made their last stand. Now a scenic viewing point, it offers panoramas of Wexford from its summit.

Admission: £1.50 ($2.25) adults, 70p ($1.10) seniors, 30p (45¢) children.

Open: June–Oct daily 10am–6pm, Nov–May daily 2–5:30pm.

Irish Agricultural Museum, Johnstown Castle, Bridgetown Road, off Wexford/ Rosslare Road, Wexford. ☎ **053/42888.**

The importance of farming in Wexford's history is the focus at this museum, on the Johnstown Castle Demesne, two miles southwest of Wexford town. In historic farm buildings, the museum contains exhibits relating to rural transport, planting, and the diverse activities of the farm household. There are also extensive displays on dairying, crafts, and Irish country furniture. Large-scale replicas illustrate the workshops of the blacksmith, cooper, wheelwright, harness maker, and basket maker. The 19th-century Gothic-Revival castle on the grounds is not open to the public—except for its entrance hall where tourist information is available. Visitors can enjoy the 50 acres of ornamental gardens that include over 200 different kinds of trees and shrubs, three lakes, a tower house, hothouses, a statue walk, and a picnic area.

Admission: Museum £1.75 ($2.63) adults, £1 ($1.50) children; gardens £1.50 ($2.25) adults, 50p (75¢) children.

Open: Museum June–Aug Mon–Fri 9am–5pm, Sat–Sun 2–5pm; Apr–May and Sept to mid-Nov Mon–Fri 9am–12:30pm and 1:30–5pm, Sat–Sun 3–5pm; Mid-Nov–Mar Mon–Fri 9am–12:30pm and 1:30–5:30pm. Gardens year-round daily 9am–5:30pm.

Ballyhack Castle, off R 733, Ballyhack, Co. Wexford. ☎ **051/89468.**

On a steep slope overlooking the Waterford estuary, about 20 miles west of Wexford, this castle is a large tower house. It's thought to have been built about 1450 by the Knights Hospitallers of St. John, one of the two great military orders founded at the beginning of the 12th century during the Crusades. Hence this building is considered a Crusader castle. It's currently being restored but will open as a heritage information center with displays on the Crusader knights, medieval monks, and Norman nobles.

Admission: £1 ($1.50) adults, 50p (75¢) seniors, students, and children.

Open: Apr–June and Sept Wed–Sun noon–6pm; July–Aug daily 10am–6pm.

Ballylane Farm, off the New Ross/Wexford Road (N 25), New Ross, Co. Wexford. ☎ **051/21315.**

In the heart of County Wexford's verdant countryside, this 200-acre farm is owned by the Hickey family, who invite visitors to get a first-hand look at their farm life— from tillage and sheep-raising to deer and pheasant husbandry. Guided tours, lasting about an hour, are given on a set route covering fields of crops, woodlands, boglands, ponds, and farm buildings. It's located 19 miles east of Wexford Town and one mile east of New Ross. It's sign-posted from the main road.

Admission: £2 ($3) adults, £1 ($1.50) children.

Open: May–Aug daily 10am–6pm.

Yola Farmstead, Wexford/Rosslare Road (N 25), Tagoat, Co. Wexford. ☎ **053/31177.**

A voluntary community project, this theme park depicts a Wexford farming community as it would have been 200 years or more ago. Thatched-roof buildings have been constructed, including barns housing farm animals. Bread- and butter-making is demonstrated. Craftsmen can be seen at work blowing and hand-cutting crystal at

Wexford Heritage Crystal, an on-site glass production enterprise. A small area is devoted to endangered species. Future plans call for a genealogy center. It's located about ten miles south of Wexford Town.

Admission: £2 ($3) adults, £1 ($1.50) seniors, and 50p (75¢) children.
Open: June–Sept daily 10am–5pm.

SPORTS & RECREATION

BEACHES   County Wexford's beaches at Courtown, Curracloe, Duncannon, and Rosslare are ideal for walking, jogging, or swimming.

BICYCLING   Rent a bike at the following shops for £7 ($10.50) per day: The Bike Shop, 9 Selskar St. (☎ 053/22514); Hayes' Cycle Shop, 108 S. Main St. (☎ 053/22462); or the Wexford Cycle Shop, 86 S. Main St. (☎ 053/22516). The local cycling club, the Wexford Wheelers, meet every Sunday morning between 9 and 9:30am, and welcome visitors to join them.

GOLF   In recent years, Wexford has blossomed as a golfing venue. The newest development is an 18-hole championship seaside par-72 course at St. Helens Bay Golf Club, Kilrane, Co. Wexford (☎ 053/33234), with greens fees of £15 ($22.50) on weekdays and £22 ($33) on weekends. Other courses that welcome visitors are the Wexford Golf Club, Mulgannon, Co. Wexford (☎ 053/42238), a par-70 inland course, with greens fees of £12 ($18) on weekdays and £15 ($22.50) on weekends; Rosslare Golf Club, Rosslare, Co. Wexford (☎ 053/32113), a par-74 seaside championship course, with greens fees of £18 ($27) on weekdays, and £23 ($34.50) on weekends; and the Enniscorthy Golf Club, Knockmarshall, Enniscorthy, Co. Wexford (☎ 054/33191), an inland par-70 course with greens fees of £10 ($15) on weekdays and £12 ($18) on weekends.

HORSEBACK RIDING   With its verdant valleys, fields, and trails, the Wexford countryside is known as good turf for horseback riding. An hour's ride averages £10 ($15) per at the following establishments: Horetown House Equestrian Centre, Foulksmills, Co. Wexford (☎ 051/63786); Boro Hill Equestrian Centre, Clonroche, Enniscorthy, Co. Wexford (☎ 054/44117); and Shelmalier Riding Stables, Trinity, Taghmon, Co. Wexford (☎ 053/39251).

SAVVY SHOPPING

Shops in Wexford are open Monday through Thursday from 9am to 5:30pm, Friday and Saturday from 9am to 6pm; some shops stay open until 8pm on Friday.

Barkers, 36–40 S. Main St. ☎ 053/23159.

Established in 1848, this has long been a mainstay in Wexford for a large selection of Waterford Crystal, Belleek China, and Royal Irish Tara China, as well as Irish linens and bronze, and international products such as Aynsley, Wedgwood, and Lladro.

The Book Centre, 5 S. Main St. ☎ 053/23543.

For books and maps on Wexford and Ireland in general, this shop offers a wide selection. It also carries cards, stationery, and music tapes and cassettes, and has a literary-theme coffee shop.

Faller's Sweater Shop, 39 N. Main St. ☎ 053/24659.

As its name implies, this shop specializes in a large selection of Aran handknit sweaters, as well as mohair knits, and cotton and linen knits, as well as ties, scarves, wool socks, and tweed caps.

Ferrycarrig Crystal, 115 N. Main St. ☎ 053/43211.

Ferrycarrig Crystal, a new name in an ancient craft, was conceived by a former Waterford craftsman, and has quickly developed into one of Wexford's great enterprises. Visitors can watch as crystal is mouth-blown, hand-crafted, and hand-decorated into glasses, bowls, tankards, lamps, decanters, vases, bowls, and more.

 Wexford Silver, 115 N. Main St. ☎ 053/43211.

One of Ireland's leading silversmiths, Pat Dolan, plies his craft at this shop, along with his sons. They are members of a long line of Dolans who trace their silversmithing connections back to 1647. The Dolans create gold, silver, and bronze pieces by hand using traditional tools and techniques. A second workshop is located at Kinsale (see "Kinsale Silver" in County Cork, below).

The Wool Shop, 39–41 S. Main St. ☎ 053/22247.

In the heart of the town's main thoroughfare, this is Wexford's long established best source for handknits, from caps and tams to sweaters and jackets, as well as tweeds, linens, mohairs, and knitting yarns.

WHERE TO STAY

Expensive/Moderate

Ferrycarrig, P.O. Box 11, Wexford/Enniscorthy Road (N 11), Wexford, Co. Wexford. ☎ 053/22999. Fax 053/41982. 40 rms (all with bath). TV TEL

Rates (including full breakfast): £40–£80 ($60–$120) single, £40–£140 ($60–$210) double. No service charge. AE, DC, MC, V.

Situated next to the Ferrycarrig Bridge and opposite the Irish National Heritage Park about two miles north of town, this contemporary four-story hotel overlooks the River Slaney estuary and fertile Wexford countryside. Guest rooms are furnished in soft pastel tones with light woods and modern art, with picture windows that look out onto the river and well-cultivated gardens. Facilities include the Conservatory restaurant noted for its seafood, the Boathouse Bistro for light fare, and the Dry Dock Bar, two tennis courts, and a river walk.

 Marlfield House, Courtown Road, Gorey, Co. Wexford. ☎ (055) 21124 or toll free **800/223-6510** in U.S. Fax 055/21572. 19 rms (all with bath). TV TEL

Rates (including full breakfast): £75–£84 ($112.50–$126) single, £120–£140 ($180–$210) double. Service charge 10%. AE, MC, V.

Originally a dower house and then the principal residence of the Earl of Courtown, this splendid Regency manor home was built around 1850. Thanks to the current owners, Ray and Mary Bowe, it has been masterfully transformed into a top-notch country inn with award-winning gardens. Although guest rooms have every modern convenience (including fully carpeted bathrooms), they retain an old-world charm with individualized decors, many with half-tester beds, four-posters, or canopies, hand-carved armoires, and one-of-a-kind antiques. The public rooms and lounge have comfortable and inviting furnishings plus gilt-edge mirrors, crystal chandeliers, and marble fireplaces. Marlfield has earned many plaudits for its cuisine, using organically grown fruits and vegetables from the garden, served either in the main dining area or in a fanciful skylit Victorian-style conservatory room. Outdoor facilities include a tennis court and croquet lawn. It is located 40 miles north of Wexford Town in the northernmost part of the county.

Moderate

Great Southern, Wexford/Rosslare Harbor Road (N 25), Rosslare Harbour, Co. Wexford. ☎ 053/33233 or toll free **800/44-UTELL** in the U.S. Fax 053/33543. 99 rms (all with bath). TV TEL

Rates: £64 ($96) single or double. Service charge 12.5%. AE, DC, MC, V.

For travelers taking the ferry to/from Britain or France or for anyone fond of sea views, this modern three-story hotel is an ideal overnight stop. It is positioned on a cliff top overlooking the harbor, less than a mile away from the ferry terminals. With a bright and airy decor, it has lots of wide floor-to-ceiling windows and colorful contemporary furnishings in the guest rooms and public areas. It's approximately 12 miles south of Wexford town.

Dining/Entertainment: The Norman Room Restaurant serves meals throughout the day, overlooking the water, and the lounge offers evening entertainment in the summer.

Facilities: Conservatory, indoor heated swimming pool, sauna, gym, and tennis court.

Moderate/Inexpensive

★ **The Talbot,** Trinity Street, Wexford, Co. Wexford. ☎ **053/22566** or toll free **800/223/6764** in U.S. Fax 053/23377. 96 rms (all with bath). TV TEL

Rates (including full breakfast): £30–£38.50 ($45–$57.75) single, £60–£77 ($90–$115.50) double. No service charge. AE, DC, MC, V.

On the western end of the quays, this modern six-story hotel has the advantage of overlooking the harbor while still being within a block from the town's main shopping street. The guest rooms are outfitted with light woods and bright floral fabrics; many rooms have river views and all have extra amenities such as hair dryers and coffee/tea-makers.

Dining/Entertainment: The Guillemot Restaurant offers formal dining for lunch or dinner, while lighter fare is available all day at the Pike Grill. For drinks with traditional music, try the Tavern, while the Trinity Lounge offers liquid refreshment with jazz or 60s music.

Services: Room service, concierge, valet/laundry.

Facilities: Indoor heated swimming pool, gym, saunas, squash court, solarium, table tennis, and hairdressing salon.

Wexford Lodge, Wexford Bridge, Wexford, Co. Wexford. ☎ **053/23611** or toll free **800/365-3346** in U.S. Fax 053/23342. 18 rms (all with bath). TV TEL

Rates (including full breakfast): £25–£70 ($37.50–$105) single or double. No service charge. AE, MC, V.

Facing south on Wexford Harbour, this small family-run two-story hotel is situated across from town on the River Slaney via the Wexford Bridge, off R 471. A handy choice if you want to be close to town but in a more peaceful setting, it's next to a former U.S. air force station. The interior is furnished in contemporary style. Both the public rooms and guest rooms have lovely views of the river. Facilities include the Beann Abu restaurant, known for good local seafood, and the River Bar, decorated with pictures of the air force station dating back to 1918.

White's, George and Main Streets, Wexford, Co. Wexford. ☎ 053/22311 or toll free 800/528-1234 in the U.S. Fax 053/45000. 82 rms (all with bath). TV TEL

Rates: (including full breakfast) £37.25–£74 ($55.88–$111) single, £52.50–£112 ($55.88–$168). No service charge. AE, DC, MC, V.

Dating back to 1779, this vintage hotel is situated right in the middle of town, with its older section facing North Main Street. Over the years it has been expanded and updated, resulting in lots of connecting corridors and bedrooms of varying size and standards, some with four poster or canopy beds and others with modern light-wood furnishings. For the most part, the public rooms reflect the aura of an old coaching inn and are a delight to browse around.

Dining/Entertainment: Top-class meals are served in the main restaurant, Captain White's, and lighter fare is available all day in the Country Kitchen. There are two bars, The Shelmalier, where jazz and folk music is often on tap on weekends, and Speakers, a contemporary watering hole.

Services: 24-hour room service, one-day dry cleaning, concierge.

Facilities: Jacuzzi, gym, sauna, steam room, solarium.

Inexpensive

McMenamin's Townhouse, 3 Auburn Terrace, Redmond Road, Wexford. ☎ 053/46442. Fax 053/46442. 6 rms (all with private bath).

Rates (including full breakfast): £18.50 ($27.75) single, £35 ($52.52) double. No service charge. MC, V.

Situated at the west end of town, opposite the railroad station, this lovely Victorian-style town house offers up-to-date accommodations at an affordable price. Guest rooms are individually furnished with local antiques, including brass beds and caned chairs; all have coffee/tea-making facilities. Some have television and all are getting in-room phones by 1995. This is one of the town's newest guesthouses, operated by Seamus and Kay McMenamin, who formerly ran the Bohemian Girl pub/restaurant, so Kay puts her culinary skills to work by providing gourmet breakfast for guests.

WHERE TO DINE

Expensive/Moderate

Lobster Pot, Carne, Co. Wexford. ☎ 053/31110.

Cuisine: SEAFOOD. **Reservations:** Recommended for dinner.

Prices: Appetizers £1.20–£5.95 ($1.80–$8.93); main courses £8.95–£13.95 ($13.43–$20.93), lobster dishes £18–£19 ($27–$28.50). AE, MC, V.

Open: June–Sept Mon–Sat 10:30am–11:30pm, Sun noon–2pm and 4–11pm; Oct–May Mon–Sat 10:30am–11pm, Sun noon–2pm and 4–11pm. **Closed:** Jan.

Situated about ten miles south of Wexford Town near the sea, this thatched-roof cottage restaurant is a popular spot for dining indoors and outdoors. The atmosphere is rustic, with a decor of local memorabilia, from crocks, kettles, and jars to framed newspaper clippings, pictures, and seafaring equipment. The menu, which is the same all day, features wild fresh salmon, pan-fried Dover sole, grilled trout meunière, baked crab or Kilmore scallops mornay, and a house special of Lobster Pot Pourri (lobster and seafood in a creamy white wine sauce). For non-seafood eaters, there are steaks, chicken Kiev, and roast duckling. Lighter items, popular at lunchtime, include seafood salads and chowders.

★ **Granary,** West Gate, Wexford. ☎ **053/23935.**
Cuisine: INTERNATIONAL. **Reservations:** Recommended.
Prices: Appetizers £2.25–£5.95 ($3.38–$8.93); main courses £10.50–£15.95 ($15.75–$23.93). AE, DC, MC, V.
Open: Mon–Sat 6–10pm.

Located in one of Wexford's most historic sections near the old city walls, this restaurant is a rustic melange of beamed ceilings, wooden pillars, and copper kettles. The menu includes dishes such as roast Kilmore scallops poached in white wine; farmyard duck with honey and lime sauce; chicken Selskar, free-range chicken in parmesan cheese, almonds, baked in orange and thyme sauce; Slaney salmon baked in balsamic vinaigrette sauce; and a variety of steaks.

Moderate

La Riva, 2 Henrietta St., Wexford. ☎ **053/24330.**
Cuisine: ITALIAN. **Reservations:** Recommended.
Prices: Appetizers £1.50–£4.50 ($2.25–$7.25); main courses £5.50–£10.95 ($8.25–$16.43). MC, V.
Open: Mon–Sat 6–10:45pm, Sun 6–10pm.

Situated within a splash of the harbor, just off Crescent Quay, this upstairs restaurant is well named, near Wexford's famous River Slaney. Step inside and enjoy the rich aromas and decor that convey the Mediterranean in the heart of Wexford. On the menu are pastas and pizzas, as well as pork alla marsala, eggplant parmigiana, garlic chicken, prawns in cream and basil sauce with courgettes (zucchini), and the ever-present steak.

★ **The Neptune,** Ballyhack Harbor, Ballyhack, Co. Wexford. ☎ **051/89284.**
Cuisine: INTERNATIONAL/SEAFOOD. **Reservations:** Required for dinner and Sunday lunch.
Prices: Appetizers £2.50–£4.90 ($3.75–$7.35); lunch main courses £2.90–£8.50 ($4.35–$12.75); dinner main courses £9.50–£11.50 ($14.25–$17.25). AE, DC, MC, V.
Open: April–Oct Tues–Sat lunch noon–2:30pm and dinner 6–10pm, Sun lunch 12:30–3pm; July–Aug daily lunch noon–2:30pm and dinner 6–10pm.

Situated in a sheltered harbor town on the western edge of County Wexford, about 20 miles from Wexford Town, this restaurant is located in an old house on the waterfront. The interior has an airy modern motif, with paintings and pottery by Irish artisans; tables are also set up outside for sunny days. The lunch menu often includes such items as asparagus quiche, crab salad, or seafood omelets. Dinner ranges from scallops in orange and ginger sauce, filet of hake in citrus sauce, to hot buttered lobster, Ballyhack wild salmon baked in cream, or the house signature dish, hot crab Brehat (crab sautéed in port, and baked with mushrooms, béchamel sauce, and cheese). For meat lovers, there are T-bone and filet steaks, as well as international favorites like Hungarian goulash or breast of chicken thermidor. You can reach this little gem easily from Waterford (via the Ballyhack-Passage East car ferry) or by road from Wexford. It's worth the trip from any direction.

Moderate/Inexpensive

Robertino's, 19 S. Main St, Wexford. ☎ **053/23334.**
Cuisine: ITALIAN. **Reservations:** Recommended.
Prices: Appetizers £1.10–£3.15 ($1.65–$4.73); main courses £2–£8.95 ($3–$13.43). No credit cards.

Open: Mon–Thurs 10:30am–midnight, Fri–Sat 10:30am–12:30am, Sun 7pm–midnight.

This informal restaurant prides itself as being an Italian oasis in the heart of Wexford, known for freshly made pastas and pizzas. The menu also includes a fine selection of steaks, quiches, omelets, and curries. The wine list is particularly extensive.

Budget

Bohemian Girl, North Main and Monck Streets, Wexford. ☎ **053/23596.**

Cuisine: PUB GRUB. **Reservations:** Not necessary.
Prices: All items £1.30–£4.95 ($1.95–$7.43). MC, V.
Open: Pub lunches 12:30–3pm.

Named for an opera written by William Balfe, a onetime Wexford resident, this is a Tudor-style pub, with hanging plants on the outside wall and an interior of lantern lights, barrel-shaped tables, and matchbook covers on the ceiling. It is known for excellent pub lunches including fresh oysters, pâtés, combination sandwiches, and homemade soups.

Cellar Restaurant, Cornmarket at Abbey Street, Wexford. ☎ **053/24544.**

Cuisine: IRISH/VEGETARIAN. **Reservations:** Not accepted.
Prices: All items £2–£5 ($3–$7.50). No credit cards.
Open: Daily 10am–6pm.

Housed in the Wexford Arts Centre, this charming eatery has a country kitchen atmosphere, with stone walls, pine furnishings and home-cooking prepared by Chef Caroline. Selections include salads, soups, quiches, pizzas, and chili, with particular emphasis on vegetarian items.

★ **Kate's Kitchen,** Henrietta Street, Wexford. ☎ **053/22456.**

Cuisine: IRISH/SELF-SERVICE. **Reservations:** Accepted for breakfast.
Prices: All items £1–£3.95 ($1.50–$5.93). No credit cards.
Open: Daily 7am–7pm.

For meals and snacks throughout the day, this is a favorite gathering spot for Wexford folk and visitors alike. Kate welcomes everyone like a long-lost friend at this shopfront cafe, situated between Crescent Quay and S. Main Street. The menu changes daily but includes homemade soups, salads, and meat pies, as well as quiches, crêpes, curries, pastas, and many tempting pastries, cakes, and desserts.

EVENING ENTERTAINMENT

Famed for its Opera Festival each October, Wexford is a town synonymous with music and the arts. Year-round performances are given at the Theatre Royal, High Street, Wexford (☎ **053/22240**), a beautiful hall dating back to 1832.

Alternatively, there is usually something going on at the Wexford Arts Centre, Cornmarket, Wexford (☎ **053/23764**). Built as the market house in 1775 at the Cornmarket, this building has served as a dance venue, concert hall, and municipal offices. Since 1974, it has provided a focal point for all of the arts in Wexford. It now houses art galleries and showcases artistic events.

To see traditional Irish music and dancing, head ten miles south of Wexford to the Yola Farmstead, Wexford/Rosslare Road (N 25), Tagoat, Co. Wexford (☎ **053/ 31177**). It stages traditional ceili evenings of Irish music, song, dance, and recitations, during July and August, on Thursday and Saturday at 7:30pm. Admission is £3 ($4.50) per person.

PUBS

Antique Tavern, 14 Slaney St., Enniscorthy. ☎ 054/33428.

It's worth a 15-mile trip to Enniscorthy to see this unique Tudor-style pub, located off the main Dublin/Wexford Road (N 11). The walls are lined with memorabilia from the Wexford area—old daggers, pikes, farming implements, lanterns, pictures, and prints. You'll also see mounted elk's heads, an antique wooden bird cage, and a glass case full of paper money from around the world.

Con Macken's, The Cape of Good Hope, The Bull Ring, off North Main Street, Wexford. ☎ 053/22949.

Long a favorite with photographers, this pub is unique for the trio of services it offers, aptly described by the sign outside the door: "Bar—Undertaker—Groceries." Hardly any visitor passes by without a second look at the windows, one displaying beer and spirit bottles, the other featuring plastic funeral wreaths. An alehouse for centuries, The Cape has always been at the center of Wexford political events, and the bar walls are lined with rebel souvenirs, old weapons, and plaques.

The Crown Bar, Monck Street, Wexford. (No phone)

Once a stagecoach inn, this tiny pub in the center of town has been in the Kelly family since 1841. Besides its historical overtones, it is well known for its museumlike collection of antique weapons. You'll see 18th-century dueling pistols, pikes from the 1798 rebellion, powder horns, and blunderbusses, as well as vintage prints, military artifacts, and swords. Unlike most pubs, it may not always be open during the day, so it is best to save a visit for the evening hours.

Oak Tavern, Wexford/Enniscorthy Road (N 11), Ferrycarrig, Wexford. ☎ 053/24922.

Dating back over 150 years and originally a tollhouse on the River Slaney, this pub is delightfully situated two miles north of town, overlooking the River Slaney and near the Ferrycarrig Bridge. Bar lunches are served during the day, with the choices ranging from beef and vegetable hot pot to shepherd's pie. There is also seating outdoors on a riverside patio. Traditional music sessions are held most evenings in the front bar.

Thomas Moore Tavern, The Cornmarket, Wexford. ☎ 053/24348.

This pub is named for the famous Irish composer and poet Thomas Moore for good reason—his mother was born in the living quarters upstairs, when the pub was known as The Ark. Although Moore never lived here, he returned to his mother's town on many occasions and to visit, and played music nearby. It's a good spot for a quiet drink in a literary ambience.

The Wren's Nest, Custom House Quay, Wexford. ☎ 053/22359.

Situated along the harborfront near the John Barry Memorial, this pub has a nautical theme, with a bar shaped like a ship, plus a fishnet ceiling and furnishings with a seagull motif. The varied pub grub includes Wexford mussel platters, house pâtés, soups, salads, and sandwiches. There is free traditional Irish music on Tuesday and Thursday nights.

2 County Waterford

Waterford City is 40 miles W of Wexford, 33 miles W of Rosslare Harbour, 98 miles SW of Dublin, 78 miles E of Cork, 95 miles SE of Shannon Airport

GETTING THERE • By Plane   Air service from Britain is operated into Waterford Airport, off R 675, Waterford (☎ **051/71701**), by Manx Airlines from London (Stansted) and Orient Air from Gloucester.

• By Rail   Irish Rail offers daily service from Dublin and other points into Plunkett Station, at Edmund Ignatius Rice Bridge, Waterford (☎ **051/73401**).

• By Bus   Bus Eireann operates daily services into Plunkett Station Depot, Waterford (☎ **051/73401**), from Dublin, Limerick, and other major cities throughout Ireland.

• By Car   These major roads lead into Waterford—N 25 from Cork and the south; N 24 from the west; N 19 from Kilkenny and points north; and N 25 from Wexford.

• By Ferry   The Passage East Car Ferry, Barrack Street, Passage East, Co. Waterford (☎ **051/82488** or **82480**), operates a car ferry service across Waterford Harbour, linking Passage East, about ten miles east of Waterford, with Ballyhack, about 20 miles southwest of Wexford. This shortcut saves about an hour's driving time between the two cities. Crossing time averages ten minutes and service is continuous. It's a drive-on, drive-off service, with no reservations required. The fares for car and passengers are £3.50 ($5.25) one-way, £5.50 ($8.25) round-trip. It operates April through September on Monday through Saturday, 7:20am until 10pm, and on Sunday, 9:30am until 10pm; October through March, Monday through Saturday, 7:20am until 8pm, and Sunday, 9:30am until 8pm.

TOURIST INFORMATION   Year-round information services are provided by the Waterford Tourist Office, 41 The Quay, Waterford (☎ **051/75788**). It's open April through October on Monday through Saturday from 9am to 6pm; January–March and November–December it's open Monday through Friday from 9am to 5:15pm. In July and August, it's open Monday through Saturday from 9am to 6pm, and on Sunday from 10am to 5pm. Seasonal offices, open mid-June through August, are maintained at Dungarvan Town Centre (☎ **058/41741**) and The Square at Tramore (☎ **051/81572**).

TOWN LAYOUT   Rimmed by the River Suir, Waterford is a small and compact city. The main commercial hub sits on the south bank of the river. Traffic from the north, west, and east enters from the north bank via the Ignatius Rice Bridge and onto a series of four quays (Grattan, Merchants, Meagher, and Parade), but most addresses simply say "The Quay." The majority of shops and attractions are concentrated near the quay area or on two thoroughfares which intersect with the quays—The Mall and Barronstrand Street, which changes names to Broad/Michael/John Streets.

GETTING AROUND • By Public Transport   Bus Eireann operates daily bus service within Waterford and its environs. The flat fare is 70p ($1.05). Taxi ranks are located outside of Plunkett Rail Station and along the Quay opposite the Granville Hotel. If you need to call a taxi, try A.B. Cabs (☎ **051/79100**), Dial A Cab (☎ **051/53333**), Five O Cabs (☎ **051/50000**), or Parnell Cabs (☎ **051/77710**).

• By Car   To see most of Waterford's sights with the exception of Waterford Glass, it is best to walk. Park your car along the Quays; parking is operated by machines at 30p (45¢) for two hours, or by the disc system at 40p (60¢) per hour. Discs are on sale at the tourist office or many of the shops. You'll need a car to reach the Waterford Glass Factory and Waterford County attractions outside of town.

     If you need to rent a car, contact Budget, 41 The Quay, Waterford (☎ **051/21670**); Hertz, Dublin Road, Waterford (☎ **051/78737**); or Murrays Europcar, Cork Road, Waterford (☎ **051/73144**)

• **On Foot**   The best way to see the city is by walking along the quays and taking a right at Reginald's Tower on The Mall, which becomes Parnell Street and then turning right onto John Street, which becomes Michael/Broad/Barronstrand Streets, which brings you back to the quays. The tourist office will supply you with a free map.

Fast Facts: Waterford

Area Code   The telephone area code for Waterford City and the surrounding area is **051**. County Waterford area codes include **052** and **058**.

Drugstores   Gallagher's Pharmacy, Barronstrand St. (☎ **78103**), and Mulligan's Chemists, with shops at 40-41 Barronstrand St. (☎ **75211**) and at Unit 12A of City Square Shopping Centre (☎ **53247**).

Dry Cleaning and Laundry   Eddie's Dry Cleaners, 82 The Quay (☎ **77677**), and Boston Cleaners, 6 Michael St. (☎ **74487**).

Emergencies   Dial **999.**

Hospital   Holy Ghost Hospital, Cork Road (☎ **74397**).

Local Newspaper and Media   The weekly newspaper covering local events and entertainment is the *Waterford News & Star.*

Waterford Local Radio (WLR) broadcasts on 97.5 FM and 95.1 FM.

Police   Phone the Garda Headquarters (☎ **74888**).

Photographic Supplies   Hennebry Camera, 109 The Quay (☎ **75049**).

Post Office   General Post Office, Parade Quay (☎ **74444**). It's open Monday through Friday from 9am to 5:30pm and Saturday from 9am to 1pm.

Mention Waterford and most people think glass. There's no question that beautiful hand-cut Waterford crystal is known and treasured around the world. But, as you'll find out when you visit this part of Ireland, Waterford is more than just the trademark of a leading Irish industry—it's also the name of a county and a city on the Emerald Isle's southeast coast—both of which have a lot to offer in their own right.

Waterford City (population 50,000) is the main seaport of the southeast. The city was known in Irish as Port Lairge, which means Lairge's Landing Place. It sits on the south bank of the River Suir (pronounced Sure) at the estuary of Waterford Harbour. The city's present name dates back to the ninth century when it was an important Danish settlement, known as Vadrefjord.

South of Waterford City is beach country. One of Ireland's premier seaside resorts, Tramore is located just eight miles away. A favorite with Irish vacationers, Tramore has a three-mile-long sandy beach, a boardwalk, and a string of amusement arcades—ideal for families.

Other coastal highlights include Passage East, a tiny seaport from which you can catch a ferry across the harbor and cut your driving time from Waterford-to-Wexford in half; Dunmore East, a picturesque fishing village; Dungarvan, a major town with a fine harbor; and Ardmore, a quiet beach resort. Ardmore, which in Irish means the great height, is also the setting for a seventh-century monastic settlement founded by St. Declan. At Ardmore stands a 97-foot-tall round tower, one of the most perfect of its kind in this part of Ireland; a 12th-century cathedral; ancient grave sites; and a

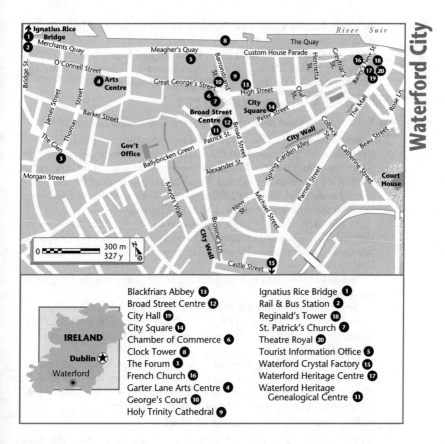

Blackfriars Abbey **13**
Broad Street Centre **12**
City Hall **19**
City Square **14**
Chamber of Commerce **6**
Clock Tower **8**
The Forum **3**
French Church **16**
Garter Lane Arts Centre **4**
George's Court **10**
Holy Trinity Cathedral **9**

Ignatius Rice Bridge **1**
Rail & Bus Station **2**
Reginald's Tower **18**
St. Patrick's Church **7**
Theatre Royal **20**
Tourist Information Office **5**
Waterford Crystal Factory **15**
Waterford Heritage Centre **17**
Waterford Heritage
    Genealogical Centre **11**

IRELAND

Dublin ★

Waterford ◉

IMPRESSIONS

We are one of the great stocks of Europe. We are the people of Burke; we are the people of Grattan; we are the people of Swift; the people of Emmet, the people of Parnell. We have created most of the modern literature of this century. We have created the best of its political intelligence.

—W.B. Yeats (1865–1939) Senate Debate, June 11, 1925

holy well. Portally Cove, near Dunmore East, is the home of Ireland's only Amish-Mennonite community.

In west County Waterford, Lismore Castle is a regal fortress built in 1185. It's said to have inspired Edmund Spencer, whose masterpiece is the *Faerie Queene.* Still inhabited today, it's the Irish home of the Duke of Devonshire.

WHAT TO SEE & DO IN WATERFORD CITY

⭐ **Waterford Crystal Factory and Gallery,** Cork Road, Waterford. ☎ **73311.**

Without a doubt, this is Waterford's number-one attraction. Founded in 1783, this glass-making enterprise thrived and Waterford became the crystal of connoisseurs. The factory was forced to close in 1851, due to the devastating effects of the Irish famine. Happily, it was revived in 1947, and Waterford has since regained the lead among prized glassware. With more than 2,000 employees, Waterford is now the largest crystal factory in the world, and the major industry in Waterford.

Visitors are welcome to watch a 17-minute audio-visual presentation on the glass-making process and then to take a 35-minute tour of the factory to see process first-hand—from the mouth-blowing and shaping of the molten glass to the delicate hand-cutting.

Note: children under 10 are not permitted on the factory tour. Reservations are not required.

You can stroll around the Waterford Crystal Gallery, a bilevel showroom containing the most comprehensive display of Waterford Crystal in the world, from all the glass-ware patterns to elaborate pieces like trophies, globes, and chandeliers. Crystal is on sale in the gallery.

Admission: £2 ($3) per person for the tour; free to the audio-visual and gallery.

Open: April–Oct Mon–Sat 8:30am–5pm, Sun 10am–5pm; Nov–Mar Mon–Fri 9am–5pm. Tours given on continuous first-come basis Apr–Oct Mon–Sat 8:30am–3:15pm, Sun 10am–3:15pm; Nov–Mar Mon–Fri 9am–3:15pm.

Reginald's Tower, The Quay, Waterford. ☎ **73501.**

Circular, topped with a conical roof, and having walls 10 ft. thick—this mighty tower stands at the eastern end of the Quay beside the river. It's said to have been built in 1003 by a Viking governor named Reginald. Still dominating the Wexford skyline, it's particularly striking at night when fully floodlit. Over the centuries, it's been a fortress, prison, military depot, mint, and air-raid shelter. Now it's the home of Waterford's Civic Museum; on display are medieval charters. As of this writing, the tower is closed for restoration. When it reopens in the spring of 1995, it will contain items recovered during city excavations from 1986 to 1992.

Note: Hours and admission may change after reopening.

Admission: 75p ($1.08) per person; in conjunction with Waterford Heritage Centre, £1 ($1.50) for both.

Open: Apr–Oct Mon–Fri 10am–8pm, Sat 10am–6pm; Nov–Mar to be advised.

City Hall, The Mall, Waterford. ☎ **73501.**

Headquarters of the local Waterford city government, this late 18th-century building houses various local memorabilia, including information on the city's charter which was granted in 1205. In addition, a display is dedicated to Thomas Francis Meagher, a leader in an 1848 Irish insurrection. Meagher was sentenced to death, but he es-caped to America where he fought in the Civil War, earning the rank of a brigadier general. Eventually he became acting Governor of Montana. City Hall's other treasures include an 18th-century Waterford glass chandelier, a complete dinner service of priceless antique Waterford glasses, and a painting of Waterford City in 1736 by the Flemish master, William Van der Hagen.

Admission: Free.

Open: Mon–Fri 9:30am–5pm.

Waterford Heritage Centre, Greyfriars St., Waterford. ☎ **71227.**

A half-block away from Reginald's Tower at the former Greyfriars church, this center houses a fine collection of Viking and medieval artifacts recovered from a recent archaeological dig. Waterford's early days of Viking and Norman settlements are also focused on.

Admission: 75p ($1.08) adults; in conjunction with Reginald's Tower Museum £1 ($1.50) adults.

Open: April–May Mon–Fri 10am–1pm and 2–6pm, Sat 10am–1pm; June–Sept Mon–Fri 10am–8pm, Sat 10am–1pm and 2–5pm.

Waterford Heritage Genealogical Centre, Jenkins Lane, Waterford. ☎ **76123.**

Did your ancestors come from Waterford? Then follow the small laneway between George's and Patrick's Streets to this historic building adjoining St. Patrick's Church, one of Ireland's oldest churches. This center specializes in tracing County Waterford ancestry. Church registers dating from 1655 and other surveys, rolls, and census lists are used as resources. An audiovisual presentation examines the heritage of the people of the area.

Admission: Free, but minimum search fee is £30 ($45).

Open: Mon–Thurs 9am–5pm, Fri 9am–2pm.

Garter Lane Arts Centre, 5 and 22a O'Connell St. ☎ **55038.**

One of Ireland's largest arts centers, the Garter Lane occupies two buildings on O'Connell Street—#5, the site of the former Waterford Library, and now the setting for exhibition rooms and artists' studios; and #22a, the former Friends Meeting House, now home of the Garter Lane Theatre, with an art gallery and outdoor courtyard. The gallery showcases works by contemporary and local artists. In July and August a crafts fair usually takes place, with works by artists from all over Ireland.

Admission: Free.

Open: Gallery Mon–Sat 10am–6pm.

Sightseeing Tours

★ **Walking Tours of Historic Waterford,** Waterford Tourist Services, Jenkins Lane, Waterford. ☎ **73711** or **51043.**

Local Waterford residents, well versed in the history, folklore, and wit of the city, conduct one-hour walking tours of Waterford, including two cathedrals and four national monuments. Tours depart from the Granville Hotel, The Quay.

Price: £3 ($4.50) adults, £2 ($3) students and seniors.

Schedule: Mar–Oct daily noon and 2pm.

Waterford Viking River Cruises, 4 Gladstone St., Waterford. ☎ **72800.**

See the Waterford sights from the water on board the *Viking I,* a luxury two-deck cruiser with bar and refreshment facilities. The trip leaves from the Waterford Quay opposite Reginald's Tower and goes downriver to Passage East and Ballyhack, passing rolling parkland, glens, fishing villages, cliffs, and the island where Waterford Castle is nestled, returning in just under two hours. Details and reservations are available from the office or the Tourist Office.

Fare: £5 ($7.50) adults, £2.50 ($3.75) children age 14 and under.

Schedule: May–Sept daily 3:30pm and 8pm; June–Aug daily noon, 3:30pm, and 8pm.

ATTRACTIONS IN NEARBY COUNTY WATERFORD

Celtworld, Tramore, Co. Waterford. ☎ **86166.**

South of Waterford in a seaside setting, this purpose-built indoor attraction reflects life in Ireland more than 1,500 years ago during Celtic times. Exhibits and animated displays re-create famous legends, myths, and folklore—from Finn MacCumaill and Cuchulainn to Oisin and Lir.

Admission: £3.95 ($5.93) adults, £3.25 ($4.88) seniors and students, £2.95 ($4.43) children.

Open: April Mon–Fri noon–5pm, Sat–Sun 10am–6pm; May and late Sept daily 10:30am–6pm; June daily 10am–8pm; July–Aug daily 10:30am–10pm; early Sept daily 10:30am–7pm; Oct Sat–Sun 10am–6pm.

★ **Lismore Castle**, Lismore, Co. Waterford. ☎ **058/54424.**

Perched high on a cliff above the River Blackwater, this multi-turreted castle has a long history, dating back to 1185 when Prince John of England built a similar fortress on this site. Local lore says that Lismore Castle was once granted for £12 ($18) a year to Sir Walter Raleigh, although he never occupied it. One man who did choose to live here was Richard Boyle, the 1st Earl of Cork, who rebuilt the castle in 1626, including the thick defensive walls that still surround the garden. Richard's son Robert, who was born at the castle in 1627, is the celebrated chemist whose name lives on in Boyle's Law. Most of the present castle was added in the mid-19th century. Today this 8,000-acre estate of gardens, forests, and farmland is the Irish seat of the Duke and Duchess of Devonshire, whose primary home is at Chatsworth in England. Although the castle itself is not open for tours, the splendid walled and woodland gardens are open.

Admission: £2 ($3) adults, £1 ($1.50) children under 16.

Open: End-April to mid–Sept daily 1:45–4:45pm.

Lismore Heritage Centre, Lismore. ☎ **058/54975.**

Where is the only Hindu Gothic bridge in Ireland located? Step inside this building and find out. This new interpretative center, housed in the town's Old Courthouse, will not only answer that question but also tells the history of Lismore, a charming town founded by St. Carthage in the year 636. The Lismore Experience is a multimedia presentation on the town's unique treasures including the *Book of Lismore,* dating back 1,000 years, and the Lismore Crozier from 1116—both of which were discovered hidden in the walls of Lismore Castle in 1814.

Admission: £2 ($3) adults, £1.50 ($2.25) seniors, £1 ($1.50) children.

Open: April and Oct Sun 2:30–5:30pm; May–Sept Mon–Fri 10am–5:30pm, Sat–Sun 2:30–5:30pm.

SPORTS & RECREATION

BEACHES   For walking, jogging, or swimming, visit one of County Waterford's wide sandy beaches at Tramore, Ardmore, Clonea, or Dunmore East.

BICYCLING   Rent a bicycle for £7 ($10.50) per day at Wright's Cycle Depot Ltd., Henrietta Street, Waterford (☎ 74411) or B 'n' B Cycles, 9 Ballybricken Waterford (☎ 70356).

GOLF   County Waterford's golf venues include three 18-hole championship courses: Faithlegg Golf Club, Faithlegg House, Co. Waterford (☎ 82241), a par-72 parkland course beside the River Suir, with greens fees of £16–£23 ($24–$34.50), depending on the time of day; Dungarvan Golf Club, Knocknagranagh, Dungarvan, Co. Waterford (☎ 058/41605), a parkland par-72 course with greens fees of £12 ($18) on weekdays and £15 ($22.50) on weekends; and Waterford Castle Golf & Country Club, The Island, Ballinakill, Waterford (☎ 71633), a par-72 parkland course with greens fees of £22.50 ($33.75) for overnight guests at the castle or £45 ($67.50) for visitors. In addition, there is the 18-hole par-71 inland course at Waterford Golf Club, Newrath, Waterford (☎ 76748), a mile from the center of the city, with greens fees of £17 ($25.50) on weekdays and £20 ($30) on weekends.

HORSEBACK RIDING   County Waterford is filled with trails for horseback riding, with fees averaging £10 ($15) per hour. You can arrange to ride at Killoteran Equitation Centre, Killoteran, Waterford (☎ 84158) or Melody's Riding Stables, Ballmacarberry, Co. Waterford (☎ 052/3647).

SAVVY SHOPPING

Most people come to Waterford to buy Waterford crystal, but there are many other fine products in the shops and in the three multilevel enclosed shopping centers—**George's Court,** off Barronstrand Street, **Broad Street Centre** on Broad Street, and **City Square** off Broad Street. Hours are usually Monday through Saturday from 9am or 9:30am to 6pm or 6:30pm. Some shops are open until 9pm on Thursday and Friday.

Aisling, Barronstrand Street at George's Court, Waterford. ☎ 73262.

Located opposite the city's Catholic cathedral, this small but interesting shop (the Gaelic name means dream) offers an assortment of unique crafts, from quilts, tartans, and kilts, to miniature paintings and watercolors of Irish scenes and subjects and floral art.

The Book Centre, 25 Broad St. ☎ 73823.

This huge four-level bookstore sells all types of books, newspapers, and magazines, as well as posters, maps, and music tapes and CDs. On-premises services include photocopying and fax transmission.

Kelly's, 75/76 The Quay. ☎ 73557.

Dating back to 1847, this store offers a wide selection of Waterford crystal, Aran knitwear, Belleek china, Royal Tara china, Irish linens, and other souvenirs.

Joseph Knox, 4 Barronstrand St. ☎ 75307 and 72723.

For visitors to Waterford, this store has long been a focal point, offering a large selection of Waterford crystal, particularly in specialty items like chandeliers.

Penrose Crystal, John Street, Waterford. ☎ 76537.

Established in 1786 and revived in 1978, this is Waterford's other glass company, turning out delicate hand-cut and engraved glassware. The craftsmen here practice the stipple engraving process, the highest art form in glass. A retail sales outlet is also located at Unit 8 of the City Square Shopping Centre. Both the factory and the retail shop are open usual hours but the factory is also open on Sunday from June to August from 2 to 5:30pm.

Woolcraft, 11 Michael St., Waterford. ☎ **74082.**

For more than 100 years, the Fitzpatrick family has operated this midcity shop, a reliable source for bainin and colored Aran sweaters. It also stocks hand-loomed knits, lightweight and cotton-and-linen sweaters, ladies' jackets, and knitting yarn, plus tweed hats and caps, pottery, decorative chess sets, *Book of Kells*–inspired jewelry, and other gifts.

WHERE TO STAY
Very Expensive/Expensive

★ **Waterford Castle,** The Island, Ballinakill, Waterford, Co. Waterford. ☎ 051/78203 or toll free **800/221-1074** in U.S. Fax 051/79316. 19 rms (all with bath). TV TEL

Rates: £115–£185 ($172.50–$277.50) single, £135–£205 ($202.50–$302.50) double. No service charge. AE, DC, MC, V. **Closed:** Dec 23–Jan 1.

Dating back 800 years, this is the most secluded of Ireland's castles—situated on a private 310-acre island in the River Suir two miles south of Waterford and reached by private chain-link car ferry. Comprising an original Norman keep and two Elizabethan-style wings, it is built entirely of stone with a leaded roof, mullioned windows, granite archways, ancient gargoyles, and fairy-tale turrets, towers, and battlements. Fully restored and refurbished in 1988, the castle's interior is full of oak-paneled walls, ornate plaster ceilings, colorful tapestries, spacious sitting areas with huge stone fireplaces, original paintings, and antiques. Each guest room is decorated with four-poster or canopied beds, hand-carved armoires, designer fabrics, and other regal accessories.

    Dining/Entertainment: Choices include the The Leinster Room restaurant and the Fitzgerald Room bar.

    Services: 24-hour room service, concierge, laundry and valet service.

    Facilities: 18-hole championship golf course, indoor heated pool and fitness center, tennis court, horseback riding, fishing, watersports.

Moderate

The Bridge, 1 The Quay, Waterford, Co. Waterford. ☎ **051/77222** or toll free **800/221-2222** in U.S. Fax 051/77229. 80 rms (all with bath). TV TEL

Rates (including full breakfast): £35–£45 ($47.50–$67.50) single, £60–£80 ($90–$120) double. Service charge 10%. AE, DC, MC, V.

Taking its name from its location—right on the waterfront at the foot of the Ignatius Rice Bridge—this three-story vintage hotel is one of the city's oldest, but it has been updated in recent years. Rooms have light wood furnishings and bright floral fabrics. Facilities include the Ignatius Rice Restaurant for formal dining, the Kitchen for light meals in an Irish country kitchen setting, and Crokers Bar and Timber Toes Lounge for liquid refreshment.

Granville, Meagher Quay, Waterford, Co. Waterford. ☎051/55111 or toll free **800/538-1234** in U.S. Fax 051/70307. 74 rms (all with bath). TV TEL

Rates (including full breakfast): £45–£71.50 (67.50–$107.25) single, £73–£124 ($109.50–$186) double. No service charge. AE, DC, MC, V. **Closed:** Dec 24–27.

Located along the quayside strip of Waterford's main business district, this hotel looks out onto the south side of the River Suir. Full of history, part of the Granville was originally a coaching inn, and an adjacent section was the home of Irish patriot Thomas Francis Meagher and a meeting place for Irish freedom fighters. In 1980 it was purchased by the Cusack family who have totally restored, refurbished, and enlarged it. The architecture is a blend of many centuries, but the furnishings are modern and functional. The bedrooms are bedecked with bright floral fabrics and the front rooms look out onto the river.

Dining/Entertainment: Amenities include Bells, a small gourmet restaurant, the Bianconi grill room, and a large lounge bar which is popular with a local clientele.

Services: Room service, concierge, laundry and valet.

⭐ **Jurys**, Ferrybank, Waterford, Co. Waterford. ☎ **051/32111** or toll free **800/44-UTELL** in the U.S. Fax 051/32863. 98 rms (all with bath). TV TEL

Rates: £62 ($93) single or double. Service Charge 10%. AE, DC, MC, V. **Closed:** Dec 24–27.

Set amid 38 acres of gardens and lawns, this modern six-story hotel is perched on a hill along the River Suir's northern banks. With such a commanding position, it's no wonder that each guest room enjoys a sweeping view of Waterford city. Recently refurbished, the rooms offer a Victorian-style decor of frilly floral fabrics, dark woods, and brass trim. In-room amenities include a hair dryer, built-in luggage rack, and coffee/tea-maker.

Dining/Entertainment: Bardens Restaurant and the Conor Bar both face the river and cityscape.

Services: 24-hour room service, concierge, same-day dry-cleaning/laundry, babysitting service.

Facilities: Indoor heated swimming pool, Jacuzzi, 2 saunas, steam room, gymnasium, 2 floodlit outdoor tennis courts, hairdressing salon.

Tower, The Mall, Waterford, Co. Waterford. ☎ **051/75801.** Fax 051/70129. 141 rms (all with bath). TV TEL

Rates: £80–£110 ($120–$165) single or double. No service charge. AE, DC, MC, V.

In an historic section of the city overlooking the River Suir, this contemporary four-story hotel is named after Reginald's Tower across the street and is within walking distance to all major downtown attractions. A popular base for bus tours, it was completely refurbished and enlarged in 1991. The bedrooms are standard but comfortable, with an eclectic mix of colors and furnishings. The public rooms have been recently extended, with emphasis on lovely wide-windowed views of the harbor. Amenities include a full-service restaurant, lounge overlooking the river, and a leisure center with indoor swimming pool, whirlpool, steam room, saunas, and exercise room.

Inexpensive

⭐ **Three Rivers Guesthouse**, Cheekpoint, Co. Waterford. ☎ **051/82520.** Fax 051/82542. 15 rms (all with bath). TEL

💲 **Rates** (including full breakfast): £17–£25 ($25.50–$37.50) single, £34–£50 ($51–$75) double. No service charge. MC, V.

This relatively new purpose-built guesthouse enjoys a serene waterfront setting, yet it's just seven miles from downtown Waterford. Aptly named, it sits on the harbor at the point where three rivers meet—the Suir, Nore, and Barrow. The guest rooms are bright and contemporary, with pastel tones, rattan furnishings, framed prints, floral fabrics and duvets. Most rooms have lovely views of the water, and all are smoke-free. Public areas include a bright multiwindowed dining room overlooking the rivers, where breakfast is served, and a large plant-filled conservatory-style TV/reading room. Innkeepers Rita and John Fitzgerald enthusiastically provide local sightseeing guidance.

WHERE TO DINE
Moderate

★ Dwyer's, 8 Mary St., Waterford. ☎ 77478 or 71183.
Cuisine: INTERNATIONAL. **Reservations:** Recommended.
Prices: Appetizers £2.50–£4.50 ($3.75–$7.25); main courses £12–£13 ($18–$19.50). AE, DC, MC, V.
Open: Mon–Sat 6–10pm.

Situated on a quiet back street near the northern entrance to the city at Ignatius Rice Bridge, this small restaurant is owned and operated by Martin and Sile Dwyer, who cook everything to order in a homey 30-seat setting with orchestral music in the background. The menu changes often, but choices often include wild salmon in pastry with cucumbers and fennel; roast filet of John Dory meunière; medaillons of filet with mushrooms, bacon, and red wine; spring lamb with mint butter sauce; honey-glazed breast of duck with lemon sauce.

★ Jade Palace, 3 The Mall, Waterford. ☎ 55611.
Cuisine: CHINESE/IRISH. **Reservations:** Recommended.
Prices: Set lunch £5.95 ($8.93); appetizers £2–£6.95 ($3–$10.43); dinner main courses £7.50–£12.95 ($11.25–$19.43). MC, V.
Open: Lunch Mon–Fri noon–2:30pm; dinner daily 6–10pm.

Some of Waterford's best cuisine is served at this reliable restaurant, on the upstairs level above a Victorian-style bar. The menu, which has garnered several awards, is attentively served amid a setting of pink linens, red velvet seats, Oriental statuary, library books, gilt-framed paintings, fresh flowers, and silver cutlery (or chopsticks, if you prefer). Dishes include king prawns, duck Cantonese, filet steak cooked at the table, lemon chicken, sweet-and-sour pork, baked lobster, and steamed fish with ginger.

Prendivilles, Cork Road, Waterford. ☎ 78851.
Cuisine: IRISH/INTERNATIONAL. **Reservations:** Recommended.
Prices: Set lunch £8.35–£10.75 ($12.53–$16.13); appetizers £2–£5 ($3–$7.50); main courses £8–£15 ($12–$22.50). AE, DC, MC, V.
Open: Mon–Sat lunch 12:30–2:15pm; dinner 6:30–9:45pm.

Located midway between downtown and the Waterford Crystal Factory, this restaurant is housed in a 19th-century Gothic-style stone gate lodge. The light and airy interior is enhanced by modern Irish art. The menu blends innovative cuisine with fresh local ingredients, offering dishes such as free-range chicken cooked with bacon and served on pasta with wild mushroom sauce; poached wild salmon with peach cream and mint sauce; breast of duck with honey and rosemary glaze; and roast lamb with herb juice.

The Reginald, The Mall, Waterford. ☎ 051/55087.
Cuisine: IRISH. **Reservations:** Recommended for dinner.
Prices: Bar food £2–£6 ($3–$9) all items; appetizers £1.65–£3.75 ($2.48–$5.63); main courses £8.25–£13.95 ($12.38–$20.93). DC, MC, V.

Open: Mon–Sat bar food noon–2:30pm, dinner 5:30–10:30pm; Sun lunch noon-2:30pm and dinner 5:30–9:30pm.

One of the city's original walls (circa A.D. 850) is part of the decor at this pub/restaurant next to Reginald's Tower. In keeping with its Viking-inspired foundations, the Reginald is laid out in a pattern of caverns, alcoves, and arches. The restaurant offers innovative choices using local ingredients such as filet steak Aoife, topped with avocado, chives, tomatoes, and green peppercorn sauce; filet of pink trout with vermouth sauce; half of roast duck with three peppercorns; pork steak and sorrel sauce; and chicken stuffed with cream cheese on noodles and tomato sauce. Buffet-style pub grub is available in the bar at lunchtime (Mon–Sat), and jazz is on tap during Sunday afternoon lunch from 12:30–2:30pm.

The Seanachie, Waterford/Cork Road (N 25), Pulla, Ring, Dungarvan, Co. Waterford. ☎ **058/46285.**

Cuisine: IRISH. **Reservations:** Recommended for dinner.
Prices: Appetizers £2.50–£6 ($3.75–$9); lunch main courses £3–£7.95 ($4.75–$11.83); dinner main courses £11–£15 ($16.50–$22.50).
Open: April–mid-Nov daily noon–10pm.

Located five miles west of Dungarvan and about 32 miles west of Waterford City, this cozy thatched-roof pub sits off the main road in a farmyard setting. It takes its name from the Irish word meaning storyteller—and storytelling as well as Irish music is usually on tap here, day and night. This pub/restaurant is also known for its good food. Lunch or snack choices include soups, sandwiches, omelets, and Irish stew plus seafood salads. Entrees at dinner have more of a gourmet flair, such as noisettes of lamb with apple mint or red wine sauce; pan-fried rainbow trout; chicken mornay; seafood pancake; or stuffed breast of duck; as well as a variety of steaks.

Moderate/Inexpensive

The Olde Stand, Michael Street, Waterford. ☎ **051/79488.**

Cuisine: IRISH/SEAFOOD. **Reservations:** Recommended.
Prices: Appetizers £1.25–£4.95 ($2.25–$7.43); dinner main courses £7.95–£12.95 ($11.83–$19.43); bar food all items £1.65–£6.95 ($2.48–$10.43). MC, V.
Open: Mon–Sat bar food 12:30–2:30pm, restaurant dinner 5:30–10:15pm, Sun lunch/dinner 12:30–9:30pm.

Overlooking the busy center of the city at the corner of Lady Lane, this upstairs restaurant is part of a Victorian-style pub, with a decor of old paintings and maps of Waterford. The restaurant, open only for dinner and Sunday lunch, features steaks and seafood, with choices ranging from surf-and-turf to salmon in pastry, sole on the bone, and seafood pancakes, as well as traditional dishes such as chicken Maryland. The lower-level pub also offers morning coffee, a self-service carvery lunch, and snacks throughout the day.

Suir Inn, Cheekpoint, Co. Waterford. ☎ **82119** or **82220.**

Cuisine: SEAFOOD. **Reservations:** Not accepted.
Prices: Appetizers £2–£3.75 ($3–$5.63); main courses £4.95–£10.95 ($7.43–$16.43). MC, V.
Open: Dinner only, June–Sept Tues–Sat 6–9:30pm; mid-Jan to June and Oct to mid-Dec Wed–Sat 6–9pm. **Closed:** Mid-Dec to mid-Jan.

With a reputation for freshly prepared to order food, this small 17th-century tavern/ restaurant is a local favorite. Situated beside the water seven miles east of Waterford, it has a simple decor of copper pots and mugs hanging from the ceiling, and informal seating on stools and benches. The menu is also simple—the local catch of the day is the specialty here, with choices such as baked crab topped with fennel sauce and crusty breadcrumbs; prawns in garlic butter; king scallops in cheese and wine sauce; and a very popular seafood pie brimming with salmon, scallops, cod, shrimp, and prawns with a cheese topping and potato crust; as well as seafood platters (smoked salmon and mackerel, prawns, mussels, crab, cockles, and more). For landlubbers, there are also beef, chicken, and vegetarian dishes.

Inexpensive/Budget

Poppy's, 25 Barronstrand St., Waterford. ☎ 70008.

Cuisine: INTERNATIONAL. **Reservations:** Not necessary.
Prices: Breakfast £1.30–£2.95 ($1.95–$4.42); all items lunch/snacks £1.30–£4.95 ($1.95–$7.43). No credit cards.
Open: Mon–Sat breakfast 9–11am, lunch and afternoon meals noon–6pm.

Poppy's is located on the fifth floor above the four-story Book Centre. There is no elevator as we go to press, but one is supposed to be installed shortly. It is worth the climb, however. Tables overlook the book shop or, on the outdoor roof, have views of the city. All food is prepared and cooked on the premises, including soups, breads, pastries, biscuits, and cakes. The menu offers an eclectic array of choices such as baked potatoes stuffed with ham, cheese, mushrooms, and chives; chicken Oriental with stir-fried vegetables; Italian-style stuffed mushrooms filled with three cheeses and served with pasta; California meatloaf stuffed with bacon and cheddar cheese; honey roast pork; spinach and mushrooms wrapped in puff pastry, plus sandwiches and salads.

Bewley's, Broad Street, Waterford. ☎ 70506.

Cuisine: IRISH/SELF-SERVICE. **Reservations:** Not necessary.
Prices: All items 80p–£3.95 ($1.20–$5.93).
Open: Mon–Sat 8am–6pm.

Located on the second level of the Broad Street Shopping Centre, this is a branch of the famous Dublin coffeehouse of the same name. It's open for breakfast, lunch, and coffee and tea all day. Homemade scones, fresh pastries, and soups are a specialty.

A Floating Restaurant

★ **Galley Cruising Restaurants,** New Ross Quay, New Ross, Co. Wexford. ☎ 051/21723.

Cuisine: IRISH. **Reservations:** Required.
Prices: Lunch £11 ($16.50); afternoon tea £5 ($7.50); dinner £17–£20 ($25.50–$30); cruise only £5 ($7.50) at 12:30pm, £4 ($6) at 3pm, and £9 ($13.50) at 5:30pm or 7pm.
Open: Apr–Oct daily from New Ross at 12:30pm (lunch), Apr–Sept daily from New Ross at 5:30pm or 7pm (dinner); June–Aug from Waterford at 3pm (afternoon tea) or cruise only.

This is Ireland's only floating restaurant, based 15 miles northeast of Waterford at New Ross, Co. Wexford, but considered part of the Waterford experience. Capt. Dick Fletcher welcomes guests aboard to enjoy a full bar service and a meal while cruising the sylvan waters of the Rivers Suir, Nore, or Barrow. The menu is limited in choice, but the food is freshly prepared, and the views can't be equalled. Cruises last from two to three hours, and are timed for lunch, afternoon tea, or dinner departures. Boats normally leave from New Ross, but during the summer months, trips are also scheduled from Waterford.

EVENING ENTERTAINMENT

Waterford has two main entertainment centers. The **Garter Lane Theatre,** 22a O'Connell St. (☎ **77153**) presents the work of local production companies such as the Red Kettle and Waterford Youth Drama. Visiting troupes from all over Ireland also perform contemporary and traditional works at this 170-seat theater, housed in one of Ireland's largest arts centers. Performances are usually on Tuesday through Saturday; tickets average £3 to £5 ($4.50–$7.50) for most events. Box office is open Monday to Saturday from 10am to 6pm.

When big-name Irish or international talent comes to Waterford, they usually perform at **The Forum** at The Glen (☎ **71111**), a large hall off Bridge Street. Tickets average £8 to £15 ($12–$22.50) depending on the event. The box office is open from Monday through Saturday, 11am to 1pm and 2 to 4pm.

Otherwise, Waterford's nightlife is centered in the hotel lounges and on the city's interesting assortment of pubs.

PUBS

T. & H. Doolan, 32 George's St. ☎ **72764.**

Once a stagecoach stop, this 170-year-old pub in the center of town claims to be Waterford's oldest public house. It is a favorite venue for evening sessions of ballad, folk, and traditional music. It is lantern lit, with white-washed stone walls, and a collection of old farm implements, crocks, mugs, and jugs.

Egan's, 36/37 Barronstrand St. ☎ **75619.**

Situated in the heart of the city center, this friendly pub is a showcase of Tudor style and decor, from its neat black and white facade to its cozy interior.

The Kings, 8 Lombard St. ☎ **74495.**

Situated just off The Mall, this pub dates back to 1776 when it was called the Packet Hotel because of its proximity to the Waterford docks and the packet ships sailing to England. It was often a send-off point for people leaving Ireland to emigrate to new shores. Today it retains its original Georgian-style facade and the interior reflects an old-world charm, particularly in the cozy 20-seat front bar. Check out the mid-19th–century bar counter—it has panels that used to hold sandpaper for customers to strike a match.

★ **Jack Meades,** Cheekpoint Road, Halfway House, Ballycanavan, Co. Waterford. ☎ **73187.**

Waterford's most unusual pub is not in the city at all, but nestling beneath an old stone bridge in an area known as Halfway House, four miles south of Waterford. Dating back to 1705, this old pub is widely known by the locals as Meade's Under the Bridge, or Ireland's only fly-over pub. As a public house with a forge, it was a stopping-off point for travelers between Waterford and Passage East in the old days. The facade and interior haven't changed much in the intervening years—wooden beams, historical paintings, antiques, and crackling open fireplaces. From May through September, there is music with sing-along sessions on Wednesday, Friday, Saturday, and Sunday evenings. The grounds include an icehouse, corn mill, lime kilns, a viaduct, and a beer garden/barbecue area. On Sundays in summer, barbecues with outdoor music are held from 6pm.

⭐ **The Munster,** Bailey's New Street. ☎ 051/74656.

The flavor of old Waterford prevails in this 300-year-old building, which also can be entered from The Mall. Often referred to as Fitzgerald's (the name of the family who owns it), this pub has a decor rich in etched mirrors, antique Waterford glass sconces, and dark wood walls, some of which are fashioned out of timber from the old Waterford Toll Bridge. Among the many rooms are an original "Men's Bar" and a lively modern lounge (which often features traditional Irish music on weekends).

Easy Excursions from Waterford to Tipperary

It's not such a long way to Tipperary from Waterford. In fact, it's less than 50 scenic miles from Waterford City to Cashel. Deep in the Irish inland countryside, Cashel is not to be missed. Since it's right on the main N 8 road, most people pass through Cashel en route from Dublin to Cork. If your travels do not take you to Cashel, then a side trip from Waterford is well worth the drive. In particular, two scenic routes are well worth a detour:

At Cahir, embark in a northerly direction through the ⭐ **Galtee Mountains** to the Glen of Aherlow. Often called Ireland's Greenest Valley, the seven-mile Glen of Aherlow is a secluded and scenic area that was an important pass between the plains of counties Tipperary and Limerick. In ancient times the Glen was the scene of many battles.

If you're trekking south after a visit to Cashel, then head for the Vee. This 11-mile-long road winds through the Knockmealdown Mountains from Clogheen to Lismore and Cappoquin in County Waterford. It's named the Vee because as you drive the horizon before you looks like a V-shaped formation. The highest point of this zig-zag course is 1,114 ft. This road offers magnificent views at different levels. It's said that you can see five counties at various points along the drive.

WHAT TO SEE & DO

The Rock of Cashel, Cashel, Co. Tipperary. ☎ 062/61437.

When you reach the town of Cashel, look for signs to the Rock of Cashel. This mound or raised area dominates the Tipperary countryside for miles. An outcrop of limestone reaching 200 ft. into the sky, the Rock of Cashel tells the tales of 16 centuries. It was the seat of the Kings of Munster at least as far back as A.D. 360. They built a castle here, and it remained a royal fortress until 1101, when King Murtagh O'Brien granted it to the church. Among Cashel's many great moments was the baptism of King Aengus

IMPRESSIONS

Then came Cashel!... 'the great vision of the guarded mount' stood directly poised on the chimney-pots of the gay painted street. Below everything was Georgian; shadowed, solid, decorous and domestic to the last degree, and above each outline from the lifted finger-tip of the belfry to the toy towers of Cormac's Chapel was remote, romantic and insubstantial.

It was all grey, the cathedral with its angle tower, the belfry with its conical top, even the steep flagged roof of Cormac's Chapel was remote; a pure, pearly, translucent grey which seemed to float and melt into the evening sky, as though it were in another dimension; an Irish Olympus.
—Frank O'Connor (1903–1966), *Irish Miles*

by St. Patrick in 448. Remaining on the rock are the ruins of a two-towered chapel, a cruciform cathedral, a 92-ft. round tower, and a cluster of other medieval monuments.

Admission: £2 ($3) adults, £1.50 ($2.25) seniors, £1 ($1.50) students and children.

Open: Mid-Sept to mid-Mar daily 9:30am–4:30pm; mid-Mar to early June daily 9:30am–5:30pm; mid-June to mid-Sept daily 9am–7:30pm.

★ **Bru Boru,** Rock Lane, Cashel, Co. Tipperary. ☎ **062/61122.**

At the foot of the Rock of Cashel, this modern complex adds a whole new dimension to the historic Cashel area—music. Bru Boru is operated by Comhaltas Ceoltoiri Eireann, Ireland's traditional music organization. Performances of authentic Irish traditional music are presented throughout the day at an indoor theater, and on many summer evenings concerts are given at an open-air amphitheater. A heritage center, a book-cum-music shop, a restaurant, and a self-service snackery are also found here.

Admission: Free to center; £5 ($7.50) per person for music performances.

Schedule: Daily 10am–6pm or later; evening music shows May–Sept Tues–Sat at 9pm.

GPA-Bolton Library, John Street, Cashel. ☎ 062/61944.

In this library you'll see the smallest book in the world and other rare, antiquarian, and unusual books dating from the 12th century. Ensconced here are works by Dante, Swift, Calvin, Newton, Erasmus, and Machiavelli. Also on display are some silver altar pieces from the original cathedral on the Rock of Cashel.

Admission: £1.50 ($2.25) adults, £1 ($1.50) seniors and students, 50p (75¢) children.

Open: Mar–Oct Mon–Sat 9:30am–5:30pm, Sun 2:30–5:30pm.

Cahir Castle, Cahir, Co. Tipperary. ☎ 052/41011.

On a rock in the middle of the River Suir, this is one of Ireland's largest medieval fortresses. Its origins can be traced back to the third century when a fort was built on the rock—hence the town's original name, City of the Fishing Fort. The present structure, which belonged to the Butler family from 1375 to 1961, is Norman and dates to the 13th and 15th centuries. It has a massive keep, high walls, spacious courtyards, and a great hall, all fully restored. So impressive is this site that it has been used often as a movie location. *Barry Lyndon, Catholics, Tristan and Isolde,* and *Excalibur* were partially filmed here. Guided tours are available on request.

Admission: £1.50 ($2.25) adults, £1 ($1.50) seniors, 60p (90¢) students and children.

Open: April to mid-June and mid-Sept to mid-Oct daily 10am–6pm; mid-June to mid-Sept daily 9am–7:30pm; Nov–Mar daily 10am–1pm and 2–4:30pm.

Swiss Cottage, off Dublin/Cork Rd. (N 8), Cahir. ☎ 052/41144.

The Swiss Cottage was used as a hunting and fishing lodge by the Earls of Glengall as far back as 1812. It's an example of cottage orne, a rustic house that embodied the ideal of simplicity that so appealed to the Romantics of the early 19th century. It's believed to have been designed by John Nash, a Royal Architect. The thatched-roof cottage has extensive timberwork, usually not seen in Ireland. The interior has some of the first wallpaper commercially produced in Paris. Access is by guided tour only.

Admission: £1.50 ($2.25) adults, £1 ($1.50) seniors, 40p (60¢) students and children.

Open: Mid-Mar, Oct–Nov Tues–Sun 10am–1pm and 2–4:30pm; April Tues–Sun 10am–5pm; May–Sept Tues–Sun 10am–6pm.

★ **Tipperary Crystal,** Waterford/Limerick Road (N 24), Ballynoran, Carrick-on-Suir, Co. Tipperary. ☎ 051/41188.

If you're nearby, don't miss this crystal factory, laid out in the style of traditional Irish cottages complete with thatched roofs. Visitors are welcome to watch master craftsmen as they mouth-blow and hand-cut crystal. The facility also includes a showroom and restaurant.

Unlike at other crystal factories, there's no restrictions on photographs and video recorders here.

Admission: Free.

Open: Mon–Sat 8am–7pm, Sun 10am–6pm.

WHERE TO STAY

Very Expensive/Expensive

★ **Cashel Palace,** Main Street, Cashel, Co. Tipperary. ☎ 062/61411 or toll free 800/221-1074 or 800/223-6510 in the U.S. Fax 062/61521. 20 rms (all with bath). TV TEL

Rates: £85–£195 ($127.50–$192.50) single, £105–£225 ($157.50–$337.50) double. Service charge 10%. AE, DC, MC, V.

Originally built in 1730 as a residence for Church of Ireland archbishops, this stately red-brick Palladian mansion has been a hotel for the last 30 years. Recent owners have thoroughly updated the property and filled it with antiques and designer-coordinated fabrics. It has an ideal location—right in the middle of Cashel town, yet within its own walled grounds, with a well-tended back garden that includes mulberry bushes planted in 1702 to commemorate the coronation of Queen Anne, and a private pathway, known as the Bishop's Walk, up a hill to the Rock of Cashel. The house itself is a proud display of Corinthian pillars, mantelpieces of Kilkenny marble, and a paneled early Georgian staircase of red pine.

Dining/Entertainment: The Four Seasons restaurant offers splendid views of the revered Rock, especially at night when it is floodlit. Other choices include the lower-level coffee shop/pub, The Buttery, and the Cellar Bar.

Moderate

Dundrum House, Dundrum, Co. Tipperary. ☎ 062/71116 or toll free 800/447-7462 in U.S. Fax 062/71366. 55 rms (all with bath). TV TEL

Rates (including full breakfast): £45–£50 ($67.50–$75) single, £78–£84 ($117–$126) double. Service charge 10%. AE, DC, MC, V.

Located six miles northwest of Cashel, this impressive Georgian country manor is nestled in the fertile Tipperary countryside, surrounded by 100 acres of grounds and gardens, with the River Multeen running through the property. Originally built as a residence in 1730 by the Earl of Montalt, then used as a convent school, it was renovated, updated, and turned into a hotel in 1978 by local residents Austin and Mary Crowe. It is furnished with assorted heirlooms, vintage curios, Victorian pieces, and reproductions. Each bedroom is individually decorated, some with four-posters or hand-carved headboards, armoires, vanities, and other traditional furnishings.

Dining/Entertainment: Choices include the elegant high-ceiling dining room and a unique bar lounge with stained-glass windows (formerly a chapel).

Facilities: championship 18-hole golf course, 2 tennis courts, riding stables, trout fishing privileges.

★ **Kilcoran Lodge,** Dublin/Cork Road (N 8), Cahir, Co. Tipperary. ☎ **052/41288** or toll free **800/447-7462** in U.S. Fax 052/41994. 22 rms (all with bath). TV TEL

Rates (including full breakfast): £40–£47.50 ($60–$70.25) single, £60–£90 ($90–$120) double. Service charge 10%. AE, DC, MC, V.

A former hunting lodge nestled on 20 acres of wooded grounds, this old Victorian treasure is set on a hillside set back from the main road a few miles west of Cahir. It has been totally renovated and refurbished in recent years, but still retains old-world charm in the public areas. Step inside and relax amid open fireplaces, grandfather clocks, antique tables and chairs, brass fixtures, and tall windows which frame expansive views of the Suir Valley and Knockmealdown Mountains. Each of the guest rooms is outfitted with traditional furnishings as well as modern conveniences such as a hair dryer, coffee/tea-maker, and garment press.

Dining/Entertainment: The choices include a formal restaurant with lovely views of the countryside and a bar/lounge, noted for its daytime pub grub, from Irish stew and traditional boiled bacon and cabbage, to homemade soups and hot scones.

Facilities: Indoor swimming pool, Jacuzzi, sauna, solarium.

Rectory House, Dundrum, Co. Tipperary. ☎ **062/71266** or toll free **800/528-1234** in U.S. Fax 062/71115. 10 rms (all with bath). TV TEL

Rates (including full breakfast): £35–£42 ($52.50–$63) single, £50–£68 double ($75–$102). No service charge. AE, MC, V. **Closed:** Dec–Feb.

Located about five miles northwest of Cashel, this mid–19th-century house is surrounded by ancient trees and lovely gardens. It has a storied past, having been built by Viscount Hawarden and then used as a Church of Ireland pastor's house until a few years ago. Totally renovated and updated by owners Stephanie and Paul Deegan, it is outfitted with all the modern conveniences, yet is a very homey place to stay. The candlelit dining room has earned a reputation for fine French/Irish cuisine, and the bar is full of old-world atmosphere, a favorite gathering spot for the locals.

WHERE TO DINE

Chez Hans, Rockside, Cashel, Co. Tipperary. ☎ **062/61177.**

Cuisine: FRENCH/IRISH. **Reservations:** Required.
Prices: Set dinner £22–£25 ($33–$37.50). MC, V.
Open: Tues–Sat 6:30–9:30pm. **Closed:** Jan.

It is not surprising that the Rock of Cashel, a pivotal landmark in the course of Irish royal and ecclesiastical history, would inspire a great restaurant within its shadow. It only seems appropriate that it is housed in a former Gothic chapel at the foot of the path that leads to the mighty Rock. The cathedral-style ceiling, original stone walls, lyrical background music, and candlelight atmosphere provide the perfect setting for the cooking of chef-owner Hans Pieter Mataier. Dishes range from quenelles of sea bass and sole meunière to a succulent herb-encrusted roast lamb or free-range duckling with honey and thyme.

PUB

The Ronald Reagan, Main Street, Ballyporeen, Co. Tipperary. ☎ 052/67133.

Yes, there really is a pub named after the former U.S. President, right in the middle of the town that was home to his great-grandfather, Michael Reagan. Filled with pictures and mementos of the President's June 3, 1984, visit to Ballyporeen, this bar is part of the pub-cum–gift shop complex of local entrepreneur John O'Farrell. Even the back wall features a mural of the original Reagan homestead cottage. It's worth a stop for a toast or at least a picture.

3 County Kilkenny

Kilkenny City is 30 miles N of Waterford, 50 miles NW of Wexford, 75 miles SW of Dublin, 85 miles SE of Shannon Airport, 92 miles NE of Cork, 38 miles NE of Cashel

GETTING THERE • By Train   Irish Rail provides daily service from Dublin into the Irish Rail McDonagh Station, Dublin Road, Kilkenny (☎ 056/22024).

• By Bus   Daily bus services from Dublin and all parts of Ireland are operated by Bus Eireann, McDonagh Station, Dublin Road (☎ 056/64933).

• By Car   Many roads lead to inland Kilkenny including N 9/N 10 from Waterford and Wexford, N 8 and N 76 from Cork and the southwest, N 7 and N 77 from Limerick and the west, and N 9 and N 78 from Dublin and points north and east.

TOURIST INFORMATION   For year-round information, maps, and brochures about Kilkenny and the surrounding area, contact the Kilkenny Tourist Office, Shee Alms House, Rose Inn Street, Kilkenny (☎ 056/51500). It is open in May through September on Monday through Saturday from 9am to 6pm and on Sunday from 10am to 5pm; in April and October on Monday through Saturday from 9am to 6pm; and from January to March and November to December on Tuesday through Saturday from 9am to 5:15pm.

CITY LAYOUT   The main business district of Kilkenny sits on the west banks of the River Nore. A mile-long thoroughfare, High Street, runs the entire length of the city, in a north-south direction, although it changes its name to Parliament Street at midpoint. It starts at The Parade, on the south end near Kilkenny Castle, and continues through the city to St. Canice's Cathedral at the northern end. Most of the city's attractions are to be found along this route or on off-shoot streets such as Patrick, Rose Inn, Kieran, and John. The tourist office will supply you with a good street map.

GETTING AROUND • By Public Transport   There is no downtown bus service in Kilkenny, but local buses do run to nearby towns on a limited basis, departing from The Parade. Check with Bus Eireann (☎ 056/64933) for details.

If you need a taxi, call Seamus Brett Taxi (☎ 056/65225), Bill Delaney Cabs (☎ 056/22457), Jim Dwyer Taxis (☎ 056/51717), Mick Howe Taxis (☎ 056/65874), Michael O'Brien Taxis (☎ 056/61333), David Nagle Cabs (☎ 056/63300), or Phonecab (☎ 056/63017).

• By Car   Don't attempt to drive up and down Kilkenny's narrow medieval streets or you may get caught in slow-moving traffic. If you have a car, park it at one of the designated parking areas at The Parade, the rail station, or at shopping centers. Some parking is free and other parking is subject to coin-operated machines, usually charging 20p (30¢) per hour. If you need to rent a car to see the surrounding countryside,

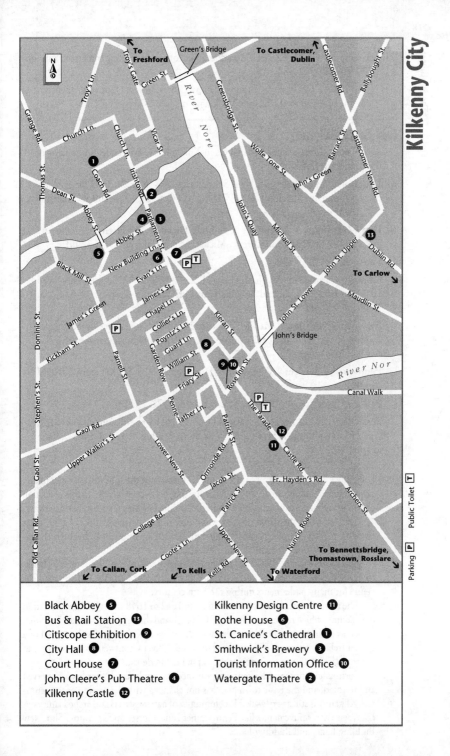

To Freshford
Green's Bridge
To Castlecomer, Dublin

N

Troy's Ln.
Troy's Gate
Green St.
Church Ln.
Church Ln.
Vicar St.
Irishtown
River Nore
Greensbridge St.
Castlecomer Rd.
Ballybought St.

Grange Rd.
Thomas St.
Dean St.
Coach Rd.
Abbey St.
Black Mill St.

① St. Canice's
② Watergate
③ Smithwick's
④ John Cleere's
⑤ Black Abbey
⑥ Rothe House
⑦ Court House

Parliament St.
Abbey St.
New Building Ln.
Evan's Ln.
James's St.
Chapel Ln.
Collier's Ln.
Poyntz's Ln.
Guard Ln.
Garden Row
William St.
Friary St.
James's Green

Wolfe Tone St.
John's Green
Barrack St.
Castlecomer New Rd.
John's Quay
Michael St.
John St. Upper
⑬
Dublin Rd.
To Carlow
John St. Lower
Maudlin St.

P T

⑥
⑦

Kieran St.
⑧
⑨ ⑩
Rose Inn St.

John's Bridge
River Nore
Canal Walk

P
T

⑫
⑪
Castle Rd.

Dominic St.
Kickham St.
Parnell St.
Stephen's St.
Gaol Rd.
Upper Walkin's St.
Gaol St.
Old Callan Rd.
College Rd.
Coote's Ln.
Lower New St.
Penne... father Ln.
Patrick St.
Ormonde Rd.
Jacob St.
Patrick St.
Upper New St.
Kells Rd.
Fr. Hayden's Rd.
Nuncio Road
Archer's St.
The Parade

To Callan, Cork
To Kells
To Waterford
To Bennettsbridge, Thomastown, Rosslare

Parking P   Public Toilet T

Black Abbey ⑤
Bus & Rail Station ⑬
Citiscope Exhibition ⑨
City Hall ⑧
Court House ⑦
John Cleere's Pub Theatre ④
Kilkenny Castle ⑫

Kilkenny Design Centre ⑪
Rothe House ⑥
St. Canice's Cathedral ①
Smithwick's Brewery ③
Tourist Information Office ⑩
Watergate Theatre ②

check at the EuroDollar Rent A Car desk at the tourist office, Rose Inn Street, Kilkenny (☎ **056/63994**).

• **On Foot**   The best way to see Kilkenny City is on foot. Plot your own route or join one of the guided Kilkenny Walking tours (see "Sightseeing Tours," below).

Fast Facts: Kilkenny

Area Code   Most telephone numbers in Kilkenny use **056** code. Some parts of the county use **0505**.

Drugstores   Sean Foley, 75 High St., Kilkenny (☎ **62422**); John Street Pharmacy, 47 John St., Kilkenny (☎ **65971**); John O'Connell, 4 Rose Inn St., Kilkenny (☎ **21033**).

Dry Cleaning and Laundry   Ormonde Cleaners, 29 High St., Kilkenny (☎ **21949**), or Brett's Launderette, Michael Street, Kilkenny (☎ **63200**).

Emergencies   Dial **999**.

Library   Carnegie Library, John's Quay, Kilkenny (☎ **22021**). Open Tues–Wed 10:30am–1pm, 2–5pm, and 7–9pm; Thurs–Fri 10:30am–1pm and 2–5pm; Sat 10:30am–1:30pm.

Newspapers and Local Media   The *Kilkenny People* is the weekly newspaper covering local events and entertainment. Radio Kilkenny broadcasts on 96.6 FM and 96 FM.

Photographic Services   White's One-Hour Photo, 5 High St., Kilkenny (☎ **056/ 21328**).

Police   Garda Station, Dominic Street, Kilkenny (☎ **22222**).

Post Office   Kilkenny District Post Office, 73 High St., Kilkenny (☎ **21813**). Open Monday through Friday from 9:30am to 5:30pm, Saturday from 9:30am to 1pm.

Kilkenny City, the centerpiece of County Kilkenny and the southeast's prime inland city, is considered the medieval capital of Ireland, because of its remarkable collection of well-preserved medieval castles, churches, public buildings, streets, and laneways.

Situated along the banks of the River Nore, Kilkenny (population 11,000) takes its name from a church founded in the sixth century by St. Canice. In the Irish language, *Cill Choinnigh* means "Canice's Church."

Like most Irish cities, Kilkenny fell into Norman hands by the 12th century. Thanks to its central location, it became a prosperous walled medieval city and served as the venue for many parliaments during the 14th century.

The town's most glorious period was from 1642 to 1648 when the Confederation of Kilkenny, which represented both the Old Irish and the Anglo-Irish Catholics, functioned as an independent Irish Parliament. In essence, Kilkenny was the capital of a united Ireland, although it was to be short lived. Oliver Cromwell's army swept into the town in 1650, and the once-proud capital fell in defeat.

Fortunately, much of Kilkenny's great medieval architecture has been preserved and restored, and the basic town plan has not changed with the passing of the centuries. Kilkenny is still a very walkable community of narrow streets and arched laneways, many with descriptive names like Pennyfeather Lane, Horseleap Slip, Butter Slip, New Building Lane, and Pudding Lane.

The main thoroughfare is High Street, which—after changing its name at mid-point to Parliament Street—runs from the grounds of the massive 13th-century Kilkenny Castle, on the southeastern corner of the city, to St. Canice Cathedral, on the northern end of town.

The oldest house in town is purported to be Kyteler's Inn on St. Kieran Street. It was once the home of Dame Alice Kyteler, a lady of great wealth who was accused of witchcraft in 1324. She escaped and forever disappeared, but her maid, Petronilla, was burned at the stake. Now restored, the inn is currently used as a pub/restaurant, but it retains an eerie air, with appropriately placed effigies of witches and other memorabilia and decorations.

One building that really stands out on the Kilkenny streetscape is the Tholsel on High Street, with its curious clock tower and front arcade. Otherwise known as the Town Hall or City Hall, it was erected in 1761 and served originally as the tollhouse or exchange. Milk and sugar candy were sold at the Tholsel. Dances, bazaars, and political meetings were held here, too. Completely restored after a fire in 1987, today it houses the city's municipal archives.

Kilkenny is often referred to as the Marble City. Fine black marble used to be quarried on the outskirts of town. Up until 1929, some of the city streets also had marble pavements.

Primarily a farming area, the surrounding County Kilkenny countryside is dotted with rich river valleys, rolling pasture lands, gentle mountains, and picture-postcard towns. Don't miss Inistioge, about 15 miles southeast of Kilkenny City. This village has a tree-lined square and an 18th-century bridge of nine arches spanning the River Nore.

The town of Graiguenamanagh—its name means village of the monks—is home to Duiske Abbey. Surrounded by vistas of Brandon Hill and the Blackstairs Mountains, Graiguenamanagh is situated at a bend of the River Barrow, about 20 miles to the southeast of Kilkenny City.

Kells, about six miles south of Kilkenny City, is the only completely walled medieval town in Ireland. The extensive curtain walls, seven towers, and some of the monastic buildings have been well preserved.

WHAT TO SEE & DO

★ **Kilkenny Castle,** The Parade, Kilkenny. ☎ **21450.**

Majestically standing beside the River Nore on the south side of the city, this landmark castle remained in the hands of the Butler family, the Dukes of Ormonde, from 1391 until 1967 when it was given to the Irish government to be preserved as a national monument. From its sturdy corner towers, three of which are original and date back to the 13th century, to its battlements—Kilkenny Castle retains the lines of an authentic medieval fortress and duly sets the tone for the entire city. What's the secret to the castle's longevity? Parts of it were renewed in the 17th century and again in the 19th century. The well-preserved interior features a fine collection of Butler family portraits, some from the 14th century. On the grounds are a riverside walk and extensive gardens.

Admission: £2 adults ($3), £1.50 ($2.25) seniors, £1 ($1.50) children and students.

Open: Apr–May daily 10:30am–5pm; June–Sept daily 10am–7pm; Oct–Mar Tues–Sat 10:30am–12:45pm and 2–5pm, Sun 11am–12:45pm and 2–5pm.

St. Canice Cathedral, Coach Road, Irishtown, Kilkenny. ☎ 21516.

At the northern end of the city, this is the church that gave Kilkenny its name. The St. Canice's Cathedral that stands today is actually a relative newcomer, built in the 13th century, but it occupies the site of the 6th-century church of St. Canice. The current church, which has benefited from much restoration work in recent years, is noteworthy for many of its interior timber and stone carvings and colorful glasswork. The hammer barn roof dates back to 1863 and its marble floor is composed of the four marbles of Ireland. The massive round tower—100 ft. high and 46 ft. in circumference—is believed to be a relic of the ancient church, although its original conical top has been replaced by a slightly domed roof. The steps that lead to the cathedral were constructed in 1614. The library contains 3,000 volumes from the 16th and 17th centuries.

Admission: Free, donations welcome.

Open: Easter–Oct Mon–Sat 9am–6pm, Sun 2–6pm; Oct–Apr Mon–Sat 10am–1pm and 2–4pm, Sun 2–4pm.

Black Abbey, Abbey Street, off Parliament Street, Kilkenny. ☎ 21279.

Why is this Dominican church founded in 1225 named Black Abbey? Two possible reasons are given. First, the Dominicans wore black capes over their white habits. Second, the Black Plague claimed the lives of eight priests in 1348. The Black Abbey's darkest days came in 1650 when it was used by Cromwell as a courthouse; by the time he left, all that remained were the walls.

The abby was reopened in 1816 for public worship, a new nave was constructed by 1866, and the entire building was fully restored in 1979. An alabaster sculpture of the Holy Trinity was carved about 1400. A pre-Reformation statue of St. Dominic, carved in Irish oak, is believed to be the oldest such piece in the world. The huge Rosary Window, a stained-glass work nearly 500 sq. ft., represents the 15 mysteries of the rosary. The window was done in 1892 by Mayers of Munich.

Admission: Free, donations welcome.

Open: Mon–Sat 8am–6:30pm, Sun 9am–7pm.

★ Rothe House, Parliament Street, Kilkenny. ☎ 22893.

This fine Tudor-style home (1594) belonged to a merchant. It has an arcaded front, cobbled courtyards, and a remarkable timber ceiling. Purchased in 1961 by the Kilkenny Archeological Society, it was restored and opened to the public in 1966. Inside is a museum of Kilkenny artifacts and a collection of Elizabethan costumes. A family history research service for Kilkenny city and county has its offices here.

Admission: £1.50 ($2.25) adults, £1 ($1.50) seniors and students, 60p (90¢) children.

Open: Apr–Oct Mon–Sat 10:30am–5pm, Sun 3–5pm; Nov–Mar Sat–Sun 3–5pm and by appointment.

Cityscope Exhibition, Shee Alms House, Rose Inn Street, Kilkenny. ☎ 51500.

In the same restored building as the city's tourist office, this imaginative presentation uses an architectural scale model and lighting and sound effects to re-create the town of Kilkenny in 1640. This show lasts 20 minutes. Also exhibited are dolls and miniature paintings. The building itself was erected in 1582 by a rich merchant to provide housing for the poor of the city.

Admission: £1 ($1.50) adults, 80p ($1.20) seniors, students, and 50p (75¢) children.

Open: May–Sept Mon–Sat 9am–6pm, Sun 11am–5pm; Oct–Apr Tues–Sat 9am–5pm.

Smithwick's Brewery, "The Ring," St. Francis Abbey Brewery, Parliament Street, Kilkenny. ☎ **21014.**

Be sure to try the local brew, a beer called Smithwick's (pronounced Smith-icks). Established in 1710 by John Smithwick, the brewery occupies a site that originally belonged to the 12th century Abbey of St. Francis. Along with Smithwicks, Budweiser is produced here. Guided tours, ending with free samples, are given in the summer months.

Admission: Free.

Open: May–Sept Mon–Fri, tours at 3pm.

Dunmore Cave, off Castlecomer Road (N 78), Ballyfoyle, Co. Kilkenny. ☎ **67726.**

Known as one of the darkest places in Ireland, this underground cave consists of a series of chambers formed over millions of years. It contains some of the finest calcite formations found in any Irish cave. Known to man for many centuries, the cave may have been the sight of a Viking massacre in A.D. 928. Exhibits at the visitor center tell the story of the cave. It's about seven miles from Kilkenny City.

Admission: £1.50 ($2.25) adults, 60p children (90¢).

Open: Mar–June Tues–Sat 10am–5pm, Sun 2–5pm; June–Sept daily 10am–7pm; Oct daily 10am–6pm; Nov–Feb Sat–Sun 10am–5pm.

Jerpoint Abbey, Waterford Road (N 9), Thomastown, Co. Kilkenny. ☎ **24623.**

About 11 miles southeast of Kilkenny, the ruins of this 12th-century Cistercian monastery offer a splendid array of artifacts from medieval times—from unique stone carvings on walls and tombs to a 14th- or 15th-century tower and cloister as well as Irish Romanesque details of a late 12th century Abbey church.

Admission: £1.50 adults ($2.25), £1 ($1.50) seniors, 60p (90¢) children and students.

Open: May to early June and end-Sept to mid-Oct Tues–Sun 10am–1pm and 2–5pm; mid-June to end-Sept daily 9:30am–6:30pm.

 Duiske Abbey, Graiguenamanagh, Co. Kilkenny. ☎ **0505/24238.**

The Duiske Abbey (1207) has a long and colorful history. It was suppressed in 1536, but its monks continued to occupy the site for many years. In 1774 the tower of the ruined abbey church collapsed. Things took a turn for the better in 1813, when the missing roof was replaced and religious services returned to the church. The abbey never approached its former glory until the 1970s, when a group of local people pooled their time and talents to mount a major reconstruction effort. With its fine Lancet windows and a large effigy of a Norman knight, the abbey is the pride and joy of Graiguenamanagh. The adjacent visitor centre has an exhibit of Christian art and artifacts.

Admission: Free, donations welcome.

Open: Mon–Sat 10am–5pm, Sat–Sun 2–5pm.

Sightseeing Tours

⭐ **Tynan's Walking Tours,** 10 Maple Dr., Kilkenny. ☎ **65929.**

Walk the streets and lanes of medieval Kilkenny, accompanied by local historian/guides Pat or Martin Tynan. Tours depart from the Tourist Office, Rose Inn Street.

Price: £2.50 ($3.75) adults, £2 ($3) seniors and students, 60p (90¢) children.

Open: Mar–Oct Mon–Sat 9:15am, 10:30am, 12:15pm, 1:30pm, 3pm, 4:30pm, Sun 11am, 12:15pm, 3pm, 4:30pm; Nov–Feb Tues–Sat 10:30am, 12:15pm, 3pm.

SPORTS & RECREATION

BICYCLING   Rent a bike to ride around the outskirts of Kilkenny especially along the shores of the River Nore. Rates average £7 ($10.50) per day. Contact J.J. Wall, 88 Maudlin St., Kilkenny (☎ **21236**); Raleigh Cycle Centre, 5 John St., Kilkenny (☎ **62037**); or Kilkenny Rent-A-Bike, Avonmore House, Castle St., Kilkenny (☎ **51399**).

FISHING   The River Nore and the nearby River Barrow are known for good salmon and trout fishing. For advice, permits and supplies, visit the Sport Shop, 82 High Street, Kilkenny (☎ **21517**).

GOLFING   The annual Irish Open Golf Tournament, the pinnacle of the Irish golfing year, took place two years in a row (1993/1994) at the Mount Juliet Golf & Country Club, Thomastown, Co. Kilkenny (☎ **24725**), situated ten miles south of Kilkenny City. You, too, can play a round on this 18-hole par-72 championship course designed by Jack Nicklaus, for greens fees of £57 ($85.50). The price drops to £29–£41 ($43.50–$61.50) if you are overnighting at Mount Juliet.

Alternatively, try the 18-hole championship course, the Kilkenny Golf Club, Glendine, Co. Kilkenny (☎ **22125**), an inland par-71 layout one mile from the city. Greens fees are £15 ($22.50) on weekdays and £17 ($25.50) on weekends.

SAVVY SHOPPING

A haven for artisans, Kilkenny City and its surrounding area is known for good shopping. To assist visitors in discovering some of the smaller workshops, the local tourist office provides a free **Craft Trail map** and information on local craft workers.

Kilkenny shopping hours are normally Monday through Saturday from 9am to 6pm; however, many shops stay open until 9pm on Thursday and Friday. The newest addition to the Kilkenny shopping scene is **Market Cross,** a new shopping center off High/Parliament Street (☎ **65534**), with its own multistory car park.

The Book Centre, 10 High St., Kilkenny. ☎ **62117.**

This centrally located shop offers a fine selection of books about Kilkenny and the local area, as well as books of Irish interest. Current best sellers, maps, stationery, cards, and posters are sold. The Pennefeather Cafe is an upstairs eatery for daytime snacks.

Kilkenny Crystal, 19 Rose Inn St. ☎ **21090.**

Established in 1969, this is the retail shop for Kilkenny's own hand-cut crystal enterprise, specializing in footed vases, rose bowls, bells, ring holders, wine glasses, carafes, and decanters. The factory is on the Callan Road (☎ **25132**), ten miles outside of town and also welcomes visitors.

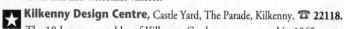 **Kilkenny Design Centre,** Castle Yard, The Parade, Kilkenny. ☎ **22118.**

The 18th-century stables of Kilkenny Castle were converted in 1965 to a workshop for craftspeople from all over Ireland. The adjacent shop, in the original coach house with an arched gateway and topped by a copper-domed clocktower, has become a showcase for the country's top hand-crafted products—jewelry, glassware, pottery, clothing, candles, linens, books, leatherwork, and furniture. An excellent coffee shop/restaurant is on the upstairs level. In additional to normal hours listed above, this shop is open on Sundays, April to September from 10am–6pm.

Liam Costigan, Colliers Lane, off High Street. ☎ **62408.**

Hand-crafted silver and gold jewelry are produced in this tiny shop by an alumnus of the Kilkenny Design Centre. As you browse here, you can also see Liam at work.

Nicholas Mosse Pottery, Bennettsbridge, Co. Kilkenny. ☎ **27126.**

In a former flour mill on the banks of the River Nore, this enterprise is the brainchild of Nicholas Mosse, a potter since age seven. Using water power from the river to fire the kilns, he produces colorful earthenware from Irish clay—jugs, mugs, bowls, and plates. All is hand-slipped and hand-turned, then decorated by hand with cut sponges and brush. A museum displays antique Irish spongewear.

P.T. Murphy, 85 High St., Kilkenny. ☎ **21127.**

The sign above the entrance says it all: Watchmaker, Jeweler, Optician, and Silver-smith. This is Kilkenny's master jeweler. The shop is a very good source for Irish Cladddagh and Heraldic jewelry.

Yesterdays, 30 Patrick St., Kilkenny. ☎ **65557.**

Porcelain dolls and miniatures, lace, teddy bears, mini-frames, perfume bottles, jew-elry, doll-house furniture, and some antiques are found at this curiosity shop. It's definitely worth a browse.

WHERE TO STAY

Very Expensive/Expensive

★ **Mount Juliet,** Thomastown, Co. Kilkenny. ☎ **056/24455** or toll free **800/447-7462** in U.S. Fax 056/24522. 53 rms (all with bath). TV TEL

Rates (includes full breakfast): £80–£135 ($120–$202.50) single, £116–£260 ($164–$390) double. No service charge. AE, DC, MC, V.

Kilkenny's top lodging facility is not in Kilkenny City at all, but ten miles south in a little country village. A winding two-mile path wends its way beside the pastures of the Ballylinch Stud Farm to this hotel; an 18th-century manor house set on a hillside overlooking the River Nore and a 1,500-acre estate of formal gardens, lawns, wood-lands, and parklands. Built in the 1760s, the house was named after Juliana (also known as Juliet), wife of the 8th Viscount Ikerrin, the first earl of Carrick. It was later owned by the McCalmont family, leaders in the Irish horse-breeding industry. The public areas are full of antiques, period pieces, and original art. Guest rooms are individually decorated with traditional dark woods, designer fabrics, and antiques.

Dining/Entertainment: The Lady Helen McCalmont Room offers formal din-ing amid a Wedgewood blue decor overlooking the river; lighter fare is served in the Old Kitchen, a basement-level bistro, and the Loft, a chalet-style lodge in the sport-ing complex. The bar has an equestrian theme.

Service: 24-hour room service, concierge, valet and laundry service.

Facilities: 18-hole championship golf course designed by Jack Nicklaus; golf club-house with indoor swimming pool, indoor and outdoor tennis courts, badminton, squash, gym, sauna, and Jacuzzi; golf and fishing academies for on-site sports instruc-tion; riding stables and ten miles of bridle paths; salmon and trout fishing on exclu-sive 1.5-mile stretch of River Nore; pheasant shooting; and fox hunting with the

Kilkenny Hunt which is headquartered on the estate. Mount Juliet is also the home of Ireland's oldest cricket club.

Moderate

Hotel Kilkenny, College Road, Kilkenny, Co. Kilkenny. ☎ **056/62000.**
Fax 056/65984. 60 rms (all with bath). TV TEL

Rates (includes full breakfast): £44–£55 ($66–$82.50) single, £82.50–£100 ($123.25–$150) double. No service charge. AE, DC, MC, V.

On the southwest edge of the city in a residential neighborhood, this hotel is a combination of a gracious country house, dating back to 1830, and a block of modern bedrooms. The main house, once the private residence of Sir William Robertson, the architect who rebuilt Kilkenny Castle, is today comprised of Gingers restaurant and the Rose Inn Bar with a sporting motif. The adjacent wing lacks the charm of the main building, but the bedrooms are comfortable and close to a health complex with indoor swimming pool, sauna, hot tub, sunbeds, gym, and two hard tennis courts.

★ **The Newpark,** Castlecomer Road, Kilkenny, Co. Kilkenny. ☎ **056/22122** or toll free **800/528-1234.** Fax 056/61111. 94 rms (all with bath). TV TEL

Rates: £35–£50 ($52.50–$75) single, £57–£75 ($85.50–$112.50) double. Service charge 10%. AE, DC, MC, V. **Closed:** Last 2 wks Dec.

A warm and friendly atmosphere is foremost at this lovely hotel situated about a mile north of the city center. Set amid 50 acres of gardens and parkland grounds, it was opened as a small Victorian-style country hotel over 35 years ago, and it has been growing in size and gaining in reputation ever since. The bedrooms are decorated in light woods with colorful Irish furnishings. The public areas have an old-world charm, especially in the Damask Restaurant. There is also a contemporary-style grill room and lounge. Facilities include an indoor heated swimming pool, sun lounge, saunas, Jacuzzi, gym, steam room, and two tennis courts.

Moderate/Inexpensive

Butler House, 16 Patrick St., Kilkenny, Co. Kilkenny. ☎ **056/65707.** Fax 056/65626.
13 rms (all with bath). TV TEL

Rates (including full breakfast): £44.50–£49.50 ($66.25–$73.25) single, £59–£69 ($88.50–$103.50) double. No service charge. AE, DC, MC, V.

Built by the 16th Earl of Ormonde circa 1770 as a dower house for Kilkenny Castle, this elegant three-story house has a front door which faces busy Patrick Street and a back yard which overlooks lovely secluded gardens and the Kilkenny Castle stables/craft center. Converted into a guesthouse in the late 1980s, it offers individualized bedrooms of various sizes and eclectic furnishings.

Inexpensive

★ **Lacken House,** Dublin/Carlow Road, Kilkenny, Co. Kilkenny. ☎ **056/65611.**
Fax 056/62435. 8 rms (all with bath). TV TEL

 Rates (including full breakfast): £31–£34 ($46.50–$51) single, £50–£56 ($75–$84). No service charge. AE, MC, V.

A husband-wife duo, Eugene and Breda McSweeney, have made this restored Georgian home into one of the area's best guesthouses. Breda supervises the lodging end and keeps the rooms in tiptop shape, while Eugene, an award-winning chef, oversees

the restaurant (see "Where to Dine," below). Guest rooms are small but are comfortably decorated with colorful Irish furnishings. It is situated on its own grounds with gardens, in the northeast corner of the city, about ten minutes walking distance from High Street and within a long block of the rail/bus station.

WHERE TO DINE

Expensive

⭐ **Lacken House,** Dublin Road, Kilkenny. ☎ **61085.**
Cuisine: IRISH/INTERNATIONAL. **Reservations:** Required.
Prices: Set dinner £22–£25 ($33–$37.50). AE, DC, MC, V.
Open: Tues–Sat 7–10:30pm.

A stately Georgian house is the setting for this restaurant, on the northeast edge of the city. Chef Eugene MacSweeney, who earned international laurels as chef of the Berkeley Court Hotel in Dublin during its early years, has carved out his own niche in this lovely setting. The menu changes daily but often includes dishes such as breast of pigeon served with lentils and smoked bacon, baked crab au gratin, and filet of Nore salmon with galette of potato and celeriac with sage butter sauce.

Moderate

The Maltings, The Bridge, Inistioge, Co. Kilkenny. ☎ **58484.**
Cuisine: IRISH. **Reservations:** Required.
Prices: Set dinner £17.95 ($26.93). MC, V.
Open: Mon–Sat dinner 7–9:30pm.

Overlooking the River Nore about ten miles southeast of Kilkenny City, this long-standing restaurant offers simple but well-prepared food in an idyllic and romantic county-house setting. The menu changes daily but usually includes Nore salmon, filet steak, stuffed breast of chicken bonne femme, duckling with brandy sauce, rosettes of pork, and minted lamb cutlets.

Parliament House Restaurant, Parliament St., Kilkenny. ☎ **63666.**
Cuisine: IRISH/CONTINENTAL. **Reservations:** Recommended.
Prices: Set lunch £4.50–£9.50 ($7.25–$13.88); dinner appetizers £2.50–£6.50 ($3.75–$9.75); dinner main courses £7.50–£12.95 ($11.25–$19.43). AE, MC, V.
Open: Daily lunch 12:30–2:30pm, dinner 6–10:30pm.

Overlooking busy Parliament Street, this upstairs restaurant has a distinctive Edwardian decor, with high ceilings, chandeliers, and floral wallpaper. The menu offers a fine selection of local beef, veal, and lamb, as well as tasty combination dishes such as prawns and mussels with hazelnuts; Nore salmon in pastry with lobster sauce; duckling in wine and garlic butter; sweet-and-sour pork; vegetable nut stir-fry; and chicken Parliament, stuffed with seafood mousse and lobster sauce.

⭐ **Ristorante Rinuccini,** 1 The Parade, Kilkenny. ☎ **61575.**
Cuisine: ITALIAN/IRISH. **Reservations:** Recommended.
Prices: Appetizers £2.25–£5.75 ($3.38–$8.63); lunch main courses £3.95–£7.95 ($5.93–$11.83); dinner main courses £7.95–£14.95 ($11.83–$22.43). AE, MC, V.
Open: June–Oct daily lunch noon–3pm, dinner 6–11pm; Nov–May Mon–Sat lunch noon–3pm, dinner 6–11pm.

Situated opposite Kilkenny Castle, this romantic candlelight restaurant specializes in the best of Irish seafood and locally produced beef in dishes such as steak Diane with brandy or prawns Rinuccini with cream sauce, mushrooms, and brandy. Chef Antonio Cavaliere also presents a full range of homemade pastas and specialties of his homeland, from spaghetti and fettuccine Alfredo, to ravioli al pomodoro, lasagne al forno, and chicken cacciatore.

Moderate/Inexpensive

The Italian Connection, 38 Parliament St., Kilkenny. ☎ 64225.

Cuisine: ITALIAN/INTERNATIONAL. **Reservations:** Recommended.
Prices: Appetizers £1.50–£4.95 ($2.25–$7.43); lunch main courses £3–£4.95 ($4.50–$7.43); dinner main courses £4.95–£12.95 ($7.43–$19.43). MC, V.
Open: Daily lunch noon–3pm; dinner 3pm–midnight.

Located just a half-block from the Watergate Theatre, this small shopfront restaurant is popular for pre- and post-theater dining. The decor is appealing with dark woods, wine casks, and crisp pink linens, and the menu is noted for pasta and pizza dishes prepared on the premises. In addition, there are steaks, five variations of veal, and seafood, as well as curries.

Lautrec's, 9 St. Kieran St., Kilkenny. ☎ 62720.

Cuisine: FRENCH/INTERNATIONAL. **Reservations:** Recommended.
Prices: Appetizers £1.45–£2.95 ($2.18–$4.43); main courses £4.95–£10.95 ($7.43–$16.43). MC, V.
Open: Mon–Fri lunch 12:30–2pm, dinner 5:30pm–12:30am, Sat lunch/dinner 12:30pm–12:30am.

With a skylit and plant-filled decor, this informal bistro-style restaurant offers an eclectic menu ranging from steaks and nachos, to char-grilled salmon, brochette of lamb, and chicken Lautrec, a breast of white meat filled with cheesy white wine and mushroom sauce.

Budget

$ Kilkenny Design Restaurant, The Parade, Kilkenny. ☎ 22118

Cuisine: IRISH/SELF-SERVICE. **Reservations:** Not accepted.
Prices: All items £1.25–£4.95 ($1.93–$7.43). AE, DC, MC, V.
Open: Apr–Sept Mon–Sat 9am–6pm, Sun 10–6; Oct–Mar Mon–Sat 9am–5pm.

Located above the Kilkenny Design shop, this spacious Georgian-style restaurant is an attraction in itself, with white-washed walls, circular windows, beamed ceilings, framed art prints, and fresh and delicious food. The ever-changing menu often includes local salmon, chicken and ham platters, salads, and homemade soups. Pastries and breads offer some unique choices, such as cheese and garlic scones.

EVENING ENTERTAINMENT

Kilkenny is home to one of Ireland's newest theaters (opened in 1993), the **Watergate Theatre,** Parliament Street (☎ 61674). This modern 328-seat showplace presents a variety of classic and contemporary plays, concerts, opera, ballet, one-person shows, and choral evenings. Local talent and visiting professional troupes perform here. Ticket prices average £4–£10 ($6–$15), depending on the event. Most evening shows start at 8pm or 8:30pm, matinees at 2pm or 3pm.

Across the street is **John Cleere's Theatre,** 28 Parliament Street (☎ 62573), a small pub theater that presents a variety of local productions. Tickets average £2–£5 ($3–$7.50), and most shows start at 8:15pm or 9:30pm.

PUBS

Caislean Ui Cuain (The Castle Inn), Castle Street, Kilkenny. ☎ **65406.**

A striking facade with a mural of Old Kilkenny welcomes guests to this pub, founded in 1734 as a stagecoach inn. The interior decor is equally inviting, with dark wood furnishings, globe-style lights, a panelled ceiling, and local memorabilia. Scheduled and spontaneous Irish traditional music is often on tap, and Irish is spoken by patrons and staff.

Kyteler's Inn, St. Kieran Street, Kilkenny. ☎ **21064.**

If you are in a medieval mood, try this stone-walled tavern in the center of town. An inn since 1324, it was once the home of Dame Alice Kyteler, a colorful character who was accused of being a witch. The decor is full of caverns and arches. The art and memorabilia has a witchcraft theme.

 Edward Langton, 69 John St., Kilkenny. ☎ **21728.**

A frequent Pub of the Year winner. Pub-enthusiasts delight in Edward Langton's rich wood tones, etched mirrors, stained-glass windows, the brass globe lamps, green velour banquettes. On cool evenings, the hand-carved limestone fireplace is warming. On summer days, a conservatory/garden area is open; it's backed by the old city walls. Pub meals are a specialty here.

Marble City Bar, 66 High St., Kilkenny. ☎ **62091.**

One of the best shopfront facades in Ireland belongs to this pub in the middle of the city. It is a showcase of carved wood, polished brass, and globe lamps, with flower boxes overhead. Needless to say, the interior is equally inviting. Even if you don't stop for a drink here, you'll certainly want to take a picture.

 Tynan's Bridge House, 2 Horseleap Slip, Kilkenny. ☎ **21291.**

A classic establishment, situated next to St. John's Bridge, along the River Nore, on a street that was once used as an exercise run for horses. The Tynan family cheerfully welcomes all comers to this award-winning 225-year-old pub, with its horseshoe-shaped marble bar, gas lamps, shiny brass fixtures, and silver tankards. Side drawers marked "mace," "citron," and "sago" are not filled with exotic cocktail ingredients, but remain from the years when the pub also served as a grocery and pharmacy. Shelves display 17th-century weighing scales, shaving mugs, and teapots; there is even a tattered copy of Chaucer's *Canterbury Tales* for rainy days.

7

Cork City

T HAS BEEN SAID THAT CORK CITY IS THE IRISH VERSION OF MANHATTAN. CORK IS built on an island, too, but that's about the extent of the similarity. Cork sits between two channels of the River Lee. The Irish city's midtown area spills over onto the elongated north and south banks of the Lee, with no less than 25 bridges spanning the narrow strips of water. Many of the bridges are so short it hardly seems that you've crossed over water at all, so Cork seems far more unified and walkable than Manhattan and its neighboring boroughs and the state of New Jersey.

The best place to begin a tour of Cork is on the south bank of the river, at least that's what St. Finbarr thought. He's credited with laying the foundation of the city by starting a church and school here in the 6th century. At that point, the area was a wetland and St. Finbarr identified it as Corcaigh, or "marshy place." In time, the school flourished and a considerable town grew up.

By the ninth century, Cork was a Danish stronghold, and then it fell to an Anglo-Norman invasion in 1172. The city's first charter was granted by King Henry II in 1185.

Because of its relatively remote location and the spunky attitude of its citizens, Cork asserted a remarkable independence from outside authority over the years—gradually earning the title "Rebel Cork." This was carried through to the 1919 to 1921 Irish War of Independence when Corkmen figured prominently in the struggle.

Today, as the Republic of Ireland's second largest city, Cork (population 136,000) is a busy commercial hub for the south of Ireland. Be warned that the traffic moves fast and the people talk even faster, with their almost sing-song accent. Walk cautiously amid the traffic of the one-way streets and take a few days to savor the lilting conversations, and you'll soon feel at home in Cork. Be sure to taste the local brews, Beamish and Murphy's. If you're a tea-totaler, ask for Barry's Tea, blended in Cork since 1901.

And lastly, you must kiss the Blarney Stone, the legendary landmark on the outskirts of the city. In many ways, the Blarney Stone is to Ireland what Big Ben is to Britain or the Eiffel Tower to France. No tour of Cork or indeed of Ireland is complete without a visit to the Blarney Stone.

1 Orientation

Cork is 160 miles SW of Dublin, 128 miles SE of Galway, 63 miles S of Limerick, 76 miles S of Shannon Airport, 78 miles W of Waterford, 54 miles E of Killarney

GETTING THERE • By Air   Flights via Aer Lingus from Dublin are scheduled regularly into Cork Airport, Kinsale Road (☎ 021/313131), eight miles south of the city. From Britain, there is service into Cork via British Airways from Birmingham, Bristol, Manchester, and Plymouth; via Orient Air from Coventry; via Manx Airlines from Jersey; via Ryanair from London; and via Air South West from Cornwall. From the Continent, there is service to Cork via Aer Lingus from Amsterdam, Paris, and Rennes; via Brit Air from Brest and Nantes; via KLM from Amsterdam.

Bus Eireann (☎ 021/506066) provides bus service from the airport to Parnell Place Bus Station in the city center; the fare is £1.70 ($7.55) one-way, £2.50 ($3.75) round trip.

• By Ferry   Car ferry routes into Cork from Britain include service from Swansea via Swansea/Cork Ferries; and from the Continent from LeHavre and Cherbourg via Irish Ferries and from Roscoff and St. Malo via Brittany Ferries. All ferries arrive at Cork's Ringaskiddy Ferryport (☎ 021/276484).

Locally, there is a car-ferry service operating in Cork Harbour, linking Glenbrook, east of Cork City, and Carrigaloe, outside of Cobh. It saves at least an hour's driving

What's Special About Cork City

Museums/Galleries
- Cork Museum, displays of locally produced silver, glass, and lace.
- Cork City Gaol, a museum in a jail.
- Crawford Municipal Gallery, home of paintings by 20th-century Irish artists.

Parks
- Cork Heritage Park, for insight into Cork's maritime history.

Buildings
- University College Cork, for its quadrangle of Gothic Revival buildings.
- Firkin Crane Cultural Centre, an 1840's rotunda-shaped building that was part of Cork's original butter market.

Ace Attractions
- Blarney Castle, Blarney, offering the "gift of eloquence" to all who kiss the stone of this famed 15th-century castle.
- St. Anne's Shandon Church, with its giant pepperpot steeple and eight melodious bells.
- Old English Market/City Market, to experience the aromas, sights, and sounds of Old Cork.
- St. Finbarr's Cathedral, founded on the site of the first settlement of Cork in the year 600.

Shopping
- Shandon Craft Centre, Cork's original butter market and now a center for a dozen working craftspeople.
- Antique Row, along Paul's Lane.
- Mercier Bookshop, home of Ireland's oldest independent publishing house.

time between the east and west sides of Cork Harbour, avoiding Cork City traffic. The trip lasts less than five minutes, with continuous service daily from 7:15am to 12:45am. Fare is £2 ($3) one-way and £3 ($4.50) round-trip; no reservations are required. For more information, contact Cross River Ferries, Ltd., Atlantic Quay, Cobh (☎ 021/811223).

• **By Train** Trains from Dublin, Limerick, and other parts of Ireland arrive into Kent Station, Lr. Glanmire Rd., Cork (☎ 021/506766), on the city's eastern edge.

• **By Bus** Buses from all parts of Ireland arrive into the Bus Eireann Passenger Depot, Parnell Place, Cork (☎ 021/506066), in the downtown area, three blocks from Patrick Street.

• **By Car** Many main national roads lead into Cork including N 8 from Dublin, N 25 from Waterford, N 20 from Limerick, N 22 from Killarney, and N 71 from West Cork.

TOURIST INFORMATION For brochures, maps, and other information about Cork, visit the Cork Tourist Office, Tourist House, 42 Grand Parade, Cork (☎ 021/273251). It's open in July and August on Monday through Saturday from

9am to 7pm and Sunday from 3 to 5pm; September through June it's open Monday through Friday from 9:30am to 5:30pm and Saturday from 9:30am to 1pm.

CITY LAYOUT   Cork is divided into three sections.

South Bank   Running south of the River Lee, South Bank encompasses the grounds of St. Fin Barre's Cathedral, the site of St. Finbarr's sixth-century monastery. This area also includes the remnants of Elizabeth Fort, 17th-century city walls, and City Hall, built in 1936 and Cork's chief administrative center.

Flat of the City   This is the downtown core of Cork, surrounded on both north and south sides by channels of the River Lee. This area includes the South Mall, a wide tree-lined street, with mostly Georgian architecture and a row of banks, insurance companies, and legal offices; the Grand Parade, a spacious thoroughfare which blends the remains of the old city walls and 18th-century bow-fronted houses with modern offices and shops; and a welcome patch of greenery, the Bishop Lucey Park, a fairly new (1986) addition to the cityspace.

Extending from the northern tip of the Grand Parade is the city's main thoroughfare, St. Patrick Street. Referred to simply as Patrick Street by Corkonians, this broad avenue was formed in 1789 by covering in an open channel in the river. It is primarily a shopping street, but it is also a place for the Cork folks to stroll and be seen and to greet friends. Patrick Street is also the site of one of the city's best-known meeting places, a statue of a 19th-century priest, Fr. Theobald Matthew, a crusader against drink who is fondly called the apostle of temperance. The statue, or The Stacha, as the locals call it, stands at the point where Patrick Street reaches St. Patrick's Bridge, and is the city's most central point of reference.

North Bank   St. Patrick's Bridge (or Patrick's Bridge), opened in 1859, leads over the river to the north side of the city, a hilly and terraced section where the continuation of Patrick Street is called St. Patrick's Hill. And is it ever a hill—with an incline so steep that it is usually compared to San Francisco. If you climb the stepped sidewalks of St. Patrick's Hill, you will be rewarded with a sweeping view of the Cork skyline.

To the east of St. Patrick's Hill is MacCurtain Street, a busy commercial thoroughfare that goes one-way in an easterly direction, leading to Summerhill Road and up into the Cork hills to the residential districts of St. Luke's and Montenotte. To the west of St. Patrick's Hill is one of the city's oldest neighborhoods, home of St. Ann's Shandon Church and the city's original Butter Market building.

2   Getting Around Cork City

BY PUBLIC TRANSPORT   Bus Eireann operates double-decker bus service from Parnell Place Bus Station (☎ **021/506066**) to all parts of the city and its suburbs including Blarney. Service is frequent and the flat fare is 70p ($1.05). Buses from 7am to 11pm Monday through Saturday, and slightly shorter hours on Sunday.

BY TAXI   Taxis are readily available throughout Cork. The chief taxi ranks are located along St. Patrick's Street, the South Mall, and outside of major hotels. To call for a taxi, try Shandon Cabs (☎ **021/502255**), Super Cabs (☎ **021/500511**) or Tele Cabs (☎ **021/506488**).

BY CAR   If you drive into Cork, most hotels will have parking lots or garages for guests' use, so it is best to park your car and explore the city on foot or by public transport. If you must park your car in public areas, it will cost 40p (60¢) per hour to park in one of the city's two multistory car parks, at Lavitt's Quay and Merchant's Quay. There are also at least a dozen ground-level parking lots throughout the city. It also costs 40p (60¢) per hour to park on the street, using the disc system. Parking discs are sold singly or in books of ten for £4 ($6), at many shops and newsstands.

Many international car rental firms maintain rental desks at Cork Airport including Avis/Johnson & Perrott (☎ 021/281166), Budget (☎ 021/314000), Hertz (☎ 021/965849), and Europcar (☎ 021/966736. Avis/Johnson & Perrott also has a large depot in Cork City at Emmet Place (☎ 021/273295).

ON FOOT   The best way to see Cork is on foot, but try not to do it all in one day. The South Bank and the central part, or flat, of the city can easily take a day to explore; save the Cork Hills and the North Bank for another day. You may wish to follow the signposted Tourist Trail of the city, to guide you to all of the major sights.

Fast Facts: Cork City

Area Code   The area code for most Cork City numbers is **021,** unless indicated otherwise.

Car Rentals   See "Getting Around Cork," above.

Drugstores   Duffy's Dispensing Chemists, 95/96 Patrick St. (☎ 272566); Hayes Conyngham & Robinson, Merchants Quay Shopping Centre (☎ 272230); and Murphy's Pharmacy, 48 N. Main St. (☎ 274121).

Emergencies   Dial **999.**

Hospitals   Bon Secours Hospital, College Road (☎ 542807), and Cork Regional Hospital, Wilton Road (☎ 546400).

Information   See "Tourist Information," above.

Laundry and Dry Cleaning   Castle Cleaners, 90 N. Main St. (☎ 277603) and Winthrop Cleaners, Winthrop Street (☎ 276383).

Library   Cork Central Library, Grand Parade (☎ 277110).

Local Newspapers and Media   The *Cork Examiner* is Cork's daily morning newspaper; the *Evening Echo* is a daily afternoon paper. Local Cork radio stations are Radio Cork 89 FM, 96 FM and 103 FM.

Photographic Needs   Cork Camera Services, 16 Academy St. (☎ 270937) and John Roche Ltd., 55A Patrick St. (☎ 272935).

Police   Garda Headquarters, Barrack Street (☎ 271220).

Post Office   General Post Office, Oliver Plunkett Street (☎ 272000), open Monday through Saturday 9am–5:30pm.

3   Where to Stay

Moderate

Arbutus Lodge, St. Luke's Hill, Montenotte, Cork, Co. Cork. ☎ 021/501237.
    Fax 021/502893. 20 rms (all with bath). TV TEL

Rates (including full breakfast): £42 ($63) single, £72 ($108) double. No service charge. AE, DC, MC, V.

The views of Cork city are hard to beat from the vantage point of this restored 1802 Georgian town house, perched high in the hills overlooking the north bank of the River Lee. Taking its name from the arbutus tree which grows in its prize-winning gardens, it was once the home of the Lord Mayor of Cork, and converted by the Ryan family into a comfortable hotel with antique furnishings, modern Irish art, and Wedgwood trim. This hotel's main claim to fame, however, is its award-winning restaurant (see "Where to Dine," below). Other facilities include the Gallery bar and patio for lighter meals.

★ **Fitzpatrick Silver Springs,** Dublin Road, Tivoli, Cork, Co. Cork. ☎ **021/507533** or toll free **800/367-7701.** Fax 021/507641. 109 rms (all with bath). TV TEL

Rates: £70–£78 ($105–$117) single, £70–£95 ($105–$142.50) double. Service charge 12.5%. AE, DC, MC, V.

Set on a hillside overlooking the River Lee and surrounded by 42 acres of gardens and grounds, this modern seven-story hotel is two miles east of the main business district. Like its sister properties in Dublin and Bunratty, it is personally managed by the Fitzpatrick family, so in spite of its size, a friendly and attentive atmosphere prevails. Each guest room, furnished with hand-crafted Irish furniture and designer fabrics, has lovely views of the river, city, or gardens; plus little extras such as a hair dryer and coffee/tea-maker. Guests are transported from the lobby to their rooms via a unique glass-walled skylift that offers views of the surrounding countryside between floors.

Dining/Entertainment: Choices include Truffles Restaurant for gourmet dining; the Waterfront Grill for meals or snacks all day; the Flyover Bar; and Thady Quill's, a pub that offers live music on Thursday through Saturday nights and a jazz brunch on Sunday mornings.

Services: Concierge, room service, laundry and dry cleaning, courtesy minibus service.

Facilities: Indoor heated Olympic-size swimming pool, Jacuzzi, sauna, steam room, gym, aerobics room, indoor and outdoor tennis courts, squash court, 9-hole golf course, and helipad.

★ **Jurys,** Western Road (N 22), Cork, Co. Cork. ☎ **021/276622** or toll free **00/44-UTELL** in U.S. Fax 021/274477. 185 rms (all with bath). TV TEL

Rates: £87.50 ($131.25) single, £100 ($150) double. Service charge 12.5%. AE, DC, MC, V.

Situated on the western edge of town, this is the only five-star hotel in this busy southern coastal city. Built on the site of the former Muskerry Railway station, it is well positioned in its own gardens, next to University College of Cork and along the banks of the River Lee, yet just a five-minute walk from the city center. A modern two-story multiwinged structure, it was recently refurbished. The public areas are light and open and include a skylit atrium and a wall-length mural of Cork characters in the lobby. Guest rooms are furnished in traditional dark woods with designer fabrics, and have views of either the central courtyard gardens or the river and city.

Dining/Entertainment: Choices include the Fastnet, a seafood restaurant with a nautical theme open only for dinner; the Glandore for meals throughout the day; the skylit atrium-like Pavilion piano bar, and Corks Bar, an in-house pub that combines views of the river with an old-Cork ambience, with free ballad music entertainment performed by The Weavers, a local group, Wednesday through Sunday nights.

Services: Concierge, 24-hour room service, laundry and dry cleaning.

Facilities: Indoor-outdoor heated swimming pool, sauna, gym, squash court.

Imperial Hotel, South Mall, Cork, Co. Cork. ☎ **021/274040** or toll free **800/44-UTELL.** Fax 021/274040 ext. 2507. 101 rms (all with bath). TV TEL

Rates (including full breakfast): £63–£75 ($94.50–$112.50) single, £85–£110 ($127.50–$165) double. Service charge 10%. AE, DC, MC, V.

Within easy walking distance of Cork's major attractions and shops, this vintage four-story lodging is the most conveniently situated in the heart of the city's business district. With Waterford crystal chandeliers, marble floors, and brass fittings, it exudes an aura of 19th-century grandeur in the reception area and public rooms. The bedrooms, however, are a mix of contemporary and traditional, some with light woods and striped pastel tones and others with dark woods, antique fixtures, and semicanopy beds. Each room has a coffee/tea-maker and garment press. Dining and entertainment outlets include The Orangery coffee shop, Clouds Restaurant and bar, and the nautical Captains Bar.

Morrison's Island Hotel, Morrison's Quay, Cork, Co. Cork. ☎ **021/275858** or toll free **800/44-UTELL** in U.S. Fax 021/275833. 40 rms. TV TEL

Rates: £73 ($109.50) single, £106 ($159) double. No service charge. AE, DC, MC, V.

Situated in the downtown area, overlooking the River Lee just off the South Mall, this six-story property is Cork's first all-suite hotel. The guest rooms, decorated with contemporary furniture and modern art, have views of the river, cityscape, and the nearby bridges. Each unit contains a hallway, sitting room, dining area, kitchen, bathroom, and one or two bedrooms. The public area include the River Bank restaurant and lounge.

Inexpensive

$ **Forte Travelodge,** Airport Rd. (R 600), Blackash, Cork, Co. Cork. ☎ **021/310730** or toll free **800/CALL-THF** in U.S. Fax 021/310707. 40 rms (all with bath). TV

Rates: £31.95 ($47.93) per room, single or double. No service charge. AE, MC, V.

Located in a grassy hillside setting 1.5 miles south of downtown, this contemporary brick-faced two-story motel is on the main road to Kinsale and the airport. The first member of this no-frills chain in Ireland, it offers standard rooms with basic furnishings and a coffee/tea-maker, providing accommodations (a double bed and a sofa bed) for up to four people for one flat rate. The public area is confined to a small reception desk, but there is an adjacent Little Chef chain restaurant.

 Jurys Cork Inn, Anderson's Quay, Cork, Co. Cork. ☎ **021/276444** or toll free **800/44-UTELL** in U.S. Fax 021/276144. 133 rms (all with bath). TV TEL

$ **Rates:** £39 ($58.50) per room, single or double. No service charge. AE, DC, MC, V.

Opened in August of 1994, this new five-story hotel is situated in the heart of the city overlooking the River Lee, next to the bus station and three blocks from Patrick Street. The brick facade, with mansard-style roof, blends in with Cork's older architecture, yet the interior is bright and modern, with contemporary light-wood furnishings. It offers amazingly good value for a city center hotel since the flat-rate room price covers one or two adults and two children. Facilities include Arches Restaurant and The Inn Pub.

Lotamore House, Dublin/Waterford Road (N 8/N 25), Tivoli, Cork.
☎ **021/822344.** Fax 021/822219. 20 rms (all with bath). TV TEL

$ Rates (including full breakfast): £25–£27 ($37.50–$40.50) single, £34–£44 ($51–$66) double. No service charge. AE, MC, V.

Overlooking the River Lee on four acres of wooded grounds and gardens two miles east of Cork City, this Georgian manor is one of Cork's best guesthouses. It is furnished with antiques, crystal chandeliers, and a fireplace dating back to 1791. An exceptionally well-run facility, it is owned by two doctors, Mareaid and Leonard Harty, who have provided extra comforts in the guest rooms, such as orthopedic beds, garment press, and hair dryer. Only breakfast is served, but even that is exceptional, with freshly squeezed juices and fruits on the menu every day.

4 Where to Dine

Expensive

Arbutus Lodge, St. Luke's Hill, Montenotte, Cork. ☎ **501237.**

Cuisine: INTERNATIONAL. **Reservations:** Required.
Prices: Set lunch £12.50 ($18.75); set dinner £21.50 ($38.25); dinner appetizers £3.50–£9 ($5.25–$13.50); dinner main courses £14–£17 ($21–$25.50). AE, DC, MC, V.
Open: Mon–Sat lunch 1–2:30pm, dinner 7–9:30pm.

Overlooking the Cork skyline from a hilltop vantage point, this lovely Georgian town-house restaurant has long been synonymous with gourmet cuisine in Cork. The menu includes such entrees as roast quail à l'Armagnac, veal kidney with mustard sauce, chicken in tomato and basil, or rib of beef with sauce Beaujolais, as well as your choice of lobster from the tank. On some evenings, the chef also prepares a tasting menu, eight courses incorporating the best of many dishes. The Ryan family, who own and operate this restaurant, have also earned a reputation for maintaining one of the best wine lists in Ireland and beyond.

Cliffords, 18 Dyke Parade, Cork. ☎ **275333.**

Cuisine: FRENCH. **Reservations:** Required.
Prices: Set lunch £13.50 ($19.95); set dinner £28.50 ($42.25). AE, DC, MC, V.
Open: Lunch Tues–Fri 12:30–2:30pm, dinner Mon–Sat 7–10:30pm.

Housed in the old County Library Building, this art deco–style restaurant offers a relaxing setting of dark woods and light lemon tones. Gastronomically, it is a trendsetter in the city, thanks to the creative cuisine of chef/owner Michael Clifford (who gained previous experience in the kitchen of the French Troisgros brothers). The menu changes daily and all dishes are cooked to order, but some favorites include ragoût of veal; filet of pork with apple and prune stuffing; breast of farmyard duck with mushroom mousse; noisettes of spring lamb; and warm salad of fresh shellfish.

Moderate

Castelli Romani, 29 Princes St., Cork. ☎ **273888.**

Cuisine: ITALIAN. **Reservations:** Recommended.
Prices: Appetizers £1.45–£3.95 ($2.18–5.93); lunch main courses £3.95–£6.50 ($5.93–$9.75); dinner main courses £5.65–£14.50 ($8.48–21.75). MC, V.
Open: Lunch Mon–Fri 12:30–2:45pm; dinner Sun–Thurs 5pm–midnight; Fri–Sat 5pm–1am.

For a sampling of the flavors, aromas, and ambience of Italy, try this small shopfront restaurant near the City Market. The menu offers a wide array of fresh pastas and pizzas, as well as steaks and seafood.

 Jacques, 9 Phoenix St., Cork. ☎ 277387.
Cuisine: IRISH/INTERNATIONAL. **Reservations:** Recommended.
 Prices: Appetizers £2.50–£5.90 ($3.75–$8.85); lunch main courses £3.90–£6.75 ($5.85–£10.13); dinner main courses £7.90–£13.90 ($11.85–$20.85). AE, DC, MC, V.
Open: Lunch Mon–Sat 11:30am–3pm; dinner Tues–Sat 6–10:30pm.

Decorated with modern art on cheery lemon, tangerine, and green walls, this small bistro is the creation of two sisters, Eithne and Jacqueline Barry. It is situated in the heart of town, on a side street near the South Mall and General Post Office. Innovative cuisine is the keynote, with featured dishes such as roast duck with an apricot and potato stuffing; rack of lamb topped with Dijon mustard and garlic breadcrumbs; breast of quail stuffed with brown rice on a bed of spring cabbage; John Dory with sun-dried tomatoes and fresh herb beurre blanc; hake with green herb and parmesan crust; and vegetable polenta with parmesan cheese, field mushrooms, tomatoes, chili, and garlic.

$ Michael's Bistro, 4 Mardyke St., Cork. ☎ 276887.
Cuisine: BISTRO/IRISH. **Reservations:** Required.
Prices: Appetizers £2.50–£3 ($3.75–$4.50); main courses £6–£12.75 ($9–$19.13). MC, V.
Open: Lunch Sun–Fri noon–3pm; dinner daily 6–10:30pm.

An offshoot of the revered Clifford's restaurant next door, this small shopfront eatery embodies the true bistro ethos—quick service and low prices—while still providing the creative cuisine of Michael Clifford. With a simple black-and-white decor, it matters little that the room is tightly packed and noisy, with small tables close together, because the food is fresh, simple, and delicious. The same menu applies all day, with straightforward choices such as Irish Stew, hamburger of prime beef with braised red onions on garlic croutons, or sirloin steak, as well as inventive combinations such as potato and crab cakes in parsley cream sauce.

Oyster Tavern, 4 Market Lane, off 56 St. Patrick St., Cork. ☎ 272716.
Cuisine: IRISH. **Reservations:** Recommended.
Prices: Appetizers £1.75–£6.25 ($2.63–$9.38); main courses £8.50–£15 ($12.75–$22.50). DC, MC, V.
Open: Mon–Sat lunch 12:30–2pm, dinner 6–9:30pm.

Nestled in a narrow alley in the heart of the city, this Cork institution is known for its seafood. With an equestrian-theme decor and old-world ambience, it's very popular with the locals, and, as its name implies, oysters are a favorite, as are other seafood dishes, from pan-fried prawns to salmon and sole. In addition, the menu offers honey-roasted breast of duck; rack of lamb with herb crust; roast stuffed pork steak with apple and brandy sauce; and a variety of steaks. Be prepared to sip an apéritif and wait in the bar area, even if you have a reservation; it's part of the tradition.

Ristorante Rossini, 34/35 Princes St., Cork. ☎ 275818.
Cuisine: ITALIAN. **Reservations:** Recommended.
Prices: Appetizers £1.90–£3.90 ($2.85–$5.85); lunch main courses £2.95–£3.95 ($4.43–$5.93); dinner main courses £5.50–£11.50 ($8.25–$17.25). MC, V.
Open: Mon–Sat noon–3pm, 6pm–12:30am, Sun 5pm–midnight.

Step inside this midcity shopfront restaurant and experience Italy in the decor—vaulted ceiling, dark wood furnishings, and pictures of Bella Italia, enhanced by an open fireplace and fresh flowers. The menu offers steaks and lamb chops, as well as a variety of pasta dishes, chicken cacciatore, pollo Regina (chicken with asparagus, artichokes, and butter sauce), and the house special, sirloin Rossini, steak prepared with prawns, cream, white wine, and peppercorns.

Moderate/Inexpensive

Bully's Restaurant & Wine Bar, 40 Paul St., Cork. ☎ **273555.**

Cuisine: IRISH/ITALIAN. **Reservations:** Suggested.
Prices: Appetizers £1.20–£3.50 ($1.80–$5.25); main courses £2.99–£11.99 ($4.49–$17.99). No credit cards.
Open: Mon–Sat noon–11:30pm, Sun 5–11pm.

Located on one of Cork's best shopping streets near antique row, this small shopfront eatery has a modern decor of black and white furnishings, enhanced by colorful plants. It offers pizzas, pastas, and burgers, as well as seafood omelets and char-grilled steaks. A second location is on the city's north side, at St. Luke's Cross (☎ **508200**).

★ **Crawford Gallery Cafe,** Emmet Place, Cork. ☎ **274415.**

Cuisine: IRISH. **Reservations:** Suggested.
Prices: All items £2–£6.50 ($3–$9.25). MC, V.
Open: Mon–Sat 9am–5pm.

Artfully ensconced amid original oil paintings and statuary in a ground floor room at the Crawford Art Gallery, this restaurant is run by the Allen family of Ballymaloe House fame (see East Cork), so it combines art in decor and food. It serves breakfast, lunch, afternoon tea. Menu items range from traditional dishes such as steak and kidney pie, Scotch eggs, and stuffed filet of pork, to open sandwiches (the smoked salmon, cheese, and pickle combination is a house favorite); as well as spinach and mushroom pancakes and scallop shells of seafood. All fish is brought in fresh daily from Ballycotton Bay and breads and baked goods from Ballymaloe kitchens.

Gino's, 7 Winthrop St., Cork. ☎ **274485.**

Cuisine: ITALIAN. **Reservations:** Not necessary.
Prices: Appetizers £1–£2 ($1.50–$3); main courses £3.50–£12 ($5.25–$18). No credit cards.
Open: Mon–Sat 11am–midnight, Sun 1pm–midnight.

Shoppers from nearby Patrick Street flock to this bright and airy cafe. It specializes in pizzas, with over a dozen extra toppings, from salami or spinach, olives or onions, pineapple or pepperoni. Fresh homemade Italian-style ice cream is the other menu feature, with exotic flavors and toppings.

Glassialley's, 5 Emmet Place, Cork. ☎ **272305.**

Cuisine: INTERNATIONAL. **Reservations:** Recommended.
Prices: Set lunch £7.95 ($11.83); dinner appetizers £1.50–£4.90 ($2.25–$7.35); dinner main courses £6.95–£11.95 ($10.43–$17.93). MC, V.
Open: Sun lunch 12:30–3pm; daily dinner 6–10pm.

Opposite the art gallery and opera house, this upstairs restaurant is a handy place to know if you are attending a show. In Cork parlance, glassialleys are marbles, and not surprisingly, they dominate the decor here, with marble-topped tables and marble-accented accessories. The menu offers an eclectic mix of dishes, such as chicken

Kiev or curry; beef stroganoff; lemon sole stuffed with prawns; mussels in garlic butter; vegetable pancake; Mexican lamb tacos; and steaks.

 Isaac's, 48 MacCurtain St., Cork. ☎ **503805.**

Cuisine: IRISH. **Reservations:** Advised for dinner.

$ **Prices:** Appetizers £2.20–£5.80 ($3.30–$8.70); lunch main courses £4.40–£6.50 ($6.60–$9.25); dinner main courses £6.50–£11.20 ($9.25–$16.80). MC, V.

Open: Mon–Sat 10am–10:30pm, Sun 6:30–9pm.

Situated on the city's north side, this restaurant is housed in a vintage warehouse-style building with tall ceilings supported by columns, stone arches, brick walls, big globe lights, and modern art. It can be noisy when busy, but the din never disturbs the enthusiastic patrons who come for the trendy food. The menu offers choices ranging from freshly prepared salads and seafood chowders, to traditional chicken and leek pie, grilled king prawns, and fish cakes, as well as international dishes such as beef bourguignon; gratin of smoked salmon and potato; spinach tagliatelle with salmon, fennel and cream; and burgers and steaks.

Budget

$ **Bewley's**, 4 Cook St., Cork. ☎ **270660.**

Cuisine: IRISH/SELF-SERVICE. **Reservations:** Not required.

Prices: All items 95p–£4.95 ($1.43–$7.43). No credit cards.

Open: Mon–Sat 8am–6pm.

A branch of the famous Dublin coffee and tea emporium of the same name, this dependable restaurant serves breakfast, lunch, snacks, or freshly brewed coffee or tea at any time of day. It is especially known for its pastries and sticky buns. A favorite meeting spot for Corkonians, it is located just off Patrick Street.

Gingerbread House, French Church Street, Cork. ☎ **276411.**

Cuisine: SELF-SERVICE/SNACKS. **Reservations:** Not accepted.

Prices: All items £1.50–£3 ($2.25–$4.50). No credit cards.

Open: Mon–Sat 9am–6pm.

Conveniently located between Patrick and Paul Streets in the main shopping area, this little shopfront pâtisserie is popular with Corkonians for its wide array of baked goods and confections, coffees and teas, as well as soups and snacks. In good weather there is seating outside on the pedestrian walk.

5 **What to See & Do**

St. Finbarr's Cathedral, Bishop Street. ☎ **963387.**

This Church of Ireland cathedral sits on the spot St. Finbarr chose in 600 for his church and school. Its three giant spires dominate the skyline. The current building dates back only to 1880 and is a fine example of early French Gothic style. The interior is highly ornamented with unique mosaic work. The bells were inherited from the 1735 church previously on this site.

Admission: Free; donations welcome.

Open: Mon–Fri 10am–1pm and 3–5:30pm.

St. Anne's Shandon Church, Church Street. ☎ **501672.**

Famous in story and song for its giant pepperpot steeple and its eight melodious bells, this is Cork's prime landmark. No matter where you stand in the downtown area,

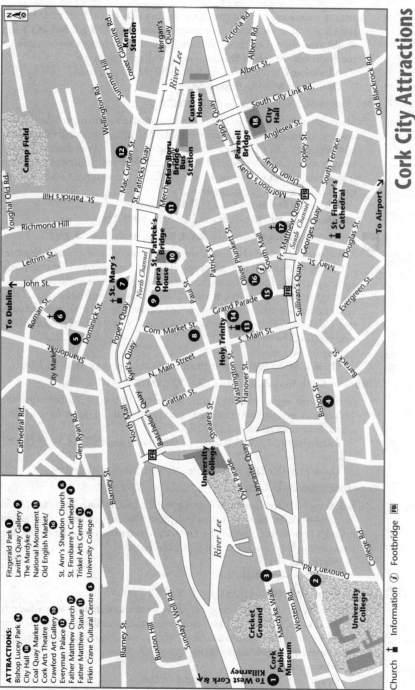

Cork City Attractions

ATTRACTIONS:

Bishop Lucey Park 14
City Hall 18
Coal Quay Market 8
Cork Arts Theatre 7
Crawford Art Gallery 10
Everyman Palace 12
Father Matthew Church 17
Father Matthew Statue 11
Firkin Crane Cultural Centre 2

Fitzgerald Park 1
Lavitt's Quay Gallery 9
The Mardyke 3
National Monument 15
Old English Market/ 16
St. Ann's Shandon Church 6
St. Finnbarre's Cathedral 4
Triskel Arts Centre 13
University College 5

Church **†**   Information *i*   Footbridge **FB**

you can usually see the 1722 church's tower, two sides of which are made of limestone and two of sandstone. The tower is crowned with a gilt ball and a fish weathervane. Visitors are often encouraged to climb to the belfry and play a tune, so you might hear the bells of Shandon ringing at all times of the day.

Admission: Church, tower, and bells £1.50 ($2.25) per person.

Open: Daily Mon–Sat 9:30am–5pm.

Cork Museum, Fitzgerald Park, Cork. ☎ 270679.

In a magnificent Georgian building set in a park on the western edge of the city, this museum has models depicting early medieval times; artifacts recovered from excavations within the city; a working model of an early flour mill with an unusual horizontal water wheel; and an archive of photographs and documents relating to Cork-born Irish patriots Terence McSwiney, Thomas MacCurtain, and Michael Collins. Antique Cork silver, glass, and lace are displayed.

Admission: Free except Sun £1 ($1.50) per person.

Open: Mon–Fri 11am–1pm and 2:15–5pm, Sun 3–5pm.

★ University College—Cork (U.C.C.), Western Road, Cork. ☎ 276871.

A component of Ireland's National University, with about 7,000 students, this center of learning is conducted in a quadrangle of Gothic Revival–style buildings. Lovely gardens and wooded grounds grace the campus. Stone Corridor is a collection of stones inscribed with the Ogham style of writing, an early form of the Irish language. Tours of the campus are conducted during the summer months and leave from the main gate. U.C.C. is celebrating its 150th anniversary in 1995 and a varied program of cultural events will be offered.

Admission: Free.

Open: Mon–Fri 9am–5pm; tours are conducted June–Sept Mon–Fri 2:30pm.

Cork City Gaol, Sunday's Well Road, Cork. ☎ 542478.

About a mile west of the city center, this restored prison was infamous in the 19th-century, housing many of Ireland's great patriots. Lifelike characters in cells and sound effects re-create the social history of Cork.

Admission: £2.75 ($4.13) adult, £2 ($3) seniors and students, £1.50 ($2.25) children.

Open: Mar–Oct daily 9:30am–8pm; Nov–Feb Sat–Sun 10am–4pm.

Crawford Municipal Gallery, Emmet Place, Cork. ☎ 273377.

Jack Yeats, Nathaniel Grogan, William Orpe, John Lavery, James Barry, and Daniel Maclise—works by these well-known Irish painters are the focal point of this gallery in Cork's 18th-century customhouse. Fine sculptures and hand-crafted silver and glass pieces are displayed too. It's next to the Opera House.

Admission: Free.

Open: Mon–Sat 10am–5pm.

Lavitts Quay Gallery, 16 Lavitts Quay, Cork. ☎ 277749.

Operated by the Cork Arts Society, this gallery promotes the contemporary visual arts of the Cork area. It's in an early 18th-century Georgian house that overlooks the River Lee. The ground floor presents a variety of work by established artists, and the upper floor showcases up-and-coming talent.

Admission: Free.

Open: Tues–Sat 10:30am–2pm and 3–5:30pm.

⭐ **Old English Market/City Market**, Grand Parade, Cork.

A Cork tradition from 1610, this huge marketplace unfolds in a relatively recent (1786) building. Colorful stands brim with meats, fish, vegetables, and fruit. You'll also see such traditional Cork foods as tripe (animal stomach), crubeens (pig's feet), and drisheens (local blood sausage). The market's name is a reflection from the days of English rule. You can enter the market from Patrick Street, Grand Parade, Oliver Plunkett Street, or Princes Street.

Admission: Free.
Open: Mon–Sat 9am–6pm.

Coal Quay Market, Cornmarket Street, Cork.

This is Cork's open-air flea market—a treasure trove of second-hand clothes, old china, used books, and memorabilia. It all happens on a street, now a little ragged, that was once Cork's original outdoor market. Happily, Cornmarket Street has been earmarked for urban renewal to the tune of £2.5 ($3.75) million—more than half of which is being provided by the European Commission. Plans call for a historically sensitive restoration and an indoor market by June of 1996.

Admission: Free.
Open: Mon–Sat 9am–5pm.

Cork Heritage Park, Bessboro Road, Blackrock, Cork City. ☎ 358854.

Two miles south of the city center, this new park is set in a 19th-century courtyard amid lovely grounds beside an estuary of Cork Harbour. The site was originally part of the estate of the Pike family, Quakers who were prominent in banking and shipping in Cork in the 1800s. The center's exhibits trace the maritime and shipping routes of Cork as well as the history of the Pike family, in a series of colorful tableaux. There is also an environmental center, an archaeology room, and a small museum dedicated to the history of Cork firefighting from 1450 to 1945, and stables that house models of a saddler and blacksmith.

Admission: £2 ($3) adults, £1.50 ($2.25) children.
Open: May–Sept daily 10:30am–5pm, Oct–April Sat–Sun 10am–5pm.

Royal Gunpowder Mills, Ballincollig, Co. Cork. ☎ 874430.

Beside the River Lee, this industrial complex was a hub for the manufacture of gunpowder from 1794 to 1903, a time of wars between Britain and France. In its heyday as Cork's prime industry, it employed about 500 men and boys as coopers, millwrights, and carpenters. Visitors can tour the restored buildings. Exhibits and an audio-visual tells the story of gunpowder production within earshot of Cork. About 5 miles west of Cork City on the main N 22/Killarney Road.

Admission: £2.50 ($3.75) adults, £2 ($3) seniors and students, £1.50 ($2.25) children.
Open: Apr–Sept daily 10am–6pm.

Blarney Castle and Stone and Blarney House, Blarney, Co. Cork. ☎ 385252.

The fabled kissing Blarney Stone is part of a 15th-century castle, originally the stronghold of the MacCarthys. All that remains of the castle today is a massive square tower, or keep, with a parapet rising 83 ft. The stone is wedged underneath the battlements; and to kiss it, visitors must bend backward to a prone position. But have no fear, a trained guide supervises all the kissing. The hardest part of the experience is climbing the ancient curved steps to the parapet.

Those who kiss the stone are said to be rewarded with eloquence. This belief harks back to the days of Queen Elizabeth I. Cormac MacDermott MacCarthy, then the Lord of Blarney, was being evasive when asked by the Queen's deputy, Carew, to renounce the traditional clan system that elected their own chief and to take the tenure of his lands from the crown. While seeming to agree to this proposal, Lord Blarney put off the fulfillment of his promise from day to day with "fair words and soft speech." Finally, the queen is reputed to have declared, "This is all Blarney—what he says, he never means!" Thus, the word *blarney* came to mean pleasant talk intended to deceive without offending, and in its modern connotation, a clever form of flattery.

After kissing the storied stone, you may wish to stroll through the gardens and a nearby dell beside Blarney Lake. You can also visit the adjacent Blarney House, a Scottish baronial mansion dating from 1874, which was recently restored. It contains a fine collection of ancestral paintings and heraldic decorations.

Admission: Castle £3 ($4.50) adults, £2 ($3) seniors and students, £1 ($1.50) children; house £2.50 ($3.75) adults, £2 ($3) seniors and students, £1.50 ($2.25) children; combination ticket to both castle and house £4.50 ($7.25) adults, £3 ($4.50) seniors and students, £2 ($3) children.

Open: Castle, May and Sept Mon–Sat 9am–6pm, Sun 9:30am–5:30pm; June–Aug Mon–Sat 9am–7pm, Sun 9:30am–5:30pm; Oct–Apr Mon–Sat 9am–5pm, Sun 9:30am–sundown. House, June to mid–Sept Mon–Sat noon–6pm.

Sightseeing Tours

In July and August, Bus Eireann, Parnell Place Bus Station (☎ 508188), offers narrated tours covering all of Cork's major landmarks and buildings via open-top buses. Departures are at 2:30pm on Tuesday and Saturday. The price is £5 ($7.50) per person.

6 Sports & Recreation

SPECTATOR SPORTS

GREYHOUND RACING   Go to the dogs, as they say in Cork, at Cork Greyhound Track, Western Road, Cork (☎ 543013), on Monday, Wednesday, and Saturday evenings at 8pm. Admission is £2 ($3).

GAELIC GAMES   Hurling and Gaelic football are both played on summer Sunday afternoons at Cork's Pairc Ui Chaoimh Stadium, Marina Walk (☎ 963311). Check the local newspapers for details.

HORSERACING   The nearest racetrack is Mallow Race Track, Killarney Road, Mallow (☎ 022/21338), approximately 20 miles north of Cork. Races are scheduled in mid-May, early August, and early October.

RECREATION

BICYCLING   Although walking is probably the ideal way to get around Cork, if you want to rent a bike, try The Bike Store, 48 MacCurtain St., Cork (☎ 500011). It costs £6 ($9) per day or £30 ($40) per week.

FISHING   The River Lee, which runs through Cork, the nearby Blackwater River, and the many lakes in the area present fine opportunities for fishing. Salmon licenses and lake fishing permits, as well as tackle and equipment, can be obtained from T.W. Murray & Co., 87 Patrick St., Cork (☎ 271089), and The Tackle Shop, Lavitt's Quay, Cork (☎ 272842).

GOLFING   Corkonians welcome visitors to play on the following 18-hole courses, all within a five-mile radius of the city: Cork Golf Club, Little Island, Cork (☎ 353451), five miles east of Cork, with greens fees of £23 ($34.50) weekdays and £26 (£39) weekends; Douglas Golf Club, Maryboro Hill, Douglas (☎ 895297), three miles south of Cork, with greens fees of £17 ($25.50) weekdays, £10 ($15); and Harbour Point, Little Island (☎ 353094), four miles east of Cork, with greens fees of £20 ($30).

7   Savvy Shopping

Patrick Street is the main shopping thoroughfare of Cork; many other stores are scattered throughout the city on side streets and in laneways. In general, shops are open from 9:30am to 6pm, Monday through Saturday, unless indicated otherwise. In the summer many shops remain open until 9:30pm on Thursday and Friday and some are open on Sunday.

The city's antique row is **Paul's Lane,** an offshoot of Paul Street, which sits between Patrick Street and the Quays. There are three shops along this lane, each brimming with old Cork memorabilia and furnishings—Anne McCarthy, 2 Paul's Lane (☎ 273755), Mills, 3 Paul's Lane (☎ 273528), and O'Regan's, 4 Paul's Lane (☎ 509141).

The main multilevel mall is **Merchant's Quay Shopping Centre,** Merchant's Quay and Patrick Street. This enclosed complex houses large department stores, such as Marks & Spencer (☎ 275555), as well as small specialty shops, such as Laura Ashley (☎ 274070).

Cork's legendary department store is **Cash's,** 18 St. Patrick St. (☎ 276771). Dating back to 1830, it offers three floors of wares, ranging from Waterford crystal and Irish linen to all types of knitwear, tweeds, and other gift items.

Books and Music

 The Living Tradition, 40 MacCurtain St. ☎ 502040.

Located on the city's north bank, this small shop specializes in Irish traditional music—CDs, cassettes, books, videos, sheet music, and song books—as well as instruments such as bodhrans and tin whistles. In addition, there is a good selection of world ethnic music and rare recordings of native musicians from around the world.

 Mainly Murder, 2A Paul St. ☎ 272413.

Tucked between French Church and Academy Streets, this tiny book shop is a huge treasure trove of who-done-its for amateur sleuths or anyone looking for a good read. It stocks volumes on murder, mystery, and mayhem from Ireland, England, and many other English-speaking lands. It's well worth a visit, to stock up for a rainy day.

 Mercier Bookshop, 5 French Church St. ☎ 275040.

Long a part of Cork's literary tradition, this shop stocks a variety of books including those published by Cork-based Mercier Press, founded in 1944 and now the oldest independent Irish publishing house. In particular, this shop had an extensive Irish-interest section, including volumes on Irish history, literature, folklore, music, art, humor, drama, politics, current affairs, law, and religion.

Waterstone's, 69 Patrick St. and 12 Paul St. ☎ 276522.

With entrances on two streets, this large British-owned bookshop is always busy. It has a good selection of books about Cork and of Irish interest, as well as sections on art, antiques, biography, religion, and travel. It's usually open on Sundays, too.

Crafts

⭐ **Crafts of Ireland,** 11 Winthrop St. ☎ **275864.**

Just a block off Patrick Street, this well-stocked shop presents an array of local crafts from weavings and wrought iron to batik hangings, candles, glass, graphics, leatherwork, pottery, toys, Irish wildlife mobiles, and Irish floral stationery.

Cork Candles, 36–37 Princes St. ☎ **275562.**

Festive and decorative candles of all sizes and styles are produced in this shop, with on-going demonstrations of candle-dipping and candle-carving. Other items for sale include incense and dried flowers.

House of James, 20 Paul St. ☎ **272324.**

Formerly a tea warehouse and candy factory, this store is a multilevel artistic showcase for the pottery products of Stephen Pearce from nearby Shanagarry, as well as the wares of at least 50 other local craftspeople—from tweeds and tiles to candles and cards, not to mention wooden toys and natural soaps.

⭐ **Shandon Craft Centre,** Cork Exchange, John Redmond Street. ☎ **508881.**

Cork's original Butter Market, a commercial exchange begun in 1730, is the site of this unique sightseeing and shopping experience—an enclosed emporium where 20th-century artisans practice a range of traditional trades and display their wares for sale. The crafts include porcelain dolls, jewelry, clothing, crystal, pottery, and hand-made violins, cellos, and violas. In the months of June through August, musicians offer free lunchtime concerts from 1 to 2pm, playing folk, traditional, jazz or classical music.

Tweeds and Woollens

Blarney Woollen Mills, Blarney, Co. Cork. ☎ **385280.**

Located about six miles northwest of Cork City near the famous castle of the same name, this Kelleher family enterprise is housed in an old mill dating back to 1824. It is a one-stop source for all kinds of Irish products, from cashmeres to crystal glassware, hats to heraldry, and tweeds to tee shirts, as well as the distinctive Kelly green Blarney Castle–design wool sweaters, made on the premises. Best of all, it's open daily until 10pm every night in summer.

Carraig Donn, Cook Street. ☎ **274050.**

This shop, which has branches all over Ireland, is known for its wide selection of knitwear, particularly Aran sweaters. In addition, the stock includes mohair garments, Irish tweeds, fashion knitwear, as well as glassware and china, jewelry, and pottery. For mark-downs and seconds, there is a bargain loft.

House of Donegal, 7 Paul St. ☎ **272447.**

"Tailoring to please" is the theme of this showroom/workshop, located one block north of St. Patrick Street, off the Grand Parade. You can buy readymade or specially tailored raincoats, classic trench coats, jackets, suits, and sportwear, for men and women. The handsome rainwear, with Donegal tweed linings, is a special find.

Quills, 107 Patrick St. ☎ **271717.**

For tweeds, woolens, and knits at the best prices, don't miss this family-run enterprise on Cork's busy main thoroughfare. It is a branch of a woollen shop that started small over 20 years ago at Ballingeary, in the heart of the West Cork Gaeltacht, and has since grown to have similar shops in Killarney, Kenmare, and Sneem.

8 Evening Entertainment & Pubs

PERFORMING ARTS CENTERS

Cork Opera House, Emmet Place. ☎ **270022.**

Situated just off Lavitt's Quay along the River Lee, this is the major venue in southwest Ireland for opera, drama, musicals, comedies, dance, concerts, and variety nights.
Admission: Tickets £5–£12.50 ($7.50–$18.25).
Open: Box office 10:15am–7pm; curtain 8pm or 8:30pm; matinees on Sat at 3pm; schedule varies.

Firkin Crane Cultural Centre, John Redmond Street, Shandon, Cork. ☎ **507487.**

Dating from the 1840s, this unique rotunda was part of Cork's original Butter Market, and the building's name is derived from Danish words pertaining to measures of butter. Although destroyed by fire in 1980, the site was completely rebuilt and opened as a cultural center in 1992. It is now a venue for live theater, ballet, concerts, dance, poetry readings, and art exhibitions. In the summer, the center hosts evenings of Irish traditional music.
Admission: Tickets £5–£10 ($7.50–$15).
Open: Most events 8pm, traditional music July–Aug 9pm.

Triskel Arts Centre, Tobin Street, off Main S. Street. ☎ **272022.**

This ever-growing arts center presents a variety of entertainment, from drama to poetry readings, musical recitals, opera, and popular Irish and traditional music concerts. There is also a full program of daytime art workshops and gallery talks.
Admission: Tickets £2–£6 ($3–$9), depending on act.
Open: Box office Mon–Sat 10:30am–5:30pm; performances Tues–Sun 8pm, Sat–Sun matinees 1:15pm or 1:30pm.

THEATERS

Cork Arts Theatre, Knapp's Square. ☎ **508398.**

Situated across the river from the Opera House, this theater presents a variety of contemporary dramas, comedies, and comedies with music, using local talent including the Dress Circle Theatre Company.
Admission: Tickets £5 ($7.50) adults, £4 ($6) seniors.
Open: Shows Tues–Sat at 8pm.

Everyman Palace, 17 MacCurtain St. ☎ **501673.**

This theater is well known as a showcase for new plays, both Irish and international. The Irish National Ballet also performs here regularly.
Admission: Tickets £8 ($12).
Open: Box office Mon–Fri 10am–6pm; curtain at 8pm.

HOTEL/BAR SCENE

Jurys Cabaret, Jurys Hotel, Western Road. ☎ **276622.**

Presented in the ballroom of Jurys Hotel, this is a foot-tapping, fast-paced evening of live entertainment with a Cork slant, including music, comedy, drama, song, and dance.
Admission: £6 ($9).
Open: July–Sept Tues–Wed 8:45pm.

The Lobby Bar, 1 Union Quay. ☎ **311113.**

Situated opposite City Hall, this bar presents a variety of musical entertainment, from traditional and folk to jazz, gypsy, blue grass, blues, rock, classical, and new age.

Admission: £2–£5 ($3–$7.50) cover charge, depending on the act.

Open: Nightly, with music starting at 9pm for most performances.

Midnight Court, Cork Opera House, Emmet Place. ☎ **270022.**

After the main stage empties, the Cork Opera House Bar swings into action on Friday nights, with an ever-changing program of contemporary music from blues and ragtime to pop and rock.

Admission: £5 ($7.50).

Open: Fri 11:30pm–2am.

PUBS

An Bodhran, 42 Oliver Plunkett St. ☎ **274544.**

Irish traditional music is on tap at this friendly pub on Monday through Thursday nights at 9pm. The old world decor includes stone walls, dark woods, and a huge stained-glass window with *Book of Kells*–inspired designs depicting Irish monks playing traditional Irish instruments.

Henchy's, 40 St. Luke's. ☎ **501115.**

It's worth a walk up the steep Summerhill Road, a northeast continuation of busy MacCurtain Street, to reach this classic and well-maintained pub (near the Arbutus Lodge Hotel). Originally established by John Henchy in 1884, it looks just the same as it did then, with lots of polished brass fittings, leaded-glass windows, silver tankards, thick red curtains, and a small snug. The original Henchy family grocery store still operates adjacent to the pub.

Le Chateau, 93 Patrick St. ☎ **203701.**

Established in 1793, this is one of Cork's oldest pubs of great character, located right in the middle of the city's main thoroughfare. As pubs go, it's a large specimen, with a choice of various rooms and alcoves filled with Cork memorabilia. Irish Coffee is a specialty here.

Maguire's, Daunt Square, Grand Parade. ☎ **502825.**

Located just off Patrick Street in the heart of town, this Edwardian-style pub has a conversation-piece decor of vintage bicycles, unicycles, and lots of old brass fixtures.

 Mutton Lane Inn, 3 Mutton Lane, off Patrick Street, Cork. ☎ **273471.**

Old Cork is alive and well at this tiny pub down an alley which was first trod as a pathway for sheep going to market. Begun in 1787 as a public house by the Ring family, who used to make their own whiskey, it is now the domain of Maeva and Vincent McLoughlin, who have preserved the old world aura, including lantern lights, dark wood-paneled walls, exposed beam ceilings, and an antique cash register.

⭐ **An Spailpin Fanac (The Loft),** 28–29 S. Main St. ☎ **277949.**

For traditional Irish music, this place is one of the choice spots in Cork, Sunday through Friday starting at 9:30pm. Situated opposite Beamish's Brewery, it was established in 1779, making it one of Cork's oldest pubs. The decor retains much of the furnishings of yesteryear, from brick walls and flagstone floors to open fireplaces and an authentic snug.

The County Cork Coast

8

Wʜᴇɴ ɪᴛ ᴄᴏᴍᴇs ᴛᴏ ʀᴀɴᴋɪɴɢ Iʀɪsʜ ᴄᴏᴜɴᴛɪᴇs ʙʏ sɪᴢᴇ, Cᴏʀᴋ ɪs ɴᴜᴍʙᴇʀ ᴏɴᴇ. Within Cork's boundaries is the Blarney Stone, Ireland's most popular tourist attraction. Cork is home of the transatlantic port of Cobh and the world's oldest yacht club at Crosshaven. Mizen Head in Cork is the most southerly point in the whole country. And that's just for starters.

Situated between the Atlantic Ocean and the Celtic Sea, Cork shares the southwest coast of Ireland with Kerry. These neighboring counties have craggy coastlines, mighty mountains, and gentle Gulf Stream breezes in common. Cork place-names like Baltimore and Long Island ring familiar to visiting Americans, while Leap, Ovens, Owenahincha, Dripsey, Crookhaven, Barleycove, and Ballycotton appeal to the ears with their fancifulness. There's no better place to start a tour of County Cork than in Kinsale, a small harbor town directly south of Cork City.

1 Kinsale

18 miles S of Cork, 54 miles SE of Killarney, 97 miles SE of Shannon Airport, 177 miles SW of Dublin, 20 miles E of Clonakilty

GETTING THERE Bus Eireann (☎ **021/506066**) operates regular daily service from Cork City to Kinsale. The arrival/departure point is on Pier Road, opposite the Tourist Office. By car, Kinsale is 18 miles south of Cork City via the Airport Road; it is reached from the west via N 71. From East Cork, the Cross River Ferries provide regular service via Cork Harbour (see "Cork City" chapter).

GETTING AROUND Kinsale's streets are so narrow that walking is the best way to get around. There is no local transport, but if you need a taxi to take you to outlying areas, call Kinsale Cabs (☎ **021/772642**).

ESSENTIALS • Tourist Information The Kinsale Tourist Office, Pier Road, Kinsale (☎ **021/774026** and **021/772234**) is open March through October.

• Area Code The telephone code for Kinsale numbers is 021.

Less than 20 miles south of Cork City, Kinsale is a small sea-fishing village with a sheltered semicircular harbor rimmed by hilly terrain. Considered the gateway to the western Cork seacoast, this compact little town of 2,000 residents has also made a big name for itself as the "gourmet capital" of Ireland. Home to more than a dozen award-winning restaurants and pubs, Kinsale draws lovers of good food year-round but particularly each October during a three-day Gourmet Festival.

Kinsale fits the picture-postcard image of what a charming Irish seaport should look like—narrow, winding streets; well-kept 18th-century houses; imaginatively painted shopfronts; windowboxes and street stanchions brimming with colorful flowers; and a harbor full of sailboats. Just for good measure, Kinsale also has a medieval church, a 16th-century castle, and two 17th-century star-shaped fortresses.

History buffs find Kinsale a mecca. In 1601 the town was the scene of the Battle of Kinsale, a turning point in Irish history. This defeat of the Irish helped to establish English domination. After the battle a new governor representing the British crown, William Penn, was appointed. For a time, Penn had his namesake son serve in Kinsale as clerk of the admiralty court. But William Penn, Jr., did not stay long—he was soon off to the New World to found the state of Pennsylvania.

What's Special About the County Cork Coast

Beaches
- Wide and sandy strands of Youghal and Barleycove.

Buildings
- Charles Fort, Kinsale, a 17th-century star-shaped fort.

Parks/Gardens
- Fota Island Wildlife Park & Arboretum, home of rare and endangered species.
- Garinish Island, a subtropical island where G. B. Shaw wrote parts of *St. Joan* under the palm trees.

Ace Attractions
- Cobh: The Queenstown Story, the hub of Ireland's emigration saga.
- Jameson Heritage Centre, home of the largest pot still in the world, with a capacity of over 30,000 gallons.
- Bantry House, an 18th-century home on Bantry Bay with objets d'art from all over Europe.

Activities
- Fishing, windsurfing, or sailing off the coast of Kinsale.
- Learn to cook at Ballymaloe Cookery School.

TV and Film Locations
- Castletownhend, setting for *The Experiences of an Irish R.M.*
- Youghal, where *Moby Dick* was filmed.

Great Towns/Villages
- Kinsale, gourmet capital of Ireland.
- Ballydehob, a town with artistic streetscapes.
- Schull, an old-world yachting town.

Offbeat/Oddities
- Mizen Head, Ireland's southernmost tip.
- Longueville House, Mallow, with a working winery—one of only a few in Ireland.

Just off the coast of the Old Head of Kinsale—about five miles west of the town—the *Lusitania* was sunk by a German submarine in 1915. More than 1,500 people were killed, and many are buried in a local cemetery.

WHAT TO SEE & DO

⭐ **Charles Fort**, off the Scilly Rd. ☎ 772263.

Southeast of Kinsale at the head of the harbor, this coastal landmark dates back to the late 17th century. A classic star-shaped fort, it was constructed to prevent foreign naval forces from entering the harbor of Kinsale, then an important trading town. Additions and improvements were made throughout the 18th and 19th centuries, and the fort remained garrisoned until 1921. Across the river is James Fort (1602).

Admission: £1.50 ($2.25) adults, £1 ($1.50) seniors and students, 60p (90¢) children.

Open: Mid-Apr to mid-June Tues-Sat 9am–4:30pm, Sun 11am–5:30pm; mid-June to mid-Sept daily 9am–6pm; mid-Sept to early Oct Mon–Sat 9am–5pm, Sun 10am–5pm.

★ **Desmond Castle**, Cork Street. ☎ **774855.**

A customhouse built by the Earl of Desmond around 1500, this tower house has had a colorful history. It was occupied by the Spanish in 1601 and later used as a prison for captured American sailors during the War of Independence. Locally it's known as "French Prison," because 54 French seamen prisoners died here in a 1747 fire. During the years of the Great Famine, the castle became a workhouse for the starving populace. At various times, the vaults of the castle have also been used as a wine storage depot. The castle is currently undergoing restoration, with plans to turn it into a permanent heritage center by 1995, depicting Kinsale's maritime and cultural heritage. (*Note:* times of opening and admission charges may change in 1995 when the castle is fully restored.)

Admission: £1 ($1.50) adults, 70p ($1.05) seniors and students, 40p (60¢) children.

Open: June to late-Sept daily 9am–6pm; mid-Sept to early Oct Mon–Sat 9am–5pm, Sun 10am–5pm. **Closed:** Mon, Fri.

Kinsale Crystal, Market St. ☎ **774463.**

Started in 1991 by a former Waterford Crystal master-craftsman, this small workshop produces a traditional full-lead, mouth-blown, and hand-cut crystal, with personalized engraving. Visitors are welcome to watch the entire process.

Admission: Free.

Open: Mon–Sat 9:15am–1pm and 2–6pm.

Kinsale Regional Museum, Market Square. ☎ **772044.**

This museum tells the town's story from its earliest days, with exhibits, photos, and memorabilia. It's in the Market House (1600), to which an arched facade was added in 1706.

Admission: 50p (75¢) adults, 20p (40¢) children.

Open: Daily 10am–6pm.

Kinsale Silver, Pearse St. ☎ **774359.**

Silvermaking is a craft that traces its origins back more than 300 years; this local silversmithing workshop is run by the Dolan family (see Wexford shopping, above). Visitors can watch as each piece is wrought and forged by hand, using tools of yesteryear.

Admission: Free.

Open: Daily 9:30am–6pm.

SPORTS AND RECREATION

BICYCLING   Biking along Kinsale Harbour is an exhilarating experience. To rent a bike, contact Deco's Cycles, 18 Main St., Kinsale (☎ **774884**). A day's rental averages £7 ($10.50), depending on equipment. Open Monday through Saturday from 9am to 6pm.

FISHING   Kinsale Holiday Activities, 8 Main St. (☎ **774355**), arranges sea fishing from Kinsale Harbour or game fishing for salmon and trout in nearby rivers. The fee for sea fishing averages £20 ($30) per day, and river fishing is £39 ($58.50) per

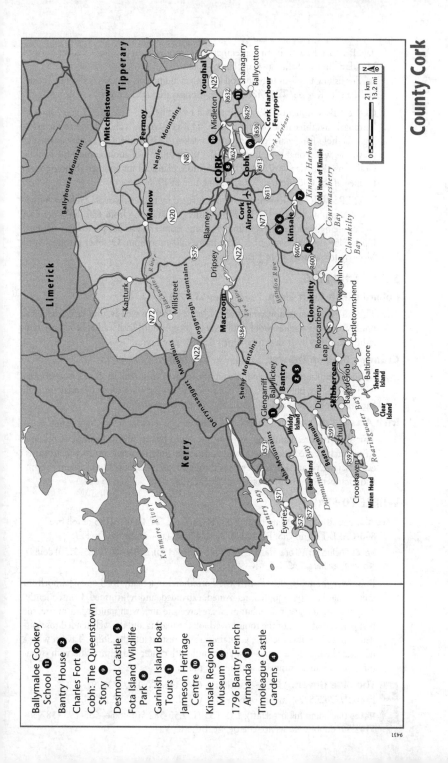

County Cork

Ballymaloe Cookery School ⑪
Bantry House ②
Charles Fort ⑦
Cobh: The Queenstown Story ⑨
Desmond Castle ⑤
Fota Island Wildlife Park ⑧
Garinish Island Boat Tours ①
Jameson Heritage Centre ⑩
Kinsale Regional Museum ⑥
1796 Bantry French Armada ③
Timoleague Castle Gardens ④

0   21 km
     13.2 mi

9431

day. It's open May through September daily from 9:30am to 8pm; October to April Monday through Saturday from 10am–6pm.

For fishing tackle or to rent a rod and other equipment, try Deco's Fishing Tackle, 18 Main St., Kinsale (☎ 774884). Open Monday through Saturday from 9am to 6pm.

GOLF   By summer of 1995, Kinsale will have a new 18-hole par-71 golf course at Farrangalway, three miles north of town. This new course is an addition to the existing nine-hole Ringenane course, dating back to 1930. Greens fees, not yet final at presstime, will probably be about £20 ($30); for full information, contact the Kinsale Golf Club, Kinsale (☎ 772197). In addition, plans call for another 18-hole course to open at the Old Head of Kinsale sometime in 1996.

WATERSPORTS   Kinsale Harbour is favored by boaters. Kinsale Holiday Activities, 8 Main St., Kinsale (☎ 774355), offers scuba diving from £30 ($45) per day; and canoeing, windsurfing, or dinghy sailing, from £7 ($10.50) per activity per day. Open May through September daily from 9:30am to 8pm; October through April Monday to Saturday from 10am to 6pm.

SAVVY SHOPPING

Boland's Irish Craft Shop, Pearse Street. ☎ 772161.

This is a good spot to buy a traditional Kinsale smock, as well as Aran knit vests, local pottery, Ogham plaques, wooly and ceramic sheep, quilts, Irish leather belts, and miniature paintings by Irish artists. Open daily 8am to 6pm.

Granny's Bottom Drawer, 53 Main St. ☎ 774839.

Ireland's traditional linens and lace are the focus of this small shop. It's well-stocked with tablecloths, pillow cases, and hand-crocheted placemats. Open Monday through Saturday from 10am to 6pm and Sunday from noon to 2pm.

Irish Arts & Crafts, 8 Main St. ☎ 774355.

This shop features hand-crafted items produced by artisans in Counties Cork and Kerry, such as needlepoint art, handmade shoes, pottery, scenic prints and art cards, candles, jewelry, and kites. Open May through September daily from 9:30am to 8pm, and October to April Monday through Saturday from 9:30am to 8pm.

WHERE TO STAY

Acton's, Pier Road, The Waterfront, Kinsale, Co. Cork. ☎ 021/772135 or toll free 800/CALL-THF in U.S. Fax 021/772231. 57 rms (all with bath). TV TEL

Rates (including full breakfast): £55–£80 ($82.50–$120), £70–£100 ($105–$150) double. No service charge. AE, DC, MC, V.

Built over the years, this Trusthouse Forte hotel is actually six 3-story harborfront houses that have been joined, renovated, expanded, and refurbished. Consequently, the guest rooms vary in size, but most are large and airy, with standard furniture; the best part is that most of the rooms overlook the marina and the well-tended rose gardens. Amenities include The Captain's Table restaurant, the Ships' Tavern with a nautical-theme, and a brand-new adjacent health center and leisure club with swimming pool, saunas, sunbeds, and billiard room.

The Blue Haven, 3 Pearse St., Kinsale, Co. Cork. ☎ 021/772209. Fax 021/774268. 21 rms (all with bath). TV TEL

Rates (including full breakfast): £35–£55 ($52.50–$82.50) single, £55–£95 ($82.50–$142.50) double. No service charge. AE, DC, MC, V.

In the heart of town on the old Fish Market, the Blue Haven is an old-world inn meticulously run by Brian and Anne Cronin. This hardworking duo has won accolades for their top-notch seafood restaurant (see "Where to Dine," below). In 1994, the Cronins expanded their inn to include an adjacent building, adding 11 new rooms, an elevator, a ground-floor resident's lounge, and a roof garden.

All the guest rooms are individually furnished in a bright and contemporary decor, with local crafts and artwork. Views are of the town or the back gardens. Rooms in the new wing are named for the Wild Geese who left from Kinsale and established wineries in Europe, such as Chateau McCarthy or Chateau Dillon. These rooms have a more traditional decor with canopy beds, window seats, armoires, and brass fixtures.

The inn has the aforementioned restaurant, a pub with a nautical theme, and a wine and cheese shop.

⭐ **The Moorings,** Scilly, Kinsale, Co. Cork. ☎ **021/772376.** Fax 021/772675. 8 rms (all with bath). TV

Rates (including full breakfast): £40–£75 ($60–$112.50) single, £60–£100 ($90–$150) double. No service charge. MC, V.

Overlooking the harbor and marina, this new two-story guesthouse has a bright and contemporary decor with lots of wide-windowed views of the water. The guest rooms are individually furnished, with brass beds, pastel-colored quilts, light woods, and modern art, plus the added convenience of over-the-bed reading lamps and a coffee/tea-maker. Five rooms with balconies face the harbor, while the rest overlook the garden. Guests enjoy use of a cozy traditional-style parlor and a large sunlit conservatory with wrap-around views of the water. Pat and Irene Jones are the innkeepers.

Trident, World's End, Kinsale, Co. Cork. ☎ **021/772301.** Fax 021/774173. 58 rms (all with bath). TV TEL

Rates (including full breakfast): £66–£118 ($99–$177) single or double. No service charge. AE, DC, MC, V.

Situated right on the harbor at the west end of the marina, this modern three-story hotel has been updated and refurbished in recent years. The bedrooms feature wide-window views of the harbor, with modern furnishings of light woods, floral fabrics, and art deco–style fixtures. Facilities include the Savannah Restaurant overlooking the water, Fisherman's Wharf Bar, plus a health center with sauna, steam room, gym, and Jacuzzi.

WHERE TO DINE

Expensive/Moderate

⭐ **Blue Haven,** 3 Pearse St., Kinsale. ☎ **772209.**
Cuisine: SEAFOOD/IRISH. **Reservations:** Recommended.
💲 **Prices:** Bar: appetizers £1.95–£7.25 ($2.93–$10.88), lunch main courses £1.85–£9.90 ($3.78–$14.85), dinner main courses £4.25–£12.50 ($6.38–$18.25); restaurant: appetizers £2.25–£7.50 ($3.38–$11.25), dinner main courses £9–£16.50 ($13.50–$24.75). AE, MC, V.
Open: Bar: lunch 12:15–3pm, dinner 5:30–9:30pm; restaurant: dinner 7–10pm.

Of all the restaurants in Kinsale, this one is the benchmark, and it has a huge following. To suit every budget and appetite, there are two menus, one for the top-of-the-line pub food in the atmospheric bar and a full à la carte menu for the lovely skylit restaurant. The bar food ranges from smoked seafood quiches and seafood pancakes to garlic mussels, oak-smoked salmon, steaks, pastas, and salads. The restaurant offers a wide array of fresh seafood including a house special of salmon slowly cooked over oak chippings. Other specialties include seafood thermidor, Dover sole on the bone, brill and scallop bake, fisherman's platter, and pasta seafood de mer (a variety of seafood in herby tomato sauce on a bed of pasta ribbons). For game lovers, there is farmyard duck with sage and onion stuffing as well as local venison in season. Steaks are prepared, too. Wines served at the Blue Haven have Irish connections—they come from many of the wineries in France started by Irish exiles, such as Chateau Dillon, McCarthy, Barton, Kirwan, Lynch, and Phelan. These wines are also on sale in the Blue Haven's adjacent wine and cheese shop.

★ **The Vintage,** 50/51 Main St., Kinsale. ☎ **772502.**
Cuisine: CONTINENTAL. **Reservations:** Required.
Prices: Appetizers £3.95–£10.50 ($5.93–$15.75), main courses £16.95 ($25.43). AE, MC, V.
Open: Mar–Dec Mon–Sat 6:45–10:30pm.

Marie and Michael Riese, from Cork and Hamburg, respectively, enliven this charming 200-year-old house in the heart of town with a repertoire of Irish and German recipes. Some of the specialties include carpetbag steak stuffed with oysters; rack of lamb; breast of chicken with smoked salmon and tarragon sauce; sea bass with trout mousseline; mussels with garlic and white wine sauce; weiner schnitzel; and hot oak-smoked salmon steak. Be sure to top off your meal with the Rieses' unique rum and brandy truffles.

Moderate

Le Bistro, Market Street, Guardwell, Kinsale. ☎ **774193.**
Cuisine: FRENCH. **Reservations:** Recommended.
Prices: Appetizers £3.50–£7 ($5.25–$10.50), main courses £9.50–£14 ($14.25–$21). MC, V.
Open: Dinner daily 6:30–11pm, lunch Sun 1–3:30pm.

As its name implies, this colorful building in the middle of town has a French atmosphere and decor. Specialties include "three-way mussels"—farci, marinière, and provençale; fresh and smoked salmon salad with sweet pepper and lime dressing; filet steak on a polenta base with green-peppercorn sauce; and crêpes stuffed with mussels and prawns.

Chez Jean-Marc, Lower O'Connell St., Kinsale. ☎ **774625.**
Cuisine: INTERNATIONAL. **Reservations:** Recommended.
Prices: Appetizers £3.50–£7 ($5.25–$10.50); Chinese lunch appetizers £3–£4.50 ($4.50–$6.75), lunch main courses £5.50–£7.50 ($8.25–$11.25); dinner main courses £13.50–£15 ($19.75–$22.50). AE, DC, MC, V.
Open: Mid-Mar to mid-Dec Tues–Sun dinner 7–10:30pm; Sun noon–3pm.

Although most of the cooking at this restaurant is French and continental, the chef Jean-Marc Tsai offers a stir-fry Chinese menu often on Sundays at lunchtime. The regular evening menu includes dishes such as duck with black-currant liqueur; turbot filled with vegetable salsa and smoked salmon and baked in pastry; salmon poached in court bouillion with crab toes and vermouth butter–cream sauce; and filet of beef in red wine sauce. It is located on the upper west end of town, near the Trident Hotel.

Cottage Loft, 6 Main St., Kinsale. ☎ 772803.

Cuisine: IRISH/INTERNATIONAL. **Reservations:** Recommended.
Prices: Appetizers £2–£5.50 ($3–$8.25); main courses £13.95–£14.50 ($20.93–$21.75). AE, MC, V.
Open: May–Oct daily dinner 6–10pm; Nov–Apr Tues–Sun dinner 6–10pm.

Housed in a 200-year-old building in the heart of town, this shopfront restaurant has a cottage-style decor, with pink linens, antiques, caned-chairs, leafy hanging plants, and wooden ceiling beams. The eclectic menu ranges from rack of lamb and farm-yard duck in apple brandy sauce to filet of lemon sole rolled in smoked salmon and prawns with lobster sauce, and a house specialty of seafood Danielle salmon stuffed with crab, prawns, and peppers with a prawn or nettle sauce.

★ **Jim Edwards**, Market Quay, off Emmet Place, Kinsale. ☎ 772541.

Cuisine: IRISH. **Reservations:** Recommended for dinner.
Prices: Appetizers £1.95–£5.95 ($2.93–$8.93); lunch main courses £3.95–£6.95 ($5.93–$10.43); dinner main courses £10–£14.95 ($15–$22.43). MC, V.
Open: Daily, lunch 12:30–3pm, and dinner 6–10:30pm.

A classy nautical theme dominates the decor of this pub/restaurant, with colored-glass windows, ship's wheels, sailing-ship art, plush red cushioned seating, and a clock over the door that tells time by letters instead of numbers. Located in a lane between the Methodist Church and the Temperance Hall, it is known for its good food, including such dishes as chicken Kiev, boneless duck with cassis and red-currant sauce; rack of lamb; salmon en croûte; king prawns in light basil cream sauce; médaillons of monkfish with fresh herbs; and a variety of steaks.

Man Friday, Scilly, Kinsale. ☎ 772260.

Cuisine: INTERNATIONAL. **Reservations:** Recommended.
Prices: Appetizers £2.95–£6.45 ($4.45–$9.68); main courses £12.95–£14.95 ($19.43–$22.43). MC, V.
Open: Feb–May and Oct–Dec Tues–Sat dinner 7–10:30pm; June–Sept Mon–Sat dinner 7–10:30pm.

Situated in a hilly area overlooking Kinsale harbor, this restaurant exudes a tropical garden ambience, including a bamboo-covered entrance and lots of leafy plants. The rustic bar area is a blend of exposed beam ceilings, stone walls, and tree-stump stools, while the dimly lit pine-paneled restaurant has a romantic display of fine artwork. The menu offers six varieties of steak and beef, as well as rack of lamb and dishes such as black sole on the bone; Swiss veal with gruyère cheese sauce; chicken Newport (stuffed with crab, thyme, and mushrooms); and free-range duck with nectarine and brandy sauce.

Seasons, Milk Market Street, Kinsale. ☎ 772244.

Cuisine: IRISH/INTERNATIONAL. **Reservations:** Recommended.
Prices: Appetizers £2.20–£5 ($3.30–$7.50), lunch main courses £3.95–£7.95 ($5.93–$11.83); dinner main courses £8.50–£15 ($12.75–$22.50). AE, DC, MC, V.
Open: May–Sept daily lunch 12:30–3pm; dinner 6–10:30pm. Oct–Apr Sun lunch 12:30–3pm; Wed–Mon dinner 7–10:30pm.

Nestled in the old market area of Kinsale in a 16th-century building, this restaurant features a varied and tasty menu, with dishes ranging from vegetable pancakes, farm-yard duck, stir-fried pork steak, or lemon-and-garlic chicken, to salmon filled with scallops and fresh herbs or hickory-flavored cod topped with bacon, cheddar, and herbs.

Moderate/Inexpensive

Max's Wine Bar, Main Street, Kinsale. ☎ 772443.

Cuisine: INTERNATIONAL. **Reservations:** Recommended.
Prices: Appetizers £2.50–£5.50 ($4.25–$8.25); lunch main courses £3–£6 ($4.50–$9); dinner main courses £6.50–£12.50 ($9.75–$18.75). MC, V.
Open: Mar–Oct lunch Mon–Sat 12:30–3pm, Sun 1–3:30pm; dinner Mon–Sat 6:30–10:30pm.

For more than 20 years, this old-world townhouse with an outdoor patio has been a local favorite for a light snack as well as a full meal. Grilled mussels are a specialty here, as are beefburgers. Other dishes offered include salmon in dill sauce, scallops poached in vermouth and cream, breast of chicken with mushroom sauce, duck with orange and ginger sauce, rack of lamb, and pasta with sun-dried tomatoes, black olives, and parmesan cheese.

Budget

Pancake Paradise, Pearse Street, Kinsale. ☎ 774811.

Cuisine: INTERNATIONAL. **Reservations:** Not necessary.
Prices: All items £1.10–£3.50 ($1.65–$5.25). No credit cards.
Open: Mon–Sat 10am–6pm, Sun noon–7pm.

With a decor of light woods, blue walls, and plants, this airy bistro specializes in pancakes with various fillings and toppings, such as ham, cheese, spinach, mushrooms; or sweet variations with sugar and banana, chocolate, or almonds. There is also a good selection of pastries, soup, sandwiches, quiches, salads, and ice cream sundaes.

PUBS

The Dock, Castlepark, Kinsale. ☎ 772522.

On the outskirts of town, this pub overlooks the inner harbor. The walls are lined with fishing-theme posters and equipment, and the windows give views of the water. If the weather is nice, you can step out onto the front deck with its row of inviting tables and chairs.

The Greyhound, Marian Terrace, Kinsale. ☎ 772889.

Photographers are enchanted with the exterior of this pub, with its neat flower boxes, rows of stout barrels, and handmade signs depicting the swift Irish racing animal. The interior rooms are cozy and known for hearty pub grub, such as farmhouse soups, seafood pancakes, shepherd's pie, and Irish stew.

Lord Kingsale, Main Street, Kinsale. ☎ 772371.

A touch of elegance prevails at this handsome pub, decorated with lots of polished horse brass and black and white Tudor-style trappings. It takes its name (and ancient spelling) from the first Anglo-Norman baron who took charge of this Irish port in 1223. You'll often find evening sing-alongs here, and the soup-and-sandwich pub grub is very good.

The Shanakee, Market Street, Kinsale. (No phone)

With an Anglicized name (derived from the Irish word *seanachie,* which means storyteller), this vintage pub is known for its music—traditional tunes and ballads nightly.

The Spaniard, Scilly, Kinsale. ☎ 772436.

Named for Don Juan de Aguila, who rallied his fleet with the Irish in an historic but unsuccessful attempt to defeat the British in 1601, this old pub is full of local seafaring memorabilia. With a much-photographed facade, it has a great location in the hills overlooking Kinsale, with tables outside for sunny day snacks. It draws large crowds for live music nightly in the summer months, and on weekends at other times of the year. On Sunday afternoons year-round there is a jazz/blues session at 5pm.

The White House, end of Pearse Street. ☎ **772125.**

With its Georgian facade and distinctive name over the front entrance, this is one pub that tempts nearly every American visitor to take a photograph. The inside is more pubby, with a motif that focuses on local sporting memorabilia.

2   East Cork

GETTING TO EAST CORK • By Car   From Cork City, take the main Waterford Road (N 25) eastward, exiting at R 624 for Fota and Cobh, or R 632 for Shanagarry and Ballycotton. Midleton and Youghal have their own signposted exits. To bypass Cork City, take the car ferry operated by Cross River Ferries Ltd., Atlantic Quay, Cobh (☎ **021/811223**). It links Carrigaloe near Cobh with Glenbrook south of Cork City. Ferries run daily from 7:15 to 12:45am, with average crossing time of five minutes. No reservations are necessary and the fares, payable on the ferry, are £3 ($4.50) round-trip and £2 ($3) one-way.

• **By Public Transport**   Irish Rail (☎ **021/506766** or **021/811655**) operates daily train service between Cork City and Cobh via Fota Island; the fare is £2 ($3) one-way or £2.40 ($3.60) round-trip. Bus Eireann (☎ **021/506066**) also provides daily service from Cork City to Cobh and other points in East Cork.

ESSENTIALS • Tourist Information   Seasonal (May or June to September) tourist offices operate at Cobh Harbour (☎ **021/813591**); 4 Main St., Midleton (☎ **021/631821**); and Market Square, Youghal (☎ **024/92390**).

• **Area Codes**   Telephone area codes for East Cork are 021 and 024.

Lying 15 miles east from Cork City is the harbor town of Cobh (pronounced cove, and meaning "haven" in the Irish language). In the days before airline travel, Cobh was Ireland's chief port of entry, with about three or four transatlantic liners calling here a week. For thousands of Irish emigrants, particularly during the famine years and in the early part of this century, Cobh was the last sight of Ireland they'd ever see. Cobh is still an important port, and the new visitor attraction "Cobh: The Queenstown Story" tells the city's history.

With a landscape of terraces rising from the sea, the Cobh skyline is dominated by the magnificent St. Colman's Cathedral, a Gothic-Revival structure with elaborate flying buttresses, columns of polished marble, mosaic flooring, and moulded arches. The fine-tuned cathedral carillon of 47 bells is said to be one of the best in the world. About five miles north of Cobh is Fota Island, a 70-acre harborside estate and wildlife park. Farther southeast in the little village of Shanagarry is the Ballymaloe Cooking School, a culinary trendsetter for the entire country.

The county's major coastal town is Youghal (pronounced yawl), 30 miles to the east of Cork City, near the Waterford border. A leading beach resort and fishing port, Youghal is loosely identified with Sir Walter Raleigh, who was once the town mayor. According to tradition, it was here that Raleigh first grew the first potatoes in Ireland. Youghal—with its red sandstone 18th-century clock tower straddling the main street—provided a memorable seaport setting for the movie, *Moby Dick*. East County Cork is also the home of the Jameson Heritage Centre at Midleton, the hub of Ireland's whiskey-production enterprises.

WHAT TO SEE & DO

★ **Cobh: The Queenstown Story**, Cobh Railway Station, Cobh. ☎ **021/813591.**

This new heritage center commemorates the days when Cobh (then known as Queenstown) was a vital link in transatlantic liner traffic, particularly in the years of high emigration, 1848 to 1950. Because more than $2^{1}/_{2}$ million people from all over Ireland departed from Cobh for new lives in the U.S., Canada, and Australia, the city became synonymous with emigration. In the former railway station, the center tells the story of the city, its harbor, and the exodus of the Irish in a series of displays, with an audio-visual presentation. The center also offers exhibits that re-create the age of luxury-liner travel and special events in Cobh's waters such as the sinking of the *Titanic* and the *Lusitania*.

Admission: £3.50 ($5.25) adults, £2 ($3) children.

Open: Mar–Dec, daily 10am–5pm.

★ **Fota Island Wildlife Park & Arboretum**, Fota Island, Carrigtwohill. ☎ **021/812678.**

Located 10 miles east of Cork on the Cobh Road, this wildlife park was established in 1983. It's home of rare and endangered species of giraffe, zebra, ostrich, antelope, cheetah, flamingo, penguin, and peafowl. The animals and birds roam in natural wildlife settings, with no obvious barriers. Monkeys swing through the trees. Kangaroos, macaws, and lemurs have the complete run of the 40 acres of grasslands. Only the cheetahs are bounded by conventional fencing. Admission charges include entrance to the adjacent Fota Arboretum. First planted in the 1820s, it contains trees and shrubs from the temperate and subtropical regions of the world, from China to South America and the Himalayas. A coffee shop, a tour train, picnic tables, and a shop are on the grounds.

Admission: £3.30 ($4.95) adults, £3 ($4.50) students, £1.90 ($2.85) seniors and children age 14 and under. Tour train, 40p (60¢) per ride. **Parking:** £1 ($1.50) per car.

Open: Mid-Mar to early Nov, Mon–Sat 10am–5pm, Sun 11am–5pm.

Jameson Heritage Centre, Distillery Rd., off Main St., Midleton. ☎ **021/682821.**

If you've always wanted to know what makes Irish whiskey different from Scotch, you can find out at this hub of whiskey making. This production center for John Jameson Whiskey and other leading Irish brands has the largest pot still in the world (it has a capacity of more than 30,000 gallons). Many of the original 1825 structures have been preserved—the mill building, maltings, corn stores, still houses, warehouses, kilns, a water wheel, and the last copper stills manufactured in Ireland.

High-tech methods are now used in a modern distillery. Visitors are not allowed into the production areas, but the whiskey-making process is illustrated by an audio-visual presentation, photographs, working models, and a demonstration. A whiskey tasting follows a tour.

Admission: £3.50 ($5.25) adults, £1.50 ($2.25) children.

Open: Mar–Nov, daily 10am–4pm.

Ballymaloe Cookery School, Kinoith, Shanagarry. ☎ **021/646785.**

Come to Ireland and learn to cook? Yes, if you head to this mecca of fine food, offering more than 35 different courses a year. The success of the Ballymaloe restaurant (see "Where to Stay & Dine," below) led to the founding of this cooking school more than a dozen years ago. Courses, which range from a day to 12 weeks, appeal to all types of amateur and professional chefs, with topics such as breadmaking, weekend entertaining, hors d'oeuvres, seafood, vegetarian, family food, barbecue food, mushrooms, and Christmas cooking. There are also courses for absolute beginners, on new trends in cooking, and for chef certificates.

Fee: One- to four-day courses from £69 to £335 ($103.50–$502.50); 12-week certificate courses £3,475 ($5,212.50). Accommodations are £10–£12.50 ($15–$18.75) per night extra.

Open: Year-round; schedule varies.

WHERE TO STAY & DINE

★ **Aherne's,** 162/163 N. Main St., Youghal. ☎ 024/92424 or toll free **800/223-6510** in U.S. Fax 024/93633. 10 rms (all with bath). TV TEL

Rates (including full breakfast): £43 ($64.50) single, £75 ($112.50) double. No service charge. MC, V.

Located in the heart of a busy seaside resort 30 miles east of Cork City, this cozy inn has long been a focal point because of its top-class seafood, served both in the nautically themed pub and the restaurant. Now the FitzGibbon family, who have owned Aherne's for three generations, have added some excellent and very spacious bedrooms. Each unit is decorated in the finest hotel style—with traditional furnishings including antiques and designer fabrics, oversized six-foot-long beds, and extra amenities such as a hair dryer and garment press. Guest facilities include two bars and a library-style sitting room, but the main reason to stay here is to be close to the restaurant, known for concentrating on the best of the local catch, including Blackwater salmon, giant prawn tails, rock oysters, and lobsters from the tank. Even the daytime bar food is worth a detour—seafood pies, chowders, crab sandwiches, and crisp salads.

★ **Ballymaloe House,** Ballycotton Road, Shanagarry, Co. Cork. ☎ 021/652531 or toll free **800/223-6510** in U.S. Fax 021/652021. 29 rms (all with bath). TEL

Rates (including full breakfast): £56–£90 ($84–$135) single, £88–£129 ($132–$193.50) double. No service charge. AE, DC, MC, V.

Combining a Georgian farmhouse facade with the tower of a 14th-century castle, this ivy-covered enclave of hospitality run by the Allen family is situated on a 400-acre farm, with grazing sheep and cows. The only road sign you'll see is one that alerts you to the importance of four-legged traffic: "Drive Slow: Lambs crossing." The bedrooms are furnished in an informal, comfortable style, and the guest facilities include a heated outdoor swimming pool, hard tennis courts, trout pond, nine-hole golf course, and a craft shop emphasizing local wares.

The biggest draw to Ballymaloe, however, is the Dining Room, a trendsetter for much of Ireland's imaginative cookery, relying on local seafood and produce, accompanied by fresh vegetables from the garden. The success of the kitchen also spawned Ireland's first year-round, country-inn cooking school (see "What to See & Do," above), and a shelf-load of Allen family cookbooks. Ballymaloe is located about 20 miles southeast of Cork City, less than two miles from Ballycotton Bay.

Bayview Hotel, Ballycotton, Midleton, Co. Cork. ☎ 021/646746 or 021/646824. 35 rms (all with bath). TV TEL

Rates (including breakfast): £50 single ($75), £80 ($120) double. No service charge. AE, DC, MC, V.
Open: Apr–Oct.

If location is everything, then this hotel has a lot to offer. Set high on a hillside overlooking Ballycotton Bay, this sprawling three-story property is an ideal waterside retreat, yet within 25 miles of Cork City. Recently refurbished and updated from top to bottom, it offers a spacious lobby, restaurant, and lounge with wide-windowed views of the bay, traditional furnishings, and contemporary art. Guest rooms have modern light-wood furniture, pastel and sea-toned fabrics, and most have panoramic views.

3 West Cork

GETTING THERE • By Car   N 71 is the prime road leading into West Cork from north and south; from Cork and points east, N 22 also leads to West Cork.

• By Public Transport   Bus Eireann (☎ 021/518188) provides daily bus service to the principal towns in West Cork.

ESSENTIALS • Tourist Information   For information on West Cork, contact the Skibbereen Tourist Office, North Street, Skibbereen, Co. Cork (☎ 028/21766). It is open year-round, on Monday through Friday from 9am to 6pm and on Saturday from 9am to 1pm, with expanded hours in the summer, according to demand. There are seasonal (May/June to August/September) tourist offices in The Square, Bantry (☎ 027/50229), Rossa Street, Clonakilty (☎ 023/33226); and Main Street, Glengariff (☎ 027/63084).

• Area Codes   Telephone area codes for West Cork include 023, 026, 027, and 028.

Some people say that you haven't really seen Cork until you drive westward along the coast into an area simply referred to as West Cork. The area is rimmed by a half-dozen beautiful bays. It's rich in subtropical vegetation, gardens, and palm trees. The coast is dotted by a string of intriguing little harbor towns—all with very memorable names—such as Courtmacsherry, Clonakilty, Rosscarbery, Castletownshend, Skibbereen, Timoleague, and Owenahincha. All of these towns are within easy reach of the major N 71 route.

Of all of the towns in West Cork, Castletownshend has probably received the most prominence because it was the home of Edith Somerville and "Martin" (Violet Florence) Ross, the 19th-century writing team who produced the classic *The Experiences of an Irish R.M.*

IMPRESSIONS

With deep affection and recollection
I often think of the Shandon bells,
Whose sounds so wild would, in days of childhood,
Fling around my cradle their magic spells.
And this I ponder, where'er I wander,
And thus grow fonder, sweet Cork of thee.
—Francis Mahoney (pseudonym: Father Prout) (1804–1866), "The Bells of Shandon"

Ballydehob, a small town pleasantly plunked between Mt. Gabriel and Roaringwater Bay, has an artistic flair, thanks to a cluster of artists in residence. At the local butcher, colorful drawings of cattle, pigs, and chickens indicate what meats are available. A mural on an outside wall of a pub depicts an Irish music session.

Other notable enclaves on the West Cork circuit include Schull, an old-world yachting town, and Barleycove, a remote windswept resort that's the last stop before Mizen Head and the sheer cliffs at the southernmost tip of the Emerald Isle.

Once you have filled your lungs with the bracing air of Mizen Head, you should aim to return to the N 71 road and head for Bantry. If time permits, you might like to do the 20-mile circuit around the Sheep's Head Peninsula, just south of Bantry. It's a relatively undiscovered beauty spot, with narrow roads and luscious views of Dunmanus Bay on one side and Bantry Bay on the other.

The N 71 route will next bring you to Glengariff, a village in a beautiful glen, thickly wooded with oak, elm, pine, yew, holly, and palm trees. On Bantry Bay, Glengariff looks out onto a subtropical island called Garinish.

Glengariff is the gateway to the Beara Peninsula, a 30-mile finger of land extending out into the Atlantic and surrounded by Bantry Bay and the Kenmare River. The Caha Mountains stretch almost the entire length of the peninsula, and a narrow road rims the edge along the north and south shores. If you're pressed for time, this drive can be cut in half by following the Tim Healy Pass across the mountains; this not only saves an hour or more but provides some of the most beautiful panoramas of West Cork. The Beara Peninsula also brings you to the County Kerry border (at Lauragh) and leads you into Kenmare, on the Ring of Kerry circuit (see Chapter 10, "The Kingdom of Kerry").

To see some of the inland highlights of West Cork, you should travel from Glengariff to Ballylickey and follow the scenic road northeast through the Pass of Keimaneigh to Gougane Barra. The River Lee has its source at Gougane Barra, a dramatic *corrie* lake in a wooded setting. The local legend says that St. Finbarr had a hermitage on one of the lake's islands before he moved downriver to Cork to found his great monastery. Gougane Barra is a peaceful mountain retreat with forest walks, nature trails, and lakeshore paths, tucked in a pocket of West Cork where Irish (or Gaelic) is the everyday language of the people.

Macroom is a marketing town on the main Killarney/Cork road (N 22). Like Kinsale, this place has a connection with William Penn. For a time in the mid-17th century, Penn's father owned both the town and its castle, the latter of which has since fallen into ruin. From Macroom, you are in a good position to return to Cork, or to travel onward to Killarney and County Kerry.

Before leaving this part of Ireland, however, don't overlook Mallow, a thriving agricultural town and one of the country's leading sugar producers. Sitting beside the banks of the River Blackwater, Mallow is technically not in West Cork, but it's only 22 miles northwest of Cork City and a place worth a visit.

WHAT TO SEE & DO

⭐ **Bantry House,** Bantry, Co. Cork. ☎ 027/50047.

Set on the edge of town, this house was built around 1750 for the Earls of Bantry. It has a mostly Georgian facade with Victorian additions. Open to the public since 1946, it contains many items of furniture and objets d'art from all over Europe, including four Aubusson and Gobelin tapestries, said to have been made for Marie Antoinette. Today it is the home of Mr. and Mrs. Egerton Shelswell-White, descendants of the 3rd Earl of Bantry. The gardens, with original statuary, are beautifully kept and well worth a stroll. Climb the steps behind the house for a panoramic view of the house, gardens, and Bantry Bay.

Admission: £3 ($4.50) adults, £1.75 ($2.63) seniors and students, children under 12 free.

Open: June–Sept, daily 9am–7pm; Oct–May, 9am–5:30pm.

1796 Bantry French Armada Exhibition Centre, East Stables, Bantry House, Bantry, Co. Cork. ☎ 027/51796.

This center commemorates Bantry Bay's role in the battle of 1796, when a formidable French Armada—inspired by Theobold Wolfe Tone and the United Irishmen—sailed from France to expel the British. Almost 50 warships carried nearly 15,000 soldiers to this corner of southwest Ireland. Thwarted by storms and a breakdown in communications, the invasion never came to pass. Ten ships were lost. Too storm-damaged to return to France, the frigate *Surveillante* was scuttled off Whiddy Island, to lay undisturbed for almost 200 years. The remains of that ship are now the centerpiece here.

Admission: £2.50 ($4.25) adults, £1.50 ($2.25) seniors and students, £1 ($1.50) children under 14.

Open: Daily 10am–6pm.

★ Garinish Island, Glengariff, Co. Cork. ☎ 027/63040.

Officially known as Ilnacullin, but usually referred to as "Garinish," this balmy island was once barren. In 1919 it was transformed into an elaborately planned Italianate garden with classical pavilions and myriad unusual plants and flowers from many continents. It's said that George Bernard Shaw wrote parts of *St. Joan* under the shade of the palm trees here.

The island is reached via a short ride on a covered ferry operated by **Blue Pool Boats,** The Pier, Glengariff (☎ 027/63333), or one of the other local services. Boats operate every 20 minutes, during the island's visiting hours.

Admission: Island, £2 ($3), adults, £1.50 ($2.25) seniors, £1 ($1.50) children and students; boat trips, £4 ($6) per person.

Open: Island, Mar and Oct, Mon–Sat 10am–4pm, Sun 1–4:30pm; Apr–June and Sept, Mon–Sat 10am–6:30pm, Sun 1–7pm; July–Aug, Mon–Sat 9:30am–6:30pm, Sun 11–7pm.

Timoleague Castle Gardens, Timoleague, Bandon, Co. Cork. ☎ 023/46116.

On the banks of the River Argideen, 15 miles west of Kinsale, these gardens have been cultivated by five generations of the Travers family since 1818. A feast of palm trees and other frost-tender plants are nurtured by the Gulf Stream. Resident peacocks wander around the ruins of a 13th-century tower and a 1920s house.

Admission: £1.50 ($2.25) adults, £1.20 ($1.80) seniors and students.

Open: June–Aug, Mon–Sat 11am–5:30pm, Sun 2–5:30pm.

SAVVY SHOPPING

Bandon Pottery, 83 N. Main St., Bandon, Co. Cork. ☎ 023/41360.

An 18th-century townhouse is the setting for this pottery workshop. The potters produce a colorful line of hand-thrown tableware, vases, bowls, and other accessories.

Open: Feb–March Sat–Sun noon–6pm; Apr–June Mon–Sat 9am–6pm; July–Aug Mon–Sat 9am–6pm and Sun noon–6pm; Sept–Jan Mon–Sat 9am–6pm.

Courtmacsherry Ceramics, Main Street, Courtmacsherry, Co. Cork. ☎ **023/46239.**

Overlooking the sea, this studio/shop offers an array of porcelain animals, birds, butterflies and tableware, all inspired by the flora and fauna of West Cork. Visitors are welcome to watch potter Peter Wolstenholme at work on new creations. Open mid-March to October daily from 10am to 6pm.

Prince August, Kilnamartyra, Macroom, Co. Cork. ☎ **026/40222.**

Prince August is Ireland's only toy soldier factory. The shop produces and displays a huge collection of metal miniatures based on J. R. R. Tolkien's classic books *The Hobbit* and *The Lord of the Rings*. Located off the main N 22 Road, northwest of Kinsale.

Open: Jan–June Mon–Fri 10am–5pm; July–Aug Mon–Fri 10am–5pm and Sat 10am–4pm; Sept–Dec Mon–Fri 10am–5pm.

Quills Woollen Market, Main Street, Ballingeary, Co. Cork. ☎ **026/47008.**

In the heart of West Cork's Gaelic-speaking area, this shop stocks hand-knit, as well as hand-loomed, woollens. Lambswool and mohair sweaters, vests, mittens, and hats are for sale. Open year-round Monday to Saturday 9am to 6pm, with extended hours in the summer.

WHERE TO STAY

Expensive/Moderate

Ballylickey Manor, Bantry/Glengariff Road (N 71), Ballylickey, Co. Cork.
☎ **027/50071** or toll free **800/223-6510** from U.S. Fax 027/50124. 11 rms (all with bath). TV TEL

Rates (including full breakfast): £71–£100 ($106.50–$150) single, £88–£165 ($132–$247.50) double. No service charge. AE, MC, V.
Open: Mid-Mar through Sept.

Overlooking Bantry Bay in a ten-acre setting of lawns and gardens, this well-established retreat offers a choice of accommodations in a 300-year-old manor house or in modern wooden cottages which surround the swimming pool. The units in the main house have a separate sitting room. All are decorated with country-style furnishings. This inn has an international ambience, thanks to the influence of its owners, the French-Irish Graves family, and a largely European clientele.

★ **Longueville House,** Killarney Road (N 72), Mallow, Co. Cork. ☎ **022/47156** or toll free **800/223-6510.** Fax 022/47459. 18 rms (all with bath). TV TEL

Rates: £51–£77 ($76.50–$115.50) single, £102–£154 ($153–$231) double. No service charge. AE, DC, MC, V.
Open: Mid-Mar to mid-Dec.

No chapter to the County Cork area would be complete without mentioning Longueville House. Geographically it's hard to classify—it's not really in West Cork, but northwest of Cork City. Built about 1720, and situated on a 500-acre farmland estate with its own winery, this convivial country retreat is the pride and joy of the O'Callaghan family. It produces a fine white wine, unique in this land known for its beers and whiskies. But most of all it is a very welcoming and homey place to stay—convenient to both Cork City and West Cork. Guest rooms are furnished in old-world style, with family heirlooms and period pieces; most have bucolic views of the gardens, grazing pastures, or vineyards. Most of all, this house is distinguished by its award-winning restaurant, The Presidents' Room, adorned with portraits of Ireland's past heads of state. The menu offers produce and vegetables from the hotel's own farm and gardens. In the summer months, meals are also served in a festive and skylit Victorian conservatory.

Moderate

 Sea View, Bantry/Glengariff Road (N 71), Ballylickey, Co. Cork. ☎ **027/50073** or toll free **800/447-7462** from U.S. Fax 027/51555. 17 rms (all with bath). TV TEL

$ **Rates** (including full breakfast): £35–£55 ($52.50–$82.50) single, £60–£100 ($90–$150) double. Service charge 10%. AE, DC, MC, V.
Open: Mid-Mar to mid-Nov.

Like a dove proudly spreading its wings on the horizon, this snowy white structure stands tall amid verdant gardens rimming the shores of Bantry Bay. Aptly named, Sea View is homey and full of heirlooms, antiques, lots of tall windows, and a cheery decor. The guest rooms are individually furnished with traditional dark woods and designer fabrics. It is best known, however, for the award-winning cuisine of proprietor Kathleen O'Sullivan. Besides the restaurant, there is also a cozy lounge bar and an outdoor patio. It is located off the main road three miles from Bantry.

West Lodge, Off Bantry/Glengariff Road (N 71), Bantry, Co. Cork. ☎ **027/50360.** Fax 027/50438. 90 rms (all with bath). TV TEL

Rates (including full breakfast): £40–£50 ($60–$75) single, £60–£80 ($90–$120) double. Service charge 12.5%. AE, DC, MC, V.
Open: Jan to mid-Dec.

Set on a hillside overlooking Bantry Bay, this modern three-story hotel is surrounded by gardens and woodlands. The public areas and guest rooms are bright and airy, enhanced by wide windows, light wood furnishings, and colorful Irish fabrics. The facilities include a restaurant, tavern, indoor heated swimming pool, tennis and squash courts, sauna, and gym.

WHERE TO DINE

Expensive

Blair's Cove, Barley Cove Road, Durrus, Co. Cork. ☎ **027/61127.**
Cuisine: INTERNATIONAL. **Reservations:** Required.
Prices: Dinner with starter buffet, £23 ($34.50); buffet and dessert only, £18 ($27). AE, DC, MC, V.
Open: Mar–June and Sept–Oct, dinner Tues–Sat 7–9:30pm, July–Aug, Mon–Sat 7–9:30pm.

A grassy country lane leads you to this romantic restaurant overlooking Dunmanus Bay, less than ten miles from Bantry. Owners Philip and Sabine de Mey have converted a stone barn with a 250-year-old Georgian courtyard and terrace into one of the best dining experiences in southwest Ireland amid high ceilings, stone walls, open fireplaces, and contemporary art. Each meal starts with a buffet of appetizers (from salmon fume to prawns, pâtés, oysters, and mousse), a display large enough to satisfy some dinner appetites. But, if you decide to have an entree as well, rack of lamb, confit of duck, grilled rib of beef, sole amandine, monkfish filet flambéed in Pernod, and bouillabaisse. For dessert, step up to the grand piano that doubles as a sweet trolley.

Chez Youen, The Pier, Baltimore, Co. Cork. ☎ 028/20136.

Cuisine: BRETON/SEAFOOD. **Reservations:** Required.
Prices: Set lunch £12.50 ($18.75); set dinner £21.50 ($32.25); dinner main courses £9.50–£32 ($14.25–$48). AE, DC, MC, V.
Open: Mar–May and Sept–Oct, dinner 6:30–11pm; June–Aug, lunch 12:30–3pm and dinner 6:30pm–midnight.

Set overlooking the marina of this small harbor town, this restaurant of Brittany-born Youen Jacob has been drawing people to West Cork since 1978. The decor is relaxing, with beamed ceilings, candlelight, floral pottery, and an open copper fireplace. Lobster is the specialty, fresh from local waters, but the poached wild salmon in fennel, leg of lamb, and steaks are also very good. The chef's signature dish (and the one that commands the £32 price tag) is a gourmet shellfish platter, piled high with rare specimens not usually seen on ordinary menus—Galley Head prawns, Baltimore Shrimp, and Velvet crab, as well as local lobster and oysters, all served in a shell.

Moderate

The Altar, Toormore, Schull, Co. Cork. ☎ 028/35254.

Cuisine: IRISH/SEAFOOD. **Reservations:** Recommended.
Prices: Bar food items £1.10–£7.50 ($1.65–$11.25); set traditional lunch £7.95 ($11.83); appetizers £1.50–£4.50 ($2.25–$7.25), dinner main courses £6–£12 ($9–$18). AE, DC, MC, V.
Open: May–Oct, Mon–Sat noon–midnight, Sun noon–3pm.

Situated deep in the West Cork countryside, this rustic cottage suddenly appears on the horizon out of nowhere. It has all the trappings of a rustic retreat inside—a glowing open fireplace and stone walls. The menu, which changes daily, emphasizes local seafoods, with choices such as seafood chowder, crab salad, oysters, and seafood plates. On Sundays, a traditional Irish lunch is served and there is Irish music on Wednesday nights.

Mary Ann's, Castletownshend, Skibbereen, Co. Cork. ☎ 028/36146.

Cuisine: IRISH. **Reservations:** Recommended for dinner.
Prices: Bar food £1.20–£6.95 ($1.80–$10.43); appetizers £1.45–£6.95 ($2.18–$10.43); main courses £7–£14 ($10.50–$21). MC, V.
Open: Apr–Oct, lunch daily 12:30–2:30pm, dinner Mon–Sat 6–10pm; Nov–Mar, lunch Tues–Sun 12:30–2:30pm, dinner Tues–Sat 6–10pm.

Dating back to 1844, this rustic pub is decorated with the wheels, lanterns, and bells of ships. The menu offers salads and West Cork cheese plates. More ambitious dishes such as scallops meunière, sirloin steak with garlic butter, chicken Kiev, and deep fried prawns are served, too. On fine days, patrons can sit in the outside courtyard.

Inexpensive

Bunratty Inn, Main Street, Schull, Co. Cork. ☎ 028/28341.

Cuisine: PUB GRUB. **Reservations:** Not necessary.
Prices: All items £1.35–£6.95 ($2.03–$10.43). MC, V.
Open: Mon–Sat noon–5pm, Sun 12:30–2pm.

Located in the center of town, this pub is a good place for a light meal or refreshment. It has a mostly seagoing decor, with agrarian touches, such as bar stools made from old milk cans. In the summer, an adjacent stableyard is outfitted with picnic tables for outdoor imbibing and snacks. Try the toasted smoked salmon sandwich with Cashel

Bleu cheese or ploughman's platter (Irish farm cheeses with country pâté, pickles, and crusty bread). Other favorites are seafood chowder or seafood pie, crab claws, vegetable or beef lasagne, or shepherd's pie.

Casey's Cabin, Baltimore, Co. Cork. ☎ **028/20197.**

> **Cuisine:** IRISH. **Reservations:** Recommended for dinner.
> **Prices:** All items £1.50–£10 ($2.25–$15). AE, DC, MC, V.
> **Open:** Bar snacks Mon–Sat 10:30am–11pm; lunch daily noon–3pm; dinner daily 6–9pm.

Overlooking Church Strand Bay, this nautical pub/restaurant has lovely views of the water and a cottagelike interior with open peat fires. It specializes in simple fare, such as local seafood and steaks.

Wine Vaults, 73 Bridge St., Skibbereen, Co. Cork. ☎ **028/22743.**

> **Cuisine:** INTERNATIONAL. **Reservations:** Not required.
> **Prices:** All items £1.40–£5 ($2.10–$7.50). No credit cards.
> **Open:** Year-round, daily noon–2:30pm and 5:30–8pm.

Situated in the heart of a busy market town, this restaurant has a classy winery-style decor. It is a handy place for lunch or a light meal in transit. The menu includes soups, sandwiches on pita bread, ham and tuna melt, crêpes, and pizzas, including a house-special pizza topped with mushrooms, peppers, onions, ham, and salami. There is live traditional music on Thursday through Sunday nights.

Killarney Town

9

AN OLD SONG ASKS, HOW CAN YOU BUY KILLARNEY? THE ANSWER IS THAT YOU can't buy it—Killarney belongs to the people of Ireland as the country's foremost National Park. Celebrated in copious prose, poetry, and song, Killarney has modestly been called Beauty's Home and Heaven's Reflex. It's a wondrous natural blend of three legendary lakes, floating islands, craggy mountains, ancient trees, lush foliage, cascading waterfalls, and rare wildlife.

Above all, the lakes are Killarney's main attraction. The first of these, the Lower Lake, is sometimes called "Lough Leane" or "Lough Lein," which mean the "lake of learning." It's the largest, more than four miles long, and dotted with 30 small islands. The second lake is aptly called the Middle Lake or Muckross Lake, and the third simply, Upper Lake. The last is the smallest and replete with storybook islands covered with a variety of trees—evergreens, Cedars of Lebanon, Juniper, Holly, and Mountain Ash.

The lakes and the surrounding woodlands are all part of the 25-square-mile Killarney National Park. Found within its borders are two major estates, the Muckross and Knockreer demesnes, and the remains of major medieval abbeys and castles. Blossoming in season is a profusion of foliage such as rhododendrons, azaleas, magnolia, camelias, hydrangeas, and tropical plant ferns. At almost every turn, you'll see Killarney's own botanical wonder, the arbutus, or strawberry tree, plus eucalyptus, redwoods, and native oak.

The place-name of Killarney is derived from *Cill Airne,* meaning "church of the sloe" in Irish. Many sloe trees, or blackthorn, rise toward heaven in the area. Killarney wildlife includes rare red deer, the only native Irish herd, plus fallow and Japanese sika deer, all-black Kerry cattle, and more than 100 species of bird.

The most noteworthy of Killarney's islands is Innisfallen, which seems to float peacefully in the Lower Lake. St. Fallen founded a monastery here in the 7th century, and it flourished for 1,000 years. Brian Boru, the great Irish chieftain, and St. Brendan the Navigator are said to have been educated here. From 950 to 1320, the "Annals of Innisfallen," a chronicle of early Irish history, was written at the monastery; it's now in the Bodlein Library at Oxford University. Traces of an 11th-century church and a 12th-century priory can still be seen today.

Near the point where the Lower Lake meets the Middle Lake is Muckross Abbey, a medieval monastery founded in 1448 for the Observantine Fathers and then suppressed in 1652. Designed in the Irish Gothic–style, it has a cloister with 22 arches, each one framing a view of a giant yew tree that's said to have been growing in the center of the courtyard since the abbey was built. Buried at the abbey are some of County Kerry's great early chieftains, the MacCarthys, O'Donoghues, and O'Sullivans (surnames that still predominate in the county). This is also the final resting place for four of the county's most cherished 17th- and 18th-century poets, Egan O'Rahilly, Geoffrey O'Donoghue, Owen Roe O'Sullivan, and Pierce Ferriter.

IMPRESSIONS

The counties of Cork and Kerry are my favorites of all. They are unbelievably beautiful. Going from Glengariff when I caught my first sight of the Lakes of Killarney, with their natural bulwark of mountains, I stopped in breath-taking wonder and found myself saying, 'My God, how lovely!'
—John Cyril Maude, MP, in *Irish Press,* September 1951

What's Special About Killarney Town

Buildings
- Ross Castle, a 15th-century fortress on the edge of the lower lake.
- St. Mary's Cathedral, a Gothic Revival edifice designed by Pugin and built of limestone in the mid-19th century.

Museums
- Museum of Irish Transport, housing a vast collection of classic cars, bicycles, and carriages.

Parks/Gardens
- Killarney National Park, a 25,000-acre expanse of natural lakeland and mountain scenery.
- Knockreer Estate, with riverside gardens and 200-year old trees.

For the Kids
- Muckross Traditional Farms, a 70-acre working farm in the style of the 1930s.
- Kennedy's Open Farm, 75-acre dairy and sheep farm with a bevy of animals and horse-drawn machinery.
- Crag Cave, over a million years old, with some of the largest stalactites in Europe.

Ace Attractions
- Muckross House & Gardens, a 19th-century Elizabethan house with gardens that reflects 200 years of Kerry folklife.

Natural Spectacles
- The Three Killarney Lakes, set amid craggy mountains, floating lakes, ancient trees, lush foliage, and rare wildlife.
- The Torc Waterfall, a 60-foot cascade set in a forest.

Activities
- Jaunting-car rides around the Lakes of Killarney.
- A Gap of Dunloe tour via horseback or horse-cart and boat, through a mountain pass and across the three lakes.
- Walking, jogging, biking and following nature trails along the Killarney lakeshore.
- A waterbus trip on the Killarney Lakes.
- Fish for salmon or trout on the Killarney lakes and rivers.

Shopping
- Kerry Glass, Killarney's own distinctive colored glass made by local craftsmen.

A forest setting surrounds the Torc Waterfall, a roaring cascade of waters dashing down a 60-foot path to the Middle Lake. If you climb the adjacent footpath to the top, you'll be rewarded with a fine view of the lake district.

The town of Killarney, located at the junction of the Kenmare and Killorglin roads, sits at the edge of the largest of three lakes. It's surrounded by mountains with names like Purple, Torc, Mangerton, and Tomie. Many horse-drawn jaunting cars clip-clop down Killarney's streets. Dating back to Victorian times, these one-horse open-carriages are the traditional mode of transport in the Killarney Lake District—parts of which are closed to vehicular traffic. So unless you prefer to walk or rent a bike, you'll need to take a jaunting car ride to see the prime scenic attractions around the three lakes.

Before you leave Killarney Town, there are two vantage points that you should not miss—both give spectacular views of the Killarney panorama—Ladies' View and Aghadoe Heights. Ladies View, about 12 miles southwest of town on the Kenmare Road, is a mountaintop look-out point that gives a broad survey of all three lakes and the surrounding mountains. The spot earned its name in 1861 at the time of Queen Victoria's visit to Ireland, when her ladies-in-waiting expressed great delight with the view. Aghadoe Heights, about two miles north of town, is a 400-foot hill looking out onto the whole Killarney spectrum—the lakes, mountains, parklands, the entire town, and the surrounding farmlands.

1 Orientation

Killarney is 84 miles SW of Shannon, 192 miles SW of Dublin, 54 miles W of Cork, 69 miles SW of Limerick, 120 miles SW of Galway

GETTING THERE • By Air   Aer Lingus offers nonstop daily flights from Dublin into Kerry County Airport, Farranfore, Co. Kerry (☎ **066/64644**), about ten miles north of Killarney.

• **By Train**   Irish Rail services from Dublin, Limerick, Cork, and Galway arrive daily at the Killarney Railway Station, Railway Road, off East Avenue Road (☎ **064/31067** or **066/26555**).

• **By Bus**   Bus Eireann operates regularly scheduled bus services into Killarney from all parts of Ireland. The bus depot is adjacent to the train station at Railway Road, off East Avenue Road (☎ **064/34777**).

• **By Car**   The Kerry people like to say that all roads lead to Killarney, and at least a half-dozen major national roads do go there, including N 21 and N 23 from Limerick, N 22 from Tralee, N 22 from Cork, N 72 from Mallow, and N 70 from the Ring of Kerry and West Cork.

TOURIST INFORMATION   The Killarney Tourist Office is located in Town Hall, Church Place, off Main Street, Killarney (☎ **064/31633**). It is open from Monday to Saturday from 9:15am to 6pm in June, 9:15am to 8pm in July and August, and from 9:30am to 5pm during the rest of the year. It offers many helpful booklets, including the *Tourist Trail* walking-tour guide and the Killarney Area Guide with maps.

Useful local publications include *Where: Killarney,* a quarterly magazine distributed free at hotels and guesthouses. It is packed with all types of current information on tours, activities, events, and entertainment.

TOWN LAYOUT   Killarney is a relatively small town by Irish standards, with a population of approximately 7,000 people, although this figure more than doubles in the summertime with the constant influx of visitors from all over the world.

The town itself is built around one central thoroughfare, Main Street, which changes its name to High Street at midpoint. The principal offshoots of Main Street are Plunkett Street, which becomes College Street at midpoint, and New Street, which, as its name implies, is still growing. The Deenagh River edges the western side of town and East Avenue Road rims the eastern side. It's all very walkable in an hour or two.

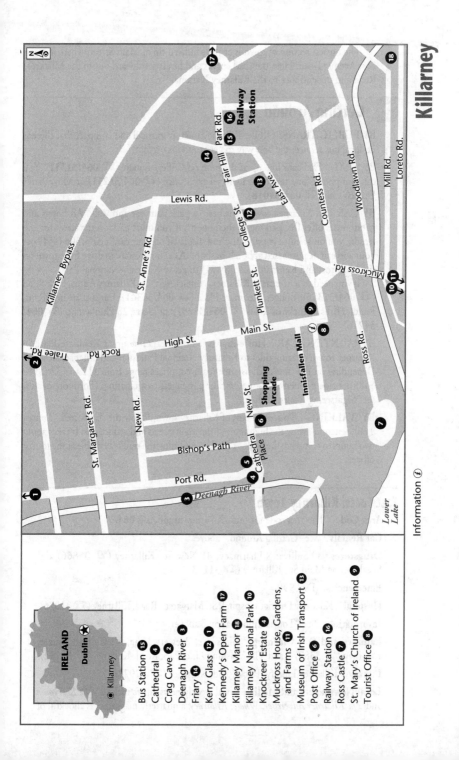

Killarney

Information *i*

IRELAND
Dublin ✪
● Killarney

Bus Station **15**
Cathedral **4**
Crag Cave **2**
Deenagh River **3**
Friary **14**
Kerry Glass **12**
Kennedy's Open Farm **17**
Killarney Manor **18**
Killarney National Park **10**
Knockreer Estate **4**
Muckross House, Gardens, and Farms **11**
Museum of Irish Transport **13**
Post Office **6**
Railway Station **16**
Ross Castle **7**
St. Mary's Church of Ireland **9**
Tourist Office **8**

The busiest section of town is at the southern tip of Main Street, where it meets East Avenue Road. Here the road curves and heads southward out to the Muckross Road and the entrance to the Killarney National Park.

2 Getting Around

BY PUBLIC TRANSPORT   Killarney town is so small and compact that there is no local bus service; the best way to get around is on foot.

BY TAXI   Taxi cabs line up at the rank on College Square (☎ **064/31331**). You can also phone for a taxi from Dero's Taxi Service (☎ **064/31251**) or Moynihan's Express Cab (☎ **064/34018**).

BY CAR   In Killarney town, it is best to park your car and walk. All hotels and guesthouses offer free parking to their guests; if you must park on the street for any reason, you must buy a parking disc and display it on your car; it costs 30p (45¢) per hour and can be purchased at hotels or shops. A car is necessary to drive from town on the Muckross and Kenmare Road (N 71) to get to Killarney National Park.

If you need to rent a car in Killarney, contact Avis, c/o Killarney Autos, Park Road (☎ **064/31355**); Budget, Kenmare Place (☎ **064/34341**); EuropeCar InterRent, Randles Bros., Muckross Road (☎ **064/31237**); or Hertz, 28 Plunkett St. (☎ **064/34216**).

BY JAUNTING CAR   Horse-drawn jaunting cars line up at Kenmare Place in Killarney town, offering rides to Killarney National Park sites and other scenic areas. Depending on the time and distance required, prices range from £12 to £32 ($18–$48) per ride per person, based on four passengers participating. (For more details, see "Sightseeing Tours," below.)

BY WALKING   To see the best of Killarney town, follow the signposted "Tourist Trail," encompassing the highlights of the main streets and attractions. It takes about two hours to complete the walk. A booklet outlining the trail is available at the tourist office.

Fast Facts: Killarney Town

Area Code   The area code for most Killarney numbers is **064**.

Car Rentals   See "Getting Around," above.

Drugstores   O'Sullivan's Pharmacy, 81 New St., Killarney (☎ **35866**) and Sheahans, 34 Main St., Killarney (☎ **31113**).

Emergencies   Dial **999**.

Hospital   Killarney District Hospital, St. Margaret's Road, Killarney (☎ **31076**).

Information   See "Tourist Information," above.

Laundry and Dry Cleaning   Gleeson's, Brewery Lane, off College Square, Killarney (☎ **33877**), and The Washing Line, Park Road, Killarney(☎ **35282**).

Library   Killarney Library, Rock Road, Killarney (☎ **32972**).

Local Newspapers and Media   Local weekly newspapers include *The Kerryman* and *The Killarney Advertiser*. *Where: Killarney,* a quarterly magazine, is chockful of helpful up-to-date information for visitors; it is distributed free at hotels and guesthouses. The local radio station is Radio Kerry, 97 FM.

Photographic Needs   Killarney Photographic Centre, 105 New Street, Killarney (☎ **32933**) and Moriarty Photographic Stores, New Street, Killarney (☎ **31225**).

Police   Killarney Garda Station, New Road, Killarney (☎ **31222**).

Post Office   Killarney Post Office, New Street, Killarney (☎ **31051**). It's open 9am to 5:30pm Monday, Tuesday, and Thursday through Saturday, and 9:30am to 5:30pm on Wednesday.

Shoe Repairs   The Cobbler, 24 High St., Killarney (no phone).

3 Where to Stay

Expensive/Moderate

Aghadoe Heights, off Tralee Road (N 22), Aghadoe, Killarney, Co. Kerry.
☎ **064/31766** or toll free **800/44-UTELL** in U.S. Fax 064/31345. 57 rms (all with bath). TV TEL

Rates (including full breakfast): £72–£100 ($108–$150) single, £105–145 ($157.50–$217.50) double. No service charge. AE, DC, MC, V.

For a total Killarney perspective—overlooking the town, lakes, mountains, and surrounding countryside, this modern two-story hotel couldn't be in a better spot. It is situated on 8.5 acres of high ground two miles northwest of Killarney town. Guest rooms offer contemporary furnishings with floor-to-ceiling window views of the Killarney kaleidoscope.

Dining/Entertainment: The main dining room is Frederick's, a rooftop restaurant with great views and an adjacent bar.

Facilities: Indoor heated swimming pool with waterfall, Jacuzzi, sauna, steam room, solarium; tennis court; salmon fishing on a private stretch of river.

Cahernane, Muckross Road (N 71), Killarney, Co. Kerry. ☎ **064/31895** or toll free **800/447-7462** in U.S. Fax 064/34340. 49 rms (all with bath). TEL

Rates (including full breakfast): £65–£75 ($102.50–$112.50) single, £85–£136 ($127.50–$204) double. No service charge. AE, DC, MC, V. **Closed:** Nov–Mar.

Originally built in 1877 as a manor home for the Herbert family (the Earls of Pembroke), this country house hotel is situated less than a mile from town, along the shores of the Lower Lake in a sylvan setting of ancient trees and well-tended rose gardens. As befits its Victorian heritage, it is furnished with antiques and period furniture both in its public areas and in most of its guest rooms.

Dining/Entertainment: Choices include The Herbert, a gracious old-world main dining room, and The Pembroke, for lighter fare.

Facilities: Two tennis courts, pitch and putt, croquet, shop, and fishing privileges for salmon and trout fishing.

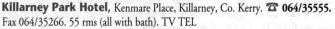 **Killarney Park Hotel,** Kenmare Place, Killarney, Co. Kerry. ☎ **064/35555.** Fax 064/35266. 55 rms (all with bath). TV TEL

Rates (including full breakfast): £60–£85 ($90–$127.50) single, £80–£130 ($120–$195) double. No service charge. AE, MC, V.

With a striking yellow neo-Georgian facade, this new four-story property is located on its own grounds on the eastern edge of town, between the railway station and the tourist office. Guests are greeted by posh and spacious public rooms, including a lobby and lounges with open fireplaces, brass fixtures, oil paintings, wainscot paneling, and deep-cushioned seating, as well as a sunlit conservatory-style lounge overlooking the gardens. Guest rooms are decorated in a contemporary style with dark and light wood furnishings, quilted designer fabrics, and marble-finished bathrooms. Public areas include a restaurant, piano bar, patio, indoor heated swimming pool, gym, and steam room.

⭐ **Muckross Park,** Muckross Road, Killarney, Co. Kerry. ☎ **064/31938.** Fax 064/31938. 27 rms (all with bath). TV TEL

Rates (including full breakfast): £50–£75 ($75–$112.50) single, £70–£130 ($105–$195) double. No service charge. AE, DC, MC, V. **Closed:** Jan–Feb.

Located just off the main road, about two miles outside of town, this hotel takes its name from the fact that it sits across the road from Muckross House and Killarney National Park. Although fairly new, it incorporates parts of the oldest hotel in Killarney, dating back to 1795, and is furnished in an old-world country-house style with paneled walls, open fireplaces, and equestrian-theme oil paintings. The rooms, which vary in size and decor, have period furniture, including some semicanopy beds, quilted fabrics, frilly draperies, and Victorian-style ceiling fixtures, plus modern amenities such as a garment press and hair dryer. Facilities include an old world–style restaurant and Molly Darcy's, a traditional thatched-roof pub (see "Entertainment & Pubs," below).

Moderate

Castlerosse, Killorglin Road, Killarney, Co. Kerry. ☎ **064/31114** or toll free from U.S. **800/528-1234.** Fax 064/31031. 65 rms (all with bath). TV TEL

Rates (including full breakfast): £62–£92 ($93–$138) single, £68–£98 ($102–$147) double. Service charge 10%. AE, DC, MC, V. **Closed:** Nov–Mar.

Set on its own parklands between the Lower Lake and surrounding mountains, this modern rambling ranch-style inn is two miles from the heart of town and next to Killarney's two golf courses. The guestrooms, recently refurbished, offer contemporary furnishings and views of the lake. Facilities include a restaurant, lounge, gym, sauna, two tennis courts, putting green, walking paths, and jogging trails.

Dunloe Castle, off the Killorglin Road, Beaufort, Killarney, Co. Kerry. ☎ **064/44111** or toll free in U.S. **800/221-1074.** Fax 064/44583. 120 rms (all with bath). TV TEL

Rates (including full breakfast): £62–£80 ($93–$120) single, £96–£122 ($144–$183) double. No service charge. AE, DC, MC, V. **Closed:** Oct–Apr.

Located on its own extensive tropical grounds about six miles west of town near the entrance to the Gap of Dunloe, this is not really a castle, in the medieval sense. Instead it's a contemporary-style five-story hotel that takes its name from a ruined 15th-century fortress nearby. Entirely renovated in 1993, it has traditional-style furnishings with many valuable antiques. Surrounded by broad mountain vistas, the Dunloe has a certain agrarian ambience, with horses, ponies, and cows grazing in the adjacent fields. It's a place to come to unwind and to spend a few days; you'll need a car to get to town or to sightsee in the area.

Dining/Entertainment: Restaurant and cocktail bar.

Facilities: Heated indoor swimming pool, sauna, tennis courts, horseback riding, fishing, putting green, and fitness track.

Europe, off the Killorglin Road, Fossa, Killarney, Co. Kerry. ☎ **064/31900** or toll free in U.S. **800/221-1074.** Fax 064/32118. 205 rms (all with bath). TV TEL

Rates (including full breakfast): £62–£92 ($93–$138) single, £84–£122 ($126–$183) double. No service charge. AE, DC, MC, V. **Closed:** Nov–Feb.

One of the most picturesque settings in Killarney belongs to this modern five-story property sitting right on the shores of the Lower Lake three miles west of town, adjacent to Killarney's two 18-hole championship golf courses and surrounded by dozens of mountain peaks. The hotel's public areas are spacious, open, and filled with antiques, while the guest rooms offer contemporary furnishings, all enhanced by spectacular lakeside vistas; most of the bedrooms have private balconies. The hotel also has its own stables with Haflinger horses.

Dining/Entertainment: Choices include the aptly named Panorama Restaurant, an alpine-themed Lakeside cafe and two lounges for light refreshment.

Facilities: Olympic-size indoor pool, saunas, gym, tennis, boating, fishing, horseback riding, bicycling, and hairdressing salon.

★ **Great Southern,** Railway Road, off East Avenue Road, Killarney, Co. Kerry. ☎ **064/31262** or toll free **800/44-UTELL** in the U.S. Fax 064/31642. 180 rms (all with bath). TV TEL

Rates: £90–£102 ($135–$153) single or double. Service charge 12.5%. AE, DC, MC, V. **Closed:** Jan–Feb.

Set amid 36 acres of gardens and lush foliage on the eastern edge of town, this four-story ivy-covered landmark is the grande dame of Killarney hotels. Dating back to 1854, it was built around the time of Queen Victoria's visit to Killarney and has since been host to presidents, princes, and personalities from all over the world, as well as many a modern-day travel group. While the guest rooms offer every modern convenience, including garment press, hairdryer, and sometimes a minibar, the public areas retain the charm of yesteryear with high ceilings rimmed by ornate plasterwork, tall paned windows looking out onto nearby mountain vistas, glowing open fireplaces, and Waterford crystal chandeliers.

Dining/Entertainment: The classic main dining room overlooks the gardens, while the smaller Malton Room provides à la carte service in a clubby setting (dinner only). Light refreshments and snacks are available in The Lounge and The Punch Bowl Bar.

Services: Concierge, room service, laundry, and dry cleaning.

Facilities: Indoor heated swimming pool, sauna, Jacuzzi, steam room, gym, two tennis courts, hairdressing salon, gift shop.

Killarney Ryan Hotel, Park Road, Killarney, Co. Kerry. ☎ **064/31555** or toll free **800/44-UTELL** in the U.S. Fax 064/32428. 168 rms (all with bath). TV TEL

Rates: £40–£90 ($60–$135) single or double. No service charge. AE, DC, MC, V. **Closed:** Dec–Feb.

Sports-minded travelers flock to this modern motel-style inn on the outskirts of town. The facilities include two outdoor tennis courts; outdoor nine-hole pitch and putt course; indoor leisure center with swimming pool, saunas, steam room, and Jacuzzi;

and a sports hall equipped for basketball, volleyball, soccer, badminton, and table tennis. Guest rooms have standard furnishings and in-room garment press and hair dryer. There is also a restaurant and lounge on the premises.

Killarney Towers, College Square, Killarney, Co. Kerry. ☎ **064/32522.** Fax 064/31755. 157 rms (all with bath). TV TEL

Rates (including full breakfast): £55–£85 ($82.50–$127.50) single, £70–£130 ($105–$195) double. No service charge. AE, MC, V. **Closed:** Dec–Feb.

Built on the site of the former Imperial Hotel in the heart of town, this three-story property incorporates a gracious Georgian facade with a contemporary interior and new wings of modern bedrooms. Guest rooms are furnished with light woods, pastel tones, and modern art; each unit offers added in-room amenities such as coffee/tea-maker and hairdryer.

Dining/Entertainment: Choices include a traditional dining room and two bars, Scruffy's, which features live traditional music most nights, and O'Donoghue's Lounge.

Clarion Hotel Randles Court, Muckross Road, Killarney, Co. Kerry. ☎ **064/35333** or toll free in the U.S. **800/4-CHOICE.** Fax 064/35206. 37 rms. TV TEL

Rates (including full breakfast): £45–£105 ($72.50–$157.50) single, £60–£120 ($90–$180) double. Service charge 12.5%. AE, DC, MC, V. **Closed:** Jan–Feb.

A former rectory dating back to the turn of the century, this multigabled four-story house sits on its own grounds in a raised site off the main road outside of Killarney town on the road to Muckross House. Totally restored, enlarged, and refurbished, it opened as a hotel in 1992. The public areas hark back to the house's earlier days, with a decor of marble floors, mantled fireplaces, chandeliers, gilt mirrors, tapestries, and old prints. Of the bedrooms, three are in the original building and the rest in a new wing, all with distinctive furnishings, including some armoires and antique desks or vanities. Facilities include a restaurant, lounge, and outdoor patio.

Moderate/Inexpensive

★ **Killeen House,** Aghadoe, Killarney, Co. Kerry. ☎ **064/31711.** Fax 064/31811. 15 rms (all with bath). TV TEL

Rates (including full breakfast): £35–£45 ($52.50–$67.50) single, £46–£66 ($69–$99) double. Service charge 10%. AE, DC, MC, V.

Dating back to 1838 and set on high ground overlooking Killarney's lakes and golf courses, this rambling country manor house is surrounded by mature gardens in a quiet residential area about two miles northwest of town. Completely refurbished and opened for guests in 1992, it offers a relaxed and homey feeling, with all the comforts of a hotel. The bedrooms, which vary in size and decor, feature semiorthopedic beds and standard furniture. The public areas include an intimate 24-seat restaurant, fireside lounge, and a golf-themed bar with sporting posters and photos and a wall collage displaying over 800 golf balls from all over the world.

Torc Great Southern, Cork Road, Killarney, Co. Kerry. ☎ **064/31611** or toll free in U.S. **800/44-UTELL.** Fax 064/31824. 91 rms (all with bath). TV TEL

Rates: £68 ($102) single or double. Service charge 12.5%. AE, DC, MC, V. **Closed:** Nov–Mar.

This contemporary two-story inn is positioned on its own grounds in a residential area less than a mile east of town. The guest rooms are sleek and bright, with large window views of adjacent gardens and nearby mountains; in-room amenities include coffee/tea-maker and hairdryer. There is a full-service restaurant and cocktail lounge, plus indoor heated swimming pool, sauna, tennis court, and outdoor patio.

Inexpensive

 Kathleen's Country House, Madam's Height, Tralee Road (N 22), Killarney, Co. Kerry. ☎ **064/32810.** Fax 064/32340. 16 rms (all with bath). TV TEL

Rates (including full breakfast): £25–£55 ($37.50–$82.50) single, £40–£60 ($60–$90) double. No service charge. AE, MC, V. **Closed:** Early Nov to mid-Mar.

Of the many guesthouses in this area, this one stands out. Located about a mile north of town on its own grounds next to a dairy farm, it is a two-story contemporary house, with a modern mansard-style roof and many picture windows. Enthusiastic and efficient hostess Kathleen O'Regan-Sheppard has also outfitted all the bedrooms with orthopedic beds, hair-dryers, coffee/tea-makers, and cheery furnishings enhanced by local art.

Inexpensive/Budget

Killarney Town House, 31 New St., Killarney, Co. Kerry. ☎ **064/35388.** Fax 064/35382. 11 rms (all with bath). TV TEL

Rates (including full breakfast): £15–£30 ($22.50–$45) single, £30–£50 ($45–$75) double. No service charge. MC, V.

This recently built three-story guesthouse is situated in the heart of town on one of the busiest streets. It's ideal for those who want a good clean room and don't need a bar or restaurant on the premises. The guest rooms, each identified by a Killarney flower rather than a number, offer all the basic comforts. Breakfast is served in a bright and airy ground-floor dining room.

4   Where to Dine

Expensive/Moderate

Gaby's, 27 High St., Killarney. ☎ **32519.**
Cuisine: SEAFOOD. **Reservations:** Recommended.
Prices: Appetizers £2.80–£6.90 ($4.20–$10.35); lunch main courses £3.40–£5.30 ($5.10–$7.95); dinner main courses £11.20–£25.80 ($16.80–$38.20). MC, V.
Open: Lunch Tues–Sat 12:30–2:30pm; dinner Mon–Sat 6–10pm.

One of Killarney's longest established restaurants, this nautically themed place is a mecca for lovers of fresh seafood. It is known for its succulent lobster, served grilled or in a house sauce of cognac, wine, cream, and spices. Other choices include turbot; haddock in wine; local salmon; and a giant Kerry shellfish platter, a veritable feast of prawns, scallops, mussels, lobster, and oysters.

Strawberry Tree, 24 Plunkett St., Killarney. ☎ **32688.**
Cuisine: IRISH. **Reservations:** Recommended.
Prices: Appetizers £2.95–£4.95 ($4.43–$7.43); main courses £11.95–£16.95 ($17.93–$25.43). AE, DC, MC, V.
Open: June–Aug, dinner daily 6–10pm; Feb–May and Sept–Nov, Mon–Sat dinner 6–10pm.

Named for Killarney's signature plant, this lovely shopfront restaurant is in the heart of town, yet it has a serene old-fashioned atmosphere, with a decor of soft pastel tones and an open hearth. The menu blends the produce of local farmers and suppliers with creative sauces and presentation. Entrees include farm duck; free-range beef from Thady Crowley's farm; free-range chicken from Michael Barry's farm, with wild-nettle mousse stuffing; sole baked in crisp potato crust and smoked salmon sauce; and rack of mountain lamb with wild garlic sauce.

Moderate

Dingles, 40 New St., Killarney. ☎ **31079.**
Cuisine: INTERNATIONAL. **Reservations:** Suggested.
Prices: Appetizers £2.20–£5.50 ($3.30–$8.25); main courses £9.50–£13.50 ($14.25–$20.25). AE, DC, MC, V.
Open: Mar–Oct, dinner daily 6–10pm.

Located near St. Mary's Cathedral, this bistro-style restaurant is furnished with recycled church pews, wooden benches, and choir stalls, enhanced by arches and alcoves and an open turf fireplace. The menu includes such dishes as chicken curry, beef Stroganoff, Irish stew, vegetable casserole, and seafood like Dingle Bay prawns in Creole sauce.

Foley's, 23 High St., Killarney. ☎ **31217.**
Cuisine: IRISH. **Reservations:** Recommended for dinner.
Prices: Appetizers £2–£6.90 ($3–$10.35); main courses £8.80–£14.50 ($13.20–$21.75). AE, DC, MC, V.
Open: Lunch daily 12:30–3pm, dinner daily 5–10pm. **Closed:** Dec 22–27.

A Georgian country home atmosphere prevails at this restaurant in the heart of town. The ever-changing menu features such items as Dingle Bay scallops mornay, rainbow trout, and fresh salmon, as well as breast of pheasant in port wine, duck in black-currant sauce, steaks, and Kerry mountain lamb. Don't pass up the home-baked brown bread scones that accompany each meal.

Picasso, 10 College St., Killarney. ☎ **31329.**
Cuisine: INTERNATIONAL. **Reservations:** Suggested.
Prices: Appetizers £1.75–£5.25 ($2.63–$7.88); main courses £7–£14 ($10.50–$21). MC, V.
Open: Mon–Sat, dinner 6–11pm.

A bistro atmosphere prevails at this small bi-level candlelit restaurant. Adorning the walls are a few reproductions of Picasso's works and paintings done by local artists. The decor has art deco influence and country music plays in the background. The menu ranges from Irish stew to smoked salmon pizza, as well as spareribs with barbecue sauce, charcoal-grilled German meatloaf, steaks, and seafood choices such as sea trout with lemon butter, crab toes tossed in garlic, and Killarney salmon hollandaise.

Swiss Barn, 17 High St., Killarney. ☎ **36044.**
Cuisine: SWISS/CONTINENTAL. **Reservations:** Recommended.
Prices: Set lunch £4.95–£7.95 ($7.43–$11.83); dinner appetizers £2.50–£6.50 ($4.25–$9.75); dinner main courses £10–£14 ($15–$21). MC, V.
Open: Mon and Wed–Sun lunch 12:30–3pm, dinner 6–10pm.

With a rustic Alpine decor, this restaurant aims to bring the taste of Switzerland and the Continent to Killarney. The menu offers Swiss favorites such as émincé of veal Zurichoise, pork filet in morrel sauce, and fondue bourguignonne, as well as veal Cordon Bleu, beef Stroganoff, steaks, seafood, and vegetarian platters.

Moderate/Inexpensive

 Bricin, 26 High St., Killarney. ☎ **34902.**
Cuisine: IRISH. **Reservations:** Suggested for dinner.
Prices: Snacks £1.50–£5 ($2.25–$7.50); dinner appetizers £1.90–£4.50 ($2.85–7.25); dinner main courses £6.90–£12.50 ($10.35–$18.75). MC, V.
Open: Mon–Sat snacks 10am–6pm, dinner 6–10pm; Sun snacks noon–6 and dinner 6–10pm.

Traditional Kerry boxty dishes (potato pancakes with various fillings, such as chicken, seafood, curried lamb, or vegetables) are the trademark of this upstairs restaurant positioned over a very good craft and bookshop. The menu also offers a variety of fresh seafood, pastas, Irish stew, and specials such as médaillons of beef in peppercorn sauce; filet of pork with sage and apricot stuffing; and chicken Bricin, breast of chicken in red-currant and raspberry sauce. This eatery is housed in one of Killarney's oldest buildings, dating back to the 1830s, sporting original stone walls, pine furniture, and turf fireplaces. Snacks and light fare are served during the day.

Robertino's, 9 High St., Killarney. ☎ **34966.**
Cuisine: ITALIAN. **Reservations:** Recommended.
Prices: Appetizers £2.30–£5.75 ($3.45–$8.63); main courses £5.75–£14.95 ($8.63–$22.43). MC, V.
Open: Dinner daily 6–10:30pm.

Step through the wrought-iron gates of this restaurant and experience the ambience of Italy—operatic arias playing in the background, and a Mediterranean-style decor of statues, murals, marble columns, hanging plants and palms, and brick walls. There are five separate dining areas including a "green zone" for nonsmokers. The menu offers dishes such as veal saltimbocca, roast rib of lamb flamed in Marsala wine sauce, and steaks, as well as a variety of local seafood and homemade pastas.

Kiwi's, St. Anthony's Place, Killarney. ☎ **34694.**
Cuisine: IRISH. **Reservations:** Recommended.
Prices: Appetizers £1.75–£3.95 ($2.63–$5.93); main courses £6.95–£12.95 ($10.43–$19.43). MC, V.
Open: April–Nov dinner daily 6–10pm.

A winding staircase from the ground floor leads to this restaurant, tucked in a laneway between College Street and East Avenue Road. The kitchen, although small, is known for innovative cooking, presenting dishes such as Atlantic salmon with seafood and martini cream sauce; filet of beef with black pudding and gingery corn and mushroom sauce; chicken, asparagus, and corn boxty; chicken Creole; lentil nut loaf with tomato pesto; and a classic Irish stew.

5 What to See & Do

THE TOP ATTRACTIONS

⭐ **Killarney National Park**, Kenmare Road (N 71), Killarney. ☎ **31440.**

This is Killarney's centerpiece—a 25,000-acre area of natural beauty, including three storied lakes, the Lower Lake or Lough Leane, the Middle Lake or Muckross Lake, and the Upper Lake. A myriad waterfalls, rivers, islands, valleys, mountains, bogs, and woodlands add to the wonderment. The park is enhanced by lush foliage and trees including oak, arbutus, holly, and mountain ash, as well as a variety of wildlife, including a rare herd of red deer. No automobiles are allowed within the park, so touring is best done on foot, bicycle, or via horse-drawn jaunting car. The park offers four sign-posted walking and nature trails along the lakeshore.

Access is available from several points along the Kenmare Road (N 71); the main entrance is at Muckross House, where there is a new visitor center featuring background exhibits on the park and a 15-minute audio-visual film, *Killarney: A Special Place.*

Admission: Free.
Open: Year-round daylight hours.

⭐ **Muckross House & Gardens**, Kenmare Road (N 71), Killarney. ☎ **31440.**

The focal point of the Middle Lake—and, in many ways, of the entire national park—is the Muckross Estate, often called "the jewel of Killarney." It consists of a gracious ivy-covered, Elizabethan-style residence with colorful and well-tended gardens. Dating back to 1843, this 20-room house has been converted into a museum of County Kerry folklife, showcasing locally carved furniture, prints, maps, paintings, and needlework. Imported treasures like Oriental screens, Venetian mirrors, Chippendale chairs, curtains woven in Brussels, and Turkish carpets are also displayed.

The house's cellars have been converted into craft shops with local artisans demonstrating traditional trades, such as bookbinding, weaving, and pottery. The adjacent gardens, known for their fine collection of rhododendrons and azaleas, can also be explored.

Admission: £3 ($4.50) adults, £2 ($3) seniors, £1.25 ($2.25) children. *Note:* a joint ticket, entitling the buyer to admission to both Muckross House and Muckross Traditional Farms, is available for £1 ($1.50) extra per person.

Open: Jan–June and Sept–Dec, daily 9am–6pm; July–Aug, daily 9am–7pm.

Muckross Traditional Farms, Kenmare Road (N 71), Killarney. ☎ **31335.**

Adjacent to the Muckross House estate, this is a 70-acre farm, maintained and operated like a Kerry farm of the 1930s. Farming is done with horse-drawn equipment. Visitors can watch sowing and harvesting or potato-picking and haymaking, depending on the season. Farmhands—continuously at work—tend the cattle, the pigs, and the hens, while the blacksmith, carpenter, and wheelwright ply their trades in the old manner. Women draw water from the wells and cook meals in traditional kitchens, with authentic utensils, crockery, and household items.

Admission: £3 ($4.50) adults, £2 ($3) seniors, £1.25 ($2.25) children. *Note:* a joint ticket, entitling the buyer to admission to both Muckross House and Muckross Traditional Farms, is available for £1 ($1.45) extra per person.

Open: Jan–April and Nov–Dec, daily 9am–5:30pm; May, daily 2–6pm; June–Oct, daily 11am–7pm.

Ross Castle, Ross Road, off Kenmare Road (N 71), Killarney. ☎ **35851.**

Newly restored, this 15th-century fortress sits on the edge of the Lower Lake, two miles outside of Killarney town. Built by the O'Donoghue chieftains, this castle distinguished itself in 1652 as the last stronghold in Munster to surrender to Cromwell's forces. All that remains today is a tower house, surrounded by a fortified bawn with rounded turrets. The tower has been furnished in the style of the late 16th and early 17th centuries and offers a magnificent view of the lakes and islands from its top. Access is by guided tour only. A lovely lakeshore walk stretches for two miles between Killarney and the castle.

Admission: £2 ($3) adults, seniors £1.50 ($2.25), £1 ($1.50) children.

Open: Daily Mar–May and Sept–Oct 10:30am–5pm, June–Aug 9am–6pm.

Knockreer Estate, Cathedral Place, off New Street, Killarney. ☎ **31440.**

Lovely views of the Lower Lake can be enjoyed in this setting, a part of the National Park grounds most recently opened to the public (1986). Once the home of Lord Kenmare, the estate has a turn-of-the-century house and a pathway along the River Deenagh. The gardens are a mix of 200-year-old trees with flowering cherries, magnolias, and azaleas. The house, not open to the public, is now a field study center for the National Park. The main access to Knockreer is via Deenagh Lodge Gate opposite the cathedral, in town.

Admission: Free.

Open: Daily, daylight hours.

St. Mary's Cathedral, Cathedral Place, off Port Road, Killarney. ☎ **31014.**

Officially known as the Catholic Church of St. Mary of the Assumption, this limestone cathedral is the town's most impressive building. Designed in the Gothic Revival style by Augustus Pugin, it's cruciform in shape. Its construction was begun in 1842, interrupted by the Irish famine years, and finished in 1855. The magnificent central spire was added in 1912. The entire edifice was extensively renovated from 1972 to 1973. It's situated at the edge of town on the far end of New Street.

Admission: Free, donations welcome.

Open: Daily 10:30am–6pm.

MORE ATTRACTIONS

Museum of Irish Transport, East Avenue Road, Killarney. ☎ **32638.**

This museum presents a unique collection of vintage and classic cars, motorcycles, bicycles, carriages, and fire engines. Displayed are a 1907 Silver Stream, the only model ever built; a 1904 Germain, one of four remaining in the world; and a 1910 Wolseley Siddeley, once driven by the poet William Butler Yeats. Lining the walls are early motoring and cycling periodicals and license plates from all over the world.

Admission: £2.50 adults ($3.75), £1.50 ($2.25) seniors and students, £1 ($1.50) children.

Open: Daily 10:30am–6:30pm or later.

St. Mary's Church, Church Place, Killarney. ☎ **31832.**

It's commonly believed that St. Mary's, an 1870 neo-Gothic church, stands on the site of the original "Church of the Sloe Woods" (in Irish called *Cill Airne*—the anglicanization of which is Killarney). It's located in the heart of town, across from Town Hall.

Admission: Free, donations welcome.

Open: Sun 10:30am–7pm.

⭐ **Kerry Glass Studio & Visitor Centre,** Killorglin Road, Fossa, Killarney. ☎ **44666.**

This studio produces Killarney's distinctive colored glass. Visitors are welcome to watch—and photograph—the craftsmen firing, blowing, and adding color to the glass as it is shaped into vases, paperweights, candleholders, and figurines. Free guided tours are conducted according to demand. The center includes a factory shop and snack bar. Located 4 miles west of the town.

Admission: Free.

Open: Daily 9am–4:30pm.

Kennedy's Open Farm, Brewsterfield, Glenflesk, Killarney. ☎ **54054.**

This 75-acre dairy and sheep farm is surrounded by mountain vistas. Visitors can see cows being milked and the piglets being fed. Roaming among the usual farm animals, peacocks spread their fantails. Horse-drawn machinery is displayed. Six miles east of Killarney, off the main Cork Road (N 22).

Admission: £3 adults ($4.50), £2 ($3) children.

Open: Daily.

Crag Cave, off Limerick Road (N 21), Castleisland, Co. Kerry. ☎ **41244.**

Believed to be more than a million years old, this limestone cave is one of the longest in Ireland; it extends for 12,510 feet. Guides accompany you on a well-lit tour of its passageways, which contain some of the largest stalactites in Europe. Exhibits, a crafts shop, and a restaurant are on the premises, 15 miles north of Killarney Town.

Admission: £3 ($4.50) adults, £1.50 ($2.25) children over 6.

Open: Mar–June and Sept–Nov, daily 10am–6pm; July–Aug, daily 10am–7pm.

Sightseeing Tours

BUS TOURS To get your bearings in Killarney, consider one of these sightseeing tours:

Killarney Highlights, Dero's Tours, 7 Main St., Killarney. ☎ **31251** or **31567.**

Besides showing off Killarney's Lakes from the best vantage points, this three-hour tour takes you to Aghadoe, the Gap of Dunloe, Ross Castle, Muckross House and Gardens, and Torc Waterfall.

Price: £7.50 ($11.25).

Schedule: May–Sept daily at 10am and 2pm, but schedules vary, so check in advance.

Lakeland Tour, Castlelough Tours, 7 High St., Killarney. ☎ **32496** or **31115.**

This tour, approximately 3.5 hours in duration, includes a visit to Muckross House and Gardens by bus and a tour of the lakes via Killarney Water Bus.

Price: £10 ($15).

Schedule: May–Sept, daily at 10:30am and 2pm.

In addition to Killarney's main sights, some bus tours also venture into the two prime scenic areas nearby, the Ring of Kerry and Dingle Peninsula. In the May to September period, tours are offered daily; prices average £10 ($15) per person. The following companies operate bus tours of the Ring of Kerry and Dingle Peninsula: Bus Eireann, Bus Depot, Railway Road, off East Avenue Road (☎ **34777**); Castlelough Tours, 7 High St. (☎ **32496**); Corcoran's Tours, Kilcummin (☎ **43151**); and Dero's Tours, 7 Main St. (☎ **31251**).

⭐ **JAUNTING CAR TOURS** You might say that a jaunting car is to Killarney what a cable car is to San Francisco or a gondola to Venice. Jaunting cars are the preferred mode of transportation in much of the Killarney sightseeing area.

Once you board a jaunting car, you'll have a tartan blanket tucked on your lap, "just in case" there's a mist or a cool breeze. The jarvey will give you a running commentary on the sights along the way, complete with local legends and, with the slightest encouragement, a song or two.

Be warned that jarveys can be a bit aggressive in soliciting your business. If you prefer to walk or bicycle around the lakes, a polite but firm "No, thank you" is all you need to say.

Take comfort in the fact that jaunting car rates are set and carefully monitored by the Killarney Urban District Council. Current rates, all based on four persons to a jaunting car, range from £3 ($4.50) per person for a round-trip to Ross Castle, to £6 per person ($9) for a round-trip to Muckross House & Gardens and Torc Waterfall, to £8 per person ($12) for round-trips to Muckross Abbey, Dinis Island, and Torc Waterfall, or a round-trip to Kate Kearney's Cottage, gateway to the Gap of Dunloe.

To arrange for a jaunting car trip, go to where the jaunting cars and drivers line up in a taxi-rank fashion: Kenmare Place in Killarney town; the first entrance to Killarney National Park, Muckross Road; Muckross Abbey Entrance to Killarney National Park, Muckross Road; Muckross House; or Kate Kearney's Cottage. If you need help or guidelines for prices, don't hesitate to go to the tourist office.

⭐ **GAP OF DUNLOE TOURS** Amid mountains and lakelands, the winding and rocky Gap of Dunloe is situated about six miles west of Killarney. Several Killarney-based companies offer all-day Gap of Dunloe excursions (see below). Journeys through the famous gap usually begin with a bus or jaunting-car ride from Killarney to Kate Kearney's Cottage, a pub that marks the starting point of the gap. From here, you'll go either by horseback or pony-and-trap through the seven-mile gap. The narrow dirt path is closed to motor traffic; those who are hale and hearty may choose to walk it.

The route through the gap passes a kaleidoscope of craggy rocks, massive cliffs, meandering streams, and deep valleys. Serpent Lake is the spot where St. Patrick is said to have drowned the last snake in Ireland. To this day, the lake has no fish. The road through the gap ends at Upper Lake, and most tours make a stop by the lakeside for a picnic, which can be supplied by your hotel or guesthouse.

The next phase of most tours is by water. A boat will glide you across the three Lakes of Killarney; then it pulls ashore at Ross Castle, where another jaunting cart or bus will return you to Killarney town.

Gap of Dunloe excursions are offered by Castlelough Tours, 7 High St. (☎ **32496** or **31115**); Corcoran's Tours, Kilcummin (☎ **43151**); Dero's Tours, 22 Main St. (☎ **31251**); and O'Donoghue's Tours, 3 High St. (☎ **31068**). A tour will cost about £20–£25 ($30–$37.50).

BOAT TOURS There is nothing quite like being in a boat on the Lakes of Killarney to enjoy all of the many shoreland and water sights. Two companies operate regular boating excursions, with full commentary:

M.V. _Pride of the Lakes_ Tours, Scotts Gardens, Killarney. ☎ **32638.**

This enclosed waterbus offers daily sailings from the pier at Ross Castle. The trip lasts just over an hour and reservations are suggested.

Fare: £5 ($7.50) adults; £2.50 ($3.75) children.
Schedule: Apr–Oct, 11am, 12:30pm, 2:30pm, 4pm, and 5:15pm.

M.V. *Lily of Killarney* Tours, 3 High St., Killarney. ☎ **31068.**

Departing from the pier at Ross Castle, this enclosed watercoach cruises the lakes for just over an hour. Reservations are suggested.

Fare: £5 ($7.50) adults; £2.50 ($3.75) children.

Schedule: Apr–Oct 10:30am, noon, 1:45pm, 3:15pm, 4:30pm, and 5:45pm.

6 Sports & Recreation

SPECTATOR SPORTS

GAELIC GAMES   The people of Killarney are passionately devoted to the national sports of hurling and Gaelic football. Games are played almost every Sunday afternoon during the summer at **Fitzgerald Stadium,** Lewis Road, Killarney (☎ **31700**). For complete details, consult the local *Kerryman* newspaper or the Killarney tourist office.

HORSE RACING   Killarney has two annual horse-racing events in early May and mid-July. Each event lasts for three or four days and is very heavily attended. For more information, contact the **Killarney Racecourse,** Ross Road, Killarney (☎ **064/31125**) or the Killarney tourist office.

RECREATION

BICYCLING   The **Killarney National Park,** with its many lakeside and forest pathways, trails, and byways, is a paradise for bikers. Various types of bikes are available, from tourers to 21-speeds, mountain bikes, and tandems. Rental charges average £5 ($7.50) per day or £25 ($37.50) per week. Bicycles can be rented from the following shops: **Cycle Ireland,** St. Mary's Terrace (☎ **32536**); **Killarney Rent-a-Bike,** High Street (☎ **064/32578**); **O'Neill Cycle Shop,** 6 Plunkett St., Killarney (☎ **064/ 31970**); and **O'Sullivan's Bike Shop,** High Street, Killarney (☎ **064/31282**). Most shops are open from 9am to 6pm daily all year, with extended hours until 8 or 9pm in the summer months.

FISHING   Fishing for salmon and brown trout is a big attraction in Killarney's unpolluted lakes and rivers. Brown trout fishing is free on the Lakes of Killarney, but a permit is necessary for the Rivers Flesk and Laune. A trout permit costs £2 to £5 ($3 to $7.50) per day.

Salmon fishing anywhere in Ireland requires a license; the cost is £3 ($4.50) per day or £10 ($15) for 21 days. In addition, some rivers also require a salmon permit, costing £8 ($12) per day. Permits and licenses can be obtained at the Fishery Office at the **Knockreer Estate Office,** New Street, Killarney (☎ **064/31246**).

For fishing tackle, bait, rod rental, and other fishing gear, as well as permits and licenses, try **O'Neill's Fishing Tackle Shop,** 6 Plunkett St., Killarney (☎ **064/31970**). This shop also arranges the hire of boats and ghillies (fishing guides). Gear and tackle can also be purchased from **Handy Stores,** Kenmare Place, Killarney (☎ **064/31188**) and from Michael O'Brien at **Angler's Paradise,** Loreto Road, Killarney (☎ **064/ 33818**).

GOLF   Visitors are always welcome at the twin 18-hole championship courses of the **Killarney Lake & Fishing Club,** Killorglin Road, Fossa, Killarney (☎ **064/ 31034**), located three miles west of the town center. Widely praised as the most scenic golf setting in the world, these courses, known as "Killeen" and "Mahony's Point," are surrounded by lake and mountain vistas. Greens fees are £26 ($39) on either course.

HORSEBACK RIDING   Many trails in the Killarney area are suitable for horse-back riding. The cost of hiring a horse ranges from £8 to £10 ($12 to $15) per hour at the following establishments: **Killarney Riding Stables,** R 562, Ballydowney, Killarney (☎ 064/31686); **O'Donovan's Farm,** Mangerton Road, Muckross, Killarney (☎ 064/32238); and **Rocklands Stables,** Rockfield, Tralee Road, Killarney (☎ 064/32592). Lessons and week-long trail rides can also be arranged.

WALKING   Killarney is ideal for walking enthusiasts. On the outskirts of town, the **Killarney National Park** offers four signposted nature trails. The Mossy Woods Nature Trail starts near Muckross House near Muckross Lake and rambles through yew woods along low cliffs (1¹/₂ miles). Old Boat House Nature Trail begins at the 19th-century boathouse below Muckross Gardens and leads around a small peninsula by Muckross Lake (¹/₂ mile). Arthur Young's Walk starts on the road to Dinis, traverses natural yew woods, and then follows a 200-year-old road on the Muckross Peninsula (3 miles). The Blue Pool Nature Trail goes from Muckross village through woodlands and past a small lake known as the Blue Pool (1¹/₂ miles). Leaflets with maps of these four trails are available at the park visitor center.

In addition to walking independently, visitors can also join in regularly scheduled organized guided walks. Priced from £12 ($18) per person a day, these walks are operated by **Kerry Country Rambles,** care of Tracks and Trails, 53 High St. (☎ 064/35277). The walks vary in duration from one day to a weekend or a full week. Reservations are required.

For long-distance walkers, there is the 125-mile "Kerry Way," a signposted walking route that extends from Killarney around the Ring of Kerry (see "Ring of Kerry" in the next chapter).

7 Savvy Shopping

Vying for the business of tourists, the shops of Killarney keep their prices competitive. Shopping hours are usually from Monday through Saturday 9am to 6pm; but during May through September or October, most stores are open every day from 9am until 9pm or 10pm. Almost all stores carry Kerry Glass products, a unique Killarney-made souvenir.

Although there are literally dozens of souvenir and craft shops in Killarney, here are a few of the best.

Blarney Woollen Mills, 10 Main St. ☎ 33222.

A branch of the highly successful County Cork–based enterprise, this large store occupies a beautiful shopfront on the corner of Plunkett Street in the center of town. The wares range from hand-knit or hand-loomed Irish-made sweaters to tweeds, crystal, china, pottery, and souvenirs of all sizes, shapes, and prices.

Danu Crafts, 4 Plunkett St. (No phone).

This little shop specializes in jewelry, stationery, and clothing with Celtic design imprints and engravings. The designs are inspired by the original art of Newgrange, the *Book of Kells,* and other historic symbols. The items range from T-shirts and art cards to jewelry made from stone, brass, ceramics, bronze, and silver.

Frank Lewis Gallery, 6 Bridewell Lane. ☎ 34843.

Housed in one of Killarney's enchanting laneways in a restored artisan's dwelling near the post office, this gallery shows and sells a wide variety of contemporary and traditional paintings, sculptures, and photographic work of the highest quality by some of Ireland's most acclaimed emerging artists. Exhibits change monthly.

Kerry Glass, College Street. ☎ 32587.

If you can't get to the Kerry Glass Factory outside of town (see "The Top Attractions," above), then stop at this outlet store for Killarney's colorful and distinctive glass, available in paperweights, figurines, vases, bowls, pendants, and more.

Killarney Art Gallery, 52 High St. ☎ 34628.

This shopfront gallery features original paintings from leading Killarney-area and other Irish artists, as well as art supplies, Irish prints and engravings.

Killarney Book Shop, 32 Main St. ☎ 34108.

Stop into this shop for books and maps on the history, legends, and lore of Killarney and Kerry. It also stocks good maps of the area and other books of Irish and international interest.

Quill's Woollen Market, 1 High St. ☎ 32277.

This is one of the best spots in town for hand-knit sweaters of all colors, sizes, and types, plus tweeds, mohair, and sheepskins. If you miss this one, there are also branches in Sneem and Kenmare on the Ring of Kerry, in Cork City, and the "original" shop at Ballingeary, Co. Cork.

Serendipity, 15 College St. ☎ 31056.

The shelves of this tidy shop feature a wide range of unusual crafts from local artisans, such as copper leprechauns mounted on aged bogwood and ceramic sheep and goats, to miniature oil paintings, pressed flowers and shamrocks, crochet work, and lace.

Words 'N' Music, 12 College St. ☎ 33664.

This small shop specializes in Irish traditional music and other folk music. In addition to CDs and tapes, it sells instruments, books, videos, and T-shirts for music lovers.

8 Evening Entertainment & Pubs

The highlight of the town's evening entertainment is the Killarney Manor Banquet, Loreto Road, Killarney (☎ 31551). This five-course dinner is done in 19th-century style with a complete program of songs, ballads, and dance. It's held in a stately 1840s stone-faced mansion that was built as a hotel and later served as a convent and school. The mansion is set on a hillside two miles south of town overlooking the Killarney panorama.

The evening starts in the Gallery, formerly a chapel replete with stained-glass windows. A welcoming drink of mulled wine provided by the "lord" of the manor, the host who then leads the guests into the Great Hall for the feasting and entertainment. The menu offers a choice of traditional Irish spiced sirloin of beef, roast Kerry lamb, or poached local salmon, with all the trimmings. The meal is accompanied and followed by traditional Irish music including the melodies of Thomas Moore, Percy French, and other celebrated Irish songwriters.

Open from April through October, the banquet is staged five nights a week (usually closed on Sunday and Thursday) starting at 8pm. The price is £26 ($39) per person for complete banquet and dinner. It's also possible to attend the entertainment segment only for £9 ($13.50) from 9pm to 10:30pm. Reservations are required. AE, DC, MC, V.

PUBS

Buckley's, 2 College St. ☎ **31037.**

For a quiet drink and some convivial conversation, don't miss this well-kept pub. Established in 1926, it has a Georgian facade. Inside, you'll see football trophies, uniforms, and team photos, plus some intriguing pictures and paintings of old Killarney. There's a session of traditional music every Monday, Tuesday, and Friday, April through September, starting at 9:30pm.

Danny Mann, 97 New St. ☎ **31640.**

Known for its traditional music, this pub attracts locals and visitors alike. The music usually starts at 9pm, but check in advance to see what's on.

Dunloe Lodge, Plunkett St. ☎ **32502.**

This simple pub in the heart of town has a friendly and comfortable atmosphere. Don't be surprised if some of its local patrons spontaneously pull out a harmonica, an accordion, a banjo, or a fiddle and start to play. You'll hear anything from Irish ballads to folk or rock music.

Kate Kearney's Cottage, Gap of Dunloe. ☎ **44146.**

Almost everyone who ventures through the famous Gap first visits this former coaching inn, which is named for a woman who was believed to be a witch. Today this outpost nine miles west of town is a refreshment stop at the start of the gap, with souvenirs on sale. From May through September, traditional music is performed on Sunday, Wednesday, and Friday evenings from 9 to 11:30pm.

The Laurels, Main St. ☎ **31149.**

The rafters ring here to the lilt of Irish song each evening. Ballad singers are slated nightly from April through October starting at 9pm.

Molly Darcy's, Muckross Village, Muckross Rd. ☎ **31938.**

Located across from Muckross House, this is one of Killarney's best traditional pubs—with a thatched roof, stone walls, an oak-beamed ceiling, open fireplaces, alcoves, snugs, and lots of Killarney memorabilia. There's set dancing on Sunday evenings.

Scotts Beer Garden, College Street. ☎ **31060.**

On a warm summer's night, this is the place to enjoy a drink in an outdoor beer garden. Music ranges from ballads to piano or jazz.

Tatler Jack, Plunkett Street. ☎ **32361.**

This traditional pub is a favorite gathering place for followers of Gaelic football and hurling. Traditional music or ballads are on tap from June through September, nightly from 9:30pm.

10

The Kingdom of Kerry

Nоt only does it shelter Ireland's number-one scenic attraction, Killarney (see Chapter 9), County Kerry also possesses the highest mountain peaks in Ireland, Macgillycuddy's Reeks and Mount Brandon. The county is the home of the two most-heralded touring routes, the Ring of Kerry and the Dingle Peninsula. No wonder its residents refer to their county as "The Kingdom."

On Ireland's extreme southwest coast, County Kerry extends into the Atlantic with a coastline dominated by two finger-shaped peninsulas. A series of smaller curves project into the ocean, too. Warmed by the Gulf Stream, the county has a mild, neutral climate throughout the year. Temperatures average from 40° to 45°F in winter and 55° to 65°F in summer.

It's said that there's not much climate in County Kerry, just weather. And thanks to the strong winds blowing off the Atlantic, that weather is "changeable." It can be beautifully sunny in the morning and very wet in the afternoon, and vice versa. On a winter day, it can feel like four seasons in one day. If Kerry didn't have its rain, it wouldn't be nearly as lush and colorful as it is. Nor would the clouds so dramatically shroud the tops of mountains and hover over the lakes and bays.

Thanks to its remoteness, County Kerry has always been an outpost of Gaelic culture. Poetry and music are intrinsic to Kerry lifestyle, as is a love of the outdoors and sports. Gaelic football is an obsession in this county, and Kerry wins most of the national championships. You'll also find some of Ireland's best golf courses here, and the fishing for salmon and trout is equally hard to resist.

1 The Ring of Kerry

GETTING THERE • Bus Eireann (☎ 064/34777) provides limited daily service from Killarney to Caherciveen, Waterville, Kenmare, and other towns on the Ring of Kerry. The best way to get to the Ring of Kerry is by car, via the N 70 and N 71 roads. Some Killarney-based companies provide daily sightseeing tours of the Ring (see Killarney chapter).

ESSENTIALS • Tourist Information For year-round information, stop in at the Killarney Tourist Office, Town Hall, Main Street, Killarney (☎ 064/31633), before you embark on the Ring (for hours open, see Killarney chapter). From May through September, the Kenmare Tourist Office, Market Square, Kenmare (☎ 064/41233) is open.

• **Area Code** Most telephone numbers on the Ring of Kerry use the 064 or 066 code.

Undoubtedly Ireland's most popular scenic drive, the Ring of Kerry is a 110-mile panorama of seacoast, mountain, and lakeland vistas. For the most part, the Ring follows the N 70 road and circles the Iveragh Peninsula; it starts and finishes at Killarney, but you can also use Kenmare as a base. Although a little rain or passing showers should not deter you from embarking on this drive, it's best not to set out in heavy sea mist or continuous rain. If the clouds are moving, however, that usually means you'll have a good day for the Ring.

The drive can be undertaken in either direction, but we recommend a counterclockwise route. The duration can be anything from four hours to a full day, depending on how many stops you make for picture-taking, beach-walking, hill-climbing, pubbing, and shopping.

What's Special About the Kingdom of Kerry

Beaches
- Rossbeigh Strand, a duney beach on the Ring of Kerry.
- Inch Strand, a wide curve of sandy beach on the Dingle Peninsula.

Monuments
- Gallarus Oratory, Ballyferriter, one of Ireland's best-preserved early Christian buildings, made of unmortared stone and watertight after 1,000 years.

Museums
- Kerry Bog Village Museum, Glenbeigh, a cluster of thatched cottages evoking life in Kerry during the 1800s.

Parks/Gardens
- Derrynane House National Historic Park, a park on the edge of the Atlantic and once home of Ireland's "Great Liberator," Daniel O'Connell.

For the Kids
- Hop aboard the Tralee Steam Railway for a scenic trip through the countryside.

Ace Attractions
- The Skellig Experience, Valentia Island, for a close-up view of the storied Skellig Rocks.
- Kerry the Kingdom, Tralee, an in-depth look at County Kerry via an audio-visual show, interactive museum, and a ride through a recreation of Tralee in the Middle Ages.
- Blennerville Windmill, the largest working windmill in both Ireland and Britain.
- Blasket Centre, Dunquin, a showcase of history on the storied Blasket Islands.

Natural Spectacles
- Ring of Kerry, a 110-mile panorama of seacoast, mountain, and lakeland vistas.
- Carrantuohill and Mount Brandon, Ireland's two tallest mountains.
- Dingle Peninsula, 100 miles of dramatic seascapes, rocky mountain cliffs, and Irish-speaking towns.
- The Blasket Islands, seven uninhabited islands off the Atlantic coast.

Activities
- Ply the waters of Kenmare Bay on a Scenic Safari and Wildlife Cruise.
- Tee off at some of Ireland's greatest golf courses at Waterville Lake, Tralee, or Ballybunion.
- Walk the Kerry Way, a 125-mile signposted scenic circuit.
- Swim with Fungie the dolphin at Dingle.
- Walk the Dingle Way, a 100-mile signposted scenic route through the Irish-speaking region of the Dingle Peninsula.

After Dark
- Siamsa Tíre, Ireland's National Folk Theatre at Tralee, for music, singing, mime, dance, and humor in the Irish tradition.

TV and Film Locations
- *Ryan's Daughter* at Inch Strand and other Dingle Peninsula locations.

Great Towns/Villages
- Glenbeigh, a palm tree–lined fishing resort.
- Waterville, once the favorite beach haunt of Charlie Chaplin.
- Sneem, with gaily painted houses.
- Kenmare, a 17th-century "planned town" and the Ring of Kerry's "little nest."
- Dingle, a seaport and seafood enclave.

WHAT TO SEE & DO

Departing Killarney, follow the signs for Killorglin. When you reach this little town, you're on the N 70 road. You may wish to stop and walk around Killorglin, a spot that's known far and wide for its annual mid-August horse, sheep, and cattle fair. It's officially called the Puck Fair, because the local residents capture a wild goat from the mountains and enthrone it in the center of town as a sign of unrestricted merry-making.

Continue on the N 70 road and soon vistas of Dingle Bay appear on your right. Carrantuohill, Ireland's tallest mountain (3,414 ft.), is to your left. The open bogland constantly comes into view. From it, the local residents dig pieces of peat, or turf, to burn in their fireplaces for warmth. Formed thousands of years ago, these boglands are mainly composed of decayed trees. They tend to be bumpy if you attempt to drive over them too speedily, so do be cautious.

You'll find that the Ring winds around cliffs and the edges of mountains, with nothing but the sea below—another reason that you will probably average only 30 miles an hour, at best. Last, you'll notice the remains of many abandoned cottages. These date from the famine years, in the mid-1840s, when the Irish potato crop failed and millions of people starved to death or were forced to emigrate. This peninsula alone lost three-fourths of its population.

The next town on the Ring is Glenbeigh, a palm tree–lined fishing resort, with a lovely duney beach called Rossbeigh strand. You may wish to stop here or continue the sweep through the mountains and along the sea's edge to Cahirciveen. From here, you can make a slight detour to see Valentia, an offshore island seven miles long and one of the most westerly points of Europe. Connected to the mainland by a bridge at Portmagee, this was the site of the first telegraph cable laid across the Atlantic in 1866. In the 18th century, the Valentia harbor was famous as a refuge for smugglers and privateers; it's said that John Paul Jones, the Scottish-born American naval officer in the War of Independence, also anchored here quite often.

Head next for Waterville, an idyllic spot wedged between Lough Currane and Ballinskelligs Bay off the Atlantic. For years, it was known as the favorite retreat of Charlie Chaplin, but today it's the home of the only Irish branch of Club Med.

If you follow the sea road north of town out to the Irish-speaking village of Ballinskelligs, at the mouth of the bay, you can also catch a glimpse of the two Skellig

Rocks. Continuing on the N 70 route, the next point of interest is Derrynane at Caherdaniel, the home of Daniel O'Connell, remembered as "the Liberator" who freed Irish Catholics from the last of the penal restraints in 1829. Derrynane is now a national monument and park, and a major center of Gaelic culture.

Watch for signs to Staigue Fort, about two miles off the main road. One of best preserved of all Irish ancient structures, this circular fort is constructed of rough stones without mortar of any kind. The walls are 13 feet wide at its base, and the diameter is about 90 feet. Not much is known of its history, but experts think it probably dates back to around 1,000 B.C.

Sneem, the next village on the circuit, is a colorful little hamlet with twin parklets. Its houses are painted in vibrant shades of blue, pink, yellow, purple, and orange, almost like a Mediterranean cluster.

As you continue on the Ring, the foliage becomes lusher, thanks to the warming waters and winds of the Gulf Stream. When you begin to see lots of palm trees and other subtropical vegetation, you'll know you are in Parknasilla, once a favorite haunt of George Bernard Shaw.

The final town on the Ring of Kerry route is by far the most enchanting, Kenmare. Originally called Neidin, which in the Irish language means "Little Nest," Kenmare is indeed a little nest of verdant foliage nestled between the River Roughty and Kenmare Bay. Well laid out and immaculately maintained by its proud residents (population: 1,200), Kenmare easily rivals Killarney as an alternative base for County Kerry sightseeing.

On the return to Killarney, the final lap of the Ring road takes you through a scenic mountain stretch known as Moll's Gap.

★ **The Skellig Experience,** Skellig Heritage Centre, Valentia Island, Co. Kerry. ☎ **066/76306.**

Situated seven miles off the mainland Ring of Kerry route on Valentia Island, this new attraction blends right in with the terrain, with a stark stone facade framed by grassy mounds. Inside, through a series of displays and audio-visuals, the center presents a detailed look at birds and plant life of the Valentia area. In particular, it gives the story of the Skellig Rocks—Skellig Michael and Little Skellig—two rocky islands that sit off the coast in Atlantic waters. In the 6th century, Skellig Michael, the larger of the two, was the home of a small group of monks who founded a monastery that survived for more than 600 years. It became recognized as a hub of learning in the early Christian church of Europe. Today, the other Skellig is one of the largest breeding grounds for the gannet in western Europe.

If you'd like a closer look at the rocks, you can also board a boat for an optional 1¹/₂-hour cruise with a commentary that lets you see, hear, and smell the Skellig world first-hand.

Admission: £3 ($4.50) adults, £2.70 ($4.05) seniors and students, £1.50 ($2.25) children under 12; cruise is an extra £12 ($18) adults, £10.80 ($16.20) seniors and students, £6.50 ($10.25) children.

Open: May–June and Sept, daily 10am–7pm; July–Aug, daily 9:30am–7pm.

Derrynane House National Historic Park, Caherdaniel, Co. Kerry. ☎ **066/75113.**

Situated on a 320-acre site along the Ring of Kerry Coast between Waterville and Caherdaniel, this is where Ireland's Great Liberator, Daniel O'Connell, lived for most of his life. The house is maintained as a museum by Ireland's Office of Public Works.

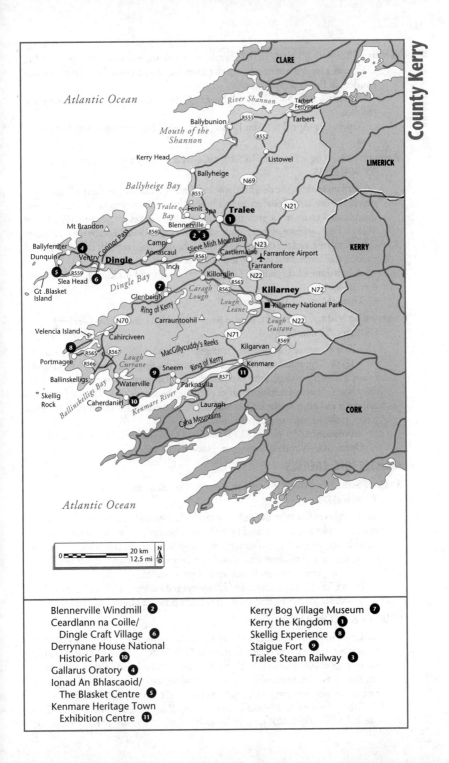

County Kerry

Atlantic Ocean

CLARE

River Shannon

Tarbert Ferryport
Tarbert

Mouth of the Shannon

Ballybunion

R551

R552

LIMERICK

Kerry Head

Listowel

Ballyheige

N69

Ballyheige Bay

KERRY

R551

Tralee Bay

Fenit Spa

Tralee ①

N21

Mt Brandon △

Blennerville

②③

Connor Pass

R560

Camp

Slieve Mish Mountains

N23

Ballyferriter ④

Dunquin

Ventry

Dingle

Annascaul

R561

Castlemaine

Farranfore Airport

Farranfore

N22

Slea Head ⑤ ⑥ R559

Inch

Killorglin

R563

Killarney

N72

Gt .Blasket Island

Dingle Bay

⑦

R562

Lough Leane

Killarney National Park

Glenbeigh

Caragh Lough

Ring of Kerry

Carrauntoohil △

N71

Lough Guitane

N22

Velencia Island

N70

MacGillycuddy's Reeks

R569

Cahirciveen

Kilgarvan

Portmagee

R565 R567

Lough Currane

Ring of Kerry

Kenmare ⑪

Ballinskelligs

R566

⑨ Sneem

R571

Skellig Rock

Ballinskelligs Bay

Waterville

Parknasilla

Caherdaniel ⑩

Kenmare River

Lauragh

CORK

Caha Mountains

Atlantic Ocean

0 ▬▬▬▬ 20 km
       12.5 mi

N

Blennerville Windmill ②
Ceardlann na Coille/
   Dingle Craft Village ⑥
Derrynane House National
   Historic Park ⑩
Gallarus Oratory ④
Ionad An Bhlascaoid/
   The Blasket Centre ⑤
Kenmare Heritage Town
   Exhibition Centre ⑪

Kerry Bog Village Museum ⑦
Kerry the Kingdom ①
Skellig Experience ⑧
Staigue Fort ⑨
Tralee Steam Railway ③

It's filled with all kinds of documents, illustrations, and memorabilia related to O'Connell's life. Visitors can also watch a 25-minute audio-visual about the great leader entitled *Be You Perfectly Peaceable.*

Admission: £1.50 ($2.25) adults, £1 ($1.50) seniors, 60p (90¢) students and children.

Open: Oct–Apr, Tues–Sun 1–5pm, May–Sept, Mon–Sat 9am–6pm, Sun 11am–7pm.

Kenmare Heritage Town Exhibition Centre, The Square, Kenmare, Co. Kerry. ☎ 064/41233.

To learn more about the delightful town of Kenmare, the Ring of Kerry's "little nest," step inside this new visitor center. Kenmare's history is recounted through exhibits; this planned estate town grew up around the mineworks founded in 1670 by Sir William Petty, ancestor of the Landsdownes, the local landlords. Locally made Kenmare lace is displayed, and the story of the woman who originated the craft is told. A scripted walking trail around the town is also under development.

Admission: £2 ($3) adults, £1.50 ($2.25) seniors and students, £1 ($1.50) children under 12.

Open: Mon–Sat 10am–6pm.

Kerry Bog Village Museum, Ring of Kerry Road (N 71), Ballycleave, Glenbeigh, Co. Kerry. ☎ 066/69184.

This little cluster of thatched-roof cottages shows what life was like in Kerry in the early 1800s. This museum village has a blacksmith's forge and house, a turf cutter's house, a laborer's cottage, a thatcher's dwelling, a tradesman's house, and a stable and dairy house. Stacks of newly cut turf sit piled high beside the road. There's also a football pitch and other recreational facilities. The interiors are furnished with authentic pieces, gathered from all parts of Kerry.

Admission: £2.50 adults ($3.75), £1.50 ($2.25) students, £1 ($1.50) children.

Open: Mar–Nov daily 9am–6pm, Nov–Mar by appointment.

SIGHTSEEING CRUISES

Seafari Scenic & Wildlife Cruises, Kenmare Pier, Kenmare, Co. Kerry. ☎ 064/83171.

See the sights of Kenmare Bay on board this 50-ft. covered boat. The two-hour cruises cover ten miles and are narrated by well-versed guides who provide information on local history, geography, and geology. Sightings of sea otters, gray seals, herons, oystercatchers, and kingfishers are pointed out. Boats depart from the pier next to the Kenmare suspension bridge. Reservations recommended.

Fare: £7.50 ($11.25) adults, £6 ($9) seniors and students, £4.50 ($7.25) children.

Schedule: May–Sept, daily every two hours between sunrise and sunset.

SPORTS & RECREATION

GOLF Home to myriad seascapes and sand dunes, the Ring of Kerry is known for its great golf courses, particularly **Waterville Golf Club,** Waterville (☎ 064/74102) on the edge of the Atlantic. On huge sand dunes and bounded on three sides by the sea, this 18-hole championship course is one of the longest in Ireland (7,234 yards). Visitors are welcome every day; greens fees are approximately £35 ($52.50).

Other challenging 18-hole courses on the Ring include **Dooks Golf Club,** Glenbeigh (☎ 066/68205), a seaside par-70 course on the Ring of Kerry Road, with a fee of £15 ($22.50); and the newly expanded Kenmare Golf Club, Kenmare (☎ 064/41291), a parkland par-71 course with greens fees from £10 ($15).

WALKING   Ireland's longest low-level long-distance path, **the Kerry Way,** traverses the Ring of Kerry. The first stage from Killarney National Park to Glenbeigh is inland through wide and scenic countryside, while the second stage provides a circuit of the Iveragh Peninsula, linking Cahirciveen, Waterville, Caherdaniel, Sneems, and Kenmare, with a farther inland walk along the old Kenmare Road back to Killarney, for a total of 125 miles. The route consists primarily of paths and "green roads" (unsurfaced), such as old driving paths, butter roads, and routes between early Christian settlements. A leaflet outlining the route is available from the Killarney or Kenmare tourist office.

SAVVY SHOPPING

Many good craft and souvenir shops are found along the Ring of Kerry, but those in **Kenmare** offer the most in terms of variety and quality. Kenmare shops are also open year-round, usually Monday through Saturday from 9am to 6pm. In May through September, many shops remain open till 9pm or 10pm and some open on Sunday from noon to 5 or 6pm.

Avoca Handweavers at Moll's Gap, Ring of Kerry Road (N 71), Moll's Gap, Co. Kerry. ☎ 064/34720.

Located in one of the most scenic of settings, this shop is set on a high mountain pass (960 ft. above sea level) between Killarney and Kenmare. It is a branch of the famous tweedmakers of Avoca, Co. Wicklow, dating back to 1723. The wares range from colorful handwoven capes and jackets to throws, knitwear, pottery, and jewelry. There is an excellent coffee shop on the premises, staffed by chefs trained at the Ballymaloe Cookery School. Closed November to mid-March.

Cleo, 2 Shelbourne Road, Kenmare. ☎ 064/41410.

A branch of the long-established Dublin store of the same name, this trendy women's wear shop is known for its colorful tweed and linen fashions, as well as specialty items like Kinsale cloaks.

D. J. Cremin & Sons, 20 Henry St., Kenmare. ☎ 064/41597.

Founded in 1906 as a general drapery store, this family-run business is a haven for limited Waterford Crystal items like lamps, globes, candelabras, wall brackets, and chandeliers. You will also find unusual Irish dolls, locally made handknits and other giftware.

Kenmare Book Shop, Shelbourne St., Kenmare, Co. Kerry. ☎ 064/41578.

This shop specializes in books on Ireland, particularly Irish biographies and books by Irish writers, as well as guides and maps about the local area. There are also art cards and craft items relating to the *Book of Kells.* In an upstairs room, there is a display and audio-visual presentation on the *Book of Kells,* for those who can't get to Dublin to see the real thing; there's an admission charge of £2 ($3) adults, £1 ($1.50) children for the upstairs exhibit.

Nostalgia, 27 Henry St., Kenmare, Co. Kerry. ☎ 064/41389.

In a town known for its lace, it's a natural to stop into this shop and view the new and antique lace, table and bed linens, traditional teddy bears, and accessories.

Quills Woolen Market, Market Square and Main Street, Kenmare, Co. Kerry. ☎ **064/41078;** and North Square, Sneem, Co. Kerry. ☎ **064/45277.**

This is a branch of the store of the same name in Killarney, known for Aran handknits, Donegal tweed jackets, Irish linen, Celtic jewelry, and colorful hand-loomed knitwear.

⭐ **Stone Circle Crafts,** 18 Henry St., Kenmare. ☎ **064/41212.**

This shop offers unique crafts, most of which are made in the area, including decorative candles, handknit sweaters, stationery, pottery, watercolor paintings, and sculptures.

WHERE TO STAY

Very Expensive/Expensive

⭐ **The Park,** Kenmare, Co. Kerry. ☎ **064/41200** or toll free **800/223-6764** in U.S. Fax 064/41402. 48 rms (all with bath). TV TEL

Rates (including full breakfast): £110–£252 ($165–$378) single, £110–£264 ($165–$396) double. No service charge. AE, DC, MC, V. **Closed:** Mid-Nov to mid-Dec and Jan to mid-Apr.

Dating back to 1897, this Victorian-style chateau is a haven of impeccable service and luxurious living. Augustly ensconced amid palm tree–lined gardens beside Kenmare Bay, it originally served as a Great Southern Railway hotel, but was totally restored and refurbished about 20 years ago, under the masterful owner/management of Francis Brennan. The interior is rich in high-ceilinged sitting rooms and lounges, crackling open fireplaces, original oil paintings, tapestries, plush furnishings, and museum-worthy antiques, including an eye-catching cistern decorated with mythological figures and supported by gilded seahorses and dolphins. The individually decorated bedrooms are decked out in a mix of Georgian and Victorian styles, many with four-poster or canopy beds, hand-carved armoires, china lamps, curios, and little extra touches like telephones in the bathroom and towel warmers. Most have views of river and mountain vistas. Yet amid all of the elegance, this hotel exudes an intrinsically welcoming atmosphere. It's not surprising that it is often rated Ireland's best hotel.

Dining/Entertainment: The elegant dining room, with romantic views of the water and the palm tree–lined gardens, is one of the most highly acclaimed hotel restaurants in Ireland, meriting a Michelin star. Other public areas include a hexagonal-shaped bar and a drawing room where a pianist plays each evening.

Services: Concierge, 24-hour room service, laundry and dry cleaning, nightly turn-down.

Facilities: 18-hole golf course, joggers' trail, tennis court, croquet lawn, and salmon fishing.

Sheen Falls Lodge, Kenmare, Co. Kerry. ☎ **064/41600** or toll free **800/221-1074** in U.S. Fax 064/41386. 40 rms (all with bath). TV TEL

Rates (including full breakfast): £155–£175 ($232.50–$362.50) single, £190–£220 ($285–$330) double. No service charge. AE, DC, MC, V. **Closed:** Jan to mid-Mar.

Originally the 18th-century home of the Earl of Kerry, this relatively new resort sits beside a natural waterfall amid 300 acres of lawns and semitropical gardens where the River Sheen meets the Kenmare Bay estuary. The public areas are spacious and graceful with pillars and columns, open fireplaces, traditional furnishings, and original oil paintings. The guest rooms are large and spacious, decorated in contemporary style;

each overlooks the falls or bay. The hotel also maintains a vintage 1922 Buick to provide local excursions for guests.

Dining/Entertainment: The Cascades is a wide-windowed restaurant facing the falls, which are floodlit at night.

Services: 24-hour room service, concierge, laundry and dry cleaning, nightly turn-down.

Facilities: Leisure center with Jacuzzi, sauna, and steam room, billiard room, 1,000-volume library, a 15-mile stretch of private salmon fishing, horseback riding, tennis, croquet, golf on a nearby course, helicopter pad.

Expensive/Moderate

⭐ **Great Southern,** Ring of Kerry Road (N 70), Parknasilla, Co. Kerry.
☎ **064/45122** or toll free **800/44-UTELL.** Fax 064/45323. 84 rms (all with bath). TV TEL

Rates: £104–£124 ($156–$186) single or double. Service charge 12.5%. AE, DC, MC, V. **Closed:** Jan to mid–Mar.

Facing one of the loveliest seascape settings in Ireland, this chateau-style hotel is nestled amid 300 acres of lush subtropical foliage, palm trees, and flowering shrubs. Thanks to the warming influence of the Gulf Stream, it enjoys a year-round temperate climate. The present structure, an outgrowth and expansion of a former private mansion, was built with a fanciful Victorian stone facade in 1896. Over the years, it has been a favorite with visiting royalty and celebrities, including Nobel prize–winning dramatist, George Bernard Shaw. It's not surprising that he found the inspiration here to write much of his play *St. Joan.* Today's traveler is inspired, most of all, to have a memorable vacation, thanks to such amenities as a private nine-hole golf course, heated indoor saltwater swimming pool, saunas, horseback riding, tennis, fishing, boating, outdoor and indoor sundecks, a pubby lounge bar, and an award-winning restaurant. The bedrooms, which vary in size, are individually furnished with reproduction pieces; most look out onto broad vistas of the Kenmare River and the Atlantic.

Club Med Waterville, off the Ring of Kerry Road (N 70), Waterville, Co. Kerry.
☎ **066/74133** or toll free **800/CLUB-MED** in U.S. Fax 066/74483. 80 rms (all with bath). TV TEL

Rates (including full board/all meals): £75–£95 ($112.50–$142.50) single, £130–£180 ($195–$270) double. No service charge. AE, DC, MC, V. **Closed:** Nov–Mar.

Located on the western sweep of the Iveragh Peninsula just south of the village of Waterville, on the shores of Lough Currane, this is Club Med's first venture into Ireland. It is a well-kept and up-to-date two-story hotel with a bright and airy decor, and lots of wide windows to show off the surrounding lake and mountain views. The public areas include a restaurant, piano bar, pub, bridge room, and shop. As for sports and outdoor activities, there is an 18-hole championship golf course (greens fees extra), heated indoor swimming pool, thermal spa pool, sauna, solarium, three tennis courts, bicycling, guided nature walks, aerobics classes, and exercise room. The hotel also holds exclusive rights to some of the best salmon and sea-trout fishing in Ireland. Rates include meals with beer or wine, most sports, and nightly entertainment.

Moderate

Butler Arms, Waterville, Co. Kerry. ☎ **066/74144.** Fax 066/74520 or toll free **800/447-7462** in U.S. 31 rms (all with bath). TV TEL

> **Rates** (including full breakfast): £60–£70 ($90–$105) single, £80–£99 ($120–$148.50). No service charge. AE, DC, MC, V. **Closed:** Nov–Mar.

Once a favorite vacation retreat of Charlie Chaplin, this grand old inn is now run by the third generation of the Huggard family. Located on the edge of town and partially facing the sea, it has a sprawling and semiturreted white facade. The refurbished guest rooms are functional and pleasant; many have views of the water or the palm tree–studded gardens. An old-world charm emanates from the public rooms and bars, most of which have open turf fireplaces. Other facilities include a full-service restaurant, a nautically themed bar, sun lounge, tennis court, free salmon and sea trout fishing on Lough Currane and private lakes.

Dromquinna Manor Country House, Blackwater Bridge P.O., off Ring of Kerry Road (N 71), Kenmare, Co. Kerry. ☎ **064/41657.** Fax 064/41791. 27 rms (all with bath). TV TEL

> **Rates** (including full Irish breakfast): £37.50–£80 ($56.25–$120); double £55–£100 ($82.50–$150); tree house £100–£150 ($150–$225). No service charge. AE, DC, MC, V.

Situated a little over two miles west of Kenmare, this newly opened Victorian-style hotel dates back to 1850 and was originally a private home. It is situated on 42 acres of woodland with almost a mile of land facing the Kenmare River. Totally refurbished in recent years, it still retains an old world ambience, with log fireplaces, original oak paneling, ornate ceilings, and authentic bric-a-brac. Each bedroom is individually furnished, some with four-poster beds or Victorian-style beds, and some modern with light woods and frilly floral fabrics; some face the water. The grounds include a tree house, said to be the only one in Ireland or Britain, situated 15 feet above ground, with two bedrooms, bathroom, and large balcony. Public areas offer a restaurant and boathouse-style bistro, while sporting facilities include a tennis court, croquet, and rowboats for hire (£12 [$18]) per day.

Kenmare Bay, Sneem Road, Kenmare, Co. Kerry. ☎ **064/41300** or toll free **800/528-1234** in U.S. Fax 064/41541. 136 rms (all with bath). TV TEL

> **Rates** (including full breakfast): £42–£45 ($63–$67.50) single, £64–£70 ($96–$105) double. Service charge 10%. AE, DC, MC, V. **Closed:** Mid–Dec through Mar.

Situated on a hillside at the edge of town, just off the main road that winds around the Ring of Kerry, this modern hotel was recently expanded and refurbished. The guest rooms are furnished with light woods and tweedy or quilted fabrics, with large windows that look out onto the mountainous countryside. Facilities include a full-service restaurant and a spacious lounge bar that is the setting for traditional Irish music sing-alongs on most evenings.

Moderate/Inexpensive

Derrynane Hotel, off Ring of Kerry Road (N 71), Caherdaniel, Co. Kerry. ☎ **066/75136** or toll free **800/528-1234.** Fax 066/75160. 75 rms (all with bath). TV TEL

> **Rates** (including breakfast): £35–£40 ($52.50–$60) single, £56–£66 double ($84–$99). Service charge 10%. AE, DC, MC, V. **Closed:** Nov–Mar.

You can really get away from it all at this contemporary style three-story hotel, set deep in the outer reaches of the Ring of Kerry between Waterville and Sneem on the edge of the Atlantic. It is surrounded by beautiful beaches, hills, and the nearby Derrynane National Historic Park. The standard furnishings of the guest rooms are enhanced by the great views from every window. The public areas include a restaurant and lounge, while a heated swimming pool is available outside.

Towers, Ring of Kerry Road (N 70), Glenbeigh, Co. Kerry. ☎ **066/68212** or toll free **800/447-7462.** Fax 066/68260. 28 rms (all with bath). TV TEL

> **Rates** (including full breakfast): £33–£42 ($49.50–$63) £46–£60 double ($69–$90). Service charge 12.5%. AE, DC, MC, V. **Closed:** Jan–Mar.

If you'd like to be right in the heart of one of the Ring of Kerry's most delightful towns, then this vintage brick-faced country inn is for you. Shaded by ancient palms, it sits in the middle of a small fishing village, yet within a mile of the sandy Rossbeigh strand and 20 miles west of Killarney. Recently refurbished and updated, most of the guest rooms are in a contemporary-style new wing with lovely views of the nearby waters. Facilities include a lively old-fashioned pub and good seafood restaurant.

WHERE TO DINE

Mode rate

The Blue Bull, South Square, Ring of Kerry Road (N 70), Sneem, Co. Kerry. ☎ **064/45382.**

> **Cuisine:** SEAFOOD/INTERNATIONAL. **Reservations:** Recommended for dinner.
> **Prices:** Lunch/snack items £1.95–£5.95 ($2.93–$8.93); dinner appetizers £2.50–£4.95 ($3.75–$7.43); dinner main courses £9.95–£13.95 ($14.93–$20.93). AE, DC, MC, V.
> **Open:** Daily bar food, noon–3pm and dinner 6–10:30pm.

With a blue straw bull's head resting over the doorway, this old pub/restaurant has long been a favorite on the Ring of Kerry route. There are three small rooms, each with an open fireplace and walls lined with old prints of Co. Kerry scenes and people, plus a skylit conservatory room in the back. The menu offers dishes such as salmon Hollandaise; salmon stuffed with spinach and smoked salmon in white wine sauce; Valencia scallops in brandy; chicken stuffed with prawns; chicken Kiev; steaks; and Irish stew.

D'Arcy's Old Bank House, Main Street, Kenmare, Co. Kerry. ☎ **064/41589.**

> **Cuisine:** IRISH. **Reservations:** Recommended.
> **Prices:** Appetizers £2.25–£5.75 ($3.38–$8.63); main courses £9.50–£13.75 ($14.25–$20.63). MC, V.
> **Open:** Mar–Oct, dinner daily 6–10:30pm, Nov–Feb, dinner Wed–Sat 7–10:30pm.

Situated in a two-story stone house at the top end of Kenmare, this restaurant has a homey atmosphere, with a big open fireplace. The chef/owner, Matt d'Arcy, who formerly presided at the kitchens of the nearby Park Hotel, has branched out to make his own culinary mark in this restaurant-rich town. Using fresh local ingredients, the creative menus include dishes such as baked sea trout in pastry with smoked salmon; whole prawns on a courgette (zucchini) cream sauce; filet of beef in pastry with a stuffing of mushrooms, roast garlic, and shallots; veal with mushroom timbale and caper sauce; loin of Kerry lamb with aubergine (eggplant), tomato, and garlic.

★ **Lime Tree,** Shelbourne Road, Kenmare, Co. Kerry. ☎ **064/42225.**
Cuisine: IRISH. **Reservations:** Recommended.
Prices: Appetizers £2.25–£5.25 ($3.38–$7.88); main courses £8.50–£13.25 ($12.75–$20.88). AE, DC, MC, V.
Open: Mar–Oct, dinner daily 6:30–10pm.

Innovative cuisine is the focus at this restaurant in a landmark renovated schoolhouse (1821), next to the grounds of the Park Hotel. The decor includes a skylit gallery and stone walls lined with paintings by local artists. The menu offers such dishes as breast of chicken with apple rosemary marmalade; char-grilled filet of beef with homestyle horseradish mustard; lambs liver with bacon, shallots, and crumb stuffing; twice-seared pork chop with ginger rhubarb chutney; beefburger with confetti salsa; seafood fettuccine; warm smoked salmon salad with gingered starfruit and lime; monkfish tail with warm herb vinaigrette; and vegetarian stir-fry in pastry.

The Huntsman, The Strand, Waterville, Co. Kerry. ☎ **066/74124.**
Cuisine: INTERNATIONAL. **Reservations:** Recommended.
Prices: Lunch/bar food items £2.25–£9.95 ($3.75–$14.93); dinner appetizers £3.50–£7.50 ($5.25–$11.25); dinner main courses £7.95–£16.95 ($11.83–$25.43). AE, DC, MC, V.
Open: Apr and Oct, Wed–Sun lunch noon–4pm and dinner 6–10pm; May–Sept, daily lunch noon–4pm and dinner 6–10pm. **Closed:** Nov–Mar.

It's worth a trip to Waterville just to dine at this contemporary restaurant on the shores of Ballinskelligs Bay. The Huntsman has sweeping picture-window vistas of the Atlantic and a welcoming decor of plush red-cushioned seating, wrought-iron fixtures, and lots of leafy plants. The menu concentrates on using the freshest of the local catch, including Skellig lobster and Kenmare Bay scampi, but also offers a wide choice of meat dishes, such as Chateaubriand, rack of lamb, Irish stew, and seasonal pheasant, rabbit, and duck. Daytime fare includes burgers, omelets, stews, goulash, and pastas, as well as seafood salads and platters.

★ **Loaves & Fishes,** Caherdaniel, Co. Kerry. ☎ **066/75273.**
Cuisine: INTERNATIONAL. **Reservations:** Required.
Prices: Appetizers £2–£5.75 ($3–$8.63), main courses £11.75–£13.90 ($17.63–$20.85). MC, V.
Open: Easter to May and Sept, Wed–Sun 7–10pm; June–Aug, Tues–Sun 7–10pm. *Note:* in the summer, there are usually two seatings, at 7pm and 9:30pm.

Run by the award-winning team of Helen Mullane and Armel White, this shopfront restaurant consists of two small rooms, with a homey decor of knotty pine furniture, shelves lined with books, and candlelight. The menu changes often but can include dishes such as steamed breast of chicken with a wild mushroom sauce; pan-fried goujons of monkfish with a warm red-currant vinaigrette; prime filet of beef with a soft garlic sauce; and pan-roasted breast of duck with a pink peppercorn and port sauce; as well as fish of the day and lobster from the tank.

The Smuggler's Inn, Cliff Road, Waterville, Co. Kerry. ☎ **066/74330.**
Cuisine: SEAFOOD. **Reservations:** Recommended for dinner.
Prices: Lunch/snack items £1.95–£11 ($2.93–$16.50); dinner appetizers £2.20–£6.50 ($3.30–$9.75); dinner main courses £11.95–£16 ($17.93–$24). AE, MC, V.
Open: Mar–Oct, daily lunch noon–2:30pm, dinner 6–10pm.

Positioned a mile north of the town along the Ballinskelligs Bay beach, this renovated farmhouse is across the road from the entrance to the Waterville Golf Course. As could be expected, the decor is nautical, with fine sea and beach views from the dining room windows. The menu offers the freshest of seafood with dishes such as seatrout in capers and lemon butter; Ballinskelligs Bay black sole; Valencia scallops au gratin; sweet seafood curry; lobster from the tank; seafood brochettes; and steaks.

Moderate/Inexpensive

$ **Packie's,** Henry Street, Kenmare, Co. Kerry. ☎ **064/41508.**
Cuisine: IRISH. **Reservations:** Recommended.
Prices: Appetizers £1.80–£4.90 ($2.70–$7.35), main courses £4.90–£12.90 ($7.35–$19.85). MC, V.
Open: Easter to mid–Nov, Mon–Sat 5:30–10pm.

With windowboxes full of colorful seasonal plantings, this informal, bistro-style restaurant exudes a welcoming atmosphere. It's in the middle of town. The interior has a slate floor, stone walls, dark oak tables and chairs. On the walls is a collection of wonderful contemporary Irish art. On the menu are tried-and-true favorites—Irish stew and rack of lamb. Also offered are creative combinations such as gratin of crab and prawns; scallops in vermouth; beefburgers with green peppercorns, cream, and brandy sauce; breast of chicken in fruity curry sauce with lemongrass; beef braised in Guinness with mushrooms; and blackboard fish specials. Chef/owner Maura Foley uses herbs from her own garden to enhance each dish.

Red Fox Inn, Ring of Kerry Road (N 71), Ballycleave, Glenbeigh, Co. Kerry.
☎ **066/69184.**
Cuisine: IRISH. **Reservations:** Recommended for dinner.
Prices: Appetizers £1.60–£5.50 ($2.40–$8.25); main courses £4.95–£9.50 ($7.43–$14.25). No credit cards.
Open: Daily lunch noon–3pm, dinner 6–9pm.

Situated adjacent to the Kerry Bog Museum, this restaurant has an old Kerry cottage atmosphere, with open turf fireplaces, family heirloom pictures on the walls, and local memorabilia. There are picnic tables outside for good weather dining. The menu includes hearty traditional dishes such as Irish stew, seafood pie, chicken and ham, leg of lamb, and steaks. In the summer (May–September), there is Irish ceili band entertainment Wednesday through Sunday from 9:30 to 11:30pm. Snacks are served all day in the bar.

The Vestry, Ring of Kerry Road (N 71), Templenoe, Kenmare, Co. Kerry.
☎ **064/41958.**
Cuisine: IRISH. **Reservations:** Recommended for dinner.
Prices: Bar snack/lunch items £2–£5 ($3–$7.50); dinner appetizers £2–£4.25 ($3–$6.38); dinner main courses £7.50–£12.90 ($11.25–$19.85). MC, V.
Open: Daily lunch/bar snacks 10am–5:30pm, dinner 6:30–10pm. MC, V.

As its name implies, this building is a former Church of Ireland edifice, constructed between 1790 and 1816, and in use for services until 1987. In 1993 it was tastefully converted into a restaurant, retaining many of its original decorations and fixtures. The menu offers dishes such as escalope of salmon with prawn sauce; monkfish with smoked salmon sauce; noisette of lamb with mushrooms and garlic tomato sauce; duck with black-cherry sauce; filet of pork with cider and pear sauce; and a variety of steaks. It is situated on Kenmare Bay about four miles west of Kenmare.

Inexpensive

Purple Heather, Henry Street, Kenmare, Co. Kerry. ☎ **064/41016.**

Cuisine: IRISH. **Reservations:** Not necessary.
Prices: All items £1.70–£7.95 ($2.55–$11.83). No credit cards.
Open: Mon–Sat 11am–7pm. **Closed:** Christmas week.

Situated in the heart of town, this dependable pub/restaurant is a great place to stop for a snack or light meal with a gourmet flair, such as wild smoked salmon or prawn salads, smoked trout pâté, vegetarian omelets, and Irish cheese platters, as well as homemade soups.

2 Tralee

20 miles NW of Killarney

GETTING THERE • By Plane   Aer Lingus operates daily nonstop flights from Dublin into Kerry County Airport, Farranfore, Co. Kerry (☎ **066/64644**), about 15 miles south of Tralee.

• By Bus   Buses from all parts of Ireland arrive daily at the Bus Eireann Depot, John Joe Sheehy Road, Tralee (☎ **066/23566**).

• By Train   Rail services from major cities into Tralee arrive at the Irish Rail Station, John Joe Sheehy Road, Tralee (☎ **066/23522**).

• By Car   Four major national roads converge on Tralee, N 69 and N 21 from Limerick and the north, N 70 from the Ring of Kerry and points south, and N22 from Killarney, Cork, and the east.

GETTING AROUND   The best way to get around Tralee's downtown area is to walk. If you prefer to take a taxi, call Speedy Cabs, 4 Bridge Place, Tralee (☎ **27411**) or Kingdom Cabs, Boherbee, Tralee (☎ **066/27828**).

TOURIST INFORMATION   The Tralee Tourist Office, Ashe Memorial Hall, Denny Street, Tralee (☎ **066/21288**), offers information on Tralee and the Dingle Peninsula. It is open year-round from Monday to Friday from 9am to 6pm and on Saturday from 9am to 1pm, with extended hours in the summer season. There is also a first-rate cafe on the premises.

Fast Facts: Tralee

Area Code   The area code for most numbers in the Tralee area is **066.**

Drugstore   Kelly's Chemist, The Mall, Tralee (☎ **21302**).

Dry Cleaning and Laundry   The Laundry, Pembroke Street, Tralee (☎ **23214**), and True Care Dry Cleaners, 3 High St. (☎ **23245**).

Hospital   Bon Secours Hospital, Strand Street, Tralee (☎ **21966**), and Tralee General Hospital, Killarney Road (N 22), Tralee (☎ **26222**).

Library   County Kerry Library, Moydewell Road, Tralee (☎ **21200**).

Newspapers and Local Media   The weekly newspaper, *The Kerryman,* covers all local events. The local radio station, Radio Kerry/97FM, broadcasts from Park View, Tralee (☎ **23666**).

Police   Garda Station, off High Street, Tralee (☎ **22022**).

Photographic Supplies   Kennelly's One Hour Photo, 6 Castle St. (☎ **21042**).

The gateway to the Dingle Peninsula, Tralee (pronounced "Trah-lee") is the chief town of County Kerry. Its population of 22,000 is twice that of Killarney. The town lies in the center of a rich limestone farm belt known as the Vale of Tralee.

Dating back more than 800 years, Tralee was prominent during the Middle Ages as headquarters of the powerful Desmond Geraldines. Perhaps Tralee's greatest claim to fame, however, is that it served as inspiration for the song, "The Rose of Tralee," composed by local resident William Mulchinock more than 100 years ago.

Consequently, Tralee is now the setting for the Rose of Tralee Festival, the country's largest annual festival. It's the permanent home of the National Folk Theatre of Ireland, Siamsa Tire.

The harbor of Tralee is located four miles northwest of the town, at Fenit. A major sailing center, Fenit is the spot where St. Brendan the Navigator was born in 484, it's said. Brendan is credited with sailing the Atlantic in a leather boat and discovering America long before Columbus.

WHAT TO SEE & DO

★ **Kerry the Kingdom,** Ashe Memorial Hall, Denny Street, Tralee. ☎ **27777.**

One of Ireland's largest indoor heritage centers, the Kingdom offers three separate attractions that give an in-depth look at 7,000 years of life in County Kerry. *Kerry in Colour* is a 10-minute video that presents the sea- and landscapes of Kerry. With interactive and hands-on exhibits, the Kerry County Museum chronologically examines the county's music, history, legends, and archaeology. The exhibit on Gaelic football is quite unique. Many items of local origin that were previously on view at the National Museum in Dublin are now here. Complete with lighting effects and aromas, Geraldine Tralee is a theme park–style ride through a recreation of Tralee's streets, houses, and abbeys during the Middle Ages.

Admission: £3.90 adults ($5.85); £2.20 ($3.30) children.

Open: Daily Mar–Oct 10am–6pm; Nov–Dec 2–5pm; closed in Jan–Feb.

Blennerville Windmill, R. 559, Blennerville, Co. Kerry. ☎ **21064.**

Located just three miles west of Tralee and reaching 65 feet into the sky, this landmark mill is the largest working windmill in Ireland and Britain. Built in 1800 by Sir Rowland Blennerhasset, it flourished until 1850. After decades of neglect, it was restored in the early 1990s and is now fully operational, producing five tons of ground wholemeal flour per week. The visitor complex has an emigration exhibition center, an audio-visual theater, craft workshops, and a café.

Admission: £2.50 adults ($3.75), £2 ($3) seniors and students, £1.50 ($2.25) children over 5.

Open: Apr–Oct Mon–Sat 10am–6pm, Sun 11am–6pm.

★ **Tralee Steam Railway,** Ballyard, Tralee. ☎ **28888.**

Europe's most westerly railway, this restored steam train offers two-mile narrated scenic trips from Tralee's Ballyard Station to Blennerville. It uses equipment that was once a part of the Tralee & Dingle Light Railway (1891–1953), one of the world's most famous narrow-gauge railways. Trains run on the hour from Tralee and on the half-hour from Blennerville.

Fare: £2.50 adults ($3.75); £1.50 children ($2.25).

Schedule: April Sun 11am–5:30pm, May and Sept daily noon–5:30pm, June–Aug daily 11am–5:30pm. Closed on 2nd Mon of each month for maintenance.

Sightseeing Tours

During July and August, **Tralee Tourism,** Ostendia, Oakpark, Tralee (☎ 28077) sponsors guided walks around Tralee—taking in the local churches, the Square, Market Lane, Ashe Hall, Siamsa Tire, the Town Park, and principal streets. Departures are from the Brandon Hotel nightly at 7:45pm and at other times by appointment; duration 1 hour and 15 minutes and the cost is £1 ($1.50) adult 50p (75¢) students.

SPORTS & RECREATION

Spectator Sports

HORSE-RACING   Horse-racing takes place twice a year (in early June and late August) at Ballybeggan Park, Racecourse Road, Tralee (☎ 26188). Post time is usually 2:30pm. Admission is £7 ($10.50) adults, £3.50 ($5.25) seniors and students, and free for children under 14.

DOG RACING   Greyhounds race year round on Tuesday and Friday nights from 8pm at the Kingdom Greyhound Racing Track, Oakview, Brewery Road, Tralee (☎ 24033). Admission is £3 ($4.50) per person including program.

Recreation

GOLF   Like its neighbor Killarney, Tralee is great golfing turf, particularly at the **Tralee Golf Club,** Fenit/Churchill Road, West Barrow, Ardfert (☎ 36379). Overlooking the Atlantic eight miles northwest of Tralee, this was the first Arnold Palmer–designed golf course in Europe. One of Ireland's newer courses, it's expected in time to rank among the great courses of the world. Greens fees are £25 ($37.50) on weekdays and £30 ($45) on weekends.

About 25 miles north of Tralee in the northwest corner of County Kerry is the famous **Ballybunion Golf Club,** Ballybunion, Co. Kerry (☎ 068/27146). This facility offers visitors the chance to play on two challenging 18-hole seaside links, both on the cliffs overlooking the Shannon River estuary and the Atlantic. The "old" course is rated by Tom Watson as one of the finest in the world, while the "new" one was designed by Robert Trent Jones, Sr. Greens fees are £20 ($30) on the New Course, £30 ($45) on the Old Course, or £40 ($60) to play both courses.

HORSEBACK RIDING   If you'd like to see the Tralee sights from horseback, you can hire a horse from **El Rancho Riding Stables,** Ballyard, Tralee (☎ 21840) or **Kennedy's Equine Centre,** Caherwisheen, Tralee (☎ 26453). Prices start at £10 ($15) per hour for one- or two-hour rides. Both places also offer extended three-day or one-week trail rides.

WHERE TO STAY

Moderate

Abbey Gate Hotel, Maine St., Tralee, Co. Kerry. ☎ **066/29888.** Fax 066/29821. 100 rms (all with bath). TV TEL

Rates (including full breakfast): £32–£90 ($48–$135) single; £56–£90 ($84–$135) double. No service charge. AE, DC, MC, V.

Scheduled to open early in 1995, this modern three-story property is the first new hotel to open in Tralee for many years. It brings some much-needed quality accommodations and a broader dimension of social activity to the center of town. The guest rooms, like the public areas, are furnished new reproductions and fabrics, art, and accessories that convey an air of Georgian/Victorian Tralee. The Vineyard Restaurant has a decorative theme that matches its name, and the Old Market Place Bar is a convenient place to have a pint of Guinness. The hotel is ideally located within walking distance of Tralee's prime attractions, shops, and pubs.

Ballyseede Castle Hotel, Tralee/Killarney Road, Tralee, Co. Kerry. ☎ **066/35799** or toll free **800/223-5695** in U.S. Fax 066/25287. 12 rms (all with bath). TV TEL

Rates: £35–£60 ($52.50–$90) single, £55–£113 ($82.50–$169.50) double. Service charge 12.5%. MC, V.

What's a castle without a resident ghost roaming the halls? Well, that's what they ask you at this 15th-century, multi-turreted, four-story castle. Ballyseede Castle was once the chief garrison of the legendary Fitzgeralds, the Earls of Desmond. Later the Blennerhassett family occupied it until 1966. In 1985, it was turned into a hotel. The lobby has Doric columns and a hand-carved oak staircase. Decorated with cornices of ornamental plasterwork, two drawing rooms are warmed by marble fireplaces. Residents feel like royalty in the elegant bedrooms and in the Regency Restaurant, with its huge oil paintings and fabric-lined walls. A library and piano lounge are open to guests. And we mustn't forget the ghost. The castle and ghost are two miles east of Tralee, on 30 acres of parkland.

★ **Brandon,** Princes Street, Tralee, Co. Kerry. ☎ **066/23333** or toll free in the U.S. **800/44-UTELL** in U.S. Fax 066/25019. 158 rms (all with bath). TV TEL

Rates (including full breakfast): £30–£90 ($45–135) single, £56–£98 ($84–$147) double. No service charge. AE, DC, MC, V. **Closed:** Dec 23–28.

Named for nearby Mount Brandon, this is a modern and dependable five-story hotel at the west edge of town, with vistas of the Dingle Peninsula in the distance. There is nothing unique about the guest rooms, but they are functional and well kept. The facilities include the Galleon restaurant, a coffee shop, two bars, and a leisure center with indoor heated swimming pool, sauna, steam room, and gym. Best of all, the hotel is just a block from the National Folk Theatre and tourist office, and within easy strolling distance of all the shops and downtown restaurants. Convenience is its forte.

Inexpensive

Ballygarry House, Tralee/Killarney Road, Leebrook, Tralee, Co. Kerry. ☎ **066/21233.** Fax 066/27630. 16 rms (all with bath). TV TEL

Rates (including full breakfast): £50–£60 ($75–$90) single or double. Service charge 10%. AE, MC, V.

Located one mile south of town, this country inn is on the edge of a residential neighborhood, surrounded by well-tended gardens and sheltering trees. Recently updated, the bedrooms vary in size; each is individually furnished and decorated to reflect different aspects of County Kerry, with names on the doorways that characterize the interiors, such as Arbutus, Muckross, Valentia, or Slea Head. The public areas have a horsey theme, with pictures of prize-winning thoroughbreds, horse brass, and other equestrian touches. Amenities include the Monarchs restaurant and old-world–style lounge bar.

WHERE TO DINE
Moderate

The Tankard, Kilfenora, Fenit. ☎ 066/36164.
Cuisine: SEAFOOD/IRISH. **Reservations:** Recommended.
Prices: Appetizers £1.80–£6.50 ($2.70–$9.75); main courses £7.50–£13.95 ($11.25–$20.93). AE, DC, MC, V.
Open: Dinner daily 6–10pm.

Located six miles northwest of Tralee, this is one of the few restaurants in the area that capitalizes on sweeping views of Tralee Bay. Situated right on the water's edge, it is outfitted with wide picture windows and a sleek contemporary decor. The straightforward menu primarily features local shellfish and seafood such as lobster, scallops, prawns, and black sole, as well as rack of lamb, duck, quail, and a variety of steaks. Bar food is available all day, but this restaurant is at its best in the early evening, especially at sunset.

⭐ **The Tilley Lamp,** 14 Princes St., Tralee. ☎ 21300.
Cuisine: INTERNATIONAL. **Reservations:** Recommended.
Prices: Appetizers £1.50–£5.50 ($2.25–$8.25); lunch main courses £3.25–£5.95 ($4.88–$8.93); dinner main courses £8.95–£12.50 ($13.43–$18.75).
Open: Daily lunch 12:30–2:30pm and dinner 6:30–10pm.

Situated in town just a few doors west of the Brandon Hotel in a row of Georgian town houses, this homey basement restaurant is known for its innovative cooking and decor of stone walls and light woods, enhanced by modern art and pink linens. The specialties include kebab of beef, lamb, and chicken; filet of duck with strawberry and green pepper sauce; char-grilled filet of lamb with light garlic cream sauce; chicken Scandinavian, breasts filled with smoked ham, Danish blue cheese, bread crumbs, almonds, and poppy and caraway seeds, in a tarragon sauce, as well as steaks, seafood, and vegetarian dishes.

Moderate/Inexpensive

💲 **Fuchsia,** 14 Russell St., Tralee. ☎ 28170.
Cuisine: INTERNATIONAL. **Reservations:** Recommended.
Prices: Appetizers £1.50–£3.95 ($2.25–$5.93); lunch main courses £2.75–£4.95 ($4.13–$7.43); dinner main courses £7.50–£9.50 ($11.25–$14.25). MC, V.
Open: Mon–Sat, morning coffee 10am–noon; lunch noon–6pm, dinner 6–10pm.

Situated in the heart of town just off The Mall, this modern shopfront restaurant has a contemporary decor of bold salmon-colored walls, floral art, and candlelight. The menu is known for its innovative sauces and stuffings, including dishes such as roast poussin stuffed with pistachio nuts in a red wine sauce; pan-fried duck breast in a strawberry and passion fruit sauce; tagliatelle of seafood with tomato and Pernod sauce; noisette of lamb with mushroom and brandy sauce; filet of salmon baked in tomato and tarragon sauce, and steaks. Lunch choices include crêpes, pasta, steak sandwiches, and seafood salads.

EVENING ENTERTAINMENT

Tralee is the home of Siamsa Tire, the National Folk Theatre of Ireland; it's located at Town Park, Tralee (☎ 23055). Founded in 1974, Siamsa (pronounced Sheem-sha) offers a mixture of music, dance, and mime. The various programs focus on three different themes—Fado Fado/The Long Ago, Sean Agus Nua/Myth and Motion, and Ding Dong Dedero/Forging the Dance. The scenes depict old folk tales and farmyard activities, such as thatching a cottage roof, flailing sheaves of corn, and twisting a sugan rope.

In addition to these folk theater entertainments, Siamsa presents a full program of drama and musical concerts (from traditional to classical) performed by visiting amateur and professional companies. Admission is £8 ($12) for adults, £6 ($9) for seniors and children. The schedule is Tuesday, Thursday, and Saturday in May; Monday, Tuesday, Thursday, and Saturday in June and September; and Monday through Saturday in July and August; curtain time is 8:30pm. The schedule in October through April varies.

PUBS

An Blascaod (The Blasket Inn), Castle Street, Tralee. ☎ 23313.

Named for the Blasket Islands, this pub has a lovely modern facade and interior using a stark red and black color scheme. The inside includes a two-story atrium with an open fireplace, plus shelves lined with old books and plates.

Harty's Lounge Bar, Castle Street, Tralee. ☎ 25385.

This pub is celebrated as the original meetinghouse where the Rose of Tralee festival was born. It is also known for its traditional pub grub such as steak and kidney pie, shepherd's pie, and Irish stew.

Kirby's Brogue Inn, Rock Street, Tralee. ☎ 22126.

This pub has a barnlike layout, with an interior that incorporates agricultural instruments, farming memorabilia, and rushwork tables and chairs. Good pub grub is served.

Oyster Tavern, Fenit Road, Spa, Tralee. ☎ 36102.

The nicest location of any pub in the Tralee area belongs to this tavern, just three miles west of downtown, overlooking Tralee Bay. The pub grub available includes seafood soups and platters.

3 The Dingle Peninsula

Dingle Town is 30 miles W of Tralee and 50 miles NW of Killarney

GETTING THERE • By Bus   Bus Eireann (☎ 066/23566) provides daily coach service to Dingle from all parts of Ireland. The boarding and drop-off point is on Upper Main Street.

• **By Car**   From Tralee to Dingle, follow R. 559, or take R. 561 from Castlemaine.

GETTING AROUND • By Public Transport   Dingle Town has no local bus service, although Bus Eireann (☎ 066/23566) provides service from Dingle to other towns on the peninsula. For local taxi transport, contact Moran's Taxis (☎ 066/51155).

• **By Foot**   The best way to get around Dingle Town, with its narrow, winding, or hilly streets, is to walk. The town is small and compact and easy to get to know.

• **By Car**   To see the sights beyond the town, you will need to drive westward along R. 559 or to take one of the sightseeing tours suggested below.

TOURIST INFORMATION   The Dingle Tourist Office is located on Main Street, Dingle (☎ 066/51188). It is open seasonally, usually from early April through October.

Fast Facts: The Dingle Peninsula

Area Code   The area code for most Dingle numbers is **066**.

Hospital   Dingle District Hospital, Upper Main Street, Dingle (☎ **51455**).

Library   Dingle District Library, Green Street, Dingle (☎ **51499**).

Local Newspapers and Media   "In & About Dingle Peninsula" is a newspaper-style publication, distributed free at hotels, restaurants, shops, and at the tourist office. It lists events, attractions, activities, and more.

Police   Garda Station, Holy Ground, Dingle (☎ **51522**).

WHAT TO SEE & DO

Similar to the Ring of Kerry, the Dingle Peninsula conveys a more rugged and remote beauty. The movie *Ryan's Daughter,* which won rave reviews for its scenery, was filmed here.

You can enter the Dingle Peninsula from Castlemaine or Tralee. The preferred route is via the Camp Road from Tralee, which travels along Tralee Bay, with the Slieve Mish Mountains rising on your left. Narrower than the Ring of Kerry, the peninsula reaches about 40 miles out into the sea and requires about 100 miles of slow and sometimes tedious driving to see it all—but it will be a day to be remembered long afterward.

From Camp, the road hugs the shore and you can see vistas of Brandon Mountain, Ireland's second highest mountain, named for the navigator saint. Follow the signs for Connor Pass, a spectacular drive through the mountains that reaches a height of 1500 feet. On a clear day, you can enjoy views of Tralee Bay, north Kerry, and the mouth of the Shannon as it meets the Atlantic. Rising steeply, the road covers a panorama of rocky mountain slopes and cliffs, including one point named Faill na Seamrog, "the shamrock cliff." The final descent will bring you to the sheltered fishing port of Dingle.

With a charter dating back many centuries, Dingle was the principal harbor in County Kerry during medieval times. Even though it's just a small town (population 1,500), Dingle has more fine restaurants than many of Ireland's major cities, rivaling Kinsale as a gourmet enclave.

Beyond Dingle are a trio of remote towns—Ventry, Dunquin, and Ballyferriter—where Irish (or Gaelic) is the spoken language. A lay-by at Slea Head overlooks a mountainous curve at the end of the peninsula; it's been the setting for many a picture postcard and sea-splashed landscape painting. From Slea Head, you can usually get a good view of the seven Blasket Islands sitting out in the Atlantic. Until the 1950s the largest of these, the Great Blasket, was inhabited.

East of Ballyferriter is Gallarus Oratory, one of the best preserved early Christian church buildings in Ireland. With a shape much like an overturned boat, it's constructed of unmortared stone, yet completely watertight after more than 1,000 years.

After Ballyferriter, the road returns inland to Dingle town. From here, take the R 561 route eastward along Dingle Bay through the villages of Lispole and Annascaul to Inch, one of Dingle's most beautiful seascapes. This is a four-mile stretch of sandy beach, with distant views of the Ring of Kerry and Killarney. From Inch, return via Camp to Tralee or continue to Castlemaine and onward to Limerick or other parts of Kerry and Cork.

Before leaving the Dingle coast, inquire about Fungie, the adult male bottlenosed dolphin that swam solo into the waters of Dingle harbor in 1984 and has remained—until the time of this writing—frolicking off the coast. No one knows where he came from, how long he will stay, or even how old he is. He shows great interest in boats and regularly swims alongside them. Showing great sensitivity and gentleness, he interacts with people in the water.

⭐ **Ionad An Bhlascaoid Mhoir/The Blasket Centre,** Dunquin, Co. Kerry. ☎ 56371.

This newly opened T-shaped heritage center is perched on the westerly tip of the Dingle Peninsula. It overlooks the Atlantic waters and the distant vistas of the remote Blasket Islands. The Great Blasket was once an outpost of Irish civilization and nurturing ground for a small group of great Irish-language writers. Its inhabitants abandoned the island in 1953. Through a series of displays, exhibits, and a video presentation, this center celebrates the cultural and literary traditions of the Blasket Islands and the history of Corca Dhuibhne, the Gaeltacht area. This center also has a research room, a bookshop specializing in local literature, and a wide-windowed restaurant with views of the Blaskets.

Admission: £2 ($3) adults, £1.50 ($2.25) seniors, £1 ($1.50) children and students.

Open: Easter–Sept, daily 10am–6pm.

⭐ **Ceardlann Na Coille,** The Wood, Dingle. ☎ 51797.

Just west of the Dingle Marina, this cluster of traditional cottages is a circular craft village, set on a hillside above the town and harbor. Each workshop is staffed by a local craftworker who produces and sells his or her craft. Knitwear, feltworks, leather goods, handweaving, and woodturning are offered. A café on the premises serves excellent homemade soups, salads, and hot dishes.

Admission: Free.

Open: Daily 10am–6pm.

Fionan Ferries Ltd., The Marina, Dingle. ☎ 76306.

This company operates cruises across Dingle Bay via the 175-passenger *Fionan of Skellig,* from Dingle to Valentia and Caherciveen on the Ring of Kerry. The route passes the storied Skellig Islands, with an opportunity to visit the Skellig Experience at Valentia (see "Ring of Kerry," above).

Fare: Cruise only £10 ($15); cruise with Skellig Experience £20 ($30).

Schedule: June–Aug, Tues–Thurs and Sat–Sun. Departure times vary.

Sightseeing Tours

Sciuird Tours, Holy Ground, Dingle. ☎ 51937.

These archaeological tours, lasting 2 to 3 hours, are led by a local expert. They involve a short bus journey and some easy walking. Four or five monuments from the Stone Age to medieval times are visited. All tours start from the top of the Pier. Reservations suggested.

Price: £5 ($7.50) per person.

Schedule: May–Sept, daily 11am, 2pm, and 5pm.

Celtic Nature Expeditions, The Old Stone House, Claddaun, Dingle. ☎ 59882.

This company offers guided nature walks over Dingle's less traveled paths, from quiet green roads to the ancient boreens. Walks take about 2¹/₂ hours, and each guide is well versed in 4,000 years of Dingle history. All walks start and finish at the Ventry Inn, five miles west of Dingle town. Reservations suggested.

Price: £5 ($7.50) per person, free for children under 12.

Schedule: May–Sept, daily; call in advance for exact departure times.

★ Fungie The Dolphin Tours, The Pier, Dingle. ☎ 51967.

Visitors are ferried out into the nearby waters, via fishing boats, to see the famous Dingle dolphin, Fungie. Trips last about one hour and depart on the hour.

Fare: £5 ($7.50) adults, £2.50 ($3.75) children under 12.

Schedule: Year-round daily 10am–5pm.

Hidden Ireland Tours, Dingle. ☎ 066/51868.

Con Moriarty, a local exponent of active travel, conducts a variety of walking tours around the cliff walks, hills, mountains, woods, and lakelands of Dingle. Commentaries on local history, archaeology, folklore, and culture are given. Participants are advised to bring sturdy footwear and rain/wind-proof clothing. Tours can also be custom-designed for those who prefer to travel by bike or car. Reservations necessary.

Prices: £10–£35 ($15–$52.50) depending on tour.

Schedule: May–Sept, daily half-day walks from 9:30am–1:30pm and 2–6pm; full day walks from 10am–5pm.

Moran's Slea Head Tours, Moran's Garage, Mail Road, Dingle. ☎ 51129.

This narrated three-hour coach tour of the Dingle Peninsula covers all the highlights—from views of Slea Head, the Blasket Islands, and the Skellig Rocks to Coumeenole, the location for the film *Ryan's Daughter*, as well as old forts and beehive huts.

Price: £6 ($9) per person.

Schedule: June and Sept daily 2:15pm; July–Aug daily 10:15am and 2:15pm.

SPORTS & RECREATION

BICYCLING Dingle is ideal territory for bicycling, along the bay and in the hillsides. Rentals cost £5 ($7.50) per day or £25 ($37.50) per week. Touring bikes are available, as are mountain bikes. To rent a bike, contact **John J. Moriarty,** Main Street, Dingle (☎ 51316), open year-round; or **An Siopa Rothar,** Dykegate Street, Dingle (no phone), open April through September.

GOLF Situated ten miles west of Dingle town on the western edge of the Dingle Peninsula overlooking the waters of the Atlantic, the **Dingle Golf Club** (Golf Chumann Ceann Sibeal), Ballyferriter (☎ 56255) welcomes visitors to play its 18-hole par-72 course. Greens fees are £18 ($24) per round.

HORSEBACK RIDING **Thompson's Horse Riding Centre,** Dunquin, Co. Kerry (☎ 56144) offers trails rides along beaches and through the coastal and mountain scenery of the Dingle Peninsula's western edge. An hour's ride averages £10 ($15).

SAILING Sailing the beautiful waters of Dingle Bay is a relaxing way to enjoy the coastline. John Doyle, 3 John Street, Dingle (☎ 51174) offers skippered sailing trips from Dingle Marina on board his 32-foot sailing cruiser, *Canna.* The price is £60 ($90) for a half-day and £120 ($180) for a full day, for up to four persons. All cruises are dependent on the weather and advance reservations are required.

Capt. Michael O'Connor, The Old Stone House, Cliddaun, Dingle (☎ 59882) offers seven-hour trips from the Marina on board the *Kimberly Laura,* a 41-foot cutter-rigged sailing yacht. The price is £40 ($60) per person including lunch and snacks, for up to eight persons. Reservations are required.

SWIMMING WITH A DOLPHIN   The prime watersport in Dingle Bay is to swim with the resident dolphin, known as Fungie. Although Fungie can swim about 25 mph, he is happy to slow down and romp at slower speeds in the waters with human visitors. To arrange a dolphin encounter, contact **Seventh Wave,** Milltown, Slea Head Road, Dingle (☎ **51548**). This ecologically attuned company will advise and outfit you in preparation for a dolphin encounter. You can rent a wet-suit, mask, snorkel, foot fins, and holdall for £9 ($13.50) for three hours or £14 ($21) overnight. The office, which is open year-round daily from 10am–2pm and 3–6pm, also includes an exhibition center on dolphins and whales and their place in our environment.

WALKING   Walking in Dingle town and along the nearby beaches is popular with visitors. For those who seek a sign-posted long-distance path into the hills and hinter-lands, there is the Dingle Way/Sli Corcha Duibhne, a 100-mile route around the entire peninsula. The walk actually begins in Tralee and continues via Inch and Annascaul to Dingle Town, followed by Ventry, Slea Head, Ballyferriter, and then back to Tralee via Cloghane, Castlegregory and Killelton. The route traverses paths and unsurfaced roads, passing panoramic scenery and a wealth of archaeological and historical sites. A leaflet outlining the walk is available at the Dingle or Tralee tourist office.

SAVVY SHOPPING

Annascaul Pottery, Green Street Courtyard, off Green Street, Dingle. ☎ **57186.**

Colorful locally made pottery and ceramics, with wildflower designs, are on sale here, in all sizes and shapes, including jewelry. Open daily Easter through October from 10:30am to 6pm. The factory at nearby Annascaul is open year-round.

Brian De Staic, The Wood, Dingle, ☎ **51298.**

Considered by many as Ireland's leading goldsmith, Brian de Staic plys his trade in his workshop, located just west of the Dingle Pier. He specializes in unusual Irish jew-elry, hand-crafted and engraved with the letters of the Ogham alphabet, an ancient Irish form of writing dating back to the 3rd century. The collection includes pendants, bracelets, earrings, cuff links, brooches, and tie clips. There are two other retail shops: Green Street, Dingle (☎ **51298**) and 18 High St., Killarney (☎ **064/33822**). Open: Nov–May, Mon–Sat 9am–6pm; June–Oct, daily 9am–6pm.

Green Lane Gallery, Green Street, Dingle. ☎ **066/51013.**

This gallery/shop offers a wide selection of modern painting and sculpture created by local artists. Open daily 11am–7pm.

★ **Holden Leathergoods/Sparan Sioda** (The Silk Purse), Main Street, Dingle, Co. Kerry. ☎ **066/51896.**

Established in 1989 by Jackie and Conor Holden, this shop offers beautiful hand-crafted leather handbags lined with suede and silk pockets; suede and leather pouches; and duffel and travel bags, as well as briefcases, belts, wallets, key cases, and billfolds. Visitors are also welcome to visit their workshop in a converted schoolhouse, four miles west of town on the Ventry Road (R 559), Baile an Ghoilin, Dingle Harbour (☎ **066/51796**). Open Easter to May, Monday to Saturday 9:30am to 6pm and Sunday, noon to 5pm; June, Monday–Saturday 9am to 7pm, Sunday 11am to 6pm; July–August, Monday–Saturday, 9am to 9pm, Sunday 11am to 6pm; September through March, Monday to Saturday 10am to 6pm.

Leac A Re, Strand Street, Dingle. ☎ **51138.**

The dolphin arts and crafts in the window of this shop began to attract customers even before a sign was put up (at presstime, there is still no name over the door). In addition to dolphin-related items, it offers a unique array of local crafts, from woolens and blankets to pottery and posters. There is a local specialty footwarmer known as "The Brandon sock."

⭐ **Lisbeth Mulcahy/The Weavers' Shop,** Green Street, Dingle. ☎ **066/51688.**

One of Ireland's leading weavers, Lisbeth creates fabrics and tapestries inspired by seasonal changes in the Irish land- and seascape. Pure Irish wool, linen/cotton, and alpaca are used in the weaving of scarves, shawls, and knee rugs, as well as wall hangings, tapestries, tablemats, and napkins. Open October through May, Monday to Saturday 9am to 6pm; July and August, Monday to Friday 9am to 8pm, and Saturday and Sunday 10am to 8pm.

Louis Mulcahy Pottery, Clogher, Ballyferriter, Co. Kerry. ☎ **066/56229.**

Located north of Dunquin, this is a working pottery studio, producing a range of pottery made from local clay and glazes devised at the shop. The finished products include vases, teapots, and platters. Local weavings and other crafts are also for sale. Hours vary with the seasons.

WHERE TO STAY

Moderate

Benner's Hotel, Main Street, Dingle, Co. Kerry. ☎ **066/51638.** Fax 066/51412. 25 rms (all with bath). TV TEL

Rates (including full breakfast): £33–£42 ($49.50–$63) single, £56–£90 ($84–$135) double. Service charge 10%. AE, DC, MC, V.

One of the few hostelries that is open year-round, this hotel is in the heart of town. The lovely Georgian doorway with fanlight at the front entrance sets the tone for guests checking in. The hotel is a blend of old world charm with modern comforts. Dating back over 250 years and totally updated in recent years, it is furnished with Irish antique pine furniture throughout, including four-poster beds and armoires in the guest rooms. Facilities include a restaurant with tall and wide-paned windows overlooking a walled garden, and two bars including the Boston Bar.

Dingle Sceilig (Ostan Na Sceilge), Annascaul Road, Dingle, Co. Kerry. ☎ **066/51144** or toll free **800/528-1234.** Fax 066/51501. 100 rms (all with bath). TV TEL

Rates (including full breakfast): £45–£55 ($67.50–$82.50) single, £70–£90 ($105–$135) double. Service charge 10%. AE, DC, MC, V. **Closed:** Mid–Nov to mid–Mar.

Named for the fabled Sceilig Rocks off the coast, this modern three-story hotel enjoys an idyllic location next to Dingle Bay on the eastern edge of town. Expanded and totally refurbished in recent years by the Cluskey family, it has a pleasing facade with a mansard-like roof that fits well in the local panorama of mountain and sea. The public areas are decorated with Irish pine and brass touches. The guest rooms, with lovely views of the bay and countryside, are modern with light woods and pastel-toned fabrics and wall coverings.

Dining/Entertainment: The Coastguard Conservatory Restaurant and Gallarus Lounge both offer good views of Dingle Bay; the Bistro Restaurant serves bar food all day; and a nautical atmosphere pervades The Blaskets Bar.

Facilities: Indoor heated swimming pool, sauna, tennis court, snooker room, table tennis, guest laundry.

Moderate/Inexpensive

 Doyle's Townhouse, 5 John St., Dingle, Co. Kerry. ☎ **066/51174** or toll free **800/223-6510** in U.S. Fax 066/51816. 12 rms (all with bath). TV TEL

Rates (including full breakfast): £39 single ($58.50), single, £62 ($93) double. Service charge 10%. DC, MC, V. **Closed:** Mid–Nov to mid–Mar.

An outgrowth of the successful Doyle's Seafood Restaurant next door, this three-story guesthouse is our favorite Dingle hideaway. Designed to reflect an old-world ambience, it has a lovely Victorian fireplace in the main sitting room area and many of the antique fixtures date back 250 years or more. Period pieces and country pine predominate in the bedrooms, although the accoutrements are totally up-to-date, with semi-orthopedic beds, bathrooms of Italian marble, towel warmers, and hair dryer. Front rooms look out onto the town while the back rooms have either a balcony or patio and face a garden, with mountain vistas in the background. At presstime, a nearby building on the same street is being refurbished and fashioned into an "annex," adding four new suites that include a sitting area for each room.

Inexpensive

Bambury's Guest House, Mail Road, Dingle, Co. Kerry. ☎ **066/51244.** Fax 066/51786. 12 rms (all with bath). TV TEL

Rates (including full breakfast): £15–£28 ($22.50–$42) single, £26–£40 ($39–$60) double. No service charge. MC, V. **Closed:** Jan 1–12.

This lovely two-story pink-toned guesthouse stands out as you enter Dingle from the east. It has a modernized Tudor-style facade, with wide-paned windows. Guest rooms are bright and contemporary, with lovely views of the town or bay. It's an easy two-minute walk to the center of town.

$ **Barnagh Bridge Country Guesthouse,** Cappalough, Camp, Dingle, Co. Kerry. ☎ **066/30145.** Fax 066/30299. 5 rms. TEL

Rates (including full breakfast): £16–£20 ($24–$30) single, £32–£40 ($48–$60) double. No service charge. MC, V. **Closed:** Dec.

Opened in 1993, this stunning two-story modern house was purposely built as a guesthouse by the Williams family. It sits on a hillside overlooking Tralee Bay, almost equidistant between Tralee and Dingle, and an ideal touring base for those who prefer a country setting to a town. Each guest room is named and furnished with the theme and colors of flowers from the surrounding gardens, such as Fuschia, Blue Bell, Rose. Rooms have modern light wood furnishings, and most have views of the mountains and sea.

 Scanlons, Mail Road, Dingle, Co. Kerry. ☎ **066/51883.** Fax 066/51297. 7 rms (all with bath). TV TEL

Rates (including full breakfast): £25 ($37.50) single, £27–£40 ($40.50–$60) double. No service charge. AE, MC, V.
Open: Year-round.

Built and opened as a guesthouse five years ago by the Scanlon family, this lovely lodging is situated less than a mile east of Dingle town on a hill overlooking Dingle Bay and the surrounding countryside. The guest rooms, furnished in tones of pink and burgundy, offer every modern convenience, including in-room hairdryers. About half of the rooms face the bay and the rest have views of the gardens and mountains.

Budget

$ **Greenmount House,** John Street, Dingle, Co. Kerry. ☎ **066/51414.** 6 rms (all with bath). TV TEL

Rates (including full breakfast): £15–£18 ($22.50–$27) single, £30–£35 ($45–$52.50) double. No service charge. No credit cards. **Closed:** Last week of Dec.

Perched on a hill overlooking Dingle Bay and town, this modern bungalow-style bed-and-breakfast home is a standout in its category. It has all the comforts of a hotel at bargain prices, including bedrooms decorated with contemporary furnishings and public areas where a sitting room has an open fireplace and a sunlit conservatory is filled with plants. The breakfasts, ranging from smoked salmon omelets to ham-and-pineapple toasties, have garnered many an award for enthusiastic proprietors Mary and John Curran.

WHERE TO DINE

Expensive/Moderate

Beginish, Green Street, Dingle. ☎ **066/51588.**

Cuisine: SEAFOOD. **Reservations:** Recommended.
Prices: Appetizers £1.50–£6.50 ($2.25–$9.75); lunch main courses £3.50–£6.95 ($5.25–$10.35), dinner main courses £7.50–£14.50 ($11.25–$21.75). AE, DC, MC, V.
Open: Tues–Sun lunch 12:30–2:15pm, dinner 6–10pm. **Closed:** Mid–Nov to mid–Mar.

Situated in a Georgian town house in the heart of Dingle, this restaurant is named for one of the Blasket Islands off the coast, and the paintings on the walls show the seascapes that surround the island. There are two dining rooms, one a traditional room with a fireplace and the other a conservatory overlooking the back gardens. The varied menu offers dishes such as seafood à la nage (salmon, mussels, prawns, scallops, monkfish in Pernod-scented juice); black sole on the bone; escalope of wild salmon with tarragon sauce; mussels with almonds and garlic butter; potpourri of vegetables in pastry; breast of duck with honey and mustard; and filet of beef with cognac and grilled peppercorn sauce. For dessert, chef Pat Moore's hot rhubarb soufflé tart is legendary in these parts.

★ **Doyle's Seafood Bar,** 4 John St., Dingle. ☎ **51174.**
Cuisine: SEAFOOD. **Reservations:** Necessary.
Prices: Appetizers £2.90–£6.50 ($4.35–$9.75); main courses £10.90–£16 ($16.35–$24). DC, MC, V.
Open: Mon–Sat dinner 6–10pm. **Closed:** Mid–Nov to mid–Mar.

It is almost 25 years since John and Stella Doyle left Dublin and settled in Dingle to open the town's first seafood bar. With John meeting the fishing boats each morning and bringing in the best of the day's catch and Stella plying her culinary skills in the kitchen, this winning combination has achieved international acclaim and is the benchmark of all of Dingle's eateries.

The atmosphere is homey, with walls and floors of stone, sugan chairs, tweedy placemats, and old Dingle sketches. All the ingredients come either from the sea, the Doyles' own gardens, or nearby farms; and the Doyles also smoke their own salmon. Specialties include baked filet of lemon sole with prawn sauce; grilled mussels with garlic stuffing; baked filet of cod stuffed with crab and topped with mornay sauce; salmon filet with puff pastry with sorrel sauce; rack of lamb, crab claws beurre blanc; hot poached lobster; and a signature platter of seafood (sole, salmon, lobster, oysters, and crab claws). Don't miss Stella Doyle's scrumptious brown bread.

The Half Door, 3 John St., Dingle. ☎ **066/51600.**

Cuisine: SEAFOOD/INTERNATIONAL. **Reservations:** Recommended.
Prices: Appetizers £2.50–£6.75 ($3.75–$10.13); lunch main courses £5–£20 ($7.50–$30); dinner main courses £11–£20 ($16.50–$30). AE, DC, MC, V.
Open: Easter–Oct, Wed–Mon lunch 12:30–2:30pm, dinner 6–10pm. **Closed:** Nov–Easter.

Aptly named, with a traditional half-door at the entrance, this restaurant exudes a country cottage atmosphere, with exposed walls, low ceilings, arches, and vintage furnishings that include copper pots and an original stove, yet there is also a bright and airy conservatory at the back. The menu combines old and new, with dishes such as lobster thermidor; salmon en croûte; sautéed John Dory sole; filet of plaice in savory crust with mustard sauce; roast farm duck with honey and lime sauce; steamed mussels with garlic and cream; and a chilled shellfish platter of lobster, prawns, oysters, mussels, and crab.

★ **Lord Baker,** Main Street, Dingle. ☎ **51277.**
Cuisine: IRISH/SEAFOOD. **Reservations:** Suggested for dinner.
Prices: Bar food £1.50–£9.90 ($2.25–$14.85); appetizers £1.90–£6.90 ($2.85–$10.35), dinner main courses £9.90–£18.50 ($14.85–$27.75). AE, MC, V.
Open: Daily lunch 11:30am–2:30pm, dinner 6–10pm. **Closed:** Christmas.

Named after a 19th-century Dingle poet, politician, and publican, this restaurant is part of a building that is supposed to be the oldest pub in Dingle. The decor blends an old world stone fireplace and cozy alcoves with a sunlit conservatory and Art Deco touches. The menu offers bar food such as seafood salads, soups, and sandwiches, as well as crab claws or prawns in garlic butter, fried scampi, Kerry oysters, seafood Mornay, and steaks. The full dinner specialties include sole stuffed with smoked salmon and spinach in cheese sauce; lobster thermidor; hot seafood platter; black sole on the bone; or rack of lamb.

Moderate

Fenton's, Green Street, Dingle. ☎ **066/51209.**
Cuisine: INTERNATIONAL. **Reservations:** Recommended.
Prices: Appetizers £1.95–£5.95 ($2.93–$8.93); lunch main courses £3.50–£4.95 ($5.25–$7.43), dinner main courses £8.95–£13.95 ($13.43–$20.93). AE, DC, MC, V.
Open: Tues–Sun lunch 12:30–3:30pm, dinner 6–10pm. **Closed:** Nov to mid–Mar.

Situated in the heart of town, this restaurant combines a country cottage interior of pine furniture and stone walls with a bright and airy garden courtyard patio setting. The diverse menu offers dishes such as hot buttered lobster; mussels in garlic with white wine sauce; and seafood pasta; as well as pork, beef, and chicken satay with peanut dipping sauce; and médaillons of filet steak on a garlic croûte and topped with Cashel Bleu cheese.

Islandman, Main Street, Dingle. ☎ **51803.**

Cuisine: INTERNATIONAL. **Reservations:** Recommended.
Prices: Appetizers £1.95–£6.50 ($2.93–$9.75); lunch main courses £2.75–£6.50 ($4.13–$9.75); dinner main courses £5.50–£13.50 ($8.25–$20.25). AE, DC, MC, V.
Open: Daily 10am–10pm. **Closed:** Christmas.

It's hard to pass this small shopfront restaurant without noticing the unique collection of Dingle Bay rocks piled artistically in the window. The interior is equally interesting with shelves and shelves of books at this café that doubles as a bookstore. The menu offers simpler fare such as burgers, steaks, lamb chops, pastas, crab claws, club sandwiches, baked potatoes filled with meat and cheese stuffings, and seafood pancakes stuffed with salmon, crab, prawns, and mussels and topped with cheese.

Waterside, Strand Street, Dingle. ☎ **51458.**

Cuisine: INTERNATIONAL. **Reservations:** Recommended for dinner.
Prices: Cafe items £1.50–£9.50 ($2.25–$14.25); restaurant main courses £8–£12 ($12–$18). MC, V.
Open: Easter–Sept, cafe daily 10am–6pm; restaurant June–Aug, 7–10pm. **Closed:** Oct–Easter.

For a daytime snack with a Dingle ambience, this restaurant offers a setting opposite the busy town marina. It is a bright and airy place with a decor of blue and white, enhanced by seasonal flowers and plants. There is seating in a sunlit conservatory-style room as well as on an outdoor patio. It operates as a cafe by day and as a full-service restaurant on summer nights. The choices include oysters on the half-shell, cockles and mussels sandwiches, prawn and crab seafood salads, and soups, as well as quiches, omelets, crêpes, and pastries. The evening menu concentrates on local seafood and steaks.

Whelan's, Main Street, Dingle. ☎ **51622.**

Cuisine: IRISH. **Reservations:** Recommended.
Prices: Appetizers £2.10–£5.75 ($3.15–$8.63), main courses £9.75–£13.55 ($14.63–$20.33). Set dinner £15.50 ($23.25). MC, V.
Open: Daily dinner 6–9:30pm.

For those who crave a good old-fashioned Irish stew, this is the place. The menu also offers an eclectic blend of other dishes, from flaming Gaelic steak and beef stroganoff to seafood mixed grills and seafood pancakes. The setting is cottage-like, with stone walls trimmed in dark wood wainscoting, lanterns, and handmade woven tablecloths.

Inexpensive/Budget

★ **An Cafe Liteartha,** Dykegate Street, Dingle. ☎ **51380.**

Cuisine: IRISH/SELF-SERVICE. **Reservations:** Not necessary.
Prices: All items 50p–£5.25 (75¢–$7.88). No credit cards.
Open: Mon–Sat 9am–6pm with extended hours in summer.

A combination bookstore and cafe, this is a treasure trove for all types of books and maps of Irish interest, and particularly on life in this corner of County Kerry. The cafe section features freshly baked scones and cakes, soups, salads, and seafoods, as well as traditional dishes such as Irish stew. It's an ideal spot to browse and to enjoy a quick lunch or snack in the middle of town.

Old Smokehouse, Main Street, Dingle. ☎ **51147.**

> **Cuisine:** INTERNATIONAL/SELF-SERVICE. **Reservations:** Not necessary.
> **Prices:** All items £1–£4.95 ($1.50–$7.43). No credit cards.
> **Open:** Daily 9am–9pm.

Situated in the heart of town beside a flowing stream, this restaurant is housed in an old stone building with a country kitchen decor, including a turf fireplace, pinewood hutch with antique crockery, and paintings of the Dingle area. There is also an outdoor patio for alfresco dining in good weather. Breakfast, snacks, morning coffee, evening meals, lunch, and take-out service are all available. The menu ranges from freshly made salads and seafood sandwiches to hot dishes such as chicken Kiev, beef lasagne, or deep fried cod.

PUBS

An Droichead Beag/The Small Bridge, Lower Main Street, Dingle. ☎ **51723.**

> With an old-Dingle decor and a friendly atmosphere, this pub in the heart of town draws crowds each night throughout the year for its spontaneous sessions of traditional Irish music, usually starting at 9:30pm.

Kruger's, Ballinaraha, Dunquin, Co. Kerry. ☎ **56127.**

> Deep in the outer reaches of the Dingle Peninsula, this pub is a social center of the Irish-speaking district. The unusual name is attributed to its former owner, Muiris "Kruger" Kavanagh, a local man who was known as a fighter at school, so he was nicknamed "Kruger" after Paulus Kruger, a famous Boer leader. He eventually emigrated to the U.S., where he worked variously as a bodyguard, truck driver, male nurse, journalist, and then as PR man of the Schubert Theater Company of New York City. After 16 years, he returned to Dunquin and opened this pub, to which he then drew his great circle of friends from the entertainment field on visits. Although Kruger is gone now, his pub is still an entertainment hub, with nightly performances of the "sean-nos" Irish singing (an old, unaccompanied style) plus step dancing on Saturday nights.

O'Flaherty's, Bridge Street, Dingle. ☎ **51461.**

> The true flavor of the Dingle Peninsula is reflected in this rustic pub. The walls are lined with old posters, prints, clippings, and photos of Irish literary figures of long ago. You'll also see poems on the Dingle area by local authors and favorite Gaelic phrases, many of which are just tacked up and curling at the edges. In the evenings, traditional music sessions are usually on tap.

Richard MacDonnell/Dick Mack's "Haberdashery," Green Street, Dingle. ☎ **51070.**

> Although Richard "Dick" Mack died a few years ago, his family keeps on the traditions of this unique pub where Dick handcrafted leather boots, belts, and other items in between his pub chores. The small leather shop is still on the left, opposite a tiny bar. The walls are lined with old pictures, books, and mugs, all part of the Dick Mack legend. This pub is a favorite with the locals.

11

Limerick City

SITUATED ALONG THE MIDWEST COAST OF IRELAND, LIMERICK IS THE THIRD LARGEST city in the Republic, with a population of 76,000. It is also the chief city of County Limerick and the major urban center of the Shannon Airport region. After landing at Shannon, chances are that Limerick is the first city you will encounter.

More than any other part of Ireland, Limerick is defined by the Shannon River. The county of Limerick is cut into two parts by the Shannon River and Limerick City is likewise divided by the river.

Because of its position on the Shannon, Limerick City has always been an important port, dating back at least to the 9th century, when the Danes made it a base for plundering the hinterland. Even before that, it is said that these riverbanks were home to the early Christian settlements dating from the 5th century, the time of St. Patrick and St. Munchin, the city's patron saint.

Limerick began to develop as a city around the island of Inisbhton (now known as King's Island). It was named for King John of England, who, as Lord of Ireland, granted Limerick its first charter in 1197.

In 1210 King John asked that a castle be built strategically on the banks of the Shannon River. This royal fortress survives today and is now the centerpiece of Limerick's historic area. The nearby St. Mary's Cathedral, built in 1172, adds an ecclesiastical dimension to this historic end of the city, now usually referred to as the Heritage Precinct. Later, the Normans established a garrison and built the city walls, part of which also survive today in this area.

Just across the Thomond Bridge from the castle is Limerick's symbolic "Treaty Stone," a rock on a pedestal overlooking the west bank of the Shannon. It is the site of an historic 1691 treaty between England and Ireland that guaranteed religious tolerance, but was never ratified by the British Parliament. Afterward Limerick was often referred to as "the city of the violated treaty."

Limerick's development beyond the medieval area came in the 18th and 19th centuries when a "new city" emerged south of King's Island. This is the area that today rims O'Connell Street, the city's wide main thoroughfare, with rows of Georgian public buildings, town houses, and shops.

The countryside around Limerick also has much to offer, from Adare, known as "the prettiest village in Ireland," to Glin Castle, home to the Knights of Glin for the past 700 years, as well as historic and cultural centers at Lough Gur and Rathkeale, and the "first" Shannon Airport at Foynes.

Although many people think that Limerick got its name from the five-line rhyme known as a "limerick," that is not true. The origin of the city's name actually comes from the Irish "Luimneach," meaning "bare spot." It seems that when Limerick was founded it was just a barren spot beside the Shannon. And how it has changed!

1   Orientation

Limerick is 15 miles E of Shannon Airport, 123 miles SW of Dublin, 65 miles N of Cork, 69 miles NE of Killarney, 65 miles S of Galway.

GETTING THERE • By Plane   From the U.S., Aer Lingus, Aeroflot, and Delta Airlines provide regularly scheduled flights into Shannon Airport, off Limerick/Ennis Road (N 18), Co. Clare (☎ 061/471444), 15 miles west of Limerick. From Britain, flights into Shannon are provided from London by Aer Lingus (Heathrow) and Ryanair (Stansted). From the Continent, flights to Shannon are operated by Aer Lingus from Dusseldorf, Paris, and Zurich.

What's Special About Limerick City

Monuments
- Treaty Stone, the symbol of an ancient treaty and Limerick's historical icon.

Buildings
- Glin Castle, home of the Knights of Glin for the last 700 years, with a fine collection of 18th-century furniture and memorabilia.

Museums/Galleries
- Hunt Museum, Ireland's finest collection of Celtic-to-medieval treasures outside of Dublin.
- Limerick Museum, for insight into the city's great history.
- Limerick Gallery of Art, Limerick's artistic focal point.
- Foynes Flying Boat Museum, home of the "first" Shannon airport and Irish coffee.

Ace Attractions
- King John's Castle, a 13th-century fortress and one of the oldest examples of medieval architecture in Ireland.
- St. Mary's Cathedral, a 12th-century church with many fine antiquities and the nightly setting for "Son et Lumière" productions.
- Lough Gur, the county's prime archaeological site.

Great Towns/Villages
- Adare, fondly called "the prettiest village in Ireland."

Bus Eireann (☎ 061/313333) provides bus service from Shannon Airport to Limerick's Railway Station. The fare is £3.40 ($5.10) one-way and £4.50 ($7.25) round-trip.

• **By Train** Irish Rail operates direct trains from Dublin, Cork, and Killarney, with connections from other parts of Ireland, arriving at Limerick's Colbert Station, Parnell Street (☎ 315555).

• **By Bus** Bus Eireann provides bus services from all parts of Ireland into Limerick's Colbert Station, Parnell Street (☎ 313333).

• **By Car** Limerick City can be reached via N 7 from the east and north, N 20, 21, 24, and 69 from the south, and N 18 from the west and north.

TOURIST INFORMATION The Limerick Tourist Information Office is located on Arthurs Quay, Limerick (☎ 061/317522). It is open Monday through Friday from 9am to 6pm and Saturday from 9am to 1pm, with extended hours in the summer season. Ask for a free copy of the "Shannon Region Visitors Guide," packed with helpful information about activities and events in Limerick and the surrounding areas. A seasonal (May–October) tourist office is also operated at Adare in the Adare Heritage Centre, Main Street, Adare (☎ 061/396255).

CITY LAYOUT

Rimmed by the River Shannon, Limerick is a city of two main parts—King's Island, on the older north end, where King John's Castle, St. Mary's Cathedral, and other

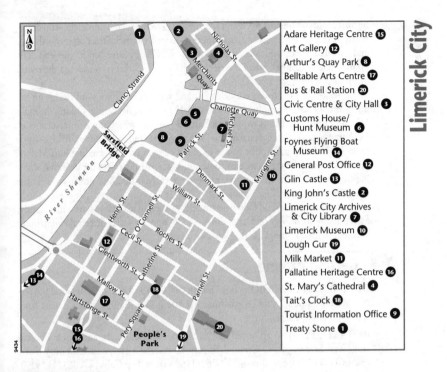

Adare Heritage Centre **15**
Art Gallery **12**
Arthur's Quay Park **8**
Belltable Arts Centre **17**
Bus & Rail Station **20**
Civic Centre & City Hall **3**
Customs House/
  Hunt Museum **6**
Foynes Flying Boat
  Museum **14**
General Post Office **12**
Glin Castle **13**
King John's Castle **2**
Limerick City Archives
  & City Library **7**
Limerick Museum **10**
Lough Gur **19**
Milk Market **11**
Pallatine Heritage Centre **16**
St. Mary's Cathedral **4**
Tait's Clock **18**
Tourist Information Office **9**
Treaty Stone **1**

IMPRESSIONS

Oh, Limerick is beautiful,
As everybody knows,
And by that city of my heart
How proud old Shannon flows.
—Michael Scanlan (1833–1917)

Oh, Ireland! thou emerald of the ocean . . .
—Percy Bysshe Shelley (1792–1822)

historic buildings hug the river, and Downtown, a rectangular commercial strip dominated by O'Connell Street, which changes its name to Patrick Street on its north end, and Sarsfield Street, which changes its name to William Street on its east end. The point where O'Connell Street intersects with Sarsfield Street is considered the center of the city.

Three bridges connect Limerick's east and west shores: Thomond Bridge on the north end, beside King John's Castle; Sarsfield Bridge in the center, linking the main (N 18) Ennis Road to downtown's Sarsfield Street, which, as it intersects with O'Connell Street, changes its name to William Street; and the Shannon Bridge which connects N 18 by-pass traffic to the southern edge of the city, feeding into Mallow Street. This latter bridge is used by those coming from or going to the west, but wanting to avoid mid-city traffic. Two smaller bridges, Matthew and Beal's, connect the downtown area with King's Island.

Streets have names and follow no particular order, so it's best to have a map handy. Streets follow a one-way traffic pattern, with O'Connell/Patrick Streets flowing south. Sarsfield/William Streets go one-way west to east.

2 Getting Around

BY PUBLIC TRANSPORT   Bus Eireann (☎ 061/313333) operates local bus service around Limerick and its environs; flat fare is 70p ($1.05). Buses depart from Colbert Station, Parnell Street.

BY TAXI   Taxis line up outside of Colbert Station, at hotels, and along Thomas and Cecil Streets, off O'Connell Street. To reserve a taxi, call Economy Taxis (☎ 061/411737); Speeditaxis (☎ 061/318844); or Top Cabs (☎ 061/417417).

BY CAR   Driving around Limerick can be a little confusing, with all of the one-way streets. It is best to park your car and walk to see the sights, although you may want to drive to King's Island for King John's Castle and the other historic sights (there is a free parking lot opposite the castle). If you must park downtown, head for the multistorey car park at Arthur's Quay, very convenient to all sightseeing and shopping and well signposted. Parking is 60p (90¢) per hour.

If you need to rent a car in Limerick, contact Alamo/Treaty Rent A Car (☎ 061/416512) or Thrifty Irish Car Rentals, Ennis Road, Limerick (☎ 061/453049). In addition, all major international car rental firms maintain desks at Shannon Airport (see County Clare Chapter).

BY FOOT   The best way to get around Limerick is to walk. Follow the signposted "Tourist Trail" to see most of the city's main attractions; a booklet outlining the trail is available at the tourist office or in bookshops. Guided walking tours are also available in the summer months (see "What to See & Do," below).

Fast Facts: Limerick City

Area Code   The telephone area code for most numbers in the Limerick area is **061.** Some County Limerick numbers have the codes **063, 068,** or **069.**

Car Rentals   See "Getting Around, above."

Drugstores   Hogan's Pharmacy, 45 Upper William St., Limerick (☎ 415195).

Emergencies   Dial **999.**

Hospital   St. John's Hospital, St. John's Square, Limerick (☎ **415822**).

Information   See "Tourist Information, above."

Laundry and Dry Cleaning   Gaeltacht Cleaners, 58 Thomas St. (☎ **415124**), and Speediwash Laundrette & Dry Cleaners, 11 St. Gerard St., Limerick (☎ **319380**).

Library   Limerick County Library, 58 O'Connell St., Limerick (☎ **318477**).

Local Newspapers and Media   Local papers include *The Limerick Leader,* published four times a week, and the *Limerick Chronicle,* a weekly. The weekly *Clare Champion,* published in Ennis, is also widely read in Limerick. *The Limerick Events Guide,* issued free every two weeks, gives news of entertainment. Radio Limerick broadcasts on 95 FM.

Parks   Limerick's People's Park is located on Pery Square off Upper Mallow Street, one block east of O'Connell Street. Other smaller parklets include Arthur's Quay Park at Arthur's Quay and the Custom House Park on the south side of Matthew Bridge.

Photographic Needs   Whelan's Cameras, 30 O'Connell St. (☎ **415246**) and Photoworld, 3 William St. (☎ **417515**).

Police   Garda Headquarters, Henry Street (☎ **414222**).

Post Office   The General Post Office is on Post Office Lane, off Lower Cecil Street, Limerick (☎ **314636**). There is a branch of the post office at Arthur's Quay Shopping Centre, Patrick St. (☎ **415538**).

---

3   Where to Stay

Very Expensive/Expensive

★ **Castletroy Park Hotel,** Dublin Road (N 7), Castletroy, Co. Limerick.
☎ **061/335566** or toll free **800/838-7100** in U.S. Fax 061/331117. 107 rms (all with bath) TV TEL
Rates: £91–£249 ($136.50–$373.50) single, £119–£249 ($178.50–$373.50) double. No service charge. AE, DC, MC, V.

Set amid 14 acres of gardens adjacent to an 18-hole golf course, this three-story hotel is two miles east of the city, next to the University of Limerick. Opened in 1991, it has a modern red brick–fronted facade, but inside there is an old world aura, with a decor of rich mahogany wood paneling, Oriental rugs, and antiques. The spacious guest rooms are decorated with traditional dark wood furniture, brass fittings, and designer fabrics. Most rooms overlook the gardens, where there is a unique Ogham walk, a pathway lined with stones engraved in the early Irish stick-form of writing.

   Dining/Entertainment: Choices include McLaughlin's Restaurant with a library-style format; the Merry Pedlar Pub, which usually offers live piano music each evening; and a sunlit conservatory lounge.

   Facilities: Indoor swimming pool, sauna and steam room, Jacuzzi, gym, aerobics area, and outdoor jogging trails; adjacent golf course.

Moderate

⭐ **Jurys,** Ennis Road (N 18), Limerick, Co. Limerick. ☎ **061/327777** or toll free **800/44-UTELL.** Fax 061/326400. 95 rms (all with bath). TV TEL

Rates: £71 ($106.50) single, £89 ($133.50) double. Service charge 10%. AE, DC, MC, V.

Situated on the banks of the Shannon across the Sarsfield Bridge in a residential section of the city, this contemporary-style hotel is just a three-minute walk from O'Connell Street. Recently renovated, it is laid out in a bright and airy style, with a skylit atrium-style foyer. The up-to-date bedrooms are spacious and practical, with traditional dark wood furniture and brass fixtures, and wide-windowed views of the gardens and river.

Dining/Entertainment: The choices include The Copper Room, a gourmet restaurant open only for dinner; an all-day coffee shop; and Limericks Bar, a pub with walls full of quotable and lyrical limericks.

Facilities: Indoor heated swimming pool, sauna, steam room, Jacuzzi, and tennis court.

Limerick Inn, Ennis Road (N 18), Limerick, Co. Limerick. ☎ **061/326666** or toll free **800/223-0888.** Fax 061/326281. 153 rms (all with bath). TV TEL

Rates: £77–£84 single ($115.50–$126), £90–£99 ($135–$148.50) double. No service charge. AE, DC, MC, V.

A country club atmosphere permeates this rambling and modern hotel, located in a pastoral setting three miles west of the city. It is handsomely decorated with bright-toned designer furnishings and fabric-textured wall coverings. Guest facilities include a leisure center with swimming pool, fitness equipment, hairdressing salon, and a billiards room. There is also a full-service restaurant, "The Burgundy Room," a coffee shop, piano lounge, and spacious drawing rooms with views of the nearby grassy hills.

Moderate/Inexpensive

Castle Oaks House, off the Dublin Road (N 7), Castleconnell, Co. Limerick. ☎ **061/377666** or toll free **800/223-6510** from U.S. Fax 061/377717. 11 rms (all with bath). TV TEL

Rates (including full breakfast): £42–£60 ($53–$90) single, £54–£80 ($81–$120) double. Service charge 10%. AE, DC, MC, V.

Set on 25 acres of mature oak woodlands along the Shannon River six miles east of Limerick City, this two-story Georgian manor house dates back more than 150 years. Among the fittings that the original owners installed were classic bow windows, a decorative staircase, and a skylit central dome. Later used as a convent, it has also been left with such unique features as stained-glass windows and a chapel that is now used as a banqueting room. It was restyled, expanded, and opened as a hotel in 1987 by the Hanrahan family. The bedrooms are furnished with crown-canopy beds, soft pastel fabrics, and choice antiques from the area. Facilities include a restaurant, lounge bar, and tennis court. It is located six miles east of Limerick.

Limerick Ryan Hotel, Ennis Road, Limerick, Co. Limerick. ☎ **061/453922** or toll free **800/44-UTELL** in the U.S. Fax 061/326333. 166 rms (all with bath). TV TEL

Rates: £40–£120 ($60–$180) single or double. No service charge. AE, DC, MC, V.

Situated on the main (N 18) road a mile west of the city center, this hotel combines one of Limerick's oldest buildings, Ardhu House, dating back to 1780, with a modern wing of new bedrooms. The public areas, part of the original manor house, are decorated in classic Georgian style. Facilities include the Ardhu Restaurant, Ardhu Bar, and a sports bar with giant screen for viewing all major sporting events.

Inexpensive/Budget

Shannon Grove, Athlunkard, Killaloe Road (R. 463), Limerick. ☎ **061/345756** or **343838.** 9 rms (all with bath). TEL

Rates (including full Irish breakfast): £17 ($25.50). single, £30 double ($45). No credit cards. **Closed:** Christmas week.

Situated in a quiet residential area a mile north of the city center, this modern two-story guesthouse is surrounded by lovely gardens and is just a quarter-mile walk from a curve of the Shannon River. The bedrooms, individually decorated in light tones of pink, blue, and peppermint, have contemporary furnishings and extra amenities such as a hairdryer; there is one room on the ground floor. Facilities include a guest TV lounge with coffee/tea-maker and two cheery breakfast rooms. There are also tables and chairs for outdoor seating in fine weather. Proprietor Noreen Marsh provides a particularly warm welcome and will help you plan an insider's tour of Limerick. If you don't have a car, local bus service stops nearby.

4   Where to Dine

Expensive/Moderate

De La Fontaine, 12 Upper Gerald Griffin St., Limerick. ☎ **414461.**
   Cuisine: FRENCH. **Reservations:** Recommended.
   Prices: Appetizers £2.50–£5 ($3.75–$7.50); main courses £11–£15 ($16.50–$22.50); set six-course dinner £21.50 ($32.25). DC, MC, V.
   Open: Mon–Sat 7–10pm.

Situated on the east end of the downtown area, this upstairs restaurant brings the aromas and ambience of France to Limerick. Chef Alain Bras-White changes the menu often depending on the season and what is fresh in local markets, but his specialty dishes include filet of lamb with red wine and herbs, breast of duck with walnut-scented sauce; médaillons of pork with ginger and exotic fruits; breast of chicken stuffed with smoked salmon and topped by a whiskey and hazelnut cream sauce; farm-venison T-bone with balsamic vinegar; and filet of beef flambéed with peppercorns and foie gras.

★ **The Silver Plate,** 74 O'Connell St., Limerick. ☎ **316311.**
   Cuisine: INTERNATIONAL. **Reservations:** Required.
   Prices: Appetizers £2–£6.50 ($3–$9.75); main courses £8–£14 ($12–$21). AE, CB, MC, V.
   Open: Tues–Sat 6–11pm.

Situated in the heart of Limerick's Georgian streetscape, this small, 40-seat restaurant occupies the basement of a restored 18th-century townhouse, near the Crescent and Pery Square. Rich in dark woods and silver accessories, the decor is dominated by a blend of pastel tones. The menu emphasizes seafood, with such specialties as lobsters from the tank, Kenmare Bay in garlic, and wild Shannon salmon, along with meat choices such as rack of Adare lamb, breast of chicken in pastry with mushroom purée; and médaillons of beef au poivre.

Moderate/Inexpensive

$ **Piccola Italia,** 55 O'Connell St., Limerick. ☎ **315844.**
Cuisine: ITALIAN. **Reservations:** Recommended.
Prices: Appetizers £2–£4 ($3–$6); main courses £5–£10.50 ($7.50–$15.75).
Open: Daily 6pm–midnight.

With a name that means "Little Italy," this basement *ristorante* adds a touch of the Mediterranean to the heart of Limerick. The tables have red-and-white check cloths, and chianti baskets hang from the ceiling. The menu is also unmistakably Italian, from zuppa de funghi, cannelloni, lasagne, and fettuccine, to scampi, salmon alla griglia, and steak pizzaiola.

Patrick Punchs, O'Connell Avenue (N 20), Punchs Cross, Limerick. ☎ **229588.**
Cuisine: IRISH/INTERNATIONAL. **Reservations:** Suggested for dinner.
Prices: Appetizers £2–£3.75 ($3–$5.63); main courses £8.25–£12.75 ($12.38–$19.13). MC, V.
Open: Daily 11am–11pm.

Situated on the southern edge of town, this popular pub-restaurant is on the main road, surrounded by gardens, ancient trees, and lots of parking. It offers a variety of settings to dine, ranging from a three-tier lounge area and a glass-enclosed conservatory overlooking the gardens to a clubby main room with an eclectic decor of Tiffany-style lamps, dark woods, an open turf fireplace, and photos of movie stars of yesteryear. Antique unicycles and model airplanes are suspended from the old tin ceiling. The menu is equally varied, with dishes such as filet of beef Wellington; chicken Cleopatra, with lemon and prawn sauce; rack of lamb with rosemary and creamed mint sauce; roast duck with black cherry sauce; filet of baked salmon with seafood sauce; prime ribs; steaks, and vegetable lasagne.

Budget

Cafe Vienna, 67 William St., opposite archway to Cruises Street. ☎ **411720.**
Cuisine: CONTINENTAL/COFFEE SHOP. **Reservations:** Not necessary.
Prices: All items £1–£4 ($1.50–$6). No credit cards.
Open: Mon–Sat 8am–6pm.

Situated opposite the main archway entrance to Cruises Street shopping complex, this European-style coffeehouse offers breakfast, lunch, and snacks on a self-service and counter-service basis, amid a classy decor of deep green colored walls, brass fixtures, and framed-flower modern art. The food choices range from pastas, pizzas, soups, salads, sandwiches, quiches, and meat pies to pastries and creamy cakes.

$ **Bewley's,** 10 Cruises St., Limerick. ☎ **414739.**
Cuisine: IRISH/SELF-SERVICE. **Reservations:** Not accepted.
Prices: Breakfast £1.99–£2.95 ($2.93–$4.43), lunch £2.95–$4.95 ($4.43–$7.43); evening meal £1.95–£4.95 ($2.93–$7.43). No credit cards.
Open: Mon–Sat 8am–6pm.

A branch of the Dublin institution of the same name that dates back to 1840, this dependable restaurant occupies prime space in the new Cruises Street shopping complex in the middle of town. It's a handy spot for coffee, tea, or a meal at any time of day.

5   What to See & Do

In addition to the attractions described below, see the "Easy Excursions" section at the end of this chapter for more suggestions about sightseeing when based in Limerick.

★ **King John's Castle**, Nicholas Street, Limerick. ☎ **411201.**
Strategically built on the banks of the Shannon River, this royal fortress is the center-piece of Limerick's historic area. It is said to date back to 1210 when King John of England visited and was so taken with the site that he ordered a "strong castle" to be built here. It survives today as one of the oldest examples of medieval architecture in Ireland, with rounded gate towers and curtain walls. Thanks to a recent $7 million restoration, the interior includes an authentic on-site archaeological excavation dating back to Hiberno/Norse times, as well as gallery displays, and an audio-visual presentation portraying Limerick's 800 years of history. On the outside, the impressive facade has battlement walkways along the castle's walls and towers, offering sweeping views of the city.
   Admission: £3.30 ($4.95) adults, £3.10 ($4.15) seniors, £1.70 ($2.55) children and students.
   Open: Daily 9:30am–5:30pm.

★ **St. Mary's Cathedral**, Bridge Street, Limerick. ☎ **413157.**
Founded in the 12th century on a hill on King's Island, this site originally held a palace belonging to one of the Kings of Munster, Donal Mor O'Brien. In 1172 he donated it for use as a church. Currently in the process of restoration, the building contains many fine antiquities including a Romanesque doorway, a pre-Reformation stone altar, and a huge stone coffin lid, said to be that of Donal Mor O'Brien himself. Features added in later years include 15th-century misericords, with carvings in black oak, and a reredos on the high altar carved by the father of Irish patriot, Padraic Pearse. Now a Church of Ireland property, St. Mary's is the site of nightly "Son et Lumière" presentations during the summer season (see "Evening Entertainment," below).
   Admission: Free; donations welcome.
   Open: May–Sept, Mon–Sat 9am–1pm and 2:30–5:30pm; Oct–Apr, Mon–Sat 9am–1pm and 2:15–5pm.

Limerick City Gallery of Art, Pery Square, Limerick. ☎ **310633.**
Founded in 1948 and expanded in 1985 to occupy the whole of the neo-Romanesque Carnegie Building (1903), this gallery is situated in the People Park's, on the corner of Mallow Street. It houses a permanent collection of 18th-, 19th-, and 20th- century art. It also plays host to a wide range of traveling contemporary art exhibitions, in-cluding touring exhibitions from the Irish Museum of Modern Art. On some eve-nings, the gallery holds literary readings or traditional or classical music concerts at 8pm.
   Admission: Free.
   Open: Mon–Wed and Fri, 10am–1pm and 2–6pm; Thurs 10am–1pm and 2–7pm; Sat 10am–1pm.

Limerick Museum, St. John's Square, Limerick. ☎ **417826.**
Housed in two stone town houses dating back to 1751, this museum provides an in-sight into the history of Limerick. It contains displays on Limerick's archaeology, natural history, civic treasures, traditional crafts of lace, silver, furniture, and

printing; plus historical paintings, maps, prints, and photographs. There are also sections of numismatics, labor history, and political history. Of particular interest are the city's original charters from Cromwell and King Charles II, and the civic sword presented by Queen Elizabeth I.

Admission: Free.
Open: Tues–Sat 10am–1pm and 2–5pm.

★ **Hunt Museum,** Foundation Building, University of Limerick, off the Main Dublin Road (N 7), Limerick. ☎ **333644.**

This museum is reputed to house Ireland's finest collection of Celtic to medieval treasures outside of Dublin's National Museum. It includes antiquities and art objects from Europe and Ireland, ancient Irish metalwork, medieval bronzes, ivories, and enamels. The collection was presented to the Irish nation by the late John Hunt, antiquarian and art historian. *Note:* as we go to press, plans call for this collection to be moved to newly restored quarters at the 18th-century Palladian-style Old Custom House in Limerick City.

Admission: £1.60 ($2.40) adults, 90p ($1.35) students and children.
Open: Mon–Sat 10am–5pm.

Sightseeing Tours

Gray Line Tours, Arthur's Quay, Limerick. ☎ **413088** or **416099.**

This company operates a full-day seven-hour tour of the scenic areas surrounding Limerick, including the Cliffs of Moher, the Burren, and Galway Bay. Pickups are made from various Limerick area hotels and from the Limerick Tourist Office.

Fare: £27 ($40.50) per person.
Schedule: May–Oct, Wed–Sun 10am.

Shannonside Tours, "Reboge," Dublin Road, Limerick. ☎ **311935.**

Get to know the city by participating in a walking tour of Old Limerick. Conducted by specially trained local guides, these tours are two hours in duration. All tours depart from the Tourist Office, Arthur's Quay.

Admission: £3.50 ($5.25) adults, £2.50 ($3.75) students and seniors, £1 ($1.50) children.
Open: Mid–June–Aug, Mon–Fri at 11am and 2:30pm.

6 Sports & Recreation

SPECTATOR SPORTS

GREYHOUND RACING Watch the sleek greyhounds race at the Limerick Greyhound Track, Market's Field, Mulgrave Street, Limerick (☎ **316788**). Races are slated on Monday, Thursday, Saturday at 8pm. Admission is £3 ($4.50) including program.

HORSE RACING Limerick has two racetracks nearby, the Greenpark Race Course, South Circular Road, Dooradoyle, Limerick (☎ **229377**) and Limerick Junction Race Course, Limerick Junction (☎ **062/51357**) about 20 miles southeast near Tipperary. There is racing throughout the year; check the local newspapers for exact fixtures and times. Admission averages £5–£6 ($7.50–$9) for most events.

RECREATION

FISHING   Visitors are welcome to cast a line in the River Shannon for trout and other freshwater fish. For information and equipment, contact Tackle Steve's Fishing Tackle, 19 Catherine St., Limerick (☎ **413484**).

GOLF   The Limerick area has three 18-hole golf courses including a championship par-72 parkland layout at the Limerick County Golf & Country Club, Ballyneety (☎ **351881**), five miles east of Limerick, with greens fee of £28 ($42). In addition, there is the par-71 inland course at the Limerick Golf Club, Ballyclough (☎ **415416**), three miles south of Limerick, charging greens fees of £20 ($30); and the par-69 inland course at Castletroy Golf Club, Castletroy, Co. Limerick (☎ **335753**), three miles east of Limerick, with greens fees of £20 ($30).

HORSEBACK RIDING   County Limerick's fertile fields provide good turf for horseback riding and pony trekking, at rates starting at about £10 ($15) per hour. The Clonshire Equestrian Centre, Adare, Co. Limerick (☎ **396770**), offers riding for all levels of ability, horsemanship classes and instruction for cross-country riding, dressage, and jumping. Clonshire is also home to the Limerick Foxhounds and in the winter months is a center for hunting in the area.

Rathcannon Equestrian Centre, Kilmallock, Co. Limerick (☎ **063/90847**) offers horseback riding, trekking, cross-country riding, and hunting, as well as instruction in the art of show-jumping.

7 Savvy Shopping

Shopping hours in Limerick are Monday through Saturday from 9:30am–5:30pm. Many stores, particularly in the Arthurs Quay Centre, also stay open late on Thursday and Friday nights until 9pm.

⭐ **Arthurs Quay Centre,** Arthurs Quay, Limerick. ☎ **419888.**
With a striking four-story brick facade, this shopping complex overlooks Arthurs Quay park and the Shannon River. It houses over three dozen shops and services, ranging from Irish handcrafts to fashions, casual wear, shoes, records and cassettes, and books.

⭐ **Cruises Street Shopping Centre,** Cruises Street, Limerick.
This is the centerpiece of Limerick's retail downtown shopping district, situated just off Patrick Street. Taking an original city street, the developers spent £18 million ($27 million) and turned it into an old-world-village–style pedestrianized shopping mall, with a total of 55 retail outlets and 20 residential apartments and offices.

Heirlooms, Cruises Street, Limerick. ☎ **419111.**
Long established in downtown Limerick, this shop moved to the new Cruises Street Shopping Centre for more space, to show off its vast stock of local collectibles, ranging from old books and maps, dolls and puppets, and biscuit tins, to frames, wood carvings, pottery, clocks, sculptures, jewelry, and candles.

Irish Handcrafts, 26 Patrick St., Limerick. ☎ **455504.**
Dating back over 100 years, this family-run business specializes in products made by people from the Limerick area, with particular emphasis on women's hand-knit and hand-loomed sweaters of all types, colors, and styles. There are also linen and lace garments.

Leonards, 23 O'Connell St., Limerick. ☎ **415721.**

This long-established shop is a good source of men's tweed jackets, hats, caps, ties, and cravats, as well as silk ties, and cashmere and lambswool knitwear.

Todd's, O'Connell Street, Limerick. ☎ **417222.**

For more than 100 years, this has been Limerick's leading department store, selling a wide array of Waterford crystal, Aran knitwear, Donegal tweeds, and ready-to-wear clothing of all types.

White and Gold, 34 O'Connell St. at Roches Street, Limerick. ☎ **419977.**

Irish Dresden figurines, the delicate porcelain pieces made at nearby Drumcollogher, are the special attraction of this chic gift shop. Other wares include fanciful European Christmas ornaments, intricate wind chimes, and Hummels.

8 Evening Entertainment & Pubs

PERFORMING ART CENTERS

Belltable Arts Centre, 69 O'Connell St., Limerick. ☎ **319866.**

Dramas, musicals, and concerts are staged year-round at this mid-city theater and entertainment center. The summer program includes presentations of Irish traditional song, dance, and poetry. By day, the building is also open for gallery exhibits showing the works of modern Irish artists and local crafts.

Admission: Tickets, £5–£7 ($7.50–$10.50).

Open: Tues–Sat 8pm for most shows; check in advance.

University Concert Hall, University of Limerick, Plassey, Co. Limerick. ☎ **331549.**

On the grounds of the University of Limerick, this hall presents a broad program of national and international solo stars, variety shows, and ballet, as well as the Irish Chamber Orchestra, RTE Concert Orchestra, University of Limerick Chamber Orchestra, the Limerick Singers, and the European Community Orchestra. It publishes a monthly list of events, available from the tourist office.

Admission: Tickets £6–£15 ($9–$22.50).

Schedule: Most performances start at 8pm.

SHOWS

⭐ **Son Et Lumière,** St. Mary's Cathedral, Merchant's Quay, Limerick. ☎ **416238.**

Housed in the historic setting of the city's oldest cathedral, this is Limerick's long-running sound-and-light show. It is comprised of a 45-minute program, using quadrophonic sound and spectacular lighting to tell the story of Limerick and the cathedral, produced by actors and lighting experts from Irish television. Reservations are not necessary.

Admission: £2.50 ($3.75) adults, £1.50 ($2.25) seniors and students.

Open: Mid–June to mid–Sept nightly at 9:15pm.

Jurys Summer Show, Jurys Hotel, Ennis Road, Limerick. ☎ **327777.**

Patterned after the famous long-running Jurys Cabaret of Dublin, this show presents the best of comedy, drama, music, song, and dance with a midwest of Ireland slant and starring Limerick-based entertainers. For those who wish to eat, there are two options—a meal of traditional Irish stew, apple pie, and Irish coffee, or a full-course dinner of choice.

Admission: £7.50 ($11.25) show only, £15 ($22.50) for show and traditional meal; £19 ($28.50) full dinner and show.

Open: June, Thurs at 8pm, July–Sept, Wed–Thurs at 8pm.

PUBS

The Locke, 3 Georges Quay, Limerick. ☎ **413733.**

Established in 1724, this is one of Limerick's oldest pubs, situated beside the east bank of the Shannon, just off Bridge Street. Although it started as a haven for sea captains visiting the port of Limerick, today it is known for its traditional Irish music, played on Sunday, Monday, and Tuesday, year-round.

Matt the Thresher, Dublin Road (N 7), Birdhill, Co. Tipperary. ☎ **379227.**

Situated about 15 miles northeast of Limerick, this roadside tavern is a replica of a 19th-century farmers' pub. A rustic, cottagelike atmosphere prevails inside, with antique furnishings, agricultural memorabilia, traditional snugs, and lots of cozy alcoves. There is music on many evenings, and this tavern is well worth the drive.

M. J. Finnegans, Dublin Road (N 7), Annacotty. ☎ **337338.**

Dating back to 1820, this restored alehouse takes its name from James Joyce's *Finnegans Wake* and the decor reflects a Joycean theme, with appropriate Limerick overtones. Special features include Irish ceili music on weekends, and picnic tables for sitting by the rose garden on warm summer days. It's located on the main road about five miles east of Limerick City.

Nancy Blake's, 19 Denmark St., Limerick. ☎ **416443.**

Situated downtown just off Patrick Street, this cozy old-world pub is known for its free traditional music sessions, year-round on Sunday through Wednesday from 9pm.

Riddler's, 9 Sarsfield St., Limerick. ☎ **414149.**

This cozy old pub sits just east of the Shannon River by the Sarsfield Bridge. The walls are wood-paneled, with shelves that are lined with brassy fixtures, old tinted bottles, and vintage crocks.

Vintage Club, 9 Ellen St., Limerick. ☎ **410694.**

Located in one of Limerick's older sections near the quays, this pub used to be a wine cellar and the decor reflects it—barrel seats and tables, oak casks, and dark-paneled walls.

---

9 Easy Excursions from Limerick City

Within a 25-mile radius of Limerick City are many historic and cultural attractions in the County Limerick countryside. Here are a few suggestions:

 Adare Heritage Centre, Main Street, Adare, Co. Limerick. ☎ **061/396666.**

Often referred to as the prettiest village in Ireland, Adare is one of County Limerick's special places, with thatched-roof and Tudor-style houses, beautiful gardens, and ivy-covered medieval churches in wooded surroundings on both sides of the street beside the River Maigue. No visit to Limerick is ever complete without a short picture-taking stop in Adare. For those who want to linger and learn more about this bucolic enclave's history, a new heritage center opened in 1994. Housed in a stone building with traditional courtyard, it offers a walk-through display on Adare's colorful history, along with a model of the town as it looked in medieval times. There is also a 20-minute audio-visual illustrating the many facets of Adare today. The center also houses a library with books on the local area, cafe, craft shop, and knitwear shop.

Admission: £2 ($3) adults, £1 ($1.50) seniors, students, and children.

Open: May–June and Sept–Oct, 9am–6pm; July–Aug, 9am–7pm.

★ **Lough Gur**, Lough Gur, Co. Limerick. ☎ **061/85186.**

Dotted with ancient monuments, this is a major archaeological site for the Limerick area. Excavations have shown that Lough Gur apparently had continuous occupation from the Neolithic period to late medieval times, and the natural caves nearby have yielded the remains of extinct animals such as reindeer, giant Irish deer, and bear. The highlights include the foundations of a small farmstead built circa A.D. 900; a lake island dwelling built between A.D. 500 and 1,000; a wedge-shaped tomb that was a communal grave circa. 2,500 B.C.; and the Grange Stone Circle, said to be the largest and finest of its kind in Ireland, built about 2,000 B.C. On the grounds is an interpretative center that features an audio-visual presentation, models of stone circles, burial chambers and facsimiles of weapons, tools, and pottery found in the area. Walking tours, covering the archaeological features of the locality, are conducted regularly. It is situated seven miles southeast of Limerick City via N 24 and R. 513.

Admission: £1.85 ($3.78) adults, £1 ($1.50) students.

Open: Mid-May–Sept, daily 10am–6pm.

Foynes Flying Boat Museum, Foynes, Co. Limerick. ☎ **069/65416.**

For aviation buffs, this museum is a must. This is the "first" Shannon Airport, the predecessor to the modern jetways of Shannon Airport in County Clare. It has now been restored and reopened as a visitor attraction, to commemorate an era begun on July 9, 1939, when Pan Am's luxury flying boat *Yankee Clipper* landed at Foynes, marking the first commercial passenger flight on the direct route between U.S. and Europe. This was followed on June 22, 1942, when Foynes was the departure point for the first nonstop commercial flight from Europe to New York. This was also the airport where Irish coffee was invented in 1942 by bartender Joe Sheridan. The complex includes a 1940s-style cinema and cafe, the original terminal building, and the radio and weather rooms with original transmitters, receivers, and Morse Code equipment. It is located 20 miles east of Limerick via N 69.

Admission: £3 ($4.50) adults, £1 ($1.50) children.

Open: April–Oct, daily 10am–6pm.

Irish Palatine Heritage Centre, Limerick-Killarney Road (N 21), Rathkeale, Co. Limerick. ☎ **069/61080.**

Ireland's unique links with Germany are the focus of this new museum, located 18 miles south of Limerick off the main road. Reflecting on the history of the several hundred Palatine families who emigrated from Germany and settled in this area of

IMPRESSIONS

Oh, sweet Adare! oh! lovely vale!
Oh, soft retreat of sylvan splendour!
Nor summer sun, nor morning gale
E'er hailed a scene more softly tender.

—Gerald Griffin (1803–1840)

Ireland in 1709, it includes an extensive display of artifacts, photographs, and graphics. In addition, the museum seeks to illustrate the Palatines' innovative contributions to Irish farming life and their formative role in the development of world Methodism.

Admission: £2 ($3) adults, £1 ($1.50) children.

Open: June–Sept, daily 2–5pm and by appointment.

★ **Glin Castle,** Limerick/Tarbert Road (N 69). ☎ 068/34112.

Lilies of the valley and ivy-covered ash, oak, and beech trees line the driveway leading to this gleaming white castle, home to the Knights of Glin for the last 700 years. Sitting on the south bank of the Shannon Estuary, this sprawling estate contains 400 acres of gardens, farmlands, and forests. Although there were earlier residences on the site, the present home was built in 1785. It is more of a Georgian house than a castle, with added crenellations and Gothic details. The current (29th) Knight of Glin, Desmond FitzGerald, a noted historian and preservationist, maintains a fine collection of 18th-century Irish furniture and memorabilia. The house also contains elaborate plasterwork, Corinthian columns, and a unique double-ramp flying staircase. The castle is protected by three sets of toy fort lodges, one of which houses a craft shop and cafe. Glin is located approximately 25 miles east of Limerick City, via the main road (N 69).

Admission: £2 ($3) adults, 50p (75¢) for students and children under 18.

Open: May, 10am–noon and 2–4pm and by appointment.

WHERE TO STAY

Very Expensive/Expensive

★ **Adare Manor,** Adare, Co. Limerick. ☎ 061/396566 or toll free **800/462-3273** in U.S. Fax 061/396124. 64 rms (all with bath) TV TEL

Rates: £112–£298 ($168–$447) single or double. Service charge 15%. AE, DC, MC, V.

Most people wouldn't expect to find a five-star hotel in a village as tiny and secluded as Adare, ten miles south of Limerick; but Ireland is surprising, with little gems tucked in all corners. This gem is a 19th-century Tudor Gothic mansion, nestled on the banks of the River Maigue amid an 840-acre estate. The former home of the Earls of Dunraven, it has been masterfully restored and refurbished as a deluxe resort, with original barrel-vaulted ceilings, 15th-century carved doors, Waterford crystal chandeliers, ornate fireplaces, and antique-filled bedrooms. The facilities include an oak-paneled restaurant with views of the river and gardens, heated indoor swimming pool, gym, sauna, plus riding stables, salmon and trout fishing, horseback riding, fox hunting, clay pigeon shooting, a variety of nature trails for jogging and walking, and an 18-hole golf course designed by Robert Trent Jones, Sr.

Beauti-ful [handwritten]

Moderate

★ **Dunraven Arms,** Main Street (N 21), Adare, Co. Limerick. ☎ **061/396633** or toll free **800/447-7462.** Fax 061/396541. 44 rooms. TV TEL

$ **Rates:** £52–£65 ($78–$97.50) single, £80–£98 ($120–$137). No service charge. AE, DC, MC, V.

Nestled on the banks of the River Maigue in one of Ireland's prettiest thatched-roof villages, this small 19th-century inn is a charming country retreat just ten miles south of Limerick City. The public areas have an old-world ambience with open fireplaces, equestrian-theme paintings, and antiques. Half of the rooms are in the original house and the other half are in a new wing, but all are furnished in traditional style with Victorian accents and period pieces. The hotel is owner-managed by Bryan Murphy, a keen horse enthusiast who gladly assists guests in making riding arrangements; in the winter months, the Fox Hunting Centre of Ireland is also headquartered here. The hotel's gardens supply fruit and vegetables for its award-winning restaurant.

WHERE TO DINE

Expensive/Moderate

★ **The Mustard Seed,** Main Street (N 21), Adare, Co. Limerick. ☎ **061/396451.**
Cuisine: IRISH. **Reservations:** Recommended.
Prices: Set 4-course dinner £25 ($37.50). AE, DC, MC, V.
Open: Tues–Sat 7–10pm. **Closed:** Feb.

Creativity is the keynote at this lovely mustard-colored cottage restaurant. Bedecked by flowerboxes overflowing with colorful blossoms, it sits in the heart of town amid its own walled garden. The menu presents a creative blend of dishes such as roulade of spinach encasing a pepper and tomato filling on warm salad of tomato and spinach; chicken coated in honey, garlic, and green peppercorns with scallion cream sauce; pan-fried veal livers on mushrooms and garden sorrel with orange butter sauce; and grilled Irish beef with onions and red wine juice.

Moderate/Inexpensive

Inn Between, Main Street, Adare, Co. Limerick. ☎ **061/396633.**
Cuisine: IRISH. **Reservations:** Recommended.
Prices: Appetizers £1.80–£4.95 ($2.70–$7.43), main courses £6.75–£11.95. ($10.13–$7.93) AE, DC, MC, V.
Open: Apr–Oct, Tues–Sat lunch 12:30–2:30pm, dinner 6:30–9:30pm.

Tucked in a row of houses and shops, this thatched-roof brasserie-style restaurant has a surprisingly airy skylit decor dominated by bright red and yellow tones, and a back courtyard for outdoor seating. The menu offers choices ranging from homemade soups and traditional dishes to innovative combinations of médaillons of beef filet with green peppercorn sauce; wild salmon on leek fondue with tomato and chive butter sauce; and sirloin steak with roasted shallots and Bordelaise sauce; as well as a classic Inn Between Burger, with homemade relish and French fries.

County Clare

12

Aᴿᴛᴇʀ ꜱᴛᴇᴘᴘɪɴɢ ᴏꜰꜰ ᴛʜᴇ ᴘʟᴀɴᴇ ᴀᴛ Sʜᴀɴɴᴏɴ, ʜɪʀᴇ ᴀ ᴄᴀʀ ᴏʀ ʙᴏᴀʀᴅ ᴀ ᴛᴏᴜʀ ʙᴜꜱ and begin your journey. Your first sights of Ireland will be the vistas of County Clare: Rich green fields and rolling hills joined by the meandering Shannon River in a pastoral tableau. If you turn left off the main road, the rocky Atlantic coast of Clare will await you; if you continue north, you'll be heading into the historic town of Ennis and then onward to the rocky outpost known as The Burren.

Contrary to popular belief, Shannon is not an Irish city like Dublin, Cork, or Limerick. It is, first of all, a river, at 230 miles the longest in Ireland and Great Britain. In 1945 this river lent its name to an airport that served for many years as the first landing point for most transatlantic flights—Shannon International Airport. In 1947 it became the world's first duty-free airport.

As the airport grew, the surrounding counties, especially County Clare, prospered. Hotels were built, new industries established, craft centers encouraged, and ancient sites rediscovered and restored. Soon the word *Shannon* meant more than an airport or a river.

The Shannon region today can best be defined as the perimeters of County Clare— a land of medieval castles, dramatic coastal scenery, and the unique terrain of The Burren. County Clare is no longer considered just a backdrop for Shannon Airport; it is indeed a destination in its own right.

GETTING THERE • By Plane   From the **United States,** Aer Lingus, Aeroflot, and Delta Airlines provide regularly scheduled flights into Shannon International Airport (☎061/471444; flight arrival and departure information ☎ 061/471582). From **Britain,** flights into Shannon are provided from London by Aer Lingus (Heathrow). From **the Continent,** flights to Shannon are operated by Aer Lingus from Dusseldorf, Paris, and Zurich. From **Russia,** Aeroflot flies to Shannon from Moscow and St. Petersburg.

• By Train   Irish Rail provides service to Ennis Rail Station, Station Road (☎ 065/24166), and Limerick's Colbert Station, Parnell Street (☎ 061/315555), 15 miles from Shannon.

• By Bus   Bus Eireann provides bus services from all parts of Ireland into Ennis Bus Station, Station Road (☎ 065/24177), and other towns in County Clare.

• By Car   County Clare can be reached via N 18. At Shannon Airport, cars can be rented from the following international firms: **Alamo** (☎ 061/472342); **Avis** (☎ 061/471094); **Budget** (☎ 061/471361); **EuroDollar** (☎ 061/472633); **Europcar** (☎ 061/471618); and **Hertz** (☎ 061/471369). Several local firms also maintain desks at the airport; among the most reliable is **Dan Dooley Rent A Car** (☎ 061/61098).

• By Ferry   From points south, County Clare can be reached directly, bypassing Limerick, via the Tarbert-Killimer car ferry, crossing the Shannon River from Tarbert, Co. Kerry, to Killimer, Co. Clare. Crossing time is 20 minutes, via a drive-on/drive-off service; no reservations are needed. Ferries operate April through September from Monday through Saturday from 7 or 7:30am until 9 or 9:30pm, Sunday from 9 or 9:30am until 9 or 9:30pm; October through March on Monday through Saturday from 7 or 7:30am to 7 or 7:30pm, Sunday from 10 or 10:30am to 7 or 7:30pm. Crossings from Tarbert are on the half-hour and from Killimer on the hour. The fares for car with passengers are £7 ($10.50) one way and £10 ($15) round-trip. For more information, contact **Shannon Ferry Ltd.,** Killimer/Kilrush, Co. Clare (☎ 065/53124).

What's Special About County Clare

Buildings
- Cratloe Woods House, one of Ireland's finest "longhouses."
- Ennis Friary, a 13th-century abbey that was the focal point of learning for all of Europe in medieval times.

Museums
- De Valera Library & Museum, Ennis, commemorating Eamonn de Valera, Ireland's American-born president.

Parks/Gardens
- Burren National Park, one of Ireland's newest national parks.

Ace Attractions
- Bunratty Castle & Folk Park, medieval fortress in the setting of a 19th-century walk-around village.
- Knappogue Castle, 15th-century Norman castle.
- Craggaunowen Bronze-Age Project, a lakeside dwelling, ring fort, and other structures from Ireland's early Christian past.

Natural Spectacles
- The Burren, 100 square miles of rocky lunarlike landscape.
- Cliffs of Moher, 700-foot cliffs that stretch five miles along the Atlantic coast.

Activities
- Learn to paint at the Burren College of Art.
- Float in a sulphur bath at the Spa Wells Centre.
- Ride the Doolin Ferry to the Aran Islands.
- Tee off on the great golf course at Lahinch.

After Dark
- Dine like a king or queen at a medieval banquet at Bunratty or Knappogue Castle.
- Tap your feet to the tunes of traditional music at an Irish ceili at Bunratty Folk Park or at Gus O'Connor's Pub in Doolin.

Shopping
- Shannon Duty Free Shops, the "grand-daddy" of duty-frees.

Great Towns/Villages
- Doolin, the traditional music capital of Ireland.

ESSENTIALS • Tourist Information   As soon as you land in Ireland, you will find a **tourist office** in the Arrivals Hall of Shannon Airport (☎ **061/471644** or **061/471004**). It's open year-round, with hours timed to coincide with flight arrivals and departures. The **Ennis Tourist Office,** Clare Road, Ennis, Co. Clare (☎ **065/28366** or **065/28308**), is also open year-round. It's located about one mile south of town on the main N 18 road. Hours are normally on Monday through Friday from 9am to 6pm and Saturday from 9am to 1pm, with extended hours during summer.

Seasonal tourist offices in County Clare are maintained at the Cliffs of Moher (☎ 065/81171); O'Connell Street, Kilkee (☎ 065/56112); and at Town Hall, Kilrush (☎ 065/51577). These offices are usually open May or June through early September.

• **Area Codes**   Telephone area codes for County Clare are 061 and 065.

1 From Shannon Airport to Ennis

One of the most-traveled roads in Ireland is the the 15-mile road from Shannon Airport to Ennis, a well-signposted route that is part of the main Limerick/Galway road (N 18). It's been said that this road is truly the gateway to all of Ireland. No matter which way you turn, you'll find a unique experience: Turn right, proceed for five miles, and the fairy-tale village of Bunratty is before you, with its 15th-century medieval castle and theme park. Turn left, heading toward Ennis, and you pass through the charming river town of Newmarket-on-Fergus, home of Dromoland Castle.

The main town of County Clare, Ennis (population 6,000) is a compact enclave of winding narrow streets on the banks of the River Fergus. Dating back to the 13th century, Ennis owes its origin to the O'Briens of Thomond, who moved from Limerick and settled here between 1208 and 1216.

The original site was an island on the River Fergus and hence the name "Ennis," an Anglicized form of the Gaelic word *Inis,* meaning "island." Donncadh O'Brien, king of Thomond, invited the Franciscan order of priests to establish a settlement within his domain circa 1240. Over the years, the friary grew to be a focal point of learning in the west of Ireland.

In 1609 James I issued Ennis a grant to hold fairs and markets. Markets for milk and other perishable goods were held each day, and large fairs were also held in summer. Ennis continues to be a thriving market town, with a market still held every Saturday morning.

Easily walkable, Ennis lends itself to a Walking Trail developed by the Ennis Urban District Council. A leaflet outlining the route is available free throughout the town.

WHAT TO SEE & DO

★ **Bunratty Castle and Folk Park,** Limerick/Ennis Road (N 18), Bunratty, Co. Clare.   ☎ 061/361511.

Long before you reach the village of Bunratty, vistas of this striking 15th-century fortress stand out along the main road from the airport. Nestled beside the O'Garney River, Bunratty Castle was built in 1425 and is today Ireland's most complete medieval castle. This ancient stronghold has been carefully restored, with authentic furniture, armorial stained glass, tapestries, and works of art. By day, the building's inner chambers and grounds are open for public tours; at night, the castle's Great Hall serves as a candlelit setting for medieval banquets and entertainment (see "Where to Dine," below).

Bunratty Castle is the focal point of a 20-acre theme park, appropriately known as Bunratty Folk Park. This re-creation of a typical 19th-century Irish village includes thatched cottages, farmhouses, and an entire village street with school, post office, pub, grocery store, print shop, and a hotel—all open to browsing and shopping. Fresh scones are baked in the cottages, and craftspeople ply their trades, from knitting and weaving to candlemaking, pottery, and photography.

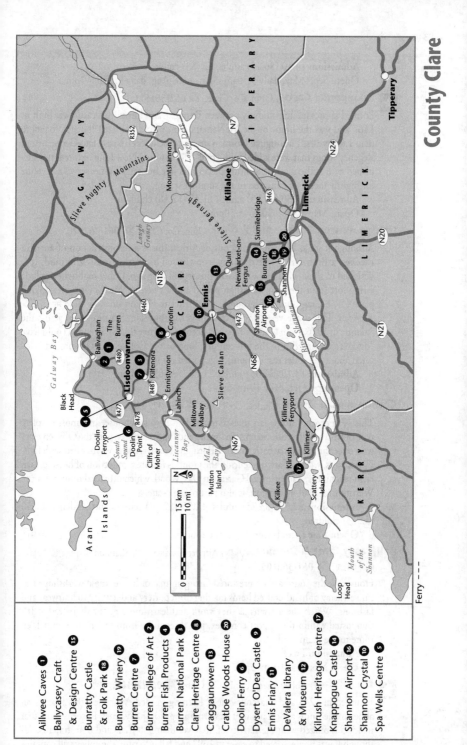

County Clare

Aillwee Caves ❶

Ballycasey Craft
& Design Centre ⓯

Bunratty Castle
& Folk Park ⓲

Bunratty Winery ⓳

Burren Centre ❼

Burren College of Art ❷

Burren Fish Products ❹

Burren National Park ❸

Clare Heritage Centre ⓭

Craggaunowen ⓴

Cratloe Woods House ⓴

Doolin Ferry ❻

Dysert O'Dea Castle ❾

Ennis Friary ⓫

DeValera Library
& Museum ⓬

Kilrush Heritage Centre ⓱

Knappogue Castle ⓮

Shannon Airport ⓰

Shannon Crystal ❿

Spa Wells Centre ❺

Ferry – – –

Admission: £4.10 ($6.15) adults, £2 ($3) children.

Open: Sept–May, daily 9:30am–5pm, June–Aug, daily 9:30am–7pm.

 Knappogue Castle, Quin, Co. Clare. ☎ **061/361511.**

Located approximately midway between Bunratty and Ennis, this castle was built in 1467 and was the home of the McNamara clan, who dominated the area for more than 1,000 years. The original Norman structure includes elaborate late-Georgian and Regency wings that were added in the mid-19th century. Now fully restored, it is furnished with authentic 15th-century pieces and, like Bunratty Castle, serves as a venue for nightly medieval banquets in the summer season.

Admission: £2.30 ($3.45) adults, £1.45 ($2.18) children.

Open: May–Oct, 9:30am–5:30pm.

Craggaunowen Bronze-Age Project, Quin, Co. Clare. ☎ **061/367178.**

Although it looks like something out of Africa, this is a reconstruction of an Irish *crannog,* a Bronze Age lake dwelling, constructed of wattles, reeds, and mud. It is designed to show what life was like in this region long ago. Other highlights include a ring fort from the early Christian period and a *Fulachta Fiadha* (ancient cooking place). The Craggaunowen grounds also shelter the history-making hide boat, *The Brendan.* This is the vessel in which explorer/author Tim Severin sailed across the Atlantic in 1976, from County Kerry to Boston, to prove that St. Brendan could have "discovered" America in the 6th century, long before Columbus. This project is located about ten miles east of Ennis, signposted off R 469.

Admission: £3.10 ($4.65) adults, £1.80 ($2.70) children.

Open: Apr–Oct, daily 10am–6pm.

Cratloe Woods House, Cratloe, Co. Clare. ☎ **061/327028.**

This 17th century house is a fine example of an Irish longhouse, an almost obsolete type of Irish architecture. Steeped in history and long associated with the O'Brien clan, who trace their ancestry back to Brian Boru, the house is still lived in, filled with family portraits, works of art, and curios; the grounds feature a collection of horse-drawn farm machinery. The primeval Garranon Oak Wood, which provided timbers for the Westminster Hall in London, is also part of the estate.

Admission: £2.50 ($3.75) adults, £1.75 ($2.63) seniors and students, £1.50 ($2.25) children.

Open: June to mid-Sept, Mon–Sat 2–6pm.

Ballycasey Craft & Design Centre, Airport Road (N 19), Shannon Airport, Co. Clare. ☎ **061/362105.**

Housed in the courtyard of a restored Georgian manor house, these workshops feature an array of hand-crafted items ranging from pottery and jewelry to knitwear and fashions. Watch the artisans as they work and learn more about their trades. It's signposted within the airport complex, just three miles from the main terminal, en route to the main road.

Admission: Free.

Open: Mon–Sat 10am–5pm.

⭐ **Ennis Friary,** Abbey Street, Ennis, Co. Clare. ☎ **065/29100.**

Founded in 1241 and a famous seat of learning in medieval times, this Franciscan abbey made Ennis a focal point of western Europe for many years. Records show that in 1375 it buzzed with the activity of no fewer than 350 friars and 600 students. Although it was finally forced to close in 1692 and fell into ruin, the abbey still contains many interesting sculpted tombs, decorative fragments, and carvings, including the famous McMahon tomb. The nave and chancel are the oldest parts of the Friary, but other structures—such as the 15th-century tower, transcept, and sacristy—are also rich in architectural detail.

Admission: £1 ($1.50) adults, 70p ($1.05) seniors, 40p (60¢) children and students.

Open: Late May to late Sept, daily 9:30am–6:30pm.

De Valera Library & Museum, Harmony Row, off Abbey Street, Ennis, Co. Clare. ☎ 065/21616.

Housed in a renovated 19th-century Presbyterian church, this museum/library pays tribute to Ireland's American-born freedom fighter and president, Eamonn de Valera (1882–1975). It contains many of de Valera's personal possessions, including his private car. There are also an art collection and interesting area relics, such as a door from a Spanish Armada galleon that sank off the Clare coast in 1588 at a place now known as Spanish Point. A bronze statue of de Valera stands several blocks away at the Ennis Courthouse.

Admission: Free.

Open: Mon and Wed–Thurs 11am–5:30pm, Tues and Fri 11am–8pm.

Bunratty Winery, Bunratty, Co. Clare. ☎ 061/362222.

Housed in a coachhouse dating back to 1816, this winery produces mead—a medieval drink made from honey, fermented grape juice, water, matured spirits, and a selection of herbs. In days long ago, it was served by the jugful at regal gatherings and at weddings. In fact, the custom required that a bride and groom continue to drink mead for one full moon in order to increase the probability of a happy marriage—legend has it that this is how the word *honeymoon* originated. Today the Bunratty Winery produces mead primarily for consumption at Bunratty Castle's medieval-style banquets. Visitors are welcome to stop by this working winery, watch the production in progress, and taste the brew.

Admission: Free.

Open: Daily 9:30am–5:30pm.

Shannon Crystal, Sandfield Road, Ennis, Co. Clare. ☎ 065/21250.

Situated on the north end of town, on the approach to Galway road, this is the Shannon area's own crystal-making enterprise, producing original handcut glassware on the premises. The showroom is open to visitors, who can watch daily demonstrations by the master cutter.

Admission: Free.

Open: Daily 9am–6pm.

SAVVY SHOPPING

As the home of Shannon Duty-Free Airport, this section of County Clare is synonymous with shopping. Here are just a few suggestions to get you started.

Avoca, Limerick/Ennis Road (N 18), Bunratty, Co. Clare. ☎ 061/364029.

This thatched-roof pink cottage shop is a branch of the legendary Co. Wicklow–based Avoca Handweavers, the oldest company of its kind in Ireland, dating back to 1723. Like its sister shops, this one carries all the colorful tweeds and mohairs that have made the Avoca line famous, plus linen-cotton fashions, stylish sweaters, tweed totes, and a wide array of hats. A coffee shop is on the premises. Open daily from 9:30am to 5:30pm.

Belleek Shop, 36 Abbey St., Ennis. ☎ **065/22607.**

Located in the heart of Ennis, this shop dates back more than 50 years and was the first Belleek china outlet in southern Ireland. In recent years, it has expanded to include other Irish products, such as handmade character dolls and turf crafts as well as crystal, pottery, pewter, and fashionable tweeds. Open Monday through Saturday from 9:30am to 6pm.

Carraig Donn, 7 O'Connell St., Ennis, Co. Clare. ☎ **065/28188.**

This shop offers a wide array of hand-crafted gifts from all over Ireland—from colorful sweaters and knitwear to pressed-flower design jewelry, linens, music boxes, and woolly sheep souvenirs. Open Monday through Saturday from 9:30am to 6pm.

Crusty's Traditional Music Shop, Francis Street, Ennis. ☎ **065/21727.**

If you'd like to bring back the melodious sounds of County Clare, this is the place to shop. The wares include a full range of traditional and folk music tapes, CDs, and books, as well as books, photos, paintings, and crafts pertaining to traditional music. You can also buy your own fiddle, tin whistle, banjo, concertina, accordion, flute, or strings. Open Monday to Friday from 9:30am to 5:30pm and Saturday from 9:30am to 4:30pm.

Dalcassian House, 61 O'Connell St., Ennis. ☎ **065/24686.**

Located opposite the Old Ground Hotel, the classy mullioned-window shopfront of this store stands out on the Ennis streetscape. You'll also be impressed by the wide array of Irish and international fine chinas, porcelain, crystal, lace, linens, knitwear, and jewelry. Open Monday to Saturday from 9:30am to 6pm.

Shannon Duty Free Shops, Shannon Airport, Co. Clare. ☎ **061/471444.**

Founded in 1947, this huge airport complex is known throughout the world as the grand-daddy of duty-free shops. It offers tax-free bargains to shoppers in transit or departing from the airport. About 65% of the products are Irish, such as Waterford crystal, Belleek china, Donegal tweeds, Aran knitwear, Connemara marble, ceramic leprechauns, shillelaghs, and smoked salmon, but you'll also find names like Wedgwood, Bing and Grondahl, Lladro, Anri, Limoges, Orrefors, and Pringle. Open daily from 9am to 7pm or later, depending on flight departures.

SPORTS & RECREATION

GOLFING Where else but in Ireland can you step off a plane and step up to the first tee? The 18-hole, par-72 championship course at the **Shannon Golf Club,** Shannon Airport (☎ **061/471020**), welcomes visitors to play, for greens fees of £22 ($33) on weekdays and £26 ($39) on weekends. Located within a half-mile of the main terminal, it is surrounded by scenic vistas of Co. Clare and the Shannon River as well as the busy jetways.

Other choices in the area include the newly expanded 18-hole, par-71 **Dromoland Golf Club,** Newmarket-on-Fergus, Co. Clare (☎ **061/368444**), with greens fees of £20 ($30) on weekdays and £22 ($33) on weekends; and the par-69 parkland course at the **Ennis Golf Club,** Drumbiggle, Ennis, Co. Clare (☎ **065/24074**), with greens fees of £15 ($22.50).

HORSEBACK RIDING Horseback riding over 40 acres of the County Clare can be arranged at the **Smithtown Riding Centre,** Ennis Road, Newmarket-on-Fergus, Co. Clare (☎ **061/3611494**). It's located two miles north of Shannon Airport. An hour's ride averages £10 to £12 ($15 to $18).

WHERE TO STAY
Very Expensive/Expensive

★ **Dromoland Castle**, Limerick/Ennis Road (N 18), Newmarket-on-Fergus, Co. Clare. ☎ **061/368144** or toll free **800/346-7007** in U.S. Fax 061/363355. 73 rms (all with bath). TV TEL

Rates: £112–£194 ($168–$281) single or double. Service charge 15%. AE, DC, MC, V.

Live like a king or queen in a fairy-tale setting of turrets and towers (but with every 20th-century luxury) at impressive castle hotel, just eight miles from Shannon Airport. It is nestled beside the River Rine, amid 400 acres of parklands and gardens that are home to varied species of wildlife, including a deer herd. In 1686 the castle was built by the O'Briens, the High Kings of Ireland, and was restored and refurbished 30 years ago as a hotel. As befits its royal exterior, the drawing rooms and stately halls are full of splendid wood and stone carvings, medieval suits of armor, rich oak paneling, and original oil paintings. The guest rooms are individually decorated with designer fabrics and reproduction furniture; many look out onto the water or the romantic walled gardens.

Dining/Entertainment: The Earl of Thomond restaurant is known for French cuisine served in a regal setting overlooking the lake. There's also a relaxing bar/lounge.

Services: Concierge, 24-hour room service, laundry and dry cleaning.

Facilities: 18-hole golf course, two tennis courts, walking/jogging trails, equipment for fishing and boating.

Moderate

Clare Inn, Limerick/Ennis Road (N 18), Newmarket-on-Fergus, Co. Clare. ☎ **061 368161** or toll free **800/528-1234.** Fax 061/368622. 121 rms (all with bath). TV TEL

Rates: £45–£60 ($67.50–$90) single, £60–£99 ($90–$148.50) double. AE, DC, MC, V. No service charge. **Closed:** Jan–Feb.

Panoramic views of the River Shannon and the Clare hills are part of the scene at this contemporary Tudor-style hotel, within eight miles of Shannon Airport and surrounded by the Dromoland Castle golf course. The public areas are bright and airy, with large picture windows framing the countryside vistas. The guest rooms are furnished in standard style with cheery colors and floral prints.

Dining/Entertainment: Choices include Deerfields restaurant, Castlefergus Bar, and the Coffee Dock café.

Facilities: 18-hole championship golf course, indoor heated swimming pool, Jacuzzi, gym, sauna, solarium, two tennis courts, jogging track, pitch and putt, games room.

★ **Fitzpatrick Bunratty Shamrock Inn**, Limerick/Ennis Road (N18), Bunratty, Co. Clare. ☎ **061/361177** or toll free **800/367-7701** in the U.S. Fax 061/471252. 118 rms (all with bath). TV TEL

Rates: £59–£75 ($88.50–$112.50) single, £75–£105 ($112.50–$157.50) double. Service charge 12.5%. AE, DC, MC, V.

Ideally located five miles from Shannon Airport, this rambling two-story ranch-style hotel sits on its own wooded grounds, set back from the main road and next to Bunratty Castle and Folk Park. The guest rooms are contemporary, with beamed ceilings, light woods, tall windows offering views of the gardens and Bunratty Castle, and multitoned

Irish fabrics and furnishings. In-room extras include a hairdryer, an ironing board and iron, and a luggage rack; some units have Jacuzzis. The public areas include a plant-filled sunlit conservatory and a spacious lobby/lounge. Like its sister hotels, Fitzpatrick's Castle in Dublin and Fitzpatrick's Silver Springs in Cork, this inn exudes a friendly atmosphere, brimming with the pervasive Fitzpatrick family finesse and hospitality.

Dining/Entertainment: Seafood and game are the specialties of Truffles Restaurant, where there is also an efficient breakfast buffet each morning; An Bruion Bar is a lively lounge with musical entertainment most evenings.

Services: Concierge, valet-laundry service, room service, courtesy minibus service to/from the airport.

Facilities: Indoor heated swimming pool, sauna.

Old Ground, O'Connell Street, Ennis, Co. Clare. ☎ **065/28127** or toll free **800/CALL-THF** in U.S. Fax 065/28112. 58 rms. TV TEL

Rates (including full breakfast): £48–£80 ($72–$120) single, £70–£100 ($105–$150) double. No service charge. AE, DC, MC, V.

Long a focal point in the busy marketing town of Ennis, this ivy-covered two-story hotel dates back to 1749. According to a citation at the front entrance, it has been known variously as the Great Inn of Jayl Street and the Kings Arms; part of the hotel was once used as the Town Hall and the Town Jail. Many of the furnishings are antiques—you'll find vintage tea chests in the halls, and there's even a 1553 fireplace that once warmed the interior of nearby Lemaneagh Castle. Most of the guest rooms have a modern decor and little extras like in-room coffee/tea-makers. Amenities include a restaurant, a grill room, and a very atmospheric pub called The Poet's Corner. In summer cabaret-style entertainment is provided on many evenings.

 Shannon Great Southern Hotel, Airport Road (N 19), Shannon International Airport, Co. Clare. ☎ **061/471122** or toll free in the U.S. **800/44-UTELL.** Fax 061/471982. 115 rooms. TV TEL

Rates: £78–£84 ($117–$126) single or double. Service charge 12.5%. AE, DC, MC, V. **Closed:** Dec 23–27.

This has to be among the most convenient airport hotels in the world, right across the street from the main Shannon departure area. You can not only walk to/from your flights but can enjoy fine views of the Irish countryside, including glimpses of the adjacent River Shannon. Best of all, this modern two-story hotel is totally soundproofed, offering contemporary guest rooms with every up-to-date convenience, including a coffee/tea-maker, hairdryer, and garment press. Public areas include a restaurant and cocktail bar.

West County Inn, Clare Road (N18), Ennis, Co. Clare. ☎ **065/28421** or toll free **800/528-1234** in U.S. Fax 065/28801. 110 rms (all with bath). TV TEL

Rates: £35–£55 ($52.50–$82.50) single, £58–£70 ($87–$105) double. No service charge. AE, MC, V.

This modern three-story hotel is set on its own grounds on the southern edge of Ennis, 17 miles from Shannon. The decor makes use of wide-windowed facades and skylights in many of the public areas. The guest rooms are roomy and functional, with traditional furnishings and quilted psastel-toned fabrics; many units have views of the nearby Clare hills. Dining and entertainment facilities include The Pine Room candlelit restaurant; the County Grill for a light meal; the Ivory Bar, a piano bar; and an Irish cabaret show in summer (see "Evening Entertainment," below).

Apple Bank for Savings

Moderate/Inexpensive

Queens Hotel, Abbey Street, Ennis, Co. Clare. ☎ **065/28963** or toll free **800/365-3346** in U.S. Fax 065/28628. 52 rms (all with bath). TV TEL

Rates (including full breakfast): £25–£40 ($37.50–$60) single, £36–£70 ($54–$105) double. No service charge. AE, DC, MC, V.

James Joyce fans will feel especially comfortable in this hotel, since the famous author referred to it as "delightful" in *Ulysses.* It is no surprise that the hotel uses this literary connection to the hilt, with a Victorian-style restaurant named Joyce's, and a bar called Bloom's. Nestled in the heart of Ennis next to the old friary, it dates back more than 100 years but was recently updated and expanded to contemporary standards, while still preserving its old-world quality. The guest rooms are furnished in traditional style, with dark woods and frilly floral fabrics, along with the modern additions of garment presses, hairdryers, and coffee/tea-makers.

Inexpensive/Budget

$ **Cill Eoin House,** Killadysert Cross, Clare Road, Ennis, Co. Clare. ☎ **065/41668** or **065/41669.** Fax 065/20224. 14 rms (all with bath). TV TEL

Rates (including full breakfast): £17.50 ($26.25) single, £35 ($52.50) double. No service charge. AE, MC, V.

Situated just off the main N 18 Road at the Killadysert Cross a half-mile south of Ennis, this newly built two-story guesthouse is a real find. It offers bright and comfortable guest rooms with hotel-quality furnishings at a very affordable price, capped by attentive service from the McGann family. Although it's within walking distance of Ennis, the rooms offer lovely views of the countryside. The house is named after the nearby medieval Killone Abbey (*Cill Eoin* is Irish for Killone).

WHERE TO DINE

Medieval Banquets & Traditional Meals with Music

The medieval banquets at Bunratty Castle and Knappogue Castle and the traditional evening at Bunratty Folk Park can be booked in advance in the United States through a travel agent or by calling toll free **800/CIE-TOUR.**

⭐ **Bunratty Castle,** Limerick/Ennis Road (N 18), Bunratty, Co. Clare. ☎ **061/361511.**

Cuisine: MEDIEVAL BANQUET. **Reservations:** Required.
Price: Dinner and entertainment £29.50 ($44.25). AE, DC, MC, V.
Open: Daily year-round; two sittings, 5:30 and 8:45pm.

Built in 1425, this splendid structure is the most complete and authentic example of a medieval castle in Ireland. Each evening a full medieval banquet is re-created with music, song, and merriment. Seated at long tables in the castle's magnificent baronial hall, you'll feast on ancient recipes using modern Irish ingredients—all served in strictly medieval use-your-fingers style. For refreshment, there's mulled wine, claret, and mugs of mead (the traditional honey-based drink). To add to the fun, at each banquet a "lord and lady" are chosen from the participants to reign over the three-hour proceedings and someone else is thrown into the dungeon.

⭐ **Knappogue Castle,** Quin, Co. Clare. ☎ **061/361511.**
Cuisine: MEDIEVAL BANQUET. **Reservations:** Required.
Price: Dinner and Entertainment £29.50 ($44.25). AE, DC, MC, V.
Open: May–Oct daily; two sittings, 5:30pm and 8:45pm.

Once the stronghold of the McNamara clan, this castle was built in 1467. Now fully restored, it's the setting for authentic medieval banquets during the summer season. This castle is smaller and more intimate than Bunratty, but you'll still feast on a medieval meal, followed by a colorful pageant of Irish history celebrating the influential role of women in Celtic Ireland. The program includes rhyme and mime, song and dance.

⭐ **Traditional Irish Night,** Bunratty Folk Park, off the Limerick/Ennis Road (N 18), Bunratty, Co. Clare. ☎ **061/361511.**
Cuisine: TRADITIONAL IRISH. **Reservations:** Required.
Prices: Dinner and entertainment £24.50 ($36.75). AE, DC, MC, V.
Open: May–Sept daily; two sittings, 5:30pm and 8:45pm.

Irish country life of yesteryear is the focus of this "at home" evening in a thatched farmhouse cottage. You'll dine on a traditional meal of Irish stew, homemade breads, and apple pie and fresh cream. Then the music begins: the flute and fiddle, accordion, bodhran, and spoons—all to a spirited, foot-tapping pace.

Expensive Restaurants

⭐ **MacCloskey's,** Bunratty House, Bunratty Folk Park, Bunratty, Co. Clare.
☎ **061/364082.**
Cuisine: IRISH/FRENCH. **Reservations:** Required.
Prices: Set dinner £26 ($39). AE, DC, MC, V.
Open: Feb–Dec, Tues–Sat dinner 6:30–9pm. **Closed:** Christmas to late Jan.

Located in the former mews and wine cellars of Bunratty House, a restored 1804 Georgian mansion, this award-winning candlelight restaurant is the creation of a hard-working duo, Gerry and Marie MacCloskey. There are four dining rooms, each with original whitewashed walls, archways, and polished slate floors. Rack of lamb, black sole, mussels in champagne, duck à l'orange, crab crêpes, and wild salmon are specialties. You can also get a masterful Caesar salad or pickled herring here, plus desserts like hot Cointreau soufflé, chocolate mousse with brandy, or baked pear puffs. It's the best in the area—don't miss it.

Moderate Restaurants

⭐ **The Cloister,** Abbey Street, Ennis. ☎ **065/29521.**
Cuisine: IRISH. **Reservations:** Recommended.
Prices: Bar food all items £2–£6 ($3–$9); dinner appetizers £2.20–£6.50 ($3.30–$9.75); dinner main courses £10–£14.50 ($15–$21.75). MC, V.
Open: Daily lunch/bar food noon–3pm, dinner 6–10pm.

Next to the remains of a 13th-century abbey, this old-world gem offers innovative Irish cuisine. The decor is warmly elegant, with open turf fireplaces and stoves, beamed ceilings, and reproductions from the *Books of Kells* adorning the walls. The menu includes grilled Dover sole on the bone; poached monkfish with red-pepper sauce; filet of beef en croûte with Madeira sauce; rack of lamb; wild venison with juniper-and-Armagnac sauce; and suprême of chicken layered with Carrigline cheese and Irish Mist. A house specialty starter is Inagh goat cheese, laced with port-wine sauce. Pub-style lunches are served in the skylit Friary Bar, adjacent to the old abbey walls. Seafood chowders, traditional Irish stew, farmhouse omelets, beefburgers, and chicken and mushroom brioches are favorite "pub grub" choices.

Moderate/Inexpensive Restaurants

Brogan's, 24 O'Connell St., Ennis. ☎ **065/29859.**

Cuisine: IRISH. **Reservations:** Recommended for dinner.
Prices: Appetizers £1.75–£4.25 ($2.63–$6.38); main courses £5.75–£12 ($8.63–$18). MC, V.
Open: Daily noon–11pm.

An oldtimer in the center of town, this pub is known for its hearty meals, including Irish stew, beef stroganoff, chicken curry, or a variety of steaks. In addition, there are roast duck, chicken, and ham; Dover sole; and local salmon. The atmosphere is casual and the decor cozy, with brick walls, a copper-fluted fireplace, and ceiling fans. On Tuesday and Thursday nights ballad music is usually offered.

Cruise's Pub Restaurant, Abbey Street, Ennis. ☎ **065/41800.**

Cuisine: IRISH. **Reservations:** Recommended for dinner.
Prices: Bar food £1.25–£8.50 ($1.93–$12.75); dinner appetizers £2.50–£5.25 ($3.75–$7.88); dinner main courses £5.50–£12.50 ($8.25–$18.75). AE, DC, MC, V.
Open: Lunch noon–3pm, dinner 5:30–10:30pm.

Housed in a 1658 building, this relatively new eatery has low beamed ceilings, timber fixtures and fittings, crackling fires in open hearths, lantern lighting, a rough flagstone floor strewn with sawdust, memorabilia from crockery to books, and a snug appropriately dubbed "the Safe Haven." On warm days, seating is extended into an outdoor courtyard overlooking the friary. The menu offers a good selection of pub grub, from a specialty dish called Friars Irish Stew, to steaks, club sandwiches, and seafood soups and sandwiches. There are often impromptu music sessions. Evening meals range from seafood and steaks to vegetarian stir-fry or chicken Kiev.

EVENING ENTERTAINMENT

In addition to the medieval banquets and traditional ceili evenings that are synonymous with this area, County Clare offers much to delight the visitor in the evenings. Many hotels, such as the **West County,** Clare Road, Ennis (**065/28421**), present music or shows, particularly in the high season. It offers Summer Cabaret, 2$^{1}/_{2}$ hours of traditional music, drama, comedy, and step dancing. Running each Tuesday from June through September, the show can be enjoyed with or without dinner. Dinner starts at 7:30pm, the show at 8:30pm. Admission is £5 ($7.50) for the show only, £12 ($18) for dinner and the show.

For pure traditional entertainment, try **Cois na hAbhna** (pronounced *Cush-na howna*), Gort Road, Ennis (☎ **065/20996**). This center stages sessions of music, song, and dance, followed by ceili dancing with audience participation. Tea and brown bread

IMPRESSIONS

Stoney seaboard fair and foreign
Stoney hills poured over space,
Stoney outcrop of the Burren,
Stones in every fertile place. . . .
—Sir John Betjeman (1906–1984)

are served. Sessions run June through September, Wednesday and Thursday from 8:30 to 11:30pm. Admission ranges from £1.50 to £3 ($2.25–$4.50), depending on the event.

This region has many fine pubs, but one definitely should not be missed—**Durty Nelly's,** Limerick/Ennis Road (N 18), Bunratty, Co. Clare (☎ **061/364861**). Established in 1620 next door to Bunratty Castle, this cottage tavern was originally a watering hole for the castle guards. Now, with a mustard-colored facade and palm trees at its entrance, it's a favorite before-and-after haunt of local folk and of tourists who join the nightly medieval banquets at the castle. With mounted elk heads and old lanterns on the walls, sawdust on the floors, and open turf fireplaces, the decor hasn't changed much over the centuries. This is a also good spot for a substantial pub lunch; spontaneous Irish music sessions erupt here on most evenings.

2 The Burren

Moving westward from Ennis into the heart of County Clare, you'll come to an amazing district of 100 square miles called The Burren. The word *burren* is derived from the Irish word *boirreann,* which means a rocky place.

It is a strange, lunarlike region of bare carboniferous limestone, roughly bordered by the towns of Corofin, Ennistymon, Lahinch, Lisdoonvarna, and Ballyvaughan. Massive sheets of rock, jagged and craggy boulders, caves, and potholes are visible for miles in a moonscapelike pattern, yet this is also a setting for little lakes and streams and an amazing assemblage of flora. Experts say there is always something in bloom, even in winter—from fern and moss to orchids, rock roses, milkworts, wild thyme, geraniums, violets, and fuchsia. The Burren is also famous for its butterflies, which thrive on the rare flora. Such animals as the pine martin, stoat, and badger, rare in the rest of Ireland, are also common here.

The story of The Burren began more than 300 million years ago when layers of shells and sediment were deposited under a tropical sea, only to be thrust above this surface many millions of years later and left open to the erosive power of Irish rain and weather, producing the limestone landscape that appears today.

As early as 7,000 years ago, humans began to leave their mark on this landscape in the form of Stone Age burial monuments such as the Poulnabrone Dolmen and Gleninsheen wedge tomb.

In addition to rock, The Burren area does have other unique attractions. Lisdoonvarna, on the western edge, is a town known for its spa of natural mineral springs. Each summer it draws thousands of people to bathe in its therapeutic waters of sulphur, chalybeate (iron), and iodine. Lisdoon, as the natives call it, is also known worldwide for hosting an annual Matchmaking Festival.

One of the most scenic Burren drives is the corkscrew-shaped road (R 480) that leads from Corofin to Ballyvaughan, a delightful little village overlooking Galway Bay.

WHAT TO SEE & DO

⭐ **Burren National Park,** The Burren, Co. Clare.

Currently under development as a national park, the confines of this park encompass the entire Burren area (100 square miles): a remarkable limestone plateau dotted with ruined castles, cliffs, rivers, lakes, valleys, green road walks, barren rock mountains, and plant life that defies all of nature's conventional rules. The area is particularly rich in archaeological remains—dolmens, stone arches, round towers, ancient churches, high crosses, crannogs, tombs, monasteries, and holy wells. In recent years there has been some local controversy with regard to the defining of the park and the place-ment of a permanent visitor/interpretative center, such as those centers at Connemara and Glenveagh National Parks. Until these issues are resolved, the park remains with-out an official entrance point, with no admission charges or restrictions to access.

The Burren Centre, Kilfenora, Co. Clare. ☎ **065/88030.**

Established in 1975 in the heart of The Burren as a community development coop-erative, this building is the best place to acquaint yourself with all facets of this area. The facility includes a 25-minute audiovisual and landscape models and interpretive displays that highlight the unique features of the region's geology and geography, as well as the various types of flora and fauna. Also here are tearooms, a shop stocked with Burren-made crafts and products, and picnic tables outside.

Admission: £2 ($3) adults, £1.50 ($2.25) seniors, £1 ($1.50) children over age 8.

Open: Mar–May and Sept–Oct, daily 10am–5pm; June–Aug, daily 9:30am–6pm.

★ **Aillwee Cave,** Ballyvaughan, Co. Clare. ☎ **065/77036.**

One of Ireland's oldest underground sites, Aillwee was formed millions of years ago, although it was discovered less than 50 years ago by local farmer Jacko McGann. The cave has over 3,400 feet of passages and hollows running straight into the heart of a mountain. Its highlights are bridged chasms, deep caverns, a frozen waterfall, and the Bear Pits, hollows scraped out by the brown bear, one of the cave's original inhab-itants. Guided tours, which last approximately half an hour, are conducted continu-ously. Among facilities are a café and craft shop, as well as a unique farmhouse cheese-making enterprise near the cave's entrance, Burren Gold Cheese, and an api-ary where honey is produced.

Admission: £3.85 ($5.78) adults, £2.20 ($3.30) children aged 4–16.

Open: Daily mid-Mar to June and Sept to early Nov, 10am–5:30pm; July–Aug, 10am–6:30pm.

Clare Heritage Centre, Corofin, Co. Clare. ☎ **065/37955.**

If you have Clare family roots, you'll be fascinated by this genealogical research cen-ter. Even if you don't have Clare ancestry, this center is worth a visit to learn about the history of the county. Housed in a former Church of Ireland edifice, it has exhib-its on Clare farming, industry, commerce, education, forestry, language, and music, all designed to reflect life in County Clare during the last 300 years. There's also a tea room and gift shop.

Admission: £1.75 ($2.63) adults, 75p ($1.08) children under 12.

Open: Apr–Oct, daily 10am–6pm.

Dysert O'Dea Castle & Archaeology Centre, Corofin, Co. Clare. ☎ **065/37722.**

Built in 1480 by Diarmaid O'Dea on a rocky outcrop of land, this castle was badly damaged during the Cromwellian years but was restored and opened to the public in 1986 as an archaeology center and museum, with exhibitions on the history of the area, plus an audiovisual show. The castle is also the starting point for a signposted trail leading to 25 sites of historical and archaeological interest within a two-mile ra-dius, including a church founded by St. Tola in the 8th century; it contains a unique Romanesque doorway surrounded by a border of 12 heads carved in stone. The O'Deas, who were chieftains of the area, are buried under the church. Also here are a round tower from the 10th or 12th century, a 12th-century high cross, holy well, a 14th-century battlefield, and a stone fort, believed to date back to the Iron Age.

Admission: £1.80 ($2.70) adults, 80p ($1.20) children.

Open: May–Sept, daily 10am–6pm.

Spa Wells Centre, Kincora Road, Lisdoonvarna, Co. Clare. ☎ 065/74023.

Nestled in a shady parkland on the edge of town, this is Lisdoonvarna's famous Victorian-style spa complex, dating from the 18th century. The sulphur-laced mineral waters are served hot or cold in the pump room, drawn from an illuminated well. Sulphur baths can also be arranged. Videos of the Burren and the Shannon area are shown continuously in the visitor center.

Admission: Free.

Open: June–Oct, daily 10am–6pm.

Burren College of Art, Newtown Castle, Ballyvaughan, Co. Clare. ☎ 065/77200.

If there ever was a great place for an artist to paint or a photographer to take a picture, it has to be The Burren. Bearing this in mind, this new center of artistic learning has sprung up in the midst of the dramatic Burren landscapes. Set on the grounds of a 16th-century castle, this newly constructed college was opened in 1993. Although geared to granting full four-year Bachelor of Fine Arts degrees or 15-week semester programs, it also offers shorter summer school courses that are ideal for a visitor. The facilities include bright modern studios for sculpture, painting, photography, and drawing, plus top-class lecturers.

Admission: Fees vary, according to courses.

Open: Year-round.

Burren Fish Products, Kincora Road, Lisdoonvarna, Co. Clare. ☎ 065/74432.

Aficionados of smoked salmon flock to this place to see the fish-smoking process first-hand and to buy right from the source. Visitors are welcome to watch as fresh Atlantic salmon is sorted, hand-treated, salted, and then slowly smoked over Irish oak chippings in the traditional way. Each side of salmon is then vacuum sealed and chilled. Tours are given continually. Smoked mackerel, eels, and trout are also produced here.

Admission: Free.

Open: Daily 10am–6pm.

SPORTS & RECREATION

WALKING   With its unique terrain and pathways, The Burren lends itself to walking. Visitors who want to amble through the hills and turloughs, limestone pavements and terraces, shale uplands and inland lakes, should follow The Burren Way, a 26-mile signposted route stretching from Ballyvaughan to Liscannor. An information sheet outlining the route is available from any tourist office.

SAVVY SHOPPING

Manus Walsh Art Gallery & Craft Workshop, Main Street, Ballyvaughan, Co. Clare. ☎ 065/77029.

This shop in the center of town features a wide range of colorful hand-crafted enamel jewelry of Celtic and early Irish designs. Visitors are welcome to watch Manus work as they browse or buy. Items for sale include pendants, brooches, earrings, ornate boxes, dishes, and plaques made by Manus, as well as crafts by other local artisans, from art prints depicting the flowers of Clare coast and posters of the Clare hills to perfumes made from the scents of Burren flora and whiskey marmalades. Open April through October, Monday through Saturday from 10am to 6pm.

WHERE TO STAY & DINE
Moderate

⭐ **Gregan's Castle**, Ballyvaughan/Lisdoonvarna Road (N67), Ballyvaughan,
Co. Clare. ☎ **065/77005** or toll free **800/223-6510** in U.S. Fax 065/77111. 22 rms
(all with bath). TEL

Rates (with full breakfast): £76–£89 ($114–$133.50) single, £99 ($148.50). Service
charge 12.5%. MC, V. **Closed:** Nov–Mar.

Located in the northern part of County Clare, just over three miles outside of
Ballyvaughan, this two-story country house is in the heart of the rocky Burren country,
with distant views of Galway Bay. Although not strictly a castle in the architectural sense,
it is built on the site of the ancient family estates of the Martyn family and the
O'Loughlens, Princes of The Burren. Owner-managed by the Hayden family, it's surrounded by beautiful gardens. The public areas, which include a traditional drawing room
and library, are furnished with heirlooms and period pieces, antique books, and Raymond
Piper's mural paintings of Burren flora. The Corkscrew Bar is a particular delight, with
copper and brass hangings and an open turf fireplace. Each bedroom is individually
decorated in country-house style, with designer fabrics, dark woods, and brass accents;
some have four-poster or canopied beds. The restaurant, with distant views of Galway
Bay, has a reputation for fine seafood and creative cookery.

WHERE TO STAY
Inexpensive

Carrigann Hotel, Lisdoonvarna, Co. Clare. ☎ **065/74036** or toll free **800/989-7676** in
U.S. Fax 065/74567. 14 rms (all with bath). TV TEL

Rates (including full breakfast): £29–£37 ($43.50–$55.50) single, £44–£60 double ($66–
$90). MC, V. **Closed:** Nov–Feb.

Situated on a hillside just off the main road on the outskirts of town, this country
house–style hotel is surrounded by rose bushes and flower-filled gardens. Most of the
guest rooms, which have standard furnishings, are enhanced by views of the gardens.
Facilities include a restaurant, lounge bar, and sun lounge.

⭐ **Rusheen Lodge**, Knocknagrough, Ballyvaughan, Co. Clare. ☎ **065/77092.**
Fax 065/77152. 6 rms (all with bath). TV TEL

Rates (including full breakfast): £32–£36 ($48–$54) single or double. No service charge.
MC, V. **Closed:** Mid-Dec to Feb.

On the main road just south of Ballyvaughan village, this modern two-story
bungalow-style guesthouse is surrounded by flowers, both in the garden and hanging
from baskets in front of the house. The innkeepers are Rita and John McGann, whose
father, Jacko McGann, discovered the nearby Aillwee Caves, one of the area's most
remarkable natural attractions. The guest rooms are individually furnished with light
woods, semicanopied beds, and floral fabrics and include a coffee/tea-maker and
hairdryer. Breakfast, served in a cheery pastel-toned room overlooking the gardens,
presents freshly caught local fish as an option. Dried and fresh Burren flowers enhance
the decor throughout the house.

WHERE TO DINE

Moderate

Claire's, Main Street, Ballyvaughan, Co. Clare. ☎ **065/77029.**

Cuisine: IRISH. **Reservations:** Required.
Prices: Appetizers £2–£4.95 ($3–$7.43); main courses £6.95–£12.95 ($10.43–$19.43). MC, V.
Open: July–Aug, Mon–Sat 7–10pm; May–June and Sept, Mon–Fri 7–10pm; and Mar–Apr, some weekends 7–10pm.

A favorite place with regular visitors to The Burren, this homey and intimate restaurant in the middle of the village is the domain of Claire Walsh, whose husband, Manus, operates an adjacent craft shop (see "Savvy Shopping," above). Just as Manus is creative with enamel designs, so Claire is equally clever in the kitchen. The menu often includes such dishes as Burren rack of lamb with rosemary; sirloin steak with Irish whiskey mustard sauce; half duckling with pineapple sauce; baked salmon with hollandaise sauce; baked Ballyvaughan crab with garlic bread crumbs; and vegetarian bean Provençale with rice or vegetable curry.

⭐ **Whitethorn,** Galway Road (N 67), Ballyvaughan. ☎ **065/77044.**

Cuisine: IRISH. **Reservations:** Recommended for dinner.
Prices: Buffet items £1.50–£6.95 ($2.25–10.43); appetizers £1.50–£3.95 ($2.25–$5.93); main courses at lunch £4.50–£6.95 ($7.25–$10.43), at dinner £8.95–£12.95 ($13.43–$19.43). MC, V.
Open: Lunch and snacks: Mar–Oct, daily 10am–6pm; dinner: Mar–May and Oct, Fri–Sat 6–9pm; June–Sept, Wed–Sat 6–9pm.

With a sailboat-shaped weathervane on the roof, it's not surprising that this site was once a coastguard station and then a fish-processing factory. Totally rebuilt in 1989 as a restaurant, it has a stone facade that blends right in with The Burren's terrain. The interior has a refreshing decor of ketchup-colored paneling, black tables and chairs, old photographs, fresh Burren flowers, and floor-to-ceiling slanted windows that provide spectacular views of Galway Bay and distant shores. There is seating outside as well, particularly popular in the evening for sunset-watching over Galway Bay. Lunch items, served buffet style, include fresh seafood salads, pastas, soups, and meat casseroles or platters. The dinner menu offers such choices as rack of lamb with rosemary-and-almond sauce; grilled sirloin steak with Irish whiskey sauce; duck with fruit sauce; salmon with herb-and-cream sauce; and wholemeal crêpes filled with mixed vegetables. It's located about a mile east of the village on the main road.

Moderate/Inexpensive

Bofey Quinn's, Main Street, Corofin, Co. Clare. ☎ **065/27627.**

Cuisine: IRISH. **Reservations:** Not necessary.
Prices: Appetizers £1.75–£5 ($2.63–$7.50); main courses £7–£10.50 ($10.50–$15.75). MC, V.
Open: Daily 6–10pm.

An informal atmosphere prevails at this pub/restaurant in the center of town. Dinner specialties include fresh wild salmon; scallops in white wine; whole black sole on the bone, and stuffed chicken and ham, as well as a variety of steaks, chops, and mixed grills. Pub grub lunches are also available throughout the day.

3 | The Clare Coast

One of Ireland's most photographed scenes, the Cliffs of Moher draw busloads and carloads of visitors to Clare's remote reaches every day of the year. Rising sheer above the Atlantic Ocean to over 700 feet and extending about five miles along the coast, these cliffs are County Clare's foremost natural wonder.

The Cliffs are only the beginning, however. Other highlights of the Clare Coast include the world-renowned golf resort at Lahinch, praised by ace golfers as the "St. Andrews of Ireland" and the paradigm of Irish links golf.

Farther up the coast is the secluded fishing village of Doolin, often referred to as the unofficial capital of Irish traditional music. Doolin, like Galway to the north, is also a departure point for a short boat trip to the Aran Islands.

The Clare Coast is dotted with a variety of seaside resorts, such as Kilrush, Kilkee, Miltown Malbay, and Ennistymon, that are particularly popular with Irish families. As you drive around this craggy coastline, you'll find many other off-the-beaten-path delights, some with intriguing placenames—Pink Cave, Puffing Hole, Intrinsic Bay, Chimney Hill, Elephant's Teeth, Mutton Island, Loop Head, and Lovers Leap.

WHAT TO SEE & DO

⭐ **Cliffs of Moher,** R 478, Co. Clare. ☎ 065/81171.

Hailed as one of Ireland's natural wonders, these 700-foot cliffs stretch for over five miles along Clare's Atlantic coast. They offer panoramic views, especially from the 19th-century O'Brien's Tower at the northern end. On a clear day you can see the Aran Islands, Galway Bay, and many distant vistas. The visitor center includes a tea room, an information desk, and a craft and souvenir shop. The Cliffs are located about five miles north of Lahinch.

Admission: Free to Cliffs; £1 ($1.50) to O'Brien's Tower.

Open: Cliffs visitor center, daily 10am–6pm; O'Brien's Tower, May–Oct, daily 10am–6pm.

Kilrush Heritage Centre, Town Hall, Market Square, off Henry Street, Kilrush. ☎ 065/51577 or 51047.

Housed in the town's historic Market House, this center provides historic and cultural background on Kilrush, often called the "capital of West Clare," and the south Clare coast. An audiovisual, *Kilrush in Landlord Times,* tells of the struggles of tenant farmers of this area during the 18th and 19th centuries and particularly during the Great Famine years. The museum is also the focal point of a signposted heritage walk around the town. The building itself, erected in 1808 by the Vandeleur family, the area's chief landlords, was burned to the ground in 1892 and rebuilt in its original style in 1931.

Admission: £1 ($1.50) adults, 50p (75¢ p) children.

Open: May–Sept, Mon–Sat 9:30am–5:30pm, Sun noon–4pm.

Trips to the Aran Islands

Doolin Ferry Co., The Pier, Doolin, Co. Clare. ☎ 065/74455.

Although many people come to Doolin to see the local sights and enjoy the music, they also come to board this ferry to the Aran Islands. The three fabled islands, sitting out in the Atlantic, are closer to Doolin than they are to Galway (five miles and a 30-minute journey). Service is provided to both Inisheer and Inishmore. (For more information about excursions to the Aran Islands, see Chapter 14, "Galway City.")

Fares: Inisheer £13 ($19.50) round-trip, Inishmore £18 ($27) round-trip.

Schedule: Mid-Apr to mid-May, daily 11am to both islands; rest of May, daily 10am, 11:30am, and 6:30pm to Inisheer, 10am and 11am to Inishmore; June–Aug, daily 9:30am, 11am, 1pm, 2:30pm (July–Aug only), 5:15pm, 6:30pm, and 7:30pm to Inisheer, 10am and 11am to Inishmore; Sept, daily 10am and 11:30am to both islands.

SPORTS & RECREATION

BOATING & FISHING   The waters of the lower Shannon estuary and the Atlantic coastline are known for good fishing for shark, skate, turbot, ray, conger eel, tope, pollack, and more. The new Kilrush Creek Marina, an attraction in itself, is the base for **Atlantic Adventures Sea Angling,** Cappa, Kilrush, Co. Clare (☎ 065/52133), a company that offers boat charters and rentals for fishing in these waters. Prices start at £25 ($37.50) per person for a day's fishing or £200 ($300) for an eight-hour boat charter. Drive-yourself fishing boats are also available from £75 ($112.50) per day; rods and reels can be hired for £5 ($7.50) per day.

GOLFING   For golfers coming to Clare's Atlantic coast, a day at **Lahinch Golf Club,** Lahinch (☎ 065/81003), is not to be missed. There are two 18-hole courses here, but the longer championship links course is the one that has given Lahinch its far-reaching reputation. This course's elevations, such as the 9th and 13th holes, reveal open vistas of sky, land, and sea; they also make the winds an integral part of the scoring. Watch out for the goats—they're Lahinch's legendary weather forecasters: If they huddle by the clubhouse, it means a storm is approaching. Visitors are welcome to play any day, especially on weekdays; greens fees range from £25 ($37.50) on weekdays to £30 ($45) on weekends.

SAVVY SHOPPING

Crafts Gallery, Ballyvoe, Doolin, Co. Clare. ☎ 065/74309.

Since 1982 this has been an oasis of fine craftsmanship in the heart of the Clare coast. Surrounded by gardens on the edge of the village next to the churchyard, this shop is the brainchild of two artisans—Matthew O'Connell, who creates batik work with Celtic designs on wall hangings, cushion covers, ties, and scarves; and Mary Gray, who hand-fashions contemporary gold and silver jewelry, inspired by The Burren's rock, flora, and wild flowers. There are also products by other Irish craftspeople, from sweaters and fashion separates to ceramics, leatherwork, crystal, linen, and lace. A good coffee shop is on the premises. Open daily from 8:30am to 8pm.

Traditional Music Shop, Doolin, Co. Clare. ☎ 065/74407.

In this town known for its traditional music, this small shop is a center of attention. It offers all types of Irish traditional music on cassette tape and compact disc, as well as books and instruments from tin whistles to bodhrans. Open Easter to mid-October daily from 10am to 6pm or later.

WHERE TO STAY

Moderate

Aberdeen Arms, Main Street, Lahinch, Co. Clare. ☎ 065/81100. Fax 065/81228. 55 rms (all with bath). TV TEL

Rates (including full breakfast): £40–£55 ($60–$82.50), £66–£88 ($99–$132) double. Service charge 10%. AE, DC, MC, V.

In the heart of town yet within view of the golf course that has made Lahinch famous, this hotel dates back over 140 years and is said to be the oldest golf links hotel in Ireland. It's an ideal base for golfers and for vacationers touring the Clare coast. The bedrooms are contemporary and functional, and the public rooms have a country-inn atmosphere. Facilities include a restaurant, coffee shop, and a golf-theme lounge bar where the chat is usually centered on golf. For nongolfers, there's a tennis court, squash court, and gym.

Moderate/Inexpensive

Aran View House, Doolin, Co. Clare. ☎ **065/74061** or **065/74420.** Fax 065/74540. 16 rms (all with bath). TV TEL

Rates (including full breakfast): £25–£35 ($37.50–$52.50) single, £45–£60 ($67.50–$90) double. AE, DC, MC, V. Closed: Nov–Mar.

Dating back to 1736, this three-story Georgian-style stone house stands on a hill on the main road, overlooking panoramic views of the Clare coastline. On a clear day you can see the Aran Islands—hence the house's name. In recent years, innkeepers John and Theresa Linnane have thoroughly updated and refurbished it as a hotel in traditional Irish style. The guest rooms are decorated with dark woods, and some have four-poster beds and armoires. Facilities include a restaurant and lounge. It's situated on 100 acres of farmland just north of town.

Inexpensive

Doolin House, Doolin, Co. Clare. ☎ **065/74259.** Fax 065/74474. 6 rms (all with bath). TEL

Rates (including full breakfast): £28–£36 ($42–$54) single or double. No service charge. MC, V. Closed: Dec 20–26.

Built as a guesthouse in 1991, this two-story traditional stone house sits on the main road on the edge of Doolin, with views of the countryside and the sea. The guest rooms have traditional dark-wood furnishings, with floral and pastel fabrics and accessories. Two rooms are on the ground floor. Facilities include a TV lounge for guests.

Doonmacfelim House, Doolin, Co. Clare. ☎ **065/74503.** Fax 065/74421. 8 rms (all with bath). TEL

Rates (including full breakfast): £20–£25 ($30–$37.50), £30–£36 ($45–$54) double. No service charge. MC, V.

Situated on the main street a few hundred feet from the famous Gus O'Connor's Pub, this modern two-story guesthouse is a great value in the heart of Doolin. Although it's in the center of everything, the house is also surrounded by a dairy farm. Guest rooms have standard furnishings and nice views of the neighboring countryside and town. Facilities include a hard tennis court.

WHERE TO DINE

Expensive/Moderate

Barrtra Seafood Restaurant, Barrtra, Lahinch, Co. Clare. ☎ **065/81280.**
Cuisine: SEAFOOD/VEGETARIAN. **Reservations:** Recommended.
Prices: Lunch main courses £1.50–£5 ($2.25–$7.50) except Sun; set lunch £8 ($12); set 4-course dinners £14–£17 ($21–$25.50). AE, DC, MC, V.
Open: May–Sept, lunch Mon–Sat 12:30–2:30pm; Sun lunch 12:30–3pm; dinner Mon–Sat 6–10pm.

Set in a country house overlooking Liscannor Bay, this wide-windowed restaurant is one of the few good coastal eateries with ocean views that serves lunch as well as dinner. Lunch items include mussels, oysters, soups, and salads, while dinner choices range from turbot with mushroom and sherry sauce to wild Irish salmon with white-wine sauce, black sole on the bone with parsley sauce, monkfish with wholegrain mustard sauce, and scallops au fromage bleu, plus rack of lamb with rosemary for those who prefer meat. In the vegetarian category are tomato-and-courgette (zucchini) roulade mornay; pastry filled with spinach, cream cheese, and sage; and stuffed aubergine (eggplant) with fresh tomato sauce. The menu also features house-smoked salmon and local Clare cheeses like Kilshanny in five flavors (garlic, pepper, herb, cumin, plain) Poolcoin (Burren goat's cheese), and Cratloe Hills Gold (sheep's cheese).

Moderate

Captain's Deck, R 478, Liscannor, Co. Clare. ☎ 065/81385.

Cuisine: IRISH. **Reservations:** Recommended.
Prices: Appetizers £1.50–£4.50 ($2.25–$7.25); main courses £8.50–£13.50 ($12.77–$20.25). AE, DC, MC, V.
Open: Easter–Sept, Tues–Sun dinner 6–10pm.

Looking out over Liscannor Bay, this nautical-theme restaurant sits up over an antiques shop, less than five miles south of the Cliffs of Moher. The menu offers such choices as lobster thermidor; sautéed skate with lemon and capers; médaillons of monkfish in garlic sauce; sirloin steak au poivre; stuffed quail with port wine; pan-fried escalope of veal; chicken Kiev; and honey-baked duckling.

★ **Manuel's**, Corbally, Kilkee, Co. Clare. ☎ 065/56211.

Cuisine: INTERNATIONAL. **Reservations:** Required.
Prices: Appetizers £1.75–£4.75 ($2.63–$7.13); main courses £9.50–£17.50 ($14.25–$26.25). DC, MC, V.
Open: Easter to mid–Sept, daily 7–10pm.

With wide windows on two sides looking out onto the Atlantic coast, this restaurant has a nautical ambience and decor. It's on high ground off the main road, about a mile north of Kilkee. Chef Manuel di Lucia relies heavily on local seafood, with choices like Clare lobster, served grilled or thermidor; baked Atlantic salmon stuffed with seafood mousseline in pastry with tomato-butter sauce; black sole on the bone; king prawns flame-grilled in garlic butter; chicken filet in tarragon sauce; and a selection of steaks.

The Setting Sun (Lui Na Greine), Spanish Point, Co. Clare. ☎ 065/84107.

Cuisine: IRISH. **Reservations:** Required.
Prices: Appetizers £2–£2.50 ($3–$3.75); main courses £9–£15 ($13.50–$22.50). MC, V.
Open: June–Sept, 6–10pm.

On the coast road just outside of Miltown Malbay, this seasonal restaurant is aptly named, as it provides great sunset views each evening, weather permitting. It has a country-cottage ambience, with a decor of pine antiques, tweedy plaid tablemats, and Irish art. The menu changes each evening but some specialties are hot seafood plate (prawns, scallops, mussels, salmon, and cod); breast of chicken with smoky bacon and mushroom sauce; vegetarian lasagne; turbot with lentil-and-coconut sauce; and wild Quilty salmon poached in white-wine dill sauce.

Moderate/Inexpensive

Ilsa's Cottage, Doolin, Co. Clare. ☎ 065/74244.

Cuisine: IRISH. **Reservations:** Required.
Prices: Appetizers £1.70–£5.40 ($2.55–$8.10); main courses £7.90–£10.90 ($11.85–$16.35). MC, V.
Open: May–Sept, daily 6–9pm.

Located just a few doors from Gus O'Connor's famous pub, this restaurant is housed in an ivy-covered thatched-roof stone cottage (dating back to 1901), with a skylight, sugan chairs, a turf fireplace, and pictures of Burren flora on the inside. The simple menu concentrates on local seafood, with such dishes as lemon sole steamed with herbs and cream-wine sauce; fisherman's casserole of cod with leeks, tomato, and cheese; Burren lamb chops; chicken roasted with rosemary and wine; and a vegetarian platter.

Bruach na hAille, Roadford, Doolin, Co. Clare. ☎ 065/74120.

Cuisine: IRISH/SEAFOOD. **Reservations:** Recommended.
Prices: Appetizers £1.50–£2.75 ($2.25–$4.13); main courses £7.50–£12 ($11.25–$18). No credit cards.
Open: Apr–Oct, daily 6–9:30pm.

Beside the bridge over the River Aille, this restaurant has a name that literally means "bridge of the River Aille." It is a cozy cottage-style place with an emphasis on seafood—lobster, crab, and other local fish. Signature dishes include filet of sole in cider with shellfish cream sauce; ragoût of seasonal fish and shellfish; and baked seafood au gratin. In addition, there's a choice of steaks, chicken, lamb, and veal dishes.

PUB

No description of the Clare coast would be complete without mention of ★ **Gus O'Connor's Pub,** Doolin, Co. Clare (☎ 065/74168). Situated in a row of thatched fishermen's cottages less than a mile from the roaring waters of the Atlantic, this simple pub beckons people from many miles each evening. Besides its historic charm (dating back to 1832), its big draw is music—from flute and fiddle to bodhran and concertina. This is the spot in western County Clare for Irish traditional music sessions.

13

Along the River Shannon's Shores

THE SHANNON RIVER, AT 230 MILES IN LENGTH, IS THE LONGEST RIVER IN IRELAND or Great Britain. It influences and defines more of the Irish landscape than any other body of water. Rising in County Cavan, it flows south through the heartland of Ireland, touching nine other counties—Leitrim, Roscommon, Longford, Westmeath, Offaly, Galway, Tipperary, Clare, and Limerick—before reaching its mouth and separating Counties Kerry and Clare as the Shannon estuary waters meet the Atlantic.

The Shannon takes many shapes and forms as it flows through the Irish landscape. At some points it's almost ten miles across, at others it narrows to a few hundred yards. For years the river was primarily a means of transportation and commerce, fondly referred to as Ireland's ancient highway, but now it's chiefly a source of enjoyment and recreation.

The river can be divided into three segments: the Lower Shannon and Lough Derg, stretching from Killaloe to Portumna; the Middle Shannon, a narrow passage from the Birr/Banagher area to Athlone; and the Upper Shannon, from Lough Ree to Lough Allen and the river's source in County Cavan. In this chapter we explore the river from the south end, working our way northward. This is not to imply the river flows in that direction; it's designed to help you start off touring in the area where there is the greatest number of things to do and see.

While it isn't likely that a visitor will follow the Shannon for all of its 214 navigable miles; we'll give an overview of some of the many delights to be found along the Shannon's shores, whether you rent a boat and navigate your own course or drive along the nearby roads.

As you drive across Ireland, you may not necessarily be heading for the Shannon River, but you'll encounter it in almost every cross-country route you take. Parts of the river will be along your route between Dublin and all the major roads to and from the west, so this chapter also presents some ideas for good stopping points and activities.

Just as the Shannon reaches out geographically to so many Irish counties, it will also influence your visit to Ireland in an aesthetic and refreshing way.

1 Lower Shannon—The Lough Derg Drive

Killaloe is 16 miles NE of Limerick and 25 miles E of Ennis; Portumna is 40 miles SE of Galway and 27 miles E of Gort

GETTING TO & AROUND THE LOUGH DERG AREA   The best way to get to the Lough Derg area is by car or boat. Although there are some limited public transporation services, you'll need a car to get around the lake. Major roads that lead to Lough Derg are the main Limerick/Dublin (N 7) road from points east and south, N 6 and N 65 from Galway and the west, and N 52 from northerly points. The Lough Derg Drive itself, which is well signposted, is a combination of R 352 on the west bank of the lake and R 493, R 494, and R 495 on the east bank.

ESSENTIALS   Since Lough Derg unites three counties—Clare, Galway, and Tipperary—there are several sources of information, including the **Shannon Development Tourism Group,** Shannon, Co. Clare (☎ 061/361555), and **Ireland West Tourism,** Victoria Place, Eyre Square, Galway (☎ 091/63081), both of which are open year-round. **Seasonal information offices** include the Nenagh Tourist Office, Connolly Street, Nenagh (☎ 067/31610), open April through September; Killaloe Tourist Office, The Bridge, Co. Clare (☎ 061/376866), open May through

What's Special About the River Shannon's Shores

Buildings
- Athlone Castle, a mighty fortress on the Shannon dating back to 1210.
- Portumna Castle, one of the finest 17th-century manor houses ever built in Ireland.

Parks/Gardens
- Lough Key Forest Park, 840 acres of woodlands, lakelands, and islands.
- Portumna Forest Park, a 1,400-acre natural expanse along Lough Derg's northern shore.
- Raheen Oakwoods, home of Ireland's oldest (1,000 years) oak tree.

For the Kids
- Ride a narrow-gauge railway around the boglands at Shannonbridge.

Ace Attractions
- Clonmacnois, the 6th-century monastic city of St. Ciaran.
- Birr Castle, site of a great astronomical exhibit and 100 acres of award-winning gardens.
- Strokestown Park House, an 18th-century Palladian-style house that shelters the Irish Famine Museum.
- Clonalis House, ancestral home of the O'Conors, the last high kings of Ireland.
- Tullynally Castle, a Gothic Revival manor dating back to 1655.
- Lough Rynn House & Gardens, a 19th-century great house with one of Ireland's largest terraced walled gardens.

Natural Spectacles
- Lough Derg Drive, a 95-mile panorama of unspoiled lakeshores, farm-lands, mountains, and forests.

Activities
- Cruise Lough Derg or Lough Ree on board a sightseeing boat.
- Fish for brown trout, pike, bream, and perch on the Shannon.
- Rent a cabin cruiser, powerboat, canoe, sail boat, kayak, or rowboat to ply the Shannon's waters.

Great Towns/Villages
- Killaloe, a picture-postcard lakeside town and home of Ireland's largest inland marina.
- Terryglass and Mountshannon, two of Ireland's "Tidy Town" winners.
- Woodford, home of great Irish traditional music sessions.

September; Tipperary Lakeside Ltd., The Old Church, Borrisokane, Co. Tipperary (☎ **067/27155**); open May through August; and the East Clare Tourist & Development Association, Holiday East Clare, Drewsboro, Scarriff, Co. Clare (☎ **061/921433**), open May through September.

AREA CODES   The area codes for this region are 061 for Co. Clare numbers, 067 for Tipperary numbers, and 0509 for Co. Galway numbers.

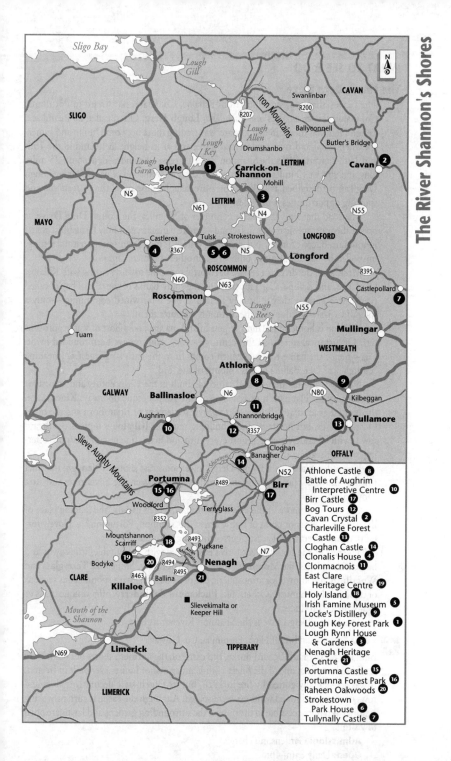

Athlone Castle **8**
Battle of Aughrim Interpretive Centre **10**
Birr Castle **17**
Bog Tours **12**
Cavan Crystal **2**
Charleville Forest Castle **13**
Cloghan Castle **14**
Clonalis House **4**
Clonmacnois **11**
East Clare Heritage Centre **19**
Holy Island **18**
Irish Famine Museum **5**
Locke's Distillery **9**
Lough Key Forest Park **1**
Lough Rynn House & Gardens **3**
Nenagh Heritage Centre **21**
Portumna Castle **15**
Portumna Forest Park **16**
Raheen Oakwoods **20**
Strokestown Park House **6**
Tullynally Castle **7**

WHAT TO SEE & DO
The Lough Derg Drive

The Lower Shannon, stretching from Killaloe, Co. Clare, northward to Portumna, Co. Galway, encompasses one huge lake, **Lough Derg.** Often called an inland sea, Lough Derg was the main inland waterway trading route between Dublin and Limerick when canal and river commercial traffic was at its height in Ireland in the 18th and 19th centuries. It is the Shannon River's largest lake and widest point: 25 miles long and almost 10 miles wide, with more than 25,000 acres of water. Today Lough Derg can be described as Ireland's pleasure lake, because of all the recreational and sporting opportunities it provides.

The road that rims the lake, a perimeter of 95 miles, the **Lough Derg Drive,** is one of the most scenic routes in Ireland—where panoramas of hilly farmlands, gentle mountains, bucolic forests, and glistening waters. It is one continuous natural setting, unspoiled by condominiums, billboards, or other commercialization.

Most of all, the drive is a collage of colorful shoreline towns, starting with Killaloe, Co. Clare, and Ballina, Co. Tipperary, on the south banks of the lake. They're called twin towns because they're usually treated as one intertwined community—only a splendid 13-arch bridge over the Shannon separates them.

Killaloe is home to Ireland's largest inland marina and a host of watersport centers. Of historical note is an 9th-century oratory, said to have been founded by St. Lua—hence the name Killaloe, which comes from the Irish language *Cill* (meaning "church") of Lua. Ballina means "mouth of the ford."

Nearby is another oratory and cathedral, built in the 12th century and named for 6th-century St. Flannan; it boasts an exquisite Romanesque doorway. **Kincora,** on the highest ground at Killaloe, was the royal settlement of Brian Boru and the other O'Brien kings, but no trace of any building remains. **Killaloe** is a picture-postcard town, with lakeside views at almost every turn and many fine restaurants/pubs offering outdoor seating on the shoreline.

Five miles inland from Lough Derg's lower southeast shores is **Nenagh,** the chief town of north Tipperary, lying in a fertile valley between the Silvermine and Arra Mountains.

On the north shore of the lake is **Portumna,** which means "the landing place of the oak tree." A major point of traffic across the Shannon, Portumna has a lovely forest park and a remarkable castle currently being restored.

The rest of the Lough Derg Drive is scattered with memorable little towns and harborside villages like **Mountshannon** and **Dromineer.** Some, like **Terryglass** and **Woodford,** are known for atmospheric old pubs bursting with spontaneous sessions of traditional Irish music. Others, like **Puckane** or **Ballinderry,** offer unique crafts or locally made products.

The Lough Derg Drive is the Shannon River at its best.

★ **Portumna Castle,** off N 65, Portumna, Co. Galway.

Built in 1609 by Earl Richard Burke, this castle on the northern shores of Lough Derg is said to have been one of the finest 17th-century manor houses ever built in Ireland. It was accidentally gutted by fire in 1826, but its Dutch-style decorative gables and rows of stone mullioned windows were spared. Although the castle is currently being restored and not accessible to the public, the surrounding gardens and lawns are open to visitors.

Admission: Gardens, no charge.
Open: Daily 8am–4pm.

Portumna Forest Park, off N 65, Portumna, Co. Galway.

On the shores of Lough Derg, this 1,400-acre park is east of the town, off the main road. It offers miles of nature trails and signposted walks, plus viewing points and picnic areas.

Admission: £1 ($1.50) adults.

Open: Daily, dawn–dusk.

East Clare Heritage Centre/Holy Island Tours, Tuamgraney, Co. Clare. ☎ 061/921351.

Housed in the restored 10th-century church of St. Cronan, this center explains the heritage and history of the East Clare area through a series of exhibits and an audiovisual presentation. In addition, a pier across the road from the center is the starting point for a 15-minute boating excursion to nearby Inishcealtra (Holy Island), in Lough Derg. The trip includes a 45-minute guided tour of the island.

Admission: Center £1 ($1.50) adults, 50p (75¢) children; Holy Island Tours £5 ($7.50) adults, £3 ($4.50) children.

Open: Center, May–Sept Mon–Sat 9am–5pm, Sun 1–5pm; Holy Island Tours, May–Sept 11am–3pm, weather permitting.

Raheen Oakwoods, Tuamgraney, Scariff, Co. Clare. ☎ 061/921351.

This ancient forest, part of a 500-acre estate on the shores of Lough Derg, is one of the last primeval woodlands of Ireland. A mixture of acid and limestone soil, edged by streams and waterfalls, has given this forest a diverse plant life, with oaks, holly, ash, hazel, birch, and alder trees sheltering a carpet of mosses, ferns, and wildflowers. The centerpiece is the Brian Boru Oak, said to be Ireland's oldest oak tree, estimated at 1,000 years old and a massive 32 feet in circumference. Legend has it that the tree was sown by the High King of Ireland, who ruled from a nearby fort. Entrance to the forest includes a touring map with a signposted trail to follow at your leisure; the full trail takes one to two hours to walk. It's situated on the main road, opposite St. Cronan's Church, site of the East Clare Heritage Centre.

Admission: £2 ($3), adults, £1 ($1.50) children ages 5–12, 80p ($1.20) students and seniors.

Open: June to early Sept daily 10am–5:30pm.

Nenagh Heritage Centre, off Kickham Street, Nenagh, Co. Tipperary. ☎ 067/32633.

Models of the whole Lough Derg area, with its main port villages, are on display at this center, five miles east of the lakeshore. Located in two stone buildings dating from about 1840, this site was once a jail, then a convent and a school. Now, as a museum, it showcases collections of local arts, crafts, photography, and memorabilia. It's also the family history research center for northern Tipperary.

Admission: £1.50 ($2.25) adult, £75p ($1.08) seniors, students, and children.

Open: Mid-May through Sept Mon–Fri 10am–5pm, Sun 2:30–5pm.

SIGHTSEEING CRUISES

Derg Marine, Killaloe, Co. Clare. ☎ 061/76364.

Enjoy a cruise of Lough Derg on board the 48-seat *Derg Princess,* a covered riverbus. Departing from Killaloe marina, the cruise takes 1¹/₂ hours, traveling past the fort of Brian Boru and into Lough Derg.

Fare: £5 ($7.50) adults, £3 ($4.50) children.
Schedule: May–Sept daily at 3pm.

Shannon Sailing Ltd., New Harbour, Dromineer, Nenagh, Co. Tipperary.
☎ **067/24295.**

This company operates a covered 53-seat waterbus, the *Ku-ee-tu,* sailing from the southeastern shore of Lough Derg at Dromineer on a 1¹/₂-hour cruise; there's full commentary on local sights.

Price: £5 ($7.50) adults, £3 ($4.50) children.
Open: May–Sept daily; schedule varies.

SPORTS & RECREATION

BICYCLING Bicycling is a great way to enjoy Lough Derg's many shoreline paths, nature trails, and forest parks. The **Shannonside Activity Center,** Killaloe/Scariff Road, Ballycuggeran, Killaloe, Co. Clare (☎ **061/376622**), rents standard bikes from £2 ($3) per hour or £8 ($12) per day; mountain bikes rent from £4 ($6) per hour or £12 ($18) per day. Hours are Monday through Friday from 10am to 9pm, Saturday and Sunday from 10am to 8pm.

CRUISING The following companies rent cabin cruisers along this section of the Shannon: **Derg Line Cruisers,** The Marina, Killaloe, Co. Clare (☎ **061/76364**); **Emerald Star Line,** The Marina, Portumna, Co. Galway (☎ **0509/41120**); **Shannon Castle Line,** The Marina, Williamstown, Co. Clare (☎ **061/927042**); and **Shannon Sailing,** The Marina, Dromineer, Co. Tipperary (☎ **067/24295**). The craft range from two- to eight-berths; rates average £60 to £100 ($90 to $150) per person a week.

FISHING Often called an angler's paradise, Lough Derg has good stocks of brown trout, pike, bream, and perch. Fish ranging in weight from 36 to 90 pounds have been caught in this lake. Brown trout average one to six pounds. For tackle and guidance on local fishing, visit one of these shops: **Eddie Fahey,** Ballyminogue, Scariff, Co. Clare (☎ **061/921019**); **Norrie Guerin,** Ivy House, Mountshannon, Co. Clare (☎ **061/927184**); **Whelan's,** Summerhill, Nenagh, Co. Tipperary (☎ **067/31301**); **D & H Clarke Ltd.,** Portumna, Co. Galway (☎ **0509/41049**); and the **Open Season Shop,** Friar Street, Nenagh, Co. Tipperary (☎ **0509/41071**).

GOLF Lovely parkland and woodland golfing in the Lough Derg area is offered at 18-hole clubs, such as **Portumna Golf Club,** Portumna, Co. Galway (☎ **0509/41059**), with greens fees of £10 ($15), and **Nenagh Golf Club,** Beechwood, Nenagh (☎ **067/33242**), with greens fees of £12 ($18) on weekdays and £15 ($22.50) on weekends. In addition, the **East Clare Golf Club,** Scariff/Killaloe Road, Bodyke, Co. Clare (☎ **061/921322**), is expanding from nine holes to an 18-hole championship course. It currently costs £7 ($10.50) to play 9 holes.

SWIMMING Lough Derg is known for its clear and unpolluted water, ideal for swimming, particularly at Castle Lough, Dromineer, and Portumna Bay; the latter has changing rooms and showers.

WALKING There are some excellent walks in Portumna Forest Park, Raheen Woods, and along the shoreline of Lough Derg.

WATERSPORTS Watersports are the pièce de résistance of a visit to Lough Derg. If you enjoy boating, tubing, waterskiing, windsurfing, canoeing, or other water-based sports, this is the place for you. Here are a few of the businesses that specialize in these activities.

Shannonside Activity and Sailing Centre, Killaloe/Scariff Road, Ballycuggeran, Co. Clare. ☎ **061/376622.**

If you want to enjoy the great outdoors around Lough Derg, this is the place to come to rent a boat or other equipment. Set on a 22-acre shoreline site about two miles north of Killaloe, this center hires sailing dinghies and windsurfers, canoes, kayaks, rowboats, and more.

Prices: Sailing dinghies from £10 ($15) per hour or £30 ($45) a day; windsurfers from £8 ($12) per hour or £36 ($54) per day; canoes or kayaks from £2 ($3) per hour or £8 ($12) per day; rowboats from £8 ($12) per day or £25 ($37.50) per hour.

Open: May–Sept Mon–Fri 10am–9pm, Sat–Sun 10am–8pm.

Lough Derg Sailing, Mountshannon Harbour, Mountshannon, Co. Clare. ☎ **061/927131.**

With its nontidal waters and numerous bays, islands, and harbors, Lough Derg is ideal for sailing. This company offers daily sailing trips on the 29-foot yacht *Sangazure,* with instruction and training on board. The activities are especially geared toward beginners who want to learn the basics of sailing.

Prices: £10 ($15) for two hrs, £35 ($52.50) per day.

Open: May–Sept daily; times of departure by appointment.

Haskett's Boat Hire, at the Bridge, Killaloe, Co. Clare. ☎ **061/376693.**

Located opposite the tourist office, this firm rents 19-foot lake boats with outboard motors for fishing or pleasure cruising. If you hire a boat for a minimum of two hours, you get two complimentary Irish coffees at a nearby pub.

Prices: £7 ($10.50) per hour or £30 ($45) per day.

Open: June–Sept daily 10am to 6pm or later.

Whelan's Boat Hire, at the Bridge, Killaloe, Co. Clare. ☎ **061/376159.**

Whelan's rents 19-foot lake boats with outboard engines, for sightseeing or fishing in the waters of Lough Derg. Prices include fuel, fishing gear, and rainwear.

Prices: £6 ($9) per hour or £25 ($37.50) per day.

Open: June–Aug daily 9am–9pm.

Watersports Lough Derg, Two Mile Gate, Killaloe, Co. Clare. ☎ **088/588430** (mobile phone).

This outdoor center offers waterskiing, speed boat rides, tubing, and jetskiing.

Prices: Waterskiing from £12 ($18), speed boat rides from L3 ($4.50) per person, tubing from £6 ($9), jetskis from £12 ($18).

Open: May–Oct, daily 11am–dusk.

SAVVY SHOPPING

Eugene & Anke McKernan, Handweavers, Main Street, Tuamgraney, Co. Clare. ☎ **061/921527.**

A husband-and-wife team, Eugene and Anke offer a colorful array of distinctive tweed scarves, jackets, vests, and blankets. The couple hand-weaves all items on the premises, which were formerly police barracks. Visitors are welcomed to the workshop to see the weaving process. Open daily May through September; hours vary October through April.

Old Church Craft Shop & Gallery, The Old Church, R 493, Terryglass, Co. Tipperary. ☎ **067/22209.**

Built on the site of the original abbey of St. Columba, dating back to A.D. 549, this current stone-faced building dates from 1838. Transformed into a craft shop in 1984, it is a treasure trove of locally produced crafts and products, ranging from Terryglass pottery and Rathbone traditional beeswax candles, to Irish bonsai plants, bog oak pendants, wildlife mobiles, boxwood products from Birr castle, Jerpoint glass, decorated horseshoes, miniature watercolors of Shannon River scenes; and books about the Shannon. Open Tuesday to Sunday from 10am to 6pm.

Walsh Crafts, R 493, Puckane, Nenagh, Co. Tipperary. ☎ **067/24229.**

A rustic thatched-roof cottage, complete with traditional half-door, serves as the workshop for Paddy Walsh, a craftsman who carves and paints on natural wood. His works depict Ireland past and present, from Celtic and rural scenes to heraldic and religious themes. The pieces range from pendant-size figurines and symbols, such as St. Patrick, the harp, or a dove, to portrait-size scenes of Irish music sessions, pub facades and interiors, farmyards, cottages, castles, sporting events, and Christmas tableaux. The craft is ingenious and truly Irish—a great souvenir. Visitors are welcome to watch Paddy and his staff as they carve the wood and then paint the colorful motifs. Open daily from 9:30am to 6pm or later.

WHERE TO STAY

Moderate

Gurthalougha House, Ballinderry, Terryglass, Nenagh, Co. Tipperary. ☎ **067/22080** or toll free in the U.S. **800/223-6510.** Fax 067/22154. 8 rms (all with bath). TV TEL

Rates (including full breakfast): £34–£40 ($51–$60) single, £68–£80 ($107–$120) double. No service charge. AE, MC, V.

Open: Jan and Mar–Dec. **Closed:** Feb and Christmas.

A mile-long winding driveway leads through 150 acres of forest to this two-story early 19th-century Georgian house, set on the northwest edge of Lough Derg. Originally a hunting lodge, it's built around a cobbled courtyard bursting with flowers. The public areas include an antique-filled drawing room, a library, and a dining room, all of which have views of the lake across to the mountains of Clare and Galway. Guest rooms are individually decorated with period pieces and antiques. Innkeeper/chef Michael Wilkinson is known for his innovative country-house cooking; sumptuous breakfasts are brought to the guest rooms or served beside the peat fire in the dining room. Facilities include two hard tennis courts, signposted woodland walks, use of boats and windsurfers, swimming from the jetty, and croquet; fishing can be arranged for an extra fee.

Lakeside Hotel, Killaloe, Co. Clare. ☎ **061/376122** or toll free in the U.S. **800/447-7462.** Fax 061/376431. 36 rms (all with bath). TV TEL

Rates (including full breakfast): £35–£45 ($52.50–$67.50) single, £55–£75 ($82.50–$112.50) double. No service charge. AE, DC, MC, V.

Perched on the southern banks of Lough Derg and shaded by ancient trees, this two-story country house–style hotel has one of the loveliest settings of any property in the area. It was completely refurbished in 1994 in a bright contemporary style. The guest rooms have standard furnishings but are greatly enhanced by wide-windowed views of the lake or gardens. The facilities include a restaurant and bar lounge overlooking the Shannon, an indoor heated swimming pool with waterslide, a Jacuzzi, a sauna, a gym, a steam room, and a tennis court. The hotel is on the Ballina side of the Bridge, on the edge of town next to the marina.

Inexpensive

Dromineer Bay Hotel, Dromineer Bay, Nenagh, Co. Tipperary. ☎ **067/24114.** Fax 067/24288. 10 rms (all with bath).

Rates (including full breakfasts): £50–£58 ($75–$87) single or double. No service charge. AE, MC, V.

Tucked along the shores of Lough Derg beside the Dromineer Yacht Club, this two-story hotel has long been a favorite with fishermen and now also appeals to tourists seeking an informal riverside retreat. Dating back more than 100 years, it was originally a coastguard inn. Recently expanded and renovated by innkeepers Denis and Lily Collison, the rooms are small and simply furnished, although some have four-poster beds and antiques. Facilities include the Moorings restaurant, open for dinner; the Boat House bar/coffee shop/delicatessen for snacks and lunch; and the Captain's Deck Bar, with an open-air deck upstairs offering fine views of the water. For a little local color, browse at the bar walls; they're decorated with photographs telling the history of the hotel and the village.

Lantern House, Ogonnelloe, Tuamgraney, Co. Clare. ☎ **061/923034.** Fax 061/923139. 9 rms (all with bath). TV TEL

Rates (including full breakfast): £20–£24 ($30–$36) single; £32–£36 ($48–$54) double. AE, DC, MC, V.
Open: Mid-Feb to Nov.

This modern guesthouse, where guests receive a warm welcome from proprietors Liz and Phil Hogan, overlooks wide vistas on Lough Derg. Palm trees grow on the well-tended but "hard-to-march" high grounds. All the public rooms overlook the Shannon, as do some of the bedrooms. Furnishings are comfortable and "home-style." The cozy lounge has a fireplace, and residents can enjoy a drink at at a small bar. Widely acclaimed is the restaurant (see "Where to Dine," below). Lantern House is six miles north of Killaloe on the main road.

Portumna Park Hotel, Portumna, Co. Galway. ☎ **0509/41121.** Fax 0509/41357. 29 rms (all with bath). TV TEL

Rates (including full breakfast): £33.50–£35 ($50.25–$52) single, £47–£50 ($70.50–$75) double. No service charge. DC, MC, V.

Set back from the main road in a garden setting on the western edge of Portumna, this contemporary rambling ranch-style inn is the prime hotel on Lough Derg's north shore. Under new ownership and totally refurbished in 1994, it offers standard guest rooms with light woods, floral fabrics, and floor-to-ceiling windows. Most rooms look out on the surrounding gardens and forest. A patio has outdoor seating. The public areas include a chalet-style restaurant with a knotty-pine decor and an old-world pub with paneled walls, lantern lights, and dark-wood trim.

Rent-a-Cottage

For an area of such amazing beauty and wide-open spaces, the Lough Derg region has surprisingly few hotels. In many ways, that's part of its alluring attraction—natural lakelands and forests unspoiled by condos, hotels, motels, and fast-food eateries. This area, perhaps more than most other parts of Ireland, calls out for visitors to settle in and become part of the way of life. And that is why the "Rent an Irish Cottage plc." program was pioneered here almost 30 years ago.

The Shannon Development Company came up with the idea of building small rental cottages in these rural areas where other types of satisfactory accommodations were scarce. The cottages were designed in traditional style, with exteriors of white stucco, thatched roofs, and half-doors, but all of the furnishings, plumbing, heating, and kitchen appliances inside were totally up-to-date, along with a real turf fireplace. The cottage rental idea was an instant success with Irish people from Dublin and other large cities wanting to get away from it all, and it is becoming equally popular with visitors from abroad who want to live like the Irish.

The cottages, built in groups of 8 to 12, are set on picturesque sites in remote villages such as Puckane, Terryglass, and Whitegate, either overlooking or close to Lough Derg's shores. There are no restaurants or bars on site, and guests are encouraged to shop in the local grocery stores and cook their own meals and to congregate in the local pubs each evening. In other words, after a day or two the visitors become part of the community. Rates range from £140 to £410 ($210 to $615) per cottage per week, depending on the size of the cottage (one to four bedrooms) and time of year. Rental rates include bed linen and color TV; metered electricity is extra. For more information, contact **Rent an Irish Cottage plc.,** 85 O'Connell St., Limerick, Co. Limerick (☎ **061/411109;** fax 061/314821).

In recent years, cottages with slate or tile roofs and modern designs have been built by individual owners. One of the loveliest cottage settings belongs to the **Mountshannon Village Cottages,** Mountshannon, Co. Clare, a cluster of nine pastel-toned one- and two-story cottages perched on a hill overlooking Lough Derg at Mountshannon Harbour. Grouped like a private village around a garden courtyard, these cottages cost £130 to £430 ($195 to $645) per week depending on the time of year and number of bedrooms required. Some weekend rentals are also available, from £80 to £220 ($120 to $330) per cottage. For more information, contact Bridie Cooke, Gortatleva, Bushypark, Galway, Co. Galway (☎ and fax **091/25295**).

WHERE TO DINE
Moderate

★ **Brocka-on-the-Water,** Kilgarvan Quay, Nenagh, Co. Tipperary. ☎ **067/22038.**
Cuisine: INTERNATIONAL. **Reservations:** Required.
Prices: Set dinner £20 ($30). No credit cards.
Open: May–Oct, Mon–Sat 7–9:30pm.

A small country lane, signposted off the Lough Derg Drive, leads to this country-house restaurant in a garden setting near the shores of Lough Derg. Rather than seeking waterside views, people flock here for the Byrne family's innovative cuisine and warm hospitality. As you browse through the menu, you'll also take delight at the antique furnishings and the Irish traditional music playing in the background. In the dining room, each table is set with care, using Waterford crystal lamps, Newbridge silver, hand-embroidered linens, and fresh flowers from their garden. The menu changes nightly, but specialties often include baked stuffed sole with a sauce of dill and lemon cream; pan-fried sirloin steak Gaelic-style (flamed in whiskey); grilled lamb chops with fresh mint or black-currant sauce; ribbons of chicken breast with root ginger and honey;

and pork médaillons with herb breadcrumbs and plum sauce. Many of the dishes are decorated with or use fresh edible flowers from the garden as part of the recipe. To finish off the meal, don't miss the carragin mousse or Farmhouse cheeses from local farms.

Goosers, Killaloe/Ballina, Co. Clare. ☎ **061/376791.**

Cuisine: IRISH. **Reservations:** Recommended for dinner.
Prices: Bar food, all items £1.80–£9 ($2.70–$13.50); set lunch £12.50 ($18.75); appetizers £1.60–£7 ($2.40–$10.50); dinner main courses £10.50–£14.50 ($15.75–$21.75). MC, V.
Open: Daily 11am–11pm.

With a thatched roof and bright mustard-colored exterior, this popular pub/restaurant sits on the Ballina side of the Shannon, looking out at the river and the broad vista of Killaloe. Its informal two rooms have open fireplaces, stone walls and floors, and beamed celings. The pub area contains window seats, sugan chairs, and lots of nautical and fishing memorabilia, from anchors and old pictures to fishing flies and rods. The restaurant has booth seating and windows that overlook an adjacent garden; there are also picnic tables outside. The bar food menu lists seafood chowder, salads, sandwiches, steaks, burgers, and such traditional dishes as bacon and cabbage and Irish stew. Dinner entrees include scampi, scallops in cream sauce, crab salad with avocado and crab claws, rack of lamb, roast duck in fruit sauce, salmon with sorrel sauce, black sole on the bone, and a variety of steaks.

Lantern House, Ogonnelloe, Co. Clare. ☎ **061/923034.**

Cuisine: IRISH. **Reservations:** Recommended.
Prices: Appetizers £1.50–£3.95 ($2.25–$5.93); main courses £9–£14.50 ($13.50–$21.75). AE, MC. V.
Open: Mid-Feb to May and Sept–Oct, Tues–Sat 6–9:30pm, Sun 7–8:30pm; June–Aug, Mon–Sat 7–9:30pm, Sun 7–8:30pm. **Closed:** Nov to mid-Feb.

Perched high on a hillside amid palm tree–lined gardens just north of Killaloe, this country-house restaurant enjoys panoramic views of Lough Derg and the verdant hills of the surrounding countryside. Host Phil Hogan extends a warm welcome to all comers. The candlelit dining room exudes old-world charm, with a beamed ceiling, wall lanterns, and lace tablecloths. Menu choices might be poached fresh local salmon with hollandaise; pan-fried sole on the bone with almonds; scallops mornay; pork steak with white wine; chicken curry; duck à l'orange; pepper steak; or smoked salmon and prawn salads.

Peter's Restaurant, Killaloe/Ballina, Co. Clare. ☎ **061/376162.**

Cuisine: CONTINENTAL. **Reservations:** Recommended.
Prices: Set lunch £9 ($13.50); dinner appetizers £2.25–£5.50 ($3.38–$8.25), main courses £8.25–£14.90 ($12.38–$22.35). AE, MC, V.
Open: Dinner daily 7–10pm; lunch Sun 1–3pm.

Set in a restored old railway station, this restaurant sits beside Lough Derg, overlooking the water, on the Ballina side of the Killaloe bridge. The plant-filled conservatory-style room has a patio/terrace for fair-weather dining. The menu offers a variety of steaks as well as such dishes as beef stroganoff, duck à l'orange, noisettes of lamb, salmon in butter, scampi, brochette of monkfish, filet of trout amandine, and pork marsala.

Inexpensive

$ **Irish Molly's**, Killaloe/Ballina, Co. Clare. ☎ 061/76632.

Cuisine: IRISH. **Reservations:** Recommended for dinner.
Prices: All items £1.25–£10.95 ($2.25–$16.43). MC, V.
Open: Daily 12:30–11:30pm.

Next to the Killaloe bridge, this brightly colored pub/restaurant offers views of Killaloe Harbour from most of its windows. The informal interior is like that of a comfortable cottage, with beamed ceilings, wall shelves lined with old plates, vintage clocks, pine and mahogany furnishings, period pictures and prints of the Shannon area, and a stove fireplace. The menu, which is the same all day, offers such light fare as soups and chowders, seafood salads and sandwiches, burgers, and lasagne. More substantial choices include mussels steamed in garlic or cider; deviled crab claws; seafood platter (salmon, prawns, crab); baked Limerick ham; grilled trout amandine; steak-and-mushroom pie; and chargrilled steaks. The open-face fresh crab sandwich on brown bread especially is worth a stop. Outdoor seating is available on picnic-style tables.

Lakeside Cottage, Tea House and Wine Bistro, Coolbawn, Ballinderry Village, Nenagh, Co. Tipperary. ☎ 067/22094.

Cuisine: IRISH. **Reservations:** Not necessary.
Prices: All items £1.50–£5 ($2.25–$7.50). No credit cards.
Open: May–Sept daily snacks 11am–6pm, lunch 12:30–2:30pm.

Originally the village forge, this old building was restored in 1991 in traditional Irish cottage style, with a half-door and stone floor. It's decorated with old-fashioned pine furniture and provides seating outdoors in good weather. All food is prepared on the premises using local ingredients, such as smoked fish, Farmhouse cheeses, homemade preserves, chutneys, breads, and cakes. The menu also features Lakeshore Foods wholegrain mustards and honey, produced at the adjacent factory shop. An ideal stop for a cup of coffee or tea, snack, or light meal, it's on the Lough Derg Drive, between the villages of Puckane and Terryglass. Lakeshore Foods products are also for sale.

PUBS

Although there are public houses in every town around the Lough Derg route, the pubs of Terryglass, Co. Tipperary, on the east shore, and the pubs of Woodford, Co. Galway, on the west shore, are particularly well known for their lively sessions of Irish traditional music.

✪ **The Derg Inn,** Terryglass, Co. Tipperary (☎ 067/22037), with three cozy rooms inside, has a beer garden courtyard. It's worth a visit just to see this pub's decor of Tipperary horse pictures, old plates, books, beer posters, vintage bottles, hanging tankards, and lanterns; however, most people come for the free traditional music on Wednesdays and Sundays.

Paddy's Bar, Terryglass, Co. Tipperary (☎ 067/22147), is known for its fine display of antiques as well as traditional music seven nights a week in summer.

On Lough Derg's western shores, the town of Woodford, Co. Galway, is particularly celebrated as a mecca for Irish traditional music of the old style. Fiddler and tin-whistle player Anthony Coen, born in Woodford of a musical family that includes six traditional musicians out of nine children, is one of the best at his instruments, often accompanied by his own talented daughters Dearbhla on the flute and tin whistle and Eimer on the concertina and bodhran. They can often be heard at **J. Walsh's**

Forest Bar, Woodford (☎ **0509/49012**), or at **Moran's,** Woodford (☎ **0509/49063**), overlooking the Woodford River. The latter establishment is a curiosity in itself since it's probably the only pub in Ireland where you'll find two clerics serving drinks at the bar during summer. Both Carmelite Order priests, they are the sons of the owner and spend their vacation time helping out in the family business. Only in Ireland!

2 Middle Shannon—From Birr to Athlone

Birr is 15 miles E of Portumna; Athlone is 60 miles E of Galway

GETTING TO & AROUND THE MIDDLE SHANNON   The best way to get to the Middle Shannon area is by car or boat. Although there's public transportation, you'll need a car to get around the river banks. Major roads that lead to this area are the main Galway/Dublin Road (N 6) from points east and west, N 62 from the south, and N 55 and N 61 from the north.

ESSENTIALS   Information on this area can be obtained year-round from the **Ireland West Tourism Office,** Victoria Place, Eyre Square, Galway (☎ **091/63081**), and the **Midlands Tourism Office,** Clonard House, Dublin Road, Mullingar, Co. Westmeath (☎ **044/48761**). Both are open Monday through Friday from 9am to 6pm and Saturday from 9am to 1pm, with extended hours in summer.

    Seasonal Tourist Information points are also operated from May or June to September at signposted sites in the following locations: Athlone (☎ **0902/94630**); Aughrim (☎ **0905/73939**); Ballinsloe (☎ **0905/42131**); Birr (☎ **0509/20110**); and Clonmacnois (☎ **0905/74134**).

AREA CODES   Telephone area codes for this region of the Shannon include 044, 091, 0506, 0509, 0902, and 0905.

WHAT TO SEE & DO

The middle of the Shannon River is the home of one of Ireland's greatest historic sites—the early Christian settlement of **Clonmacnois,** a spot that has been drawing visitors since the 6th century.

    This region also includes vast stretches of boglands, as well as the inland town of **Birr,** known for its magnificent and historic gardens, and **Banagher,** a river town with a picturesque harbor.

    In addition, this stretch of the river curves into **Athlone,** the largest town on the Shannon and a leading inland marina for mooring and hiring boats. Athlone's other claim to fame is that it produced Ireland's most famous operatic tenor, the late John McCormack.

Clonmacnois, Shannonbridge, Co. Offaly. ☎ **0905/74195.**

Standing silently on the east bank of the Shannon, this is one of Ireland's most significant ancient monuments. Founded as a monastery by St. Ciaran in 548, the site was one of Europe's great centers of learning for nearly 1,000 years, flourishing under the patronage of many Irish kings. The last High King, Rory O'Conor, was buried here in 1198. In its later years, Clonmacnois was raided many times by native chiefs, Danes, and Anglo-Normans, until it was finally abandoned in 1552. Today's visitor can see the remains of a cathedral, a castle, eight churches, two round towers, three sculpted high crosses, and over 200 monumental slabs. The site includes a visitor center with an exhibition, an audiovisual program, and tea rooms.

Admission: £1.50 ($2.25) adults, £1 ($1.50) seniors, 60p (90¢) students and children.

Open: Mid-Mar to May and Sept–Oct daily 10am–6pm, June to early Sept, daily 9am–7pm; Nov to mid-Mar, daily 10am–5pm.

Birr Castle, Rosse Row, Birr, Co. Offaly. ☎ **0509/20056.**

The main attraction of this inland estate 12 miles east of the river is its 100-acre garden. The demesne of the Parsons, otherwise known as the Earl and Countess of Ross, it's laid out around a lake and along the banks of the two adjacent rivers and contains more than 1,000 species of trees and shrubs, from magnolias and cherry trees to chestnut and weeping beech. The hornbeam alleys and box hedges are featured in the *Guinness Book of Records* as the tallest in the world. Farther along the path you can combine a bit of star-gazing with the garden stroll, because the grounds also contain an astronomical exhibit, thanks to the efforts of the third Earl of Rosse, who in 1845 built a six-foot reflecting telescope. It was then the largest in the world and remained so for more than 75 years. The display area also contains astronomical artifacts, drawings, photographs, and a scale model of the original telescope. As a bonus during summer, you can usually find additional rotating exhibits dealing with the history of Birr Castle and its residents. The 17th-century castle/residence itself is not open to the public.

Admission: Jan–Mar and Nov–Dec £2.60 ($3.90) adults, £1.30 ($1.95) children over 5; Apr–Oct £3.20 ($4.80) adults, £1.60 ($2.40) children over 5.

Open: Jan–Apr and Oct–Dec daily 9am–1pm and 2–5pm; May–Sept daily 9am–6pm.

⭐ **Bog Tours,** Bord na Mona/The Irish Peat Board, Blackwater Works, Shannonbridge, Co. Offaly. ☎ **0905/74114.**

Bogland discoveries are the focus of this tour in the heart of the Irish midlands on the east bank of the Shannon. Visitors are invited to board the narrow-gauge Clonmacnois and West Offaly Railway for a five-mile circular ride around the Blackwater bog. The commentary explains how the bogland was formed and became a vital source of fuel for Ireland. The route includes a first-hand look at turf cutting, stacking, and drying, and close-up views of bog plants and wildlife. Participants can even take a turn at digging the turf or pick some bog cotton en route. The ride lasts approximately 45 minutes. The visitor center also offers an audiovisual story about the bog.

Admission: Tours £3 ($4.50) adults, £2.20 ($3.30) seniors and students, £2 ($3) children.

Open: Daily 10am–5pm; tours on the hour.

Athlone Castle, Athlone, Co. Westmeath. ☎ **0902/92912.**

Built in 1210 for King John of England, this mighty stone fortress sits on the edge of the Shannon. It played an important part in Athlone's history, first as the seat of the Presidents of Connacht and later as the headquarters of the Governor of Athlone during both the first Siege of Athlone in 1690 and the second in 1691. Declared a national monument in 1970, it was recently restored and adapted for use as a visitor center,

IMPRESSIONS

The very stones speak.
—Pope John Paul II, speaking at Clonmacnois, 1979

museum, gallery, and tea room. The exhibition area offers an audiovisual presentation on the Siege of Athlone, plus displays on the castle itself, the town of Athlone, the flora and fauna of the Shannon region, and John McCormack, the great Irish tenor and Athlone's most-honored son. The castle's original medieval walls have been preserved, as have two large cannons dating from the reign of George II and a pair of ten-inch mortars, which were cast in 1856. Located on the riverbank, it's signposted from all directions.

Admission: £2.20 ($3.30) adults, £1.60 ($2.40) for youth ages 12–18, 80p ($1.20) children to age 12.

Open: May–Sept Mon–Sat 10am–5pm, Sun noon–5pm.

Locke's Distillery, Kilbeggan, Co. Westmeath. ☎ 0506/32134.

Established in 1757, this 18th- and 19th-century enterprise was one of the oldest licensed pot-still whiskey distilleries in the world. Unfortunately, after producing whiskey for almost 200 years, it closed in 1953; but in the past 10 years a local group has succeeded in restoring it as a museum. A 25-minute tour will not only tell you how whiskey was distilled, using old techniques and machinery but also inform you about the area's social history. It's located east of Athlone on the main road (N 6), almost midway between Dublin and Galway, making it a good stopoff point while you're on a cross-country journey or touring in the area. On the premises are a restaurant, coffee shop, and craft shop.

Admission: £2 ($3) adults, £1.80 ($2.70) seniors and students, £1 ($1.50) children.

Open: Apr–Oct daily 9am–6pm; Nov–Mar daily 10am–4pm.

Battle of Aughrim Interpretative Centre, Galway/Dublin Road (N 6), Aughrim, near Ballinsaloe, Co. Galway. ☎ 0905/73939.

Using a high-tech three-dimensional audiovisual display, this center invites visitors to relive the July 12, 1691, Battle of Aughrim. On that day the army of James II of England confronted the forces of his son-in-law, William of Orange, and staged the bloodiest battle in Irish history. The confrontation involved 45,000 soldiers from eight European countries and cost 9,000 lives, but it changed the course of Irish and European history. The center—also housing a bookshop, craftshop, and café—is adjacent to the actual Aughrim battlefield, which is now signposted for visitors. Aughrim is about 12 miles west of the Shannonbridge/Clonmacnois area.

Admission: £2.50 ($3.75) adults, £.50 ($1.00) seniors and students, 75p ($1.08) children.

Open: Easter–Sept daily 10am–6pm.

Cloghan Castle, Lusmagh, Banagher, Co. Offaly. ☎ 0509/51650.

Located three miles south of Banagher, this fortress is said to date back to the 13th century and has been inhabited for 800 years. The castle structure consists of a large stone keep with walls 10 feet thick in places. A Georgian addition was built around 1800 and other additions accrued over the last 300 years. The keep stands within four stone towers that originally were joined by a huge bawn wall. Guided tours of the interior include a look at the stark medieval stone walls, enhanced by hand-carved oak furniture, and at paintings and accessories from the colorful Georgian period. The great hall is 50 feet long and 40 feet high, with a fine plaster ceiling and galleries at either end. The castle sits in a lovely 60-acre parkland setting that's grazed by a flock of Jacob sheep.

Admission: £3 ($4.50) adults, £2 ($3) seniors and students.
Open: May–Sept Wed–Sun 2–6pm

Charleville Forest Castle, off N 52/Birr Road, Tullamore, Co. Offaly.
☎ **0506/21279.**

Designed in 1798 by Francis Johnston, one of Ireland's foremost architects, this castle took 12 years to build and was the first of the great Gothic houses. Today it's considered one of the the best of the early 19th-century castles remaining in Ireland. The castle has a fine limestone exterior, with fanciful towers, turrets, and battlements. The rooms inside have spectacular ceilings and plasterwork and great hand-carved stairways, as well as secret passageways and dungeons. Admission includes a guided tour.

Admission: £2.50 ($3.75) adults, $2 ($3) seniors and students, £1.50 ($2.25) children.
Open: April–May Sat–Sun 2–5pm; June–Sept Wed–Sun 11am–5pm.

Sightseeing Cruises

Rosanna Cruises, Cranagh, Galway Road, Athlone, Co. Westmeath. ☎ **0902/92513.**

Cruises of the inner lakes of Lough Ree or to Clonmacnois are offered by this company on board the 71-passenger *MV Avonree.* A live commentary is given and refreshments are offered. Trips to Lough Ree, which last about 1 1/2 hours, depart from The Strand, and trips to Clonmacnois, lasting 4 hours, depart from Navigation Lock.

Fare: Lough Ree trip £3.50 ($5.25) adults, £2.50 ($3.75) children; Clonmacnois trip £5 ($7.50) adults, £3.50 ($5.25) children.
Schedule: July–Sept Lough Ree trip, Mon–Tues and Thurs–Sun 11am and 2:30 and 4:30pm, and Wed at 4:30pm; Clonmacnois trip, Wed 10am.

Shannon Holidays, Jolly Mariner Marina, Athlone, Co. Westmeath. ☎ **0902/72892.**

This company operates cruises around Lough Ree on board the 60-passenger *MV Ross.* Average cruising time is 90 minutes, and the boat has a sundeck and a covered deck with a bar and coffee shop.

Fare: £3.50 ($5.25) adults, £2.50 ($3.75) children.
Schedule: May–Sept, times vary.

Silver Line Cruisers Ltd., The Marina, Banagher, Co. Offaly. ☎ **0509/51112.**

This company operates 90-minute cruises via the *River Queen,* a 54-seat enclosed riverbus. The trip starts out by passing under the seven-arched Banagher Stone Bridge and then via Martello towers and fortresses, downstream to Victoria Lock, the largest lock on the entire Shannon system. The taped commentary covers all the historical aspects of the route. There's a bar on board.

Fare: £3.50 ($5.25) adults, £2 ($3) children.
Schedule: May–Sept Sun 3:30pm; other times vary.

SPORTS & RECREATION

Spectator Sports

HORSE RACING Horse racing is held in July, August, and September at the **Kilbeggan Racecourse,** Loughnagore, Kilbeggan, Co. Westmeath, located off the main Mullingar Road (N 52), a mile from town, on Mullingar Road. Admission is £5 ($7.50) for adults and £2.50 ($3.75) for students.

Recreation

CRUISING   The following companies rent cabin cruisers along this section of the Shannon: **Athlone Cruisers,** Jolly Mariner Marina, Athlone, Co. Westmeath (☎ 0902/72892); **Carrick Craft Cruisers,** The Marina, Banagher, Co. Offaly (☎ 0509/51187); **Silver Line,** The Marina, Banagher, Co. Offaly (for reservations ☎ 0902/51112); and **S.G.S. Marine,** Ballykeeran Marina, Athlone, Co. Westmeath (☎ 0902/85163). Craft range from two- to eight-berth; rates average £60 to £100 ($90 to $150) per week per person.

GOLF   **Birr Golf Club,** Birr, Co. Offaly (☎ 0509/20082), is an 18-hole course set amid 112 acres of parkland countryside; the greens fees are £10 ($15) on weekdays and £12 ($18) on weekends.

In the Athlone area are the 18-hole **Athlone Golf Club,** Hodson Bay, Athlone, Co. Roscommon (☎ 0902/92073), with greens fees of £12 ($18) on weekdays and £15 ($22.50) on weekends; and the new 18-hole championship **Mount Temple Golf Club,** Moate, Co. Westmeath (☎ 0902/81545), five miles east of Athlone, charging greens fees of £7 ($10.50) on weekdays and £10 ($15) on weekends.

WHERE TO STAY & DINE

Moderate

★ **Hodson Bay Hotel,** Roscommon Road, Athlone, Co. Westmeath. ☎ 0902/92444. Fax 0902/92688. 46 rms (all with bath). TV TEL

Rates (including full breakfast): £40–£57 ($60–$85.50) single, £60–£90 ($90–$135) double. No service charge. AE, DC, MC, V.

On the shores of Lough Ree, this four-story hotel stands out on the harborfront with a new pale lemon–colored facade. Totally renovated and extended in 1992, the guest rooms have a contemporary decor of light-wood furnishings and pastel-toned quilted fabrics. The public areas and most of the bedrooms overlook the marina and Hodson's Pillar, a stone monument located on an island offshore and reputed to mark the center of Ireland. At press time, plans called for an additional 50 rooms to be added.

Dining/Entertainment: Facilities include L'Escale Restaurant for formal dining and the Waterfront Bar & Buttery for light fare.

Facilities: Indoor heated swimming pool, sauna, steam room, gym, solarium; adjacent to 18-hole golf course.

Prince of Wales, Church Street, Athlone, Co. Westmeath. ☎ 0902/72626. Fax 0902/75658. 72 rms (all with bath). TV TEL

Rates (including full breakfast): £35–£65 ($52.50–$97.50) single, £60–£80 ($90–$120) double. No service charge. AE, DC, MC, V.

Dating back to the 1780s and originally known as Rourke's Hotel, this three-story property is in the center of Athlone on a busy street. In spite of its age, it has a modern interior with tasteful brass touches and paneled walls. The guest rooms offer contemporary Irish furnishings with light woods and multitoned fabrics, plus all modern conveniences, including coffee/tea-makers and garment presses. A historical note: The hotel took its present name in 1863 to mark the marriage of the heir to the British throne.

Dining/Entertainment: Choices include the Beech Tree restaurant, the Cherry Tree coffee shop, and the old-world Hunters bar.

Inexpensive

★ **Brosna Lodge,** Main Street, Banagher, Co. Offaly. ☎ **0902/51350.**
Fax 0509/51521. 14 rms (all with bath). TEL

$ **Rates** (including full breakfast): £20–£26 ($30–$39) single, £35–£48 ($52.50–$72) double. No service charge. DC, MC, V. **Closed:** Dec 24–Jan.

Although it sits along the main thoroughfare in a busy river town near Clonmacnois, this two-story hotel has a warm country atmosphere, thanks to a beautiful flower-filled front garden and the enthusiastic innkeeping of owners Geraldine and Aidan Hoare. The public areas, which include Snipes Restaurant, a cozy old-world bar, and a TV lounge, are furnished with traditional period pieces and local antiques. The guest rooms are bright and airy and overlook the gardens or the town. Best of all, it's just a short walk to the riverfront.

Dooly's Hotel, Emmet Square, Birr, Co. Offaly. ☎ **0509/20032.** Fax 0509/21332. 18 rms (all with bath). TV TEL

Rates (including full breakfast): £29 ($43.50) single, £50 ($75) double. No service charge. AE, DC, MC, V.

Dating back to 1747, this three-story Georgian hotel is located in the center of town. Although one of Ireland's oldest former coaching inns, it's been thoroughly restored and refurbished in recent years. The public areas retain their Georgian charm, while the guest rooms offer all the modern conveniences, such as tea/coffee-makers; rooms have views of the town or back garden. Facilities include the Emmet Restaurant for international fare; the old-world Coach House Bar; and an all-day coffee shop (open 10am to 10pm), handy for onward travelers in search of a meal at odd hours.

PUBS

Of all the river towns in this section of the Shannon, Banagher is particularly well known for lively Irish traditional music sessions at two of its pubs: **J. J. Hough's,** Main Street (☎ **0509/51499**), with music every night during summer and Friday to Sunday during the rest of the year; and the **Vine House,** West End (☎ **0902/51463**), with music every night during summer.

---

3 Upper Shannon—From Lough Ree to Lough Allen

Roscommon is 51 miles NE of Galway, 91 miles NW of Dublin; Longford is 80 miles NW of Dublin, 27 miles NE of Athlone; Carrick-on-Shannon is 35 miles SE of Sligo; Cavan is 65 miles NW of Dublin

GETTING TO & AROUND THE UPPER SHANNON The best way to get to the Upper Shannon area is by car or boat. Although there's public transportation, you'll need a car to get around the riverbanks and to the various attractions. Among major roads that lead to this area are the main Dublin/Sligo Road (N 4); the main Dublin/Cavan Road (N 3); N 5, and N 63 from Castlebar and the west; N 61 and N 55 from the south.

ESSENTIALS Year-round information on **County Roscommmon** is available from the **Ireland West Tourism Office,** Victoria Place, Eyre Square, Galway (☎ **091/ 63081**); on **County Longford** from the Midlands East Tourism Office, Clonard House, Dublin Road, Mullingar, Co. Westmeath (☎ **044/48761**); on **County Cavan** from the Cavan Tourist Office, Farnham Street, Cavan, Co. Cavan (☎ **049/31942**);

and on **County Leitrim** from the North-West Tourism Office, Aras Reddan, Temple Street, Sligo (☎ **071/61201**).

Seasonal information points, operating from June through August, are signposted in the following towns: Boyle (☎ **079/62145**), Carrick-on-Shannon (☎ **078/20170**), Longford (☎ **043/46566**), and Roscommon (☎ **0903/26342**).

AREA CODES   Telephone area codes in the Upper Shannon region include 043, 044, 049, 071, 078, 091, and 0903.

WHAT TO SEE & DO

The Upper Shannon River region is home to a remarkable assortment of castles, great houses, and museums, including one of Ireland's newest and most significant collections, the **Irish Famine Museum,** at Strokestown, Co. Roscommon. It chronicles the great tragedy that changed the course of history in Ireland and the world, sending forth the Irish diaspora to England, the United States, Canada, and Australia.

In addition, the shores of the Upper Shannon encompass **Lough Ree,** the second-largest of Shannon's lakes. Considered almost an inland sea, it's distinguished by long, flat vistas across the farming countryside of Counties Roscommon, Westmeath, and Longford.

Of these, Longford also gives the river its literary associations. This eastern bank of the Shannon is often referred to as Goldsmith country because 18th-century dramatist, novelist, and poet Oliver Goldsmith was born here at Pallas, near Ballymahon. Although Goldsmith did much of his writing in London, it's said that he drew on many of his Irish experiences for his works, including *She Stoops to Conquer.*

Between Lough Ree and Carrick-on-Shannon, the river is relatively narrow. The town of **Carrick-on-Shannon,** in County Leitrim, is situated on one of the great ancient crossing places of the River Shannon and is particularly known as a center for boating. There is a vast marina in the middle of the town and many local companies rent cabin cruisers.

The whole county of **Leitrim** is uniquely affected by the Shannon's waters. It's divided into two parts, almost wholly separated from one another by Lough Allen. A storage reservoir for a nearby hydroelectric plant, Lough Allen is the Shannon's third-largest lake, seven miles long and three miles wide. North of Lough Allen, in County Cavan, is the source of the Shannon River—the **Shannon Pot** on the southern slopes of the Cuilcagh Mountain.

The scope of the Shannon has been broadened in recent years so it's now possible to travel from the Shannon River to Lough Erne, using a stretch of water known as the Ballinamore–Ballyconnell Canal. Following a painstaking restoration, it was reopened in the spring of 1994, after a lapse of 125 years. Because it provides a clear path from the Shannon in the Republic of Ireland to Lough Erne in Northern Ireland, the new passage is officially designated the Shannon-Erne Waterway. It symbolizes yet another facet of cross-border cooperation and ease of travel. This is seen as a touchstone in a new golden age of Irish waterways travel.

Tullynally Castle, Castlepollard, Co. Westmeath. ☎ **44/61159.**

A turreted and towered Gothic-Revival manor, this house has been the home of the Pakenham family, the Earls of Longford, since 1655. The highlights include a great hall that rises through two stories, with a ceiling of plaster Gothic vaulting, and a collection of family portraits, china, and furniture. There's also a collection of 19th-century gadgets. The 30-acre grounds are an attraction in themselves, with various woodland walks, a linear water garden, a Victorian grotto, and an avenue of 200-year-old Irish yew trees. Tullynally is near Lough Derravaragh, an idyllic spot featured in the legendary Irish tale *The Children of Lir*. It's located about 20 miles east of Longford and 13 miles north of Mullingar, off the main Dublin/Sligo (N 4) road.

Admission: Castle, £2 ($3) adults, 50p ($1) children; castle and gardens, £3 ($4.50) adults, £1.50 ($2.25) children.

Strokestown Park House, Strokestown, Co. Roscommon. ☎ 078/33013.

A Georgian Gothic arch at the end of Ireland's widest main street leads into this estate, the seat of the Pakenham-Mahon family from 1600 to 1979. The present 45-room Palladian house, designed for Thomas Mahon by German architect Richard Castle in the 1730s, incorporates parts of an earlier tower house. The center block is fully furnished as it was in earlier days, surrounded by two wings. The north wing houses Ireland's last galleried kitchen (a kitchen gallery allowed the lady of the house to observe the culinary activity without being part of it); while the south wing is an elaborate vaulted stable, often described as an equine cathedral. It's situated on the main Dublin/Castlebar (N 5) road, less than ten miles from the west bank of the Shannon.

Admission: £3 ($4.50) adults, £2 ($3) seniors, £1 ($1.50) students and children.

Open: June to mid–Sept, Tues–Sun noon–5pm.

★ The Irish Famine Museum, Strokestown Park, Strokestown, Co. Roscommon. ☎ 078/33013.

One of the most defining events of Ireland's history—the Great Potato Famine of the 1840s—is the focus of this museum opened in 1994. Housed in the stableyards of Strokestown Park House (see above), this museum illustrates how and why the famine started, how English colonial officials failed to prevent its spread, and how it reduced the Irish population of 8.1 million by nearly 3 million through death and mass emigration. The exhibits range from photographs, letters, documents, and satirical cartoons to farm implements and a huge cauldron that was used for soup to feed the people in a famine-relief program. This museum is particularly interesting for Irish Americans, tens of millions of whom trace their ancestry to the those who left the country during and after the famine, the great Irish diaspora. The museum also seeks to relate the events of the Irish famine to contemporary world hunger and poverty.

Admission: £2.50 ($3.75) adults, £2 ($3) seniors and students, £1 ($1.50) children.

Open: May–Oct, Tues–Sun 11am–5pm.

★ Clonalis House, Castlerea, Co. Roscommon. ☎ 0907/20014.

Standing on land that has belonged to the O'Conors for more than 1,500 years, this is one of Ireland's great houses. It's ancestral home of the O'Conors, kings of Connaught, and the home of the O'Conor Don, the direct descendant of the last high king of Ireland.

The house itself, built in 1880, is a combination of Victorian, Italianate, and Queen Anne architecture, with mostly Louis XV–style furnishings, plus antique lace, horsedrawn farm machinery, and other memorabilia. It's primarily a museum of the O'Conor (O'Connor) family, with portraits, documents, and genealogical tracts dating back 2,000 years. Displays also include a rare ancient harp, said to have belonged to Turlough O'Carolan (1670–1738), the blind Irish bard who composed songs still sung today. The grounds, with terraced and woodland gardens, also hold the O'Conor inauguration stone, similar to the Stone of Scone of Westminster Abbey. The house is located about 10 miles off the main Dublin/Longford/Castlebar Road (N 5).

Admission: £2.50 ($3.75) adults, £1.75 ($2.63) seniors and students, £1 ($1.50) children over 7.

Open: June to mid–Sept Tues–Sun noon–5pm.

Lough Key Forest Park, Boyle, Co. Roscommon. ☎ 079/62363.

Spanning 840 acres along the shores of Lough Key, this is one of Ireland's foremost lakeside parks, comprising mixed woodlands, a lake, and more than a dozen islands. The grounds include nature walks, tree identity trails, ancient monuments, ring forts, a central viewing tower, picnic grounds, a restaurant, and a shop. In addition to cypress groves and other diverse foliage, you'll find a unique display of bog gardens, where a wide selection of peat-loving plants and shrubs flourishes. Fallow deer, otters, hedgehogs, birds, pheasants, and many other forms of wildlife also roam the park. The lake is navigable from the Shannon via the Boyle River. In summer, boat trips are offered by Lough Key Boat Tours (☎ 079/62214). The park entrance is located on the main Dublin/Sligo Road (N 4), two miles east of the town of Boyle.

Admission: Park £1 ($1.50) adults, free for children under 12; boat trips £3 ($4.50) adults, £1.50 (2.25) children.

Open: Park, year-round daily dawn–dusk; boat trips, May–Sept, noon–5 or 6pm, on the hour.

Lough Rynn House & Gardens, Mohill, Co. Leitrim. ☎ 078/31427.

Seat of the Clements, the earls of Leitrim, this estate comprises 100 acres of woodland, ornamental gardens, open pastures, and lakes. Of particular interest is the terraced walled garden dating from 1859 and comprising three acres—it's one of the largest of its kind in the country, laid out in the manner of a Victorian pleasure garden. The arboretum contains specimens of the tulip tree, California redwood, and other exotic species, including the oldest monkey puzzle tree in Ireland. History buffs also point out that 4,000 years of history can be seen in one 180-degree sweep of the eye at the rear of the Lough Rynn House. The neolithic burial tomb atop Druids Hill was constructed about 2,000 B.C.; Reynolds Castle, a lonely sentinel by the lakeshore, dates from the 16th century; and Lough Rynn House itself was built in 1832. It's situated south of Carrick-on-Shannon, on the outskirts of Mohill, 3¹/₂ miles from the main Dublin/Sligo (N 4) Road.

Admission: £1.25 ($1.93) adults, 70p ($1.05) seniors and students, or maximum of £3.50 ($5.25) per car; £1 ($1.50) extra per person for guided tour.

Open: May–Sept 10am–7pm.

Cavan Crystal, Dublin Road (N 3), Cavan, Co. Cavan. ☎ 049/31800.

One of the top three crystal companies of Ireland, this establishment is known for its delicate glassware, mouth-blown and hand-cut by skilled craftspeople. Visitors are invited to watch as skilled master blowers fashion the molten crystal into intricate shapes and designs, followed by the precision work of the master cutters. The glassware is for sale in the factory shop.

Admission: Free.

Open: Factory shop, Mon–Fri, 9am–5:30pm; Sat, 10am–5pm, Sun 2–5pm; factory tours, Mon–Fri 10:30am–3:30pm at regular intervals.

SPORTS & RECREATION

CRUISING The following companies rent cabin cruisers along this part of the Shannon: **Athlone Cruisers,** The Marina, Carrick-on-Shannon, Co. Leitrim

(☎ **0902/72892**); **Carrick Craft,** The Marina, Carrick-on-Shannon, Co. Leitrim (☎ **078/21248**); and **Emerald Star Line,** The Marina, Carrick-on-Shannon, Co. Leitrim (☎ **078/20234**).

GOLFING There are two 18-hole championship golf courses in the area that should not be missed. Opened in 1993, the **Glasson Golf and Country Club,** Glasson, Co. Westmeath (☎ **0902/85120**), is situated on the shores of Lough Ree, six miles north of Athlone. Greens fees are £25 ($37.50) on weekdays and £30 ($45) on weekends. Equally new is the **Slieve Russell Hotel Golf Club,** Cranaghan, Ballyconnell, Co. Cavan (☎ **049/26444**). Greens fees for those not staying at the hotel are £20 ($30) on weekdays and £30 ($45) on weekends.

Two other 18-hole courses in the area are **County Cavan Golf Club,** Arnmore House, Drumellis, Co. Cavan (☎ **049/31283**), and **County Longford Golf Club,** Dublin Road, Longford (☎ **043/46310**). Both charge greens fees of £10 ($15) on weekdays and £12 ($18) on weekends.

WHERE TO STAY & DINE
Expensive/Moderate

 Slieve Russell Hotel, Ballyconnell, Co. Cavan. ☎ **049/26444.** Fax 049/26474. 151 rms (all with bath). TV TEL

Rates (including full breakfast): £65–£80 ($97.50–$120) single, £110–£140 ($165–$210) double. No service charge. AE, DC, MC, V.

Set on 400 acres of parklands and gardens, including 50 acres of lakes and ponds, this impressive four-story hotel is named after a nearby mountain, originally known in the Irish language as Slieve Rushen. Although relatively new, it captures the opulence and charm of a bygone era, with public areas that boast marbled colonnades, huge open fireplaces, plush carpets, marble staircases, and wrought-iron trim. The conservatory-style Fountain Room exudes a country garden atmosphere, with its skylit glass dome and array of leafy plants. Guest rooms are modern and large, with light-wood furnishings, pastel-toned fabrics, and brass accessories. Each room has a garment press, coffee/tea-maker, and hairdryer. Situated near the new Shannon-Erne Waterway, this hotel is a good base for touring not only the upper Shannon area but also the attractions of Enniskillen and Northern Ireland.

Dining/Entertainment: Choices include the Conall Cearnach Restaurant for gourmet cuisine; the brasserie-style Brackly Restaurant for light fare; The Kells Bar with a stunning decor of illustrations from the *Book of Kells;* and the intimate Pike Bar for residents.

Services: Concierge, room service, babysitting, laundry and dry-cleaning service.

Facilities: 18-hole championship golf course; heated indoor swimming pool, sauna, steam room, Jacuzzi, exercise room, two squash courts, four all-weather tennis courts, hairdressing salon, gift shop, walking trails.

Inexpensive

Hotel Kilmore, Dublin Road (N 3), Cavan, Co. Cavan. ☎ **049/32288.** Fax 049/32458. 39 rms (all with bath). TV TEL

Rates (including full breakfast): £34–£36 ($46–$54) single, £58–£62 ($87–$93) double. No service charge. AE, DC, MC, V.

Located two miles south of Cavan town, this modern hotel was built in the early 1980s and has recently been totally refurbished. The public areas are airy and bright, overlooking the garden with its trio of fountains. Guest rooms have standard furnishings. Facilities include the Annalee Restaurant specializing in fish and game dishes.

Park Hotel, Cavan/Dublin Road (N 3), Virginia, Co. Cavan. ☎ **049/47235.**
Fax 049/47203. 19 rms (16 with bath). TV TEL

Rates (including full breakfast): £35 ($52.50) single, £55 ($82.50) double. No service charge. AE, DC, MC, V. **Closed:** Oct–Mar.

Set on 100 acres of woodlands and gardens beside Lough Ramor, this hotel dates back to 1751. It was originally known as Deer Park Lodge, a sporting and summer residence of the marquis of Headfort, and was converted into a hotel in the 1930s. It has since had a number of renovations and extensions, making for lots of connecting corridors and varying standards of bedrooms. The public areas retain a definite 18th-century charm, with high ceilings, elaborate chandeliers, period furnishings, and original oil paintings. The amenities include a restaurant, a lounge bar, a nine-hole golf course, a hard tennis court, fishing privileges, boating equipment, and forest walking trails. As a point of interest, this hotel and its kitchen are used as the Irish campus for the Baltimore International Culinary College in the off-season.

A PUB

Although there are many good pubs in the area, don't miss the **Derragarra Inn,** Butlersbridge, Co. Cavan (☎ **049/31003**), for a snack or a drink. Dating back over 200 years, it's full of local farm implements and crafts as well as exotic souvenirs collected by owner John Clancy during his travels around the world. Relax by the old turf fireplace or on the garden patio. It's located four miles north of Cavan town.

Along the River Shannon's Shores   Upper Shannon—From Lough Ree to Lough Allen

14

Galway City

Galway City (pronounced *Gawl-way*) is the focal point and gateway of County Galway and the west of Ireland. Situated beside the River Corrib and at the mouth of Galway Bay off the Atlantic, it's just a little over an hour's drive from Shannon Airport. With a population of 50,000, this principal city of Connaught is among the top five Irish cities. Most of all, Galway is Ireland's Renaissance City—a blend of many traditions and yet always keeping pace and boldly moving ahead.

A popular notion holds that Galway was named after some foreigners, or Galls, who had settled in the region. The earliest historically dated references to the area date back to 1124 A.D. and describe it as a Gaelic hinterland.

Because of its position on the Atlantic, Galway emerged as a thriving seaport and developed a brisk trade with Spain. Close to the city docks, you can still see the area where Spanish merchants unloaded cargo from their galleons. The Spanish Arch was one of four arches built in 1594, and the Spanish Parade is a small open square where the visitors strolled in the evening.

Tradition has it that Christopher Columbus attended Mass at Galway's St. Nicholas Collegiate Church before setting sail for the New World in 1492. Originally built in 1320, the church has been enlarged, rebuilt, and embellished over the years. It has also changed denominations at least four times.

From medieval times, Galway has been known as the City of Tribes, thanks to 14 wealthy merchant families—the Athys, Blakes, Bodkins, Brownes, Darcys, Deanes, Fonts, Frenchs, Joyces, Kirwans, Lynches, Martins, Morrises, and Skerrets—mostly of Welsh and Norman origins who ruled the town for many years as an oligarchy.

By far the most important of these families were the Lynches, who not only gave the city its first mayor in 1484, but an additional 83 other mayors during the next 169 years. In the center of town, on Shop Street, is Lynch's Castle, dating from 1490 and renovated in the 19th century. It remains the oldest Irish medieval town house used daily for commercial purposes (now the Allied Irish Bank). The exterior is full of carved gargoyles, impressive coats of arms, and other decorative stoneworks.

In more recent centuries, two developments in the city have earned it a place of prominence in the west—the founding of the Queens' College (now University College—Galway) in 1848, and the establishment of a permanent rail-link with Dublin in 1854.

Today the activity of the city revolves around a pedestrian park at Eyre Square (pronounced "air"), originally a market area known as the Fair Green. It's officially called the John F. Kennedy Park in commemoration of his visit here in June 1963. A bust of President Kennedy shares space in the park with a statue of a man sitting on a limestone wall. This statue depicts Galway-born local hero Padraig O'Conaire, a pioneer in the Irish literary revival of the early 20th century and the epitome of a Galway Renaissance man.

IMPRESSIONS

Galway is Irish in a sense in which Dublin and Belfast and Cork and Derry are not Irish but cosmopolitan. Its people, their speech, their dress, their swarthy complexions, their black hair, their eyes like blue flames, excite the imagination with curious surmises. Galway city—technically, it is only Galway town—is to the discoverer of Ireland something like what Chapman's 'Homer' was to Keats. It is a clue, a provocation, an enticement.
—Robert Wilson Lynd (1879–1949), "Galway of the Races"

What's Special About Galway City

Monuments
- Spanish Arch and Spanish Parade, dating back to 16th-century trading days with Spain.

Buildings
- Lynch's Castle, Ireland's oldest Irish medieval town house.
- St. Nicholas Collegiate Church, where it's said that Columbus prayed before setting sail for the New World in 1492.
- Galway Cathedral, built in 1965 of local marble, with statues, stained glass, and mosaics all designed by contemporary Irish artists.
- Thoor Ballylee, Gort, a restored 16th-century Norman tower house, and once the summer home of poet W. B. Yeats.

Parks/Gardens
- Eyre Square, Galway's "Central Park."
- Coole Park, Gort, a national forest and wildlife park once owned by Lady Gregory, a founder of the Abbey Theatre.

Natural Spectacles
- Sunset over Galway Bay.
- Salmon leaping upstream under the Salmon Weir Bridge.

Activities
- Take a "Ramble in Historic Galway."
- Board the "Corrib Princess" for a floating tour.
- Take a boat or plane excursion to the Aran Islands.
- Fish for salmon in the River Corrib.

After Dark
- An Taibhdhearc, Ireland's national stage of the Irish language, for traditional plays and music.
- Dun Guaire Castle, Kinvara, for 16th-century–style medieval banquets.

Shopping
- Galway Irish Crystal, Galway's distinctive glassware.
- Royal Tara China, one of Galway's oldest enterprises.
- Kenny's Book Store, a local favorite for books of all kinds and an art gallery, too.
- Fallers of Galway, known for Claddagh rings.

Next to the downtown area, on the west bank of the River Corrib, is the Claddagh, originally a fishing village, thought by many to predate Galway itself. Its name is taken from the Irish *An Cladach,* which means "a flat stony shore." The Claddagh people were descendants of early Gaelic families and spoke only the Irish language. Their stone streets were haphazardly arranged, with small squares rimmed by thatched mud-walled houses. But this old-world scene came to an end in 1934, with the construction of a modern housing development.

One Claddagh tradition, however, survives, and that's the Claddagh ring, cast in the form of two hands clasping a heart, with a crown at the top. For the people of the

Claddagh, their ring symbolized trust or plighted troth. Many Galwegians and other Irish folk still choose a Claddagh ring as a wedding band, and visitors also seek out these rings as souvenirs.

1 Orientation

Galway is 57 miles N of Shannon Airport, 136 miles W of Dublin, 65 miles NW of Limerick, 130 miles NW of Cork, 120 miles N of Killarney.

GETTING THERE • By Air   Aer Lingus operates daily service from Dublin into Galway Airport, Carnmore (☎ **091/755569**), about ten miles east of the city.

• **By Train**   Irish Rail trains from Dublin and other points arrive daily into Ceannt Station (☎ **091/564222**), off Eyre Square, Galway.

• **By Bus**   Buses from all parts of Ireland arrive daily into Bus Eireann Travel Centre, Ceannt Station, Galway (☎ **091/563555**).

• **By Car**   As the gateway to the West of Ireland, Galway is the terminus for many national roads, leading in from all parts of Ireland, including N 84 and N 17 from northerly points, N 63 and N6 from the East, and N 67 and N 18 from the south.

TOURIST INFORMATION   For information about Galway and the surrounding areas, contact or visit Ireland West Tourism, Aras Failte, Victoria Place, off Eyre Square, Galway (☎ **091/563081**). Hours are May, June, and September from Monday through Saturday, 9am to 5:45pm; July and August daily from 9am to 6:45pm; and, the rest of the year, Monday through Friday from 9am to 5:45pm and Saturday from 9am to 12:45pm.

TOWN LAYOUT   The core of downtown Galway lies between Eyre Square on the east and the River Corrib on the west. To the west of Eyre Square, Galway's main thoroughfare begins—a street that changes its name four times (from William to Shop, Main Guard, and Bridge), before it crosses the River Corrib and changes again. If that sounds confusing, don't worry. The streets are all very short, well marked, and, with a map in hand, easy to follow.

2 Getting Around

By Public Transport   Galway has an excellent local bus service, with buses running from the Bus Eireann Travel Centre, Galway (☎ **091/563555**) or Eyre Square to various suburbs, including Salthill and the Galway Bay coastline. The flat fare is 70p ($1.05).

By Taxi   There are taxi ranks at Eyre Square and all the major hotels within the city. If you need to call a cab, try Galway Taxi Co-op (☎ **091/561111**), Apollo-Corrib Taxis (☎ **091/564444**), or Big O Taxis (☎ **091/566166**).

By Car   A town of medieval arches, alleyways, and cobblestone lanes, Galway is at its best when explored on foot (with comfortable shoes). Once you check in to your hotel or guesthouse, it is best to leave your car and tour by walking. If you must bring your car into the center of town, park it and then walk. There is free parking in front of Galway Cathedral but the majority of street parking follows the disc parking system. It costs 20p (40¢) for one hour; a book of 10 discs costs £2 ($3). Multistory parking garages average £1 ($1.50) per hour or £3.50 ($5.25) per day.

To rent a car, contact one of the following firms with offices in Galway: Budget Rent-A-Car, Eyre Square (☎ **091/566376**); Hertz Rent-a-A-Car, 88 Fr. Griffin Rd. (☎ **091/561837**); or Murrays Europcar, Headford Road ☎ **091/562222**).

On Foot   To see the highlights of the city, follow the signposts on the Tourist Trail of Old Galway. The tour is explained in a handy 32-page booklet, available at the tourist office and most bookshops.

Fast Facts: Galway City

Area Code   The area code for most Galway city numbers is **091**. Area code for the Aran Islands is **099**.

Car Rentals   See "Getting Around," above.

Drugstores   Commins Pharmacy, 32 Shop St., Galway (☎ **562924**), Matt O'Flaherty Chemist, 16/18 William St., Galway (☎ **566670**) and 39 Eyre Sq., Galway (☎ **562927**), and Whelan's Chemist, Williamsgate St., Galway (☎ **562291**).

Emergencies   Dial **999.**

Hospital   University College Hospital, Newcastle Road (☎ **24222**).

Information   See "Tourist Information," above.

Laundry and Dry Cleaning   Shannon Dry Cleaners, Cross Street and Prospect Hill, Galway (☎ **565930**); Launderette & Dry Cleaners, Olde Malte Arcade, off High Street, Galway (no phone); and Heaslips Dry Cleaners, William Street and Prospect Hill, Galway (☎ **568944**).

Library   Galway Library/An Leabhar, Hynes Building, Augustine Street, Galway (☎ **561666**). Open Monday 2–5pm, Tues–Thurs 11am-8pm, Fri 11am–5pm, Sat 9am–1pm and 2–5pm.

Local Newspapers and Media   The weekly *Connacht Tribune,* published in Galway, is the largest newspaper covering the west of Ireland. Other weeklies include the *City Tribune* and the *Connacht Sentinel.* Free weekly publications that cover the arts and entertainment include the *Galway Advertiser* and the *Galway Observer.* Local radio stations are Galway Bay FM 95.8 and FM 96.8, and Raidio na Gaeltachta, an Irish language and music station broadcasting on M.W. 556.

Photographic Needs   Fahyfoto Camera Shop, 13 High St., Galway (☎ **562283,** Galway Camera Shop, 58 Dominick St., Galway (☎ **565678**), and One Hour Photo, Eglinton Street, Galway (☎ **562682**).

Police   Garda Station, Mill Street, Galway (☎ **563161**).

Post Office   Post Office, Eglinton Street, Galway (☎ **562051**). Hours are 9am to 6pm, Monday through Saturday.

Shoe Repairs   Hill & Son, 4 William St., Galway (☎ **564908**) and Olde Malte Cobblers, Olde Malte Arcade, off High Street, Galway (no phone).

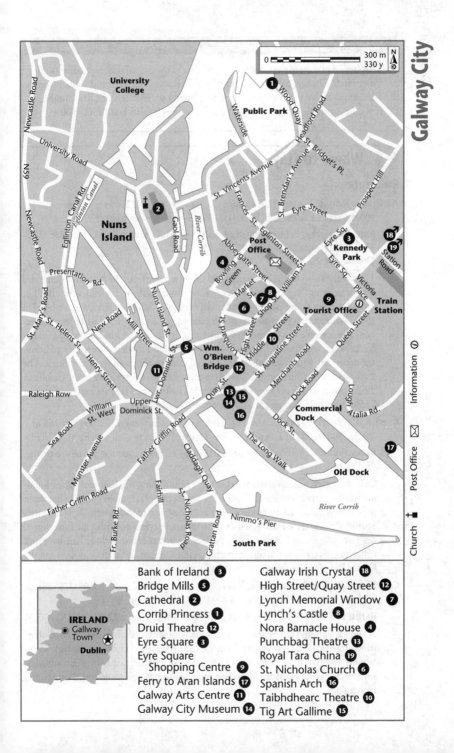

Galway City

Scale: 0 — 300 m / 330 y

University College

Public Park

Nuns Island

River Corrib

Post Office ✉

Kennedy Park

Eyre Square

Bowling Green

Market St.

High Street/Shop St.

Lynch's Castle

Tourist Office ⓘ

Train Station

Wm. O'Brien Bridge

Middle Street

St. Augustine Street

Merchants Road

Quay St.

Commercial Dock

Spanish Arch

Dock St.

The Long Walk

Old Dock

River Corrib

Nimmo's Pier

South Park

Roads and Streets
Newcastle Road · University Road · N59 · Newcastle Road · St. Mary's Road · St. Helens St. · Henry Street · Raleigh Row · Sea Road · Munster Avenue · William St. West · Upper Dominick St. · Father Griffin Road · Father Griffin Road · Fr. Burke Rd. · Fairhill · St. Nicholas Road · Claddagh Quay · Grattan Road · Eglinton Canal Rd. · Eglinton Canal · Presentation Rd. · New Road · Mill Street · Nuns Island St. · Gaol Road · Tower Dominick St. · Waterside · Wood Quay · St. Vincents Avenue · Frances St. · St. Brendan's Avenue · Headford Road · St. Bridget's Pl. · Eglinton Street · William Street · Eyre Street · Prospect Hill · Eyre Sq. · Victoria Place · Queen Street · Dock Road · Lough Atalia Rd. · Station Road · Abbeygate Street

Legend
- Information ⓘ
- Post Office ✉
- Church ✝■

IRELAND
Galway Town · Dublin

Listings
- Bank of Ireland ③
- Bridge Mills ⑤
- Cathedral ②
- Corrib Princess ①
- Druid Theatre ⑫
- Eyre Square ③
- Eyre Square Shopping Centre ⑨
- Ferry to Aran Islands ⑰
- Galway Arts Centre ⑪
- Galway City Museum ⑭
- Galway Irish Crystal ⑱
- High Street/Quay Street ⑫
- Lynch Memorial Window ⑦
- Lynch's Castle ⑧
- Nora Barnacle House ④
- Punchbag Theatre ⑬
- Royal Tara China ⑲
- St. Nicholas Church ⑥
- Spanish Arch ⑯
- Taibhdhearc Theatre ⑩
- Tig Art Gallime ⑮

3 Where to Stay

Moderate

Ardilaun House, Taylor's Hill, Galway, Co. Galway. ☎ **091/21433** or toll free **800/44-UTELL** in the U.S. Fax 091/21546. 89 rms (all with bath). TV TEL

Rates: (including full breakfast) £38–£50 ($57–$150) single; £60–£95 double ($90–$142.50). Service charge 10%. AE, DC, MC, V.
Closed: Dec 23–28.

This Georgian-style country house hotel takes its name from the Irish placename *Ard Oilean* meaning "high island," a picturesque island nearby in Lough Corrib. Built in 1840 as a town house for a prominent Galway family, it was converted into a hotel in 1962. With ancient trees and extensive gardens, it is located in a hilly residential section, about a mile west of the downtown area. It has been expanded and updated in recent years, and most of the guest rooms, situated in a modern three-story addition, are decorated with traditional furnishings, dark woods, and quilted fabrics. The atmosphere of an old mansion prevails in the public areas, especially in the Camilaun dining room, and in the hunting-theme bar, The Blazers, a favorite local rendezvous. Facilities include a sauna and steamroom.

Brennan's Yard Hotel, Lr. Merchant's Rd., Galway, Co. Galway. ☎ **091/568166** or toll free **800/44-UTELL** in the U.S. Fax 091/568262. 24 rms (all with bath). TV TEL

Rates: (including full breakfast) £60–£90 ($90–$135) single or double. No service charge. AE, DC, MC, V.

One of the cleverest restorations in Galway's historic area, this four-story stone building was formerly a warehouse. Opened as a hotel in 1992, it offers compact but skylit public areas enhanced by modern Irish art. The guest rooms, overlooking the city's Spanish Arch area, are decorated in contemporary style with Irish pine furnishings, designer fabrics, and locally made pottery. In-room extras include hairdryer and coffee/tea-maker. The restaurant specializes in European and seafood dishes; and the Oyster Bar offers bar food and snacks all day.

Corrib Great Southern, Dublin Road (N 6), Galway, Co. Galway. ☎ **091/755281** or toll free **800/44-UTELL** in U.S. Fax 091/751390. 180 rooms. TV TEL

Rates: £86–£94 ($129–$141) single or double. Service charge 12.5%. AE, DC, MC, V.

Set on high ground two miles east of Galway City, this modern five-story hotel offers panoramic views of Galway Bay, from its skylit atrium-style lobby to the wide wrap-around windows in all of the public areas. Guest rooms are equally bright and airy, with lovely bay views enhanced by contemporary furnishings, pastel-toned fabrics, and modern art.

Dining/Entertainment: Enjoy views of Galway Bay while dining in The Currach, the hotel's main restaurant, or at O'Malley's Pub.

Services: Concierge, room service, laundry and dry cleaning, babysitting, children's program (July–Aug).

Facilities: Indoor heated swimming pool, sauna, Jacuzzi, steam room, table tennis.

⭐ **Glenlo Abbey,** Bushy Park, Galway, Co. Galway. ☎ **091/26666.** Fax 091/27800. 42 rms (all with bath). TV TEL

Rates (including full breakfast): £65–£80 ($97.50–$120) single, £96–£115 ($144–$172.50) double. No service charge. AE, DC, MC, V.

Situated about two miles outside of Galway on the main Clifden Road, this secluded hotel overlooks Lough Corrib in a tranquil and sylvan setting, surrounded by a nine-hole golf course. Dating back to 1740, it was originally the ancestral home of the Ffrench and Blake families, two of Galway's 14 great tribes who ruled over the city for centuries. Totally restored and opened as a hotel in 1993, it has retained the aura of grandeur in all of the public areas, with hand-carved wood furnishings, hand-loomed carpets, ornate plasterwork, and an extensive collection of Irish art and antiques. The guest rooms, which have lovely views of Lough Corrib and the surrounding countryside, are similarly decorated with traditional furnishings as well as marbled bathrooms; each room has a personal safe and garment press.

Dining/Entertainment: Choices include the Ffrench Room for fine dining; the Kentfield Bar, decorated with a unique collection of pen-and-ink drawings of Irish writers; and the Oak Cellar Bar.

Services: Concierge, room service, laundry/dry cleaning.

Facilities: Nine-hole golf course, fishing in Lough Corrib.

⭐ **Great Southern Hotel,** 15 Eyre Sq., Galway, Co. Galway. ☎ **091/564041** or toll free **800/44-UTELL** in the U.S. Fax 091/566704. 114 rms (all with bath). TV TEL

Rates: £90–£102 ($135–$153) single or double. Service charge 12.5%. AE, DC, MC, V.

Dating back to 1845, this handsome five-story hotel is truly the grande dame of the Galway area. Positioned in the heart of the city overlooking the landmark Eyre Square, it is next to the bus/rail station and within walking distance of all the major sights. The spacious public areas have high ceilings, elaborate plasterwork, crystal chandelier, and original Connemara marble fireplaces. Recently refurbished, the guest rooms have traditional dark woods, semicanopy beds, designer fabrics, and brass accoutrements, with extras such as hair dryer, garment press, and coffee/tea-maker; rooms overlooking Eyre Square have views of the whole city and beyond.

Dining/Entertainment: Choices include the Oyster Room restaurant for fine dining and O'Flaherty's Pub, an Old Galway bar that serves excellent pub grub.

Services: Concierge, room service, dry cleaning and laundry, babysitting.

Facilities: Rooftop indoor heated swimming pool, sauna, and steam room.

Victoria Hotel, Victoria Place, Eyre Square, Galway, Co. Galway. ☎ **091/567433.** Fax 091/565880. 57 rms (all with bath). TV TEL

Rates (including full breakfast): £70–£75 ($105–$112.50) single or double. No service charge. MC, V.

Tucked in a peaceful corner of the city, opposite the Tourist Office and just a block from Eyre Square, this new hotel has a great location. The interior is designed in a modern Art Deco style, enhanced by lots of plants and mirrors. Guest rooms are compact and contemporary, with light wood furnishings and pastel-toned fabrics, as well as in-room amenities such as coffee/tea-maker, hairdryer, and garment press. There is a restaurant/bar and 24-hour room service.

Inexpensive

$ **Jurys Inn**, Quay Street, Galway, Co. Galway. ☎ **091/566444** or toll free **800/44-UTELL** in the U.S. Fax 091/568415. 128 rooms. TV TEL
★ **Prices:** £39–£51 ($58.50–$76.50) single, double, or triple. No service charge. AE, DC, MC, V.

Situated beside the River Corrib and opposite the Spanish Arch, this is a new four-story hotel designed in keeping with the area's historic character. Geared to the cost-conscious traveler, it the first of its kind for Galway's downtown area, providing quality hotel lodgings at guesthouse prices. The guest rooms, all with double-glazed windows, look out on expansive views of the river or nearby Galway Bay; each room is decorated in modern art deco style, with light wood furniture and pink- and gray-toned fabrics, enhanced by pictures of Old Galway and Connemara. There are coffee/tea-makers in the rooms, and ice machines, a rarity in Ireland, on the first and third floors. Facilities include a moderately priced restaurant, The Arches, and the Inn Pub.

Adare Guest House, 9 Fr. Griffin Place, Galway, Co. Galway. ☎ **091/566421** or **091/562638.** Fax 091/563963. 9 rms (all with bath). TV TEL
Rates (including full breakfast): £20–£22 ($30–$33) single, £30–£35 ($45–$52.50) double. No service charge. MC, V.

Situated west of the River Corrib in a quiet residential area, this modern three-story guesthouse is within a comfortable walking distance (two blocks) from the Wolf Tone Bridge and the Spanish Arch area of the city. It offers modern accommodations with orthopedic beds and standard furnishings. Breakfast is served in a cheery dining room, using Royal Tara china and other Galway-produced accessories. Innkeepers are Padraic and Grainne Conroy.

4 **Where to Dine**

Expensive

Casey's Westwood, Dangan, Upper Newcastle Road, ☎ **21442.**
Cuisine: INTERNATIONAL. **Reservations:** Recommended.
Prices: Appetizers £3.20–£6.20 ($4.80–$9.30); lunch main courses £4.50–£8.50 ($7.25–$2.77); dinner main courses £7.50–£14.50 ($11.25–$21.75), lobster £21.50 ($32.25). AE, MC, V.
Open: Daily lunch 12:30–2:30pm, dinner 5:30–10:15pm.

Situated on the Clifden Road (N 59) about 1.5 miles from Eyre Square, this restaurant is set back from the main road amid flowering gardens and tall trees. Owner Bernie Casey has converted an old brick house into a modern Georgian-style dining experience. The creative Irish menu includes parcel of turbot wrapped in pastry with spring onions; pan-fried sole on the bone; ravioli of lobster and Galway Bay prawns; breast of chicken and fish on a skewer; filet of salmon with herbs and crab claws; steak Diane; and guinea fowl wrapped in pastry. Light pub meals are available all day in the Elm bar including a stew of the day.

⭐ **deBurgos**, 15/17 Augustine St. ☎ **562188.**
Cuisine: INTERNATIONAL. **Reservations:** Recommended.
Prices: Set lunch £9.50 ($14.25) or bar menu items £1.50–£5.95 ($2.25–$8.93); dinner appetizers £1.75–£5.50 ($2.63–$8.25); dinner main courses £10.75–£14.95 ($16.13–$22.43). AE, MC, V.
Open: Mon–Sat lunch noon–3pm; dinner 6:30–10:30pm.

Named after one of Galway's most important Norman tribes, deBurgos is found in what was originally the wine vault of a 16th-century merchant's house. It has an impressive interior of white-washed walls, caverns, arches, turreted dividers, Oriental carpets, and medieval-style wall hangings. All is enhanced by flickering candles, fresh flowers, pink linens, and Irish music playing in the background. The imaginative menu offers dishes such as deBurgos three fillets (pork, veal, beef) on a confit of shallots; surf-and-turf Hollandaise; filet of beef with jumbo prawns; chicken Nicole, stuffed with farci of chicken, shrimp and chervil cream sauce; rack of Conemara lamb; breast of duck in orange, lime, and brandy sauce; and Galway salmon with cream dill sauce. The bar lunch menu includes sandwiches, salads, seafood, and steaks.

Eyre House & Park House Restaurant, Forster Street ☎ **564924.**
Cuisine: INTERNATIONAL. **Reservations:** Recommended.
Prices: Set lunch £6–£8 ($9–$12); set dinner Eyre House £16.75–£18.75 ($25.13–$28.13); set dinner Park House £17.45–£20.45 ($26.18–$30.63). AE, DC, MC, V.
Open: Daily lunch noon–4pm, dinner 6–10pm.

Just a half-block east of Eyre Square, these twin restaurants are housed in a lovely old five-story stone building. Eyre House has an old-world decor of stained glass, dark woods, oil paintings, and plants, while the Park Room is more elegant, with Georgian-style windows, pink walls, and modern Art Deco fittings. The menus are similar, with slightly higher prices in the Park Room. Entrees include sirloin steak au poivre; roast duckling with peach and brandy sauce; honey-glazed rack of lamb with tomato flavored garlic sauce; chicken Kiev; grilled Galway salmon with Marchand de Vin sauce; fresh Carna scallops Mornay; and Dublin Bay prawns thermidor.

Moderate

Bridge Mills Restaurant, O'Briens Bridge. ☎ **566231.**
Cuisine: INTERNATIONAL. **Reservations:** Recommended.
Prices: Appetizers £1.50–£5.50 ($2.25–$8.25); dinner main courses £9.50–£12.50 ($14.25–$18.75). MC, V.
Open: Dinner daily 5:30–10:30pm.

Located on the lower ground floor (riverbank level) in a restored mill building beside the Corrib, this restaurant allows the diner the charm of sitting beside the rhythmic flow of the river or by the gently turning original mill wheel. Menu choices are such as escalope of turkey breast; stuffed noisettes of lamb; chicken Milano with ham, cheddar and garlic butter; seafood platter; trout amandine; and a variety of pastas.

The Grapevine, 2 High St. ☎ **562438.**
Cuisine: IRISH/VEGETARIAN. **Reservations:** Recommended.

Prices: Appetizers £1.95–£4.25 ($2.93–$6.38); lunch main courses £1.20–£3.25 ($1.80–$4.88); dinner main courses £8.95–£12.25 ($13.43–$18.38). MC, V.
Open: Daily lunch 12:30–2:30pm, dinner 6–11pm.

Situated above the Bunch of Grapes pub, this small, ten-table restaurant has an elegant nautical decor of natural stone and white-washed walls, ships' wheels, lantern and candle lighting, and fresh and dried flower arrangements. Escalope of salmon in fresh salmon or herb cream sauce might tempt you, or grilled médaillons of monkfish in chive butter sauce; loin of lamb on port wine sauce; breast of duck on orange and lemon sauce; prime Irish beef with green peppercorn sauce; or a few vegetarian dishes such as vegetable pancakes and vegetable cannelloni in noodle pastry on carrot sauce. Fresh vegetables, such as carrots or cucumbers in star-shaped slices, are also used as decorations to enhance other dishes. Lunch items include Irish stew, smoked salmon plate, seafood chowder, and fresh local oysters or mussels.

★ **The House of Bards,** 2 Market St. ☎ 568414.
Cuisine: IRISH. **Reservations:** Recommended.
Prices: Appetizers £2–£4.95 ($3–$7.43); lunch main courses £1.35–£4.25 ($2.03–$6.38), dinner main courses £6.95–£14.95 ($10.43–$22.43). MC, V.
Open: Daily lunch 12:30–2:30pm, dinner 6–11pm.

One of Galway's newest restaurants, the House is lodged in one of the city's oldest buildings, with a fireplace oven dating back to 1589. The crest over the fireplace is the marriage stone of Joyce and Skerret, two of the tribes of Galway. White-washed walls, arches, flagstone floors, candle wall sconces, medieval art, and the menu itself add to the 16th-century atmosphere. What choices! There's Lady Jane Darcy's fancy, chicken with Irish cheese stuffing; the Chieftain's Choice, pork filled with cheese and apples in rosemary sauce; Knight's Armour, sirloin steak with Irish whiskey sauce; Jester's Leap, salmon stuffed with creamy dill sauce; and King's Ransom, seafood trio of baked scallops, mussels, and prawns in white wine cheese sauce. Lunch items range from soups and salads, to a medley of seafood au gratin, chicken cordon bleu, or lasagne.

Tigh Neachtain, 2 Quay St. and 17 Cross St. ☎ 566172.
Cuisine: IRISH/INTERNATIONAL. **Reservations:** Required.
Prices: Appetizers £1.95–£5 ($2.93–$7.50); main courses £7.50–£14.50 ($11.25–$21.75). MC, V.
Open: Mon–Sat 6:30–10:30pm.

Situated above a vintage pub of the same name, this restaurant exudes an intimate of days past atmosphere, with a glowing open fireplace, wood paneled walls, and Victorian-style furnishings, enhanced by live guitar music strumming in the background. The menu's offerings are a variety or fresh seafood as well as breast of chicken in saffron sauce; médaillons of pork in onion cream sauce; marinated filet of beef in brandy sauce; and vegetable chili.

Moderate/Inexpensive

The Chestnut, 3 Eyre Sq. ☎ 565800.
Cuisine: IRISH/SEAFOOD. **Reservations:** Recommended.
Prices: Set lunch £8.75 ($13.13); appetizers £2–£5 ($3–$7.50); dinner main courses £6.95–£10.95 ($10.43–$16.43). AE, MC, V.
Open: Mon–Sat lunch 12:30–3pm, dinner 6:30–10pm.

Located on the second floor (first floor in Irish terms) of a small shopfront building, this restaurant overlooks Eyre Square. The rich decor gleams with mahogany furnishings and cathedral stained-glass windows. A variety of steaks and traditional dishes can be had, stuffed turkey and ham and leg of lamb, or perhaps seafood crêpe mornay with cod, turbot, salmon, and mussels; Galway Bay plaice; grilled sea trout with prawn butter; or an Aran seafood platter.

Conlon & Sons, 8 Eglinton St. ☎ 562268.

Cuisine: SEAFOOD. **Reservations:** Not accepted.
Prices: Seafood bar items £1.20–£7.95 ($1.80–$11.93), restaurant appetizers £1.20–£4.30 ($180–$6.45), main courses £4.90–£9.90 ($7.35–$14.85). MC, V.
Open: Daily 11am–11pm.

Located in the heart of the city opposite the post office, this restaurant, known for its fresh fish, serves its meals in a ground-level cafe/take-away bar and downstairs in a long, narrow basement restaurant. Treasures of the deep await: grilled wild salmon; steamed Galway Bay mussels; grilled silver hake; curried monkfish; fishermen's platters (smoked salmon, mussels, prawns, smoked mackerel, oysters, crab claws); smoked salmon omelet; and prawn and smoked salmon salads:

$ G.B.C./Galway Bakery Company, 7 Williamsgate St. ☎ 563087.

Cuisine: INTERNATIONAL. **Reservations:** Not necessary.
Prices: Coffee shop all items £2–£6 ($3–$9); restaurant appetizers £1.40–£3.50 ($2.10–$5.25); lunch main courses £2.50–£6.50 ($3.75–$9.75); dinner main courses £4.50–£13 ($7.25–$19.50). AE, DC, MC, V.
Open: Coffee Shop Mon–Sat 8am–9pm, Sun 9am–9pm, restaurant daily noon–10pm.

With a distinctively Old Galway shopfront facade, this building is two eateries in one—a ground level self-service coffee shop and a full-service restaurant upstairs. On the restaurant menu a variety of dishes appear, priced to every budget, from steaks and seafood dishes, to chicken Oscar, Kiev, or cordon bleu, as well as quiches, crêpes, omelets, salads, and stir-fried vegetable platters. Baked goods, particularly the homemade brown bread, are an added attraction.

Hooker Jimmy's Steak & Seafood Bar, The Fishmarket, Spanish Arch. ☎ 568351.

Cuisine: SEAFOOD/IRISH. **Reservations:** Recommended for dinner.
Prices: Appetizers 85p–£4 ($1.28–$6); main courses £3.95–£15.25 ($5.93–$22.88). AE, MC, V.
Open: Daily 11am–11pm.

Housed in an old stone building beside the Spanish Arch and the River Corrib, this informal restaurant offers the same menu all day in a nautical atmosphere: mussels in cream sauce; lobster thermidor; West coast platter (crab claws, lobster tail, salmon, mussels); Galway Bay salmon with stir-fry vegetables; smoked salmon platter with prawns; and a variety of steaks and pastas.

★ McDonagh's Seafood Bar, 22 Quay St. ☎ 565001.

Cuisine: SEAFOOD. **Reservations:** Not Accepted.
Prices: Appetizers £1.95–£4.50 ($2.93–$7.25); main courses £5.50–£13.95 ($8.25–$20.93). AE, MC, V.
Open: Daily 11am–10pm.

For fresh seafood in an authentically sea-going atmosphere, Galway's best choice is this little shopfront eatery, divided into a fish market, a fish-and-chip shop, and a full-service restaurant. The McDonagh family, fishmongers for more than four generations, buy direct from local fishermen every day—and it shows, as crowds line up every night to get in. The menu presents the names of available fish in Irish, English, German, French, Dutch, Italian, and Japanese. The choice usually includes salmon, trout, lemon and/or black sole, turbot, and silver hake, all cooked to order. In addition, you can crack your own prawns' tails and crab claws in the shell; break open steamed wild mussels cooked in wine and garlic; or tackle a whole lobster. For hearty appetites, there is McDonagh's house special (a platter of smoked salmon, mussels, crab claws, salmon pate, smoked mackerel, and cod).

Budget

$ **Bewley's Cafe,** The Cornstore, Middle Street. ☎ **565789.**
Cuisine: IRISH/SELF-SERVICE. **Reservations:** Not accepted.
Prices: All items 95p–£4.25 ($1.43–$6.38). MC, V.
Open: Oct–May, Mon–Sat 8:30am–6pm; June–Sept, Mon–Sat 8:30am–8:30pm, Sun noon–6pm.

For a cup or coffee or a snack, this is a favorite spot for Galwegians and visitors. A branch of the famous Dublin institution established in the 1840s, this new location has been designed to re-create the 19th-century with rounded Georgian windows, dark wood furnishings, and brass fixtures. But the menu is modern: sandwiches, salads, soups, and quiches, as well as the famous Bewleys's cakes and sticky buns.

Grainstore Cafe, Lower Abbeygate St. ☎ **566620.**
Cuisine: IRISH/SELF-SERVICE. **Reservations:** Not accepted.
Prices: All items £1–£5 ($1.50–$7.50). No credit cards.
Open: Oct–May, Mon–Sat 9:30am–5:30pm, June–Sept, 9:30am–9pm.

Set amid a gallery of contemporary Irish art, this little cafe offers snacks and light meals, ranging from homemade soups and pastries to pastas and stir-fry dishes, as well as stuffed eggplant, pizzas, quiches, salads, and hummus plates. Traditional fare, such as bacon and cabbage, is also prepared.

5 What to See & Do

Some of Galway's greatest attractions are not within four walls and require no admission charge, but are out in the open, always there for partaking. Leading the list is Galway Bay—just about every visitor who comes to this city yearns "to see the sun go down on Galway Bay." And no one should miss a stroll around the Spanish Arch and Spanish Parade, Eyre Square and the John F. Kennedy Park, or upon the banks of the River Corrib, which glistens at all hours as salmon playfully leap upstream under the Salmon Weir Bridge.

For a change of pace, or if it rains, here are some of the more conventional indoor attractions:

 St. Nicholas' Collegiate Church, Lombard Street. ☎ **566784.**
It is said that Christopher Columbus prayed here before setting out to discover the New World. Established about 1320, it has changed from Roman Catholic to Church of Ireland (Episcopal) at least four times and is currently under the aegis of the latter

denomination. Highlights include an authentic crusader's tomb, dating back to the 12th or 13th centuries, with a rare Norman inscription on a grave slab. In addition, there is a free-standing benitier, or holy water stoup, unique in Ireland, as well as a carved font dating back to the 16th or 17th century, and a stone lectern with barley-sugar twist columns dating back to the 15th or 16th centuries. The belfry contains ten bells, some of which date back to 1590. Guided tours, conducted by a knowledgeable and enthusiastic church representative, Declan O Mordha, depart from the south porch according to demand, except Sunday morning.

Admission: Free to the church, but donations welcome; tours £1.50 ($2.25) adults, £1 ($1.50) students.

Open: May–Sept, daily 9am–5:30pm.

Galway Cathedral, University and Gaol Roads. ☎ 563577.

Dominating the city's skyline, Galway Cathedral is officially known as the Cathedral of Our Lady Assumed into Heaven and St. Nicholas. Mainly in the Renaissance style, it's constructed of fine-cut limestone from local quarries with Connemara marble floors. Completed in 1965, it took eight years to build. Contemporary Irish artisans designed the statues, stained-glass windows, and mosaics. It's beside the Salmon Weir Bridge on the west bank of the River Corrib.

Admission: Free. Donations welcome.

Open: Daily 8am–6pm.

Tig Art Na Gaillime, Flood Street. ☎ 563553.

Located near the Spanish Arch, this is Galway's House of Art, displaying oils, watercolors, and pen and pencil work by native artists. Many pieces are on display for the first time.

Admission: Free.

Open: Mon–Sat 9:30am–5:30pm

Galway Arts Centre, 47 Dominick St. and 23 Nuns Island ☎ 565886.

Originally the town house of W. B. Yeats' patron, Lady Augusta Gregory, then for many years the offices of the Galway Corporation, this arts center offers concerts, readings, and exhibitions by Irish and international artists.

Admission: Free.

Open: Mon–Sat 10am–6pm or later.

Galway City Museum, off Quay Street. ☎ 568151.

Located next to the Spanish Arch, this little museum offers a fine collection of local documents, photographs, and city memorabilia.

Admission: 60p (90¢) adults, 30p (45¢) children

Open: Daily 10am–1pm and 1:15–5:15pm.

Nora Barnacle House, Bowling Green. ☎ 564743.

Opposite St. Nicholas's church clock tower, this restored terrace house was once the home of Nora Barnacle, wife of James Joyce. It contains letters, photographs, and other exhibits on the lives of the Joyces and their connections with Galway.

Admission: £1 ($1.50) per person.

Open: May–Sept, Mon–Sat 10am–5pm.

★ Galway Irish Crystal Ltd., Merlin Park. ☎ 757311.

Visitors to this distinctive crystal manufacturer are welcome to watch the craftsmen at work—blowing, shaping, and hand-cutting the glassware. Demonstrations are continuous weekdays. The shop is open daily. It's located east of the city on the main road (N 6).

Admission: Free.

Open: Mon–Sat 9am–5pm, Sun noon–5pm; demonstrations Mon–Fri 9am–5pm.

★ **Royal Tara China Ltd.,** Tara Hall, Mervue. ☎ **751301.**

One of Galway's oldest enterprises, this company manufactures fine bone china gift and tableware, distinguished by delicate shamrock patterns and designs inspired by the *Book of Kells,* Tara brooch, and the Claddagh ring. Guided factory tours are conducted on weekdays. Look for the sign, a mile east of Galway City off the main Dublin Road.

Admission: Free.

Open: Jan–June and Sept–Dec, daily 9am–6pm; July–Aug daily 9am–9pm; tours, Mon–Fri 11am and 3pm.

Sightseeing Tours & Cruises

Duchas Tours, Swan House, Flood Street. ☎ **566784.**

See the best of this city by taking a Ramble in Historic Galway, a series of walking tours that focus on the the historical, literary, cultural, and maritime traditions of Galway. All walks depart from the Tourist Office or the Galway City Museum.

This company also offers the two guided bus tours, described below, of the city and surrounding area, with emphasis on history, literature, and archaeology. Both tours leave from the Tourist Office.

The **City and South County Tour** covers Galway City and the southern part of Galway county, with its many literary associations including Coole Park, and also the Burren area.

The **Corrib Country and Connemara Tour** goes along Lough Corrib to Cong, and into the Maam Valley of Connemara. On the itinerary are Bronze Age Stone Circles made famous by Sir William Wilde, Oscar Wilde's father; the monastic village of Cong; and mountain bogs with rare fly-eating plants.

Prices: Guided walks £3.50 ($5.25) adults, £3 ($4.50) students; bus tours £10 ($15) adults, £8 ($12) students.

Schedules: May–Sept, daily guided walks at 9:15am, 11:15am, 2:15pm, 4:15pm, and 6:15pm; City and South County Tour at 9:30am; Corrib Country and Connemara at 2:30pm.

Western Heritage Sightseeing, Galway Tourist Office, Victoria Place, off Eyre Square, Galway. ☎ **21699.**

Walking tours of Galway are conducted by local guides, with emphasis on the city's medieval history and connections. Tours last for $1\frac{1}{2}$ hours and depart from the Tourist Office.

For those who prefer to ride, there is also a half-day bus trip taking in the major sights of Galway City and the Thoor Ballylee area. Highlights are Galway Cathedral, the Church of St. Nicholas, the Nora Barnacle house, and the Fishery walk beside the banks of the River Corrib. The tour last for three hours and departs from the Tourist Office and major hotels.

Prices: Walking tour, £3.50 ($5.25) adults, £2.50 ($3.75) students; bus tour, £8 ($12) adults, £7 ($10.50) children.

Schedule: Walking tour, May–Sept daily, departs at 2:30pm; bus tour, departs at 9:50am from the Tourist Office and on demand from hotels.

★ *Corrib Princess*, Woodquay, Galway. ☎ **568903.**

See the sights of Galway from afloat, aboard this 157-passenger two-deck boat that cruises along the River Corrib, with a commentary on all points of interest. The trip lasts 90 minutes, passing castles and various sites of historical interest and wildlife. There is full bar and snack service. Tickets can be bought at the dock or at the *Corrib Princess* desk at the Tourist Office.

Fare: £5 ($7.50) per person.
Schedule: May–Sept daily 2:30 and 4:30pm.

6   Sports & Recreation

SPECTATOR SPORTS

GREYHOUND RACING   The hounds race year-round every Tuesday and Friday at 8:15pm at the Galway Greyhound Track, College Road, off Eyre Square, Galway (☎ **562273**). The admission price of £3 ($4.50) includes a racing card.

HORSE RACING   Each year at the end of July for six days, thoroughbreds ply the track at the Galway Racecourse, Ballybrit, Galway (☎ **753870**), less than two miles east of town. Shorter two-day race meetings are scheduled in early September and late October. Admission is £5–£8 ($7.50–$12), depending on the event.

RECREATION

BICYCLING   To rent a bike, contact **Galway Cycle Hire,** Victoria Place, off Eyre Square (☎ **561600**), situated opposite the Tourist Office. It hires touring and mountain bikes, from £3 ($4.50) for four hours or £6 ($9) per day. It's open daily from 9am to 7pm in summer, 9am to 5pm the rest of the year.

FISHING   Sitting beside the River Corrib, Galway City and nearby Connemara are popular fishing centers for salmon and seatrout in the west of Ireland. For latest information on requirements for state licenses and local permits, check with the **Western Regional Fisheries Board,** Weir Lodge, Earl's Island, Galway (☎ **563118**). For gear and equipment, try **Duffy's Fishing,** 5 Mainguard St., Galway (☎ **562367**); Freeney's Sport Shop, 19–23 High St., Galway (☎ **568794**); or **Great Outdoors Sports Centre,** Eglinton Street, Galway (☎ **562869**).

GOLF   Less than five miles east of Galway is the 18-hole par-72 championship Galway Bay Golf & Country Club, Renville, Oranmore, Co. Galway (☎ **590500**), with greens fee of £25 ($37.50), and less than two miles west of the city is the 18-hole par-69 seaside course at Galway Golf Club, Blackrock, Galway (☎ **22169**), with greens fees of £15 ($22.50).

HORSEBACK RIDING   Riding enthusiasts head to **Aille Cross Equitation Centre,** Aille Cross, Loughrea, Co. Galway (☎ **41216**), about 20 miles east of Galway. Run by personable Willy Leahy (who has appeared often on American television programs), this facility is one of the largest in Ireland, with 50 horses and 20 Connemara ponies. For about £10 ($15) an hour, you can arrange to ride through nearby farmlands, woodlands, forest trails, and mountain lands. Week-long trail rides in the scenic Connemara region are also a specialty of this riding center, as is hunting with the Galway Blazers in the winter months.

7 Savvy Shopping

Galway offers malls with small shops, clustered in some of the city's well-preserved and restored historic buildings, such as the **Cornstore** on Middle Street, the **Grainstore** on Lr. Abbeygate Street, and the **Bridge Mills,** a 430-year-old mill building beside the River Corrib.

Eyre Square Centre, the downtown area's largest shopping mall with 50 shops, has incorporated a major section of Galway's medieval town wall as part of its complex.

Most shops are open Monday through Saturday from 9am or 10am to 5:30pm or 6pm. In July and August, many shops stay open late, usually till 9pm on weekdays, and some also open on Sunday from noon to 5pm.

Here is a sampling of some of Galway's best shops.

Antiques and Curios

Cobwebs, 7 Quay La. ☎ **564388.**

Established almost 25 years ago, this little shop is located across from the Spanish Arch. It offers a variety of antique toys and rarities from all parts of Ireland.

Curiosity Corner, Cross St. (no phone)

Located on a corner opposite the Spanish Arch, this shop has a wide variety of unusual Irish-made gifts, from curios and ceramics, to scents, pot pourri, and dried flowers.

Books

Charlie Byrne's Bookshop, 4 Middle St. ☎ **561766.**

Situated opposite the Cornstore, this small but well-organized shop presents a large selection of second-hand books on Irish literature and poetry.

Hawkins House Bookshop, 14 Churchyard St. ☎ **567507.**

Visit this shop for new books concentrating on Irish poetry, drama, fiction, history, art, archaeology, genealogy, mythology, and music. It's located beside the Collegiate Church of St. Nicholas, off Shop Street.

 Kennys Book Shop and Gallery, Middle and High Streets. ☎ **562739.**

A Galway fixture for over 50 years, this shop is a sightseeing attraction unto itself. You'll find old maps, prints, and engravings. Books of all topics—many on local history, as well as a Yeats and a Joyce section—are wedged on shelves and window ledges, and piled in crates and turf baskets. Lining the walls are signed photos of more than 200 writers who have visited the shop over the years. In addition, Kenny's is famous for its antiquarian department, a book-binding workshop, and an ever-changing gallery of watercolors, oils, and sculptures by local talent. Enough goes on here to keep eight members of the Kenny family busy.

Crystal, China, and Souvenirs

Moons, William Street at Eglinton Street. ☎ **565254.**

This is Galway's long-established mid-city department store, with crystal, china, linens, and gifts, as well as clothing and household items.

 Treasure Chest, 31 William Street at Castle Street. ☎ **563862.**

For more than 25 years, this attractive shop with a Wedgwood-style exterior has been a treasure trove of top quality crafts, fashions, and gifts. You'll find everything from

Waterford Crystal chandeliers to Royal Tara and Royal Doulton china, Irish Dresden figurines, Lladro figures, and Belleek China, as well as Irish designer clothing, Aran knitwear, lingerie, and swimwear, not to mention hand-made leprechauns and Irish whiskey marmalade.

Jewelry

Hartmann's, 27-29 William St. ☎ 562063.

The Hartmann family, who began in the jewelry business in the late 1800s in Germany, brought their skills and wares to Ireland in 1895, eventually opening this Galway shop in 1942. They still enjoy a far-reaching reputation as watchmakers, goldsmiths, and makers of Claddagh rings. This store also stocks Celtic crosses, writing instruments, crystal, silverware, and unusual clocks. It's in the heart of town, just off Eyre Square.

★ **Fallers of Galway**, Williamsgate St., Galway. ☎ 561226.

Dating back to 1879, Fallers has long been a prime source of Claddagh rings, many of which are made on the premises. It also sells Celtic crosses, some inlaid with Connemara marble, as well as gold and silver jewelry.

Handcrafts

★ **Design Ireland Plus**, The Cornstore, Middle St. ☎ 567716.

Ceramics, pottery, linen, lace, jewelry, leather bags, rainwear, blankets, stationery, candlesticks, multi-colored sweaters and capes, and hand-crafted batik ties and scarves—all designed and made in Ireland are sold here.

Judy Greene Pottery, 11 Cross St. ☎ 561753.

Don't miss this small shop for hand-thrown pottery painted by hand with colorful Irish floral designs. Wares include goblets, vases, candleholders, dinner and tea services, garden pots, cut-work lamps, miniatures, and jewelry. Pieces can be specially commissioned.

Kevin McGuire & Son, Prospect Hill. ☎ 568733.

Housed in a white-washed cottage and gray stone building, a block from Eyre Square, this specialty leather shop offers Celtic and modern handbags, briefcases, music cases, wallets, watch straps, belts, pendants, sheepskin rugs.

Meadows & Byrne, Castle Street, Galway. ☎ 567776.

Earthenware pottery and hand-blown glass have long been featured at this store, as well as silk paintings, batik prints, tableware, scented beeswax candles, Irish preserves and honey, toys, and designer knitwear.

Music and Musical Instruments

Mulligan's, 5 Middle St. Court, Middle Street. ☎ 564961.

Mulligan's boasts of having Ireland's largest stock of records, CDs, and cassettes of Irish and Scottish traditional music. There is also a good selection of folk music from all over the world including Cajun, Latin American, and African, as well as country music, blues and jazz.

⭐ **P. Powell & Sons/The Music Shop,** The Four Corners, William Street.
☎ 562295.

Located opposite Lynch's Castle, where William Street meets Abbeygate Street, this shop is known for Irish traditional music. In addition to cassettes and CDs, tin whistles, flutes, bodhrans, accordians, and violins are sold. Also available are sheet music and a full range of music books are available.

Tweeds, Woolens and Clothing

⭐ **O Maille (O'Malley),** Dominick Street. ☎ 562696.

Established in 1938, this family-run shop is located on the west side of the River Corrib, slightly off the beaten track, but customers from far and near flock here for quality Irish clothing, including Irish-designed knitwear, traditional Aran knits, and tweeds for men and women. There is always a good selection of sweaters, jackets, coats, suits, capes, kilts, caps, and ties.

Mac Eocagain/Galway Woollen Market, 21/22 High St. ☎ 562491.

This shop brims with traditional Aran hand-knits and colorful hand-loomed sweaters and capes, as well as linens, lace, sheepskins, jewelry, and woolen accessories.

---

8 Evening Entertainment & Pubs

THEATERS

Druid Theatre, Chapel Lane. ☎ 568617.

Irish folk dramas, modern international dramas, and Anglo-Irish classics are the focus at this professional theater in the heart of Galway. Started in 1975, it is housed in a converted grain warehouse, configured with 65 to 115 seats, depending on the production. Lunchtime performances are often staged during the summer months.

 Admission: Tickets, evening £5–£7 ($7.50–$10.50), lunchtime £3–£4 ($4.50–$6).

 Open: Mon–Sat, box office noon to 8pm; evening shows at 8pm, lunchtime shows at 1:10pm.

Punchbag Theatre, Quay Lane. ☎ 565422.

Located opposite the Spanish Arch in the city's historic section, this newly renovated theater presents contemporary plays from Ireland and abroad. In May through September, the emphasis is on staging the works of new writers.

 Admission: Tickets, £7 ($10.50).

 Open: Box office, Mon–Sat noon–6pm; shows, Tues–Sun 8pm.

⭐ **An Taibhdhearc Theatre,** Middle Street. ☎ 562024.

Pronounced *Thive-yark* and officially known as An Taibhdhearc na Gaillimhe (the Theatre of Galway), this is Ireland's national stage of the Irish language. Founded in 1928, it is a 108-seat, year-round venue for both Irish plays and visiting troupes (such as ballet). In the summer months, the theater presents Siamsa, a program of traditional music, song, dance, and folk drama.

 Admission: Tickets, £7 ($10.50).

 Open: Box office, daily 11am–6pm; shows nightly, 8pm; Siamsa, July–Aug, Mon–Fri 8:45pm.

A MEDIEVAL BANQUET

On the shores of Galway Bay, **Dun Guaire** is a splendid 16th-century castle that features a medieval banquet with a literary-themed show. Located in south County Galway on Ballyvaughan Road (N 67), Kinvara, Co. Galway (☎ **091/37108**), the castle is a nightlife option for people staying in Galway City—just a half-hour drive away (see "Easy Excursions," below). The show features the work of Synge, Yeats, Gogarty, and other Irish writers who knew and loved this area of western Ireland. Banquets are staged from May to September, twice nightly at 5:30 and 8:45pm, priced at £27.50 ($42.25). Reservations can be made by calling the castle directly or the Shannon Medieval Castle Banquets (☎ **061/360788** or toll free **800/CIE-Tour** in the U.S.).

PUBS

Busker Browns, Cross Street, Galway. ☎ **563101.**

Alcoves, nooks and crannies, and a choice of bars fill this pub, one of the city's newest but with an Old Galway ambience. Traditional music is performed Sunday through Thursday nights from 9pm and on Saturday afternoon. The place swings to Dixieland jazz on Sunday from noon to 2pm.

Crane Bar, 2 Sea Rd. ☎ **567419.**

In the southwestern part of Galway at the corner of an open market area called "the Small Crane," this rustic pub is known for its nightly musical entertainment. From 9pm every night, it's country/western downstairs and traditional Irish tunes upstairs.

Hole in the Wall, Eyre St., ☎ **565593.**

Topped with a thatched roof, this old-world pub stands out on a busy shopping street one block from Eyre Square. The interior has a low beamed ceiling, open fireplaces, old sporting prints, and an old-fashioned juke box. Cable TV screens show major sports events in this regular gathering spot for fans of Gaelic football and horse racing. In between the sports talk, traditional Irish music starts nightly in the summer months at 9:30pm.

McSwiggans, 3 Eyre St., Woodquay. ☎ **568917.**

The walls of this grand old pub range from brick, stone, tin, and wood paneling, and they're covered with vintage ale posters. The ceilings above the pub's nooks and crannies are beamed, and a skylight encloses a veranda. Live music is on tap Sunday nights from 8pm.

O'Malleys, 30 Prospect Hill. ☎ **564595.**

Claiming to be Galway's oldest music pub, this informal watering hole has traditional Irish music sessions nightly at 9:15pm. In the July and August, there is also Irish music at 4pm on Wednesday through Sunday.

An Pucan, 11 Forster St. ☎ **561528.**

Located a block east of Eyre Square, this old-fashioned nautical theme pub features free traditional Irish music nightly, from 9pm.

The Quays, Quay Street and Chapel Lane. ☎ **561771.**

This little treasure is in the heart of the city, a half block from the Druid Theatre. The decor is decidedly nautical, with pictures of sailing ships and other seafaring memorabilia. The bar area is quite small, but there is also an enclosed skylit back courtyard. Evening music ranges from traditional Irish to Dixie and usually starts at 9pm.

Rabbitt's, 23–25 Forster St. ☎ **562215.**

Dating back to 1872, this pub is much the way it was a century ago. Old lanterns hang in the corners, skylights brighten the bar area, and the walls are lined with pictures of Galway in horse-and-carriage days. A hefty bucket of ice sits on the counter. Run by the fourth generation of the Rabbitt family, it's located just a block east of Eyre Square.

---

9 Easy Excursions from Galway City

THE ARAN ISLANDS

West from the mouth of Galway Bay 30 miles out at sea, the storied Aran Islands—Inis More (Inishmore), Inis Meain (Inishmaan), and Inis Oirr (Inisheer)—are outposts of Gaelic culture and language. The vibrant islanders have been immortalized in John Millington Synge's play *Riders to the Sea* and Robert Flaherty's film *Man of Aran*. In currachs, little craft made of tarred canvas stretched over a timber frame, the fishermen pilot their way through the turbulent waters that crash around the islands.

The island's 1500 inhabitants live in simple stone cottages and get around in pony-drawn transport. The classic hand-knit bainin sweaters originated here. The islanders' rawhide shoes are ideal for the rocky terrain. *Crios* are finger-braided belts made of colored wool worn by the islanders. Brightly colored petticoats and elaborately hand-crocheted shawls are traditional garb for women.

Dun Aengus is a stone cliff fortress on Inishmore that extends more than 11 acres. Dating back to the fifth century, the fort is believed to have been of great maritime significance. It's set on the edge of a cliff that drops 250 feet to the sea, and it offers a spectacular view of Galway Bay.

The new heritage center, Ionad Arann, Kilronan, Inishmore (☎ **099/61355**), tells the history and culture of these islands. Exhibits examine the harsh yet beautiful landscape, the Iron Age forts, the churches of the first Christians. It's open from April through September daily from 10am to 7pm. Admission is £2 ($3) adults, £1.50 ($2.25) students, £1 ($1.50) children and seniors.

Here are the best ways to arrange an excursion to the Aran Islands:

Aer Arann, Connemara Airport, Inverin, Co. Galway. ☎ **593034.**

The fastest way to get from the mainland to the Aran Islands is via this local airline, which departs from a new airport approximately 20 miles west of Galway City. Flight time is only six minutes, and bus service between Galway City and the airport is available. Flights can be booked at the Aer Arann desk at the Galway Tourist Office.

Fares: £33 ($49.50) roundtrip, £17 ($25.50) one way per person; if booked at least a week in advance, £25 ($37.50) roundtrip.

Schedule: June–Sept daily at 9:30am, 11am, 2pm, and 5pm, returning at 9:45 and 11:15am, 4:15 and 5:15pm; Oct–May schedule varies.

Aran Ferries, Galway Tourist Office, Eyre Square, Galway. ☎ **568903.**

Galway Bay, a triple-deckered, 290-passenger ferry, cruises to Kilronan on Inishmore in a 90-minute trip from the Galway Docks. From Rossaveal in Connemara—23 miles west of the city, a connecting bus is available from downtown Galway—the *Aran Flyer,* a double-deckered, 218 passenger ferry, will take you to Kilronan in 20 minutes. Both ships have a bar, snack service, and a sundeck.

Fares: Round-trip Apr–June and, Sept £12–£15 ($18–$22.50); July–Aug £15–£18 ($22.50–$27).

Schedule: From Galway, June and Sept at 10:30am, July–Aug at 9:30am and 1:30pm; from Aran, June and Sept at 4:30pm; July–Aug at 11:30am and 4:30pm. From Rossaveal Apr–Oct at 10:30am, 1:30 and 6pm, returning at 12:30, 5, and 7pm.

Island Ferries, Victoria Place, off Eyre Square, Galway. ☎ 561676.

Year round, the double-deckered *Aran Seabird* ferries between Rossaveal, 23 miles west of downtown Galway, and the Aran Islands. The trip takes 35 minutes. Buses depart for Rossaveal from the ferry office opposite the tourist office in Galway an hour before each sailing. The boat has indoor and outdoor seating for all passengers. The snack bar serves alcohol.

Fares: £15 ($22.50) per person with bus connection; £12 ($18) without bus.

Schedule: Year-round from Rossaveal at 10:30am, 1:30 and 6:30pm, returning at noon, 5, and 7:30pm; June–Sept extra sailings are scheduled; check for times.

O'Brien Shipping, Galway Docks, Galway. ☎ 567283.

The *M.V. Oileain Arann,* a 191-passenger, air-conditioned, three-deck ship, launched in 1993, is one of the newest on the Galway/Aran Islands route. It has a full bar, snack bar, and a public telephone on board. Sailing time is 90 minutes. Booking office is at the Galway Tourist Office. **Note:** this company also operates a "fly/sail" arrangement in conjunction with Aer Arann, offering a boat/plane combination trip.

Fares: £15 ($22.50) per person roundtrip; £8 ($12) one-way; fly/sail £26 ($39) per person.

Schedule: From Galway, June and Sept at 10am, July–Aug 10:30am; from Aran, June and Sept at 5:30pm, July–Aug at 4:30pm. Oct–May schedule varies.

OYSTER COUNTRY

South of Galway on the main road south (N 18) are the two small fishing villages, Clarenbridge and Kilcolgan. Each year, at the end of September, these two villages host the annual Galway Oyster Festival. Launched in 1954, this five-day festival is packed with traditional music, song, dancing, sports, art exhibits, and, above all, oyster-tasting events and oyster-opening competitions. A Galway beauty is crowned Oyster Pearl, and she reigns over the festival.

Even if you can't be there for the festival, you can still enjoy some of Ireland's best oysters during any other month with an "r" in it.

If you continue southward on N 18 for another ten miles, you'll see signs to Coole Park (☎ 091/31804). This national forest is populated by Irish red deer, pine martens, red squirrels, and badgers. It was once the summer home of Lady Augusta Gregory, dramatist and folklorist. Along with W. B. Yeats and Edward Martyn, she founded the Abbey Theatre. Her house no longer stands, but an "autograph tree" bears the signatures and sets of initials carved by George Bernard Shaw, Sean O'Casey, John Masefield, Oliver St. John Gogarty, and Douglas Hyde, the first president of Ireland. The restored courtyard has a visitor center, tearooms, picnic tables, and a garden. Admission is £1 ($1.50) adults, 70p ($1.05) seniors and students, and 40p (60¢) children. It's open from mid-April to mid-June and September on Tuesday through Sunday from 10am to 5pm, and mid-June to the end of August daily from 9:30am to 6:30pm.

Also in Gort on the N 18 is Thoor Ballylee (☎ **091/31436**). This restored 16th-century Norman tower house was the summer home of the Nobel Prize–winning poet, William Butler Yeats. Yeats described the house as "a tower set by a stream's edge"; it served as the inspiration for his poems "The Winding Stair" and "The Tower." In the interpretative center, an audio-visual examines the poet's life. Also on the grounds are the original Ballylee Mill, partially restored and a bookshop specializing in Anglo-Irish literature. Admission is £2.50 ($3.75) adults, £2 seniors and students ($3), and 75p (1.08) children. It's open from Easter to September daily from 10am to 6pm.

West off the main road, between Gort and Kilcolgan, is Dunguaire Castle, Kinvara (☎ **091/37108**). Reached via R 347, this tower house and bawn sits on the south shore of Galway Bay. It was erected in the 16th century by the O'Heynes family at the royal seat of the 7th-century King Guaire of Connaught. The castle was later the country retreat of Oliver St. John Gogarty, Irish surgeon, author, poet, and wit. Admission is £2.10 ($3.15) adults, £1.60 ($2.40) seniors, and £1.15 ($1.68) students and children. It's open daily from late April through September from 9:30am to 5:30pm. Medieval banquets are held here in the evenings (see "Evening Entertainment," above).

Where to Eat Oysters

Paddy Burkes, Ennis/Galway Road (N 18), Clarenbridge, Co. Galway. ☎ **091/96107.**
Cuisine: SEAFOOD. **Reservations:** Recommended for dinner.
Prices: Appetizers £2–£5 ($3–$7.50); lunch main courses £1.50–£11.50 ($2.25–$17.25), dinner main courses £8.95–£14.50 ($13.43–$21.75). AE, DC, MC, V.
Open: Daily 10:30am–11pm.

Good

Platters of local oysters and mussels are served throughout the day at this homey tavern, with its lemon color and thatched roof, situated on the main road ten miles south Galway City. You can pick your favorite spot to relax amid a half-dozen rooms and alcoves, with a nautical decor of fish nets, original stone walls, open fireplaces, pot belly stoves, and traditional sugan chairs. In good weather, there is also seating in a back garden beside a weir bridge. Lunch and other snack items range from seafood soups and chowders to sandwiches, salads, and omelets. In the evening, you can also order full meals with choices such as whole black sole; baked salmon; king prawns thermidor; Atlantic plaice and crab with prawn sauce; rack of lamb with pepper sauce; honey roast duck with mead sauce; chicken cordon bleu; or médaillons of beef with whiskey and mustard.

★ **Moran's Oyster Cottage,** The Weir, Kilcolgan, Co. Galway. ☎ **091/96113.**
Cuisine: SEAFOOD. **Reservations:** Recommended.
Prices: Appetizers £1.60–£4.85 ($2.40–$7.28); main courses £1.20–£9.80 ($1.80–$14.70). AE, MC, V.
Open: Daily 10:30am–11pm.

As presidents, prime ministers, and movie stars who have visited here can testify, it's worth the drive down a twisting lane, 12 miles south of Galway, to reach this 220-year-old thatched-roof pub. And it's not just a thirst that draws visitors from all walks of life. Moran's is known first and foremost for its nautical traditions and excellent seafood—succulent Galway Bay oysters plucked from the waters outside, fresh and smoked salmon, prawns, and crab claws, all accompanied by heaping platters of crusty brown bread, garden salad, and the drink of your choice. Amble into one of the cozy snugs, sit by the fireside, or take a place at one of the outdoor tables and watch the sun go down on Galway Bay. It's an experience worth planning your whole day around!

Savvy Shopping

Clarenbridge Crystal Shop, Clarenbridge, Co. Galway. ☎ 091/596178.

Housed in a early 19th-century building that was once a church and then a school, this shop features all types and styles of Clarenbridge crystal, a local glass product that has been hand-cut, engraved, and decorated at a factory a mile away. In addition to the crystal, other wares for sale include locally made woolens, sweaters, framed prints and watercolors, and jewelry. Open Monday through Friday from 9am to 7pm, Saturday from 10am to 6pm, and Sunday from noon to 6pm.

15

The West

"**T**HE WEST'S AWAKE!" INTONES THE OLD SONG. INDEED, THE WEST—THE counties of Galway and Mayo—is not only awake but thriving. And that's a remarkable achievement, considering the turbulent and painful past of these two counties.

Situated along the rocky western coast, Galway and Mayo are Ireland's second- and third-largest counties, together forming the heart of the province of Connaught. "To hell or Connacht!" was the dubious choice that Oliver Cromwell offered to the Irish in the 17th century. Ravaging the land and chopping down choice trees, he attempted to push the native population westward, far away from the more valuable midland farms.

The displaced Irish chose to till the west's poor soil and eke out a living from the rocky land. Just as they were managing to raise a decent potato crop, the blight struck and the famine years of 1845 through 1849 took a further toll. Galway and Mayo were Ireland's most devastated regions during the famine, as thousands of people either starved or took off on ships sailing westward, never to return.

You'll be amazed to see the miraculous recovery that has been made in Galway and Mayo today. But, most important, you'll be glad to know that the progress has not interfered with the cherished ways of the people. Some of the country's greatest hotels, restaurants, and sports and shopping opportunities are here, all a part of a setting in which Ireland's traditional customs, crafts, music, and lifestyle still thrive.

1 The Galway Bay Coast

From Galway City to Inverin is 20 miles

GETTING TO & AROUND   The best way to see the sights along the Galway Bay coast is to drive, departing Galway City and following the Coast Road (R 336).

ESSENTIALS • Tourist Information   Contact or visit the **Ireland West Tourist Office,** Aras Failte, Victoria Place, Galway, Co. Galway (☎ **091/563081**), open year-round (see Chapter 14, "Galway City," for hours). In addition, a seasonal office, open from late May to mid-September, is maintained at Salthill (☎ **091/563081**).

• **Area Code**   Most numbers in this region have the area code 091.

Almost everyone heading to Ireland dreams of watching "the sun go down on Galway Bay," as the old song suggests. Well, once you've arrived in Galway City, you'll find Galway Bay just down the road.

It's certainly worth a trip to see the bay's wide blue waters, with the Aran Islands sitting 30 miles off the coast like three giant whales at rest on the sea. With vistas of Galway Bay on your left, the drive along the coast from Galway City is so spectacular that you'll want to turn around and do it all again, retracing your way back to Galway, with Galway Bay on your right.

WHAT TO SEE & DO

Head west, following the signs for the Coast Road (R 336). Within two miles you'll be in Salthill, a modern Irish beach resort that's somewhat along the lines of the Jersey shore in the U.S., with a boardwalk and fine beach, plus lots of bars, fast food, amusement rides, and arcades of games. This is a summer mecca for Irish families, but we prefer to continue on this scenic road to the little towns like Barna and Spiddal, both of which are considered to be Irish-language towns. Spiddal, 12 miles west of

What's Special About the West

Beach
- Salthill, a resort with a long boardwalk and a fine sandy beach.

Buildings
- Aughnanure Castle, Oughterard, a 16th-century tower house with an unusual double bawn (a fortified enclosure) and a watchtower.
- Westport House, one of the few great 18th-century houses in Connaught.

Parks/Gardens
- Connemara National Park, 3,800 acres of mountains, bogs, heaths, and grasslands that are home to Connemara ponies and Irish red deer.

For the Kids
- Dan O'Hara's Farm, an eight-acre farm operated in the style of the 1840s.

Ace Attractions
- Ceide Fields, Co. Mayo, a 5,000-year-old farm preserved in a blanket of bog, believed to be the most extensive Stone Age monument in the world.
- Foxford Woollen Mills, Co. Mayo, a 100-year-old local industry known the world over.
- Kylemore Abbey, a 19th-century Neo-Gothic house with a Gothic chapel, working pottery studio, and craft center.
- Leenane Cultural Centre, for the history of the Irish wool industry.

Natural Spectacles
- Connemara, a tableau of white-washed thatched cottages, rock-strewn land, an open bog, lakes, rivers, and mountains.
- The Twelve Bens, Connemara's glorious mountain range.

Activities
- Cruise Lough Corrib and visit Inchagoill Island.
- Fish for salmon at Mayfly time in Connemara rivers or on the River Moy at Ballina, "home of the Irish salmon."

Shopping
- Spiddal Craft Village, to see artisans at work.
- Connemara Marble Industries, Moycullen, to see the quarrying, cutting, and finishing of the unique green marble of this land.
- Millar's Connemara Tweed, Clifden, for skeins of wool and ready-made apparel.
- Roundstone Musical Instruments, for a bodhran made-to-order.

Religious Shrines
- National Shrine of Our Lady of Knock, Ireland's Lourdes.
- Croagh Patrick, St. Patrick's Holy Mountain, a 2,510-foot peak that dominates the Mayo coast and is a place of pilgrimage to this day.
- Ballintubber Abbey, in continuous use for the last 800 years.

TV and Film Locations
- *The Quiet Man* at Cong, Co. Mayo.
- *The Field* at Leenane, Co. Galway.
- *Year of the French* at Killala, Co. Mayo.

Great Towns/Villages
- Clifden, the "capital" of Connemara.
- Westport, Co. Mayo, a tree-lined "planned town," with rows of Georgian buildings and an octagonal central mall.

Galway City, is also an ideal spot to shop for locally made Aran knit sweaters and other handcrafts made by the people in the surrounding cottages.

The road continues as far as Inverin and then turns northward, with signposts for Rossaveal. From **Rossaveal,** you can make the shortest sea crossing from the Galway mainland to the Aran Islands (see "Easy Excursions from Galway," in Chapter 14). You may wish to combine this coastal drive with a trip to the islands.

If you continue on R 336, you'll leave the Galway Bay coast and travel amid the rocky and remote scenery approaching the center of Connemara. **Casla (Costelloe)** is the home of Raidio na Gaeltachta, the Irish-language radio station, and **Rosmuc** is the site of the **Padraic Pearse Cottage.** This simple thatched-roof cottage served as a retreat for Dublin-based Pearse, who was one of the leaders of Ireland's 1916 Rising. He used his time here to improve his knowledge of the Irish language. Now a national monument, the cottage contains various documents, photographs, and other Pearse memorabilia. Admission is £1 ($1.50) for adults, 70p ($1.05) for seniors, and 40p (60¢) for students and children. It's open from mid-June until mid-September, daily from 9:30am to 1:30pm and 2 to 6:30pm.

At this point you can continue northward into the heartland of Connemara or retrace your route so you can have another look at Galway Bay. Try to time your drive so that you can "watch the sun go down on Galway Bay" from a good vantage point. All this activity can easily take a full morning or afternoon, so it is best to save a new day for Connemara.

SPORTS & RECREATION

FISHING   Rimmed by the waters of Galway Bay and the Atlantic, this area is prime territory for sea fishing, especially for mackerel, pollock, cod, turbot, and shark. **Spiddal Sea Angling,** Craigmore, Greenhill, Spiddal (☎ 091/83535), offers fishing trips on board the *Thresher 1,* a 33-foot catamaran designed especially for sea fishing. The price averages £30 ($45) per person per day and includes rods, reels, and bait. The boat leaves from Spiddal Pier; advance reservations are required.

For those who prefer trout fishing, there's **Crumlin Fisheries,** Inverin, Co. Galway (☎ 091/93448). This fishery has a lake stocked with sea-reared rainbow trout and allows two fish per person to be taken per day. Prices range from £10 ($15) for fishing from the bank to £25 ($37.50) for fishing with a boat; ghillies (fishing guides) are available for £25 ($37.50) extra. Fishing is available from 9am daily, but reservations must be made at least a day in advance.

SWIMMING   Two clean and sandy beaches, ideal for swimming, are the Silver Strand at Barna and the beach at Spiddal.

SAVVY SHOPPING

★ **Ceardlann an Spideil/Spiddal Craft Centre,** Coast Road, Spiddal.
☎ 091/83376.

In a setting overlooking Galway Bay, this is a cluster of cottage shops where craftspeople ply their trades each day. Browse around and watch crafts in the process of being made. The selection includes pottery, weaving, knitwear, floral art, screen printing and design, jewelry, and woodturning. The art gallery features original hand-carved stonecraft, sculpture, paintings, prints, and batiks, plus a very good coffee shop. Open April through October, Monday through Saturday from 9:30am to 6pm and Sunday 2 to 6pm.

An Gallerai Beag/The Small Gallery, Pier Road, Barna, Co. Galway. ☎ 091/27534.

Nothing quite captures the beauty of Connemara like an artist's brush put to canvas. This gallery displays and sells paintings and miniatures of Connemara's scenery, villages, and people. Open May through September, Monday through Saturday from 10am to 6pm.

⭐ **Mairtin Standun,** Coast Road, Spiddal, Co. Galway. ☎ 091/83102 or 83108.

A fixture on the Connemara coast since 1946, this shop has long been known as a good source for traditional bainin sweaters, hand-crafted by local women from the nearby Aran Islands and the surrounding Connemara countryside. Recently enlarged, it also offers colorful knits, tweeds, sheepskins, linens, glassware, china, pottery, jewelry, books, and maps. In addition there is a new wide-windowed café, facing Galway Bay and the Aran Islands. Open March through November, Monday through Saturday from 9:30am to 6:30pm.

WHERE TO STAY

⭐ **Connemara Coast,** Coast Road, Furbo, Co. Galway. ☎ 091/592108. Fax 091/592065. 112 rms (all with bath). TV TEL

Prices: (including full breakfast) £45–£77.50 ($67.50–$116.25) single, £80–£120 ($120–$180) double. No service charge. AE, DC, MC, V.

If you want to see the sun go down on Galway Bay, this is the place to stay. Located six miles west of Galway City, it's nestled right along the shores of the famous bay, with unobstructed views of the coast as well as the Aran Islands. Recently refurbished and expanded, the guest rooms are decorated in a colorful tweedy or floral style, each with a picture-window view of the water. Some units have turf-burning fireplaces and private verandas.

Dining/Entertainment: The bi-level Gallery restaurant has views of the bay, and the lounge bar has traditional entertainment nightly in summer and on weekends during the rest of the year.

Facilities: Indoor heated swimming pool, Jacuzzi, steam bath, gym, two all-weather tennis courts.

WHERE TO DINE

Expensive/Moderate

⭐ **Boluisce,** Coast Road, Spiddal, Co. Galway. ☎ 091/83286.

Cuisine: SEAFOOD. **Reservations:** Recommended for dinner.

💲 **Prices:** Appetizers £1.50–£4 ($2.25–$6); lunch main courses £1.20–£5.75 ($1.80–$8.63); dinner main courses £5.25–£18.95 ($7.88–$28.43). MC, V.

Open: Mar–Dec daily seafood bar noon–10pm, restaurant 7–10pm. **Closed:** Jan–Feb.

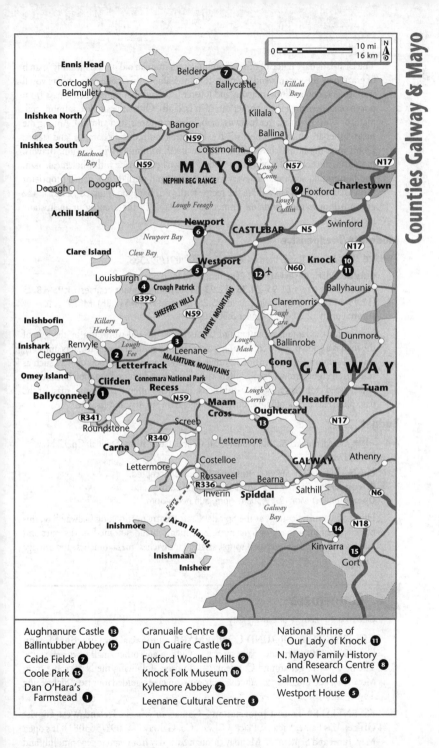

Counties Galway & Mayo

The Irish-language name of this restaurant comes from an old phrase meaning "patch of grazing by the water." And, if you're fond of seafood, this is one patch where you'll want to graze on scallops, prawns, and lobster (it is said that more lobsters pass from pot to plate here than in any other eatery in Ireland). Or try the smoked salmon, crab plate, or West Coast platter (prawns, crab, lobster, mussels, and salmon). Among the meat dishes are chicken or beef stir-fry, beef stroganoff, duck à l'orange, and steaks. Don't miss the house chowder—a meal in itself, brimming with salmon, prawns, monkfish, mussels, and more. Home-baked brown bread, made with wholemeal, bran, and buttermilk, accompanies every meal; it's rich and nutlike, and genial proprietor John Glanville will gladly share the recipe with you. Bar food is served all day in the ground-floor lounge, and full dinners are available in the evening in an upstairs restaurant.

Moderate/Inexpensive

Twelve Pins, Coast Road, Barna, Co. Galway. ☎ 091/592368.

Cuisine: IRISH. **Reservations:** Recommended for dinner.
Prices: Appetizers £1.95–£4.75 ($2.93–$7.13); lunch main courses £1.95–£8.95 ($2.93–$13.43), dinner main courses £5.25–£11.85 ($7.88–$17.88). MC, V.
Open: Lunch 12:30–3pm, dinner 6:30–10pm.

Named for the famous mountains of Connemara, this old-world inn by the side of the road is a good place to come for fresh oysters or a seafood platter (oysters, mussels, smoked salmon, and prawns), and other creatively prepared seafood choices such as scallops en croûte; trout Oisin (stuffed with almonds and seafood); salmon hollandaise; and sautéed crab claws. For non-fisheaters, the menu offers a traditional roast of the day, plus steaks, rack of lamb, duckling, vegetarian stir-fry, and lasagne.

Budget

An Caife, Ceardlann an Spideil/Spiddal Craft Centre, Coast Road, Spiddal, Co. Galway. ☎ 091/83443.

Cuisine: IRISH/SELF-SERVICE. **Reservations:** Not accepted.
Prices: All items 80p–£4 ($1.20–$6). No credit cards.
Open: Apr–Oct Mon–Sat 9:30am–6pm, Sun noon–6pm.

Housed in a rustic cottage at the Spiddal Craft Centre overlooking Galway Bay, this place is ideal for a snack or light meal. The menu includes home-baked scones and pies, as well as freshly prepared soups, salads, sandwiches, pizza, quiches, and sausage rolls.

2 Connemara

Clifden is 40 miles W of Galway City

GETTING TO & AROUND CONNEMARA From Galway City, **Bus Eireann** (☎ 091/62000) provides daily service to Clifden and other small towns en route. The best way to get around Connemara is to drive, following the N 59 route from Moycullen and Oughterard. Alternatively, you can take a guided tour (see "Sightseeing Tours," below).

ESSENTIALS • Tourist Information Contact or visit the **Ireland West Tourist Office,** Aras Failte, Victoria Place, Galway, Co. Galway (☎ 091/563081). It's open May, June, and September, Monday through Saturday from 9am to 5:45pm; July and

August, daily from 9am to 6:45pm; and, the rest of the year, Monday through Friday from 9am to 5:45pm and Saturday from 9am to 12:45pm. The **Oughterard Tourist Office,** Main Street, Oughterard (☎ **091/82224**), is also open year-round, Monday through Friday from 9:30am to 6pm and Saturday from 9:30am to 1pm, with extended hours in the summer season. In addition, a seasonal office, open from May through September, is maintained at Clifden (☎ **095/21163**).

Area Codes   Telephone area codes for numbers in the Connemara area are 091 or 095.

If you look at an average map or road sign, you won't usually see a marking or directional for Connemara. That's because it's not a city or a town—it is an area or region, much like the Burren is, in County Clare, or the Garden of Ireland, in Wicklow. In general, Connemara constitutes the section west of Galway City, starting out from Oughterard and continuing toward the Atlantic.

Although the area does have some fascinating attractions and a beautiful national park, Connemara is most of all an experience—Ireland at its natural best. Drive around Connemara and you'll see the Ireland of most people's dreams.

WHAT TO SEE & DO

The "capital," or largest town, in Connemara is **Clifden**—if you follow the signs for Clifden, you can't go wrong. The road marked N 59 will take you around the heart of Connemara and then onward to County Mayo. You can also follow many of the smaller roads and wander around Connemara for days. In fact, many people choose to stay in this region for a week or so, usually basing themselves in one or more of the fine resorts and inns that dot the countryside, especially in places like Cashel, Ballynahinch, Renvyle, and Clifden itself.

The coastline is indented with little bays and inlets, small harbors, and beaches. At almost every turn are lakes, waterfalls, rivers, and creeks, while a dozen glorious mountains, known as the **Twelve Bens,** rise at the center. All of this is interspersed with rock-strewn land and flat fields of open bog, rimmed with gorse and heather, rhododendrons, and wild flowers. The tableau presents a dramatic panorama of sea and sky, land and bog.

You'll see thatched-roof cottages in the most out-of-the-way places, sheep grazing on remote hillsides, and fences along the road that are literally made of piles of rock, one of Connemara's greatest natural resources. You can't help but wonder—if the rocks ever turned to diamonds or gold, what a rich land this would be!

Connemara's other natural wonder is the **bogland.** It is said that the bogs began forming 2,500 years ago, and, during the Iron Age, the Celts preserved their butter in the bog. Today, with one-third of Connemara classified as bog, the turf, or peat, which is cut from the bog, is an important source of fuel for the surrounding cottages.

Cutting and drying turf is an integral part of the rhythm of the seasons in Connemara. Cutting requires a special tool, a spade called a slane, which slices the chunks in a uniform size, about 18 in. long. These bricks of turf are spread out to dry and stiffen slightly, so they can be stacked in pyramids to permit air circulation for further drying. Finally they're stacked by roadside for transport to each cottage. You can always tell when a family is burning turf in a fireplace—the smoke coming out of the chimney is blue and sweet scented.

Another thing you'll notice as you drive around Connemara is an absence of trees, except in the gardens of major country inns. This is primarily attributed to the aforementioned Cromwell, who carted off some of the country's best wood for furniture and buildings in England. In recent years, however, the Irish government has undertaken an aggressive reforestation program, and vast areas of land have been set aside for planting new trees; you'll pass quite a few of these forestry nurseries.

A trademark of this region is the **donkey,** still a worker on the farms. In some places you'll see a sturdy little horse known as the **Connemara pony,** the only native Irish horse breed, though it has had an infusion of Spanish blood over the centuries. Raised in tiny fields with limestone pastures, these animals have great stamina and are invaluable for farming and pulling equipment. The Connemara pony is also noted for its gentle temperament, which makes it ideal for children's riding activities.

A major part of Connemara is designated as a **Gaeltacht,** or Irish-speaking area, so you may hear many of the people conversing in their native tongue. Traditional music thrives in this part of the countryside, as does hand-craft work and cottage industries.

The much-imitated **Aran knit sweaters** are synonymous with this region of Ireland. Made of an oatmeal-colored wool from the native sheep, these semiwaterproof sweaters were first knit by the women of the nearby Aran Islands for their fishermen husbands and sons—each family would have a different stitch or pattern. Years ago the patterns were more than just pretty designs; they served another more somber purpose—they were the chief way to identify men who had drowned in the rough waters off the coast.

Today these sweaters are knit in the homes of Connemara and the nearby Aran Islands and then sold in the many craft shops throughout the region.

★ **Connemara National Park,** Clifden/Westport Road (N 59), Letterfrack, Co. Galway. ☎ 095/41054.

Incorporating 3,800 acres of Connemara mountains, bogs, heaths, and grasslands, this beautiful park is one of Ireland's five national parks. The grounds are home to herds of Connemara ponies and Irish red deer, as well as a variety of birds and smaller mammals. To acquaint visitors with all of the aspects of the park, the exhibition center has a series of displays and an audiovisual presentation. To see the sights on foot, you can follow one or both of the two sign-posted nature trails.

Admission: £1.50 ($2.25) adults, 60p ($90¢) children or students.

Open: Park, year-round; visitor center, daily May and Sept 10am–5:30pm, June 10am–6:30pm, July–Aug 9:30am–6:30pm.

★ **Kylemore Abbey,** Kylemore, Co. Galway. ☎ 095/41146.

Originally a private residence (1868), this castellated house overlooking Kylemore Lake is a splendid example of Neo-Gothic architecture. In 1920 it was turned over to the Benedictine nuns who have since opened the grounds and part of the house to the public. The highlight is the recently restored Gothic chapel, considered a miniature cathedral. The complex also includes a café, serving produce grown on the nuns' own farm, and a shop with a working pottery studio. The visitor center has a video that gives an overview of life at Kylemore, both past and present. The abbey is most atmospheric when the bells are rung for midday office or vespers at 6pm.

Admission: £1.50 ($2.25) adults, £1 ($1.50) seniors or students, 50p (75¢) children.

Open: Easter–Oct daily 9:30am–6pm.

Leenane Cultural Center, Clifden/Westport Road (N 59), Leenane, Co. Galway. ☎ 095/42323.

Overlooking Killary Harbour, this center focuses on the history of wool and the 20 breeds of sheep in Connemara. In particular, it presents exhibits on the local wool industry, including carding, spinning, weaving, and using natural dyes. Daily demonstrations of sheep-shearing are given from June through August, and visitors are invited to try a hand at it on at spinning or weaving. In addition, a 13-minute audiovisual presentation provides background on the local history and places of interest in the area. Facilities include a wool craft shop and an octagonal café.

Admission: £2 ($3) adults, £1 ($1.50) seniors, students, and children over age eight.

Open: Mar–Oct daily 10am–7pm.

Dan O'Hara's Homestead Farm, Lettershea, Clifden, Co. Galway. ☎ 095/21246.

If you're wondering how Connemara farmers find soil to farm on this rocky land, head to this small farm about four miles east of Clifden off the main N 59 road. This eight-acre site reflects how a typical totally organic and self-sufficient 1840s farm operated, with local people using traditional tilling and farming methods. This farm was once owned by Dan O'Hara, who was forced to emigate to the United States because he couldn't pay the high rents levied by a landlord. The land also contains a reconstructed crannog, or fortified lake dwelling; an authentic megalithic tomb; and a dolmen.

Admission: £2 ($3) adults, £1.50 ($2.25) seniors and students, £1 ($1.50) children.

Open: April–Sept daily 10am–6pm.

Aughnanure Castle, Clifden Road, Oughterard, Co. Galway. ☎ 091/82214.

Standing on a rocky island close to the shores of Lough Corrib, this castle is a well-preserved example of a six-story Irish tower house, with an unusual double bawn (a fortified enclosure) and a watchtower. It was built around 1500 as a stronghold of the O'Flaherty clan.

Admission: £1.50 ($2.25) adults, £1 ($1.50) seniors, 60p (90¢) students and children.

Open: Mid-June to mid-Sept, daily 9:30am–6:30pm.

Sightseeing Tours

Several companies provide sightseeing tours of Connemara from Galway or Clifden.

Bus Eireann, Ceannt Station, Galway. ☎ 091/62000.

Departing from the bus station in Galway, this eight-hour tour of Connemara takes in Maam Cross, Recess, Roundstone, and Clifden, as well as Kylemore Abbey, Leenane, and Oughterard.

Price: £10 ($15) adults, £5 ($7.50) children.

Schedule: Mid–June to late June and late Aug to mid–Sept on Sun, Tues, and Thurs 9:45am; end of June to end of Aug, daily Mon–Sat 9:45am.

Connemara Heritage Tours, The Island House, Market Street, Clifden, Co. Galway. ☎ 095/21379.

Walking tours of Connemara with expert local guides are offered by this company, with an emphasis on history and archaeology as well as scenery. The walks cover different sections of Connemara—from the Renvyle Peninsula and Roundstone Bog, to the Kylemore Valley, Maam Turk Mountains, and the Sky Road. The tour to Inishbofin Island includes a 45-minute boat trip. All walks assemble at Island House in Clifden and include bus transportation to the walking site. Advance reservations are required.

Price: £10–£20 ($15–$30) depending on itinerary.

Schedule: June to mid–Sept, daily at 9:30am or 2pm for most tours; Inishbofin Island trip departs at 11am.

Corrib Ferries, Oughterard, Co. Galway. ☎ **091/82644.**

Departing from the pier at Oughterard, this company's sightseeing boat cruises across Lough Corrib, Ireland's second-largest lake, with a stop at Inchagoill Island, home of a 12th-century monastery that was inhabited until the 1940s. Two round-trips are offered: one to the island only, the other to the island and continuing on to Congin Co. Mayo, site of Ashford Castle and the area where the movie *The Quiet Man* was filmed.

Fare: £5 ($7.50) to island; £8 ($12) to Cong.

Schedule: May–Sept daily 11am and 2:45pm.

Duchas Tours, Swan House, Flood Street, Galway. ☎ **66784.**

This company operates a full-day bus tour of Connemara, with emphasis on history, archaeology, culture, and natural resources. It takes in Lough Corrib, Cong, and the Maam Valley.

Prices: £10 ($15) adults, £8 ($12) students.

Schedules: May–Sept daily at 2:30pm.

Inishbofin Island Tours, Kings of Cleggan, Cleggan, Co. Galway. ☎ **095/44642.**

This company's boat tours explore the island of Inishbofin, about three miles off the northwest Connemara coast. A haunt of artists, poets, and philosophers, this still-inhabited island holds the ruins of a 7th-century monastery. Trips are conducted on board the three-deck *The Queen.*

Price: £10–£12 ($15–$18) per person.

Schedule: Apr–June and Sept, 11:30am and 6:45pm; July–Aug, 11:30am, 2pm, and 6:45pm.

Western Heritage Sightseeing, Galway Tourist Office, Victoria Place, off Eyre Square, Galway. ☎ **21699.**

This full-day tour of Connemara includes a visit to Cong, with an optional boat trip to the early Christian site of Inchagoill, followed by an afternoon bus tour through the Maam Valley to Leenane, Kylemore Abbey, and Connemara National Park.

Price: £10 ($15) adults, £9 ($13.50) senior and students; boat trip extra £4 ($6) per person.

Schedule: May–Sept, daily walking tour departs at 10am from the Tourist Office and on demand from hotels.

SPORTS & RECREATION

BIKING   Bicycles can be hired year-round from **John Mannion & Son,** Bridge Street, Clifden, Co. Galway (☎ **095/21160**). The rate for a regular touring bike is £7 ($10.50) per day. Mountain bikes can be hired from May through October at the **Little Killary Adventure Centre,** Salruck, Renvyle, Co. Galway (☎ **095/43411**), at a charge of £5 ($7.50) per day.

FISHING   Lough Corrib is renowned for brown-trout and salmon fishing, with the brown-trout fishing usually good from the opening date of mid-February and salmon best from the end of May. The Mayfly fishing commences around the middle of May and continues up to three weeks, during which dapping the natural Mayfly is best, but trout can also be taken during this time on the wet and dry flies. Angling on Lough Corrib is free, except a state license is required for salmon. For expert advice and rental equipment, contact the **Cloonnabinnia Angling Centre,** Moycullen, Co. Galway (☎ **091/85555**).

GOLFING Visitors are welcome at the 18-hole, par-72 championship seaside course of the **Connemara Golf Club,** Ballyconneely, Clifden (☎ **095/23502**), nestled in the heart of Connemara and looking out into the waters of the Atlantic. Greens fees are £16 ($24).

The **Oughterard Golf Club,** Oughterard, Co. Galway (☎ **095/82131**), is an 18-hole, par-70 inland course. The greens fees are £13 ($19.50).

HORSEBACK RIDING **Cashel Equestrian Centre,** Cashel, Co. Galway (☎ **095/31082**), conducts treks of one, two, or three hours through the mountains. Beach trekking and jaunting-car rides are also available. Minimum charges average £10 ($15) per hour.

WATERSPORTS Dinghy sailing and sailboarding can be arranged at the **Little Killary Adventure Centre,** Salruck, Renvyle, Co. Galway (☎ **095/43411**). Daily rates are £15 to £17 ($20 to $25.50) per day for equipment rental. An inclusive charge of £20 to £22 ($30 to $33) per day entitles you to use the watersports equipment and participate in all the center's supervised sporting activities, including kayaking, hill and coastal walking, rock climbing, archery, and more.

SAVVY SHOPPING

Clifden Heritage Crystal, Main Street, Clifden. ☎ **095/21989.**

This crystal enterprise produces patterns that reflect the beauty of the surrounding countryside. All glass is mouth-blown and hand-cut in this workshop, led by a master cutter, formerly of Waterford Crystal. Open Monday through Saturday from 9am to 6pm, with extended hours in summer.

Connemara Handcrafts, Clifden/Leenane Road (N 59), Dooneen Haven, Letterfrack, Co. Galway. ☎ **095/41058.**

Situated six miles north of Clifden on an inlet of the bay and surrounded by colorful flower gardens, this shop has one of the loveliest and most-photographed locations in Ireland. Colorful Avoca tweeds are featured here, as are all sorts of Connemara-made marble souvenirs, candles, copperwork, wood carvings, pottery, and knits. A snack shop is on the premises. Open mid-March through October, daily from 9:30am to 6pm or later.

Connemara Marble Industries Ltd., Galway/Clifden Road (N59), Moycullen, Co. Galway. ☎ **095/85102.**

Connemara's unique green marble—diverse in color, marking, and veining—is quarried, cut, shaped, and polished here. Estimated by geologists to be about 500 million years old, the marble shows twists and interlocking bands of serpentine in various shades, ranging from light lime green to dark emerald. On weekdays, you'll see craftspeople at work hand-fashioning marble jewelry, paperweights, ashtrays, Celtic crosses, and other giftware. The shop and showroom, on the main road eight miles west of Galway City, are open daily, May through October, from 9am to 5:30pm, with reduced schedule in off-season.

 Fuchsia Craft, The Square, Oughterard, Co. Galway. ☎ **091/82644.**

Wedged in the center of Oughterard's main thoroughfare, this small shop is a treasure trove of unusual and hard-to-find crafts, produced by more than 100 craftspeople throughout Ireland. The items range from handmade fishing flies and products made from pressed Irish peat, to bronze sculptures, recycled art cards of Connemara scenes, decorative metal figurines fashioned from nails, and lithographs of early Ireland, as well as pottery, crystal, jewelry, knitwear, and much more. It's open from May through September, daily from 9am to 10pm, and from October through April, Monday through Saturday from 9:30am to 6pm.

 Millar's Connemara Tweed Ltd., Main Street, Clifden, Co. Galway. ☎ **095/21038.**

This is the home of the colorful Connemara tweeds, an industry started in 1900 by Robert Millar as a small mill to process wool from local mountain sheep. Although most people travel to Clifden just to buy Millar's skeins of wool or hand-woven materials, plus ready-made ties, hats, caps, scarves, blankets, and bedspreads, today's shop is more than just an outlet for wool. You'll also find Irish patchwork, rush baskets, Aran crios belts, embroidery work, handmade miniature currachs, tin whistles, and blackthorn pipes, plus an art gallery of regional paintings. Open Monday through Saturday from 9am to 6pm, with extended hours in summer.

 Roundstone Musical Instruments, I.D.A. Craft Centre, Roundstone, Co. Galway. ☎ **095/35808.**

Devotees of Irish traditional music come from far and near to buy a handmade bodhran (goatskin drum) at this small shop in a cottagelike setting on the grounds of a former monastery. Malachy Kearns, often fondly called Malachy Bodhran, hand-crafts and hand-decorates all instruments on the premises, with the help of his wife, Anne, an artist. In addition to bodhrans, you can buy a flute or tin whistle and choose from a fine selection of Irish music books and videos, as well as Irish music on tape and CD. Open June to October, daily from 9am to 6:30pm, November to May, Monday through Friday from 9am to 6pm.

Sila Mag Aoide Designs (Shelagh Magee), I.D.A. Craft Centre, Roundstone, Co. Galway. ☎ **095/35912.**

Situated in a stone belltower on the grounds of a former monastery and claiming to be the smallest shop in Ireland, this wee place displays the creations of resident artist Shelagh Magee. The unusual, one-of-a-kind works include watercolor prints and art cards of Connemara scenes, handmade pencils of wood, baskets, jewelry, and miniature frames. It's open daily from 10am to 10pm in May through September, with shorter hours in off-season.

Weavers Workshop, Main Street, Clifden, Co. Galway. ☎ **095/21074.**

Hand-weaving and design work are carried on at this small shop for visitors and passersby to watch or to buy. The finished products include colorful sweaters, vests, scarves, and hats, as well as rugs and wall hangings. Open Easter through October, Monday through Saturday from 9am to 6pm.

WHERE TO STAY
Expensive/Moderate

Ballynahinch Castle, Ballynahinch, Recess, Co. Galway. ☎ **095/31006** or toll free **800/447-7462** in U.S. Fax 095/31085. 28 rms (all with bath). TEL

Rates (including full breakfast): £55–£77 ($82.50–$115.50) single, £80–£120 ($120–$180) double. No service charge. AE, DC, MC, V. **Closed:** First three wks in Feb.

Set on a 350-acre estate at the base of Ben Lettery, one of the Twelve Bens mountains, this turreted and gabled manor house overlooks the Owenmore River. Dating back to the 16th century, over the years it has served as a base for such diverse owners as the O'Flaherty chieftains and the sea pirate Grace O'Malley, and as the sporting residence of the Maharajah Jans Sahib Newanagar, better known as Ranjitsinhgi, the famous cricketer. The guest rooms are individually named and decorated, many with individual fireplaces and four-poster or canopy beds. The restaurant, with its impressive Connemara marble fireplace, offers sweeping views of the countryside and the river. But most of all, this is a place for top-notch sea-trout and salmon fishing. Each evening the specimens of the day's catch are weighed in and recorded at the Fishermen's Bar, usually making a nightly cause for celebration. Other facilities include a tennis court and lovely gardens.

★ **Cashel House**, Cashel Bay, Cashel, Co. Galway. ☎ **095/31001** or toll free in the U.S. **800/223-6510** or **800/44-UTELL.** Fax 095/31077. 32 rms (all with bath). TV TEL

Rates (including full breakfast): £46–£126 ($69–$189) single, £92–£126 ($138–$189) double. Service charge 12.5%. AE, MC, V. **Open:** Mar–Oct.

Set on 50 acres of exotic gardens and woodlands, this 100-year-old country house is nestled deep in the mountains and lakelands of Connemara. Established as a hotel in 1968 by enthusiastic innkeepers Dermot and Kay McEvilly, it has attracted a wide range of discerning guests over the years, including President and Madame de Gaulle, who spent two weeks here in 1969 and literally put Cashel House on the map. Among the public rooms are an old-world lounge, a well-stocked library, and a conservatory-style restaurant that has won many awards for innovative cuisine. Guest rooms, which have wide-windowed views of the bay or the gardens, are decorated with a blend of Irish floral fabrics, European antiques, sheepskin rugs, rattan pieces, vintage paintings, and local heirlooms. Facilities include a private beach on the bay, a tennis court, fishing, boating, and sign-posted walking paths. On the grounds is a helipad; or to stay closer to the sod, Connemara pony stable.

Rosleague Manor, Clifden/Leenane Road (N 59), Letterfrack, Co. Galway. ☎ **095/41101** or toll free **800/223-6510** in U.S. 15 rms (all with bath). TEL

Rates (including full breakfast): £60–£90 ($90–$135) single, £80–£140 ($120–$210) double. No service charge. AE, MC, V. **Closed:** Nov to Easter.

Occupying a sheltered spot with views of Ballinakill Harbor and the Twelve Bens Mountains, this two-story Georgian house is surrounded by 30 acres of lush gardens and well-trimmed lawns. Brother/sister owners Paddy and Ann Foyle have decorated the interior with all sorts of antiques, polished heirloom silver, Waterford crystal chandeliers, and paintings of local scenes. The bedrooms have comfortable furnishings, mostly floral patterns, and many enjoy views of the bay. Among facilities are a fine restaurant, using produce from the garden, plus a tennis court and sauna. The manor is situated seven miles north of Clifden near the entrance to Connemara National Park.

Zetland House, Cashel Bay, Cashel, Co. Galway. ☎ 095/31111 or toll free 800/447-7462 in U.S. Fax 095/31117. 19 rms (all with bath). TEL

Rates (including full breakfast): £50–£80 ($75–$120) single, £100–£130 ($150–$195) double. Service charge 12.5%. AE, DC, MC, V. **Closed:** Mid–Oct through Mar.

Built in 1850 as a sporting lodge, this three-story manor house was named for the Earl of Zetland, a frequent visitor during the 19th century. Surrounded by lush gardens and ancient trees, the Zetland was converted into a hotel in the mid-1980s under its current owner, John Prendergast, a Paris-trained hotelier. The guest rooms, many of which look out onto the bay, have reproduction or antique furnishings. The dining room is known for its local seafood and lamb dishes; the vegetables and fruit come from the inn's own kitchen garden. If you enjoy fishing, take note that the Zetland owns the Gowla Fishery, one of the best private sea-trout fisheries in Ireland, comprised of 14 lakes and four miles of river, and the hotel staff eagerly caters to those fond of casting a rod on Irish waters. Other facilities include a tennis court, croquet, and a billiards room.

Moderate

Hotel Ardagh, Ballyconneely Road, Clifden, Co. Galway. ☎ 095/21384 or toll free 800/447-7462 in U.S. Fax 095/21314. 17 rms (all with bath). TV TEL

Rates: (including full breakfast) £42–£50 ($63–$75) single, £63–£79 ($94.50–$118.50) double. No service charge. AE, DC, MC, V. **Closed:** Nov through Mar.

Overlooking Ardbear Bay, about two miles south of Clifden, this modern two-story inn reflects a chalet-style atmosphere, with a decor of light woods and expansive windows. Many of the rooms, including the second-floor restaurant, that face the sea, and five guest rooms have individual balconies. A solarium and lovely gardens are added pleasures.

Connemara Gateway, Galway/Clifden Road (N 59), Oughterard, Co. Galway. ☎ 091/82328. Fax 091/82332. 62 rms (all with bath). TV TEL

Rates (including full breakfast): £40–£75 ($60–$112.50) single, £75–£105 ($112.50–$157.50) double. DC, MC, V.

Situated on its own grounds, less than a mile from the village of Oughterard and 16 miles west of Galway City, this contemporary two-story inn is well positioned near the upper shores of Lough Corrib and across the road from an 18-hole golf course. Although it has a rambling modern exterior, a hearthside ambience permeates the interior, with leafy plants and homey bric-a-brac in the corridors, and public rooms full of copper hangings, farming implements, and area fishing memorabilia. Guest rooms are warmly furnished with local tweed fabrics and hangings, oak dressers and headboards, and scenes of Connemara.

Dining/Entertainment: The restaurant is enhanced by a fine collection of original paintings by landscape artists John MacLeod and Kenneth Webb, while the lounge has a village pub atmosphere.

Facilities: Heated swimming pool, sauna, sun lounge, tennis court, putting green, croquet lawn, ten acres of walking trails.

Renvyle House, Renvyle, Co. Galway. ☎ **095/43511.** Fax 095/43515. 56 rms (all with bath). TV TEL

> **Rates:** £65–£105 ($97.50–$157.50) single or double. Service charge 12.5%. AE, DC, MC, V. **Closed:** Jan to mid–Mar.

Originally the residence of the Blake family, this grand old house sits on a 200-acre estate along the Atlantic shoreline in the wilds of Connemara. It was purchased in 1917 by Oliver St. John Gogarty, a leading Irish poet, wit, surgeon, and politician, who fondly called this secluded seacape and mountain setting "the world's end." And that's putting it mildly: it really is off the beaten track, ideal not for a quick overnight but for a few days' stay or longer. Updated and refurbished in recent years by current owner Hugh Coyle, it retains a turn-of-the-century ambience, particularly in its public areas. Guest rooms vary in size and decor—from rooms with balconies to attic rooms with dormer windows. Facilities include a restaurant, a lounge bar, an outdoor heated swimming pool, horseback-riding stables, a nine-hole golf course, two all-weather tennis courts, fishing, and boating.

Rock Glen Manor House, Ballyconneely Road, Clifden, Co. Galway. ☎ **095/21035** or toll free **800/447-7462** in U.S. Fax 095/21737. 29 rms (all with bath). TV TEL

> **Rates** (including full breakfast): £57–£62 ($85.50–$91) single, £79–£90 ($118.50–$135) double. Service charge 12.5%. AE, DC, MC, V. **Closed:** Oct to mid-Mar.

Originally an 18th-century hunting lodge, this rambling country house sits amid lovely gardens about 1.5 miles south of Clifden. Expanded over the years and now in the hands of John and Evangeline Roche, Rock Glen is set back from the road, with views of Ardbear Bay and the Atlantic Ocean. It's a restful spot, with tastefully furnished bedrooms and homey public areas. Most rooms, including the restaurant, face the sea, and half the bedrooms are on the ground floor. Facilities include a tennis court, a putting green, and fishing privileges.

★ **Sweeney's Oughterard House,** Galway/Clifden Road (N 59), Oughterard, Co. Galway. ☎ **091/82207.** Fax 091/82161. 20 rms (all with bath). TV TEL

> **Rates** (including full breakfast): £50–£54 ($75–$81) single, £90–£99 ($135–$148.50) double. No service charge. AE, DC, MC, V. **Closed:** Late Dec to mid-Jan.

A favorite with fishermen (and women), this ivy-covered 200-year-old Georgian house has been run by the Sweeney-Higgins family since 1913. Situated across the road from the rushing and babbling salmon-filled waters of the Owenriff River, the inn is surrounded by flowering gardens and ancient trees on the quiet western end of the village. The public rooms have an old-world charm thanks to multipaned bow windows and a decor that includes local curios, paintings by Irish artists, and comfortable deep-cushioned original furnishings. The guest rooms vary in size and decor—from antique-filled to modern light-wood styles—but all include such extras as a hairdryer and coffee/tea-maker; some have four-poster or king-size beds. It's a great spot for fishing, taking long countryside walks, or catching up on your reading. Amenities include a good dining room with an extensive wine cellar.

Moderate/Inexpensive

Abbeyglen Castle Hotel, Sky Road, Clifden, Co. Galway. ☎ **095/21201** or toll free **800/447-7462** in U.S. 46 rms (all with bath). TV TEL

> **Rates:** £52–£75 ($78–$112.50) single or double. Service charge 12.5%. AE, DC, MC, V. **Closed:** Early Jan to Feb.

Located on a hilltop overlooking Clifden and the bay, this property has a history dating back to the 1820s, although the castlelike facade was added only within the last 20 years. Happily, the turrets and battlements blend in well with the Connemara countryside. The regal facade is enhanced by the public areas, with brass candelabra chandeliers, arched windows, vintage settees, as well as a restaurant in a Gothic-theme, and guest rooms with crown canopies. Twelve acres of gardens and parklands, a heated outdoor swimming pool, a sauna, a solarium, and a hard tennis court add to the enjoyment. Personable proprietor Paul Hughes will arrange fishing trips, packed lunches, and a host of other local activities.

WHERE TO DINE

Expensive/Moderate

O'Grady's, Market Street, Clifden, Co. Galway. ☎ 095/21450.

Cuisine: IRISH/SEAFOOD. **Reservations:** Recommended for dinner.
Prices: Set lunch £10.95 ($15.44); appetizers £2–£4.95 ($3–$7.43); dinner main courses £7.25–£18.95 ($10.88–$28.43). AE, MC, V.
Open: Mon–Sat lunch 12:30–2:30pm, dinner 6–10pm. **Closed:** Nov–Mar.

Ever since the mid-1960s, this shopfront restaurant has been drawing people in search of great seafood to Clifden. The menu features all that is freshest from the sea on a daily basis, with such choices as Clifden lobster with lemon or garlic butter or a filet of Cleggan brill. For non-fisheaters there's filet of beef with radish sauce, pork with peach stuffing in peppercorn cream sauce, lamb with rosemary sauce, lamb's liver with caramelized onion and basil, and chicken with corn-and-raisin stuffing.

★ **Drimcong House,** Moycullen, Co. Galway. ☎ 091/85115.

Cuisine: IRISH/INTERNATIONAL. **Reservations:** Required.
Prices: Set dinner £14.95–£17.95 ($22.43–$26.93). AE, DC, MC, V.
Open: Tues–Sat 7–10:30pm. **Closed:** Sun–Mon and Christmas to March.

On the main Clifden Road just under ten miles west of Galway City, this restaurant, in a 300-year-old lakeside house, is the perfect setting for the quintessential Irish dining experience. As your order is taken, you relax in a book-filled drawing room/lounge with an open fireplace; then you're escorted into one of two elegant dining rooms (the back room looks out onto the lake, while the front windows have garden views). All the little touches await at your table—fresh flowers, candlelight, fine Irish silver and glassware, hot brown scones with butter twirls. The five-course dinners, to be sure, live up to the setting. Entrees range from roast local lamb with ratatouille and herbs or baked chicken breast with parsley mousse, to *bollito misto*—Drimcong's version of an Italian dish with beef, pork, and chicken; as well as roulade of John Dory and pike, or a vegetarian dinner such as herb and vegetable soufflé or smoked-cheese–and–apple ravioli.

Water Lily, Bridge Street, Oughterard, Co. Galway. ☎ 091/82737.

Cuisine: SEAFOOD/IRISH. **Reservations:** Suggested for dinner.
Prices: Appetizers £2.50–£5.50 ($3.75–$8.25); lunch main courses £1.50–£9 ($2.25–$13.50); dinner main courses £8.50–£14.50 ($12.77–$21.75), lobster £16.50–£19.50 ($24.75–$29.25). AE, DC, MC, V.
Open: Daily lunch noon–3pm, dinner 6–10pm.

Set on the edge of town beside a stream of the Corrib, this yellow-and-green cottage is a delightful stopping place en route to or from Connemara. This bi-level flower-filled restaurant offers wide-windowed river views. Lunch items range from platters of oysters, crab claws, and other seafoods to sandwiches, soups, and salads. The dinner menu offers such creative entrees as filet of trout with toasted almonds, noisettes of lamb on an island of red cabbage, suprême of chicken filled with camembert and wholegrain mustard sauce, duck with herb stuffing and peach sauce, poached salmon with sorrel sauce, and a variety of lobsters and steaks.

Moderate

★ **High Moors,** off the Ballyconeely Road, Dooneen, Clifden, Co. Galway. ☎ **095/21342.**

Cuisine: IRISH. **Reservations:** Required.
Prices: Appetizers £1.80–£4.20 ($2.70–$6.30), main courses £7.90–£10.90 ($11.85–$16.35). MC, V.
Open: Wed–Sun dinner 7pm–9:30pm. **Closed:** Nov to Easter.

Less than a mile from Clifden, a narrow country road leads to this modern bungalow-style restaurant, set high on a hill with panoramic views of the surrounding wild Connemara countryside. A homey ambience prevails inside—and well it should since this is the home of John and Eileen Griffin, host and chef, respectively. The food and menu are simple, based on what is fresh at the markets and what vegetables and herbs are in season in John's gardens. Eileen's specialties include breast of chicken with basil and tomato; filet of pork with three spices; wild salmon with sorrel butter sauce; ragoût of salmon, sole, and scallops; roast leg of Connemara lamb with red-currant and rosemary; Carna bay scallops with chive sauce; and duck breast with purée of apple, sage, and onion. Try to book a table for sunset; the views are surpassed only by the food.

Mitchell's, Market Street, Clifden, Co. Galway. ☎ **095/21867.**

Cuisine: IRISH/SEAFOOD. **Reservations:** Suggested for dinner.
Prices: Appetizers £1.30–£4.95 ($1.95–$7.43); lunch/snack main courses £1.35–£4.95 ($2.03–$7.43); dinner main courses £5.95–£10.95 ($8.93–$15.44). MC, V.
Open: Mid–Mar through Oct lunch/snacks 11:30am–6pm, dinner 6–10:30pm.

Housed in a shopfront building in the center of town, this restaurant has a turn-of-the-century decor, with brick and stone walls, local furnishings and memorabilia, and an open fireplace. The menu offers a variety of dishes, such as traditional Irish stew, burgers, scampi, chicken with blue cheese and garlic, baked stuffed cod, hot smoked trout, steak au poivre, scallops mornay, and pan-fried grilled Atlantic salmon. Lighter fare, available throughout the day, includes smoked salmon quiche or smoked mackerel pâté, salads, crab claws, and seafood pastas.

Moderate/Inexpensive

$ **Destry Rides Again,** The Square, Clifden, Co. Galway. ☎ **095/21722.**

Cuisine: INTERNATIONAL. **Reservations:** Recommended for dinner.
Prices: Appetizers £2–£4 ($3–$6); lunch main courses £3–£6 ($4.50–$9); dinner main courses £6–£12 ($9–$18). MC, V.
Open: Daily noon–10pm. **Closed:** Christmas to Feb.

Borrowing its name from the classic western movie starring James Stewart and Marlene Dietrich, this small 30-seat restaurant has a film-world–inspired funky and fun decor. One of the newest restaurants in the area, opened in 1993, it is also known for its innovative menu, ranging from a classic fish and chips to steaks char-grilled over high flames with daring flair. Other, more trendy dishes include filet of hake with a crust of black sesame seeds on gingered cabbage stir-fry; escalope of chicken with spinach and cream cheese; marinated leg of lamb with chutney sauce; and duck terrine with Cumberland sauce. All meals are accompanied by a unique olive bread served with aromatic olive oil.

Doris's, Market Street, Clifden, Co. Galway. ☎ **095/21427.**
Cuisine: INTERNATIONAL. **Reservations:** Recommended for dinner.
Prices: Appetizers £1.50–£3.90 ($2.25–$5.85); main courses £5.90–£10.90 ($5.85–$16.35). MC, V.
Open: Daily noon–10pm. **Closed:** Oct–Mar.

Occupying one of the oldest houses in town, this small shopfront restaurant has an eclectic decor of white-washed walls, natural woods, fishnets, old pictures, and fresh flowers. The menu is equally eclectic, with such dishes as grilled tuna with Provençale sauce; grilled dressed crab; swordfish in tarragon cream sauce; Asian curry with vegetables, chicken, or pork; Irish stew; beef-and-Guinness casserole; bacon and cabbage; and pastas and pizzas.

The Quay House, Clifden, Co. Galway. ☎ **095/21369.**
Cuisine: INTERNATIONAL. **Reservations:** Recommended.
Prices: Appetizers £2–£4.95 ($3–$7.43); main courses £6.50–£11.95 ($9.75–$17.93). MC, V.
Open: Daily dinner 6–10pm. **Closed:** Christmas to Feb.

Originality is the keynote of this restaurant opened in 1994. Even the bread is different—a tasty recipe of red peppers and olives. Sitting on the harborfront in Clifden, this is a sister restaurant to *Destry Rides Again,* described above. Creative cuisine is to be had, such as filet of sole with silky leek sauce; pork fillet with sesame crust and ginger sauce; tagliolini with escalope of wild salmon; warm salad of mussels and smoked bacon with anchovy-and-soy dressing; sautéed lambs kidneys and sweetbreads with a red-onion confit.

---

3 County Mayo

Mayo's chief town (Ballina) is 63 miles N of Galway, 120 miles N of Shannon Airport, 153 miles NW of Dublin, 193 miles NW of Cork

GETTING TO & AROUND COUNTY MAYO • By Air   Aer Lingus provides daily service from Dublin into Knock International Airport, Charlestown, Co. Mayo (☎ **094/67222**). In addition, charter flights operate in the summer from the United States.

From Britain, air service to Knock is provided by **Logan Air** from Glasgow and Manchester, and **Ryan Air** from London's Stansted and Luton as well as from Liverpool.

• **By Public Transport   Irish Rail** and **Bus Eireann** (☎ **096/21011**) provide daily service from Dublin and other cities into Ballina, Westport, and Castlebar, with bus connections into smaller towns. There is also express service from Galway into most Mayo towns.

• **By Car**   From Dublin and points east, the main N 5 road leads to many points in County Mayo; from Galway, take N 84 or N 17. From Sligo and points north, take N 17 or N 59. To get around County Mayo, it's best to rent a car. Two international firms with outlets at Knock International Airport are **Avis** (☎ **094/67252**) and **Hertz** (☎ **094/67404**).

ESSENTIALS • Tourist Information   For year-round information, visit or contact the **Westport Tourist Office,** The Mall, Westport (☎ **098/25711**). It's open June through September, Monday through Friday from 9am to 6pm, and from October to May, Monday through Friday from 9am to 5:15pm. The **Knock Airport Tourist Office** at Knock International Airport (☎ **094/67427**) is also open year-round, but only to coincide with flight arrivals.

Seasonal tourist offices, open from May/June to September/October, are the **Ballina Tourist Office,** Cathedral Road, Ballina, Co. Mayo (☎ **096/70848**); **Castlebar Tourist Office,** Linenhall Street, Castlebar, Co. Mayo (☎ **094/21207**); **Knock Village Tourist Office,** Knock (☎ **094/67427**); and **Louisburgh Community Tourist Office,** Bridge Street, Louisburgh (☎ **098/66394**), open June through August.

• **Area Codes**   Area codes for County Mayo include 094, 096, 097, and 098.

Rimmed by Clew Bay and the Atlantic Ocean, County Mayo boasts many diverse attractions, although it has been most readily identified as *The Quiet Man* country ever since the classic movie was filmed here in 1951. The exact setting for the film was Cong, a little village wedged between Lough Mask and Lough Corrib and back-to-back with the County Galway border.

To add to the glory of Cong, it is also the home of one of the most celebrated of Ireland's luxury hotels: Ashford Castle. This resort alone is probably enough to draw most visitors to this part of Ireland, but there are many other reasons to come here—from the 5,000-year-old farmstead settlement at Ceide Fields to the modern Christian religious mecca at Knock, not forgetting some of Europe's best fishing waters at Lough Conn, Lough Mask, and the River Moy. Ballina (pronounced Bal-in-ah), Mayo's largest town, calls itself the home of the Irish salmon.

WHAT TO SEE & DO

Unlike Counties Galway, Limerick, and Cork, County Mayo does not have one great central city. It is a county of many towns: from large market and commercial centers such as Castlebar, Claremorris, and Ballinrobe in the southern part of the county, to Ballina in the northern reaches. Most of the attractions of interest to visitors lie in the hinterlands in small communities like Knock, Foxford, Ballycastle, Louisburgh, and Newport.

County Mayo's loveliest town, **Westport,** is nestled on the shores of Clew Bay. Once a major port, it is one of the few planned towns of Ireland, designed by Richard Castle, with a splendid tree-lined mall, rows of Georgian buildings, and an octagonal central mall.

Southeast of Westport is **Croagh Patrick,** a 2,510-ft. mountain that dominates the vistas of western Mayo for many miles. It was here in A.D. 441 that St. Patrick is said to have prayed and spent the forty days of Lent. To commemorate this belief, each year on the last Sunday of July, thousands of Irish people make a pilgrimage to the site, which has become known as St. Patrick's Holy Mountain.

The rugged, bog-filled, and thinly populated coast of Mayo provides little industry for the locals but many scenic drives and secluded outposts to intrigue visitors. Leading the list is **Achill Island,** linked by a bridge to the mainland and a heather-filled bogland with sandy beaches and great cliffs dropping into the Atlantic. Clare Island, once inhabited by Mayo's amazing pirate queen, Grace O'Malley, sits south of Achill in Clew Bay.

The drive from Ballina along the edge of the northern coast to Downpatrick Head is particularly scenic and includes a visit to **Killala,** a small and secluded harbor village that came close to changing the course of Ireland's history. In August 1798 France's General Humbert landed at Killala in an abortive attempt to lead the Irish in a full-scale rebellion against the British. For this reason, the phrase "The Year of the French" is part of the folk memory of Mayo. It was also used by novelist Thomas Flanagan as the basis for his recent novel of the same name.

The county's other main attractions follow.

 Ceide Fields, Ballycastle, Co. Mayo. ☎ **096/43325.**

One of Ireland's oldest archaeological sites, this 5,000-year-old farm was preserved in a blanket of bog. Recently discovered, this 2,500-acre parcel is believed to predate the pyramids and is said to be the most extensive Stone Age monument in the world. Unearthed from the bog were stone walls, rectangular fields, a house, a hearthside, neolithic tombs, pottery, flints, and part of a polished stone ax. The visitor center shows a 20-minute video. Walking tours are conducted regularly by expert guides. Ceide Fields is situated on R 314, the coastal road north of Ballina, between Ballycastle and Belderrig.

Admission: £2 ($3) adults, £1.50 ($2.25) seniors, £1 ($1.50) students and children.

Open: Mid-Mar to May and Oct, daily 10am–5pm; June–Sept daily 9:30am–6:30pm.

 National Shrine of Our Lady of Knock, Knock, Co. Mayo. ☎ **094/88100.**

Commonly known as Knock Shrine, this is Ireland's major religious site. It was here in 1879 that local people claim to have seen an apparition of the Blessed Mother. Now considered the Lourdes or Fatima of Ireland, Knock achieved worldwide publicity in 1979 when Pope John Paul II visited it. Knock's centerpiece is a huge circular basilica that seats 7,000 people. The architecture includes objects or furnishings from every county in Ireland. The grounds also contain a folk museum and a religious bookshop.

Admission: Shrine, free; museum £1.50 ($2.25) adults, 75p ($1.08) seniors and children over age 5.

Open: Shrine and grounds, year-round, daily 8am–6pm or later; museum, May–Oct, daily 10am–6pm.

Ballintubber Abbey, Ballintubber, Co. Mayo. ☎ **094/30934.**

Situated off the main Galway/Castlebar Road (N 84) and about 20 miles west of Knock, this abbey is known as the abbey that refused to die, because it is one of the few Irish churches in continuous use for nearly 800 years. Founded in 1216 by Cathal O'Connor, king of Connaught, it survived early fires and other tragedies. Even though the forces of Cromwell took off the church's roof in 1653 and attempted to suppress services, clerics persisted in discreetly conducting religious rites through the centuries. Completely restored in 1966, the interior includes a video display and an interpretative center, and the grounds are landscaped to portray spiritual themes.

Admission: Free; donations welcome.

Open: Year-round daily 9am–midnight.

Foxford Woollen Mills, St. Joseph's Place, Foxford, Co. Mayo. ☎ **094/56756.**

Founded in 1892 by a local nun, Mother Agnes Morrogh-Bernard, to provide work for a community ravaged by the effects of the Irish famine, these woollen mills have brought prosperity to the area, as its lovely woollen products have been shipped throughout the world. Using a multimedia audiovisual presentation, the center tells the story of this local industry, then provides an on-site tour of the working mills to see the production of the famous Foxford blankets, rugs, and tweeds. Tours run every 20 minutes. A restaurant, a shop, an exhibition center, an art gallery, a prototype 19th-century schoolroom, and other craft units (including a doll-making and restoration workshop) enrich a visit.

Admission: £2.75 ($4.13) adults, £2 ($3) seniors, £1.75 ($2.63) students and children.

Open: Year-round, Mon–Sat 10am–6pm, Sun 2–6pm.

Westport House, Westport, Co. Mayo. ☎ 098/25430.

At the edge of town you can visit Westport House, a late 18th-century residence that's home of Lord Altamont, the marquis of Sligo, who is still in residence with his family. The work of Richard Cassels and James Wyatt, the house is graced with a staircase of ornate white Sicilian marble, unusual art nouveau glass and carvings, family heirlooms, and silver. Admission includes access to all the house's grounds and a zoo.

Admission: £6 ($9) adults, £3 ($4.50) children.

Open: Mid–May to June and Sept, daily 2–6pm; July–Aug, Mon–Sat 10:30am–6pm, Sun 2–6pm.

Granuaile Centre, Louisburgh, Co. Mayo. ☎ 098/66195.

Using an audiovisual display and graphic exhibits, this center tells the story of one of Ireland's great female heroes, Granuaile (Grace) O'Malley (1530–1600). Known as the pirate queen, Grace led battles against the English and ruled the Baronies of Burrishoole and Murrisk around Clew Bay. Her extraordinary exploits are recounted in Elizabethan state papers. The center also includes a craft shop and coffee shop.

Admission: £2 ($3) adults, £1.25 ($1.93) seniors and students, £1 ($1.50) children.

Open: May and Sept–Oct, Mon–Fri 10am–5pm; June, Mon–Sat 10am–5pm; July–Aug, daily 10am–6pm.

Salmon World, Farran Laboratory, Furnace, Newport, Co. Mayo. ☎ 098/41107.

In this county of great salmon fishing, it is only natural that a center would open up to provide insight on the background and life cycle of the Atlantic salmon. Operated on the shores of Lough Furnace by the Salmon Research Agency of Ireland, it presents a video show as well as freshwater and marine aquariums and fish-feeding areas, and exhibits.

Admission: £1.50 ($2.25) adults, £1 ($1.50) students, 50p ($1.00) seniors and children.

Open: June–Aug, daily 10–1pm and 2–6pm.

★ North Mayo Family History Research & Heritage Centre, Enniscoe, Castlehill, Ballina, Co. Mayo. ☎ 096/31809.

If your ancestors came from Mayo, this center will help you trace your family tree. The databank includes indices to church registers of all denominations, plus school rollbooks, leases, and wills. Even if you have no connections in Mayo, you'll enjoy the adjacent museum with its displays of rural Mayo household items, farm machinery, and farm implements, including the gowl-gob, a spadelike implement exclusive to this locality. The center is situated on Lough Conn, about two miles south of Crossmolina, off the R 315. (**Note:** If your ancestors were from the southern part of the county, try the South Mayo Family Research Centre at Town Hall, Neale Road, Ballinrobe, Co.

Mayo (☎ 092/41214). It's open Monday through Friday from 9am to noon and Saturday and Sunday from 2 to 4pm).

Admission: Museum £1 ($1.50) adults, 75p ($1.08) seniors, 50p (75¢) students and children.

Open: Oct–Apr, Mon–Fri 9am–4pm, June–Sept, Mon–Fri 9am–6pm, Sat–Sun 2–6pm.

SPORTS & RECREATION

FISHING The County Mayo waters of the River Moy and Loughs Corrib, Conn, and Mask offer some of the best fishing in Europe, and some of Ireland's premier sources for salmon and trout. For general information about fishing in County Mayo, contact the **North Western Regional Fisheries Board,** Ardnaree House, Abbey Street, Ballina (☎ 096/22788).

To arrange a day's fishing, contact ★ **Cloonamoyne Fishery,** Castlehill, near Crossmolina, Ballina (☎ 096/31851). Managed by an Irish-born former New Yorker, Barry Segrave, this professional angling service will advise and equip you to fish the local waters—for brown trout on Loughs Conn and Cullin, for salmon on Loughs Beltra, Furnace, and Feeagh, and for salmon and sea trout on the Rivers Moy and Deel. Services include the rental of fully equipped boats, flycasting tuition, tackle hire, and transport to and from all fishing. Daily rates average £10 ($15) for a boat, £20 ($30) for a boat with engine, and £45 to £50 ($67.50 to $75) for a boat with engine and ghillie (guide).

County Mayo is also home to the **Pontoon Bridge Fly Fishing School,** Pontoon, Co. Mayo (☎ 094/56120). This school offers various one- to four-day courses in the art of fly casting, as well as fly tying, tackle design, and other background information necessary for successful game fishing. Fees range from £25 to £85 ($37.50 to $127.50), depending on the duration of the course. Courses run daily from April to late September.

Permits and state fishing licenses can be obtained at the **North Mayo Angling Advice Centre** (Tiernan Bros.), Upr. Main St., Foxford, Co. Mayo (☎ 094/56731).

For fishing tackle, try **Jones Ltd., General Merchants,** Main Street, Foxford, Co. Mayo (☎ 094/56121) or Walkins Fishing Tackle, Tone Street, Ballina, Co. Mayo (☎ 096/22442).

GOLFING County Mayo has three 18-hole golf courses—a par-72 links course at **Carn Golf Course,** Carn, Belmullet, Co. Mayo (☎ 097/81051), with greens fees of £12 ($18); a par-71 inland course at **Castlebar Golf Club,** Rocklands, Castlebar, Co. Mayo (☎ 094/21649), with greens fees of £10 ($15); and a par-73 championship course at **Westport Golf Club,** Co. Mayo (☎ 098/25113), with greens fees of £15 ($22.50) on weekdays and £18 ($27) on weekends. Set on the shores of Clew Bay, the last course winds its way around the precipitous slopes of Croagh Patrick Mountain. It is one of the west of Ireland's most challenging and scenic courses.

WHERE TO STAY

Very Expensive/Expensive

★ **Ashford Castle,** Cong, Co. Mayo. ☎ 092/46003 or toll free **800/346-7007** or **800/221-1074** in U.S. Fax 092/46260. 83 rms (all with bath). TV TEL

Rates: £112–£194 ($168–$291) single or double. Service charge 15%. AE, DC, MC, V. **Closed:** Dec 22–Jan 3.

From turrets and towers to drawbridge and battlements, this castle is indeed a fairy-tale resort, dating back to the 13th century, when it was first the home of the De Burgo (Burke) family and later the country residence of the Guinnesses. A hotel since 1939, over the years it has been enlarged and updated and was the focus of worldwide media attention in 1984 when President Reagan stayed here during his visit to Ireland. Situated on the shores of Lough Corrib amid 450 forested and flowering acres, it sits in the heart of the scenic territory that provided the setting for the film classic *The Quiet Man*.

The interior is rich in baronial furniture, medieval armor, carved oak paneling and stairways, objets d'art, and masterpiece oil paintings. Guest rooms are decorated with designer fabrics and traditional furnishings, some with canopied or four-poster beds.

Dining/Entertainment: Choices include the 130-seat main dining room, for contemporary Irish cuisine, and the smaller 40-seat Connaught Room, a French restaurant. Sip a cocktail in the vaulted basement-level dungeon bar.

Services: Concierge, room service, laundry and dry cleaning service.

Facilities: Nine-hole golf course, tennis court, salmon and trout fishing, boating.

Moderate

The Downhill, Ballina, Co. Mayo. ☎ **096/21033** or toll free **800/221-1074** or **800/223-6510** in U.S. Fax 096/21338. 50 rms (all with bath). TV TEL

Rates (including full breakfast): £62–£69 ($93–$93.50) single, £108–£125 ($162–$187.50) double. No service charge. AE, DC, MC, V. **Closed:** Dec 22–27.

Incorporating a gracious 19th-century manor house with a modern new wing, this three-story hotel sits amid 40 acres of wooded grounds on the banks of the Brosna River, a tributary of the River Moy, at the northern edge of town. The public areas exude traditional charm, while guest rooms vary from contemporary to traditional, with thoughtful extras like coffee/tea-makers and hairdryers. It is situated off the Sligo Road (N 59).

Dining/Entertainment: The Brosna restaurant overlooks Brosna Falls; a bi-level piano bar, Frogs Pavilion, has a unique brass dance floor.

Facilities: Indoor heated swimming pool, two squash courts, sauna, Jacuzzi, gym, three all-weather tennis courts, hair salon, game room.

★ **Enniscoe House,** Castlehill, near Crossmolina, Ballina, Co. Mayo. ☎ **096/31112** or toll free **800/223-6510** in U.S. Fax 096/31773. 6 rms (all with bath).

Rates (including full breakfast): £48–£60 ($72–$90) single, £76–£100 ($114–$150) double. No service charge. MC, V. **Closed:** Mid–Oct to Apr 1.

Overlooking Lough Conn and surrounded by a wooded estate, this pastel-pink two-story Georgian country inn has been described as the last great house of North Mayo. Owned and managed by Susan Kellett, a descendant of the original family who settled on the lands in the 1660s, Enniscoe is filled with family portraits, antique furniture, country magazines, bric-a-brac, early drawings and pictures of the house and surrounding area, and open crackling fireplaces. Guest rooms are individually furnished, with huge hand-carved armoires and canopied or four-poster beds, and have views of parkland or lake. In the dining room, fish from local rivers, produce from the house's own farm, and vegetables and herbs from the adjacent garden are daily pleasures. Enniscoe also has its own Fishery (see Cloonamoyne Fishery, under "Fishing" in "Sports and Recreation," above). It is located two miles south of Crossmollina off R 315, next to the No. Mayo Heritage Centre.

Mount Falcon Castle, Foxford Road (N 57), Ballina, Co. Mayo. ☎ **096/21172** or toll free **800/223-6510** in U.S. Fax 096/21172. 10 rms (8 with private bath).

Rates (including full breakfast): £90 ($135) single or double. Service charge 10%. AE, DC, MC, V. **Closed:** Oct–Apr.

Built in 1876 by the same man who did much of the exterior work at Ashford Castle in Cong, this multigabled Victorian-style structure has been owned and managed as a country house inn by the Aldridge family since 1932. The decor in both the public areas and the guest rooms is an eclectic blend of comfortable old furniture with fluffy pillows, carved chests, and gilded mirrors. Mounted elk heads and local memorabilia line the entrance hall. If you're fond of fishing, this is a real find, because a stay here entitles you to salmon and trout fishing on Lough Conn and to preserved salmon fishing on the River Moy. The management enthusiastically caters to all the needs of fishing folk, even to serving the day's catch for dinner. Set in a hundred-acre wooded estate four miles south of Ballina, Mount Falcon has fine walking trails and an all-weather tennis court.

 Newport House, Newport, Co. Mayo. ☎ **098/41222** or toll free in U.S. **800/223-6510** or **800/44-UTELL.** Fax 098/41613. 19 rms (all with bath). TEL

Rates (including full breakfast): £56–£70 ($84–$105) single, £92–£120 ($138–$180) double. No service charge. AE, DC, MC, V. **Closed:** Oct to mid-Mar.

Close to the Clew Bay coast, this ivy-covered Georgian mansion sits at the edge of town along the Newport River, making it a favorite base for salmon fishermen (and women). Originally part of the estate of the O'Donnell family, ancient Irish chieftains, it has been a country-house hotel only in recent decades. The interior boasts splendid examples of ornate plasterwork and high ceilings; a skylit dome crowns a curved central staircase. The public areas are filled with antique furnishings, oil paintings, and fishing trophy cases. Guest rooms are spread among the main house and two smaller courtyard buildings.

Dining: The restaurant is known for its fish dishes, of course, including salmon smoked on the premises. If you catch a salmon, the chef will cook it for your dinner or smoke it for you to take home. There is also a small bar.

Facilities: Private salmon and sea-trout fishing on the Newport River and Lough Beltra.

Moderate/Inexpensive

Breaffy House, Claremorris Road, Castlebar, Co. Mayo. ☎ **094/22033** or toll free **800/528-1234** in U.S. Fax 094/22276. 38 rms (all with bath). TV TEL

Rates (including full breakfast): £43–£46 ($64.50–$69) single, £70–£76 ($105–$114) double. No service charge. AE, DC, MC, V.

A long paved driveway leads into this sprawling three-story château-style hotel, picturesquely ensconced amid 60 acres of gardens and woodlands. The public areas are furnished with traditional and period pieces. Guest rooms vary in size and shape, each with individual furnishings and character. Facilities include a restaurant and bar.

Westport Woods, Louisburg Road, Westport, Co. Mayo. ☎ **098/25811** or toll free **800/44-UTELL.** Fax 098/26212. 56 rms (all with bath). TV TEL

Rates: £40–£54 ($60–$81) single, £58–£74 ($87–$111) double. No service charge. AE, DC, MC, V.

Nestled in a quiet woodland setting, this two-story chalet-style hotel is conveniently situated midway between the historic town center and the quay area, which overlooks Clew Bay. The public rooms are woody, bright, and airy, with contemporary furnishings. The well-maintained bedrooms offer standard comforts plus hairdryer and garment press. Facilities include a full-service restaurant, a lounge, and a tennis court.

WHERE TO DINE
Expensive/Moderate

The Asgard Tavern, The Quay, Westport, Co. Mayo. ☎ 098/25319.

Cuisine: INTERNATIONAL. **Reservations:** Recommended for dinner.
Prices: Bar food appetizers £1–£4 ($1.50–$6); bar food main courses £3–£9 ($4.50–$13.50); dinner appetizers £2–£6 ($3–$9); dinner main courses £6–£14 ($9–$21) and £17.50 ($26.25) lobster. AE, DC, MC, V.
Open: Tues–Sun bar food noon–8:30pm, dinner 6:30–10pm.

Located in the center of the harbor strip opposite Clew Bay, this nautical pub/restaurant consists of an informal ground-floor pub and an upstairs candlelit 50-seat restaurant. Bar food, available throughout the day in the pub, includes Killary mussels in wine, crab claws, Clew Bay prawn salad, quiches, Irish stew, beef stroganoff, and steaks. In the evening the restaurant offers coquille St-Jacques; Dover sole on the bone; lobster in brandy-cream sauce; médaillons of beef in garlic sauce; traditional chicken Maryland; duck à l'orange; trout Marseilles; and a variety of steaks.

Moderate

⭐ **Ardmore House**, The Quay, Westport Harbour, Westport, Co. Mayo.
☎ 098/25994.

Cuisine: CONTINENTAL/IRISH. **Reservations:** Recommended for dinner.
Prices: Appetizers £1.95–£5.50 ($2.93–$8.25); lunch main courses/bar food £1.65–£9.95 ($2.48–$14.93); dinner main courses £7.50–£11.95 ($11.25–$17.93). AE, DC, MC, V.
Open: May–Sept, daily bar food 12:30–3pm, dinner 6:30–10pm; Oct–Apr, Mon–Sat bar food 12:30–3pm, dinner 6:30–10pm.

On high ground at the edge of town overlooking the harbor, Ardmore House enjoys grand views of Clew Bay. Lunchtime fare reaches to the bay for Clew Bay seafood chowder. Also on the menu are burgers, cottage pies, and steaks, hot seafood shell, curry chicken, and an omelet with smoked salmon and prawns. Entrees at dinner include seafood crêpes; salmon steak; pan-fried filets of brill; seafood in shell au gratin; roast duck; chicken Kiev; beef kebabs; or chicken curry.

The Moorings, The Quay, Westport, Co. Mayo. ☎ 098/25874.

Cuisine: IRISH. **Reservations:** Recommended.
Prices: Appetizers £1.50–£4.95 ($2.25–$7.43); main courses £8.50–£12 ($12.77–$18). MC, V.
Open: Mon–Sat 7–10pm.

As a change from all of the great seafood eateries in the area, this small harborfront restaurant serves six types of steaks, from pepper to plain or à la mode (with mushrooms, onions, cream, and brandy sauce), prepared by a Cordon Bleu–trained chef. In addition, meat dishes from chicken with avocado, cream cheese, garlic, and cream sauce; to pork filet in creamy mustard sauce; to charcoal-grilled lamb chops and rack of lamb are prepared. For fish eaters, there is fresh local salmon in season.

★ **The Quay Cottage,** The Quay, Westport. ☎ **096/26412.**
Cuisine: INTERNATIONAL. **Reservations:** Recommended for dinner.
Prices: Appetizers £1.60–£3.90 ($2.40–$5.85); lunch main courses £2–£5 ($3–$7.50); dinner main courses £6.90–£13.50 ($10.35–$20.25). AE, MC, V.
Open: Mon–Sat noon–10pm, Sun 1–9:30pm. **Closed:** Christmas and Jan.

Overlooking Westport Harbour, little Quay Cottage is awash with nautical bric-a-brac. The menu presents seafood such as lemon sole beurre blanc, wild local salmon, smoked haddock in cheese sauce, and monkfish Creole; a request for a plain steak will also be fulfilled. Also on the menu to tempt you are bananas and ham, sweet-and-sour pork, and black bean stroganoff.

Inexpensive/Budget

$ **The Old Mill,** St. Joseph's Place, Foxford, Co. Mayo. ☎ **094/56756.**
Cuisine: IRISH. **Reservations:** Not necessary.
Prices: All items £1–£4.50 ($1.50–$7.25). No credit cards.
Open: Mon–Sat 11am–6pm, Sun 1–6pm.

On the grounds of the Foxford Woollen Mills (see "What to See and Do," above), The Old Mill serves a wide array of light meals and snacks in a historic setting that's bright and airy. On the menu: freshly prepared soups, salads, sandwiches, and cold meat plates, as well as quiche, lasagne, sausage rolls, scones, muffins, and desserts. There are also daily hot meal specials.

The Northwest

16

I T HAS BEEN RIGHTLY SAID THAT IRELAND'S NORTHWESTERN CORNER IS THE BEST OF the Emerald Isle in miniature: panoramas of seacoast and mountain scenery, sylvan lakes and rivers, hillsides full of grazing sheep, sheltered parklands, ancient forts, historic landmarks, clusters of craft centers, walkable cities, picturesque villages, rich cultural traditions, and very friendly people.

If you're traveling from Shannon or Dublin, it'll take you a day's driving to reach Ireland's northwest. Irish roads being what they are, you just can't zip up to Sligo or Donegal, see the sights, and return southward a day or two later.

In fact, you need the better part of a week to do justice to this off-the-beaten-track part of Ireland. But if you're planning on staying two or three weeks in the country or you've already seen the south, west, and east on previous trips, then you owe it to yourself to travel the extra few miles to this special corner of the Emerald Isle.

1 Sligo & Yeats Country

136 miles NE of Shannon Airport, 135 miles NW of Dublin, 47 miles NE of Knock, 37 miles NE of Ballina, 87 miles NE of Galway, 73 miles N of Athlone, 209 miles N of Cork

GETTING THERE • By Plane   **Aer Lingus** operates daily flights into Sligo Airport, Strandhill, Co. Sligo (☎ **071/68280**), five miles south west of Sligo town.

• **By Train**   **Irish Rail,** Lord Edward Street, Sligo (☎ **071/69888**), operates daily service into Sligo from Dublin and other points.

• **By Bus**   **Bus Eireann,** Lord Edward Street, Sligo (☎ **071/60066**), operates daily bus service to Sligo from Dublin, Galway, and other points, including Derry in Northern Ireland.

• **By Car**   Three major roads lead to Sligo—the N 4 from Dublin and the east, the N 17 from Galway and the south, and the N 16 from Northern Ireland.

TOURIST INFORMATION   For information about Sligo and the surrounding area, contact the **North West Tourism Office,** Aras Reddan, Temple Street, Sligo (☎ **071/61201**). It's open on Monday through Saturday in June from 9am to 6pm; in July and August until 8pm and Sunday from 10am to 2pm; and September through May on Monday through Friday from 9am to 5pm.

TOWN LAYOUT   Edged by Sligo Bay to the west, Sligo town sits beside the Garavogue River, with most of the city's commercial district on the south bank of the river. **O'Connell Street** is the main north-south artery of the downtown district. The main east-west thoroughfare is **Stephen Street,** which changes its name to Wine Street and then to Lord Edward Street. The **Tourist Office** is in the southwest corner of the town on Temple Street, two blocks south of O'Connell Street. Three bridges span the river, but the **Douglas Hyde Bridge,** named for Ireland's first president, is the main link between the two sides.

GETTING AROUND • By Public Transport   There is no public transport in the town of Sligo, but during July and August **Bus Eireann** (☎ **071/60066**) operates service from Sligo town to Strandhill and Rosses Point. The fare is £2 ($3) round-trip.

• **By Taxi**   Taxis line up looking for fares at the Sligo taxi rank on Quay Street. If you prefer to call for a taxi, try **AAA Taxi** (☎ **071/41111**), **ABC Cabs** (☎ **071/43000**), **Cab 55** (☎ **071/42333**), or **City Cabs** (☎ **071/45577**).

What's Special About the Northwest

Beaches

- Bundoran, a wide sandy beach with amusement arcades and lots of action.
- Rossnowlagh, a two-mile-long sandy beach, shielded by curved hills—a surfer's delight.
- Rosses Point, a sandy beach resort north of Sligo.
- Strandhill, with a sand-duned beach west of Sligo.

Monuments

- Grianan of Aileach, one of Ireland's best examples of a ring fort, dating back to 1700 B.C.
- Yeats Grave at Drumcliff Churchyard, a monument to a literary giant.
- Carrowmore, Ireland's largest cemetery of megalithic tombs.
- Friary of Donegal, dating back to 1474 and now in ruins, this was a major hub of learning in medieval times.

Buildings

- Donegal Castle, the 15th-century stronghold of the O'Donnells with a large 17th-century Jacobean extension.
- Sligo Abbey, dating to 1252, with outstanding stone carvings.

Museums

- Sligo County Museum & Art Gallery, with a section devoted to the Yeats family.
- Yeats Memorial Building, with a Yeatsian library of renown.

Parks/Gardens

- Glenveagh National Park, a 24,000-acre estate of woodlands, alpine gardens, lakes, wildlife, and a baronial castle.

Ace Attractions

- Glencolumbkille Folk Village, a mini–theme park of Donegal-style thatched cottages and village buildings.
- Parke's Castle, Co. Leitrim, a 17th-century fortified manor house overlooking Lough Gill, with fine examples of Irish oak traditional craftsmanship.
- Lissadell House, a 19th-century house on Sligo Bay that was a favorite haunt of Yeats.
- Glebe House and Gallery, a world-class art gallery deep in the hinterlands of Donegal.

Natural Spectacles

- The Lough Gill Drive, a signposted 26-mile circuit around Lough Gill, a beautiful lake that Yeats immortalized in his writings.
- The Lake Isle of Innisfree, the storied island floating in Lough Gill.
- Glencar Lake and Waterfall, Co. Leitrim, the inspiration of Yeats's "The Stolen Child."
- Knockarea and Benbulben, two mountains that rim Sligo town.
- Glengesh Pass, a scenic but narrow roadway that rises to a height of 900 feet near Ardara.
- Mount Errigal, the highest mountain in Donegal.

- Sunsets over the Bloody Foreland, a stretch of land where the rock takes on a warm ruddy hue when lit by the sun.
- Gap of Mamore, a pass that rises to over 800 feet on the Inishowen Peninsula.

Activities
- Cruise Lough Gill on a narrated boat tour.
- Fish for shark and skate off the Killybegs coast.

Shopping
- Donegal Craft Village, to see artisans at work.
- Magee of Donegal, the major tweed producer of the northwest, established in 1866.
- Donegal Parian China, producing delicate wafer-thin porcelain products.

Religious Shrines
- Lough Derg, dating back to St. Patrick's time and still a place of pilgrimage.

Great Towns/Villages
- Ardara, tweed-making and weaving center in the heart of the Gaeltacht.
- Killybegs, colorful sea-fishing village on Donegal coast.

Offbeat
- Malin Head, Ireland's northernmost point on the Inishowen Peninsula.

• **By Car** You'll need a car to see the sights outside of Sligo town. If you need to hire a vehicle locally, contact **Avis** at Sligo Airport, Strandhill (☎ **071/68280**) or **Hertz,** 1 Teeling St., Sligo (☎ **071/60111**).

• **On Foot** The best way to see Sligo town is on foot. Follow the signposted route of the Tourist Trail. The walk takes approximately 90 minutes.

During July and August, guided walking tours depart from the **Tourist Office,** Temple Street, Sligo (☎ **071/61201**) on Monday through Saturday at 11am and 7pm. The tour lasts 1.5 hours and costs £1.50 ($2.25) per person. For further information, check at the Tourist Office.

Fast Facts: Sligo

Area Code The area code for most Sligo telephone numbers is **071.** Some numbers in the county use **074.**

Emergencies Dial **999.**

Hospital Sligo General Hospital, Malloway Hill (☎ **71111**).

Library County Sligo Library, Stephen Street (☎ **42212**), open Tuesday through Friday from 10am to 5pm, Saturday from 10am to 1pm and 2 to 5pm.

Newspapers and Local Media The weekly *Sligo Champion* covers most news and entertainment of the area, and the local North West Radio broadcasts from Sligo on 102.5 FM and 96.3 FM.

Police Garda Station, Pearse Road (☎ **42031**).

Post Office   Sligo General Post Office, Wine Street (☎ **42646**), open Monday through Saturday from 9am to 5:30pm.

From ancient times, the gateway to northwest Ireland has always been County Sligo (pronounced *Sly*-go), particularly its chief urban center and namesake, Sligo town.

Sligo town (population 18,000) is ideally located, nestled in a valley between two mountains, Ben Bulben on the north and Knocknarea on the south, and at the mouth of the River Garavogue, with Sligo Bay and the Atlantic on its western shores and Lough Gill to the east. The name Sligo is derived from the Irish or Gaelic word meaning the "shelly river."

It's no wonder that the poet William Butler Yeats, who spent much of his time here, called Sligo the "Land of Heart's Desire." He also took inspiration from many places in the area and wrote glowingly of them (the Lake Isle of Innisfree, Dooney Rock, Lissadell, and Ben Bulben, among others). This is why the Sligo region is usually referred to as Yeats Country.

WHAT TO SEE & DO

Much of Sligo's earliest history is reflected in the area south of the town at **Carrowmore,** Ireland's largest cemetery of megalithic tombs. It is said that the graves at Carrowmore predate those of Newgrange by more than 700 years. Over 60 tombs, many of which are small passage graves or dolmens, have been identified by archaeologists. The site is open June through September, daily from 9:30am to 6:30pm; admission is £1 ($1.50) for adults, 70p ($1.05) for seniors, and 40p (60¢) for students and children.

Nearby is **Knockarea** (1,078 ft.), the mountain that rims the southwest edge of town. On the summit is a gigantic cairn or gravesite, known as **Miscaun Meadhbh** (Maeve's Mound). It has traditionally been considered the resting place of Queen Maeve, who reigned in the first century B.C. This rocky structure is 630 feet around the base, 80 feet high, and 100 feet in diameter, and can be seen for miles around.

At the foot of Knockarea is **Strandhill,** five miles from Sligo town. This delightful resort area stretches out into Sligo Bay, with a sand-duned beach and a patch of land nearby called Coney Island, which is usually credited with lending its name to the New York beach amusement area. Across the bay, about four miles north of Sligo town, is another beach resort, Rosses Point.

In Sligo town, the earliest history can be traced to the ruins of Sligo Abbey on Abbey Street. Founded as a Dominican house in 1252 by Maurice Fitzgerald, earl of Kildare, it was accidentally destroyed by fire in 1414, then rebuilt two years later. It flourished in medieval times and was the burial place of the kings and princes of Sligo. After many raids and sackings, the abbey was eventually closed in 1641. Much restoration work has taken place in recent years, however, and the cloisters are considered to be outstanding examples of stone carving; the 15th-century altar is one of the few medieval altars still intact in Ireland.

Most of Sligo's attractions are associated in some way with the poet William Butler Yeats. If you visit the places described below, you'll have a thorough Yeatsean tour of the area.

IMPRESSIONS

Down at Sligo, one sees the whole world in a day's walk.
—William Trevor (b. 1928), Irish novelist

★ **Yeats Memorial Building,** Douglas Hyde Bridge, Sligo. ☎ **42693** or **45847.**

Located in a 19th-century red-brick Victorian building, this museum contains an extensive library with items of special interest to Yeatsian scholars. The building is also headquarters of the Yeats International Summer School and the Sligo Art Gallery, which exhibits works by local, national, and international artists.

Admission: Free.

Open: June–Aug, Mon–Fri 2–5pm.

★ **Sligo County Museum & Art Gallery,** Stephen Street, Sligo. ☎ **42212.**

Housed in a church manse of the mid-19th century, this museum exhibits material of national and local interest dating back to pre-Christian times. One section, devoted to the Yeats family, includes a display of first editions of William Butler Yeats's complete works, poems on broadsheets, letters, and his Nobel Prize for literature (1923), as well as a collection of oils, watercolors, and drawings by Jack B. Yeats and John B. Yeats. There is also a permanent collection of general 20th-century Irish art, including works by Paul Henry and Evie Hone.

Admission: Free.

Open: Museum, Mon–Fri 10:30am–12:30pm and 2:30–4:30pm. Art gallery, Apr–May, Tues, Thurs, and Sat 10:30am to 12:30pm; June–Sept, Tues–Sat 10:30am–12:30pm and 2:30–4:30pm.

★ **The Lough Gill Drive,** Co. Sligo and Co. Leitrim.

This 26-mile drive-yourself tour around Lough Gill is well signposted. Head one mile south of town and follow the signs for **Lough Gill,** the beautiful lake that figured so prominently in Yeats's writings. Within two miles you'll be on the lower edge of the shoreline. Among sites to see are **Dooney Rock,** with its own nature trail and lakeside walk (inspiration for the poem "Fiddler of Dooney"); the **Lake Isle of Innisfree,** made famous in Yeats's poetry and in song; and the **Hazelwood Sculpture Trail,** unique to Sligo, a forest walk along the shores of Lough Gill with 13 wood sculptures en route.

The storied Lake Isle of Innisfree is only one of 22 islands in Lough Gill. You can drive the whole lakeside circuit in one sweep in less than an hour, or you can stop at the east end and visit **Dromahair,** a delightful village on the River Bonet, technically part of County Leitrim.

The road along Lough Gill's upper shore brings you back to the northern end of Sligo town. Continue north on the main road (N 15) and you'll see the profile of graceful and green **Ben Bulben** (1,730 feet), part of the Dartry Mountains, rising to the right.

Yeats Grave, Drumcliffe Churchyard, Drumcliffe, Co. Sligo.

Five miles north of Sligo town is Drumcliffe, site of the Church of Ireland cemetery where William Butler Yeats chose to be buried. It's well signposted so you'll easily find the poet's grave with the simple headstone bearing the dramatic epitaph he composed: "Cast a cold eye on life, on death; Horseman, pass by." This cemetery also contains the ruins of an early Christian monastery founded by St. Columba in A.D. 745.

Lissadell House, off the main Sligo/Donegal Road (N 15), Drumcliffe, Co. Sligo. ☎ **074/63150.**

Situated on the shores of Sligo Bay eight miles north of Sligo, this large neoclassical building was another favorite haunt of Yeats. Dating back to 1830, it has long been the home of the Gore-Booth family, including Yeats's friends Eva Gore-Booth, a

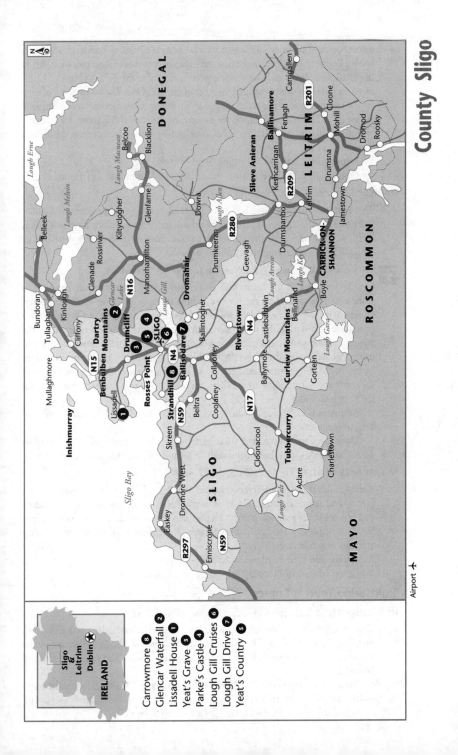

County Sligo

Carrowmore
Glencar Waterfall
Lissadell House
Yeat's Grave
Parke's Castle
Lough Gill Cruises
Lough Gill Drive
Yeat's Country

Airport ✈

fellow poet, and her sister, Constance, who became the Countess Markievicz after marrying a Polish count). One of the first truly liberated women, Constance took part in the 1916 Irish Rising and was the first woman elected to the British House of Commons and the first woman cabinet member in the Irish Dail. The house is full of such family memorabilia as the travel diaries of Sir Robert Gore-Booth, who mortgaged the estate to help the poor during the famine. At the core of the house is a dramatic two-story hallway lined with Doric columns leading to a double staircase of Kilkenny marble.

Admission: £2.50 ($3.75) adults, 50p (75¢) children.

Open: June to mid–Sept, Mon–Sat 10:30am–12:15pm and 2–4:15pm.

Glencar Lake, off N 16, Glencar, Co. Leitrim.

This Yeats Country attraction is not in Sligo at all, but just over the border in County Leitrim. Lovely Glencar Lake stretches eastward for two miles along a verdant valley, highlighted by two waterfalls, one of which rushes downward for 50 feet. Yeats's "The Stolen Child" speaks wondrously of this lake.

★ **Parke's Castle,** Lough Gill Drive, Co. Leitrim. ☎ 071/64149.

On the north side of the Lough Gill Drive, within the County Leitrim border, this stone structure appears on the horizon, a lone manmade outpost amid the natural tableau of lakeview and woodland scenery. Named after an English family who gained possession of it during the 1620 plantation of Leitrim, this castle was originally the stronghold of the O'Rourke clan, rulers of the kingdom of Breffni. Recently restored using Irish oak and traditional craftsmanship, it is a fine example of a fortified manor house. In the visitor center, exhibits and an audiovisual show illustrate the history of the castle and surrounding area. With a tea room, the castle makes an ideal stop on the Lough Gill route.

Admission: £1.50 ($2.25) adults, £1 ($1.50) seniors, 60p (90¢) students and children over age six.

Open: St. Patrick's weekend (near March 17), 10am–5pm; April 10 to late May, Tues–Sun 10am–5pm; June–Sept, daily 9:30am–6:30pm, Oct daily 10am–5pm.

Model Arts Centre, The Mall, Co. Sligo. ☎ 41405.

Although this is a relatively new development (1991) in Sligo, it carries on the Yeatsian literary and artistic traditions. Housed in an 1850 Romanesque-style stone building that was originally a school, it offers a half-dozen rooms for touring and local exhibits by artists, sculptors, writers, and musicians. In the summer, there are often poetry readings or arts lectures.

Admission: Free. Readings/lectures £2–£4 ($3–$6).

Open: Mon–Sat, 11am–6pm; evening events 8pm, dates vary.

Sightseeing Tours & Cruises

JH Transport, 57 Mountain Close, Carton View, Sligo. ☎ 42747.

This company operates narrated minibus tours of the Sligo area, departing daily from the Sligo Tourist Office. The morning tour follows the Lough Gill Drive, while the afternoon tour goes to Yeats's grave, Lissadell House, and Glencar Lake and Waterfall.

Prices: Morning tour is £5.50 ($8.25) for adults and £3 ($4.50) for children ages 6–16; afternoon tour, £6.50 ($9.75) adults, and £3 ($4.50) for children ages 6–16.

Schedule: July–Aug, 9:45am to 12:45pm, 2 to 5:45pm.

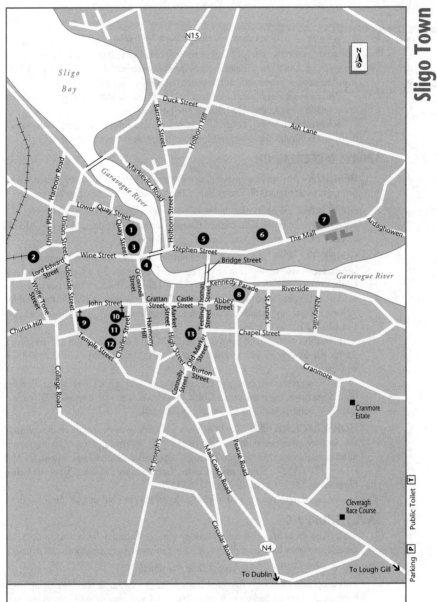

Sligo Town

Cathedral of the Immaculate
    Conception (R.C.) **9**
City Hall **1**
Courthouse **13**
General Hospital **7**
Hawks Well Theatre **11**
Model Arts Centre **6**

Post Office **3**
Railway Station & Bus Terminal **2**
Sligo Abbey **8**
Sligo County Museum & Art Gallery **5**
St. John's Cathedral (C. of I.) **10**
Tourist Information Office **12**
Yeats Memorial Building **4**

Parking **P** Public Toilet **T**

Lough Gill Cruises, Blue Lagoon, Riverside, Sligo. ☎ **64266.**

Narrated cruises (the poetry of Yeats is recited) of Lough Gill and the Garavogue River are given on board the 70-passenger *Wild Rose* waterbus. Trips to the Lake Isle of Innisfree are also scheduled. An on-board bar is open for refreshments.

Price: Lough Gill cruise, £4 ($6) adults, £1 ($1.50) children over age 10; Inishfree cruise, £3 ($4.50) adults, £1 (1.50) children over age 10.

Schedule: June–Sept, Lough Gill cruise 2:30 and 4:30pm; Inishfree tour, 12:30, 3:30, and 6:30pm. Apr, May, and Oct, Sun schedule subject to demand.

SPORTS & RECREATION

BEACHES   For walking, jogging, or swimming, there are safe sandy beaches with promenades at Strandhill, Rosses Point, and Enniscrone on the Sligo Bay coast.

BICYCLING   With its lakes and woodlands, Yeats Country is particularly good biking territory. To rent a bike, contact **Conway Bros.,** High Street, Sligo (☎ **61370**) or **Gary's Cycles Shop,** Quay Street, Sligo (☎ **45418**).

GOLFING   With its seascapes, mountain valleys, and lakesides, County Sligo is known for its challenging 18-hole golf courses. Leading the list is **County Sligo Golf Club,** Rosses Point Road, Rosses Point (☎ **77186**), overlooking Sligo Bay under the shadow of Ben Bulben mountain. It's a par-71 championship seaside links famed for its wild, natural terrain and constant winds; greens fees are £15 ($22.50) on weekdays and £20 ($30) on weekends.

Five miles west of Sligo town is **Strandhill Golf Club,** Strandhill (☎ **68188**), a seaside par-69 course, with greens fees of £10 ($15) on weekdays and £12 ($18) on weekends.

In the southwestern corner of the county overlooking Sligo Bay, about 25 miles from Sligo town, the **Enniscrone Golf Club,** Enniscrone (☎ **096/36297**), is a seaside par-72 course with greens fees of £15 ($22.50).

HORSEBACK RIDING   An hour's or a day's riding on the beach, in the countryside, or over mountain trails can be arranged at the following places, all within seven miles of Sligo town: **Moneygold Riding Centre,** off the Ballyshannon Road (N 15), Grange (☎ **63337**); **Sligo Riding Centre, Carrowmore** (☎ **61353**); or the **Celtic Horsefarm,** Derry Cross, Grange (☎ **63337**).

Riding charges average £10 to £12 ($15 to $18) per hour or £40 ($60) per day.

SAVVY SHOPPING

Most Sligo shops are open from Monday through Saturday from 9am to 6pm, although some may have extended hours during July and August, according to demand.

The Cat & The Moon, 25 Market St., Sligo. ☎ **43686.**

This shop offers uniquely designed crafts from throughout Ireland—ranging from beeswax candles and baskets to modern art, metal and ceramic work, wood-turning, hand-weaving, and Celtic jewelry.

Kate's Kitchen, 24 Market St., Sligo. ☎ **43022.**

Step into Kate's to savor the aromas of potpourri, soaps, and environmental oils, as well as Crabtree & Evelyn products. The shop also has an outstanding delicatessan section, with gourmet meats, cheeses, salads, pâtés, and breads baked on the premises, all ideal makings for a picnic by Lough Gill. Don't miss the handmade Irish chocolates and preserves.

Keohane's Bookshop, Castle Street, Sligo. ☎ **42597.**

Try this shop for works by William Butler Yeats and other Irish authors. There are also books and maps of Sligo and other Sligo-related publications.

Innisfree Crystal, The Bridge, Dublin Road (N 4), Collooney. ☎ **67340.**

Taking its name from the Lough Gill island immortalized in William Butler Yeats's poem "The Lake Isle of Innisfree," this crystal factory produces individually handcut glassware, such as punch bowls, decanters, vases, and bowls. Each piece is hand-signed by one of the craftspeople. You can watch them work (weekdays only) or browse in the showroom.

Michael Kennedy Ceramics, Church Street, Sligo. ☎ **62586.**

One of Ireland's foremost ceramic artists, Michael Kennedy produces pottery and porcelain with layers of texture markings and drawings that form a maze of intricate patterns. He then applies glazes that reflect the strong tones and shades of the Irish countryside. The results yield one-of-a-kind vases, jars, dishes, figurines, buttons, jewelry, and other pieces.

Music Room, Harmony Hill. Sligo. ☎ **44765.**

Located just off O'Connell Street, this small cottagelike store will draw you to it with the sounds of Irish music. This is a great spot to purchase musical instruments—from concertinas and cymbals to banjos, bells, bodhrans, and button accordians, from flutes and fiddles to tin whistles and unique jews harps (harmonicas) and accessories, A sister shop, the **Record Room,** a half-block away on Grattan Street (☎ **43748**), offers cassettes, CDs, videos, and records.

★ **My Lady Art Gallery,** Castle Street, Sligo. ☎ **42723.**

Established in 1932, this shop specializes in original watercolors of Sligo in standard and miniature sizes. There are also oil paintings and prints of Sligo, as well as new and used books on the history of Sligo.

★ **M. Quirke,** Wine Street, Sligo. ☎ **42624** or **45800.**

Michael Quirke started out as a butcher, but a few years ago he traded his cleaver for wood-carving tools and transformed his butcher shop into a craft studio. Step inside and watch as he transforms chunks of native timbers into Ireland's heroes of mythology—from Sligo's Queen Maeve to Cu Chulainn, Oisin, and other folklore characters. He also carves chess sets and other Irish-theme wood items.

Sligo Crystal Glass, Ballyshannon Road (N 15), Grange, Co. Sligo. ☎ **63251.**

Located six miles north of Sligo, this workshop is noted for its personalized engraving of such items as family crests on mirrors or glassware. The craftsmen also produce handcut crystal candlesticks, glasses, and curio items like crystal bells and scent bottles. If you visit on a weekday, you'll see the craftspeople at work.

Wehrly Bros. Ltd, 3 O'Connell St., Sligo. ☎ **42252.**

Established in 1875, this is one of Sligo's oldest shops, noted for a fine selection of jewelry and watches, as well as cold-cast bronze sculptures of Irish figures, silverware, Claddagh rings, Waterford crystal, Belleek china, and Galway crystal.

WHERE TO STAY
Expensive/Moderate

★ **Cromleach Lodge**, Ballindoon, Castlebaldwin, Co. Sligo. ☎ **071/65155.**
Fax 071/65455. 10 rms (all with bath). TV TEL

Rates (including full breakfast): £60–£95 ($90–$142.50) single, £90–£160 ($135–$240) double. No service charge. AE, MC, V.

One of the best places to stay in Sligo is not in the town at all, but 20 miles south at this lovely modern country-house hotel, nestled in the quiet hills above Lough Arrow. You may never want to leave as you gaze out the windows of the skylit bar and restaurant, as well as from your guest room to see the panorama of lakeland and mountain scenery. The rooms are extra large by Irish standards and have all the comforts of a top hotel, including over size beds, designer fabrics, and original oil paintings. Each room is named after a different part of the Sligo countryside (from Ben Bulben and Knocknarea to Moytura and Carrowkeel) and is decorated with colors reflecting its namesake. Half the rooms are no-smoking, there is a smoking and no-smoking lounge, still a novelty in Ireland. But the pièce de résistance here is the dining room (see "Where to Dine," below). The enthusiastic innkeepers are Moira and Christy Tighe.

Moderate

Ballincar House, Rosses Point Road, Sligo. ☎ **071/45361** or toll free **800/447-7462** in U.S. Fax 071/44198. 25 rms (all with bath). TV TEL

Rates (including full breakfast): £50–£65 ($75–$97.50) single, £85–£110 ($127.50–$165) double. Service charge 10%. AE, DC, MC, V.

Nestled on six tree-shaded pastoral acres overlooking Sligo Bay, this two-story hotel was built as a private residence in 1848, then was extended and opened as a lodging in 1969. The public rooms preserve the house's old-Ireland charm, with open fireplaces, period furnishings and original oil paintings of the area. The guest rooms are decorated in contemporary country style; most rooms look out onto the gardens or vistas of Sligo Bay. Amenities include a full-service restaurant, a bar, a hard tennis court, a sauna, and a snooker table. It is located two miles northwest of the Sligo town center.

★ **Markree Castle**, Collooney, Co. Sligo. ☎ **071/67800** or toll free **800/223-6510, 800/221-1074** or **800/44-UTELL** in U.S. Fax 071/67840. 11 rms (all with bath). TV TEL

Rates (including full breakfast): £47–£57 ($70.50–$85.50) single, £87–£97 ($130.50–$145.50) double. No service charge. AE, DC, MC, V. **Closed:** Feb to mid–Mar.

Located eight miles south of Sligo off the main Dublin Road, this is Sligo's oldest inhabited castle and the home of the Cooper family since 1640. The castle's current owner, Charles Cooper, who purchased the building from his brother a few years ago, is the tenth generation of his family to live at Markree. The original house was altered and extended over the years, but the dramatic four-story turreted stone facade still remains. Even the approach to the castle is impressive, via a mile-long driveway, along pasturelands grazed by sheep and horses and lovely gardens that stretch down to the Unsin River. Inside, the decor is equally regal, including a hand-carved oak staircase, ornate plasterwork, and a stained-glass window that traces the Cooper family tree back to the time of King John of England. The guest rooms, restored and equipped with modern facilities, have lovely views of the gardens. The restaurant, known as Knockmuldowney (see "Where to Dine," below), is a masterpiece of Louis Philippe–style plasterwork. Facilities at the castle include horseback-riding, falconry, and salmon fishing on the Ballisodare River.

Silver Swan, Hyde Bridge, Sligo, Co. Sligo. ☎ **071/43231.** Fax 071/42232. 29 rms (all with bath). TV TEL

Rates (including full breakfast): £40–£55 ($60–$82.50) single, £60–£84 ($90–$126) double. Service charge 10%. AE, DC, MC, V.

Sitting beside the Hyde Bridge, this modern four-story hotel has a rather uninteresting glass-and-concrete facade, though it does have a great location, right beside the Garavogue River in the heart of town. The recently refurbished guest rooms, which have wide-windowed views of town and river, are decorated in conventional style with dark woods and multitoned fabrics; in-room extras include a garment press, hairdryer, and hospitality tray. Most of the public areas, including the Cygnet restaurant, overlook the river. The Horse-Shoe bar is known for its traditional Irish music sessions, usually on Wednesday evenings, and jazz sessions on Sunday afternoons.

 Sligo Park Hotel, Pearse Road, Sligo, Co. Sligo. ☎ **071/60291** or toll free **800/44-UTELL** in the U.S. Fax 071/69556. 89 rms (all with bath). TV TEL

Rates: £49–£53 ($73.50–$79.50) single, £64–£80 ($96–$120) double. Service charge 10%. AE, DC, MC, V.

With a glass-fronted facade and skylit atrium lobby, this is Sligo's most contemporary hotel, set back from the road on seven acres of parkland just over a mile south of Sligo on the Dublin Road. It is surrounded by lovely gardens, with distant views of Ben Bulben to the north. The public areas are equally modern, enhanced by Irish art. Guest rooms are furnished in art deco style, with light woods, pastel-toned floral fabrics, quilted headboards, and framed scenes of the Sligo area.

Dining/Entertainment: Choices include the Hazelwood Restaurant overlooking the gardens; the Rathanna Piano Bar; and a coffee shop.

Facilities: Indoor swimming pool, whirlpool, sauna, steam room, gym, tennis court.

Southern Hotel, Lord Edward Street, Sligo, Co. Sligo. ☎ **071/62101.** Fax 071/60328. 77 rms (all with bath). TV TEL

Rates (including full breakfast): £44–£46 ($66–$69) single, £64–£68 ($96–$102) double. No service charge. AE, DC, MC, V.

This lovely old five-story hostelry in the northwest of Ireland is called Southern because it started out as part of the Great Southern chain. When it became an independent property more than a dozen years ago, it kept half its name. For visitors who travel around Ireland by train or bus, it is ideal, situated next to the train and bus station and close to the center of town. Recently refurbished, it has retained its old-world charm while rejuvenating its guest rooms with dark-wood furnishings, local art, and quilted print fabrics.

Dining/Entertainment: Choices include the Garden Room Restaurant, Orient Express Bar, and Squires nightclub.

Facilities: Indoor heated swimming pool, gym, Jacuzzi, squash court, sauna, steam room.

Moderate/Inexpensive

Yeats Country Hotel, Rosses Point Road, Rosses Point, Co. Sligo. ☎ 071/77211 or toll free **800/44-UTELL** in U.S. Fax 071/77203. 79 rms (all with bath). TV TEL

Rates: £40–£54 ($60–$71) single, £58–£74 ($77–$111) double. No service charge. AE, DC, MC, V. **Closed:** Jan.

Located five miles northwest of Sligo town next to an 18-hole golf course, this modern hilltop property overlooks several miles of sandy beach and the waters of Sligo Bay. The interior is decorated in a bright contemporary style, with light woods, soft pastels, and wide windows looking out onto the neighboring attractions. Facilities include a full-service restaurant, a lounge bar, two tennis courts, and a pitch-and-putt area.

WHERE TO DINE

Expensive

 Knockmuldowney, Markree Castle, Collooney, Co. Sligo. ☎ **67800.**
Cuisine: INTERNATIONAL. **Reservations:** Required.
Prices: Set lunch £12 ($18); set dinner £18.50–£23.50 ($27.75–$34.75). AE, DC, MC, V.
Open: Dinner daily 7–9:30pm, lunch Sun 1–2:30pm. **Closed:** Feb to mid–Mar.

Long before Charles and Mary Cooper bought Markree Castle (see "Where to Stay," above), they were winning culinary plaudits for Knockmuldowney restaurant, then situated in a small house at the base of Knocknarea Mountain on the shores of Ballisodare Bay. When they recently acquired the castle, they simply transferred the restaurant name and following with them. Although it is now housed in a more regal and spacious 60-seat setting under 19th-century Louis Philippe–style plasterwork, the spotlight is still on the food, offering such entrees as suprême of chicken with Cashel Blue cheese; escalopes of pork with Morvandelle cream sauce; grilled wild salmon with hollandaise sauce; filet steak with red-wine butter; and roast farmyard duckling with black-cherry–and–port sauce.

⭐ **Cromleach Lodge,** Ballindoon, Castlebaldwin, Co. Sligo. ☎ **65155.**
Cuisine: IRISH. **Reservations:** Required.
Prices: Set dinner £26.50 ($39.75). AE, MC, V.
Open: Dinner Mon–Sat 7–9pm, Sun 6:30–8pm.

It's worth the drive 20 miles south of Sligo town to dine overlooking Lough Arrow at this lovely country house. The panoramic views are secondary, however, to chef Moira Tighe's culinary talents. The menu changes nightly, depending on what is freshest and best from the sea and garden, but may include such dishes as escalope of veal on red and yellow pepper sauces; boned stuffed roast quail with a vintage port sauce; wild Atlantic salmon on a julienne of vegetables and saffron; loin of lamb scented with garlic and Irish Mist; and filet of beef with Roquefort cheese sauce. The dining room itself is a delight—with old-style decorated plaster moldings and chair rails, curio cabinets with figurines and crystal, ruffled valances, palm tree plants, and place settings of Rosenthal china and fine Irish linens and silver.

Moderate

Austie's/The Elsinore, Rosses Point Road, Rosses Point, Co. Sligo. ☎ 071/77111.

Cuisine: SEAFOOD/INTERNATIONAL. **Reservations:** Recommended for dinner.
Prices: Bar food £1.20–£8.95 ($1.80–$13.43); appetizers £1.20–£3.50 ($1.80–$5.25); dinner main courses £5–£14.50 ($7.50–$21.75). MC, V.
Open: Daily bar food 12:30–5pm, dinner 5–10pm.

Set on a hill with lovely views of the waters of Sligo Bay, this pub/restaurant has a seafaring decor—from nautical knick-knacks and fishnets to periscopes, corks, and paintings of sailing ships. Substantial pub grub is available during the day, ranging from open-face "sandbank" sandwiches of crab, salmon, or smoked mackerel, to crab claw, prawn, or mixed seafood salads, as well as hearty soups and chowders. The dinner menu offers such fresh seafood choices as pan-fried Dover sole, baked trout amandine, or crab au gratin, as well as steaks and chicken curry. Lobster is also available, at market prices. Outdoor seating on picnic tables is available in good weather. The restaurant is located four miles northwest of Sligo.

Glebe House, Collooney, Co. Sligo. ☎ 67787.

Cuisine: IRISH/FRENCH. **Reservations:** Recommended.
Prices: Appetizers £2.25–£4.25 ($3.38–$6.38); main courses £8.75–£12.95 ($13.13–$19.43). AE, MC, V.
Open: May–Oct daily 6:30–9:30pm; Nov–Apr, Tues–Sat 6:30–9:30pm. **Closed:** 1st two wks Jan.

Set in a restored Georgian house near Collooney village and the Owenmore River, this restaurant with a homey atmosphere is run by an Irish/French couple, Brid and Marc Torraden. They espouse a sort of *cuisine bourgeoise* and rely heavily on using fresh herbs and vegetables, picked from the gardens that surround the house. The menu changes daily but often includes symphony of the sea (the day's best catch); noisettes of lamb with garlic; chicken breast filled with basil and mustard seed; pan-fried wild salmon with sorrel; mussels with garlic and basil; roast beef and Yorkshire pudding; and pancake of vegetables in a light mustard sauce. It is south of Sligo, off the N 4 main road.

Moderate/Inexpensive

★ **Truffles,** 11 The Mall, Sligo. ☎ 44226.

Cuisine: IRISH/ITALIAN. **Reservations:** Recommended.
$ **Prices:** Appetizers £2–£5 ($3–$7.50); main courses £5–£10 ($7.50–$15). No credit cards.
Open: Tues–Sat 5–10:30pm, Sun 5–10pm.

"New age" pizzas are the specialty of this innovative restaurant on the edge of town. Chef Bernadette O'Shea is constantly experimenting to create new styles and types of pizza—from the Californian Classic, with sun-dried tomatoes and roasted garlic; to the Mexicano, with hot chile peppers and sausage; to an intrinsically Irish pizza with an assortment of local cheeses including Cashel Blue, smoked Brie, goat's cheese, cream cheese, cottage cheese, and Irish mozzarella on a bed of tomato sauce, crowned by an assortment of fresh herbs. All dishes are prepared with local organic produce, including some great main-course salads and pastas.

Budget

The Cottage, 4 Castle St., Sligo. ☎ **45319.**

Cuisine: IRISH/VEGETARIAN. **Reservations:** Not necessary.
Prices: All items £1.50–£4.50 ($2.25–$7.25). No credit cards.
Open: Mon–Fri 8:30am–9pm, Sat 8:30am–6pm.

For a light meal or snack, try this cottage-style restaurant in the heart of town. It's known for hot open sandwiches on French bread, topped with melted cheese; as well as quiche, chili, pizza, baked potatoes with different fillings, crab claws, and seafood chowders. There is either self-service and table service.

EVENING ENTERTAINMENT

Theaters/Performing Arts

The Factory, Lr. Quay Street, Sligo. ☎ **70431.**

In summer the Blue Raincoat Theatre Company presents a lunchtime series of Yeats's plays and other one-act Sligo-related plays at this small theater.
Admission: Tickets, £2–£4 ($3–$6) depending on show.
Open: July–Aug, Tues–Sat 1:10pm.

Hawk's Well Theatre, Temple Street, Sligo. ☎ **61526.**

The premier stage of Ireland's northwest region, this modern 300-seat theater presents a varied program of drama, comedy, ballet, opera, and concerts of modern and traditional music. It derives its name from *At the Hawk's Well,* a one-act play by William Butler Yeats. A resident professional group performs throughout the year, augmented by visiting troupes and individual artists.
Admission: Tickets, £5 ($7.50).
Open: Tues–Sat box office 10am–6pm; most shows at 8:30pm.

Seo Cheoil, Temple Street, Sligo. ☎ **61526.**

This is a session of Irish traditional music, song, dance, and story, presented weekly at the Hawk's Well Theatre. The program includes a portrayal of the life of St. Patrick as well as a selection of music associated with Sligo. It is produced by members of the Sligo branch of Comhaltas Ceoltoiri Eireann, Ireland's national traditional music organization.
Admission: Tickets, £4 ($6).
Open: Late June through Aug Mon 8:30pm.

PUBS

The Blue Lagoon Tudor Room, Riverside, Sligo. ☎ **42530.**

Overlooking the Garavogue River, this pub is a five-minute walk from the town center. It offers sessions of traditional Irish music on Monday night and ballads on Thursday. There is no cover charge.

Hargadon's, 4 O'Connell St., Sligo. ☎ **70933.**

More than a century old, this is the most atmospheric bar in the center of the downtown area. Although it is strictly a pub now, it also used to be a grocery shop, as you'll see if you glance at the shelves on the right. The decor is a mélange of dark-wood walls, mahogany counters, stone floors, colored glass, old barrels and bottles, genuine snugs, and alcoves lined with early prints of Sligo.

Stanford's Village Inn, Main Street, Dromahair, Co. Leitrim. ☎ **64140.**

If you're driving around Lough Gill from Sligo, this 160-year-old pub is a great midway stop for a drink or a snack. The decor is a delightful blend of old stone walls, vintage pictures and posters, oil lamps, and tweed-covered furnishings.

 The Thatch, Dublin/Sligo Road (N 4), Ballisodare, Co. Sligo. ☎ **67288.**

Established in 1638 as a coaching inn, this pub is about five miles south of Sligo on the main road. As its name suggests, it has a fully thatched roof and a whitewashed exterior, with a country-cottage motif inside. It's a good spot for taking pictures as well as refreshments. Irish traditional music is usually scheduled from 9pm on Thursday all year and on Tuesday through Friday in July and August.

Yeats's Tavern, Ballyshannon Road (N 15), Drumcliffe, Co. Sligo. ☎ **63668** or **73117.**

Located four miles north of Sligo across the road from the famous churchyard where William Butler Yeats is buried, this pub honors the poet's memory with quotations from his works, as well as photos, prints, and murals. Basically a modern tavern with a copper-and-wood decor, it is a good place to stop for a snack/refreshment when touring Yeats Country.

2 Donegal Town

138 miles NW of Dublin, 176 miles NE of Shannon Airport, 41 miles NE of Sligo, 43 miles SW of Derry, 112 miles W of Belfast, 127 NE of Galway, 250 miles N of Cork, 253 miles NE of Killarney

GETTING THERE • By Plane **Loganair** operates regularly scheduled flights from Glasgow to Donegal Airport, Carrickfinn, Kincasslagh, Co. Donegal (☎ **075/48284**), about 40 miles northwest of Donegal town on the Atlantic coast.

• By Bus **Bus Eireann** (☎ **074/21309**) operates daily bus service to Donegal town to and from Dublin, Derry, Sligo, Galway, and other points. All tickets are issued on the bus. Pickup and boarding point is in front of the Abbey Hotel on The Diamond.

• By Car From the south, Donegal is reached via N 15 from Sligo or A 46 or A 47 from Northern Ireland; from the east and north, it's N 15 and N 56; from the west, N 56 leads to Donegal town.

TOURIST INFORMATION The **Donegal Tourist Office,** Quay Street, Donegal (☎ **073/21148**), is open from May through September, Monday through Saturday from 9am to 6pm, with extended hours in July and August according to demand.

TOWN LAYOUT Donegal Town, which sits to the east of the River Eske, is laid out around a triangular central mall or market area called The Diamond. **Main Street** and **Upper Main Street,** the prime commercial strip, extend in a northeast direction from The Diamond.

GETTING AROUND • By Public Transport Easily walkable, Donegal has no local bus service within the town. If you need a taxi, call **McGroary Cabs** (☎ **073/21972** or **35162**) or **Marley Taxis** (☎ **074/33013**).

• By Car If you drive into Donegal, there is free parking along the Quay beside the Tourist Office and off Main Street.

• On Foot Follow the signposted walking tour of Donegal Town; a booklet outlining the walk is available at the Tourist Office and most bookshops.

Fast Facts: Donegal

Area Code Most telephone numbers in the Donegal town area use the code **073.**

Drugstores Begley's Pharmacy, The Diamond (☎ **21232**), and Britton's Pharmacy, Main Street (☎ **21008**).

Hospital Donegal District Hospital, Upper Main Street (☎ **21019**).

Library Donegal Library, Mountcharles Road (☎ **21105**). Open Monday, Wednesday, and Friday from 3 to 6pm and Saturday from 11am to 1pm and 2 to 6pm.

Police Garda Station, Quay Street (☎ **21021**).

Post Office Donegal Post Office, Tirconnail Street (☎ **21001**). Open Monday, Tuesday, and Thursday to Saturday from 9am to 5:30pm and Wednesday from 9:30am to 5:30pm.

Situated on the estuary of the River Eske on Donegal Bay, Donegal town is a very walkable little metropolis (population 2,000) that's a pivotal gateway for touring the county.

Like so many parts of Ireland, County Donegal (pronounced "Donny-gawl") can trace its roots back for at least a thousand years. The Vikings were among the first foreign visitors to discover the joys of Donegal, establishing a fort here in the 9th century. The native Irish soon described the fort as *Dun na nGall,* meaning "the fort of the foreigner," and that's how the name Donegal is said to have originated.

In the 13th century, Donegal town rose to prominence as the local O'Donnell clan became the ruling power in the Kingdom of Tirconnaill (the present County Donegal). The O'Donnell chieftain, known as Red Hugh, built a Norman-style tower house on the site of the old Fort of the Foreigners.

With his wife, Nuala, Red Hugh is also credited with bringing the Franciscan friars to Donegal in 1474 and constructing the Mainistir Dhun na nGall (Donegal Monastery) on the banks of the River Eske.

It was at the monastery that the *Annals of the Four Masters* were conceived and written by Franciscan lay brother Michael O'Cleary and three lay scholars. It took them at least four years to write this year-by-year narrative, which has since been recognized as the most comprehensive history of Ireland from earliest times (2242 B.C. to A.D. 1616). The *Annals* are now in Dublin's Royal Irish Academy Library, but a 25-foot-high obelisk of red granite, erected in the center of Donegal town in 1937, commemorates this literary achievement.

In 1612 Donegal town became a corporate town under royal charter and developed as an important marketplace in Ireland's northwest. As recently as the 1940s, the town's central Diamond was used as a market for trading livestock and goods. Today the marketing is more in the form of tweeds and tourist goods.

Because the area comprising Donegal town and the surrounding county is so close to Northern Ireland, it is a favorite vacation destination for people from the other side of the border, so you'll often hear a variety of accents (or brogues) in Donegal town and in nearby towns and villages.

WHAT TO SEE & DO

The greatest attraction of Donegal town is the town layout itself, a happy mix of medieval and modern buildings. And all of the structures of interest are there for you

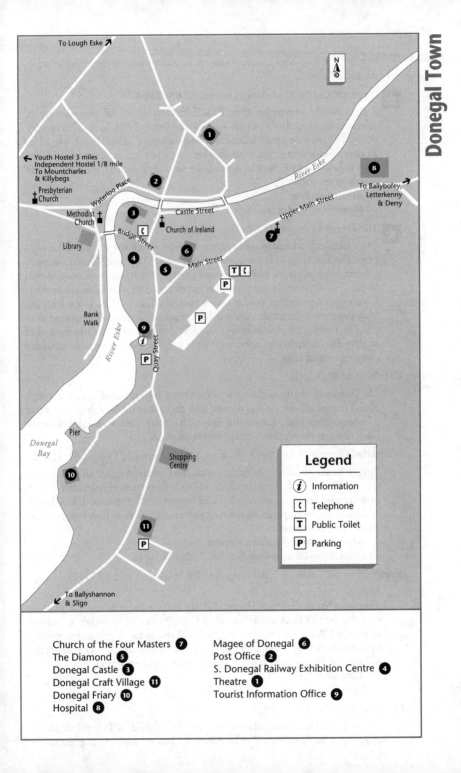

Donegal Town

To Lough Eske ↗

To Ballybofey, Letterkenny & Derry ↗

Youth Hostel 3 miles
Independent Hostel 1/8 mile
To Mountcharles & Killybegs

Presbyterian Church

Methodist Church

Waterloo Place

Castle Street

Upper Main Street

Church of Ireland

Bridge Street

Library

Main Street

Bank Walk

River Eske

River Eske

Quay Street

Donegal Bay

Pier

Shopping Centre

To Ballyshannon & Sligo ↙

Legend

i Information

C Telephone

T Public Toilet

P Parking

to enjoy at will, with no admission charges, no audiovisuals, no interpretative exhibits, and no crowds.

 Donegal Castle, Castle Street, Donegal. ☎ **073/22405.**

Built in the 15th century beside the River Eske, this magnificent castle was once the chief stronghold for the O'Donnell's, a powerful Donegal clan. In the 17th century, during the Plantation period, it came into the possession of Sir Basil Brook, who added an extension with ten gables, a large bay window, and other, smaller mullioned windows in Jacobean style. Now recognized as a national monument, the castle is in the process of restoration.

Admission: Free.

Open: Mid–June to mid–Sept, daily 10am–6pm.

★ The Friary of Donegal, The Quay, Donegal.

Often mistakenly referred to as The Abbey, this Franciscan house was founded in 1474 by the first Red Hugh O'Donnell and his wife, Nuala O'Brien of Munster. Sitting in a peaceful spot where the River Eske meets Donegal Bay, it was generously endowed by the O'Donnell family and became an important center of religion and learning. Great gatherings of clergy and lay leaders assembled here in 1539. It was from this friary that some of the scholars undertook to salvage old Gaelic manuscripts and compile *The Annals of the Four Masters* (1632–36). Unfortunately, little remains now of its glory days, except some impressive ruins of a church and a cloister. No admission charge; continual access.

The Diamond, Donegal.

The Diamond is the triangular market area of town. It's dominated by a 25-foot-high obelisk erected as a memorial to the four Irish clerics from the local abbey who wrote *The Annals of the Four Masters* in the early 17th century, the first recorded history of Gaelic Ireland. No admission charge; continual access.

Memorial Church of the Four Masters, Upper Main Street, Donegal. ☎ **21026.**

Perched on a small hill overlooking the town, this Catholic church is officially known as St. Patrick's Church of the Four Masters. It is of fairly recent vintage, built in 1935 in an Irish Romanesque style of red granite from nearby Barnesmore. It is dedicated to the four men who produced the most monumental work of Irish literature, *The Annals of the Four Masters.*

Admission: Free; donations welcome.

Open: Mon–Fri 8am–6pm, Sat–Sun 7:30am–7:30pm.

South Donegal Railway Exhibition Centre, Anderson's Yard, off The Diamond, Donegal.

This center houses displays of Donegal County's narrow-gauge railway that originally extended for 125 miles throughout all of County Donegal. Although it ceased to operate by 1960, it is currently in the process of restoration. It is hoped to restore a section of the railway that runs through the scenic Barnesmore Gap. The current displays include photographs, artifacts, posters, tickets, and equipment.

Admission: Free.

Open: June–Sept, Mon–Sat 10am–5pm.

Lough Derg, off R. 233.

This lake, filled with many islands, lies about ten miles east of Donegal. At this secluded spot, St. Patrick is said to have spent 40 days and nights fasting in a cavern.

Ever since then it has been revered as a place of penance and pilgrimage. From June 1 to August 15, thousands of Irish people take turns coming to Lough Derg to do penance for three days at a time. It's considered one of the most rigorous pilgrimages in all of Christendom. No admission; continual access.

SPORTS & RECREATION

BICYCLING   Rent a bike from **Doherty's,** Main Street (☎ **073/21119**). A day's rental costs £7 ($10.50) It's open year-round Monday through Saturday from 9am to 6pm.

FISHING   For advice and equipment for fishing in Lough Eske and other local waters, contact **Doherty's Fishing Tackle,** Main Street (☎ **073/21119**). This shop stocks a wide selection flies, reels, bait, fishing poles. It's open year-round Monday through Saturday from 9am to 6pm.

SAVVY SHOPPING

Most Donegal shops are open from Monday through Saturday from 9am to 6pm, with extended hours in summer and slightly reduced hours in winter.

 Donegal Craft Village, Ballyshannon Road, Donegal. ☎ **30017.**

You'll find this cluster of individual craftworkers' shops about a mile south of town in a rural setting. Encouraged and financed by Ireland's Industrial Development Authority and the EU, this project provides a creative environment for an ever-changing group of artisans to practice ancient and modern crafts—ranging from porcelain and ceramics to hand-weaving, batik, crystal, jewelry, metalwork, and visual art. You can buy some one-of-a-kind treasures or just browse from shop to shop and watch the craftspeople at work.

Forget-Me-Not/The Gift Shop, The Diamond, Donegal. ☎ **21168.**

This shop features a wide selection of unusual gifts: from handmade jewelry and woolly sheep mobiles, to Irish traditional music figures, tweed paintings, bog oak sculptures, beaten-copper art, Celtic art cards, and Donegal County banners and hangings.

The Four Masters Bookshop, The Diamond, Donegal. ☎ **21526.**

Facing the monument commemorating the Four Masters, this shop specializes in books of Irish and Donegal interest, plus Waterford crystal, Celtic watches, Masons Ironstone figures, Aynsley, and souvenir jewelry.

 Magee of Donegal Ltd, The Diamond, Donegal. ☎ **21100.**

Established in 1866, this shop is synonymous with fine Donegal hand-woven tweeds. Weaving demonstrations are given throughout the day. Products on sale include tweed jackets, overcoats, hats, ties, and batches of material.

Melody Maker Music Shop, Castle Street, Donegal. ☎ **22326.**

If you're enchanted by the traditional and folk music of Donegal, stop in here for tapes and recordings and posters.

Wards Music Shop, Castle Street, Donegal. ☎ **21313.**

If you'd like to take home a harp, bodhran, bagpipe, flute, or tin whistle, this is the shop for you. It specializes in the sale of Irish musical instruments and instructional books. The stock also includes violins, mandolins, and accordians.

William Britton & Sons, Main Street, Donegal. ☎ **21131.**

Established in 1874, this shop stocks antique jewelry, silver, crystal, and clocks, as well as sports-related sculptures, pens, and watches.

WHERE TO STAY & DINE
Moderate

Harvey's Point Country Hotel, Lough Eske, Donegal, Co. Donegal. ☎ **073/22208.**
Fax 073/22352. 20 rms (all with bath). TV TEL MINIBAR

Rates (including full breakfast): £50–£57 ($75–$85.50) single, £78–£90 ($117–$135)
double. Service charge 10%. AE, DC, MC, V. **Closed:** Mid–Nov to mid–Mar.

Situated four miles northwest of town, this modern rambling Swiss-style lodge is nestled
amid a 13-acre woodland setting on the shores of Lough Eske at the foot of the Blue
Stack Mountains. The guest rooms, most of which feature views of Lough Eske and
the hills of Donegal, have traditional furnishings, some with four-poster beds; a
hairdryer and coffee/tea-maker are standard equipment in each room. Public areas
include a restaurant specializing in French cuisine and a piano bar/lounge. Facilities,
available for extra fees, are two tennis courts, bicycle and boat hire, and trips on Harvey's
Jarvey, a Clydesdale horse wagon.

Hyland Central, The Diamond, Donegal, Co. Donegal. ☎ **073/21027** or toll free
800/528-1234 in U.S. Fax 073/22295. 74 rms (all with bath). TV TEL

Rates (including full breakfast): £40–£48 ($60–$72) single, £60–£75 ($90–$112.50)
double. Service charge 10%. AE, DC, MC, V. **Closed:** Dec 24–27.

Owned and operated by the Hyland family since 1941, this four-story hotel sits on
Donegal's main thoroughfare, while the back of the hotel has a modern extension that
overlooks Lough Eske. Guest rooms are outfitted with traditional furnishings of dark
woods and light floral and quilted fabrics; many rooms have views of the water. In-room
extras include a coffee/tea-maker and garment press. The public areas include a
dining room that overlooks Lough Eske and an old-world pub lounge. Among the
facilities are an indoor heated swimming pool, a Jacuzzi, a steam room, a sunbed,
and a gym.

 St. Ernan's House, St. Ernan's Island, Donegal, Co. Donegal. ☎ 073/21065 or
toll free **800/223-6510.** Fax 073/22098. 12 rms (all with bath). TV TEL

Rates (including full breakfast): £100–£112 ($150–$168) single or double. No service
charge. MC, V. **Closed:** Mid–Nov to Apr.

This is one of the area's most unusual lodgings—an 1826 country house that occupies an entire small island in Donegal Bay and is connected to the mainland by its
own causeway. The island, named for a 7th-century Irish monk, is planted with hawthorn and holly bushes that have been blooming for almost three centuries. The
Georgian-theme dining room, acclaimed for its cuisine, and the other public areas
have all been magnificently restored, with delicate plasterwork, high ceilings, crystal
chandeliers, gilt-framed oil paintings, heirloom silver, antiques, and open log fireplaces.
The guest rooms, all individually decorated by proprietors Brian and Carmel O'Dowd,
have traditional furnishings, with dark woods, designer fabrics, floral art, and period
pieces; most have views of the water. It's a delightful spot, almost like a kingdom unto
itself, yet less than two miles south of Donegal town.

Moderate/Inexpensive

The Abbey, The Diamond, Donegal, Co. Donegal. ☎ **073/21014** or toll free
800/4-CHOICE in the U.S. Fax 073/21014. 49 rms (all with bath). TV TEL

Rates (including full breakfast): £34–£40 ($51–$60) single, £55–£72 ($82.50–$108) double. Service charge 10%. AE, DC, MC, V.

Set right in the heart of town, with The Diamond at its front door and the River Eske at its back, this vintage three-story hotel has been updated and refurbished in recent years. The guest rooms, about half of which are located in a new wing overlooking the river, have standard furnishings and bright floral fabrics; in-room amenities include a hairdryer and garment press.

Dining/Entertainment: Choices include the Eske restaurant overlooking the back gardens; the modern bi-level Eas Dun Bar and Corabber Lounge with views of the River Eske; and an outdoor beer garden/patio with great waterside views.

WHERE TO DINE

In addition to the hotel dining rooms listed above, try these two restaurants for a snack or light meal.

Belshade Restaurant, Magee Tweed, The Diamond. ☎ **22660.**

Cuisine: IRISH/SELF-SERVICE. **Reservations:** Not necessary.
Prices: 80p–£3.50 ($1.20–$5.25). AE, DC, MC, V.
Open: Mon–Tues and Thurs–Fri 10am–5pm, Sat 10am–5:30pm.**Closed:** Nov–Mar.

Located upstairs from Magee's Tweed shop, this 60-seat restaurant conveys an aura of times past, with a huge mural of Donegal on the wall. The menu changes daily but usually includes prawn, cheese, and fruit salads, as well as sandwiches, soups, cakes, and tarts.

Errigal Restaurant, Upper Main Street, Donegal. ☎ **21428.**

Cuisine: IRISH. **Reservations:** Not necessary.
Prices: All items £1–£6.95 ($1.50–$10.43). No credit cards
Open: Breakfast Mon–Sat 9am–noon, lunch noon–3pm, dinner 5:30–11pm; Sun 3:30–11pm.

Opposite the Church of the Four Masters, this family-run restaurant is known for its fish and chips. It also serves fresh salmon and trout, chicken curry, steaks, chops, mixed grills, sandwiches, burgers, salads, and favorite traditional Irish dishes, such as chicken Maryland.

EVENING ENTERTAINMENT

If you're in Donegal during July and August, try to take in a performance of the Donegal Drama Circle at the **Donegal Town Summer Theatre,** O'Cleary Hall, Tirconnaill Street, Donegal (no phone). Performances are held on Tuesday, Wednesday, and Thursday at 9pm. Recent programs have included such plays as *Dancing at Lughnasa* and other works by Donegal-based playwrights. No reservations are necessary; admission is £4 ($6) for adults and £2 ($3) for students.

PUBS

Biddy O'Barnes, Donegal/Lifford Road (N 15), Barnesmore, Co. Donegal. ☎ **21402.**

It's worth a detour seven miles northeast of Donegal town to the Blue Stack Mountains and the scenic Barnesmore Gap to visit this pub, which has been in the same family for four generations. Stepping inside will be like entering a country cottage, with blazing turf fires, stone floors, wooden stools and benches, and old hutches full of plates and bric-a-brac. A picture of Biddy, who once owned this house, hangs over the main fireplace. On most evenings there'll be a session of spontaneous music in progress.

Charlie's Star Bar, Main Street, Donegal. ☎ **21158.**

The wins and losses of Donegal's hurling and Gaelic football teams are the topics of conversation at this bar. Sports fans gather amid a decor of teams' jerseys, pictures, and equipment. On some nights, there is spontaneous fiddle music.

The Olde Castle Bar, Castle Street, Donegal. ☎ **21062.**

There is an old-Donegal aura at this little pub, with a welcoming open fireplace and decor of etched glass, whitewashed walls, old jars, and crocks. In July and August, there is usually a cabaret on Monday from 9pm to midnight, with songs, dances, and stories. Cover charge is £2 ($3).

The Schooner Inn, Upper Main Street, Donegal. ☎ **21671.**

A nautical decor of model ships and seafaring memorabilia prevails at this pub. There is usually music on here most evenings, with traditional Irish music on Monday and Saturday, folk on Wednesday, and various singing acts on Thursday, Friday, and Sunday.

3 Donegal Bay Coast

The Donegal Bay Coast extends for 50 miles: from Bundoran, 20 miles S of Donegal town, to Glencolumbkille, 30 miles W of Donegal town.

GETTING TO & AROUND DONEGAL BAY • By Plane   Loganair operates regularly scheduled flights from Glasgow to Donegal Airport, Carrickfinn, Kincasslagh, Co. Donegal (☎ **075/48284**), about 40 miles north of Killybegs.

• By Bus   Bus Eireann (☎ **074/21309**) operates daily bus service to Killybegs and Glencolumbkille on the northern half of the bay and to Ballyshannon and Bundoran on the southern half of the bay.

• By Car   The best way to get to and around Donegal Bay is by car, following the main N 15 route on the southern half of the bay and the main N 56 route on the northern half of the bay.

ESSENTIALS • Tourist Information   Contact the **North West Tourism Office,** Aras Reddan, Temple Street, Sligo (☎ **071/61201**); the **Letterkenny Tourist Office,** Derry Road, Letterkenny (☎ **074/21173**); or **Bundoran Tourist Office,** Main Street, Bundoran, Co. Donegal (☎ **072/41350**). The first two are open year-round; the third office is open from June through August.

• Area Codes   The area codes for telephone numbers in this area include 072 and 073.

The Donegal Bay coast is comprised of two almost-equal parts: the area from Ballyshannon north to Donegal town (Southern Donegal Bay) and the area west of Donegal town stretching to Glencolumbkille (Northern Donegal Bay).

Quite simply, the coast resembles a lobster claw reaching out from Donegal town to hold the beautiful waters of the bay. Although beaches, watersports, and coastal scenery are the main drawing cards of this area, the Donegal Bay coast also holds many other attractions, ranging from bustling seaport towns to folk museums to craft centers.

Southern Donegal Bay

WHAT TO SEE & DO

To reach the southern section of Donegal Bay, take the N 15 road up the Atlantic coast, and at about 20 miles north of Sligo you'll come to **Bundoran,** the southern tip of the Donegal County and a major beach resort. A favorite with Irish and Northern Irish visitors, Bundoran takes on an almost carnival-like atmosphere in the middle of summer. In addition to its busy beaches and amusement arcades, there is an 18-hole golf course on the north side of the town overlooking Donegal Bay.

Continuing up the coast, you'll pass **Ballyshannon,** dating back to the 15th century and one of the oldest inhabited towns in Ireland; it's another favorite with beachgoers. At this point, leave the main road and head for the coastal resort of **Rossnowlagh,** one of the loveliest beaches in all of Ireland. At over two miles long and as wide as the tides allow, it's a flat sandy stretch, shielded by flower-filled hills, ideal for walking. You'll even see cars driving on the beach and horses racing. This wonderful spot is surely the best vantage point in Ireland for watching sunsets over the churning foam-rimmed waters of the Atlantic.

Overlooking the beach from a hilltop is the **Franciscan Friary,** Rossnowlagh (☎ 072/51342), which houses a small museum of local Donegal history. The complex also contains beautiful gardens and walks overlooking the sea, a tearoom with outdoor seating, and a craft shop. Open daily from 10am to 6pm. There is no admission charge, but donations are welcome.

From Rossnowlagh, return to the main road, via the **Donegal Golf Club** at Murvagh, a spectacular setting nestled on a rugged sandy peninsula of primeval dunesland and surrounded by a wall of dense woodlands. From here, the road curves inland and it's less than ten miles to Donegal town.

SPORTS & RECREATION

BEACHES   Donegal Bay's beaches are wide, sandy, clean, and flat—ideal for walking. The best are **Rossnowlagh** and **Bundoran.** At Rossnowlagh, surfing is a favorite pastime. When the surf is up, you can rent surfboards and wetsuits at £2 ($3) per hour per item; lessons are £5 ($7.50) per hour. For more information, phone **073/21053.**

GOLFING   The Donegal Bay coast is home to two outstanding 18-hole championship seaside golf courses. **Donegal Golf Club,** Murvagh, Ballintra, Co. Donegal (☎ 073/34054), is three miles north of Rossnowlagh and seven miles south of Donegal town. It's a par-73 course with greens fees of £13 ($19.50) on weekdays and £16 ($24) on weekends.

The Bundoran Golf Club, off the Sligo/Ballyshannon Road (N 15), Bundoran, Co. Donegal (☎ 072/41302), is a par-70 course designed by the great Harry Vardon. The greens fees are £12 ($18) on weekdays and £14 ($21) on weekends.

HORSEBACK RIDING   Stracomer Riding School, off the Sligo/Ballyshannon Road (N 15), Bundoran, Co. Donegal (☎ 072/41787), supplies horses for trekking on the surrounding farmlands, beaches, sand dunes, and mountain trails. An hour's ride averages £10 ($15).

SAVVY SHOPPING

Barry Britton, Off the Ballyshannon/Donegal Road, Rossnowlagh, Co. Donegal. ☎ **072/51974.**

Located in a cottage opposite the Sand House Hotel, this workshop is a source of unusual artistic crafts, such as mirrors or glass that have been hand-etched with heraldic crests or nautical, floral, and wildlife designs; wall hangings; and prints of Donegal, as well as posters and pottery with surfing and Irish music themes. Open daily June through September from 10am to 6pm; schedule varies the rest of the year.

Donegal Parian China, Bundoran Road (N 15), Ballyshannon, Co. Donegal. ☎ **072/51826.**

Established in 1985, this pottery works produces delicate wafer-thin china gift items and tableware in patterns of the shamrock, the rose, the hawthorn, and Irish flora. Free guided tours, commencing every 20 minutes, enable visitors to watch as vases, bells, spoons, thimbles, wall plaques, lamps, and eggshell coffee and tea sets are shaped, decorated, fired, and polished. They also have an audiovisual room, an art gallery, a tearoom, and a showroom/shop for on-the-spot purchases. Open October through April, Monday through Friday from 9am to 6pm; May and September, Monday through Saturday from 9am to 6pm; and June through September, Monday through Saturday from 9am to 6pm and Sunday from 1 to 6pm.

WHERE TO STAY & DINE

Moderate

Great Northern Hotel, Sligo/Donegal Road (N 15), Bundoran, Co. Donegal. ☎ **072/41204.** Fax 072/41114. 96 rms (all with bath). TV TEL

Rates (including full breakfast): £48–£53 ($72–$79.50) single, £76–£84 ($114–$126) double. No service charge. AE, MC, V. **Closed:** Jan to Apr.

Surrounded by 130 acres of parkland and sand dunes beside an 18-hole golf links, this sprawling multiwinged hotel is right on Donegal Bay. The hotel's interior has been recently refurbished with a bright modern Irish motif, and the guest rooms have also been stylishly redecorated; most rooms have views of the sea or the golf course. Facilities include a full-service restaurant, a grill room, a lounge, a heated outdoor swimming pool, and a lawn tennis court. A favorite hotel with Irish families, it's situated on the northern edge of Bundoran.

 The Sand House, off the Ballyshannon/Donegal Road (N 15), Rossnowlagh, Co. Donegal. ☎ **072/51777** or toll free **800/447-7462** or **800/223-6764** in U.S. Fax 072/52100. 39 rms (all with bath). TEL

Rates (including full breakfast): £35–£55 ($52.50–$82.50) single, £70–£90 ($105–$135) double. Service charge 10%. AE, DC, MC, V. **Closed:** Mid–Oct to Apr.

Set on a crescent of beach overlooking the Atlantic coast, this three-story pink-toned hotel is a standout among all the County Donegal lodgings. Although there are subtle suggestions of turreting on the roof, it does not pretend to be a castle. In fact, the Sand House had its early beginnings as a fishing lodge in 1886 and was used as a thatched pub by 1906; it was not until 1949 that Vincent and Mary Britton moved in and began their quest to create a top-notch hotel—and they've succeeded very well. With open log and turf fireplaces, the public rooms are decorated with antiques and local artwork, exuding a country-inn atmosphere, except for the sunlit and plant-filled

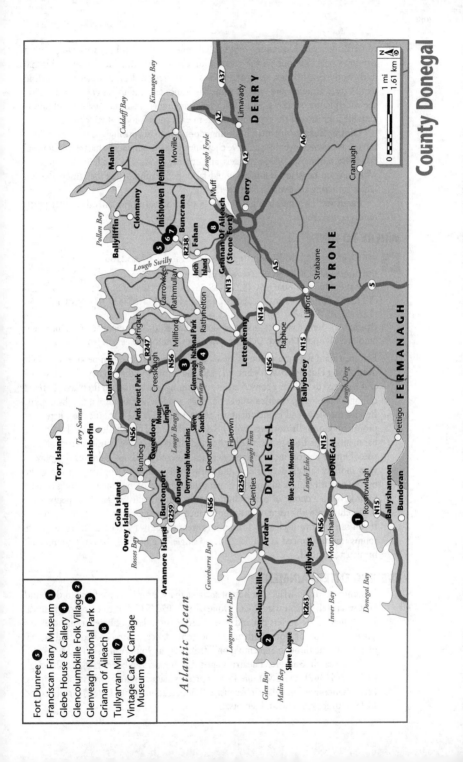

County Donegal

Fort Dunree 5
Franciscan Friary Museum 1
Glebe House & Gallery 4
Glencolumbkille Folk Village 2
Glenveagh National Park 3
Grianan of Aileach 8
Tullyarvan Mill 7
Vintage Car & Carriage Museum 6

conservatory, which is reminiscent of a contemporary ocean-liner with wraparound windows that look out on the water. Guest rooms are decorated with traditional dark-wood furnishings, designer fabrics, antiques, and period pieces including hand-carved armoires and vanities; some have canopied or four-poster beds. Of course, the wide picture windows, with their ever-changing vistas of the Atlantic and unforgettable sunsets, add the crowning touch to each room's individual tableau.

Dining/Entertainment: The dining room, which, surprisingly, does not overlook the sea, is presided over by a creative chef who specializes in locally harvested Donegal Bay lobster, oysters, scallops, mussels, and other seafoods. The resident's lounge, cozy with an open fireplace, is a relaxing old-fashioned setting, while the Surfers Bar is a larger gathering spot with a nautical decor.

Facilities: Two-mile beach for walking, swimming, surfing, and other watersports; tennis court; croquet.

WHERE TO DINE

★ **Smugglers Creek,** Rossnowlagh, Co. Donegal. ☎ 072/52366.
Cuisine: SEAFOOD/IRISH. **Reservations:** Required for dinner.
Prices: Bar food £1.50–£6.50 ($2.25–$9.75) all items; dinner appetizers £1.75–£5.50 ($2.63–$8.25); dinner main courses £7.75–£11.75 ($11.63–$17.63), lobster £18.50 ($27.75). AE, DC, MC, V.
Open: May–Sept, daily; Oct–Apr, Wed–Sun lunch 12:30–3pm, dinner 6:30–9:30pm. Bar food daily 1–6pm. **Closed:** Oct–Apr, Mon–Tues and three weeks in Jan.

For great food with grand sunset views, don't miss this little gem perched on a cliff overlooking Donegal Bay. It's housed in an 1845 stone building that has been restored and enlarged to include a conservatory-style dining area with open fireplaces, beamed ceilings, stone walls, wooden stools, porthole windows, crab traps, and lobster pots. Besides the views and homey/nautical decor, seafood is the star attraction here, and proprietor Conor Britton even pulls his own oysters and mussels from local beds. The bar menu ranges from soups, salads, and sandwiches to buttered garlic mussels or fresh pâté. Dinner entrees include Smugglers sea casserole (scallops, salmon, and prawns with mornay sauce); deep-fried squid with Provençale sauce; tiger prawns in garlic butter; pan-fried black sole on the bone; wild Irish salmon hollandaise; steaks cooked to order with a choice of parsley butter, garlic butter, whiskey sauce, or peppercorn sauce; chicken with cream of mushroom sauce; and vegetarian pasta or stir-fry dishes. If you can't tear yourself away from this romantic hideaway, there are five guesthouse rooms upstairs, priced at £30 ($45) for a single or £39 ($58.50) for a double, full breakfast included.

EVENING ENTERTAINMENT

In summer, Rossnowlagh is a hub of social activity. Many people flock to the **Sand House Hotel,** Rossnowlagh, Co. Donegal (☎ 072/51777), to enjoy the nautical atmosphere of the Surfers Bar and to see the Slice of Ireland Cabaret at the hotel. It's a two-hour show of Donegal-theme music, song, dance, poetry, comedy, and drama, presented June through September on Wednesday at 9pm. Admission is £3 ($4.50).

Nearby at the **Summer Theatre,** staged at the Franciscan Friary Hall, Rossnowlagh (☎ 072/51342), the Coolmore Players present classic dramas by Irish playwrights. Performances are Thursdays in August at 8:30pm; admission is £2 ($3) for adults and £1 ($1.50) for children and seniors.

Farther south, **Dorrian's Thatch Bar,** Main Street, Ballyshannon, Co. Donegal (☎ 072/51147), holds nightly sessions of Irish traditional music in summer.

Northern Donegal Bay

WHAT TO SEE & DO

From Donegal town follow the main road, N 56, for a very scenic (though slow) drive along the northern coast of Donegal Bay. You'll encounter narrow roads, sheer cliffs, craggy rocks, boglands, and panoramic mountain and sea views. You'll also see the thatched-roof cottages that are distinctively typical of this area—with rounded roofs, because the thatch is tied down by a network of ropes (sugans) and fastened to pins beneath the eaves, to protect it from the prevailing winds off the sea. It's only 30 miles out to Glencolumbkille, but plan on at least a couple of hours' drive, especially if you want to stop in the craft centers along the way at Kilcar or at the busy fishing port of Killybegs, where, if your timing is right, you can watch the fishing boats arriving to unload the day's catch.

Just before you come to Killybegs, the N 56 road swings inland and northward. Continue on the coastal road westward to **Glencolumbkille,** an Atlantic outpost dating back 5,000 years. It is said that St. Columba established a monastery here in the 6th century and gave his name to the glen forevermore. (*Glencolumbkille* literally means "the glen of Columba's church.")

You'll be hard-pressed to see a more beautiful landscape anywhere, and you certainly can't beat the peace and quiet. This is one spot where the sheep far outnumber the people!

While here, don't miss a visit to the **Glencolumbkille Folk Museum,** Glencolumbkille, Co. Donegal (☎ 073/30017). Built in the format of a tiny village, or *clachan,* this mini–theme park of Donegal thatched cottages is designed to reflect life in this part of the world over the years. Each house is an exact replica of a dwelling used by the local people during the last three centuries and is equipped with the furniture, artifacts, and utensils of its particular period.

✪ Founded in 1967, the Folk Village was the brainchild of the local priest, the Rev. James McDyer, who sought to create a living-history attraction in the area and thus provide jobs and turn back the tide of emigration. It was built and assembled entirely by the people of Glencolumbkille, and it is maintained by them. The complex includes a 19th-century school, plus a craft shop, a tearoom, an herb garden, and a nature walk. Museum tours are given every hour on the hour. Admission is £2.50 ($3.75) for adults and £1.75 ($2.63) for children. It's open from Easter through May on Monday through Saturday from 10am to 6pm and Sunday from noon to 6pm; June through October on Monday through Saturday from 10am to 6:30pm and Sunday from noon to 6:30pm.

To continue touring onward from Glencolumbkille, follow the signs for Ardara over a mountainous inland road. Soon you'll come to **Glengesh Pass,** a scenic but narrow roadway that rises to a height of 900 feet, then plunges in a steep descent into the valley below. It leads to **Ardara,** known for its tweed and woollen craft centers (see "Atlantic Highlands," below).

SPORTS & RECREATION

FISHING   Surrounded by waters that hold shark, skate, pollock, conger, cod, and mackerel, **Killybegs** is one of the most active sea-fishing centers on the northwest coast on a commercial and sport basis. Brian McGilloway of Killybegs (☎ **073/31144**) operates full-day fishing expeditions for visitors, on board the 34-foot *M.V. Susanne* from Blackrock Pier. Prices average £20 ($30) per person a day plus £5 ($7.50) for rods and tackle. The daily schedule and departure times vary according to demand; reservations are required.

At **Mountcharles,** a coastal town midway between Donegal town and Killybegs, deep-sea fishing trips are organized by Michael O'Boyle, Old Road (☎ **073/35257**). Outings are slated daily from 11am to 5pm and cost £15 ($22.50) per person. This company also offers guided boat trips and wildlife cruises on demand, priced from £15 ($22.50) per person with a two-hour minimum booking.

SAVVY SHOPPING

Studio Donegal, The Glebe Mill, Kilcar, Co. Donegal. ☎ **073/38194.**

Started in 1979, this hand-weaving enterprise is distinguished by its knobby tweed, subtly colored in tones of beige, oat, and ash. You can walk around both the craft shop and the mill and see the chunky-weave stoles, caps, jackets, and cloaks in-the-making. Other products fashioned of this unique tweed include tote bags, cushion covers, table mats, tapestries, and wall hangings. It's located between Killybegs and Glencolumbkille, about 20 miles west of Donegal town. Open Monday through Saturday from 10am to 6pm, with extended hours in summer.

Teresa's Cottage, Donegal/Killybegs Road (N 56), Bruckless. ☎ **073/37080.**

For more than 20 years, Teresa Gillespie and her team of local folk have been producing delicately embroidered linens and lace, crochetwork, and knitwear. If you stop at this busy shop, you not only can buy at the source but also see the craftspeople at work. Open Monday through Saturday from 10am to 6pm, with extended hours in summer.

WHERE TO STAY & DINE

Moderate

★ **Bay View Hotel,** 1–2 Main St., Killybegs, Co. Donegal. ☎ **073/31950.** Fax 073/31856. 38 rms (all with bath). TV TEL

Rates (including full breakfast): £40–£48 ($60–$72) single, £60–£76 ($90–$114) double. No service charge. MC, V.

Situated on the harbor in the middle of town, this four-story hotel was completely renovated and refurbished in 1992. Guest rooms are decorated in contemporary style with light pine furnishings, bright quilted fabrics, and brass accessories, all enhanced by wide-windowed views of the marina and fishing boats.

Dining/Entertainment: Choices include the ground-floor Bay View Brasserie for light meals all-day; the traditional first floor dining room with lovely bay views and contemporary art; and two bars, the ground-floor Fisherman's Wharf and the first-floor Upper Deck cocktail lounge.

Facilities: Indoor heated swimming pool, sauna, steam room, Jacuzzi, gym.

Moderate/Inexpensive

The Glencolumbkille Hotel, Glencolumbkille, Co. Donegal. ☎ **073/30003.** Fax 073/30003. 30 rms (all with bath). TV TEL

Rates (including full breakfast): £23–£50 ($34.50–$75) single, £30–£80 ($45–$120) double. No service charge. DC, MC, V.

If you want to get away from it all, this hotel is the most westerly outpost you can get in Donegal. Edged by Malin Bay and the Atlantic Ocean, encircled by craggy mountains that are populated mostly by meandering woolly sheep, it's a lovely spot, with warming turf fireplaces and a cottage atmosphere. There's a good dining room, with panoramic views of the countryside, and the guest rooms have standard furnishings and views of the sea or the valley. Staying here for a few days will put color in your cheeks and recharge your inner batteries.

WHERE TO DINE

★ **The Blue Haven,** Largymore, Kilcar, Co. Donegal. ☎ 073/38090.
Cuisine: IRISH. **Reservations:** Recommended for dinner.
Prices: Bar food all items £1–£5 ($1.50–$7.50); dinner appetizers £1–£4 ($1.50–$6); dinner main courses £4.50–£9.50 ($7.25–$14.25). MC, V.
Open: May–Sept, daily 11am–11pm.

Set on a broad open sweep of Donegal Bay between Killybegs and Kilcar, this modern skylit restaurant offers 180-degree views of the bay from a semicircular bank of windows. It's an ideal stop for a meal or light refreshment while touring. The bar food menu, available throughout the day, offers soups, sandwiches, and omelets with unusual fillings, such as potato and cheese. The dinner menu includes filet of rainbow trout; lemon sole bonne femme; curried beef, chicken, or pork; T-bone and sirloin steaks; beef stroganoff; cold meat buffet; and savory mushroom pancakes.

PUBS

The **Harbour Bar,** Main Street, Killybegs, Co. Donegal (☎ 073/31049), holds an Irish music night on Tuesdays during July and August.

For good conversation and atmosphere at any time, step through the half-door at the **Piper's Rest,** Kilcar, Co. Donegal (☎ 073/38205), a thatched-roof pub with original stone walls, arches, flagged floors, an open turf fire, and a unique stained-glass window depicting a piper. As its name implies, music may erupt at any time, and usually does on summer nights.

---

4 The Atlantic Highlands

The Atlantic Highlands start at Ardara 25 miles NW of Donegal Town, 10 miles N of Killybegs

GETTING TO & AROUND THE ATLANTIC HIGHLANDS • By Plane   Loganair operates regularly scheduled flights from Glasgow to Donegal Airport, Carrickfinn, Kincasslagh, Co. Donegal (☎ 075/48284), in the heart of the Atlantic coast.

• **By Bus   Bus Eireann** (☎ 074/21309) operates daily bus service to Ardara and Glenties.

• **By Car**   The best way to get to and around Donegal's Atlantic Highlands is by car, following the main N 56 route.

ESSENTIALS • Tourist Information   Contact the **North West Tourism Office,** Aras Reddan, Temple Street, Sligo (☎ 071/61201); the **Letterkenny Tourist**

Office, Derry Road, Letterkenny (☎ **074/21173**); or the **Donegal Tourist Office,** Quay Street, Donegal (☎ **073/21148**). The first two are open year-round; the third office is open from May through September.

• **Area Codes**   The area codes for telephone numbers in this region are 074 and 075.

Scenery is the keynote to the Atlantic Highlands of Donegal—vast stretches of coastal and mountain scenery, beaches and bays, rocks and ruins. It's sometimes lonely but always breathtaking. And set deep amid the coastal scenery is Mount Errigal, the highest mountain in Donegal (2,466 feet), gently sloping beside one of Ireland's greatest visitor attractions, the Glenveagh National Park, far off the beaten track.

The best place to start a tour of the Atlantic Highlands of Donegal is at Ardara, a small town on the coast about 25 miles northwest of Donegal town. From here, it's easy to weave your way up the rest of the Donegal coast. This drive can take four hours or four days, depending on your own particular time schedule and interests.

The deeper you get into this countryside, the more you'll be immersed into a section known as the Gaeltacht, or Irish-speaking area. This really should present no problems, except that most of the road signs will be only in Irish. Now, if you keep to the route of the main (N 56) road, you should have no difficulties, but if you follow little roads off to the seashore or down country paths, you may have a problem figuring out where you're going (unless you can read Irish). In many cases, the Irish word for a place bears no resemblance to the English equivalent (*An Clochan Liath* in Irish = Dungloe in English). So, our best advice is to buy a map with placenames in both languages or to stick to the main road.

WHAT TO SEE & DO

Ardara, known for its local tweed and sweater industries, is worth a stop for shoppers. North of Ardara, the route travels inland near Gweebarra Bay and passes via Dungloe to an area known as **The Rosses,** extending from Gweebarra Bridge as far north as Crolly. This stretch presents a wealth of rock-strewn land, with frequent mountains, rivers, lakes, and beaches. Here you can visit **Burtonport** (otherwise known as *Ailt an Chorrain*), one of the premier fishing ports of Ireland; it's said that more salmon and lobster are landed there than at any other port in Ireland or Britain.

North of the Rosses is an area known as the **Bloody Foreland,** between Derrybeg and Gortahork, a stretch of land that derives its name from the fact that the rock takes on a warm ruddy color when lit by the setting sun. The sunsets should not be missed.

By now, you'll be approaching the top rim of Donegal, which is dominated by a series of fingers of land or small peninsulas jutting out into the sea. Chief among these scenic areas are **Horn Head** and **Ards.** The latter contains a forest park with a wide diversity of terrain—woodlands, a salt marsh, sand dunes, seashore, freshwater lakes, and fenland.

The next spit of land to the east is **Rosguill.** The ten-mile route around this peninsula is called the Atlantic Drive. This leads you to yet another peninsula, the **Fanad,** with a 45-mile circuit between Mulroy Bay and Lough Swilly. The resort of **Rathmullan** is a favorite stopping point here.

After driving to all these scenic peninsulas, it may come as a surprise that the greatest visitor attractions of the Atlantic Highlands are not along the coast at all, but inland, a few miles off the main N 56 road near Kilmacrennan.

⭐ **Glenveagh National Park,** Church Hill, Co. Donegal. ☎ **074/37088.**

Deep in the heart of County Donegal, far off the coastal path, this 24,000-acre estate is considered by many to be Ireland's finest national park. Designed originally as the home of Lord Leitrim in the 1870s, the estate was purchased over 50 years ago by Henry McIlhenny, a distinguished Philadelphia art historian (of the Tabasco sauce family) who restored the baronial castle and planted gardens full of exotic species of flowers and shrubs.

McIlhenny subsequently gave Glenveagh to the Irish nation for use as a public park. Today this fairy-tale setting includes extensive woodlands, herds of red deer, alpine gardens, a sylvan lake, and the highest mountain in Donegal, Mount Errigal. Visitors can tour the castle and gardens and explore the parklands via a minibus or on foot. In addition, the complex includes a visitor center with a continual audiovisual show, displays on the history, flora and fauna of the area, and signposted nature trails.

Admission: Castle £1.50 ($2.25) adults, £1 ($1.50) seniors, 60p (90¢) students and children; gardens £1.50 ($2.25) adults, £1 ($1.50) seniors, 60p (90¢) students and children.

Open: Mid–Apr through May and Oct, Thurs and Sat 10am–6:30pm, Sun 10:30am–6:30pm; June–Aug, Mon–Sat 10am–6:30pm, Sun 10am–7:30pm; Sept, daily 10am–6:30pm.

⭐ **The Glebe House and Gallery,** Church Hill. ☎ **074/37071.**

Sitting in woodland gardens on the shores of Lough Gartan about four miles southwest of Glenveagh, this Regency-style house was built as a rectory in the 1820s. It was owned until recently by English artist Derek Hill, who donated the house and his own art collection to the Irish government for public use and as an enhancement to the area he loves. The house is decorated with Donegal folk art, Japanese and Islamic art, Victoriana, and William Morris papers and textiles. The adjacent stables have been converted into an art gallery housing the 300-item Hill Collection of works by Picasso, Bonnard, Kokoschka, Yeats, Annigoni, and Pasmore, as well as Hill himself. It's more than surprising to find this first-rate 20th-century art collection in this remote part of Donegal, but this is a surprising area.

Admission: £1.50 ($2.25) adults, £1 ($1.50) seniors, 60p (90¢) students and children.

Open: May–Oct Mon–Thurs and Sat 11am–6:30pm, Sun 1–6:30pm.

SPORTS & RECREATION

BEACHES   Donegal's Atlantic Highlands are dotted with secluded and sandy beaches—ideal for walking and jogging—including Carrigart, Downings, Marble Hill, and Port na Blagh.

GOLFING   One of Ireland's most challenging golf courses is the **Rosapenna Golf Club,** Atlantic Drive, Downings, Co. Donegal (☎ **074/55301**), an 18-hole championship seaside par-70 links course. In 1893 it was laid out by Tom Morris of St. Andrews. Greens fees are £12 ($18) on weekdays and £15 ($22.50) on weekends.

Other 18-hole courses in this part of Donegal are **Dunfanaghy Golf Club,** Dunfanaghy, Co. Donegal (☎ **074/36355**), a seaside par-68 course, with greens fees of £10 ($15) on weekdays and £12 ($18) on weekends; **Narin & Portnoo Golf Club,** Narin-Portnoo, Co. Donegal (☎ **075-45107**), a par-69 seaside course, with greens fees of £10 ($15) on weekdays and £12 ($18) on weekends; and **Portsalon Golf Club,**

Portsalon, Co. Donegal (☎ **074/59459**), a seaside par-69 course, with greens fees of £10 ($15).

FISHING   The rivers and lakes in this area produce good catches of salmon, sea trout, and brown trout, and the coastal waters yield flounder, pollock, and cod. Fishing expeditions are offered by charter boats, fishing boats, and trawlers. For details, contact the **Dunfanaghy Angling Association** (☎ **074/36208**), **Creeslough Angling Association** (☎ **074/38004**), or the **Downings Bay Sea Angling Club** (☎ **074/55161**).

SAVVY SHOPPING

Ardara is a hub of tweed and woollen production. Most shops are open Monday through Saturday from 9am to 5:30pm, with extended hours in summer. These shops are all on the main street of the town (N 56).

C. Bonner & Son, Ardara, Co. Donegal. ☎ **075/41303.**

This firm produces its own hand-knit and hand-loomed knitwear, including linen-cotton and colorful sheep-patterned lambswool sweaters. The shop also sells sheepskins, pottery, wildlife watercolors, wool and tweed hangings, linens, crystal, and china.

John Molloy, Ardara, Co. Donegal. ☎ **075/41243.**

In the heart of wool and weaving country, this factory shop is well stocked with handknits, homespun fashions, sports jackets, tweed scarves and rugs, and all types of caps, from kingfisher to ghillie styles. There's even a bargain bin.

Kennedy of Ardara, Ardara, Co. Donegal. ☎ **075/4116.**

Established in 1904, this family-owned knitwear company employs about 500 home workers who hand-knit or hand-loom bainin sweaters, hats, scarves, and jackets, in native Donegal patterns and colors. The shop also sells turf crafts, pottery, and dolls.

WHERE TO STAY

Moderate

Fort Royal Hotel, Rathmullan, Co. Donegal. ☎ **074/58100** or toll free **800/447-7462** in U.S. Fax 074/58103. 15 rms (all with bath). TV TEL

Rates (including full breakfast): £50–£65 ($75–$97.50) single, £70–£100 ($105–$150) double. No service charge. AE, DC, MC, V. **Closed:** Oct–Mar.

Built in 1819, this three-story rambling country house has been a hotel since 1948, owned by the Fletcher family. It is situated on 18 acres of gardens and woodlands with a small sandy beach, overlooking the water on the western shore of Lough Swilly, one mile north of the village. Both the public areas and the guest rooms are decorated with traditional furnishings, period pieces, and oil painting scenes of Donegal. The facilities include a restaurant, lounge, tennis court, squash court, and par-3 golf course.

★ **Rathmullan House,** Rathmullan, Co. Donegal. ☎ **074/58188** or toll free **800/223-6510** or **800/44-UTELL** from U.S. Fax 074/58200. 23 rms (21 with bath). TEL

Rates (including full breakfast): £30–£75 ($45–$112.50) single, £60–£110 ($90–$165) double. Service charge 10%. AE, DC, MC, V. **Closed:** Nov to mid–Mar.

Located on the western shores of Lough Swilly about a half-mile north of town, this secluded country mansion is surrounded by colorful rose gardens and mature trees.

The mostly Georgian interior features intricate ceilings, crystal chandeliers, oil paintings, white marble log-burning fireplaces, and an assortment of antiques and heirlooms collected over the years by owners Bob and Robin Wheeler. The guest rooms vary in size and style of furnishings, but most have a comfortable Irish motif and overlook the lake and gardens.

Dining/Entertainment: The restaurant, housed in a glass-enclosed pavilion crowned by a flowing silk Arabian-tent design, specializes in seafood. Light snacks and refreshment can be found in an atmospheric cellar bar.

Facilities: Indoor saltwater swimming pool, sauna, steam room, drawing room, well-stocked library, private beach, equipment for boating and sea-trout fishing.

Rosapenna Golf Hotel, Atlantic Drive, Downings, Co. Donegal. ☎ **074/55301** or toll free **800/528-1234** from U.S. Fax 074/55128. 43 rms (all with bath). TV TEL

Rates (including full breakfast): £42–£48 ($63–$72) single, £72–£84 ($108–$126) double. Service charge 12.5%. AE, DC, MC, V. **Closed:** Nov to late Mar.

Surrounded by Sheephaven Bay and the hills of Donegal, this contemporary two-story hotel is a favorite with golfers, who flock here to enjoy the hotel's 18-hole seaside course. Nongolfers come just for the scenery and seclusion, as well as the hotel's proximity to northern Donegal attractions. Other amenities include two all-weather tennis courts and wind-surfing. The bedrooms, dining area, and lounges are modern, with an emphasis on panoramic views of land and sea.

Inexpensive

Ostan Na Rosann/Hotel of the Rosses, Dungloe, Co. Donegal ☎ **075/21088.** Fax 075/21365. 48 rms (all with bath). TV TEL

Rates (including full breakfast): £30–£35 ($45–$52.50) single, £40–£50 ($60–$75) double. Service charge 10%. AE, DC, MC, V. **Closed:** Jan–Mar.

On a hill overlooking the waters of the Atlantic, this modern ranch-style hotel sits in the heart of the Rosses, a scenic Gaelic-speaking area. The guest rooms have standard furnishings with light floral fabrics and wide-windowed views of the sea. A popular hotel with Irish families, it offers a dining room, a lounge, nightclub with disco dancing, an indoor heated swimming pool, a Jacuzzi, a steam room, a sauna, and a gym.

WHERE TO DINE

Moderate

★ **Water's Edge,** The Ballyboe, Rathmullan, Co. Donegal. ☎ **074/58182.**
Cuisine: IRISH/INTERNATIONAL. **Reservations:** Recommended for dinner.
Prices: Bar menu, all items, £1.20–£5.25 ($1.80–$7.88); appetizers £1.75–£5.50 ($2.63–$8.25); main courses £5.50–£12.50 ($8.25–$18.75). MC, V.
Open: Easter–Sept, daily lunch noon–3pm, dinner 6–9:30pm; Oct–Apr, Tues–Sat lunch noon–3pm, dinner 6–9pm.

As its name implies, this restaurant is situated right on the edge of picturesque Lough Swilly, on the south end of town. Although the glassy facade on three sides gives the 70-seat dining area a modern look, the interior is actually quite traditional, with beamed ceilings, an open fireplace, nautical bric-a-brac, and watercolors of Donegal landscapes. The menu blends Irish dishes with such international favorites as wild salmon in brandy-bisque sauce, fresh scallops in wine-cheese sauce, chicken Kiev, roast Ramelton turkey with ham and stuffing, prawns Provençale, and steaks. Bar food; served all day, ranges from soups and sandwiches to pâtés, scampi, and fish and chips.

Inexpensive

Lobster Pot, Ardara, Co. Donegal. ☎ 075/41463.

Cuisine: IRISH/SEAFOOD. **Reservations:** Not necessary.
Prices: Appetizers £1.10–£3.30 ($1.65–$4.95); main courses £2.50–£9 ($3.75–$13.50). MC, V.
Open: Daily 11am–10pm.

In the heart of town, this local eatery is known for its fish and chips, lobster and chips, and sausage and chips, cooked the traditional way. The menu also offers soups, seafood chowders, burgers, mixed grills, and such dishes as smoked salmon or salmon-and-prawn salad, chicken Kiev, and steaks.

EVENING ENTERTAINMENT

Almost all the pubs in this Irish-speaking area provide spontaneous sessions of Irish traditional music in summer. Two places known for music are the **Lakeside Centre,** Dunlewey (☎ 075/31699), and **Leo's Tavern,** Meenaleck, Crolly (☎ 075/48143). The highly successful Irish group Clannad got their start at Leo's, as did the Irish folk singer Enya.

---

5 Inishowen Peninsula

Buncrana, the Inishowen's chief town, is 70 miles NE of Donegal Airport, 52 miles NE of Donegal Town, 12 miles NW of Derry, 90 miles NE of Sligo, 223 miles NE of Shannon, 161 miles NW of Dublin.

GETTING TO & AROUND THE INISHOWEN PENINSULA The **Lough Swilly Bus Company** (☎ 074/22853) operates a regular service from Buncrana to Cardonagh and Moville, with connections to other points.

The best way to get to and around the Inishowen Peninsula is by car, following the signposted 100-mile Inishowen 100 route.

ESSENTIALS • Tourist Information Contact the **North West Tourism Office,** Aras Reddan, Temple Street, Sligo (☎ 071/61201); the **Letterkenny Tourist Office,** Derry Road, Letterkenny (☎ 074/21173); or the **Inishowen Tourism Office,** Chapel Street, Cardonagh, Co. Donegal (☎ 077/74933). The first two are open year-round; the third office is open from May through September.

• Area Codes The area codes for telephone numbers in this region are 074 and 077.

Bounded by Lough Swilly on the left and Lough Foyle on the right, Inishowen is a triangular peninsula stretching from Bridgend to Ireland's most northerly point, Malin Head on the Atlantic Ocean.

The Inishowen gets its name from Eoghain, a son of King Niall of the Nine Hostages, who lived at the time of St. Patrick in the 5th century (*Inis Eoghain* means "the island of Owen"). The king named this amazing finger of land for his son.

The drive around the Inishowen is a panoramic ring of seascapes, mountains, valleys, and woodlands. Just as it has been said that Donegal is a miniature Ireland, so it is claimed by Donegal folk that Inishowen is a miniature Donegal.

WHAT TO SEE & DO

In spite of its remote location, the Inishowen Peninsula circuit is one the best-marked roads in Ireland, with all directionals clearly printed in English and Irish, as well as in miles and kilometers. Among the many features of this 100-mile route is a string of beach resorts like Ballyliffin, Buncrana, Greencastle, and Moville.

The natural wonders range from the **Gap of Mamore,** five miles north of Buncrana, a pass rising to 800 feet and then slowly descending on a corkscrew path to sea level, and **Slieve Snacht,** a 2,019-foot mountain.

The peninsula's most impressive historic monument is the hilltop fort known as ✪ **Grianan of Aileach,** ten miles south of Buncrana. One of Ireland's best examples of a ring fort, it was built as a temple of the sun around 1700 B.C. From the mid-5th century to the early 12th it was the royal residence of the O'Neills, the kings of this area.

After you've toured the Inishowen, or perhaps stayed a few days, head back south, driving through Letterkenny, the largest town in the county (population 5,000), on a hillside overlooking the River Swilly.

At Letterkenny you can link up with N 56, the main road and drive to the junction of the twin towns, Ballybofey and Stranorlar, changing here to N 15. This will take you to yet another scenic Donegal drive, the **Barnesmore Gap,** a vast open stretch through the Blue Stack Mountains, which, in turn, will lead you into Donegal town and points south.

Fort Dunree, Buncrana, Co. Donegal. ☎ **077/61817.**

Perched on a cliff overlooking Lough Swilly, this is a military/naval museum incorporating a Napoleonic martello tower at the site of World War I defenses on the north Irish coast. It features a wide range of exhibitions, an audiovisual center, and a cafeteria housed in a restored forge. Even if you have no interest in military history, it's worth a trip here for the view. Dunree has one of the best vantage points in Donegal, or in all of Ireland, for picture-taking or for just enjoying unencumbered seascapes and broad mountain vistas.

Admission: £1.50 ($2.25) adults, 75p ($1.08) seniors and children.

Open: June–Sept Tues–Sat 10am–6pm, Sun 12:30–6pm.

Tullyarvan Mill, off Main Street, Buncrana, Co. Donegal. ☎ **077/61613.**

Housed in an old mill on the northern edge of town, this is the cultural and exhibition center of the Inishowen Peninsula. The building includes a textile museum and other interpretative displays on the crafts and the wildlife of the region. On summer evenings, a program of traditional music and dancing is presented. The premises house a craft shop with items made in the area and a coffee shop.

Admission: Museum £1.50 ($2.25) adults, 75p ($1.08) students, seniors, and children over age 6; music evenings £3 ($4.50).

Open: Easter–Sept Mon–Sat 10am–6pm, Sun 2–6pm; music, Thurs evenings in Aug at 9pm.

Vintage Car & Carriage Museum, Buncrana, Co. Donegal. ☎ **077/61130.**

Transportation of yesteryear is the theme of this museum, which houses a large collection of classic cars, horsedrawn carriages, Victorian bicycles, and vintage motorcycles, as well as model-car and railway exhibits.

Admission: £1.50 adults ($2.25), 50p (75¢) children.

Open: May–Sept daily 10am–8pm; Oct–Apr Sun noon–5pm.

SPORTS & RECREATION

BEACHES   Ballyliffin, Buncrana, Greencastle, and Moville have safe and sandy beaches that are ideal for swimming or walking.

GOLFING   Donegal's northern coast is believed to be one of the first places where golf was ever played in Ireland, and it has been played on the Inishowen for more than 100 years. The Inishowen has three 18-hole golf courses. The **Ballyliffin Golf Club,** Ballyliffin, Co. Donegal (☎ 077/76119), the most northerly golf course in Ireland, is a par-71 links course, with greens fees of £8 ($12) on weekdays and £12 ($18) on weekends.

The **North West Golf Club,** Fahan, Buncrana, Co. Donegal (☎ 077/61027), founded in 1890, is a par-69 seaside course with greens fees of £10 ($15) on weekdays and £15 ($22.50) on weekends; and **Greencastle Golf Course,** Greencastle, Co. Donegal (☎ 077/81013), is a par-69 parkland course with greens fees of £9 ($13.50) on weekdays and £13 ($19.50) on weekends.

WATERSPORTS   The Inishowen's long coastline, sandy beaches, and combination of open ocean and sheltered coves offer great opportunities for watersports. One company that specializes in renting equipment for waterskiing and other sports is **Rent-a-Jet Watersports,** Quayside, Moville, Co. Donegal (☎ 077/82052). Rates for waterskiing or knee-boarding are £7.50 ($11.25) per 15 minutes; banana boat rides are £4 ($6) per person per 10 minutes. It's open Easter to September, Wednesday from 6 to 9pm, Saturday and Sunday from 2 to 9pm.

WHERE TO STAY

Moderate

Mount Errigal, Derry Road, Ballyraine, Letterkenny, Co. Donegal. ☎ 074/22700. Fax 077/25085. 82 rms (all with bath). TV TEL

Rates (including full breakfast): £42–£50 ($63–$75) single, £60–£80 ($90–$120) double. No service charge. AE, DC, MC, V.

Located south of Lough Swilly and less than a mile east of town, this contemporary two-story hotel is a handy place to stay midway between the Inishowen Peninsula and Donegal town, within 20 miles of Glenveagh National Park. Although the exterior has a rather ordinary gray facade, inside is bright and airy, with skylights, light woods, hanging plants, colored and etched glass, and brass fixtures. The bedrooms are outfitted in contemporary style, with cheerful colors and modern art, as well as good reading lights over the beds, hairdryers, garment presses, and tea-makers.

Dining/Entertainment: Choices include the full-service Glengesh Restaurant and the Buffet Counter coffee shop. The old-world lounge, Blue Stack Bar, offers piano music Monday through Thursday and live bands on the weekends.

Facilities: Indoor heated swimming pool, sauna, steam room, gym.

Redcastle Hotel, Redcastle, Moville, Co. Donegal. ☎ 077/82073. Fax 077/82214. 31 rms (all with bath). TV TEL

Rates (including full breakfast): £35–£50 ($52.50–$75) single, £50–£70 ($75–$105) double. No service charge. AE, DC, MC, V.

Set on the shores of Lough Foyle on the Inishowen's eastern coast, this country inn–style hotel offers a combination of old-world charms and modern comforts. The guest rooms are furnished with designer fabrics, and each has a view of the lake or the adjacent golf course. In-room hairdryers and coffee/tea-makers are also supplied. The public areas include the Art Gallery Restaurant, offering views and contemporary art; a coffee shop; and a lounge.

Facilities: Nine-hole golf course, two swimming pools, Jacuzzi, sauna, steam room, gym, tennis court.

INEXPENSIVE

Hotel Clanree, Derry Road, Ballaghderg, Letterkenny, Co. Donegal. ☎ **074/24369.** Fax 074/25389. 21 rms (all with bath). TV TEL

Rates (including full breakfast): £40–£50 ($60–$75) single or double. No service charge. AE, MC, V.

Opened in 1992, this contemporary red-brick two-story hotel sits on the main road near the tourist office at the eastern edge of town. It's a good central location midway between the Inishowen Peninsula and Donegal town, within twenty miles of Glenveagh National Park. The public rooms have been designed in Irish traditional style, with dark woods and rich colors, while the guest rooms have standard furnishings with scenes of Donegal and multitoned fabrics. In-room amenities include a hospitality tray, hairdryer, and garment press. Dining facilities include the Aileach Room Restaurant and Tara Lounge Bar.

 The Strand, Ballyliffin, Clonmany, Co. Donegal. ☎ **077/76107.** Fax 077/76486. 12 rms (all with bath). TV TEL

Rates (including full breakfast): £25–£30 ($37.50–$45) single, £38–£45 ($57–$67.50) double. No service charge. MC, V. **Closed:** Dec.

Set on a hillside overlooking Pollan Strand, with views of nearby Malin Head, this small family-run hotel is located on the edge of town, set apart amid its own palm tree–lined rose gardens. The decor is modern Irish, with wide windows and traditional touches. Guest rooms have standard furnishings with such extras as coffee/tea-makers and hairdryers. Amenities include a good restaurant and a lounge bar known for its local entertainment.

WHERE TO DINE

Expensive/Moderate

Restaurant St. Johns, Fahan, Co. Donegal. ☎ **077/60289.**

Cuisine: IRISH. **Reservations:** Required.
Prices: Set dinner £20–£24 ($30–$36). AE, DC, MC, V.
Open: Tues–Sat 6–10pm.

Set on its own grounds overlooking Lough Swilly, this lovely Georgian house has two dining rooms, each with a cozy elegance. Open turf fireplaces, Waterford crystal, embroidered linens, and richly textured wallpaper add to the ambience. Best of all, the food is dependably good—baked Swilly salmon with lemon sauce; roast duck with port-and-orange sauce; spiced lamb en croûte with gooseberry-and-mint sauce; sesame-crumbed filet of beef with béarnaise sauce; and John Dory with fennel.

MODERATE

 Carolina House Restaurant, Ramelton Road, Loughnagin, Letterkenny, Co. Donegal. ☎ **074/22480.**

Cuisine: IRISH/FRENCH. **Reservations:** Required on weekends.
Prices: Appetizers £1.95–£4.50 ($2.93–$7.25); main courses £8.95–£11.95 ($13.43–$17.93). AE, DC, MC, V.
Open: Tues–Sat 7–9:30pm.

On high ground overlooking Lough Swilly on the northern edge of town, this lovely restaurant stands out on the roadside, with colorful gardens and a snowy white cottage-style facade and red-tile roof. The interior is just as charming—with open turf fireplaces, turn-of-the-century furnishings, and framed local artwork. The menu changes nightly, with proprietors Mary and Charles Prendergast relying on what is fresh from their garden as well as from local markets and seaports. Specialties of the house include a traditional loin of bacon with a fresh herb crust on a caramelized Irish whiskey sauce, as well as such contemporary dishes as escalope of wild Donegal salmon with sorrel sauce; pan-fried John Dory with nutmeg sauce; confit of duck with jasmine sauce and raisins; filet of beef with a peppered crust on Madeira sauce; and chicken ballotine with a tomato-and-basil sauce.

INEXPENSIVE

Kealy's Seafood Bar, Greencastle, Co. Donegal. ☎ 077/81010.

Cuisine: SEAFOOD. **Reservations:** Not necessary.
Prices: Bar food all items 95p–£4.95 ($1.43–$7.43). MC, V.
Open: Tues–Sun bar food 12:30–5pm.

For a light meal or snack overlooking Lough Foyle and fishing boats belonging to the Foyle Fishermen's Co-op, try this little harborfront eatery. Menu items range from Greencastle seafood chowder, local oysters, and smoked-salmon salad to deep-fried plaice, southern-fried chicken, sandwiches, lasagne, and burgers.

The North

17

THE NORTH—OTHERWISE KNOWN AS NORTHERN IRELAND, ULSTER, OR THE SIX Counties—occupies the northeast corner of the Emerald Isle. Politically separate from the Republic of Ireland, the North is a part of Britain, governed from London. The people of the North have their own distinctive way with words and speech, sometimes more akin to Scotland than Ireland. Farms in the North are bigger and better equipped than in the Republic, and they're separated by neat wooden fences, not the piles of stones that often divide the small farm holdings in Ireland. Roads are better surfaced and wider in the North, and every house, place of business, or attraction has a precise address with a street and number—whether it be located in a city or far out in the countryside.

The cities and towns of Northern Ireland rely economically on industry, while the Republic depends on tourism. Although the North attracts 60,000 people annually from North America, that's a mere handful compared to the nearly half a million North Americans who vacation in the Republic.

Nature has bestowed upon Northern Ireland such wonders as the Giant's Causeway, the Glens of Antrim, the Mountains of Mourne, and Lough Neagh. Man in the North has crafted collectible marvels like Belleek china and Tyrone crystal and distilled whiskey at Old Bushmills Distillery.

In the past 26 years, many people were afraid to visit the North because of the political violence that often flared up. The tenseness in the province has been eased, however, by the good news of cease-fire declarations in 1994.

Shoppers are returning to the downtown area of Belfast; night life in the city is returning to normal. American hotel companies such as Radisson and Hilton have announced plans to build hotels in or near Belfast. Members of the RUC (Royal Ulster Constabulary) are writing parking tickets instead of patrolling with their rifles. British soldiers who once wore helmets have replaced them with berets.

At the time of this writing, the whole atmosphere in the North is changing for the better. It's hoped that more good news will come from the area as you read these pages. And this is indeed a blessing; the people of the North are longing for peace. For the traveler to get a complete picture of Ireland, a visit to the North should not be missed.

GETTING TO THE NORTH • **By Air**   From New York, American Transair operates scheduled service into Belfast International Airport (☎ **0894/22888**). Flights from Britain land at Belfast City Airport (☎ **0232/457745**) and Eglinton Airport, Derry (☎ **0504/810784**).

• **By Ferry**   The quickest crossing from Britain to Northern Ireland is the 90-minute SeaCat (☎ **0232/312002**), a catamaran service from Stranraer, Scotland. Other ferry services into Belfast include **Norse Irish Ferries** (☎ **0232/779090**) from Liverpool; and **Isle of Man Steam Packet Co.** (☎ **0232/351009**) from the Isle of Man. In

---

Telephone Number Advisory

As of this writing, telephone numbers in the United Kingdom are scheduled to change on April 16, 1995. On this date, the digit 1 will be added to the beginning of all area codes for the six counties that compose Northern Ireland. For example, Belfast's current area code of 232 will be changed to 1232. This change does not affect any of the area codes in the 26 counties of the Irish Republic.

addition, there is **Stena Sealink** (☎ 0574/273616) from Stranraer, Scotland, to Larne; and **P & O European Ferries** (☎ 0574/274321) from Cairnyan, Scotland, to Larne.

• **By Train**   Trains from the Irish Rail and Northern Ireland Railways systems travel from Dublin daily into Northern Ireland, arriving at Belfast Central Station, East Bridge Street (☎ 0232/230310). The boat train service from Stranraer, Scotland, terminates at Yorkgate Station, York Street, Belfast (☎ 0232/235282).

• **By Bus**   Ulsterbus operates buses between Belfast and all parts of Northern Ireland and the Republic. For schedules and prices, phone the Ulsterbus Enquiries Hotline (☎ 0232/333000).

• **By Car**   Northern Ireland is directly accessible from the Republic of Ireland via many main roads and secondary roads. At some points, there are border crossing checkpoints. Main roads leading to Northern Ireland from the Republic include N 1 from Dublin, N 16 from Sligo, N 15 from Donegal, and N 3 from Cavan.

GETTING AROUND THE NORTH • **By Bus   Ulsterbus** (☎ 0232/333000) runs daily scheduled services from Belfast to major cities and towns throughout Northern Ireland. From the **Europa Bus Centre,** Glengall Street, Belfast (☎ 0232/320011), there are buses leaving for destinations in Counties Armagh, Tyrone, Derry (west), Fermanagh, and Down (west); and from the **Oxford Street Bus Station,** Oxford Street, Belfast (☎ 0232/232356), for destinations in Counties Antrim, Down (east), Derry (east) and Cookstown.

To save money, ask about the Freedom of Northern Ireland bus passes, valid for unlimited travel on all Ulsterbus and Citibus services operating within Northern Ireland. A one-day pass costs £9 ($13.77) and a 7-day pass costs £28 ($42.84). Tickets can be bought at all Ulsterbus depots, but not from bus drivers.

• **By Sightseeing Tour**   From June through August, **Ulsterbus** (☎ 0232/333000) operates a wide variety of full-day and half-day coach tours from the Europa Bus Centre, Glengall Street, Belfast, to places such as the Glens of Antrim, Causeway Coast, Fermanagh Lakelands, Sperrin Mountains, the Mountains of Mourne, and Armagh. There are also tours designed to take you to specific attractions such as the Giant's Causeway, Old Bushmills Distillery in Bushmills, Navan Centre in Armagh, Ulster-American Folk Park in Omagh, and Tyrone Crystal Factory in Dungannon. Tour prices range from £3.50 to £7 ($5.36 to $10.71) for a half-day tour and £6 to £12 ($9.18 to $18.36) for full-day trips.

During July and August, **Ulsterbus** (☎ 0232/333000) also operates a daily open-top bus service from Coleraine to the Giant's Causeway and back. The journey lasts 50 minutes and may be broken at Portstewart, Portrush, Portballintrae, or Bushmills. Price is £2.60 ($3.98) round-trip or £1.90 ($2.92) one-way. For schedule, call **0265/43334.**

• **By Rail**   Northern Ireland Railways, 28 Wellington Place, Belfast (☎ 0232/230310) operates trains throughout Northern Ireland, from two stations in Belfast— Central Station, East Bridge Street (☎ 0232/230310) for all destinations except Larne; and Yorkgate Station, York Street, Belfast (☎ 0232/235282) for the Larne boat train.

IMPRESSIONS

Ulster: where every hill has its hero and every bog its bones.
—Sam Hanna Bell (b. 1909), "In Praise of Ulster"

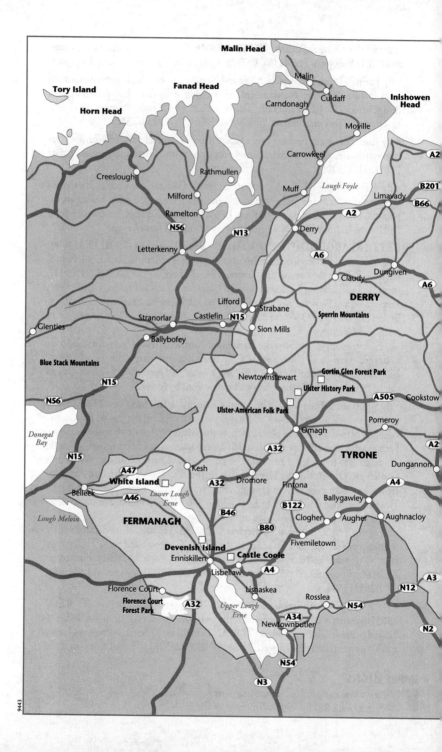

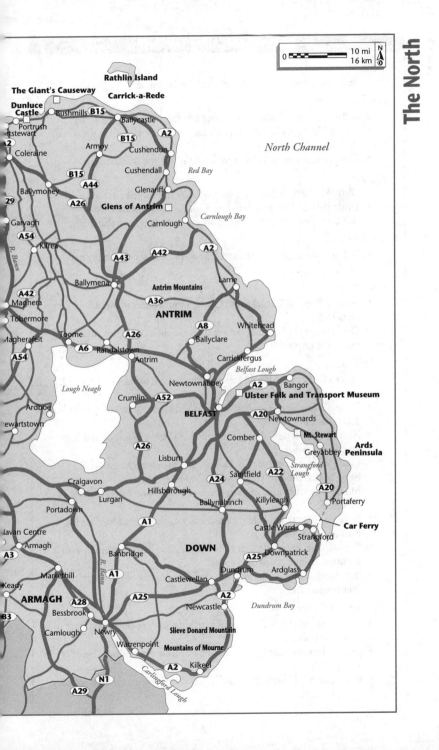

What's Special About the North

Beaches
- Ballycastle, Portrush, Portstewart, and Portballintrae.

Buildings
- Belfast City Hall, 1906, which dominates the main shopping area.
- Crown Liquor Saloon, Belfast, a classic Victorian-style pub in the care of the National Trust.
- Carrickfergus Castle, 1180, considered the first real Irish castle.

Museums
- Ulster Museum, Belfast, summarizes 9,000 years of Irish history.
- Ulster Folk & Transport Museum, Cultra, 60 acres of homes and buildings preserved from earlier days and moved intact to this site.

Parks/Gardens
- Belfast Botanic Gardens & Palm House, 1829, containing many rare tropical plants.

For the Kids
- "Knight Ride," at Carrickfergus Castle, a reenactment of history via monorail.
- Dunluce Centre, Portrush, with multimedia show, thrill ride, and interactive displays.

Ace Attractions
- Giant's Causeway, a World Heritage Site and 8th wonder of the world, a rocky landscape formed millions of years ago.
- Bushmills Distillery, Co. Antrim, the world's oldest, licensed in 1608 but dating back to 1276.
- Navan Fort, Armagh, the earliest capital of Ulster and seat of Irish kings for over 700 years.
- Castle Ward, Strangford, Co. Down, an 18th-century house—half-Classical and half-Gothic—on a 700-acre estate.
- Mount Stewart House, an 18th century house known for its great art collection.
- Florence Court, Enniskillen, 18th-century manor house famed for its Rococo plaster work.
- Castle Coole, Enniskillen, an 18th-century neo-Classical mansion with furniture dating back to the 1830s.
- Irish Linen Centre, Lisburn, traces the history of one of Northern Ireland's prime industries.

Irish/American Connections
- Ulster-American Folk Park, Omagh, tells the story of emigration from Ulster to America.
- Andrew Jackson Centre, Boneybefore, Carrickfergus, ancestral home of 7th U.S. president.
- Grant Ancestral Home, Ballygawley, Co. Tyrone, ancestral home of 18th U.S. president.

- Wilson Ancestral Home, Strabane, Co. Tyrone, ancestral home of 28th U.S. president.

Natural Spectacles

- Lough Neagh, the largest lake in the British Isles.
- Mountains of Mourne, 12 peaks in County Down including Slieve Donard, the highest mountain in Northern Ireland.
- Glens of Antrim, nine green valleys on Antrim coast.
- Marble Arch Caves, Enniskillen, among the finest caves in Europe for exploring the underground.

Shopping

- Tyrone Crystal, Dungannon, the North's own famous hand-cut crystal enterprise.
- Belleek Pottery, Co. Fermanagh, emblematic of fine Irish craftsmanship since 1857.

Zoos

- Belfast Zoo, set in a mountain park overlooking the city.

Great Towns/Villages

- Derry, one of Europe's finest walled cities.
- Armagh, the ecclesiastical capital of Ireland, with two cathedrals, and seat of both the Catholic and Anglican primates.
- Cushendun, Co. Antrim, a National Trust village with Cornish-style cottages.

If you are going to be spending a week in the North, ask about the Rail Runabout, a reduced-rate ticket, valid for seven days of unlimited travel on all scheduled rail services; the cost is £25 ($38.25).

• **By Car**   The best way to travel around the Northern Ireland countryside is by car. The roads are in extremely good condition and are very well signposted. Distances between major cities and towns are short. If you wish to rent a car—Avis, Budget, Dollar, Europacar, and Hertz all have depots in Belfast city and at least one of the Belfast airports. Alternatively, if you rent a car in the Republic, you can drive it in the North, with the proper insurance.

1 Belfast

Belfast is 103 miles N of Dublin, 211 miles NE of Shannon, 125 miles E of Sligo, 262 miles NE of Cork

GETTING AROUND • **By Bus**   Citybus, Donegall Square West, Belfast (☎ **0232/ 246495**), provides local bus services within the city. Departures are from Donegall Square East, West, and North, plus Upper Queen Street, Wellington Place, Chichester Street, and Castle Street. There is an information kiosk on Donegall Square West for guidance on where to get a bus to a certain locale.

• **By Car**   If you have brought a car into Belfast, it is best to leave it parked at your hotel and take local transport or walk around the city. If you must drive and want to park your car downtown, look for a blue "P" sign that shows a carpark or a parking area. In Belfast there are a number of control zones, indicated by a pink and yellow sign, where no parking is permitted. In general, on-street parking is limited to an area behind City Hall (south side), St. Anne's Cathedral (north side), and around Queen's University and Ulster Museum.

• **By Taxi**   Taxis are available at all main rail stations, ports, and airports. Most metered taxis are the London-type black cabs with a yellow disc on the window.

• **By Sightseeing Tour**   For an overview of the city, **Citybus Tours** (☎ **0232/ 246485**), offers a three-hour Belfast City Tour, departing daily at 2pm from late June to September on Tuesday, Wednesdays, and Thursdays. It is priced at £4.50 ($6.89) for adults, £3.50 ($5.36) for seniors, and £2.50 ($3.83) for children. In addition, there is an **evening tour** spotlighting Belfast's landmark buildings, with a commentary by a member of Belfast's Civic Trust; departures are on Wednesdays at 7pm from the end of June to September. Reservations are required for the latter tour. All tours depart from Castle Place, two blocks north of Donegall Square. Tickets can be purchased in advance from the Citybus Ticket Kiosk on Donegall Square West.

• **On Foot**   Belfast is a good city for walking. To guide visitors on the best and safest areas for a stroll, the Belfast City Council has produced five different self-guided walking tour leaflets: City center southward to Shaftesbury Square; city center northward to the *Irish News* office; Shaftesbury Square southward to the university area; city center northeast to the port area; and Donegall Square south to Donegall Pass. Each walk is about a mile in length and an hour in duration. Ask for a copy of the walk(s) that interest you at the Northern Ireland Tourist Office.

ESSENTIALS • Tourist Information   Brochures, maps, and other data about Belfast and all of the North are available from the **Northern Ireland Tourist Board,** St. Anne's Court, 59 North St., Belfast BT1 1NB (☎ **0232/246609**). It is open September through June, Monday through Saturday, from 9am to 5:15pm; July and August, Monday through Friday, 9am to 7:30pm, Saturday 9am to 5:15pm, and Sunday noon to 4pm. In addition, there is a tourist information desk at **Belfast City Airport** (☎ **0232/457745**), open year-round daily from 5:30am to 1pm; and at **Belfast International Airport** (☎ **08494/22888**), open March through October daily 24 hours and November through February daily from 7am to 11pm.

• **Area Code**   The telephone area code for Belfast numbers is 0232, unless otherwise indicated.

TOWN LAYOUT   The core of downtown Belfast sits beside the west bank of the River Lagan. The city revolves around a central point, Donegall Square, which holds the City Hall; all roads radiate out from Donegall Square. Donegall Place, which extends northward from the square, leads to Royal Avenue, a prime shopping district. Bedford Street, which extends southward from the square, becomes Dublin Road which, in turn, leads to the Queen's University area.

Nestled beside the River Lagan and Belfast Lough and ringed by gentle hills, Belfast has a lovely setting, often called a Hibernian Rio. Nearly half a million people, a third of Northern Ireland's population, reside in the Belfast city limits.

With its large port, Belfast is a very industrialized city, often referred to as the engine room that drove the whirring wheels of the industrial revolution in Ulster. Major

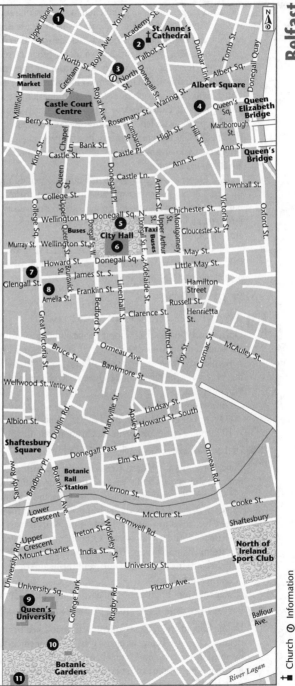

Belfast

Albert Memorial ④
Belfast Zoo ①
Botanic Gardens ⑩
City Hall ⑥
The Crown Liquor Saloon ⑧
The Grand Opera House ⑦
Linen Hall Library ⑤
Northern Ireland Tourist Office ③
Queen's University ⑨
St. Anne's Cathedral ②
Ulster Museum ⑪

✝▪ Church ⊘ Information

IRELAND

Belfast ◉

industries range from linen production to rope-making and shipbuilding. The *Titanic* was built in Belfast port, and today the world's largest dry dock is here.

The city's architecture is rich in Victorian and Edwardian buildings with elaborate sculptures over the doors and windows. Stone-carved heads of gods and poets, scientists, kings, and queens, peer down from the high ledges of banks and old linen warehouses. Some of Belfast's grandest buildings are the banks of Waring Street—the Ulster Bank, dating back to 1860, has an interior like a Venetian palace, and the Northern Bank, dating back to 1769, was originally a market house.

One person who left her mark on Belfast was Queen Victoria, who came to the city in 1849. She must have made quite a favorable impression because dozens of streets, a hospital, park, manmade island, the harbor's deepwater channel, and the university are all named after her.

The Queen's University, with its Tudor cloister, dominates the southern sector of the city. The original edifice was built in 1849 by Charles Lanyon, who designed more buildings in Belfast than anyone else. Today the university serves 12,000 students and is the setting for the annual Belfast Festival at Queen's, one of the city's major annual arts events.

Northwest of downtown is Cave Hill, at 1,182 ft. above sea level, the home of the Belfast Castle estate. This 200-acre estate is a public park, ideal for walking, jogging, picnicking, and fine overviews of the city.

WHAT TO SEE & DO

★ **City Hall**, Donegall Square. ☎ **320202**, ext. 2227.

Opened in 1906, this magnificent public building is the core of Belfast, around which the whole city radiates. It was built of Portland stone after Belfast was granted the status of a city by Queen Victoria in 1888. Similar to an American state capitol building, except for the big statue of Queen Victoria at the front, it dominates the main shopping area.

Admission: Free.

Open: For guided tours in July–Aug, Mon–Fri at 2:30pm and Sept–June, Wed at 10:30am or by appointment. Reservations required.

★ **Ulster Museum**, Stranmillis Rd. ☎ **3812251**.

Built in the grand Classical Renaissance style, with an Italian marble interior, this museum summarizes 9,000 years of Irish history with exhibits on Irish art, furniture, glass, ceramics, costume, industrial heritage, and a permanent display of products "Made in Belfast." One of the best-known exhibits is the collection of gold and silver jewelry recovered by divers in 1968 off the Antrim coast from the 1588 wreckage of the Armada treasure ship *Girona*. Other permanent collections focus on waterwheels and steam engines, making Irish linen, the post office in Ireland, coins and medals, early Ireland, Irish flora and fauna, and the living sea.

Admission: Free.

Open: Mon–Fri 10am–5pm, Sat 1–5pm, Sun 2–5pm.

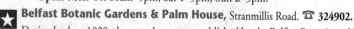

★ **Belfast Botanic Gardens & Palm House**, Stranmillis Road. ☎ **324902**.

Dating back to 1829, these gardens were established by the Belfast Botanic and Horticultural Society. Ten years later a glass house, or conservatory, was added, designed by noted Belfast architect Charles Lanyon. Now known as the Palm House, this unique building is one of the earliest examples of curvilinear cast-iron glass-house construction. It contains many rare plant specimens, including such tropical plants as sugar cane, coffee, cinnamon, banana, aloe, ivory nut, rubber, bamboo, guava, and the striking bird of paradise flower. The Tropical Ravine, also known as the fernery, provides a setting for plants to grow in a sunken glen. Take time also to stroll in the surrounding outdoor gardens of roses and herbaceous borders, established in 1827.

Admission: Free.

Open: Palm House and Tropical Ravine: open Apr–Sept, Mon–Fri 10am–noon, Sat–Sun 2–5pm; Oct–Mar, Mon–Fri 10am–noon and 1–4pm, Sat–Sun 2–4pm, gardens open 8am–sunset.

★ **Linen Hall Library,** 17 Donegall Square N. ☎ **321707.**

Established in 1788 as an independent charitable institution, this is Belfast's oldest library. It is known for its rare and old books, but also has current best sellers. Three of its most important collections are its Irish books, Robert Burns' books, and heraldry books.

Admission: Free.

Open: Mon–Wed and Fri 9:30am–5:30pm, Thurs 9:30am–8:30pm, Sat 9:30am–4pm.

Belfast Zoo, Antrim Road. ☎ **776277.**

Set in a picturesque mountain park on the slopes of Cave Hill overlooking the city, this zoo was founded in 1920 as Bellvue Gardens. A completely new and modern zoo was designed in recent years, with emphasis on conservation, education, and in breeding rare species including Hawaiian geese, Indian lions, red lechwe, and golden lion marmosets.

Admission: £4 ($6.12) adults, £2 ($3.06) children ages 4–16.

Open: Apr–Sept daily 10am–5pm; Oct–Mar 10am–3:30pm.

SAVVY SHOPPING

Shops in Belfast city center are open from on Monday through Saturday from 9am to 5:30pm, with many shops remaining open until 8pm or 9pm on Thursday.

Before you start to stop, take time to stop into the **Craftworks Gallery,** 13 Linenhall St. (☎ **0232/236334**), a display center and shop for the work of individual craftspeople from all over Northern Ireland. This gallery will also supply you with a free copy of the brochure "Crafts in Northern Ireland," detailing local crafts and where to find them. The Castle Court Shopping Centre on Royal Avenue is the main downtown multistory shopping mall, with dozen of boutiques and shops.

Belfast's leading department stores are Anderson & McAuley and Marks & Spencer, both on Donegall Place, and Debenham's in the Castle Court Shopping Centre on Royal Avenue. Some other shops to look for include:

Arts Council Gallery, 56 Dublin Rd. ☎ **321402.**

Located at the corner of Harrington Street, this shop features a wide array of art posters, books, and postcards by Irish artists.

Emer Gallery, 88 Gt. Victoria St. ☎ **231377.**

Paintings by Irish artists are displayed and sold at this little gallery, next to the Europa Bus Centre.

National Trust Gift Shop, 86 Dublin Rd. ☎ **230018.**

Operated for the benefit of the National Trust properties, this shop sells a fine assortment of books by Irish authors including Yeats and Joyce, as well as items pertaining to the *Book of Kells.* There's also a wide variety of gifts produced in Northern Ireland, from Tyrone crystal and Belleek china, to Celtic pewter jewelry, pottery, lace, linen, stationery, fine arts cards, jams, biscuits, fudge, and organically grown coffee.

Prospect House Books, 93 Dublin Rd. ☎ **245787.**

This shop features antiquarian books of paper and hard back, particularly rare, old, and out-of-print volumes. Books are bought and sold here.

Smyth's Irish Linens, 65 Royal Ave. ☎ **322983.**

If you want to stock up on fine Irish linen damask tablecloths, napkins, and handkerchiefs, head for this shop in the heart of the city's prime shopping thoroughfare. It also stocks souvenirs and other traditional gifts.

Tom Caldwell Gallery, 40 Bradbury Place. ☎ **323226.**

Come here for a selection of paintings by living Irish artists, as well as hand-crafted furnishings, rugs, pottery, and cast iron candlebras.

WHERE TO STAY

Very Expensive/Expensive

★ **Culloden Hotel,** 142 Bangor Rd., Craigavad, Holywood, Co. Down BT18 OEX. ☎ **0232/425223.** Fax 0232/426777. 85 rms, 7 suites (all with bath). TV TEL

Rates (including full breakfast): £106 ($162.18) single, £140 ($214.20) double, £185–£300 ($283.05–$459) suites. AE, DC, MC, V.

The Belfast area's finest hotel is not in Belfast at all, but five miles to the east on the southern shore of Belfast Lough, technically in County Down. Set on 12 acres of secluded gardens and woodlands, this hotel incorporates a Gothic mansion built in 1876 of Scottish stone by William Auchinleck Robinson, a government official who named it Culloden House in honor of his wife, the former Elizabeth Jane Culloden. On his death, the house passed to the Church of Ireland and was used as a residence by a succession of bishops, and later sold to private individuals until it was opened as a hotel in 1963. It was purchased in 1967 by the Hastings Hotel Group, which has extended and refurbished it in luxurious style including many fine antiques, paintings, plasterwork ceiling, and Louis XV chandeliers. Guest rooms offer contemporary furnishings with Victorian flair.

Dining/Entertainment: Choices include the elegant Mitre Restaurant overlooking the gardens; the Gothic Bar; and the Cultra Inn (☎ **425840**), a casual pub/restaurant on the grounds of the hotel.

Facilities: Octagonal-shaped ozone swimming pool, gym, Jacuzzi, steam room, all-weather tennis court, squash court, putting green, croquet lawn, hairdressing salon.

Expensive

Europa Hotel, Great Victoria Street, Belfast, Co. Antrim BT2 7AP. ☎ **0232/327000.** Fax 0232/327800. 195 rms (all with bath). TV TEL

Rates (including full breakfast): £100 ($153) single, £130 ($198.90) double. AE, DC, MC, V.

Situated in the heart of the city beside the Grand Opera House, this is Belfast's largest and most modern hotel. At presstime, it was undergoing renovation and repair resulting from a 1993 bombing, but it should be fully operational again by 1995. Facilities include a restaurant, bistro, bar, and nightclub.

Moderate

⭐ **Dukes Hotel,** 65–67 University St., Belfast, Co. Antrim BT7 1LH.
☎ **0232/236666.** Fax 0232/237177. 21 rms (all with bath). TV TEL

💲 **Rates** (including full breakfast): £76.50 ($117.05) single, £92 ($140.76) double. AE, MC, V.

Located in a tree-lined residential area near the university, this hotel is housed in a former Victorian residence. The interior decor is bright and modern with art deco furnishings, waterfalls, and plants. Guest rooms are contemporary, with double-glazed windows, light wood furnishings, floral fabrics, and modern art, with such amenities as a phone in the bathroom, mirrored closets, hairdryer, coffee/tea-maker, and a basket of fruit.

Facilities include Dukes Restaurant, Duke's Bar, 24-hour room service, and a health club with gym and sauna. It's located off Botanic Avenue, within a half-mile walk of the center of the city.

Quality Plaza Hotel, 15 Brunswick St., Belfast, Co. Antrim BT2 7GE.

☎ **0232/333555** or toll free **800/221-2222** from U.S. Fax 0232/232999. 73 rms (all with bath). TV TEL

Rates (including breakfast): £59 ($90.27) single, £69 ($105.81) double. AE, DC, MC, V.

Located in the heart of the city, less than two blocks from City Hall, this modern, nine-story hotel was opened in 1990. It is within walking distance to all major city sights. The guest rooms are contemporary in style with light woods, floral fabrics, and amenities such as hair dryer and garment press. Dining and entertainment choices include the Amelia Garden, an upstairs conservatory-style restaurant, and George C. McClatchy's Public Bar on the ground floor.

Inexpensive

Ash-Rowan Town House, 12 Windsor Ave., Belfast, Co. Antrim BT9 6EE.
☎ **0232/661758.** Fax 0232/663227. 4 rms (all with bath). TV TEL
Rates (including full breakfast): £38 ($58.14) single, £56 ($85.68) double. MC, V.

Situated on a quiet, tree-lined street in a residential neighborhood, this four-story Victorian house sits between Lisburn and Malone Roads near Queen's University. Proprietors Evelyn and Hazlett have outfitted it with country-style furnishings, family heirlooms, and antiques, along with bouquets of fresh flowers from their garden. The rates include a choice of eight different traditional breakfasts including the Ulster fry or scrambled eggs with kippers or smoked salmon. There is a private car park outside.

WHERE TO DINE

Expensive

⭐ **Roscoff,** 7 Lesley House, Shaftesbury Sq. ☎ **331532.**
Cuisine: INTERNATIONAL. **Reservations:** Required.
Prices: Appetizers £5.95–£7.95 ($9.10–$12.16); main courses £12.95–£15.50 ($19.81–$23.72). AE, MC, V.
Open: Lunch Mon–Fri 12:15–2:15pm, dinner Mon–Sat 6:30–10:30pm.

Although the decor here is simple, with frosted windows, black and white furnishings, and white walls adorned by modern art, the menu is definitely artistic at this

Michelin-starred restaurant, thanks to chef/owner Paul Rankin's penchant for using the best of Uster produce in creative combinations of taste and color. The menu offers dishes such as rack of lamb; char-grilled beef filet with bacon and roquefort sauce; sautéed turbot and prawns; whole Dover sole with grilled leeks and red wine butter; filet of Irish salmon with asparagus and chervil; and steamed symphony of seafood with salmon, mako, monkfish, brill, sole, prawns, and lobster.

Restaurant 44, 44 Bedford St. ☎ **244844.**
Cuisine: CONTINENTAL. **Reservations:** Recommended.
Prices: Appetizers £2.25–£5.95 ($3.44–$9.10); main courses £7.95–£13.95 ($12.16–$21.34). Set lunch £8.95–£13.95 ($13.69–$21.34); set dinner £10.95–£15.95 ($16.75–$24.40). AE, DC, MC, V.
Open: Lunch Mon–Fri noon–3pm, dinner Mon–Sat 6–11pm.

Defining itself as a Colonial-style brasserie, this midcity restaurant sits between City Hall and the BBC studios. The menu lists creative and dishes—chicken with basil mousse; char-grilled filet of beef with prawns and butter sauce; filet of salmon with green vegetable caviar and saffron sauce; paupiette of lemon sole with beetroot and wine sauce; and Mediterranean vegetable strudel with eggplant, artichokes, tomatoes, garlic, and herbs, wrapped in zucchini.

Moderate

★ **La Belle Epoque,** 61/63 Dublin Rd. ☎ **323244.**
Cuisine: FRENCH. **Reservations:** Suggested.
 Prices: Appetizers £1.65–£3.95 ($2.52–$6.04); lunch main courses £4.05–£5.95 ($6.20–$9.10); dinner main courses £6.50–£12.50 ($9.95–19.13). AE.
Open: Mon–Fri noon–11:30pm, Sat 6–11:30pm.

Housed in a double shopfront brick building, this brasserie-style restaurant sits at the corner of Ventry Lane. The menu offers a creative mixture of fruit and vegetable-based sauces with dishes such as chicken with almond crust and mushroom sauce; veal in creamy artichoke sauce; duck in cherry sauce; noisette of lamb with peanut butter, chicken stock, spring onion, and strawberry sauce; filet of turbot with salmon trout mousse; and pan-fried salmon with broccoli and ginger sauce, as well as lobster thermidor, vegetarian kebabs, and filets of beef, pork, and lamb kidney in three sauces.

★ **Nick's Warehouse,** 35 Hill St. ☎ **439690.**
Cuisine: INTERNATIONAL. **Reservations:** Suggested.
Prices: Appetizers £2.50–£4.95 ($3.83–$7.57), lunch or dinner main courses £5.95–£10.95 ($9.10–$16.75). DC, MC, V.
Open: Lunch Mon–Fri noon–2pm, dinner Tues–Sat 6–11pm.

Set in an old warehouse between St. Anne's Cathedral and the tourist office, this restaurant offers a wine bar setting downstairs, and a classy dining room upstairs, with brick walls and open kitchen. The offers a variety of international appetizers from gazpacho to curly kale soup to a platter of Italian salami or gravlax (cured Norwegian salmon). Main courses range from sirloin steaks to hot-and-sour beef with water chestnuts, as well as lamb chops with honey and ginger sauce; breast of duck with a hot plum sauce; calves liver with spicy port and Rosemary sauce; filet of lemon sole with basil pesto; or mixed nut bake with mushroom sauce.

Moderate/Inexpensive

Bananas, 4 Clarence St. ☎ **339999.**

Cuisine: INTERNATIONAL. **Reservations:** Suggested for dinner.
Prices: Appetizers £1.75–£5.95 ($2.68–$9.10); main courses £4.95–£11.95 ($7.57–$18.28). MC, V.
Open: Lunch Mon–Fri noon–3pm; dinner Mon–Sat 5–11pm.

Situated around the corner from Ulster Hall, this informal little restaurant blends culinary influences from Thailand, Mexico, and California, as well as other parts of Europe. The menu offers a variety of tapas, Cajun chicken or chicken Kiev, salads, steaks, sandwiches, pastas, and vegetable goulash. As might be expected, the featured dessert is roast bananas in puff pastry.

$ Saints & Scholars, 3 University St. ☎ **325137.**

Cuisine: INTERNATIONAL. **Reservations:** Not accepted.
Prices: Set lunch £4.95–£8.95 ($7.57–$13.69); dinner appetizers £1.75–£4.95 ($2.68–$7.57); dinner main courses £4.95–£8.95 ($7.57–$13.69). AE, MC, V.
Open: Mon–Sat noon–11pm, Sun 12:30–2:30pm and 5:30–9:30pm.

Situated two blocks from the Botanic Gardens and the Queen's university, this restaurant has a collegiate atmosphere, with a variety of book-filled dining rooms, eclectically decorated with rattan furnishings, ceiling fans, plants, and wall coverings of Celtic design. The blackboard-style menu offers dishes such as wok-roasted monkfish; "big bowl" of mussels, cockles, prawns, and more; salmon en croûte with spinach; trout in pastry with oranges, bananas, honey; filet of chicken sautéed with crab and prawns; pink duck breast with green peppercorn and brandy sauce; breast of chicken stuffed with garlic, cream cheese, pickle, and peppers; rack of lamb, steaks, salads, and pastas.

Skandia, 50 Howard St. ☎ **240239.**

Cuisine: IRISH. **Reservations:** Suggested for dinner.
Prices: Appetizers £1.30–£4.15 ($1.99–$6.35); lunch main courses £2.50–£5.65 ($3.83–$8.64); dinner main courses £3.95–£10.95 ($6.04–$16.75). AE, MC, V.
Open: Mon–Sat 9:30am–11pm.

Located in the heart of the city a block west of Donegall Square, this restaurant is a convenient and dependable place to dine at any time of day. It has a homey atmosphere with banquette seating and a salad bar in the middle of the room. It offers dishes such as grilled salmon, scampi, or turbot steamed with celery, mushrooms, and nuts; as well as salads such as Viking Treasure (smoked salmon, prawns, mackerel, tuna, and sardines), and fresh fruit extravaganza; pastas, vegetarian dishes, burgers, steaks, ribs, and omelets. *Note:* this restaurant is a favorite with families since it does not have a liquor license.

Inexpensive

Harveys, 95 Great Victoria St. ☎ **233433.**

Cuisine: INTERNATIONAL. **Reservations:** Not required.
Prices: Appetizers £1.35–£2.85 ($2.07–$4.36), main courses £4.95–£7.95 ($7.57–$12.16). MC, V.
Open: Mon–Thurs and Sun 5–11pm, Fri–Sat 5pm–midnight.

An American atmosphere prevails here with a decor of U.S. flags and a menu that offers choices such as steaks, burgers, salads, pizza, tacos, pastas, and a signature Frisco

Bay platter (prawns, crab claws, scampi, mussels, and langoustines), as well as beef stroganoff, chicken Kiev, and smokey pork filet stuffed with cheese and smoked bacon.

EVENING ENTERTAINMENT

The leading concert and performance halls in Belfast are the **Grand Opera House,** Great Victoria Street (☎ **241919**), presenting a wide variety of entertainment; **Ulster Hall,** Bedford Street (☎ **323900**), staging major concerts from rock to large scale choral and symphonic works by the Ulster Orchestra and Northern Ireland Symphony Orchestra; and **Kings Hall,** Lisburn Road (☎ **665225**), for superstar concerts and other musical events.

Theaters include the **Arts Theatre,** Botanic Avenue (☎ **324936**), for popular theatrical productions; **Lyric Theatre,** Ridgeway Street (☎ **381081**) for new plays by Irish and international playwrights; and the **Belfast Civic Arts Theatre,** 41 Botanic Ave. (☎ **324936**), for popular shows, musicals, and comedies.

Tickets, priced from £5 to £10 ($7.65 to $15.30) for most events, can be purchased in advance from the **Virgin Ticket Shop,** Castle Court, Belfast (☎ **323744**), and **Good Vibrations Ticket Shop,** 121 Gt. Victoria St., Belfast (☎ **233456**).

PUBS

⭐ **Crown Liquor Saloon,** Great Victoria Street. ☎ **249476.**

Dating back to 1826 and situated opposite the Grand Opera House, this gaslit pub, a feast of Victoriana, is a member of the National Trust. Step inside and see the marvelous array of ten snugs on the right, each with its own door and call bell, as well as the tin ceiling, tile floor, etched and smoked glass, beveled mirror with floral and wildlife decorations, scalloped lamps, and long bar with inlaid colored glass and marble trim.

Kelly's Cellars, Bank Street, Belfast. ☎ **324835.**

Recognized as Belfast's oldest tavern in continuous use, this pub dates back to 1720 and has had a storied history including being a headquarters for leaders in the 1798 Insurrection. Situated just off Royal Avenue, it has also been a favorite haunt for actors and novelists. The decor is rich in vaulted ceilings, paned windows, old barrels, whitewashed arches, wooden snugs, with lots of memorabilia including old ledgers, coins, china, prints, maps, and international soccer caps. There is often traditional music on tap in the evenings.

Pat's Bar, Prince's Dock Street. ☎ **744524.**

For a taste of Belfast's harbor atmosphere, step into this pub at the gates of Prince's Dock. It is frequented by sailors, dockers, and local business people. The decor includes an antique hand-carved beech bar, pine wood furnishings, red tile floor, black and white photos of the pub's earliest days, and an interesting collection of memorabilia given to the bar's owner by sailors passing through the port—from clogs, swords, tomtoms, and maraccas, to a telescope and a bayonet. There is traditional Irish music on Friday and Saturday nights from 9pm.

White's Tavern, Winecellar Entry, off High Street. ☎ **243080.**

Tucked in a historic cobblestoned trading laneway between High and Rosemary Streets, this old tavern was established in 1630 as a wine and spirit merchant shop. It's full of old barrels and hoists, ornate snugs, brick arches, large copper measures, framed newspaper clippings of 200-year-old vintage, quill pens, and other memorabilia. A good pub for conversation and browsing.

2 Excursions from Belfast

Ards Peninsula

10 miles E of Belfast

The Ards Peninsula curls around the western shore of Strangford Lough, an 18-mile-long lake and one of the largest inland sea inlets in the British Isles. A place of natural beauty, it's home to more than 100 different species of marine life and fish as well as a great bird sanctuary and wildlife reserve. Two roads traverse the peninsula—A 20 (the Lough road) and A 2 (the coast road). Of the two, the Lough road is the more scenic.

At the southern tip of the Lough, there is a continuous car ferry service connecting Portaferry with Strangford on the mainland side. It runs from 7:30am to 10:30 or 11pm each day, no reservations are needed. The one-way fare is £2.40 ($3.67) for a car and driver and 60p (92¢) for each passenger.

Sea-fishing trips from Portaferry into the waters of Strangford Lough and along the County Down coast are organized by Peter Wright, Norsemaid Sea Enterprises, 152 Portaferry Rd., Newtownards, Co. Down (☎ 0247/812081). Reservations are required.

There are two National Trust properties in this area, one on the Ards Peninsula and the other just across the lough at Portaferry.

★ **Castle Ward**, Strangford, Co. Down. ☎ 039686/204.

Situated 1.5 miles west of Strangford village, this National Trust house dates back to 1760 and is half Classical and half Gothic in architectural style. It sits amid a 700-acre country estate of formal gardens, woodlands, lakelands, and seashore. It also has a restored 1830s cornmill and a Victorian-style laundry. The theater in the stableyard is a venue for operatic performances in summer.

Admission: House, £2.50 ($3.83) adults, £1.25 ($1.91) children; estate, £1.50 ($2.30) per car in off season; £3 ($4.59) per car in high season.

Open: House Apr, Sept and Oct Sat–Sun 1–6pm; May–Aug, Mon–Wed and Fri–Sun 1–6pm; estate year-round dawn to dusk.

★ **Mount Stewart House**, Newtownards, Co. Down. ☎ 024774/387.

Once the home of Lord Castlereagh, this 18th-century house sits on the eastern shore of Strangford Lough, about 15 miles east of Belfast. It has one of the greatest gardens in the care of the National Trust, with an unrivaled collection of rare and unusual plants. The interior of the house is also noteworthy for its art works, including *Hambletonian* by George Stubbs, one of the finest paintings in Ireland, and family portraits by Batoni, Mengs, and Lazlo. The Temple of the Winds, a banqueting house built in 1785, is also on the estate.

Admission: House, garden, and temple £3.30 ($5.05) adults, £1.65 ($2.52) children; garden and temple £2.70 ($4.13) adults, £1.35 ($2.07) children; temple only 90p ($1.38) per person.

Open: House, Apr and Oct Sat–Sun 1–6pm; May–Sept Mon and Wed–Sun 1–6pm; garden, Apr–Sept daily 10:30am–6pm, Oct, Sat–Sun 10:30am–6pm; Temple same as house except hours are 2–5pm.

Armagh

40 miles SW of Belfast

TOURIST INFORMATION   Stop into the Armagh Tourist Information Office, 40 English St., Armagh (☎ **0861/527808**). It's open from April through September, Monday through Saturday from 10am to 7pm and on Sunday from noon to 7pm; from October through March, on Monday through Saturday from 10am to 5pm and on Sunday from 2 to 5pm.

One of Ireland's most historic cities, Armagh takes its name from the Irish *Ard Macha* or Macha's Height, after the legendary pagan queen Macha, who is said to have built a fortress here in the middle of the first millennium B.C.

This fort, known originally as ◘ Eamain Macha, still exists today, known simply today as Navan Fort, Killylea Road, Armagh (☎ **0861/525550**). Situated two miles west of Armagh, it reflects more than 7,500 years of Irish history, from Mesolithic hunters, Neolithic farmers, and Bronze Age people, to the Celts and eventually the Christian era.

It was the earliest capital of Ulster and seat of the kings of the province for over 700 years. Today it is a system of earthenworks, settlement sites, and grassy mounds. The story of the fort is told at a new visitors center, specially designed to be an integral part of the landscape, using a series of audio-visual presentations including the 10-minute *The Dawning,* an introduction to the history of the area; the 35-minute *Real World,* an explanation of the archaeology of the region; and the 30-minute *The Other World,* a dazzling review of all the legends of Navan. Admission is £3.50 ($5.36) for adults, £2 ($3.06) for seniors and students, £1.90 ($2.92) for children under 16. It's open from April through August on Monday through Saturday from 10am to 7pm, and on Sunday from 11am to 7pm; September through March on Monday through Friday, 10am to 5pm, and on Sunday, 11am to 5pm.

Most of Armagh's history, however, focuses on the 5th century, when St. Patrick chose this place as a base from which to spread Christianity. St. Patrick called it "my sweet hill" and built a stone church here.

Ever since then, Armagh has been considered the ecclesiastical capital of Ireland and today there are two St. Patrick's cathedrals, Catholic and Anglican, seats of the primates of both religions.

Many of the public buildings and the Georgian town houses along the Mall are the work of Francis Johnston, a native of Armagh, who also left his mark on Georgian Dublin. Buildings are made of warm-colored local limestone that make the city glow even on a dull day. This pink, yellow, and red limestone, has also been used for doorsteps and pavements, like the glowing pink pavement on the Mall.

In addition to being Ireland's spiritual capital, this area is known for its apple trees, earning Armagh the title of the Orchard of Ireland.

Carrickfergus

12 miles NE of Belfast

TOURIST INFORMATION   Stop into the Carrickfergus Tourist Information Office, Antrim Street, Carrickfergus, Co. Antrim (☎ **0960/366455**). It's open Monday through Saturday from 9am to 5pm and on Sunday from 2pm to 6pm.

Carrickfergus, Co. Antrim, was a thriving town, it is said, when Belfast was a sandbank. In 1180 John de Courcy, a Norman, built a massive keep to guard the approach to Belfast Lough at Carrickfergus, the first real Irish castle. Today visitors can tour this well-preserved ✪ Carrickfergus Castle, Antrim Street, Carrickfergus (☎ **0960/ 351273**) and enjoy an audio-visual on the castle's history. In the summer months, medieval banquets, a medieval fair, and a crafts market are held here. It's open from April through September on Monday through Saturday from 10am to 6pm and on Sunday from 2 to 6pm; from October through March on Monday through Saturday from 10am to 4pm and on Sunday from 2 to 4pm. Admission is £2 ($3.06) adults, £1 ($1.53) seniors and children.

In addition, Knight Ride, Antrim Street, Carrickfergus (☎ **0960/366455**), is an action-packed monorail that takes passengers on a re-enactment of the history of the town from A.D. 531. Admission to the ride is £2 ($3.00) adults and £1 ($1.53) seniors and children. It is open from April through September, Monday through Friday from 10am to 8pm, Saturday from 10am to 6pm, Sunday noon to 6pm; from October through March, daily from 10am to 4:30pm. Reduced rate tickets for admission to both the castle and the ride are £3.60 ($5.51) adults, £1.80 ($2.75) seniors and children.

This area is also the setting of the Andrew Jackson Centre, Boneybefore, Carrickfergus (☎ **0960/364972**), a simple one-story cottage with earthen floor and open fireplace that was the home of the parents of Andrew Jackson, 7th president of the United States. His parents left here and emigrated to the U.S. in 1765. The house now contains a display on the life and career of Andrew Jackson and Ulster's connections with America. In July and August weekends, there are craft demonstrations reflecting rural folklife, such as sampler-making, basket-weaving, griddle-making, patchwork-quilting, and lace-making. Admission is 60p (92¢) adults, 30p (46¢) seniors and children. It's open from May through October, Monday through Friday, 10am to 1pm and 2 to 6pm, Saturday and Sunday from 2 to 6pm.

Cultra

7 miles E of Belfast

One of the most popular attractions in the Belfast area is actually in County Down— ✪ the Ulster Folk & Transport Museum at Cultra, Holywood, (☎ **0232/428428**). It encompasses many parts of Ulster's past, all brought together onto one 176-acre site.

Sixty acres are devoted to a unique outdoor museum that contains a series of 19th-century buildings, all saved from the bulldozer's path and moved intact from their original sites in various parts of Northern Ireland. You can literally walk among 19th-century farmhouses, mills, churches, terraces of houses, rural schools, a forge, bank, print shop, and a small conical hut where a watchman would sit with his musket guarding the linen laid out on the green to bleach in the sun. There are demonstrations of people cooking over an open hearth, ploughing the fields with horses, thatching roofs, and practicing traditional Ulster crafts such as textile-making, spinning, quilting, lace-making, printing, spade-making, and shoe-making.

In addition, there is an exhibit on Irish railways, considered one of the top 10 of its kind in Europe. Admission is £3 ($4.59) for adults, £2 ($3.06) for children. It's open during July and August, Monday through Saturday, 10:30am to 6pm, and on Sunday, noon to 6pm; April through June and in September, Monday through Friday, 9:30am to 5pm, Saturday from 10:30am to 6pm, Sunday from noon to 6pm; and October through March, Monday through Friday from 9:30am to 4pm, and on Saturday and Sunday from 12:30pm to 4:30pm.

Lisburn

10 miles SE of Belfast

The linen industry, long synonymous with Northern Ireland, is the focus of the new Irish Linen Centre, Market Square, Lisburn, Co. Antrim (☎ 0846/663377). This museum invites visitors to trace the production of linen, from earliest days in the 17th century to the high-tech industry of today. There are opportunities to see linen in all stages of production including a weaving workshop with hand looms, and audio-visual presentations. Admission is £2.50 ($3.83) for adults, £1.50 ($2.30) for seniors and children. Hours are April through September, Monday through Wednesday and Friday and Saturday from 9:30am to 5:30pm, on Thursday from 9:30am to 9pm, and from 2pm to 5:30pm on Sunday; October through March on Monday through Wednesday and Friday and Saturday from 9:30am to 5pm, on Thursday from 9:30am to 9pm, and on Sunday from 2pm to 5pm.

Lough Neagh

10 miles W of Belfast

Lough Neagh, at 153 square miles, is the largest lake in the British Isles. Often called an inland sea, the lough is 20 miles long and 10 miles wide, with a 65-mile shore. It is famous for its eels, an Ulster delicacy. Hundreds of tons of eels from Lough Neagh are exported each year.

Lough Neagh is also a playground for Belfast residents. To sample the outdoor activity, head for the Lough Neagh Discovery Centre, Oxford Island, Craigavon, Co. Armagh (☎ 0762/322205).

Situated midway between Belfast and Armagh city, this center is on the southern shore of Lough Neagh at Oxford Island, a nature reserve with a range of habitats such as reedbeds, woodlands, and wildflower meadows. It serves as an introduction to all that the lough has to offer, with historical and geographic exhibits, and an interactive ecolab explaining the ecosystems of the lough, as well as walking trails, birdwatching observation points, and picnic areas. **Boat trips** on Lough Neagh, lasting about 45 minutes, depart regularly from the discovery center jetty. Admission is £2 ($3.06) for adults, £1.30 ($1.99) for children; boat trips cost £3 ($4.59) for adults, £1.50 ($2.30) for children. It's open in September and April, Monday through Friday 10am to 7pm, on Saturday from 10am to 8pm, and on Sunday from noon to 8pm; during May through August, daily from 10am to 9pm; and October through March, on Monday through Friday 10am to 5pm, on Saturday and Sunday from noon to 5pm.

The Mountains of Mourne

20 miles SW of Belfast

TOURIST INFORMATION   Stop into the Downpatrick Tourist Information Centre, 74 Market St., Downpatrick, Co. Down (☎ 0396/612233) or the Newcastle Centre, 10-14 Central Promenade, Newcastle, Co. Down (☎ 03967/22222). Both offices are open all year, with varying days and hours according to the season.

Sweeping down to the Irish Sea in the southeast corner of Northern Ireland, the ★ Mountains of Mourne were immortalized by songwriter Percy French. The Mournes consist of 12 shapely summits rising above 2,000 ft., dominated by the barren peak of Slieve Donard, reaching to 2,796 ft., making it the highest mountain in Northern Ireland.

It's worth the drive from Belfast to see this beautiful coastal panorama. Alternately, if you are coming from the Republic of Ireland, the A 2 drive along the coast is particularly scenic, with the mountains in the background.

The Mountains of Mourne also lead to Downpatrick, one of the north's oldest cities and a place closely identified with St. Patrick. History tell us that when Patrick came to Ireland, in 432, strong winds blew his boat into this area. He had meant to sail up the coast to County Antrim, where as a young slave he had tended flocks on Slemish Mountain. Instead he settled here and converted the local chieftain Dichu and his followers to Christianity. Over the next 30 years Patrick roamed to many other places in Ireland carrying out his work, but he wound up here to die and is said to be buried in the graveyard of Downpatrick Cathedral. A large stone marks the spot.

For an overview on St. Patrick's association with this area, stop into the St. Patrick's Centre/Down Heritage Museum, The Mall, Downpatrick, Co. Down (☎ **0396/615218**). It's open from Tuesday through Friday, 11am to 5pm, and on Saturday from 2 to 5pm; during July to mid-September, it is also open on Sunday 2 to 5pm.

This area is also home of Newcastle, a favorite seaside resort of the Irish, and site of one of the world's great golf courses, ★ Royal County Down, Newcastle, Co. Down (☎ **03967/23314**). Nestled in huge sand dunes with the Mountains of Mourne in the background, this 18-hole, par-71 championship course dates back to 1889. Greens fees range from £35 ($53.55) on weekdays to £40 ($61.20) on weekends.

---

3 The Antrim Coast

TOURIST INFORMATION   There are tourist information centers at the following locations: 7 Mary St., Ballycastle, Co. Antrim (☎ **02657/62024**); 44 Causeway Road, Bushmills, Co. Antrim (☎ **02657/31855**); and at Dunluce Centre, Sandhill Drive, Portrush, Co. Antrim (☎ **0265/823333**). All are open year-round, with varying hours according to the seasons.

Heralded in story and song, the Glens of Antrim consist of nine green valleys, sitting north of Belfast and stretching from south to north. All of these glens have individual names, each based on a local tale or legend. Although the meanings are not known for certain, the popular translations are as follows: Glenarm (glen of the army), Glencloy (glen of the hedges), Glenariff (ploughman's glen), Glenballyeamon (Edwardstown glen), Glenaan (glen of the rush lights), Glencorp (glen of the slaughter), Glendun (brown glen), Glenshesk (sedgy glen), and Glentaisie (Taisie's glen).

The people who live in the Glens of Antrim are descendants of both the ancient Irish and their cousins, the Hebridean Scots, so this area is one of the last places in Northern Ireland where Gaelic was spoken. To this day, the glen people are known to be great storytellers.

In all, the area identified as the Antrim coast is 60 miles, stretching north of Larne and then west after passing Bushmills and the Giant's Causeway to Portrush. The route takes in marine seascapes and chalky cliffs, and includes the National Trust village of Cushendun with pretty Cornish-style cottages as well as a string of beach resorts that are favored by Irish and English vacationers, such as Portrush, Portstewart, and Portballintrae. This coastal drive also meanders under bridges and arches, passing bays, sandy beaches, harbors, and huge rock formations. Two of Ireland's foremost attractions are also here—the Giant's Causeway and Old Bushmills Distillery. Each

August, the seaside town of Ballycastle plays host to one of Ireland's oldest traditional gatherings, the Oul' Lammas Fair.

WHAT TO SEE & DO

★ **Giant's Causeway Centre,** 44 Causeway Rd., Bushmills, Co. Antrim. ☎ **02657/31855.**

Declared a World Heritage Site, this natural rock formation known as the Giant's Causeway is often called the eighth wonder of the world. It consists of more than 37,000 tightly packed basalt columns that extend for three miles along the coast in a lunarlike landscape. The tops of the columns form stepping stones that lead from the cliff foot and disappear under the sea. Mostly hexagonal in shape, the columns are as tall as 40 ft. high. Scientists estimate that they were formed 60 or 70 million years ago, by volcanic explosions, a sort of geological freak, caused by volcanic eruptions and cooling lava. The ancients, on the other hand, believed the rock formation to be the work of giants and legend has it that Finn MacCool, the Ulster warrior and commander of the king of Ulster's armies, built the causeway as a highway over the sea to bring his girlfriend from the Isle of Hebrides. Start a visit to the causeway at the Visitor Centre, where there is a continuous 25-minute audio-visual show that illustrates the formation and history of the site. To reach the causeway itself, you have a choice of taking a shuttle bus or following a circular walk. The walk goes past amphitheaters of stone columns and formations with fanciful names like Honeycomb, Wishing Well, Giant's Granny, King and his Nobles, Lover's Leap, and up a wooden staircase to Benbane Head and back along the cliff top.

Admission: Causeway, free; audio-visual and exhibition, £1 ($1.53) adults over 15, 50p (75¢) children; bus is free, but donation encouraged; parking £2 ($3.06).

Open: Mid-Mar through May, daily 11am–5pm; June, daily 11am–5:30pm; July–Aug, daily 10am–7pm; Sept–Oct, Mon–Fri 11am–5pm, Sat–Sun 10:30am–5:30pm.

★ **Bushmills Distillery,** Main St., Bushmills, Co. Antrim. ☎ **02657/31521.**

Licensed to distill spirits in 1608 but with historical references dating back to 1276, this is Ireland's and the world's oldest distillery. Visitors are welcome to tour the facility and watch the whole whiskey-making process, starting with fresh water from the adjacent River Bush and continuing through distilling, fermenting, and bottling. At the end of the tour, samples can to be tasted in the Poststill Bar, where there are also some fascinating exhibits on the long history of the distillery. Tours depart regularly and last about 25 minutes.

Admission: £2 ($3.06) adults, £1.50 ($2.30) seniors and students, free for children under 18.

Open: Oct–May Mon–Thurs 9am–noon and 1:30–3:30pm, Fri 9am–12:15pm; June–Aug, Mon–Thurs 9am–noon and 1:30–4:15pm, Fri 9am–3:45pm, Sat 10am–3:45pm.

Carrick-A-Rede Rope Bridge, Larrybane, Co. Antrim. ☎ **02657/31159** or **32143.**

Located five miles west of Ballycastle, this open rope bridge spans a chasm 60 ft. wide and 80 ft. above the sea between the mainland and a small island. The bridge is put up each spring by local fishermen to give access to a salmon fishery on the island, but it can be used by visitors for a thrilling walk and the chance to call out to each other "Don't look down!"

Admission: Free; parking £1.50 ($2.30).

Open: May–June and Sept, Sat–Sun 11am–6pm, July–Aug daily 10am–6pm.

Dunluce Castle, Bushmills/Portrush Rd., Dunluce, Co. Antrim. ☎ **02657/31938.**

Situated three miles east of Portrush off the A 2 road, this site was once the main fort of the Irish MacDonnells, chiefs of Antrim. It consists of a series of fortifications built on rocky outcrops extending into the sea. The present castle incorporates two of the original Norman towers dating from 1305, and was the power base of the north coast for 400 years. The visitor center shows an audio-visual with background on the site.

Admission: £1.50 ($2.30) adults, 75p ($1.15) seniors and children under 10.

Open: April–Sept Mon–Sat 10am–7pm, Sun 2–7; Oct–Mar Tues–Sat 10am–4pm, Sun 2–4pm.

Dunluce Centre, Dunluce Ave., Portrush. ☎ **0265/834444.**

Opened in June of 1993, this new entertainment complex provides a variety of indoor activity. It offers a multimedia show, *Myths & Legends,* that illustrates the folklore of the Antrim coast, as well as *Turbo Tours,* a thrill ride that simulates a modern-day space ride, and *Earthquest,* an interactive display on the wonders of nature. There is also a viewing tower with panoramic views of the coast and a Victorian-style arcade of shops, and a restaurant.

Admission: Turbo Tours £2 ($3.06), Earthquest £1 ($1.53); Myths & Legends £2 ($3.06), Tower 50p (77¢); all four attractions £4 ($6.12).

Open: June–Aug daily 10am–10pm; Sept Mon–Thurs 11am–6pm, Fri–Sun 11am–10pm; Oct–May, Fri–Sun 2–7pm.

Rathlin Island, off the coast of Ballycastle, Co. Antrim. ☎ **02657/63917.**

For peace and solitude, plan a trip to this boomerang-shaped island, lying six miles off the coast north of Ballycastle and 14 miles south of Scotland. It is almost four miles long, yet less than a mile wide at any point, and is almost completely treeless, with a rugged coast of 200-ft. high cliffs and a small beach, and a native population of 100. It is a great bird-watching center. Boat trips are operated daily from Ballycastle pier; crossing time is 50 minutes.

Fare: Round-trip £5.40 ($8.26) adults, £4.30 ($6.58) seniors, £2.70 ($4.13) children under 14.

Schedule: Daily year-round at 10:30am and 5pm from Ballycastle; at 9am and 4pm from Rathlin.

WHERE TO STAY

Moderate

⭐ **Bushmills Inn,** 25 Main St., Bushmills, Co. Antrim BT57 8QA. ☎ **02657/32339.** Fax 02657/32048. 11 rms (all with bath). TV TEL

Rates (including full breakfast): £48 ($73.44) single, £74 ($113.22) double. MC, V.

Situated in the center of the famous whiskey-making village of the same name, this inn dates back to the 17th century. It was totally restored and refurbished in 1987.

IMPRESSIONS

> *There is something inexpressibly weird about those millions of mathematically formed pillars which thrust themselves upward at the edge of the sea. And the whole scene is a shade of metallic grey. I have never seen stones that so closely resemble iron or steel. The [Giant's] Causeway has a queerly modern look! It is Cubist.*
> —H. V. Morton, *In Search of Ireland,* 1930

The interior has a definite old-world charm, with open turf fireplaces, gas lamps, and antique furnishings. Guest rooms are contemporary in design, with country pine and caned furniture, floral wallpaper, brass fixtures, and vintage prints. Facilities include the Barony restaurant, which features recipes using Bushmills whiskey, a lounge bar, and a gallery/drawing room.

Causeway Coast Hotel, 36 Ballyreagh Rd., Portrush, Co. Antrim BT56 8LR.
☎ **0265/822435.** Fax 0265/824495. 21 rms and 20 apts (all with bath). TV TEL
Rates (including full breakfast): rooms £45 ($68.85) single, £60 ($91.80) double; apts £100 ($153) single or double. AE, MC, V.

Located opposite the nine-hole Ballyreagh Golf Course and overlooking the Atlantic coastline, this rambling resort is located between Portstewart and Portrush, but away from the bustle of both towns. Guest rooms have modern furnishings with pastel tones, and added amenities of garment press, hairdryer, and coffee/tea-maker. Some rooms have sea views and private balconies. The property also includes self-catering apartments with kitchens. Among facilities are the Dunluce restaurant, Tramways Steak Bar, and the Wine Bar.

Londonderry Arms, 20 Harbour Rd., Carnlough, Co. Antrim BT44 OEU.
☎ **0574/885255** or toll free **800/44-PRIMA** in U.S. Fax 0574/885263. 22 rms (all with bath). TV TEL
Rates (including full breakfast): £45 ($68.85) single, £65 ($99.45) double. AE, DC, MC, V.

Located at the foot of Glencloy, one of the nine Antrim glens, this ivy-covered former coaching inn dates back to 1848 and was at one point in 1921 owned by Sir Winston Churchill through a family inheritance. It has been a hotel in the hands of the O'Neill family since 1947. Today it sits in the heart of a delightful coastal town with views of the harbor across the street. The interior is rich in Georgian and Tudor-style decor including hand-carved furniture, paintings by Ulster artists, early maps of Ireland, and a unique driftwood collection. Guest rooms have traditional furnishings with dark woods and floral fabrics. A restaurant and lounge.

Magherabuoy House Hotel, 41 Magheraboy Rd., Portrush, Co. Antrim BT56 8NX.
☎ **0265/823507.** Fax 0265/824687. 38 rms (all with bath). TV TEL
Rates (including full breakfast): £50 ($76.50) single, £75 ($114.75) double. AE, DC, MC, V.

Nestled amid gardens on high grounds on the edge of town, this country manor–style hotel enjoys panoramic views of the town and seacoast, yet is away from all of the resort hubbub. The interior's traditional ambience—dark woods, gilded mirrors, and open fireplaces, contrasts with the guest rooms, which are contemporary, are smart with pastel-toned frilly fabrics, brass fittings, and floral wallpapers. Public facilities include a restaurant, lounge, snack bar, night club, and a leisure complex with Jacuzzi and gym.

Inexpensive

Marine Hotel, 1 North St., Ballycastle, Co. Antrim BT64 6BN. ☎ **02657/62222.**
Fax 02657/69507. 32 rms (all with bath). TV TEL
Rates (including full breakfast): £38 ($58.14) single, £55 ($84.15) double. AE, DC, MC, V.

Sitting right on the harbor at Ballycastle, this newly refurbished three-story contemporary-style hotel is a favorite with Irish vacationers. The guest rooms offer lovely views of the sea and bright modern furnishings. Facilities include the Glass Island restaurant, Marconi lounge bar, and Legends, a nightclub featuring a variety of music from disco to cabaret, country western, jazz, and popular tunes.

WHERE TO DINE

⭐ **Hillcrest Country House,** 306 Whitepark Rd., Giant's Causeway, Co. Antrim. ☎ 02657/31577.

Cuisine: IRISH. **Reservations:** Required.
Prices: Appetizers £2.95–£5.95 ($4.51–$9.10); main courses £7.25–£9.95 ($11.09–$15.32). MC, V.
Open: Bar food lunch Mon–Sat noon–2:30pm; dinner Tues–Sat 7:30–9:30pm.

Surrounded by lovely gardens and situated opposite the entrance to the Giant's Causeway, this restaurant offers lovely wide-windowed views of the coast particularly at sunset. The menu emphasizes local ingredients and creative sauces: salmon baked with cucumbers, mushrooms, and fennel sauce; suprême of sole Inishowen garnished with prawns and shallots; chicken breast coated in almonds and hazelnuts; grilled venison with game mousse laced with Black Bush Irish whiskey; roast N. Antrim duck with sage and onion stuffing and peach brandy; and noisettes of lamb with rosemary and garlic sauce.

⭐ **Ramore,** Ramore St., The Harbour, Portrush, Co. Antrim. ☎ **0265/824313.**
Cuisine: INTERNATIONAL. **Reservations:** Required.
Prices: Appetizers £1.95–£5.95 ($2.98–$9.10); main courses £6.95–£9.95 ($10.63–$15.22). MC, V.
Open: Tues–Sat 6:30–10:30pm.

Situated on the east end of the harbor overlooking boats and the sea, this restaurant is known for its international menu choices, such as chicken breast with fresh asparagus and vinaigrette of pine nuts, sun-dried tomatoes, parmesan, and truffle oil; duck on a bed of shredded cabbage; pork filled with Parma ham and emmenthal cheese; and tagliatelle with Roquefort cheese sauce and bacon; as well as paella, Thai chicken; tempura prawns, fish of the day, rack of lamb, and steaks.

Inexpensive

$ **Sweeney's Public House and Wine Bar,** 6 B Seaport Ave., Portballintrae, Co. Antrim. ☎ 02657/31279.
Cuisine: IRISH. **Reservations:** Recommended for dinner.
Prices: Appetizers £1.70–£3.50 ($2.60–$5.36); main courses £3.75–£5.75 ($5.74–$8.80). No credit cards.
Open: Mon–Sat 12:30–4:30pm and 5:30–8:30pm; Sun 7–8:30pm.

Situated on the coast, this informal restaurant lends a pubby setting with a conservatory-style extension. In good weather, there is also seating outside. The menu features pub grub—burgers, pastas, seafood plates (prawns, scampi, cod, and white fish), seafood pie, steak and kidney pie, and stir-fry vegetables.

Victorianna Restaurant, Dunluce Ave., Portrush, Co. Antrim. ☎ **0265/834444.**
Cuisine: SELF-SERVICE. **Reservations:** Not accepted.
Prices: Appetizers 75p–£2.20 ($1.15–$3.37); main courses £1.90–£4 ($2.92–$6.12). No credit cards.
Open: Mar–Sept, daily 10am–10pm; Oct–Feb, weekends 2–8pm.

Located in the new Dunluce Center, this Victorian-theme bilevel restaurant is a great place to stop for refreshment when touring the Antrim coast. The menu includes sandwiches, omelets, salads, pastas, and steaks, as well as "Ulster fry," a cheese and onion pie, or sausage, beans, and chips.

4 Derry & the Northwest Passage

Derry is 73 miles NW of Belfast, 39 miles SW of Portrush, 70 miles NW of Armagh, 61 miles NE of Enniskillen, 144 miles NW of Dublin, 220 miles NE of Shannon

GETTING AROUND • By Bus   Local bus services to suburban areas outside the city are operated by Ulsterbus, Foyle Street Depot, Derry (**0504/262261**). There is no bus service within the city walls since it is small and easily walkable.

• By Taxi   There are taxi ranks at the Ulsterbus, Foyle Street Depot (☎ **0504/262262**) and at the Northern Ireland Railways Station, Duke Street, Waterside, Derry (☎ **0504/42228**). To call a cab, contact Central Taxis (☎ **0504/261911**), City Radio Cabs (☎ **0504/264466**), Foyle Taxis (☎ **263905**), or Tower Taxis (☎ **0504/371944**).

• By Sightseeing Bus Tours   From June through September, Ulsterbus operates Civic Bus Tours of the Derry sights, in cooperation with the Foyle Civic Trust (☎ **0504/262211**). Tours are scheduled for Tuesday and Thursday (hours vary) and the cost is £2.50 ($3.83) for adults, £2 ($3.06) for seniors, and £1.50 ($2.30) for children under 16.

• By Walking Tour   In July and August, the Derry City Council (☎ **0504/365151**, ext. 307) sponsors Inner City Walking Tours, departing from the Tourist Information Centre, 8 Bishop St., Derry (☎ **0504/267284**). Tours are conducted Monday through Saturday at 10:30am and 2:30pm; price is £1.50 ($2.30) per person.

ESSENTIALS • Tourist Information   The Derry Tourist Information Centre is at 8 Bishop St., Derry (☎ **0504/267284**). It's open from October through June, on Monday through Friday from 9am to 5pm; and in July through September, on Monday through Saturday from 9am to 8pm, and on Sunday from 10am to 6pm.

• Area Code   The telephone area code for numbers in the Derry area is 0504, unless indicated otherwise.

CITY LAYOUT   The focal point of Derry is The Diamond, a square in the center of the city, sitting just west of the banks of the Foyle River. From the Diamond, four streets radiate—Bishop, Ferryquay, Shipquay, and Butcher. Each street extends for several blocks and ends at a walled gateway of the same name (i.e., Bishop's Gate, Ferryquay Gate, Shipquay Gate, and Butcher's Gate). The gates are all connected by a massive wall that rings the inner city.

Two bridges connect the east and west banks of the River Foyle—the Craigavon Bridge, built in 1933 and one of the few examples of a double-decker bridge in the British Isles, and the Foyle Bridge, opened in 1984, Ireland's longest bridge, providing a dual-lane carriageway about two miles north of the Craigavon Bridge. West of the river is Derry's walled inner city and an area west of the walls called Bogside. East of the Foyle are the prime residential districts, in an area usually referred to as Waterside. All of the fine hotels and restaurants are in the Waterside area.

Derry, also known as Londonderry, is the second largest city (population: 90,000) of Northern Ireland and the unofficial capital of the northwestern region of the province.

The city derives its name from the Irish words *Doire Calgach*, meaning "the oak grove of Calgach." Calgach was a pagan warrior who set up a camp here in pre-Christian times. The name survived until the 10th century when it became known as *Doire Colmcille* in honor of St. Columb, who founded his first monastery in Derry in A.D. 546. He is supposed to have written, "The angels of God sang in the glades of Derry and every leaf held its angel." Over the years the name was anglicized to Derrie or simply Derry.

Set on a hill on the banks of the Foyle estuary, Derry has often come under siege since it is strategically close to the open sea. At the time of the Plantation of Ulster in the 17th century, the City of London sent master-builders and money to rebuild the ruined medieval town and hence the name became Londonderry.

A legacy from that era is the city's great 17th-century walls, about a mile in circumference and 18-ft. thick. Although they were the focus of several seiges in 1641, 1649, and 1689, the walls have withstood the test of time and are unbroken and complete. They make Derry one of the finest examples in Europe of a walled city.

The rest of the city's architecture is largely Georgian, with brick-fronted town houses and imposing public buildings. Basement-level pubs and shops are common.

About 12 miles east of the city is another Georgian enclave, the town of Limavady in the Roe Valley. It was here that Jane Ross wrote down the tune of a lovely air that she heard as a fiddler played as he passed through town. It was to become the famous "Londonderry Air" ("Danny Boy").

Moving about 15 miles south of Derry is Strabane in County Tyrone. It begins an area known as the Northwest Passage, stretching inland from Strabane to Armagh. It is a part of Northern Ireland that has a number of unique attractions, such as the Sperrin Mountains, Ulster-American Folk Park, Tyrone Crystal, and the ancestral homes of two U.S. presidents, all well worth a detour from Derry or when en route between the eastern and western halves of Northern Ireland.

WHAT TO SEE & DO

★ **Cathedral of St. Columb,** London St. ☎ **262746.**
Located within the city walls near the Bishop's Gate, this cathedral is a fine example of Planters Gothic style of architecture, built as a Church of Ireland edifice between 1628 and 1633. It was the first cathedral in the British Isles to be built after the Reformation. Several sections were added afterward, including the impressive spire and stained-glass windows that depict scenes from the great siege of 1688–89. In the chapterhouse, there is a display of city relics, including the four original keys to the city gates, and an audio-visual presentation that provides background on the history of the building and the city.

Admission: Free to cathedral, 50p (77¢) to chapter house.
Open: Mon–Sat 9am–1pm and 2–4:30pm.

★ **St. Eugene's Cathedral,** Great James St.
Designed in the Gothic Revival style, this is Derry's Catholic cathedral, nestled in the heart of the Bogside district just beyond the city walls. The foundation stone was laid in 1851 but it took until 1873 for the work to be completed. The spire was added in

1902. It is built of local sandstone and is known for its stained-glass windows depicting the Crucifixion, by Meyer of Munich.

Admission: Free.

Open: June–Sept, daily 9am–9pm; Oct–May, 9am–8:30pm.

Tower Museum, Union Hall Place. ☎ 372411.

Occupying the ground floor of the O'Doherty Tower, a medieval-style fort, this museum presents the history of the city in walk-through format from prehistoric times to the present. In the O'Doherty Tower above the museum are artifacts from the Spanish Armada ships wrecked off the Irish coast in 1588. It's just inside the city walls next to Shipquay Gate.

Admission: £1.50 ($2.30) adults, 50p (77¢) children.

Open: Tues–Sat 10am–1pm and 2–5pm; longer hours in summer.

Heritage Library, 14 Bishop St. ☎ 269792.

Did your ancestors come from Derry or nearby? It's very likely, since Derry served as the principal port for thousands of emigrants who left Ulster for the New World in the 18th and 19th centuries. Records show that Ulster men and women became the second most numerous group in the colonial population and played an important role in the American Revolution and the settlement of the west. This genealogy center, located a block from the Cathedral of St. Columb, will help you research your roots.

Admission: Free; varying charges for research.

Open: Mon–Fri 9am–5pm.

Guildhall, Shipquay Place, Derry. ☎ 0504/365151.

Situated just outside the city walls between Shipquay Gate and the River Foyle, this Tudor Gothic–style building looks much like its counterpart in London. The original structure on this site was built in 1890, but it was rebuilt after a fire in 1908 and after a series of bombs in 1972. Distinguished by its huge four-faced clock, the hall has its stained-glass windows, made by Ulster craftsmen, that illustrate almost every episode of note in the city's history. The hall is used as a civic and cultural center for concerts, plays, and exhibitions.

Admission: Free.

Open: Mon–Fri 9am–4pm and weekends by appointment.

Amelia Earhart Centre, Ballyarnett, Co. Derry. ☎ 354040.

Located three miles north of Derry off the A 2 road, this cottage commemorates the landing of Amelia Earhart here in 1932, as the first woman to fly the Atlantic solo. The grounds encompass the Ballyarnett Community Farm and Wildlife Centre, with a range of farmyard animals and wildlife.

Admission: Free.

Open: Cottage, Mon–Fri 9am–4:30pm, June–Sept daily 9am–6pm; farm and sanctuary, Mon–Fri 10am–dusk, Sat–Sun 10am–6pm.

SAVVY SHOPPING

The inner city of Derry offers some fine shopping, including a modern multistory mall, the Richmond Centre, facing The Diamond at the corner of Shipquay and Ferryquay Streets. It houses more than 30 specialty shops and boutiques. In general, shops are open Monday through Thursday and on Saturday from 9am to 5:30pm and on Friday from 9am to 9pm.

Austins, The Diamond. ☎ **261817.**

This is the city's landmark three-story Victorian-style department store specializing in fashions, perfumes, china, crystal, and linens. The coffee shop on the third floor looks out on a panorama of the city.

Bookworm Community Bookshop, 18 Bishop St. ☎ **261616.**

This shop specializes in books of Irish interest including history, politics, poetry, art, and fiction, as well as maps, guides, and postcards. It is situated at the corner of London Street.

★ **Derry Craft Village,** Shipquay Street. ☎ **260329.**

Located in the heart of the inner city near the Tower, with entrances on Shipquay and Magazine Streets, this unique shopping complex reflects Old Derry, with architecture of the 16th to 19th centuries. It combines retail shops, workshops, residential units, and a thatched-cottage pub.

WHERE TO STAY

Moderate

Beech Hill Country House Hotel, 32 Ardmore Rd., Derry, Co. Derry BT47 3QP, Co. Derry. ☎ **0504/49279** or toll free **800/44-PRIMA** in U.S. Fax 0504/45366. 17 rms (all with bath). TV TEL

Rates (including full breakfast): £53 ($81.09) single, £70 ($107.10) double. AE, MC, V.

In a residential area southeast of the city, this country-house hotel dates back to 1729. Antiques and marble fireplaces decorate the public areas. Some of the guest rooms have four-poster beds with frilly floral covers. The hotel has the Ardmore restaurant and lounge. The wooded grounds are lovely, and the hotel is named for the arbor of beech trees.

Broomhill House Hotel, Limavady Road, Derry, Co. Derry BT47 1LT. ☎ **0504/47995.** Fax 0504/49304. 42 rms (all with bath). TV TEL

Rates (including full breakfast): £45 ($67.50) single, £60 ($91.80) double. MC, V.

Lovely views of Lough Foyle are a feature of this modern hotel, set on its own grounds in a residential area 1.5 miles east of the city on the main road near the Foyle Bridge. Guest rooms are modern, with standard furnishings, welcome tray, and garment press. Among facilities are the Garden Restaurant, with lovely views of the river and the city.

★ **Everglades Hotel,** Prehen Road, Derry, Co. Derry BT47 2PA. ☎ **0504/46722.** Fax 0504/49200. 49 rms, 3 suites (all with bath). TV TEL

Rates (including full breakfast): £65 ($99.45) single, £80 ($122.40) double, £95–£150 ($142.50–$225) suites. AE, DC, MC, V.

Set on a hill overlooking the east bank of Lough Foyle in the prosperous Waterside district, this three-story contemporary hotel takes its name from Florida's Everglades and bears the great seal of Florida as its hotel crest. Like much of Florida, the hotel is built on reclaimed waterfront land. Guest rooms have modern furnishings with light woods, floral designer fabrics, and rattan touches; extras include a garment press, hair dryer, and coffee/tea-maker. Public facilities include the Seminole Restaurant and Cibola Bar.

WHERE TO DINE

⭐ **Schooner's**, 59 Victoria Rd., Derry. ☎ **311500.**

💲 **Cuisine:** INTERNATIONAL. **Reservations:** Only for parties over seven people or for Sun lunch.

Prices: Appetizers £1.95–£2.95 ($2.98–$4.51); lunch main courses £3.95–£6.45 ($6.04–$9.87); dinner main courses £4.95–£8.95 ($7.57–$13.69). AE, MC, V.

Open: Lunch Mon–Sat 12:30–2pm, Sun 12:30–2:30pm; dinner daily 5:30–10pm.

A sea-worthy atmosphere prevails at this classy restaurant, with a 30-ft. schooner as part of the decor and a complete glass front wall overlooking the water along the east bank of the River Foyle. The menu, similar at lunch and dinner, offer innovative entrees such as paupiettes of plaice filled with smoked salmon and prawns, coated in a smoked-salmon sauce; baked filet of trout with hazelnut butter; suprême of chicken coated in a crab and bacon sauce; sweet and tangy pork with honey and apple dip; mushroom stroganoff; filet, T-bone, or minute steaks served with a choice of peppercorn, Diane, or barbecue sauce; and Schooner's Specialty, a breast of chicken stuffed with broccoli and cheddar cheese and wrapped in puff pastry.

PUBS

Derry pubs are known for their music and quiz evenings. Three of the best are right along the same street: **Dungloe Bar,** 41/43 Waterloo St. (☎ **267716**); **Gweedore Bar,** 61 Waterloo St. (☎ **263513**); and **Castle Bar,** 26 Waterloo St. (☎ **263118**).

Along the "Northwest Passage"

The many attractions along this inland corridor start at Strabane and continue through the Sperrin Mountains of County Tyrone to Armagh.

Gray's Printing Press, 49 Main St., Strabane, Co. Tyrone. ☎ **0504/884094.**

This print shop, with its attractive bow-front window, dates back to 1760. The pressroom behind the shop exhibits a collection of 19th-century hand-operated printing presses, going back to the days of hand composition of every word. John Dunlop, founder of the first daily newspaper in the U.S. and printer of the American Declaration of Independence, learned his trade here. An audio-visual show provides insight into how the original presses operated and the part played by Dunlop in America's early printing days.

Admission: £1.30 ($1.99) adults, 65p (99¢) children.

Open: Apr–Sept Mon–Wed and Fri–Sat 2–5:30pm.

Sperrin Heritage Centre, 274 Glenelly Road, Cranagh, Co. Tyrone. ☎ **06626/48142.**

Southeast of Derry the Sperrin Mountains arise with the highest mountain called Sawel. From its peak of 2,240 ft., Sawel's sweeping views reach as far as the Foyle Estuary and the Northern Ireland countryside to Lough Neagh and the Mournes. This is splendid walking country in open lands frequented by golden plover, red grouse, and thousands of sheep. In the midst of this mountain setting is the Sperrin Heritage Centre, with exhibits on natural history and gold-mining in the area. Visitors can even try a hand at panning for gold. There is also a cafe and craft shop.

Admission: Centre £1.65 ($2.52) adults, 65p (99¢) children; panning for gold 65p (99¢) adults, 35p (60¢) children.

Open: Apr–Sept, Mon–Fri 11am–6pm, Sat 11:30am–6pm and Sunday from 2–7pm.

★ **Ulster-American Folk Park,** Mellon Road, Castletown, Camphill, Omagh, Co. Tyrone. ☎ **0662/243292.**

Situated three miles north of Omagh on the A 5 road, this outdoor museum seeks to present the story of emigration from this part of rural Ireland to America in the 18th and 19th centuries. There are authentic reconstructions of the thatched cottages that the emigrants left behind, and prototypes of the log cabins that became their new homes in the frontiers of America. The park developed around the homestead where Thomas Mellon was born in 1813. He went to Pittsburgh and prospered to the point where his son Andrew became one of the world's richest men. Funding to build this park was donated in part by the Mellon family. Walk-through exhibits include a forge, weaver's cottage, smokehouse, schoolhouse, post office, and typical Ulster and American streets of the time. It takes about two hours to do a self-guided tour of all the exhibits. Various music events that tie in with the Ulster-American theme, such as a bluegrass music festival in September, are hosted on the site each year.

Admission: £3 ($4.59) adults, £1.50 ($2.30) seniors and children under 16.

Open: Oct–Mar, Mon–Fri 10:30am–5pm; Apr–Sept, Mon–Sat 11am–6:30pm, Sun 11:30am–7pm.

★ **Grant Ancestral Home,** Dergina, Ballygawley, Co. Tyrone. ☎ **066252/7133.**

Located 20 miles southeast of Omagh off the A 4 road, this farm cottage was the home of the ancestors of Ulysses S. Grant, 18th president of the United States. Grant's maternal great-grandfather, John Simpson, was born here and emigrated to Pennsylvania in 1738 at the age of 22. The cottage has two rooms with mud floors and has been restored and furnished with period pieces including a settle-bed and dresser. A collection of typical 18th-century agricultural implements is also on view, from ploughs and turf creels, to a horse cart. The site includes a visitor center with audio-visual presentation, exhibits, and tea room.

Admission: 60p (92¢) adults, 30p (46¢) children.

Open: End of Apr–Sept, Tues–Sat 10am–6pm, Sun 2–6pm.

Wilson Ancestral Home, off Plumbridge Road, Dergalt, Strabane, Co. Tyrone. ☎ **0662/243292.**

Situated on the slopes of the Sperrin Mountains, this small thatched white-washed cottage was the home of Judge James Wilson, grandfather of Woodrow Wilson, 28th president of the United States. James Wilson left the house in 1807 at the age of 20. It contains some of the original furniture of the Wilson family including a tiny outshot bed (sleeping nook) in the kitchen close to the fire, larger curtained beds, and a portrait of the president's grandfather over the fireplace. The modern farmhouse nextdoor is still occupied by Wilsons.

Admission: 50p (77¢) adults, 25p (38¢) children.

Open: Apr–Sept daily 2–6pm.

Ulster History Park, Cullion, Omagh, Co. Tyrone. ☎ **06626/48188.**

Ireland's history from the Stone Age through the 17th-century Plantation period is the focus of this outdoor theme park, located seven miles north of Omagh. There are full-scale models of homes, castles, and monuments through the ages, including a Mesolithic encampment, Neolithic dwelling, crannog lake dwelling, church settlement with round tower, and motte-and-bailey type of castle common.

Admission: £2.50 ($3.83) adults, £1.50 ($2.30) seniors, students, and children.

Open: Apr–Sept, Mon–Sat 10:30am–6:30pm, Sun 10:30am–7pm; Oct–Mar, Mon–Fri 10:30am–5pm.

⭐ **Tyrone Crystal,** Oaks Road, Killybrackey, Dungannon, Co. Tyrone.
☎ **08687/25335.**

With a tradition dating back over 200 years, this crystal factory is one of Ireland's oldest and best known. Visitors are welcome to tour the operation and see glass being blown and crafted, carved, and engraved by hand. A 25-minute audio-visual tells the story of the development of Tyrone Crystal through the years; a showroom displays the finished products, and a very good cafe adds sustenance. It is located just under two miles east of the town.

Admission: Free.

Open: Mon–Fri 9am–5pm, Sat 10am–4pm; tours Sept–June Mon–Thurs at 10:30am and 1:30pm; July–Aug Mon–Fri 10:30am and 1:30pm.

WHERE TO DINE

⭐ **Mellon Country Inn,** 134 Beltany Rd., Omagh, Co. Tyrone. ☎ **06626/61224.**
Cuisine: INTERNATIONAL. **Reservations:** Not required.
Prices: Appetizers £1.75–£3.95 ($2.68–$6.04); lunch main courses £2.95–£10.95 ($4.51–$16.75); main courses £7.95–£18.95 ($12.16–$28.99). AE, DC, MC, V.
Open: Mon–Sat lunch and snacks 10:30am–6:30pm, dinner 6:30–9:30pm; Sun lunch 12:30–5pm and dinner 6:30–8:30pm.

Located one mile north of the Ulster-American Folk Park, this old-world country inn combines an Irish theme with a connection to the Mellons of Pennsylvania. One of the dining rooms, the Pennsylvania room, has log-cabin–style decor. Simple fare is served—burgers, soup, salads, and ploughman's platters—as well as elegant dishes, from lobster newburg, beef stroganoff, and steak Diane, to coquilles St-Jacques, and sole bonne femme. The house specialty is Tyrone black steak, a locally bred hormone-free beef. Food is available all day including late breakfast and after-noon tea.

5   Enniskillen & the Fermanagh Lakelands

Enniskillen is 83 miles SW of Belfast, 61 SW of Derry, 52 miles W of Armagh, 27 miles SW of Omagh, 108 miles NW of Dublin, 168 miles NE of Shannon

GETTING AROUND   The best way to get around Enniskillen and the surround-ing lakelands of Lough Erne is by car. Enniskillen itself sits in the middle of Lough Erne, wedged between the upper and lower shores. The total signposted driving cir-cuit around the lake is 65 miles.

ESSENTIALS • Tourist Information   Contact the Fermanagh Tourist Informa-tion Centre, Wellington Road, Enniskillen, Co. Fermanagh (☎ **0365/323110**). It's open in July and August, Monday through Friday from 9am to 6:30pm, Saturday from 10am to 5pm, and Sunday from 10am to 3pm; Easter to June and in Septem-ber, Monday through Friday from 9am to 1pm and 2 to 5pm, and Saturday from 10am to 5pm; October to Easter, on Monday through Friday from 9am to 1pm and 2 to 5pm.

• Area Code   The telephone area code for the Enniskillen area is 0365, unless oth-erwise indicated.

Tucked in the extreme southwest corner of Northern Ireland, County Fermanagh is resort country, dominated by the waters of Lough Erne, a long lake dotted with 154 islands and rimmed by countless alcoves and inlets. It's 50 miles of cruising waters, from a shallow channel in some places to five miles wide in others.

The largest island in this lakeland paradise, situated right between the lower and upper branches of Lough Erne, is Enniskillen, a delightful resort town that was the medieval seat of the Maguire clan and a major crossroads between Ulster and Connaught. At the northern tip of the lake is Belleek, sitting right on the border with the Republic of Ireland, and known the world over for delicate bone chinaware. At the southern end of the lake is County Cavan and another slice of border with the Irish Republic. In the surrounding countryside there are diverse attractions, from stately homes at Florence Court and Castle Coole to the unique Marble Arch Caves.

WHAT TO SEE & DO

★ **Enniskillen Castle,** Castle Barracks, Enniskillen. ☎ **325000.**

Dating back to the 15th century, this magnificent stone fortress sits overlooking Lough Erne on the western edge of town. It incorporates three museums in one—the medieval castle itself with its unique twin-turreted Watergate tower, once the seat of the Maguires, chieftains of Fermanagh; the county museum, with exhibits on the area's history, wildlife, and landscape; and the museum of the famous Royal Inniskilling Fusiliers, with a collection of uniforms, weapons, regimental memorabilia, and medals dating back to the 17th century.

Admission: £1 ($1.53) adults, 75p ($1.15) seniors, 50p (77¢) students and children.

Open: May–June and in Sept, Tues–Fri 10am–5pm, Sat 2–5pm; July–Aug, Tues–Fri 10am–5pm, Sat–Sun 2–5pm.

★ **Belleek Pottery,** Belleek, Co. Fermanagh. ☎ **65501.**

With the possible exception of Waterford crystal, Belleek china is the name most readily identified throughout the world as a symbol of the finest Irish craftsmanship. Established in 1857, this pottery enterprise produces distinctive and delicate porcelain china, made into tableware, vases, ornaments, and other pieces. The visitor center has a museum showing the product from earliest days to the present. Tours are conducted weekdays every 20 minutes, with the last tour at 3:30pm.

Admission: Free; tours £1 ($1.53) adults and children over 12.

Open: Mar–Sept, Mon–Fri 9am–6pm, Sat 10am–6pm, Sun 2–6pm; July–Aug, Mon–Fri 9am–8pm, Sat 10am–6pm, Sun 2–6pm; Oct–Feb Mon–Fri 9am–5pm.

★ **Florence Court,** Florence Court, Co. Fermanagh. ☎ **348249.**

One of the most beautifully situated houses in Northern Ireland, this 18th-century manor is set among dramatic hills, eight miles southwest of Upper Lough Erne and Enniskillen. Originally the seat of the Earls of Enniskillen, its interior rich in Rococo plasterwork and antique Irish furniture, while the exterior has a fine walled garden, ice house, and water wheel–driven sawmill.

Admission: £2.30 ($3.52) adults, £1.15 ($1.76) children.

Open: Apr, May, and Sept Sat–Sun 1–6pm; June–Aug Mon–Wed and Fri–Sun 1–6pm.

★ **Castle Coole,** Belfast-Enniskillen Road (A 4), Enniskillen. ☎ **322690.**

Located on east bank of Lower Lough Erne about 1.5 miles southeast of Enniskillen, this neo-Classical mansion was designed by James Wyatt for the Earl of Belmore, and was completed in 1796. The rooms inside include a lavish state bedroom, hung with crimson silk, said to have been prepared for George IV. Other features include a Chinese-style sitting room, as well as magnificent woodwork, fireplaces, and furniture dating back to the 1830s. The house is surrounded by a fine woodland estate.

Admission: £2.30 ($3.52) adults, £1.15 ($1.76) children.

Open: Apr, May, and Sept, Sat–Sun 2–6pm; June–Aug, Mon–Wed and Fri–Sun 2–6pm.

★ **Marble Arch Caves,** Marlbank, Florence Court, Co. Fermanagh.
☎ **0365/348855.**

Located west of Upper Lough Erne and 12 miles from Enniskillen near the Florence Court estate, off A 32, these caves are considered among the finest in Europe for exploring underground rivers, waterfalls, winding passages, and hidden chambers. Visitors are taken underground on electrically powered boat tours led by knowledgeable guides who explain the origins of the stalactites and stalagmites.

Admission: £4 ($6.12) adults, £3.50 ($5.36) children under age 18; £3 ($4.59) seniors and students.

Open: Mid–Mar to June and Sept, daily 11am–4:30pm; July–Aug, daily 11am–5pm.

Sightseeing Cruises

Erne Tours Ltd., Enniskillen (☎ **322882**), operates **cruises on Lower Lough Erne** on board the *M.V. Kestrel,* a 63-seat cruiser, departing from the Round O Jetty, Brook Park, Enniskillen. Trips last for just under two hours; they operate daily in July and August at 10:30am, 2:15pm, and 4:15pm; in May and June on Sunday at 2:30pm; and in September on Tuesday, Saturday, and Sunday at 2:30pm. The fare is £3 ($4.59) for adults and £1.50 ($2.30) for children under 14.

Cruises on Upper Lough Erne are operated by the **Share Centre,** Smith's Strand, Lisnaskea (☎ **722122**). These 1.5-hour trips are conducted on board the *Viking,* a 30-passenger canopied long ship. Sailings are scheduled in April through June and in September, on Saturday and Sunday at 3pm; in July and August, daily (except Tuesday) at 3pm and sometimes at 11am, according to demand. The fare is £3 ($4.59) for adults, and £2 ($3.06) for seniors and children under 16.

Ferry crossings to some of the many islands in Lough Erne are also offered by independent boatmen. From April through September, a ferry runs from Devenish Island from Trory Point, four miles from Enniskillen on A 32; and from June through September, a ferry runs to White Island, departing from Castle Archdale Marina, ten miles from Enniskillen on the Kesh Road. Departures on both services are Tuesday through Saturday from 10am to 7pm, and on Sunday from 2 to 7pm. Fare is £1 ($1.53) for adults and 50p (77¢) for children.

SPORTS & RECREATION

WATERSPORTS The Lakeland Canoe Center, Castle Island, Enniskillen (☎ **324250**) is a watersports center based on an island west of downtown. It offers a full day of canoeing and other sports, including archery, cycling, dinghy sailing, and windsurfing, from £11 ($16.83) per day.

On Lower Lough Erne, north of town, **motorboats** can be hired from The Beeches, Killadeas (☎ **621557**) or Manor House Marine, Killadeas (☎ **628100**). Charges average £25 to £30 ($38.25 to $45.90) for a half day to £40 to £45 ($61.20 to $68.85) for a full day including all fuel.

SAVVY SHOPPING

Enniskillen has fine shops along its main street, which changes its name six times (from East Bridge to Townhall, High, Church, and Darling, to Ann) as it runs the length of the town. Most shops are open Monday through Saturday from 9:30am to 5:30pm.

The largest shopping complex is Erneside Shopping Center, a modern bi-level skylit mall on Shore Road, just off Wellington Road. This center stays open until 9pm on Thursday and Friday.

A unique shopping experience is had at the town's former Butter Market, dating back to 1835 and now restored and transformed into the Enniskillen Craft and Design Centre, Down Street (☎ **324499**). There are craft workshops and retail outlets, with occasional traditional music, craft fairs, and street theater to enliven the atmosphere.

WHERE TO STAY

Moderate

 Killyhevlin Hotel, Killyhevlin, Enniskillen, Co. Fermanagh BT74 4AU. ☎ **0365/323481.** Fax 0365/324726. 22 rms (all with bath). TV TEL

Rates (including full breakfast): £40–£60 ($61.20–$91.80) single, £60–£90 ($91.80–$137.70) double. AE, DC, MC, V.

Set on the shores of Upper Lough Erne, this two-story country manor–style hotel is just a mile south of town and close to the entrance for the Ardhowen Theatre. Guest rooms have contemporary furnishings, and each room has a wide window and balcony with lovely views of the lake or gardens. There is a restaurant for full-service dining, a bistro for quick meals, and a bar with resident pianist. At presstime, plans called for a leisure complex with indoor swimming pool, gym, and other amenities.

Manor House Country Hotel, Killadeas, Irvinestown, Enniskillen, Co. Fermanagh BT94 1NY. ☎ **0365/621561.** Fax 0365/621545. 10 rms (all with bath). TV TEL

Rates (including full breakfast): £50 single ($76.50), £75 ($114.75) double. AE, MC, V.

Dating back to 1860, this splendid three-story Victorian mansion has had a varied history, including use by the American forces as a base during World War II. The public areas are full of antiques and ornate plasterwork, and the windows look out to Lough Erne. Guest rooms are furnished in traditional style with dark woods, frilly fabrics, and decorative wallpaper; some rooms have four-posters or half-canopy beds, and each has a garment press and coffee/tea-maker. Facilities include a indoor heated swimming pool, gym, steam room, sauna, tennis court, marina, and beauty salon. It sits on the shores of Lower Lough Erne 5.5 miles north of Enniskillen.

Inexpensive

$ Belmore Court Hotel, Tempo Road, Enniskillen, Co. Fermanagh BT74 6HR. ☎ **0365/326633.** Fax 0365/326362. 35 units (all with bath). TV TEL

Rates (including continental breakfast): £35–£45 ($53.55–$68.85) double or single. MC, V.

One of the newest lodgings in the area, this three-story motel offers a variety of accommodations; most have kitchenettes and about a third of the rooms have two bedrooms or a bedroom and sitting room. All units have contemporary furnishings with light woods, floral fabrics, down comforters, and vanity area/desks, plus coffee/tea-maker. It is on the east edge of town, within walking distance to all the major sights and shops.

WHERE TO DINE

Moderate

⭐ **Franco's,** Queen Elizabeth Road, Enniskillen. ☎ **324424.**

Cuisine: IRISH/ITALIAN. **Reservations:** Not accepted.

Prices: Appetizers £2.75–£5.60 ($4.21–$8.57); lunch main courses £3.35–£10.50 ($5.13–$16.07); dinner main courses £6.95–£18.95 ($10.63–$28.99). AE, DC, MC.

Open: Mon–Sat noon–11pm, Sun 5–10pm.

Situated next to the Buttermarket in three converted and restored buildings that were once part of Enniskillen's working waterfront, this restaurant blends old world ambience and the legacy of the sea with contemporary recipes and fresh local ingredients. Choices might be filet of beef en croûte; black sole and salmon with sorrel sauce; lobster thermidor; jumbo prawns in the shell, grilled with garlic butter, on noodles; Lough Melvin salmon on a bed of spinach in pastry and saffron sauce; duck breast in plum sauce; and stir-fried chicken, pork or shrimp; as well as barbecued ribs, and a wide variety of specialty pastas and pizzas. From Wednesday through Sunday, there is traditional music starting at 9pm.

Moderate/Inexpensive

Saddlers, 66 Belmore St., Enniskillen. ☎ **326223.**

Cuisine: INTERNATIONAL. **Reservations:** Not necessary.

Prices: Appetizers £1.50–£3.45 ($2.30–$5.28); lunch main courses £2.45–£4.95 ($3.75–$7.57); dinner main courses £5.95–£10.95 ($9.10–$16.75). MC, V.

Open: Mon–Sat dinner 5:30–11pm; lunch Sun noon–2:30pm.

An equestrian atmosphere prevails at this restaurant over the Horse Show Bar. Barbecued pork ribs, steaks, surf-and-turf, burgers, mixed grills are the hearty choices, along with local seafoods, salads, pizzas, pastas, and a house special of sirloin Sandeman, with bacon, shallots, peppercorns, and port wine sauce.

EVENING ENTERTAINMENT

Plan an evening at the **Ardhowen Theatre,** Dublin Road, Enniskillen (☎ **325440**), also known as the Theatre by the Lakes, because of its enviable position overlooking Upper Lough Erne. It presents a varied program of concerts, drama, cabarets, jazz, gospel, blues and other types of modern music. Tickets range from £3 to £6 ($4.59 to $9.18) for most performances; curtain time is usually 8:30pm.

The outstanding public house of the area is ✪ **Blakes of the Hollow,** 6 Church St., Enniskillen (☎ **322143**). Opened in 1887, this pub has been in the Blake family ever since, retaining its original Victorian decor and ambience, with a long marble-topped mahogany bar and pinewood snugs.

Index

Now Save Money On All Your Travels By Joining FROMMER'S™ TRAVEL BOOK CLUB The World's Best Travel Guides At Membership Prices!

Frommer's Travel Book Club is your ticket to successful travel! Open up a world of travel information and simplify your travel planning when you join ranks with thousands of value-conscious travelers who are members of the Frommer's *Travel Book Club*. Join today and you'll be entitled to all the privileges that come from belonging to the club that offers you travel guides for less to more than 100 destinations worldwide. **Annual membership is only $25.00 (U.S.) or $35.00 (Canada/Foreign).**

The Advantages of Membership:

1. Your choice of **three free** books (any **two** Frommer's Comprehensive Guides, Frommer's $-A-Day Guides, Frommer's Walking Tours or Frommer's Family Guides—plus **one** Frommer's City Guide, Frommer's City $-A-Day Guide or Frommer's Touring Guide).

2. Your own subscription to the **TRIPS & TRAVEL** quarterly newsletter.

3. You're entitled to a **30% discount** on your order of any additional books offered by the club.

4. You're offered (at a small additional fee) our **Domestic Trip-Routing Kits.**

Our **Trips & Travel** quarterly newsletter offers practical information on the best buys in travel, the "hottest" vacation spots, the latest travel trends, world-class events and much, much more.

Our **Domestic Trip-Routing Kits** are available for any North American destination. We'll send you a detailed map highlighting the best route to take to your destination—you can request direct or scenic routes.

Here's all you have to do to join:

Send in your membership fee of $25.00 ($35.00 Canada/Foreign) with your name and address on the form below along with your selections as part of your membership package to the address listed below. Remember to check off your three free books.

If you would like to order additional books, please select the books you would like and send a check for the total amount (please add sales tax in the states noted below), plus $2.00 per book for shipping and handling ($3.00 Canada/Foreign) to the address listed below.

FROMMER'S TRAVEL BOOK CLUB
P.O. Box 473
Mt. Morris, IL 61054-0473
(815) 734-1104

[ ] **YES!** I want to take advantage of this opportunity to join Frommer's Travel Book Club.

[ ] My check is enclosed. Dollar amount enclosed_____*
(all payments in U.S. funds only)

Name _____

Address _____

City _____ State _____ Zip _____

Phone ( ) _____(In case we have a question regarding your order).

All orders must be prepaid.

To ensure that all orders are processed efficiently, please apply sales tax in the following areas: CA, CT, FL, IL, IN, NJ, NY, PA, TN, WA and CANADA.

*With membership, shipping & handling will be paid by Frommer's Travel Book Club for the three FREE books you select as part of your membership. Please add $2.00 per book for shipping & handling for any additional books purchased ($3.00 Canada/Foreign).

Allow 4-6 weeks for delivery for all items. Prices of books, membership fee, and publication dates are subject to change without notice. All orders are subject to acceptance and availability.

Please send me the books checked below:

FROMMER'S COMPREHENSIVE GUIDES

*(Guides listing facilities from budget to deluxe,
with emphasis on the medium-priced)*

	Retail Price	Code		Retail Price	Code
☐ Acapulco/Ixtapa/Taxco, 2nd Edition	$13.95	C157	☐ Jamaica/Barbados, 2nd Edition	$15.00	C149
☐ Alaska '94-'95	$17.00	C131	☐ Japan '94-'95	$19.00	C144
☐ Arizona '95 (Avail. 3/95)	$14.95	C166	☐ Maui, 1st Edition	$14.00	C153
☐ Australia '94'-'95	$18.00	C147	☐ Nepal, 2nd Edition	$18.00	C126
☐ Austria, 6th Edition	$16.95	C162	☐ New England '95	$16.95	C165
☐ Bahamas '94-'95	$17.00	C121	☐ New Mexico, 3rd Edition (Avail. 3/95)	$14.95	C167
☐ Belgium/Holland/ Luxembourg '93-'94	$18.00	C106	☐ New York State '94-'95	$19.00	C133
☐ Bermuda '94-'95	$15.00	C122	☐ Northwest, 5th Edition	$17.00	C140
☐ Brazil, 3rd Edition	$20.00	C111	☐ Portugal '94-'95	$17.00	C141
☐ California '95	$16.95	C164	☐ Puerto Rico '95-'96	$14.00	C151
☐ Canada '94-'95	$19.00	C145	☐ Puerto Vallarta/ Manzanillo/Guadalajara '94-'95	$14.00	C135
☐ Caribbean '95	$18.00	C148			
☐ Carolinas/Georgia, 2nd Edition	$17.00	C128	☐ Scandinavia, 16th Edition (Avail. 3/95)	$19.95	C169
☐ Colorado, 2nd Edition	$16.00	C143	☐ Scotland '94-'95	$17.00	C146
☐ Costa Rica '95	$13.95	C161	☐ South Pacific '94-'95	$20.00	C138
☐ Cruises '95-'96	$19.00	C150	☐ Spain, 16th Edition	$16.95	C163
☐ Delaware/Maryland '94-'95	$15.00	C136	☐ Switzerland/ Liechtenstein '94-'95	$19.00	C139
☐ England '95	$17.95	C159	☐ Thailand, 2nd Edition	$17.95	C154
☐ Florida '95	$18.00	C152	☐ U.S.A., 4th Edition	$18.95	C156
☐ France '94-'95	$20.00	C132	☐ Virgin Islands '94-'95	$13.00	C127
☐ Germany '95	$18.95	C158	☐ Virginia '94-'95	$14.00	C142
☐ Ireland, 1st Edition (Avail. 3/95)	$16.95	C168	☐ Yucatan, 2nd Edition	$13.95	C155
☐ Italy '95	$18.95	C160			

FROMMER'S $-A-DAY GUIDES

(Guides to low-cost tourist accommodations and facilities)

	Retail Price	Code		Retail Price	Code
☐ Australia on $45 '95-'96	$18.00	D122	☐ Israel on $45, 15th Edition	$16.95	D130
☐ Costa Rica/Guatemala/ Belize on $35, 3rd Edition	$15.95	D126	☐ Mexico on $45 '95	$16.95	D125
			☐ New York on $70 '94-'95	$16.00	D121
☐ Eastern Europe on $30, 5th Edition	$16.95	D129	☐ New Zealand on $45 '93-'94	$18.00	D103
☐ England on $60 '95	$17.95	D128			
☐ Europe on $50 '95	$17.95	D127	☐ South America on $40, 16th Edition	$18.95	D123
☐ Greece on $45 '93-'94	$19.00	D100			
☐ Hawaii on $75 '95	$16.95	D124	☐ Washington, D.C. on $50 '94-'95	$17.00	D120
☐ Ireland on $45 '94-'95	$17.00	D118			

FROMMER'S CITY $-A-DAY GUIDES

	Retail Price	Code		Retail Price	Code
☐ Berlin on $40 '94-'95	$12.00	D111	☐ Madrid on $50 '94-'95	$13.00	D119
☐ London on $45 '94-'95	$12.00	D114	☐ Paris on $50 '94-'95	$12.00	D117

FROMMER'S FAMILY GUIDES
(Guides listing information on kid-friendly hotels, restaurants, activities and attractions)

	Retail Price	Code		Retail Price	Code
☐ California with Kids	$18.00	F100	☐ San Francisco with Kids	$17.00	F104
☐ Los Angeles with Kids	$17.00	F103	☐ Washington, D.C.		
☐ New York City			with Kids	$17.00	F102
with Kids	$18.00	F101			

FROMMER'S CITY GUIDES
(Pocket-size guides to sightseeing and tourist accommodations and facilities in all price ranges)

	Retail Price	Code		Retail Price	Code
☐ Amsterdam '93-'94	$13.00	S110	☐ Montreal/Quebec City '95	$11.95	S166
☐ Athens, 10th Edition			☐ Nashville/Memphis,		
(Avail. 3/95)	$12.95	S174	1st Edition	$13.00	S141
☐ Atlanta '95	$12.95	S161	☐ New Orleans '95	$12.95	S148
☐ Atlantic City/Cape May,			☐ New York '95	$12.95	S152
5th Edition	$13.00	S130	☐ Orlando '95	$13.00	S145
☐ Bangkok, 2nd Edition	$12.95	S147	☐ Paris '95	$12.95	S150
☐ Barcelona '93-'94	$13.00	S115	☐ Philadelphia, 8th Edition	$12.95	S167
☐ Berlin, 3rd Edition	$12.95	S162	☐ Prague '94-'95	$13.00	S143
☐ Boston '95	$12.95	S160	☐ Rome, 10th Edition	$12.95	S168
☐ Budapest, 1st Edition	$13.00	S139	☐ St. Louis/Kansas City,		
☐ Chicago '95	$12.95	S169	2nd Edition	$13.00	S127
☐ Denver/Boulder/Colorado			☐ San Diego '95	$12.95	S158
Springs, 3rd Edition	$12.95	S154	☐ San Francisco '95	$12.95	S155
☐ Dublin, 2nd Edition	$12.95	S157	☐ Santa Fe/Taos/		
☐ Hong Kong '94-'95	$13.00	S140	Albuquerque '95		
☐ Honolulu/Oahu '95	$12.95	S151	(Avail. 2/95)	$12.95	S172
☐ Las Vegas '95	$12.95	S163	☐ Seattle/Portland '94-'95	$13.00	S137
☐ London '95	$12.95	S156	☐ Sydney, 4th Edition	$12.95	S171
☐ Los Angeles '95	$12.95	S164	☐ Tampa/St. Petersburg,		
☐ Madrid/Costa del Sol,			3rd Edition	$13.00	S146
2nd Edition	$12.95	S165	☐ Tokyo '94-'95	$13.00	S144
☐ Mexico City, 1st Edition	$12.95	S170	☐ Toronto '95 (Avail. 3/95)	$12.95	S173
☐ Miami '95-'96	$12.95	S149	☐ Vancouver/Victoria '94-'95	$13.00	S142
☐ Minneapolis/St. Paul,			☐ Washington, D.C. '95	$12.95	S153
4th Edition	$12.95	S159			

FROMMER'S WALKING TOURS

*(Companion guides that point out the places
and pleasures that make a city unique)*

	Retail Price	Code		Retail Price	Code
☐ Berlin	$12.00	W100	☐ New York	$12.00	W102
☐ Chicago	$12.00	W107	☐ Paris	$12.00	W103
☐ England's Favorite Cities	$12.00	W108	☐ San Francisco	$12.00	W104
☐ London	$12.00	W101	☐ Washington, D.C.	$12.00	W105
☐ Montreal/Quebec City	$12.00	W106			

SPECIAL EDITIONS

	Retail Price	Code		Retail Price	Code
☐ Bed & Breakfast Southwest	$16.00	P100	☐ National Park Guide, 29th Edition	$17.00	P106
☐ Bed & Breakfast Great American Cities	$16.00	P104	☐ Where to Stay U.S.A., 11th Edition	$15.00	P102
☐ Caribbean Hideaways	$16.00	P103			

FROMMER'S TOURING GUIDES

*(Color-illustrated guides that include walking tours,
cultural and historic sites, and practical information)*

	Retail Price	Code		Retail Price	Code
☐ Amsterdam	$11.00	T001	☐ New York	$11.00	T008
☐ Barcelona	$14.00	T015	☐ Rome	$11.00	T010
☐ Brazil	$11.00	T003	☐ Tokyo	$15.00	T016
☐ Hong Kong/Singapore/ Macau	$11.00	T006	☐ Turkey	$11.00	T013
☐ London	$13.00	T007	☐ Venice	$ 9.00	T014

*Please note: If the availability of a book is several months away, we may
have back issues of guides to that particular destination.
Call customer service at (815) 734-1104.*